CRITICAL SURVEY
OF
LONG FICTION

CRITICAL SURVEY
OF
LONG FICTION

English Language Series

REVISED EDITION

Le-Nab

5

Edited by
FRANK N. MAGILL

SALEM PRESS
Pasadena, California   Englewood Cliffs, New Jersey

SECOND PRINTING

Library of Congress Cataloging-in-Publication Data
Critical survey of long fiction. English language series/
edited by Frank N. Magill. — Rev. ed.
    p.   cm.
    Includes bibliographical references and index.
    1. English fiction—Dictionaries. 2. American
fiction—Dictionaries. 3. English fiction—
Bio-bibliography. 4. American fiction—
Bio-bibliography. 5. Novelists, English—
Biography—Dictionaries. 6. Novelists, American—
Biography—Dictionaries.
I. Magill, Frank Northen, 1907-
PR821.C7   1991
823.009′03—dc20   91-19694
ISBN 0-89356-825-2 (set)   CIP
ISBN 0-89356-830-9 (volume 5)

PRINTED IN THE UNITED STATES OF AMERICA

LIST OF AUTHORS IN VOLUME 5

CRITICAL SURVEY OF LONG FICTION

CRITICAL SURVEY
OF
LONG FICTION

JOHN LE CARRÉ
David John Moore Cornwell

Born: Poole, England; October 19, 1931

Principal long fiction

Call for the Dead, 1960; *A Murder of Quality*, 1962; *The Spy Who Came In from the Cold*, 1963; *The Looking Glass War*, 1965; *A Small Town in Germany*, 1968; *The Naive and Sentimental Lover*, 1971; *Tinker, Tailor, Soldier, Spy*, 1974; *The Honourable Schoolboy*, 1977; *Smiley's People*, 1980; *The Little Drummer Girl*, 1983; *A Perfect Spy*, 1986; *The Russia House*, 1989; *The Secret Pilgrim*, 1991.

Other literary forms

John le Carré's reputation rests exclusively on his novels. He has published a handful of articles and reviews and two short stories but no book-length works in other forms.

Achievements

Espionage fiction, the spy thriller, has a large, worldwide audience; one out of every four new works of fiction published in the United States belongs to this genre. Le Carré is preeminent among writers of espionage fiction. John Gardner, himself an espionage novelist and the author of the continuing James Bond saga, has called le Carré "the British *guru* of literary espionage fiction."

Le Carré not only constructs the intricate plots which have made his works international best-sellers but also raises complex and fundamental questions about human nature. Most espionage fiction has a rather simplistic frame of reference: right and wrong; good and evil; us and them. The hero battles it out, his victory assured as he prepares to take on another assignment to save the free world from total collapse. He is a superman and his adventures are narrated with all the razzle-dazzle and pyrotechnics of escapist fiction.

Le Carré's novels undermine all the stereotypes of spy fiction. Instead of a clear-cut conflict between right and wrong, le Carré's novels offer subtle shades of grey. Instead of a dashing James Bond figure, le Carré's most representative hero is George Smiley, fat, short, and balding, who "entered middle age without ever being young." In novel after novel, le Carré is concerned with ends and means, with love and betrayal. He is concerned with character and motive, probing the agony and tragedy of the man who betrays his country not for personal profit but for a cause in which he believes. He dramatizes the dilemma faced by men and women involved in the monotonous and often inhuman work of espionage, which leads him to raise the uncomfortable yet fundamental question: How is it possible to defend humanity in inhuman ways? Like Graham Greene, le Carré compels one to go on a journey of self-exploration, to come to grips with one's own self-delusions, fears, and anxieties. In the words of George Grella (*The New Republic*, July 31, 1976), the novels of le Carré "are not so much spy thrillers as thoughtful, compassionate meditations on deception, illusion and defeat." Le Carré's major achievement is his remarkable ability to transform espionage fiction from cliché-ridden, escapist fare to the level of great literature.

Le Carré's novels take his readers to the nerve center of the secret world of espionage. His is an authentic voice, drawing upon his own experiences. Whether it is the minutiae about an agent's training in combat and radio transmitting technique in *The Looking Glass War*, the subtleties of the "memory man" shredding classified documents in *A Small Town in Germany*, or the meticulous psychological and physical details involved in delivering a clandestine message in *Smiley's People*, le Carré's novels have, in the words of Melvyn Bragg, "the smell of insider lore . . . like a good wax polish." He gives a complete portrait of the intelligence community with all its warts and wrinkles, conveying the sheer monotony and the "measureless tedium of diplomatic life" which form the background of the deadly game of espionage. There is nothing glamorous in this limbo world of spies and double agents, a world chillingly described by Alec Leamas in *The Spy Who Came In from the Cold*: "What do you think spies are? They're a squalid procession of vain fools, traitors too, yes; pansies, sadists and drunkards, people who play cowboys and Indians to brighten their rotten lives." The British Foreign Service is involved not only in plots and counterplots to outwit the Soviets, but also in its own interdepartmental plots and counterplots within the Circus, the London headquarters of the intelligence establishment. In presenting such an uncompromisingly realistic portrait of the spy profession, le Carré has scored a significant achievement.

Finally, in his portrait of George Smiley, le Carré has created a major character in contemporary world literature. Smiley is "one of life's losers." A notorious cuckold who continues to love his beautiful, unfaithful wife, he "looks like a frog, dresses like a bookie," but has a brilliant mind. His vision of retirement is to be left alone to complete his monograph on the German baroque poet Martin Opitz. When he travels on a highly sensitive life-and-death mission, his fellow passengers think of him as "the tired executive out for a bit of fun." Smiley, however, is not one face but "a whole range of faces. More your patchwork of different ages, people and endeavours. Even . . . of different faiths." He is "an abbey, made up of all sorts of conflicting ages and styles and convictions." In spite of all the "information" the reader possesses about Smiley, he remains an elusive personality, thus reflecting a mark of great literary creations: a sense of mystery, of a life beyond the boundaries of the text.

Biography

John le Carré was born David John Moore Cornwell, the son of Ronald and Olive (Glassy) Cornwell, on October 19, 1931, in Poole, Dorset, England, "in a mouldering, artless house with a 'for sale' notice in the garden." He went to Sherborne School—where James Hilton's *Goodbye, Mr. Chips*, was filmed—but did not like Sherborne and attempted to run away. "I was not educated at all," le Carré writes in his essay "In England Now" (The New York Times Magazine, October 23, 1977), and speaks of his school as a prison. He spent much of his time "planning escapes across moonlit playing fields," thereby finding release from "those huge and lonely dormitories." He remembers the severity of the school crystallized in his being "sprawled inelegantly over the arm of the headmaster's small chair," to smart under blows from a small riding whip. Since young le Carré's father seldom paid the school fees, he was singled out even more for punishment. He was struck by the hand as well as being whipped, and le Carré attributes his "partial deafness in one ear to a Mr. Farnsworth," a teacher in school at that time. The school atmosphere was violent: rugger wars were fought "almost literally to death," boxing was a religious obligation, and instructors drummed into their pupils the notion that "to die in battle" was the highest achievement to which they could aspire.

Le Carré's father was determined to make his two sons grow up independent, so he sent them to schools thirty miles apart. Young David and his brother Tony, two years his senior, made arduous journeys to meet each other on Sundays to find the emotional nourishment they so desperately needed. Le Carré quit Sherborne two years later.

Le Carré's father had dropped out of school at the age of fourteen and ever after, as le Carré said in an interview with *Time* magazine (October 3, 1977), "lived in a contradictory world," full of credit but no cash with a "Micawber-like talent for messing up his business adventures." He finally ended up in prison for fraud. Le Carré's mother abandoned the children to live with a business associate of her husband. Le Carré did not see his mother until he was twenty-one. His father died in 1975 without reconciling with his sons. Without the support of his parents, le Carré had to depend on his elder brother. As children, they were ignorant of the whereabouts of their parents, and the young le Carré often wondered if his father were a spy on a crucial mission for England. False promises by his father made him distrustful of people, and he confesses that "duplicity was inescapably bred" into him. His childhood was therefore traumatic, and he draws upon this painful experience in *The Naive and Sentimental Lover* when he makes Aldo Cassidy, one of the heroes of the novel, tell Shamus how his mother abandoned him when he was a child. The loss "robbed him of his childhood," denying him "normal growth."

Le Carré's father was angry that his son had left Sherborne and, to punish him, sent him to Berne University, Switzerland; le Carré was sixteen at the time. At Berne, he studied German, French, and skiing. After completing his military service in Vienna with the army intelligence corps, he went to Lincoln College, Oxford, and studied Modern Languages, taking an honors degree in 1956. From 1956 to 1958, he taught languages at England's most prestigious public school, Eton.

Le Carré is fond of quoting Graham Greene's observation that "a writer's capital is his childhood." In his own case, the circumstances of his childhood led him to accept the "condition of subterfuge" as a way of life. In an interview with Melvyn Bragg (*The New York Times Book Review*, March 13, 1983), le Carré speaks again of the manner in which his childhood contributed to his secretive nature; he "began to think that [he] was, so to speak, born into occupied territory." Like the boy Bill Roach in *Tinker, Tailor, Soldier, Spy*, le Carré is the perennial clandestine watcher, observing, noting, analyzing, and piecing together the parts of the puzzle.

In 1954, le Carré married Alison Ann Veronica Sharp, daughter of an R.A.F. Marshall. He has three sons from this marriage, which ended in divorce in 1971. He is now married to Jane Eustace, formerly an editor at his British publisher, Hodder and Stoughton; they have a son, Nicholas.

In 1960, le Carré entered the British Foreign Service and served as Second Secretary in Bonn from 1960 to 1963, and as Consul in Hamburg from 1963 to 1964. Le Carré has been reticent about his actual work in the Foreign Office, and has been noncommittal about whether his Bonn and Hamburg posts were covers for duties as a secret agent. As Melvyn Bragg writes, "He used to deny having been a spy, but now it's out. He gives in gracefully—caught but too late for it to matter. His new line is a line in charming resignation, an admission of nothing very much." The tension, the drama, and the intense human conflict that pervade all his novels undoubtedly derive from le Carré's "insider lore."

Le Carré experimented with writing while he was a student at Sherborne, but abandoned it because he was discouraged in his creative attempts. After getting married and living in Great Missenden, he once again started writing. Frequently, he used the two-hour train journey he had to make every day to London to plot his stories and overcome his "restlessness as a diplomat." He chose the pseudonym "John le Carré" in order to satisfy the regulation of the British Foreign Service which forbids its employees to publish under their own names. Appropriately, the origin of le Carré's pseudonym is itself obscured in mystery and possible deception. Long ago, le Carré told interviewers that he had seen the name "Le Carré" ("The Square") on the window of a London shop, but diligent researchers have been unable to find any record of such a shop in the registry of London's businesses.

Le Carré's first two novels, *Call for the Dead*, which makes use of his German experience, and *A Murder of Quality*, which draws upon his Eton experience, had moderate success. It was with his third novel, however, *The Spy Who Came In from the Cold*, that le Carré won both fame and financial security. He gave up his job in the Foreign Office and became a full-time writer.

Le Carré leads a very private life in an elegantly furnished cliff house in Cornwall, near Land's End. He is a slow but eclectic reader and avoids novels in his own genre. He follows no writer as a model, but admires and enjoys good prose, clear, lucid, and full of subtle nuances. Joseph Conrad, Graham Greene, and V. S. Naipaul are among his favorite authors.

Analysis

In his first novel, *Call for the Dead* (which took second place in the Crime Writers Association awards for 1961), John le Carré introduced George Smiley, not only his most important character, but also one of the most fascinating and complex characters in the world of fictional espionage. In the very first chapter of the novel, aptly entitled "A Brief History of George Smiley," the reader is offered more information about Smiley than is provided in any other novel in which he appears.

Cast in the form of a detective story, even though the theme—the control of Samuel Fennan, a British Foreign Service official, by East Germany—is one of international intrigue and espionage, *Call for the Dead* is a tight, short, well-constructed novel written against the background of Britain's postwar security crisis. There is a need for men of Smiley's experience because "a young Russian cypher-clerk in Ottawa" had defected. (The cypher-clerk to whom le Carré referred was Igor Gouzenko, author of *The Fall of a Titan*, 1954; his defection set in motion a number of arrests and other defections, including the notorious cases of Guy Burgess and Kim Philby, who were revealed to have been Soviet agents.)

Smiley, who "could reduce any color to grey," and who "spent a lot of money on bad clothes," has interviewed Samuel Fennan on the basis of an anonymous letter charging Fennan with Communist party affiliations. Soon after the interview, Fennan commits suicide in suspicious circumstancs. In investigating Fennan's death, Smiley investigates himself. Smiley's self-exploration and the moral responsibility he accepts for being indirectly responsible for Fennan's death add strength to the novel. Years earlier, during a year in Germany in the Nazi era, Smiley had recruited a young man named Dieter Frey, because the handsome young German had "a natural genius for the nuts and bolts of espionage." Smiley now has to confront Dieter, who turns out to be an East German agent involved in the Fennan case. When the confrontation takes place, Dieter, out of respect for their past friendship, does not fire his gun to kill Smiley, as he could. After that momentary hesitation, Dieter and Smiley struggle, and Smiley kills his former pupil. Ever the scholar-spy, Smiley recalls a line from Hermann Hesse, "Strange to wander in the mist, each is alone," and realizes that however closely one lives with another, "we know nothing."

Call for the Dead introduces and makes reference to a number of characters who become permanent citizens of le Carré's espionage world. There is Steed-Asprey, Smiley's boss, whose secretary, the Lady Ann Sercombe, Smiley married and lost. Le Carré makes a practice of alluding to Steed-Asprey in each subsequent novel, rewarding his faithful readers with sly bits of information; in *A Small Town in Germany*, for example, a character remarks with seeming irrelevance that Steed-Asprey has become Ambassador to Peru. When Smiley is on his final hunt after Karla in *Smiley's People*, it is Steed-Asprey's training he recalls. The reader is also introduced to Peter Guillam, who plays a prominent part in assisting Smiley with tracking down the Soviet mole in *Tinker, Tailor, Soldier, Spy*. Mundt, who is a key character in *The Spy Who Came In from the Cold*, also makes a diabolical appearance in *Call for the Dead*. Le Carré's first novel makes it very clear that he was working to create a design, an oeuvre, and his later novels demonstrate that he succeeded in that attempt.

Set in an English public school, le Carré's second novel, *A Murder of Quality* (which was a finalist for the Crime Writers Association Award for 1962), is a straight mystery novel with no element of espionage or international intrigue, except that the unofficial "detective" is George Smiley, brought into the case by a friend.

Stella, the wife of Stanley Rode, a teacher at Carne, a posh public school, feels threatened by her husband. Before Smiley can meet her and inquire as to the basis for her fear, Stella is murdered. In investigating Stella's death, Smiley meets a variety of characters both within and outside the school, reflecting the rigid class structure of British society. Le Carré draws upon his own teaching experience at Eton to present a convincing picture of a public school, with its inner tensions and nuances of snobbery and cruelty. "We are not democratic. We close the door on intelligence without parentage," says one of the characters. Stanley Rode is not considered a gentleman because he did not go to the right school. Life at the school is an intensely closed society, and hence, there has not been "an original thought . . . for the last fifty years."

The least likely suspect turns out to be the murderer. Smiley faces a dilemma because the murderer is the brother of one of his best friends, a fellow agent who disappeared on a mission and is presumed dead. The irony of the situation makes Smiley say, "We just don't know what people are like, we can never tell. . . . We're the chameleons."

Le Carré's third novel, *The Spy Who Came In from the Cold*, became an international best-seller and brought him fame and financial independence. Graham Greene called it "the best spy story I have ever read." Malcolm Muggeridge praised it for "the cold war setting, so acutely conveyed." It was made into a successful film, with Richard Burton as Alec Leamas. The novel continues to sell, has been translated into more than a dozen languages, and is le Carré's masterpiece.

Le Carré has said that the novel was inspired by the sight of the Berlin Wall, which drew him "like a magnet." The plot was "devised in the shadow of the Wall." Written in a spare, athletic style (the first draft of 120,000 words was reduced to 70,000, while more than a dozen characters present in the first draft were eliminated in the final version), *The Spy Who Came In from the Cold* is the story of fifty-year-old Alec Leamas, "built like a swimmer," a veteran British agent who has lost his most important agent in East Germany. He is asked to take on one more assignment before coming "in from the cold." Tired and weary, almost burned out, Leamas accepts his terminal assignment: to get a British agent, "a mole," out of East Germany. It is, however, not until the very end that Leamas, a master spy himself, realizes that he is not involved in a mere double cross, but in a triple cross, and that *he* is to be sacrificed. *The Spy Who Came In from the Cold* is also a touching love story of two of society's outcasts, Leamas and Liz. Both are betrayed by the men and institutions in whom they have faith and hope, and to whom they have given their loyalty.

The moves and countermoves in the novel are plotted with the intricacy of a masterly chess game. "I wanted to make an equation and reverse it," le Carré has said, "make another equation and reverse that. Finally, let him think he's got nearly to the solution of the main equation, and then reverse the whole thing."

In Alec Leamas, le Carré creates a stunning portrait of an antihero. "Not accustomed to living on dreams," Leamas is a citizen of the amoral world of espionage who practices the art of self-deception so completely that he is unable to distinguish where his life begins and his deception ends. "Even when he was alone he compelled himself to live with the person he had assumed." Leamas is needed by the British Foreign Service because he is the expendable man. His boss asks him if he is tired of spying because "in our world we pass so quickly out of the register of hate or love. . . . All that is left in the end is a kind of nausea." Leamas has a sharp-edged cynicism, but when he meets Liz, a devoted but naïve Communist, in the London Library, he feels for her, believing that she can give him "faith in ordinary life." She is his tender spot; she also becomes his Achilles heel. The Service has no qualms about using her to discredit and destroy Leamas, because "In the acquisition of intelligence, the weak and even the innocent must suffer."

Le Carré makes the telling point that in condoning the sacrifice of the individual, without his consent, for the good of the masses, both East and West use the same weapons of deceit and even the same spies. Le Carré's judgment on this murky world is not reassuring: "There is no victory and no virtue in the cold war, only a condition of human illness and misery."

Mundt, whom the reader met in *A Call for the Dead*, has a prominent role in the novel as the second man in the *Abteilung*, the East German Secret Service. A loathsome figure, an ex-Nazi, he turns out to be a double agent serving the British. To rescue him is Leamas' task, and in the process, two decent human beings, both Jews, are destroyed. "I used Jewish people," le Carré writes in his article "To Russia, with Greetings" (*Encounter*, May, 1966), "because I felt that after Stalin and Hitler they should particularly engage our protective instincts." Smiley makes a brief appearance in the novel in a somewhat menacing role, the only such appearance in all of le Carré's novels—Smiley without his humane personality. There are other references to Steed-Asprey, Peter Guillam, and to the Samuel Fennan case, echoes from *A Call for the Dead*.

The time frame of le Carré's next novel, *The Looking Glass War*, is twenty years after that of *The Spy Who Came In from the Cold*. The British Military Intelligence unit, which during World War II has been vibrant, proud, and respectable, now exists as a mere remnant. Its officers and agents, nostalgic for the old days, wait for an incident to happen that could summon them to relive the past glory and regain their identity and honor. The head of this outfit is Le Clerc, a bland "precise cat of a man." When one of his agents stumbles across evidence pointing to the possible Soviet smuggling of nuclear rockets to the East Germans, Le Clerc is overjoyed. It is a British version of the Bay of Pigs. Le Clerc wants to stage an overflight to photograph the incriminating evidence. He goes about his mission with messianic zeal, because to him, the enemy is not only the Soviet Union, but the Circus—the rival British intelligence agency—as well. The Circus could take the mission away from him and destroy his unit's moment of glory. In *The Looking Glass War*, le Carré reveals the cold war professionals' lack of "ideological involvement." In his own words, "Half the time they are fighting the enemy, a good deal of the time they are fighting rival departments."

Taylor, the man sent to pick up the secret film, is killed, and Le Clerc recruits Avery, untrained for such work, to go undercover to bring back Taylor's body. Avery is a true believer; he attributes legendary qualities to his unit. He is faced with reality when he bungles the recovery mission and is saved only by a seasoned and contemptuous British diplomat, but he falls under Le Clerc's spell again in an ambitious project to train an agent—one of their own, not a Circus man—to send into East Germany to gather evidence of the rockets. His true moment of disillusionment comes when Fred Leiser, the agent in whose training he has participated, is caught inside East Germany. The Department refuses to help Leiser, who is left to fend for himself because of "some squalid diplomatic reason."

Leiser, an immigrant from Poland with wartime espionage experience, is another one of le Carré's rootless spies who is given a prepackaged identity and then discarded. Leiser's training provides the Department with its "carefree exciting days," yet in spite of his loyalty and his gentlemanly dress, Leiser is not considered by the Oxonians who run the show as "one of us." "He is a man to be handled, not known," says Haldane, a friend of Smiley. Leiser is not from the proper class nor from the proper school and hence cannot be a member of the privileged caste to which Haldane and Smiley belong. Through the character of Leiser, le Carré again analyzes the subtle nuances of the British class system.

The "town" of *A Small Town in Germany* is Bonn, "a very metaphysical spot" where "dreams have quite replaced reality." Britain is eager to get into the Common Market, so eager that she is prepared to shake hands with the devil. The devil in this case is Karfeld, a demogogue with Hitlerian overtones, fanatically anti-British and involved in forging a Russo-German alliance. Of more immediate concern to the British, however, is Leo Harting, second secretary in the political section of the British Embassy. Because of his refugee background—like that of Leiser in *The Looking Glass War*—Harting is in an "unpromotable, unpostable, unpensionable position."

At the beginning of the book, Harting is missing along with some top-secret files. Information in these files could destroy British chances to join the Common Market and compromise British-German relations. Harting must be found, but the files are more important than the man. To lead this urgent manhunt, Alan Turner is sent from London. Most of the events in the novel are seen through Turner's eyes.

"A big lumbering man," Turner walks "with the thrusting slowness of a barge; a broad aggressive policeman's walk." Like Leamas, Turner is a professional. Tough, acerbic, with a passionate obsession to get the job done, Turner shakes up the inefficient officials of the British Embassy. In his pursuit of Harting, Turner begins to see a mirror image of himself. Both are underground men. "I'll chase you, you chase me and each of us will chase ourselves," Turner soliloquizes. In Turner's view, Harting must not only be found but also protected, because he is "our responsibility." To the Oxonians, Harting, although he dresses in British style and "uses our language," is "only half tamed." He is, like Leamas and Leiser, expendable. In his minute analysis of the British Embassy officials in Bonn, le Carré portrays what Raymond Sokolov aptly calls "an encyclopedia of the English class system."

Both as an exciting tale of suspense and as a novel exploring the moral dilemma confronting men and women involved in defending Western freedom, *A Small Town in Germany* further advanced le Carré's reputation as an able chronicler of a murky world.

Tinker, Tailor, Soldier, Spy, the first volume in the trilogy concerning Smiley's pursuit of his Soviet counterpart, Karla, is the story of the exposure of a Soviet "mole" burrowed deep within the Circus. Smiley, who has been fired (officially, he has "retired") because of his close association with Control, the former head of the Circus, now dead, who was discredited by the mole because he was coming too close to the truth, is summoned "to come out of his retirement and root out as unobtrusively as possible" the Soviet mole. Smiley begins his meticulous search through the "long dark tunnel." Proust-like, he indulges in remembrance of things past to trace the identity of the mole. He even questions his own motives, part of the subtle pressure exerted on him by his adversary Karla. The search in memory takes him to Delhi, India, where the reader meets Karla for the first time. Karla, "a little wiry chap, with silvery hair and bright brown eyes and plenty of wrinkles," is imprisoned under the name of Gerstman. With characteristic frankness, Smiley tells Karla, "I can see through Eastern values just as you can through our Western ones." Trying vainly to persuade Karla to defect, Smiley offers him cigarettes and hands him his lighter, a gift inscribed with love from his wife, Ann. Karla keeps the lighter when he returns, unpersuaded, to his cell. Echoes of this prison meeting between Karla and Smiley reverberate effectively in *The Honourable Schoolboy* and *Smiley's People*.

Smiley finally captures the mole: it is suave, handsome Bill Haydon, who comes from the right background and the right school. Haydon has turned mole because he could no longer be an empire builder. Haydon not only has betrayed his country, but also has betrayed his friend Jim Prideaux by setting him up for Soviet cruelty. Further, at the command of Karla, Haydon has slept with Smiley's wife, Ann, thereby creating a doubt in Smiley's mind concerning his own motives for ferreting out Haydon. The bureaucratic world of official secrets is linked with the private world of emotional betrayal, giving le Carré's work a universality which transcends its genre.

Kim Philby, the British defector, was the prototype of Bill Haydon. In his introduction to *The Philby Conspiracy* (1968), le Carré writes that the British secret services are "microcosms of the British condition, of our social attitudes and vanities." *Tinker, Tailor, Soldier, Spy* portrays such a microcosm.

Tinker, Tailor, Soldier, Spy was a successful television mini-series with Alec Guinness as George Smiley. Le Carré admired the production, but he has remarked that Guinness "took the character away from me. Writing Smiley after Smiley-through-Guinness had entered the public domain was very difficult. In a sense his screen success blew it for me."

Set in Southeast Asia at the time of America's disastrous retreat from Vietnam, *The Honourable Schoolboy*, the second volume in the trilogy *The Quest for Karla*, is a stunning novel of contemporary history. In *The Honourable Schoolboy*, Smiley steps out of Europe: the action of the novel ranges across Southeast Asia and is centered in Hong Kong. There are two spheres of action: the Circus, where one encounters the familiar faces of Peter Guillam, Sam Collins, and Toby Esterhase; and Southeast Asia, where Smiley has sent Jerry Westerby to track down a high-ranking Chinese who is a top Soviet agent. As the novel progresses Smiley must also contend with the machinations of the "cousins" (the American Central Intelligence Agency).

Jerry Westerby is the honorable schoolboy, so called because he was called "schoolboy" in the Tuscan village where he was trying to write a novel, and given the honorific "the Honorable" because he is the son of a Press Lord. Le Carré had introduced Westerby in *Tinker, Tailor, Soldier, Spy*, and in making him the major figure in *The Honourable Schoolboy*, he demonstrated one of his techniques for developing characters. In an interview with Michael Barber (*The New York Times Book Review*, September 25, 1977), le Carré explained that he gives some of his minor characters "a variety of qualifications" so that he can later "turn them from two dimensional characters into three dimensional characters." He had provided Westerby with a Far Eastern background in the earlier novel, making him a natural for a leading role in a novel with that setting.

In *The Honourable Schoolboy*, Smiley feels compelled to restore the dignity of the Circus, lost in the aftermath of the exposure of Bill Haydon. When he spots large amounts of money from Russia pouring into Southeast Asia, his curiosity is aroused. He recruits Westerby, a newspaper writer and an "occasional" for the Circus, to go to Hong Kong. Westerby's targets are two Chinese brothers, Drake Ko and Nelson Ko. In dealing with them, Westerby is fatally attracted to Drake Ko's mistress Lizzi Worthington. Westerby, by allowing his passion—and compassion—to intrude on his sense of duty, pays a heavy price for his weakness.

The Honourable Schoolboy is a very complex novel, and there are plots within plots like ingenious Chinese boxes. Any attempt at a synopsis would be futile, and it is difficult to capture the rich texture of the novel. Le Carré peoples it with a multitude of characters, each bursting with possibilities for a separate novel. There is Craw, the Australian journalist, an old China hand, based on the London *Sunday Times* correspondent Richard Hughes (who also appears as Dikko Henderson in Ian Fleming's *You Only Live Twice*, 1964); Connie Sachs, the Circus Sovietologist; Fawn, the professional killer; and the mercenary pilot Ricardo, to mention but a few. They interact with one another in a variety of ways to dramatize a labyrinthine maze of involved relationships, both personal and political. Within this framework, le Carré again poses the questions with which he continues to be concerned: What is honor? What is loyalty? These questions, as Eliot Fremont-Smith noted, "provide the tension in the book, and are its engines of suspense."

Smiley's People, the final volume in *The Quest for Karla* trilogy, opens with the knowledge that one of Smiley's most valued and loyal "people," Vladimir, alias Colonel Miller, has been murdered. He had a message for Smiley concerning the Sandman (a code name for Karla). Once again, Smiley is called back from retirement. Smiley's quest is to find a weak spot in Karla, his Soviet counterpart. In Karla, Smiley sees his own dark and mysterious side. As Connie Sachs says to him, "You and Karla, two halves of the same apple."

In this novel, Smiley is the detective *par excellence*. He stalks Vladimir's killer with the skill and acumen of Sherlock Holmes. No James Bond, Smiley is the philosopher-spy who wants to find Karla's Achilles heel. He is convinced that Karla is not "fireproof." The tender spot turns out to be Karla's mentally defective daughter, Alexandra. Smiley plays upon this weakness, this aspect of a Karla "flawed by humanity."

Karla yields, and the final tense scene of *Smiley's People* is acted out on the same site as le Carré's masterpiece, *The Spy Who Came In from the Cold*—the Berlin Wall. Smiley sees the face of the man whose photograph had hung on the wall in the Circus, constantly reminding him of his unfinished business. They face each other, "perhaps a yard apart," Smiley hears the sound of Ann's gold cigarette lighter fall to the ground, and Karla crosses over to give Smiley the victory he has sought for so long.

In *Smiley's People*, the reader meets Ann for the first time, "beautiful and Celtic." When Smiley sees her, "Haydon's shadow" falls "between them like a sword." In the end, Smiley is alone, as he had been in his first appearance in *A Call for the Dead*, "without school, parents, regiment or trade," a man who has invested his life in institutions and realizes philosophically that all he is "left with is myself."

The women in *Smiley's People* are more fully delineated than in le Carré's previous novels. He attributes this to his second marriage. After completing *Smiley's People*, le Carré expressed the hope that the "emergence of female strength" in that novel could be carried into later writing. In *The Little Drummer Girl*, he fulfilled that ambition.

Charmian ("Charlie"), an English actress—incidentally inspired by le Carré's own sister Charlotte, a Shakespearean actress—is the heroine of *The Little Drummer Girl*. Charlie is a promoter of many causes, a grab-bag of the serious and the fashionable, "a passionate opponent of apartheid . . . a militant pacifist, a Sufist, a nuclear marcher, an anti-vivisectionist, and until she went back to smoking again, a champion of campaigns to eliminate tobacco from theatres and on the public underground." The resemblances to Vanessa Redgrave are unmistakable.

Kurtz, an Israeli intelligence agent, offers Charlie the most spectacular role of her career—an opportunity to perform in "the theatre of the real." She is transformed into a successful double agent with the task of cracking "the terror target." The target is Khalil, a Palestinian guerrilla who is bombing Jews and Israelis in Bonn and various other European cities. In her attempt to get Khalil out into the open, Charlie undergoes an astonishing change in her own character. It is hard to think of another novel that has so masterfully portrayed the destruction and reconstruction of the psyche of a person in the process of being turned into a double agent.

The Little Drummer Girl is a departure for le Carré. There are no moles here, but rather terrorists, and Britain and the Soviet Union are replaced by

Israelis and Palestinians. Le Carré made several trips to the Middle East, talking with members of Israeli intelligence and with Yasser Arafat to soak up the atmosphere and allow his characters to develop and determine the action of the novel. The characters are not only authentic but also credible. In Charlie's switching of roles and loyalties, le Carré has the opportunity to present both viewpoints, the Israeli and the Palestinian. While le Carré admires all that Israel stands for, in this book he is a partisan for the needs of the Palestinians. In *The Little Drummer Girl*, le Carré skillfully weaves a suspense tale taken from newspaper headlines, seeking out the universal themes of loneliness, alienation, exile, love, and betrayal of human beings behind those headlines. The result is a great novel.

In his next two novels, le Carré returned to the world of British espionage. *A Perfect Spy* centers on Magnus Pym, a British double agent. Here, as in previous works, le Carré considers the meaning of loyalty and betrayal, not only among spies but also in everyday life; in much of the book, espionage is peripheral. The character of Rick Pym, Magnus' charming but untrustworthy father, is clearly based on le Carré's own father, and the novel is his most autobiographical to date.

With *The Russia House*, le Carré became one of the first masters of espionage fiction to reckon with the changes wrought by Mikhail Gorbachev's policy of *glasnost*. Published in the spring of 1989, shortly before the momentous events in Germany and Eastern Europe, *The Russia House* suggests that powerful factions in the United States intelligence community and military establishment might well contrive to keep the Cold War going.

A Perfect Spy and *The Russia House* demonstrate le Carré's continuing determination to extend the boundaries of the espionage novel. Indeed, le Carré's career offers proof—if further proof is needed—that great fiction can be written in any genre, that genius is no respecter of critical categories.

K. Bhaskara Rao

Bibliography
Cawelti, John G., and Bruce A. Rosenberg. *The Spy Story*. Chicago: University of Chicago Press, 1987. This study analyzes the appeal of espionage and clandestinity, as well as their success in fiction. There is a chapter on John le Carré, "The Complex Vision." The book itself is an interesting context for le Carré's writing. Includes a bibliography of the author's works.

Lewis, Peter E. *John le Carré*. New York: Frederick Ungar, 1985. One of the most extensive criticisms of John le Carré's work, with special mention of its political context. The material is well organized and includes a useful bibliography.

Monaghan, David. *The Novels of John le Carré: The Art of Survival*. New

York: Basil Blackwell, 1985. Provides book-by-book coverage of all of le Carré's novels through *The Little Drummer Girl*. Also includes an insightful chapter on George Smiley.

Sauerberg, Lars Ole. *Secret Agents in Fiction*. New York: St. Martin's Press, 1984. A criticism and comparison of John le Carré, Ian Fleming, and Len Deighton. Although there are references to le Carré throughout the text, one chapter, "The Enemy Within," is devoted solely to his work.

Wolfe, Peter. *Corridors of Deceit: The World of John le Carré*. Bowling Green, Ohio: Bowling Green University Popular Press, 1987. An in-depth probing of le Carré's writing, this work contains many interesting insights into the author's characters. No bibliography.

JOSEPH SHERIDAN LE FANU

Born: Dublin, Ireland; August 28, 1814
Died: Dublin, Ireland; February 7, 1873

Principal long fiction

The Cock and Anchor, 1845; *The Fortunes of Colonel Torlogh O'Brien*, 1847; *The House by the Churchyard*, 1863; *Wylder's Hand*, 1864; *Uncle Silas: A Tale of Bartram-Haugh*, 1864; *Guy Deverell*, 1865; *All in the Dark*, 1866; *The Tenants of Malory: A Novel*, 1867 (3 volumes); *A Lost Name*, 1868; *The Wyvern Mystery*, 1869; *Checkmate*, 1871; *The Rose and the Key*, 1871; *Morley Court*, 1873; *Willing to Die*, 1873 (3 volumes).

Other literary forms

Joseph Sheridan Le Fanu is better known today as a short-story writer than as a novelist. His many tales first appeared in periodicals, later to be combined into collections. In addition to having genuine intrinsic merit, the stories are important to an understanding of Le Fanu the novelist, for in them he perfected the techniques of mood, characterization, and plot construction that make his later novels so obviously superior to his early efforts. Indeed, Le Fanu seems to have recognized little distinctive difference between the novel and the tale; his novels are often expansions of earlier stories, and stories reissued in collections might be loosely linked by a frame created to give them some of the unity of a novel. The major collections, *Ghost Stories and Tales of Mystery* (1851), *Chronicles of Golden Friars* (1871), *In a Glass Darkly* (1872), and *The Purcell Papers* (1880), reveal an artist who ranks with Edgar Allan Poe, Ambrose Bierce, M. R. James, and Algernon Blackwood as one of the masters of supernatural fiction in the English language. One story from *In A Glass Darkly*, "Carmilla," is reprinted in almost every anthology of horror stories and has inspired numerous film versions, the most famous being Carl Dreyer's *Vampyr* (1932).

Le Fanu wrote verse throughout his literary career. While unknown as a poet to modern audiences, in his own day at least one of his compositions achieved great popularity in both Ireland and America. "Shamus O'Brien" (1850) is a fine ballad that relates the adventures of the title character in the uprising of 1798.

Achievements

In the Preface to his most famous novel, *Uncle Silas*, Le Fanu rejects the claim of critics that he is a mere writer of "sensational novels." Pointing out that the great novels of Sir Walter Scott have sensational elements of violence and horror, he denies that his own work, any more than Scott's should be characterized by the presence of such elements; like Scott, Le Fanu too has "moral aims."

To see the truth in this self-appraisal requires familiarity with more than one of Le Fanu's novels. Singly, each of the major works overwhelms the reader with the cleverness of its plot, the depravity of its villain, the suspense evoked by its carefully controlled tone. Several novels together, however, recollected in tranquility, reveal a unity of theme. Moreover, each novel can then be seen as not merely a variation on the theme but also as a deliberate next logical step toward a more comprehensive and definitive statement. The intricacies of plot, the kinds of evil represented by the villains, the pervasive Gothic gloom are to Le Fanu more than story elements; they are themselves his quite serious comment on the nature of human existence, driven by natural and social forces that leave little room for the effective assertion of free will toward any beneficial end.

In Le Fanu's short stories more often than in his novels, those forces are embodied in tangible supernatural agents. "Carmilla," for example, is the tale of a real female vampire's attack on a young woman, but seen in the context of the larger theme, it is more than a bit of occult fiction calculated to give its readers a scare. With her intense sexuality and lesbian tendencies, the vampire is nothing less than the embodiment of a basic human drive out of control, and that drive—like the others that move society: self-preservation, physical comfort—can quite unpredictably move toward destruction. Le Fanu's most significant achievement as a novelst was to show how the horror genre could be used for serious purposes—to show that monsters are not as horrible as minds that beget monsters, and that ghosts are not as interesting as people who are haunted.

Biography

Joseph Sheridan Le Fanu was descended from a Huguenot family that had left France for Ireland in the seventeenth century. Both his grandfather, Joseph, and great uncle, Henry, had married sisters of the famous playwright, Richard Brinsley Sheridan. His father, Philip Le Fanu, was a noted scholar and clergyman who served as rector at the Royal Hibernian School, where Le Fanu was born, and later as Dean of Emly. His mother was from all accounts a most charming and gentle person, an essayist on philanthropic subjects and a leader in the movement for humane treatment of animals. With loving and indulgent parents and the excitement of life at the school, where military reviews were frequent, Le Fanu's childhood was a happy one.

In 1826, the family moved to Abington in county Limerick. Le Fanu and his brother, William, were not sent to a formal school but were tutored by their father with the help of an elderly clergyman, who gladly excused the boys from their lessons so he could pursue the passion of his life: fishing. Walking tours through the wild Irish countryside, conversations with friendly peasants, who told of fairies and pookhas and banshees, shaped very early the imagination of the boy who would become the creator of so many tales of the mysterious and supernatural. The Tithe Wars of 1831 and the resulting animosity of the peasants to the Le Fanus, who were seen as representative of the Anglo-Irish establishment, forced the young Le Fanu to examine his own Irishness. On the one hand, he was intellectually supportive of the union and convinced that the British rule was in the best interest of the Irish people; on the other, the courage and sacrifices of the bold Irish nationalists filled him with admiration and respect.

In 1837, Le Fanu was graduated from Trinity College, Dublin. He took honors in classics and was well-known for his fine orations before the College Historical Society. Called to the Irish Bar in 1839, he never practiced law but entered a productive career in journalism. His first published work, "The Ghost and the Bonesetter," appeared in the *Dublin University Magazine*, January, 1838. That magazine was to publish serially eight of Le Fanu's fourteen novels after he became its owner and editor in 1861. During the early 1840's, Le Fanu became proprietor or part-owner of a number of journals, including *The Warder*, *The Statesman*, *The Protestant Guardian*, and the *Evening Mail*.

In 1844, Le Fanu married Susan Bennett. The union was a happy one; the Le Fanus had two sons and two daughters. One son, George, became an artist and illustrated some of his father's works. Le Fanu's novels published in the 1840's, *The Cock and Anchor* and *Torlogh O'Brien*, received poor reviews, and Le Fanu turned from writing fiction to concentrate on his journalistic work. With the death of his beloved wife in 1858, he withdrew from society and became a recluse. Only a few close friends were allowed to visit "the invisible prince" at his elegant home at Merrion Square, Dublin. Emerging only occasionally to visit booksellers for volumes on ghosts and the occult, Le Fanu established a daily routine he was to follow for the remaining years of his life: writing in bed by candlelight from midnight till dawn, rising at noon, and writing all afternoon at a prized, small desk once owned by Richard Brinsley Sheridan. In this manner was produced the greatest share of a literary canon that rivals in quantity the output of the most prolific authors of the Victorian age.

At the end, under treatment for heart disease, troubled by nightmares—especially one recurring scene of a gloomy, old mansion on the verge of collapsing on the terrified dreamer—Le Fanu refused the company of even his closest friends. On the night of February 7, 1873, his doctor found him in bed, his arms flung wide, his unseeing eyes fixed in terror at something that could no longer do him harm. "I feared this," the doctor said; "that house fell at last."

Analysis

After writing two novels that failed to impress the critics, Joseph Sheridan

Le Fanu left that genre for approximately fifteen years. In his reclusive later life, he returned to long fiction to produce the fine work for which he is remembered. Le Fanu's career as a novelist reveals a marked change in his perception of humanity and the very nature of the universe itself. The development of the author's major theme can be illustrated by a survey of the major novels in his quite extensive canon.

The early works, *The Cock and Anchor* and *The Fortunes of Colonel Torlogh O'Brien*, are both historical novels dealing with the Ireland of the late seventeenth and early eighteenth centuries, the turbulent time of the Williamite wars (1689-1691). *The Cock and Anchor* presents a slice of Irish life that cuts across events and persons of real historical significance and the personal misfortunes of one fictional couple, Mary Ashewoode and Edmund O'Connor. The story of these ill-fated lovers has nothing special to recommend it. Mary is kept from Edmund first by her father, Sir Richard, who would marry her for fortune to Lord Aspenly, a conventional fop, and then by her brother, Henry, who would see her wed to one Nicholas Blarden, a conventional villain. Mary escapes these nefarious designs and flees to the protection of Oliver French, the conventional benevolent uncle. There is, however, no happy ending: Mary dies before Edmund can reach her. The designing Sir Richard suffers a fatal stroke; brother Henry finally finds the destiny for which he was born, the hangman's noose; and even Edmund's unlucky life ends on the battlefield of Denain in 1712. More interesting to the modern reader are the historical characters. The haughty Lord Warton, Viceroy of Dublin, personifies power and Machiavellian self-interest. Joseph Addison and young Jonathan Swift are also here in well-drawn portraits that demonstrate considerable historical research. Still, the novel is at best uneven, the work of an author with promise who has more to learn about his craft.

The technical obstructions, however, cannot hide Le Fanu's message: The problems of Ireland are profound and rooted deep in a history of conflict. The Anglo-Irish establishment, represented by the Ashewoode family, has lost sight of the values needed to end the strife and move the society toward peace and prosperity, values such as personal responsibility, compassion, and even love within the family. Le Fanu was unwilling to risk clouding his theme by allowing the happy marriage of Mary and Edmund, the conventional ending to which the conventional plot could be expected to lead. They die to prove the point. The Ashewoodes decay is really Ireland's decay, and the wage is death.

The Fortunes of Colonel Torlogh O'Brien, Le Fanu's second novel and the last he was to write for sixteen years, is set a few years before *The Cock and Anchor*, during the Williamite war. Again, most critics have found little to admire in the work. The historical scenes and characters show that once more Le Fanu thoroughly researched his subject, but the fictional characters reveal little improvement in their creator's art. The plot, except for some unusually

violent scenes, would hold no surprises for a reader of romances. The villainous Miles Garret, a traitor to the Protestant cause, wishes to take Glin-
darragh Castle from Sir Hugh Willoughby, a supporter of William of Orange.
Arrested on false charges created by Garret, Sir Hugh and his daughter,
Grace, are taken to Dublin for trial. Their escort is Torlogh O'Brien, a soldier
in the army of King James II, whose family originally held the estate. O'Brien
and Sir Hugh, both honorable men, rise above their political differences to
gain mutual respect. Finally, it is O'Brien who intervenes to save the Willoughbys from the designs of Garret, and of course his bravery is rewarded
by the love of Grace.

From the first novel to the second, villainy—Nicholas Blarden or Miles
Garret—remains a constant, and the agony of a torn Ireland is the common
background against which Edmund O'Connor and Torlogh O'Brien act out
their parts. The social cancer that blighted the love of Mary and Edmund is,
however, allowed a possible cure in *The Fortunes of Colonel Torlogh O'Brien*.
As the deaths of the lovers in the first novel showed Ireland as a sterile
wasteland, so the union of the Willoughbys and O'Briens in the second promises restoring rain, but when after the long hiatus Le Fanu returned to novel-
writing, he chose to let the promise go unfulfilled.

Held by many critics to be Le Fanu's finest work, *The House by the Churchyard*, the first novel of his later period, appeared in the *Dublin University
Magazine* in 1861; two years later, it was published in London as a book. The
story is set in late eighteenth century Chapelizod, a suburb of Dublin. As in
the earlier historical romances, there are villains, lovers, and dispossessed
heirs. A major plot concerns the righting of an old wrong. Eighteen years
after the death of Lord Dunoran, executed for a murder he did not commit,
his son, using the name Mr. Mervyn, returns to the confiscated family lands
hoping to establish his father's innocence. The real murderer, Charles Archer,
has also returned to Chapelizod under the alias of Paul Dangerfield. He is
soon recognized by a former accomplice, Zekiel Irons, and a witness,
Dr. Barnaby Sturk. Sturk attempts blackmail, only to have Archer beat him
severely. His victim in a coma, Archer plays benefactor and arranges for a
surgeon he knows to be incompetent to perform a brain operation, supposedly
to restore Sturk to health. To Archer's surprise, the operation gives Sturk a
period of consciousness before the expected death. Irons joins Sturk in revealing Archer as the murderer, Lord Dunoran's lands and title are restored to
Mervyn, and the family name is cleared at last.

This, however, is only one of several interrelated plots that make *The House
by the Churchyard* a marvel of Victorian complexity. To label the Archer
mystery as the major story line would be to mislead the reader who has yet
to discover the book. More accurately, the novel is about Chapelizod itself.
The discovery of a murderer stands out in the plot as, to be sure, it would
in any small community, but Le Fanu is reminding his readers that what

immediately affects any individual—for example, Mervyn's need to clear his father's name—no matter how urgently, is of limited interest to other individuals, who are in turn preoccupied with their own concerns. Mrs. Nutter has her own problem with protecting her inheritance from wicked Mary Matchwell. Captain Devereux and Lilias Walsingham have their doomed romance to concern them, as, on a more humorous note, Captain Cuffe is preoccupied with his love for Rebecca Chattesworth, who is finally joined with Lieutenant Puddock, the former suitor of Gertrude Chattesworth, who in turn has a secret romance with Mervyn. Indeed, the unsolved murder cannot totally dominate even the life of Lord Dunoran's son.

Some of the characters serve a comic purpose, and with so many complex entanglements, the comic could easily slide into complete farce. Le Fanu avoids caricature, however, by providing each comic figure with some other distinguishing quality—wit, compassion, bravery. In *The House by the Churchyard*, Le Fanu, already a master of description and mood, added the one needed skill so obviously absent in his early novels, the art of characterization.

The characterization of Archer, alias Dangerfield, is by itself sufficient to demonstrate Le Fanu's growth as a novelist. Dangerfield's evil is almost supernatural; he describes himself as a corpse and a vampire, a werewolf and a ghoul. He is incapable not only of love but also of hate, and he calmly announces before his suicide that he "never yet bore any man the least ill-will." He has had to "remove two or three" merely to insure his own safety. The occult imagery used to define Dangerfield also links him to the microcosm of Chapelizod, for Mervyn's Tiled House is reputedly haunted; the specter of a ghostly hand has frightened more than one former resident. Le Fanu allows Mervyn, like Torlogh O'Brien, his happy ending, but so powerful is the hold of Dangerfield on the novel that the possibility of colossal evil that he personifies is not totally exorcised even by his death. The fact that he was not really supernatural but was the embodiment of human depravity in no way diminishes the horror.

With his fourth novel, *Wylder's Hand*, Le Fanu left historical romances and social panoramas to study evil with a closer eye. The story, certainly Le Fanu's finest mystery, concerns the strange disappearance of young Mark Wylder, a lieutenant in the navy and rival of Captain Stanley Lake for the hand of Dorcas Brandon, a rich heiress. From several locations in Europe, Wylder has sent letters containing instructions for the conduct of his business and releasing Dorcas to marry Lake. The suspicion of Larkin, a family attorney, is aroused by a problem with the dating of certain letters, but then Wylder returns to Brandon Hall, where he is actually seen in conversation with Lake. The very next day, however, Lake is thrown from his horse as the animal is startled by the pointing hand of Mark Wylder's corpse protruding from the ground, exposed by a heavy rain. Dying, Lake confesses to having murdered his rival and himself arranging for the posting of forged letters. In fact, it was not Wylder who appeared the preceding night at Brandon but one James Dutton, the unwitting accomplice who had posted the letters and who happens to resemble Wylder. Only one person knew of Wylder's fate, having witnessed his midnight burial: Rachel Lake, the murderer's sister. Devotion to her brother and to Dorcas Brandon, who really loves Lake, compelled her silence.

The plot is a masterpiece of suspense, but still more impressive are the characterizations. Each figure is finely drawn and fits into a mosaic of human types which together pictures a species ill-equipped to deal with evil. Wylder is a swaggering braggart, crude, unfeeling, with a general air of disreputability that seems to promise some future act of monstrous brutality had not a violent death cut short his career. Like two vicious dogs claiming the same territory, Wylder and Lake cannot exist in the same world without one destroying the other. Lake's evil, however, is of a quite different nature. In many respects, he is Le Fanu's most interesting study. Wylder's is a rather directionless evil; it could as easily manifest itself in one abhorrent action as another. Dangerfield was simply amoral. Born without any sense of restraint, his natural selfishness led to murder for convenience. Lake's evil is weakness. Greed for property and position seems almost an outside force, a part of human society that can compel even murder in those who lack the strength to resist. He experiences guilt and fear and never is able to derive satisfaction from his villainy. Considering that the murdered man was certainly no credit to the human race, the reader may actually feel sympathy for Lake. In him, Le Fanu presents the criminal as victim, but the consequences of Lake's weakness affect others as well. Rachel's knowledge of the secret and Dorcas' ignorance isolate them from the man they love as much as Lake is himself isolated. Gloom, a sense of a scheme of things not quite right, permeates the texture of the entire novel. There is no happy ending. Years later, Rachel and Dorcas are seen in Venice, sad, alone.

In *Uncle Silas*, Le Fanu continued his investigation of the terrible yet tragic evil represented by Lake. Two earlier tales, "An Episode in the Secret History of an Irish Countess" (1838) and "The Murdered Cousin" (1851) provided a basic plot structure for the study, and in 1864, the same year that *Wylder's Hand* was published, *Maud Ruthyn* appeared serially in the *Dublin University Magazine*. A bound edition in three volumes with the title *Uncle Silas: A Tale of Bartram-Haugh* followed immediately. Considered by most critics Le Fanu's finest novel, it brings all the skill acquired over a productive career to a definitive study of the themes that interested its author most: the nature of evil, and the hereditary aristocracy as a paradigm for the effects of that destructive force. As usual, the study is conducted through carefully drawn characters and a plot filled with mystery and suspense.

In compliance with the will of the deceased Austin Ruthyn, his daughter, Maud, is made the ward of Austin's brother, Silas, a sinister man suspected but never convicted of a past murder. The suspicions are well-founded, for Uncle Silas will stop at nothing to gain full ownership of Maud's estate. When an arranged marriage between Maud and Silas' son, Dudley, proves impossible—the scoundrel is discovered to be already married—murder seems the only solution. Dudley botches the job, however, and kills Madame de la Rougierra, another of Silas' agents, by mistake. Maud flees to a kindly relative; Dudley flees to Australia; and Uncle Silas dies that same night from an overdose of opium.

Le Fanu called *Uncle Silas* a "tragic English romance," and indeed the novel does depict a truly tragic situation. The Ruthyns stumble blindly through situations and realities they can hardly perceive much less understand. Austin Ruthyn, heedless of the suspicions surrounding his brother, sends his daughter into the wolf's lair. Dudley, purposeless and crude, sees only the moment, and this he addresses with instinct rather than intelligent consideration of consequences. Even Maud Ruthyn, the heroine and narrator, is unaware of her perilous situation until it is almost too late. Gothic heroines are expected to be naïve, and Le Fanu uses that trait in his narrator to good advantage. Maud often tells more than she realizes, and the reader sensitive to the unspoken messages that careful diction can convey sees the closing circle of predators before she does. The rhetorical effect is a sense of foreboding, a tension that charges the entire novel.

Despite his avoidance of prosecution for an earlier crime and his careful designs for his niece's downfall, Silas is as blind as any of the lesser characters. His lust for wealth and property is virtually inherited: similar drives have directed his family for generations. His body a slave to narcotics, his mind to religious fanaticism, he is the aristocracy in decay. Le Fanu surrounds him with appropriate death imagery, and his loutish son, Dudley, married without Silas' knowledge to a barmaid, is final evidence of the collapse of the Ruthyn line. Silas' first murder-victim had been a Mr. Charke, to whom he owed gambling debts, but with the planned murder of Maud, the violence turns in upon the Ruthyns themselves. Austin's blind trust puts Maud in harm's way, and Silas' blind greed would destroy her; *Uncle Silas* is ultimately nothing less than a portrait of the aristocratic class cannibalizing itself. Maud survives and eventually marries a young lord, but her concluding words speak more of hope for happiness than happiness realized, and the death of her first child, sorrowfully remembered, strikes at the last the same note sounded throughout the novel.

That note of futility is heard most clearly in Le Fanu at the end of his career as a novelist. *Willing to Die*, first published serially in *All the Year Round* (1872-1873), is by no means his finest effort. The story, while complex, lacks the Gothic excitement of the works for which he is remembered. Still, the novel is important in a thematic study.

Ethel Ware, the heroine, is allowed to sample a full range of life's possibilities. Poverty, loneliness, love, all contribute to the growth of her character; she surmounts all obstacles to achieve great material wealth and an understanding of the meaning of life. This is a new picture; in Ethel, the reader does not meet yet another aristocrat beaten by an ignorance of the forces at work in human society. Ethel wins, in the sense that Silas Ruthyn and Stanley Lake would have liked to win, but the mature vision that comes with the material victory only shows that the quest is pointless and the victory hollow. Isolated in her accomplishment as the protagonists of earlier novels were most often isolated in their failures, Ethel sees that the human struggle is manipulated by forces of society and chance, and whether the struggle culminates in a moment that might be called success or failure is finally irrelevant, for the last force to affect the struggle, death, affects the Wares and the Ruthyns alike.

The novels of Le Fanu are the record of an artist exploring social structures and individual minds in quest of horrors natural and supernatural. With his final entry in that often brilliant record, *Willing to Die*, he penetrated at last to the very heart of darkness to discover the ultimate horror: the utter futility of it all.

William J. Heim

Other major works

SHORT FICTION: *Ghost Stories and Tales of Mystery*, 1851; *Chronicles of Golden Friars*, 1871; *In a Glass Darkly*, 1872; *The Purcell Papers*, 1880; *The Watcher and Other Weird Stories*, 1894; *A Chronicle of Golden Friars*, 1896; *Madam Crowl's Ghost and Other Tales of Mystery*, 1923 (M. R. James, editor); *Green Tea and Other Ghost Stories*, 1945; *Best Ghost Stories of J. S. Le Fanu*, 1964.

POETRY: *The Poems of Joseph Sheridan Le Fanu*, 1896.

Bibliography

Begnal, Michael. *Joseph Sheridan Le Fanu*. Lewisburg, Pa.: Bucknell University Press, 1971. Sketches Le Fanu's life up to the death of his wife in 1858 and the beginning of his seclusion in Dublin. Analyzes his work as part of the Gothic tradition to which Le Fanu makes a serious contribution, though he breaks from it to relate his ideas to his contemporary society. Focuses on his last four novels, presented as his best, which he published after emerging from his seclusion, beginning with *The House by the Churchyard*, in 1863. A brief study with a chronology and a selected bibliography.

Browne, Nelson. *Sheridan Le Fanu*. New York: Roy, 1951. Begins with an assessment of Le Fanu's reputation and provides the main facts of his life and family background. Focuses on his fourteen novels from *The Cock and Anchor*, in 1845, to *Willing to Die*, in 1873; five of the novels are said to be works of genius, and all are presented as worth reading. Also focuses on his short stories, whose plots are described, and verse, which once was very popular and deserves continued reading. Presents Le Fanu as entitled to serious reconsideration and study, and worthy of comparison with Sir Walter Scott, Edgar Allan Poe, and Wilkie Collins. A compact study of his life and writings, with an index and an appendix listing his principal works and original publication dates.

McCormack, W. J. *Sheridan Le Fanu and Victorian Ireland*. Oxford, England: Clarendon Press, 1980. After a short introductory note, analyzes Le Fanu's life and career, examining the special conditions in Victorian Ireland behind his writing. These include the clerical world of Dublin during the struggles for Catholic Emancipation, his Irish political background, and his own changing opinions with regard to the Repeal of the Act of Union. Includes a close analysis of the symbolism of *Uncle Silas* as his most complex novel. Acknowledges that his late writing is not good, but argues that study of his entire career is fundamental to study of Anglo-Irish literature. Contains illustrations, two appendices, a substantial bibliography with manuscript sources, and an index.

Melada, Ivan. *Sheridan Le Fanu*. Boston: Twayne, 1987. After summarizing Le Fanu's life, concentrates on his writing and concludes with an assessment of his literary achievements. Discusses Le Fanu's early short fiction, then his historical novels, followed by a sustained analysis of *Uncle Silas*, and then the late short fiction; Le Fanu's poetry and periodical fiction are saved for a final word on the variety of his work. Estimates his achievement by arguing that *Uncle Silas* shows him to be a master of terror literature, that his cinematic style should be attractive to a modern audience, and that his canon makes Le Fanu a major author in the Gothic tradition. Provides a prefatory chronology, supplementary notes, a selected annotated bibliography, and an index.

Sloan, Barry. *The Pioneers of Anglo-Irish Fiction 1800-1850*. Totowa, N.J.: Barnes & Noble Books, 1986. Examines the pioneering work of early nineteenth century writers who began the tradition of Anglo-Irish fiction which climaxed in the works of great twentieth century Irish writers. While Le Fanu is given focused attention for only a part of chapter 7, including comments on his novels by Mrs. S. C. Hall, Charles Lever, and William Carleton in the period between 1845 and 1850, he is nevertheless shown as making an important contribution to this tradition. His predecessor Charles Robert Maturin did not develop the subject of Irish nationalism as fully as Le Fanu in *The Cock and Anchor*, which depicts the decline and predicts the end of the Irish ruling class in Victorian Ireland. Contains prefatory chronology, notes, a bibliography, and an index.

URSULA K. LE GUIN

Born: Berkeley, California; October 21, 1929

Principal long fiction

Rocannon's World, 1966; *Planet of Exile*, 1966; *City of Illusions*, 1967; *A Wizard of Earthsea*, 1968; *The Left Hand of Darkness*, 1969; *The Tombs of Atuan*, 1971; *The Lathe of Heaven*, 1971; *The Farthest Shore*, 1972; *The Dispossessed: An Ambiguous Utopia*, 1974; *Very Far Away from Anywhere Else*, 1976; *Malafrena*, 1979; *Leese Webster*, 1979; *The Beginning Place*, 1980; *The Eye of the Heron*, 1982; *Always Coming Home*, 1985; *Catwings*, 1988; *Catwings Return*, 1989; *Tehanu: The Last Book of Earthsea*, 1990.

Other literary forms

Included in Ursula K. Le Guin's list of novels have been books specifically written for children and young adults: *A Wizard of Earthsea*, *The Tombs of Atuan*, and *The Farthest Shore* (the first three books of what is known as the Earthsea series); *Very Far Away from Anywhere Else*; *Leese Webster*; and *The Beginning Place*. Her other published works include a novella, *The Word for World Is Forest* (1972); several volumes of short stories, *The Wind's Twelve Quarters* (1975), *Orsinian Tales* (1976), *The Compass Rose* (1982), and *Buffalo Gals and Other Animal Presences* (1987); and several volumes of poetry, *Wild Angels* (1975), *Hard Words and Other Poems* (1981), *In the Red Zone* (1983), and *Wild Oats and Fireweed: New Poems* (1988). Le Guin's comments on the nature and meaning of fantasy, her own creative process, and science fiction in general are collected in *From Elfland to Poughkeepsie* (1973), *The Language of the Night: Essays on Fantasy and Science Fiction* (1979; Susan Wood, editor), *Dancing at the Edge of the World: Thoughts on Words, Women, and Places* (1988), and *Napa: The Roots and Springs of the Valley* (1989).

Achievements

The quality of Le Guin's work has been apparent from the beginning of her writing career. Brian Attebery, a fellow writer, has stated that even her first published novels are superior to most works of science fiction written at that time. Public recognition of Le Guin's work began with the Boston *Globe* Horn Book Award for *A Wizard of Earthsea* in 1969. Since then, Le Guin has amassed numerous prestigious awards. They include Nebula and Hugo Awards for *The Left Hand of Darkness* (1969, 1970); the Newbery Silver Medal Award for *The Tombs of Atuan* (1972); a Hugo Award for *The Word for World Is Forest* (1973); a National Book Award for Children's Books for *The Farthest Shore* (1973); a Hugo Award for "The Ones Who Walk Away from Omelas" (1974); Nebula, Jupiter, and Hugo Awards for *The Dispossessed*

(1974, 1975); a Jupiter Award for "The Diary of the Rose" (1976); a Gandalf Award for achievement in fantasy (1979); and, in 1986, the Kafka Award. In addition to receiving these honors, Le Guin has been a writer-in-residence at the Clarion West workshop at the University of Washington and a teaching participant in a science-fiction workshop at Portland State University. Her stature among science-fiction writers was recognized on an international scale when, in 1975, Le Guin was the Guest of Honor at the 33rd World Science Fiction Convention (Aussiecon) in Sydney, Australia. The following year, she was a Visiting Fellow in creative writing at the University of Reading, England.

Biography

Ursula Kroeber Le Guin was born into a close, intellectual family in Berkeley, California, on October 21, 1929. Her father Alfred was an anthropologist distinguished for his studies of the California Indians; her mother, Theodora Krackaw Kroeber, a respected writer with an advanced degree in psychology.

The Kroeber family seems to have enjoyed an enviable degree of closeness, reasonable financial security, and an abundance of intellectual stimulation. During the academic year, they lived in a large, airy house in Berkeley. Their summers were spent in their Napa Valley home, Kishamish. To these forty acres flocked writers, scholars, graduate students, relatives, and Indians.

Living among so many people rich in knowledge and curiosity, and having access to an almost unlimited supply of books, Le Guin began writing and reading quite young. She did not discover science fiction, however, until she was twelve. When she found, while reading Lord Dunsany one day, that people were still creating myths, Le Guin felt liberated, for this discovery validated her own creative efforts.

In 1947, Le Guin entered Radcliffe College in Cambridge, Massachusetts. After she was graduated magna cum laude in 1951, she entered Columbia University, where she majored in French and Italian Renaissance literature. After completing her master's degree in 1952, she began work on a doctoral program. En route to France as a Fulbright fellow, she met Charles Le Guin, a historian from Georgia also on a Fulbright. They were married in Paris on December 22, 1953.

When they returned from France, the Le Guins lived in Georgia. Ursula taught French at Mercer University in Macon, and Charles completed his Ph.D. in French history at Emory University. Afterward, they moved to Idaho, where their first child, Elisabeth, was born in 1957. A third child, Theodore, would be born in 1964.

Caroline, their second daughter, arrived in 1959, the year Charles accepted a position at Portland State University and the family moved to a permanent home in Oregon. Ursula, who had never stopped writing but had yet to find a proper market for her efforts, became reacquainted with science fiction when a friend encouraged her to borrow from his library. Cordwainer Smith's story "Alpha Ralpha Boulevard" proved to be a catalyst, a type of fiction approaching Le Guin's own attempts. Le Guin began thinking, not only about writing, but also about publishing her work in something other than obscure magazines.

Since she had begun to write, she had been trying to get her work published, but except for one story, "An die Musick," and a few poems, her work was returned, some of it characterized as "remote." Her breakthrough came when *Fantastic* published "April in Paris" in September, 1962. The following year, *Fantastic* published her first genuine science-fiction story, "The Masters." After that time, Le Guin's literary output steadily increased, and her recognition as one of America's outstanding writers was assured.

Throughout her career, Le Guin has been reserved about the details of her personal life, maintaining that they are expressed best through her fiction. Although she has been involved in political activities, most of Le Guin's efforts are devoted to writing. As her recognition has increased, she has become a strong advocate for improving the quality of fantasy and science fiction. She seems determined that readers of this genre will not be cheated on their voyages of discovery.

During her writing career, however, Le Guin's work has expanded significantly outside the genre of science fiction. From "pro-choice" parables reprinted in *Ms.* magazine to advice to fellow authors, both from her book of essays *Dancing at the Edge of the World*, Le Guin has been prolifically diverse in her output.

Analysis

When Ursula K. Le Guin has Genly Ai state in *The Left Hand of Darkness* that "truth is a matter of the imagination," she is indirectly summarizing the essential focus of her fiction: explorations of the ambiguous nature of truth through imaginative means. Few other contemporary authors have described this process with the force and clarity of Le Guin. Her subject is always humankind and, by extension, the human environment, since mankind cannot survive in a vacuum; her technique is descriptive, and her mode is metaphoric. The worlds Le Guin creates are authentic in a profoundly moral sense as her characters come to experience truth in falsehood, return in separation, unity in variety. Frequently using a journey motif, Le Guin sends her characters in search of shadows, rings, theories, or new worlds—all of which are metaphors for undiscovered elements of the self. Once made, these discoveries allow her characters to be integrated into themselves and their worlds.

Unity is what Le Guin's characters seek: not a simple sense of belonging but a complex sense of wholeness which recognizes paradoxes inherent in human existence. Much of her outlook is derived from the Taoist philosopher Lao-tzu, who maintained that scientific, ethical, and aesthetic laws, instead of being imposed by any authority, "exist in things and are to be discovered." Thus, Le Guin's characters must learn to recognize the true natures (or true names) of people or objects—none of which yields easily to the protagonist—before apprehending their essence and role in the world. Tao is the ultimate unity of the universe, encompassing all and nothing. Built upon paradox, Taoist philosophy proposes that apparently opposing forces actually complete each other. Discovering this in a world enamored of dualist thought, however, requires attaining an attitude of actionless activity, an emptying of the self and at the same time the fullest self-awareness. This compassionate attitude establishes a state of attraction, not compulsion; a state of being, not doing. Indeed, because the cycle of cause and effect is so strong, the Taoist sage never tries to do good at all, for a good action implies an evil action. Discovering the correlation of life/death, good/evil, light/dark, male/female, and self/other requires a relativist judgment. The Indian lore Le Guin absorbed as a child also contributed to her sense of unity. In her writing, she has drawn upon her rich knowledge of myths and the work of C. G. Jung as well as her own fertile imagination to create intricate metaphors for psychic realities. In her own words, "Outer Space, and the Inner Lands, are still, and will always be, my country."

Le Guin has described *Rocannon's World*, her first published novel, as "definitely purple," an odd mixture of space age and bronze age, the product of an author unsure of her direction and materials. Drawing heavily on Norse mythology, the novel originated from a short story, "Dowry of the Angyar," published in 1964. The story begins when a woman named Semley leaves her husband and child to claim her dowry, a gold and sapphire necklace. During her search, Semley time-travels to another planet, where Rocannon, an ethnologist, struck by her beauty and bearing, gives her the necklace, a museum piece on his planet. Semley returns home, believing that she has been gone only overnight. To her dismay, though, she discovers that she has been gone for sixteen years. Her husband is dead; her daughter a grown stranger.

The remainder of the novel concerns Rocannon's exploration of Semley's planet, known to him as Formalhaut II, with the aid of Semley's grandson Mogien. After his ship is destroyed by rebels from the planet Farady, Rocannon must warn the League of All Nations of their rebellion. To do so, he must locate the rebel ship in order to use their ansible, an instantaneous transmitter, since his has been destroyed.

This episodic tale moves from adventure to adventure, as Rocannon learns that appearance often belies reality, that knowledge is not gained without sacrifice. The price he pays for increased understanding (the gift of mind-speech through which he can hear the voices of his enemy) is costly: Mogien's life. Through his efforts, however, the planet is saved. Rocannon, a man changed forever by his knowlege, never returns to his own planet, and he dies without knowing that the planet he rescues is given his name.

Often her own best critic, Le Guin has cited this novel to illustrate the flaws of mixing science fiction with fantasy; of ignoring the limitations imposed by plausibility; of excessive caution in creating a new myth; and of reliance on stereotyped characters and situations. While this novel lacks the rich complexity of her later works, it does contain elements Le Guin develops in subsequent novels. A readily apparent trait is that her focus is not on theoretical or applied science but rather on social science: how different individuals, races, and cultures perpetuate diffusion through lack of communication and how her main character surmounts these genuine yet arbitrary barriers. For example, as an ethnologist, Rocannon is interested in learning about all kinds of human behavior; nevertheless, he assumes superiority over his "primitive" guides. Experience, however, leads him to admire the individual qualities of Mogien, Kyo, and the Fiians. During their journey, his admiration of and loyalty to them increase to such an extent that loyalty becomes a prominent theme, one developed more thoroughly in *The Left Hand of Darkness*, with the relationship of Mogien and Rocannon prefiguring that of Genly Ai and Estraven (as well as other pairs of characters).

The most important goal in the novel, though, is to locate the other, often presented as the enemy, unify it with the self, and thus receive personal gain. The mindspeech Rocannon learns to hear expresses his fear. Though once he listens to the voices of his enemies he will never regain the self-sufficient confidence he had before embarking on his journey, he earns a vital awareness of his human limitations. Rocannon's sense of adventure is tempered by responsibility; his gain requires loss. In the end, Rocannon feels that he is a temporary resident on an alien planet. His sense of displacement denotes his lack of completion as a character. The novel ends without any resolution. In her next two novels, Le Guin shows greater control over her materials: less dependence upon others' stories and more considered ideas and direction. Where *Rocannon's World* indicates a major theme of self-exploration, *City of Illusions* develops this theme, bringing it closer to its fullest realization in *The Dispossessed.*

City of Illusions begins dramatically in the blank terror of mental darkness experienced by Ramarren and ends in an even larger exterior darkness when Falk-Ramarren, returning to his home planet, departs for his unknown future. In the intervening time, Le Guin presents vivid scenes of an America largely undeveloped and peopled by disparate tribes, all of whom distrust one another and are united only in their universal fear of the Shing, an alien group who maintain division through that terror. Themes of communication, truth, self-discovery, and self-unification are central to this novel.

Using the quest motif, Le Guin has Falk nurtured by the pacific Forest Dwellers, who instill in him their set of values. When he leaves to discover his former identity, Falk confronts differing values, conflicting truths. Along the way, he receives the same warning from those who befriend him: trust no one; go alone. While he neglects to heed this advice always, these warnings prepare him in part to withstand the considerable powers of the Shing, whose authority depends on self-doubt. Falk is able to recover his past self and retain his present self when he discovers that "there is in the long run no disharmony, only misunderstanding, no chance of mischance but only the ignorant eye." Once he achieves this state of understanding, his two identities merge; he becomes Falk-Ramarren to return to his world with the truth—or rather truths—he apprehends.

Le Guin's Taoist beliefs are given full exposure in this novel, where Falk-Ramarren not only reads the *Tao Te Ching* (late third century B.C.), called the Old Canon, and looks for The Way, but also demonstrates the strength of passivity and enters a state of actionless activity to find himself. Stoical and silent, he prefigures Shevek of *The Dispossessed*. Le Guin's use of setting is also significant as it is employed to reflect psychological states. Her description of the Shing buildings in Es Toch suggests the illusory quality of this alien race and Falk's ambiguous state of mind. This novel fails, however, to measure up to later works. The Shing, for example, meant to personify evil, are all but unbelievable. Their ambiguity lapses into confusion; their "power" is unsubstantiated. Falk's sudden compassion for them is thus rather surprising. Another mark of this novel's early place in Le Guin's career is her heavy-handedness regarding her source. Not only does she thinly disguise the *Tao Te Ching*, but she also employs puns and even paraphrases passages to stress her meaning. In her later novels, she achieves better results through greater restraint and insight.

Le Guin arrived at a denser, more original expression of Taoist thought in *The Left Hand of Darkness*. In this novel, she brings together previously expressed themes in a striking metaphor. Time levels, separate in former books, coexist in this novel, as do polarized political systems, philosophies, and genders. Genly Ai, the man sent to bring the planet of Genthen into the Ekumen (formerly the League of All Worlds), must, like Falk, come to see the relativity of truth. To do so, he must cross barriers of thought, barriers he is at first incapable of recognizing. Even when he does, Ai is reluctant to cross, for he must abandon his masculine-scientific-dualist training to become a relativist. He must believe that "truth is a matter of the imagination."

Ai's difficulty in arriving at this conclusion is complicated by his alien existence on Genthen, where he is not merely an outsider; he is a sexual anomaly, a pervert as far as the natives are concerned. Being a heterosexual male in an androgynous culture adds immeasurably to Ai's sense of distrust, for he cannot bring himself to trust "a man who is a woman, a woman who is a man." The theme of androgyny enriches this novel, not simply because it develops the complex results of an androgynous culture, but also because it demonstrates how gender affects—indeed prejudices—thought and explores the cultural effects of this bias. Initially, Ai can see only one gender, one side at a time. This limited vision leaves him vulnerable to betrayal, both by himself and by others. Through his friendship with Estraven, Ai begins to respect, even require, those qualities he at first denigrates until he and Estraven become one, joined in mindspeech. Ai's varied experiences on Genthen teach him that apparently polarized qualities of light/dark, male/female, rational/irrational, patriot/traitor, life/death are necessary complements. The order of the universe requires both.

The Left Hand of Darkness consolidates Taoist ideas expressed in Le Guin's previous books, places them in a dramatically unique culture, and develops them with a finesse lacking in her earlier novels. Ai discovers what Falk does: a fuller recognition of self through merger with the other. He does so, however, in a much more complete way because Le Guin complicates *The Left Hand of Darkness* with questions of opposing political systems, the nature and consequences of sexism, the issue of personal and political loyalty, and the interrelatedness of different periods of time. While retaining her basic quest structure, Le Guin has Genly Ai construct his "report" by using multiple sources: Estraven's diary, folktales, ancient myths, reports from previous investigatory teams. This adds texture and depth by dramatizing the multiplicity of truth and the unity of time. In a sense, this mixture of sources, added to the seasonlessness of Genthen, where it is always winter, and the relentless journey over the Gobrin Ice, constructs a center of time for the reader, an objective correlative to Ai's state of mind. Within a circular framework, a sense of wholeness is achieved. Ai will set the keystone in the arch, the image which opens *The Left Hand of Darkness*, by adding Genthen to the Ekumen. Later, he cements his personal bond to Estraven by visiting his home, ostensibly to return Estraven's diary but actually to assuage a sense of betrayal for not having Estraven publicly absolved of his "crime" of supporting the Ekumen instead of his king. At the novel's end, however, when Ai meets in Estraven's son the father's limitless curiosity, Ai's journey begins anew.

Robert Scholes has stated that one of the great strengths of *The Left Hand of Darkness* is that it "asks us to broaden our perspectives toward something truly ecumenical, beyond racism and sexism, and even speciesism." Clearly, Le Guin has opened up new territory for science-fiction writers to explore. In *The Dispossessed*, her next novel in what is called her Hainish cycle, she presses even further, bringing to full realization her heroic figure of the Taoist sage in the protagonist Shevek. Stoic, persistent, curious, and humane, he shares qualities with Falk, Estraven, and Genly Ai. Shevek's character and journey, however, differ from his predecessors' in several important respects. Shevek's sense of alienation is tempered by his mature love for his partner Takver. No matter how alone he is on his journey, Shevek can and does turn to their mutually supportive relationship for solace. Shevek's sense of individual integrity is also more conscious than that of previous characters. Already aware of himself and his value, he is able to expand beyond both. Most important, Shevek has a clearly defined sense of purpose—a need to unbuild walls through communication—and a certainty of return. Early in the novel, Le Guin assures her readers that "he would most likely not have embarked on that years-long enterprise had he not had profound assurance that return was possible . . . that the very nature of the voyage . . . implied return." Buttressed by this conviction, Shevek goes forth, his empty hands signifying his spiritual values, and effects a revolution in both senses of the word: a completed cycle and a dynamic change. When he discovers his theory of temporal simultaneity, Shevek gives it away, for he knows that its value is not in its scarcity, but in its general use.

The Dispossessed is not simply a vehicle for Taoist philosophy; it is just as significantly a political novel. Le Guin subtitles the novel *An Ambiguous Utopia*, indicating her focus, and she directs her reader's attention by alternating chapters on Anarres, Shevek's home planet, and Urras, where he resides throughout much of the novel. Scenes from Anarres are recalled through flashback as Shevek, surrounded by an alien political and social system repugnant to much in his nature, reflects upon himself in relation to his culture. Anarres, founded by libertarian followers of Odo, a radical Urrasti thinker, is at once dedicated to individual freedom and the good of the whole. There is no formal government, only a system of individually initiated syndicates, a Division of Labor to keep track of job needs, and the Production Distribution Committee to oversee production loosely. On Anarres nothing is owned; everything is shared. Since everyone is equal, there is no discrimination, no exploitation; but there are stringent societal responsibilities which all Anarresti share. Because Anarres is virtually a desert, with plant life so scarce that no animals are indigenous, careful conservation, voluntary labor, and a sense of duty to the whole are required of everyone.

By contrast, Urras is wealthy, lush with water, teeming with life. Its capitalistic system, however, encourages exploitation because profit is the motivating force. As a result, Urras has an entrenched class system, with women and workers considered inferior to the intellectual and governing classes, and a power structure intent on maintaining control. While much of this authority is exerted by custom, some is imposed by force. Shevek, unaccustomed to any type of exploitation, violence, discrimination, or conspicuous waste, needs to experience fully the benefits and detriments of Urras before he can make necessary connections. Once he recognizes that the seeds of his freedom germinated in the rich soil of Urras, he can declare his brotherhood with the Urrasti and offer them what he can: a way to the only future he knows, that of Anarres. Speaking from deep within himself, Shevek tells Urrasti rebels "You must come to it alone, and naked, as the child comes into his future, without any past, without any property, wholly dependent on other people for his life. . . . You cannot make the Revolution. You can only be the Revolution."

Much of Le Guin's work has been categorized as simply children's literature, but her Earthsea series speaks to adults as well. *A Wizard of Earthsea*, the first of this series of epic fantasies, recounts the adventures of a young boy named Sparrowhawk and the young priestess named Arha whom he rescues. *The Tombs of Atuan* and *The Farthest Shore* follow their lives as they mature and develop their individual powers.

Ged is a natural-born wizard whose insensitive family does not realize Ged's innate gift. Ged becomes a sorcerer's apprentice to the mage Ogion but ultimately is forced to leave before completing his studies because he keeps casting spells before learning their complications. His inner conflicts are revealed through his struggle to find and to name what he believes to be a mysterious shadow pursuing him. Le Guin's essay "The Child and the Shadow" (in *The Language of the Night*) discusses her depiction of this archetypal Jungian "dark brother of the conscious mind."

Arha, Le Guin's main female character in the series, is as powerful as Ged in her own way. Yet, she, too, leaves her apprenticeship with Ogion before completing her training, though for a different reason. Ged is forced to leave; Arha chooses to leave for the fulfillment of married life.

Le Guin's understanding of identity and its relationship to naming is revealed in the theme that runs throughout the Earthsea series: To know the true name of someone gives power over him. Hence, characters have "use" names as well as real names. Real names are usually only told at the moment of death or to someone who is completely trusted.

In 1990, *Tehanu: The Last Book of Earthsea* was published, formally (or so Le Guin has said) bringing the adventures of Arha (now called Tenar) and Sparrowhawk (now called Ged) to an end. *Tehanu* is markedly different from the earlier books in the series, however, in that it is written for adults. Perhaps Le Guin wanted to aim it at the audience who had grown up reading her books and was now older and mature—like Tenar and Ged, no longer rash in their actions and fearless with the immortality of youth.

In *Tehanu*, the fourth book of Le Guin's Earthsea series, Tenar has been widowed and is using her Gontish name, Goha. She is called to assist in the treatment of a badly burned and sexually abused young girl, whom Tenar adopts and names Therru. A visit to the now-dying mage Ogion elicits the information that there is a powerful and dangerous presence in Therru. The dramatic return of Ged aboard the back of the dragon Kalessin, however, occupies Tenar's mind, as she must nurse him. He has lost the powers of archmagery and has returned to his former name, Sparrowhawk.

Tehanu is, like much of Le Guin's work, a careful compendium of names, spells, and physical transformations. (As a venture in world-making, *Tehanu* resembles *Always Coming Home*, a work intended primarily for adults. Purporting to write the history of several peoples in the distant future, *Always Coming Home* is accompanied by tape-recordings of poems and stories, and the text is supplemented by illustrations and glossaries of terms.) *Tehanu*, however, deals more directly with the dark themes of child molestation and abuse and death than do her earlier young-adult works.

The essence of Le Guin's novels is that she compels her characters to undergo a reductive process in order to discover their identity. In the end, her characters stand for no one, no concrete meaning; they simply are. Along the way, Le Guin demands that they learn the paradoxes inherent in life, the ambiguous nature of creation, and the interrelatedness of all that seems to be opposed. By offering her readers characters motivated by intellectual curiosity, humanism, and self-determination; a nonviolent, nonexploitative philosophy capable of encompassing the unknown; and complex cultures in relation to one another, Le Guin is far more than a science-fiction writer. She is a novelist whose contribution to American literature will be valued for generations to come.

Karen Carmean

Other major works

SHORT FICTION: *The Word for World Is Forest*, 1972; *The Wind's Twelve Quarters*, 1975; *Orsinian Tales*, 1976; *The Compass Rose*, 1982; *Buffalo Gals and Other Animal Presences*, 1987.

POETRY: *Wild Angels*, 1975; *Hard Words and Other Poems*, 1981; *In the Red Zone*, 1983; *Wild Oats and Fireweed: New Poems*, 1988.

CHILDREN'S LITERATURE: *The Visionary*, 1984; *Solomon Leviathan's 931st Trip Around the World*, 1988; *Fire and Stone*, 1989.

NONFICTION: *From Elfland to Poughkeepsie*, 1973; *The Language of the Night: Essays on Fantasy and Science Fiction*, 1979 (Susan Wood, editor); *Dancing at the Edge of the World: Thoughts on Words, Women, and Places*, 1988; *Napa: The Roots and Springs of the Valley*, 1989.

Bibliography

Bittner, James W. *Approaches to the Fiction of Ursula K. Le Guin*. Ann Arbor, Mich.: UMI Research Press, 1984. A revised version of Bittner's 1979 doctoral thesis. Discusses the difference between Le Guin's fantasy and science-fiction writing, taking into account her work up to *Orsinian Tales*. Includes notes to chapters, primary and secondary bibliographies, and an index.

Bloom, Harold, ed. *Ursula K. Le Guin*. New York: Chelsea House, 1986. A compilation of eighteen essays by different authors on Le Guin's work. Also contains a brief biographical and publishing chronology, a general bibliography, and an index.

Bucknall, Barbara J. *Ursula K. Le Guin*. New York: Frederick Ungar, 1981. Contains information about both Le Guin's life and her literary output. Includes a useful detailed chronology up to 1980, notes, primary and secondary bibliographies, and an index.

Selinger, Bernard. *Le Guin and Identity in Contemporary Fiction.* Ann Arbor, Mich.: UMI Research Press, 1988. Covers the works missed by the earlier Bittner volume, *Approaches to the Fiction of Ursula K. Le Guin.* Discusses Le Guin's work as breaking the bounds of "realistic" fiction, placing her in the same category as Stanisław Lem, Italo Calvino, and John Barth. Annotated references, primary and secondary bibliographies, and an index are included.

Spivack, Charlotte. *Ursula K. Le Guin.* Boston: Twayne, 1984. Begins with a brief chronology of important personal and professional milestones in Le Guin's life up to 1981, and then examines her background and her literary contributions. Includes annotated references, primary and secondary bibliographies, and an index.

ROSAMOND LEHMANN

Born: Bourne End, England; February 3, 1901
Died: London, England; March 12, 1990

Principal long fiction

Dusty Answer, 1927; *A Note in Music*, 1930; *Invitation to the Waltz*, 1932; *The Weather in the Streets*, 1936; *The Ballad and the Source*, 1944; *The Echoing Grove*, 1953; *A Sea-Grape Tree*, 1976.

Other literary forms

Rosamond Lehmann's preferred art form was the novel, but in addition, she published a volume of short stories, *The Gipsy's Baby and Other Short Stories* (1946), and a play, *No More Music* (1939). Her autobiography, *The Swan in the Evening: Fragments of an Inner Life*, appeared in 1967, and a memoir, *Rosamond Lehmann's Album*, in 1985.

Achievements

Lehmann's first novel, *Dusty Answer*, appeared in 1927, when the author was twenty-six years old. The novel struck a responsive chord with the post–World War I generation, and Lehmann soon found herself famous. Her subsequent novels and other works found a considerable audience, especially in England, where her writing was highly regarded by the reading public as well as critics. In 1982, Lehmann was honored as a recipient of the Order of the British Empire. Those of her novels which had been out of print were republished by Virago Press.

Biography

Rosamond Nina Lehmann was born near London on February 3, 1901. On the same day, Queen Victoria was buried, a fact that would later strike Lehmann as having symbolic significance. She received her early education at home, partly through the use of the enormous library of her father, Rudolph Lehmann, an editor of *Punch* magazine. Her later education was at Girton College of Cambridge University.

An early marriage ended in divorce, attributable, Lehmann believed, to the upheaval arising from her sudden fame. A second marriage, to the Honorable Wogan Philipps, also ended in divorce; a long relationship with the poet C. Day-Lewis also ended unhappily. Lehmann's primary bonds were with family: her brother, poet-critic John Lehmann; her sister, actress Beatrix Lehmann; and her two children, Hugo and Sally. Sally's sudden death from polio in 1958 ended Lehmann's writing for some time; when she began to write again, her works reflected her new interest in what may imprecisely be called spiritualism. In her eighties, she served as vice president of the British

College of Psychic Studies, and she counseled other parents who had lost children. Lehmann died in London in 1990, at the age of eighty-nine.

Analysis

The great theme of Rosamond Lehmann's fiction is the evanescent quality of love in a world where love is the only thing worth having. This emphasis on love and on female characters has sometimes caused her to be considered a "woman's novelist," an evaluation which would have surprised her audience early in her career. To many of her contemporaries in the 1920's, Lehmann was part of the vanguard, a peer of Virginia Woolf, Dorothy Richardson, and May Sinclair, writers who chose female characters as the voices of a new fictional style which these women, along with James Joyce and others, were creating. This style is generally called "stream of consciousness," although the term is somewhat imprecise: Lehmann's style requires neither the intense, allusive language of Joyce nor the changing viewpoints of Woolf. Lehmann learned from her contemporaries to stay within the mind of one character and to show the sensibilities and sensitivities of that character.

Lehmann's first novel, *Dusty Answer*, is a fine achievement as a novel of consciousness, especially of the special consciousness of adolescence. The novelist stays within the mind of the young Judith Earle as she grows into early adulthood. Like other popular novels of the 1920's (Michael Arlen's *The Green Hat*, 1924, is a good example), the novel traces the character's development by her relationship with a person or group of people whom the central character views as somehow enchanted. That the enchanted ones are also destructive constitutes the fascination and also the growth experience for the central character.

Judith grows up in a wealthy home, in an isolation which creates her bookishness and romantic turn of mind. Her loneliness is broken occasionally by a family of five cousins who visit next door; Judith sees them as a closed unit, incredibly mysterious and desirable. Her fascination with them continues even when she goes off to Cambridge (Lehmann herself was at Girton College, Cambridge) and meets a fellow undergraduate, Jennifer Baird, to whom she is also drawn. The novel traces Judith's intense friendship with Jennifer and with each of the cousins. As the book ends, she has been separated from all of them by the differing courses of their maturity. She believes that enchantment is gone from the world and that she must now live in the cold light of reality.

Dusty Answer had an immediate and intense popularity. For some readers, it powerfully evoked their university days, and in this regard the book bears comparison with Evelyn Waugh's *Brideshead Revisited: The Sacred and Profane Memories of Captain Charles Ryder* (1945, 1960), which is set at Oxford in the same time period, the early 1920's. A reader desiring a portrait of those days could do no better than to read these two novels. A second reason for the novel's popularity is its relative frankness with regard to sexual attitudes; Lehmann shows her heroine eager to "give herself" to the man she loves. Homoerotic relationships also abound. Although there are no explicit sexual scenes, the novel was considered shocking by many critics. Some of her contemporaries thought that *Dusty Answer* was a flash in the pan which would both begin and end Lehmann's career. On the contrary, as she continued to write, maturity deepened her powers of observation.

Lehmann's third novel, *Invitation to the Waltz*, shows her mastery of atmosphere in a novel. The main character is Olivia Curtis, an adolescent on the verge of adulthood, and it is primarily through her that Lehmann conveys a wonderful atmosphere of expectation, anticipation. The story opens on the morning of Olivia's seventeenth birthday. Her upper-middle-class home in the snug village of Little Compton is carefully described. A gentle air of mystery, however, is developed: "Something is going on. The kettle's boiling, the cloth is spread, the windows are flung open. Come in, come in! Here dwells the familiar mystery. Come and find it! Each room is active, fecund, brimming over with it." The invitation to the reader is explicit: Enter this novel, this home, to watch the dance of life. What one finds is both common and marvelous—common in the easy familiarity and give-and-take of family life and marvelous in the recurring mystery of girl growing to young woman. That Lehmann can have it both ways, in both its common and its marvelous aspects, testifies to her growth as a novelist.

An invitation necessarily inculcates expectation. At the opening of the novel, the invitation to the Spencers' dance, one week hence, has already been extended. Even as she lies in bed, reveling in its delicious warmth and in the slow, pleasant moments before the hectic day must begin in earnest, Olivia anticipates the dance. Indeed, thoughts about the dance subsume Olivia's anticipation of a more immediate event, breakfast with the family—the presents to be opened and the good wishes to be received. That the prized gift of the day turns out to be some flame-colored fabric for a new dress to wear to the Spencers' dance indicates something of Lehmann's skill in developing a sense of expectation in ever-expanding circles of anticipation. Mundane events of plot resonate with increasingly meaningful, open-ended implications, all circumferences being blurred in the subjective consciousness, the magical visionary world, of an innocent, naïve, alert, and sensitive seventeen-year-old.

After the early-morning anticipation of the birthday breakfast, the plot points to the big dance, a week away. The dress is to be readied. An escort is to be speculated on. On the night itself, Olivia and her sister Kate are to prepare themselves carefully—with long baths and manicures and attentive dressing of hair. Kate, the older sister who is at once rival and best friend, does much better in the business of appearance than Olivia, but having turned Olivia's dress around and suggested how to fashion her hair, she and

Olivia are finally ready for the dance. Part 2 of the novel explains the day's preparation for the dance, while part 3 focuses on the dance itself. Thus, the structure of the novel supports the atmosphere of anticipation.

If this were all there were to it, however, part 3 of the novel would be something of a disappointment to the reader, as it surely seems to be at times for Olivia. Reggie Kershaw, the man Olivia and Kate have invited to escort them, first asks Marigold Spencer for a dance. Olivia's dance program gradually fills, but her predominant emotion is gratitude that she will not be humiliated by being a wallflower rather than excitement over the young men with whom she will be dancing. She feels clumsy and awkward when she finally dances with Reggie; she feels intellectually inferior and unstylish with Peter Jenkin; she feels very much out of her social class with George; she feels crude and unsophisticated with Podge; and so the evening goes. She feels surprise, shock, pity, sorrow, resentment, and even repulsion at her various partners through the evening. Yet there are minor triumphs, too. When dashing Rollo Spencer returns from walking the dogs, he invites her into his father's library, where Olivia meets Sir John Spencer himself. As Olivia leaves the library, she is overwhelmed with good feeling and a sense of accomplishment: Far "from being outcast, flung beyond the furthest rim, she had penetrated suddenly to the innermost core of the house, to be in their home." At the end of the evening, sitting in the armchair, waiting for the last dancers to finish and for Kate and Reggie to appear, she reflects on the evening: "Nothing for myself really," yet "to have come to the place of not caring was very soothing, very peaceful." She anticipates "with longing . . . her dark bedroom, her bed waiting for her at home."

The power of the novel lies in the wider implications of Olivia's anticipations, for the events of the story are only the pretext for the grand anticipation of Olivia's life, the fulfillment of which the reader is left to imagine. Early in the novel, Olivia had looked at herself in the mirror, wondering if this would be one of those days when the mirror reflected back not what was familiar, but a new Olivia, a new self, a different person, a beginning life. Throughout the novel, the people whom Olivia meets and the episodes she experiences resonate as options for Olivia in her adult life. Will she become bitter and poor, like the spinster dressmaker Miss Robinson? Will scandal rob her of simple companionship and neighborly friendship, as it did Major Skinner? Will she be a victim of calculated pathos, as she is with the lace maker, who takes advantage of her pity so that she wastes the ten shillings given to her by Uncle Oswald for her birthday? Will her life be reduced to a tragedy of isolation, restriction, and emptiness, as is the life of blind Timmy Douglas, married to a former nurse in an arrangement of convenience rather than of passion?

As one anticipates Olivia's adult life, one realizes that not all options are equally available to her. The Spencers represent an aristocratic life-style that is clearly beyond the Curtises. Marigold and Rollo live in a world made brilliant and dashing by their parents' social status; theirs is a self-confidence that comes from solid and long-standing foundation in the bedrock of social place. Kate, too, may represent an option that proves not to be viable for Olivia, for Kate, during the course of the evening, becomes separated from Olivia, each sister following her individual pathway to the future. Kate falls in love with Tony Heriot and secretly makes plans to meet him in Paris; they share a vision to which Olivia is not party.

At the end of the novel, though, Olivia, too, has a vision. Running out beyond the garden, recognizing that every woman makes the trip to adulthood by herself, Olivia feels a sense of new beginning. Her future, in the image of a winged gigantic runner, hastens toward her from a great distance: "On it came, over ploughed field and fallow. The rooks flashed sharply, the hare and his shadow swerved in sudden sunlight. In a moment it would be everywhere. Here it was. She ran into it." The future is now. The girl is a young woman with a full life ahead. The dance of life is now beginning.

With good reason, Lehmann's fifth novel, *The Ballad and the Source*, is widely considered her best. It has an evocative power and strength of characterization that linger long after the book has been read. Furthermore, the narrative technique is at once complex and suggestive: Rebecca Landon tells the tale of a period during her childhood, between the ages of ten and fifteen, the years 1912 to 1917, when she first came to know a neighbor, Mrs. Jardine, and Mrs. Jardine's grandchildren. As she recalls the long afternoons at tea with Mrs. Jardine and the conversations with Maisie, the grandchild with whom she developed the closest of friendships, she seems at times to be reliving the experience, to return again to those childhood days of innocence threatened only sporadically by glimpses into the adult world of evil. Occasionally, the adult consciousness reflects on the limitations of the child's awareness and the reader is reminded of the retrospective perspective, but the child's consciousness prevails, and the movement between today's adult and yesterday's child is blurred and inconsistent.

This is not to say that the shifting consciousness is a flaw in the novel. Indeed, it is one of the novel's triumphs, for like other of Lehmann's novels, *The Ballad and the Source* creates a highly subjective consciousness that colors what it encounters. Rebecca is a sensitive, romantic child, strongly attracted to the unusual situation and the magnetic personality of the suspect Mrs. Jardine. The novel presents Rebecca's attempt to solve the puzzle that is Mrs. Jardine. In rehearsing those preadolescent years, Rebecca is even now trying to reach some resolution, some recognition that ever eludes her. The novel gains in immediacy because one is not presented with the adult's conclusions but learns the pieces of information as the child did many years ago, and one can follow her engaged understanding through the maze of hints and innuendos, biased accounts and tortured confessions, shadings and concealments to which she is subject.

The amazing thing about this novel is that Rebecca is not ultimately the main character, even though her consciousness and experience govern the reader's access to information. She is an observer of the developments in the Jardine/Thomson family and a receiver of information about their past, not an involved participant in the ongoing drama of their lives. What Rebecca says or does or thinks relative to the Jardines and Thomsons is ultimately of little importance. Sibyl Anstey Herbert Jardine is really the main character, the source, and the subject of all the ballads. It is her strong personality that so attracts the love of Rebecca and the hatred of her granddaughter Maisie.

The novel is a detective story of sorts, including all the material of high drama—adultery, abandoned children, runaway wives, insanity, lifelong hatred, empty and wasted lives, early death, kidnaping, jealousy, secrecy, plots, shifting conspiracies, and passion, as well as loyalty, dedication to truth, independence, and love. Young Rebecca has led far too sheltered a life to be able to take in what she hears, but the reader is not hindered by Rebecca's limitations. That the reader has greater understanding than does the narrator of the story is possible through Lehmann's strategy of allowing several different people to reveal what they know. Rebecca learns something about Mrs. Jardine first from Mrs. Jardine herself. In fact, Mrs. Jardine at times actually confides in Rebecca, using her as the "listener" she always needs. It is largely because Rebecca is so fascinated by Mrs. Jardine that she has difficulty accepting some of the other accounts she subsequently hears. Rebecca recognizes good qualities in Mrs. Jardine—a strong maternal instinct, a fondness for children, courage, loyalty, and strength. These are not the traits about Mrs. Jardine that most impress other people.

Tilly, for example, the poor, elderly seamstress who makes a yearly visit to the Landon family to do necessary work and who formerly was employed by Rebecca's grandmother, certainly does not share Rebecca's fondness for the woman. When Rebecca discovers that Tilly knew Mrs. Jardine years ago, she pumps her to tell her story of Mrs. Jardine's life. Part 2 of the novel is a long narration by Tilly, interrupted by prompts and questions from Rebecca. To Tilly, Mrs. Jardine is an evil woman who violated her friendship with Rebecca's grandmother by asking her to assist her in deceiving her former husband, Charles Herbert, in order to gain access to their daughter, Ianthe. Despite her loyalties toward her grandmother, Rebecca still sides with the cause of the mother deprived of her only child. When Sibyl Anstey Herbert (later Mrs. Jardine) left her husband, she had never intended to leave the child Ianthe behind as well, but Charles Herbert insisted on total estrangement between Ianthe and her mother, an estrangement Sibyl was never able to overcome, despite a life dedicated to winning Ianthe back.

Part 3 is a long conversation between Mrs. Jardine and Rebecca, during which Rebecca learns much about the life of Ianthe. In veiled suggestions of incest that Rebecca cannot quite grasp, Mrs. Jardine tells of the "sick" relationship between Charles Herbert and his daughter, when they are everything to each other. After his death, Ianthe moves in with a Mr. and Mrs. Connor. Again, there are suggestions in the narrative of illicit sex and corruption that young Rebecca does not understand; an adult world is being opened up to a child. Mrs. Jardine, aware that her daughter is involved in a scandalous situation but still unable to approach her directly, sends a male relative to Ianthe, and they run away together. Later, Mrs. Jardine admits that sending this young man was a mistake. Ianthe conceives a child and goes to Bohemia with Tilly to bear it. The long-standing enmity between Tilly and Mrs. Jardine stems from Tilly's refusal even at this point to allow Mrs. Jardine access to her daughter.

The story covers three generations, and the sins of the one are visited upon the next. As Sibyl left her child, so Ianthe, having married Thomson, leaves him and ultimately must abandon her children, Maisie, Malcolm, and Cherry, Mrs. Jardine's three grandchildren who became friends with Rebecca and Rebecca's sister Jess. Their father, Mr. Thomson, develops an intense hatred of both Ianthe and her mother, Mrs. Jardine—Ianthe for leaving him and Mrs. Jardine for having ruined Ianthe. As another husband with custody of children, he refuses to allow any contact between his children and either their mother or grandmother. Maisie tells Rebecca that her mother Ianthe is beautiful and that she loves the children very much, although she cannot be with them. It is Mrs. Jardine who tells Rebecca that Ianthe never cared for the children. As with every aspect of this complicated web of right and wrong, love and hate, Rebecca receives different and sometimes flatly contradictory information. Despite Mr. Thomson's hatred for Mrs. Jardine, he allows the children to live with her when he becomes too ill to care for them himself. Finally, upon his death, Mrs. Jardine recovers what had always eluded her with Ianthe; she gains custody of her grandchildren.

The influence of Henry James is sometimes noted in connection with this novel, and surely no more so than in the almost demonic passion with which Mrs. Jardine seeks to gain possession of the soul first of her own child, Ianthe, and then, when that fails, of her grandchildren. Jamesian, too, is the immature consciousness accosted with hints and suggestions, indirectness and obscurity, contradiction and variety. The quest for truth is not an easy one. The success of this novel depends in large measure on the reader's willingness to bear the burden of judgment and opinion, to make his or her own distillation of the facts and arrive at truth, and then to make a moral judgment if such is deemed necessary, for Lehmann does not make the moral judgment for the reader. Indeed, the need for the rights of women and their freedom from the bondage of marriage comes across strongly, especially from the mouth of Mrs. Jardine. Yet the novel unremittingly insists, too, that the consequences of such freedom are devastating and evil. Rebecca is drawn to this saga because she, too, is one of those intelligent, sensitive, strong women who may find social restrictions too binding to tolerate. An awareness of the plight of such women and a recognition of the confused and incremental way in which one learns truth are the main accomplishments of Lehmann's fifth novel.

Creating and interweaving the experiences and attitudes of both Rebecca and Mrs. Jardine, *The Ballad and the Source* attains a power that is unique in Lehmann's fiction. Her other novels are likelier to be regarded as "period pieces." Such a label does not discount the value of her work: Lehmann had the gift, shared by many other minor writers, of being able to populate a time and place—her own closely observed day, whether the 1920's or 1950's. Reading her novels, one senses instinctively that she has "gotten it right," shown the university, the seaside villa, the run-down flat, all as they must have been. The inhabitants of those locales have life in her fiction. To create such portraits is no small feat. Lehmann's work may lack the resonance and depth of that of some of her more famous contemporaries, but she contributed significantly to the British novel: All of her novels represent some experiments with the representation of consciousness, they add to the tradition of realism, and several give powerful portrayals of the anxieties of youth and love.

Deborah Core
Paula Kopacz

Other major works

SHORT FICTION: *The Gipsy's Baby and Other Short Stories*, 1946.
PLAY: *No More Music*, 1939.
NONFICTION: *The Swan in the Evening: Fragments of an Inner Life*, 1967 (autobiography); *Letters from Our Daughters*, 1972 (with C. H. Sandys); *Rosamond Lehmann's Album*, 1985.

Bibliography

Lehmann, John. *In My Own Time*. Boston: Little, Brown, 1969. Probably the most important source of information on Rosamond Lehmann's life, consisting of the three volumes of her brother's memoirs published separately in earlier editions during the 1960's. The description of Rosamond's childhood is especially revealing. Lehmann includes accounts of his sister's numerous friendships, ranging from Bernard Berenson to Guy Burgess.

Le Stourgeon, Diana E. *Rosamond Lehmann*. New York: Twayne, 1969. A standard brief survey of Lehmann's work, handicapped because it appeared before her brother's memoirs. Notes her concentration on female characters; males are relegated to minor positions. Conflicts among different generations of women often figure at the center of Lehmann's novels, which are reviewed in detail. Includes a bibliography of criticism of Lehmann with skimpy annotations.

McCormick, John. *Catastrophe and Imagination*. London: Longmans, 1957. Argues that Lehmann is a "cognitive novelist," a writer who goes beyond emotion to present a thesis about the nature of life. For Lehmann, technique is secondary; what counts most is the presentation of her ideas. Nevertheless, she was very skilled in her use of words.

Markovic, Vida E. *The Changing Face: Disintegration of Personality in the Twentieth-Century British Novel, 1900-1950*. Carbondale: Southern Illinois University Press, 1970. Important for its analysis of the theme of illusion and reality in *The Ballad and the Source*. The main character in the novel, Mrs. Jardine, acts as if it is praiseworthy to maintain appearances and conceal the real nature of one's life, a view that Lehmann wishes to prove false. The relation between truth and appearance is of vital significance in her work.

Tindall, Gillian. *Rosamond Lehmann: An Appreciation*. London: Chatto & Windus, 1985. The most comprehensive critical study. Behind the surface readability of her novels, Lehmann is a "deep writer" who writes frequently of death, trying to puzzle out its meaning. Abortion and the death of the very young, in particular, figure often in her novels, as does rivalry between children and parents and relations between sisters. Discusses each of the novels, and many of the short stories, in elaborate detail. Contains no footnotes or index.

ELMORE LEONARD

Born: New Orleans, Louisiana; October 11, 1925

Principal long fiction

The Bounty Hunters, 1953; *The Law at Randado*, 1954; *Escape from Five Shadows*, 1956; *Last Stand at Saber River*, 1959 (also known as *Lawless River* and *Stand on the Saber*); *Hombre*, 1961; *The Big Bounce*, 1969; *The Moonshine War*, 1969; *Valdez Is Coming*, 1970; *Forty Lashes Less One*, 1972; *Mr. Majestyk*, 1974; *Fifty-two Pickup*, 1974; *Swag*, 1976 (also known as *Ryan's Rules*); *The Hunted*, 1977; *Unknown Man No. 89*, 1977; *The Switch*, 1978; *Gunsights*, 1979; *City Primeval: High Noon in Detroit*, 1980; *Gold Coast*, 1980; *Split Images*, 1981; *Cat Chaser*, 1982; *Stick*, 1983; *LaBrava*, 1983; *Glitz*, 1985; *Bandits*, 1987; *Touch*, 1987; *Freaky Deaky*, 1988; *Killshot*, 1989; *Get Shorty*, 1990.

Other literary forms

Elmore Leonard has published numerous Western short stories as well as several magazine articles on crime writing and police procedure. More significantly, he has had considerable experience as a writer of screenplays, both originals and adaptations.

Achievements

Leonard has come to be widely regarded as the best crime-fiction writer in the world. He has been ranked with Dashiell Hammett and Raymond Chandler as a writer who transcends the limitations of category fiction. He has made hard-boiled crime fiction "respectable" and has influenced writers all over the world with his contributions to storytelling technique. In 1984 his novel *LaBrava* won the Edgar Allan Poe Award from Mystery Writers of America as the best mystery novel of the year.

Biography

Elmore Leonard was born in Louisiana but grew up in Detroit, Michigan, a city that forms the background for many of his crime novels. He served in the U.S. Navy during World War II and attended the University of Detroit on the GI Bill. After graduation in 1950, he went to work for a Detroit advertising agency. His growing family made it difficult for him to pursue his ambition to become a free-lance writer, but he began writing Western short stories between five and seven o'clock each morning before going to work. By 1953, he had established a reputation as a writer of Westerns. In 1965, Twentieth Century-Fox purchased the film rights to his novel *Hombre* for ten thousand dollars, and at last Leonard felt free to devote his full time to creative writing.

The market for Westerns was drying up, however, because the genre had been overly exploited by television. Leonard, in characteristically pragmatic fashion, switched to writing crime fiction. This was the turning point in his career, for he had never felt entirely at home with Westerns. He developed his unique technique of fiction writing and has been perfecting it ever since.

In 1974, after twenty years of heavy drinking, he joined Alcoholics Anonymous; in 1977 he was divorced from his first wife. He now lives quietly in Birmingham, on the outskirts of Detroit, with his second wife and writes from 9:30 to 6:00 almost every day. After thirty years of hard work, he finally began receiving widespread critical praise. He has been aptly described as "the best American writer of crime fiction alive, possibly the best we've ever had."

Analysis

Elmore Leonard's early short stories and novels were conventional in terms of plot and characterization; however, writing Westerns was good training. Knowing nothing about the West, he learned to depend on research that he could embellish with his vivid imagination; this is essentially the method he has employed throughout his writing career. Furthermore, when he switched to crime fiction, he brought some of his hair-trigger, saloon-wrecking cowboy villains into urban settings with startling effects. Examples of these "redneck monsters" are Raymond Gidre in *Unknown Man No. 89*, Clement Mansell in *City Primeval*, Roland Crowe in *Gold Coast*, and Richard Nobles in *LaBrava*. Another type of displaced Western character is Armand Degas in *Killshot*, a half-breed Indian turned Mafia hit-man.

Placing cowboys and Indians in modern cities such as Miami and Detroit is only one of the many types of contrast Leonard employs to produce effects. In his crime novels the most violent incidents occur in the most peaceful settings, such as family restaurants, supermarkets, and real estate offices, and the worst villainy is often directed against people whose lives had previously been conventional and uneventful. In *Killshot*, a working-class couple suddenly find themselves having their front windows blown out with shotgun blasts; the story ends with a double murder in the cozy breakfast nook of their model kitchen.

In 1959, there were thirty prime-time Western series on television. The public was bound to become surfeited with saloon brawls and shootouts on Main Street. It was not until this sixgun-overkill forced Leonard to turn to crime fiction that he began to develop the distinctive approach to storytelling that has brought him fame and fortune. That approach has been influenced by his own involvement in filmmaking, which has one cardinal rule for writers: "Don't tell us: *show* us."

Hollywood has long exerted a push-pull effect on fiction writers. The cinematic manner of telling stories through action and dialogue has had an incalculable influence on the conscious and unconscious minds of all creative writers, and the big money to be made from sales of motion-picture rights has been an often irresistible temptation to structure novels so that adaptation from print to film would present no problems. Leonard has been involved with filmmaking for more than three decades. The three things that distinguish his crime novels are the three things found in all good films: strong characterization, believable dialogue, and interesting visual effects.

The publication of his crime novel *Fifty-two Pickup* in 1974 was the turning point in his career. He says, "I started to realize that the way to describe anywhere, *anywhere*, was to do it from someone's point of view . . . and *leave me out of it*." Perhaps not entirely coincidentally, 1974 was also the year he separated from his first wife and began attending Alcoholics Anonymous meetings. In describing his recovery from alcoholism, he has also said: "The key is getting out of yourself." Prior to *Fifty-two Pickup*, Leonard had written his fiction in a conventional manner—that is, mostly in the "voice" of an anonymous narrator who sets the scenes, describes his characters' appearance and behavior, and quotes their verbal interchanges. This objective technique was perfected by Ernest Hemingway, whose Spanish Civil War novel *For Whom the Bell Tolls* (1940) had a permanent effect on Leonard's approach to fiction writing. Leonard has gone beyond Hemingway: he is trying as much as possible to vanish as a narrator and to let his stories be told by the characters themselves. He describes what his viewpoint characters see and hear as well as what they think and feel in language appropriate to each character, so that most of his narration and description reads like dialogue without the quotes.

It would be inaccurate to call this technique "stream of consciousness" or "interior monologue": it is a modification that Leonard has described as his unique "sound." There are no long passages in italics, no stream-of-consciousness ramblings. Nor are there "pebbles in the pond" or other old-fashioned flashback conventions. Since Leonard generally has the reader inside a character's mind, it is easy to move back and forth in time, as he frequently does. The character simply remembers an earlier event, and the reader is instantly transported back in time.

Changing from past to present is simply another of Leonard's ways of deliberately keeping the reader off balance. The one consistent feature of a Leonard novel is that nothing ever stays the same. He imitates modern American films, which create the effect of being in continuous motion with changing camera angles, jump cuts, intercuts, tracking shots, aerial shots, flashbacks, and all the other tricks of the trade. His practice of constantly shifting viewpoints is analogous to modern filmmaking, in which scenes are shot simultaneously by several cameras and strips of film are spliced together to provide visual variety as well as to highlight whatever the director considers most important.

Typically, Leonard will change points of view from chapter to chapter;

however, he can do it within chapters as well, and do it with an effortlessness that makes lesser writers envious. The average category fiction writer will describe his characters only once, when they first appear, and then rely largely on peculiarities of dialogue to differentiate them from one another for the rest of the book. A standard practice of commercial fiction writers is to give each character some "shtick"—a cane, a monocle, a pipe, a stammer, a foreign accent—to help the reader remember him or her; still, in many category novels the characters become a hopeless jumble in the reader's mind.

The reader's interest in a novel depends on the credibility of its characters. Shootings, bombings, and other forms of violence are not effective unless the reader can believe that they are happening to real people. In describing each character's appearance and actions through the eyes of another character, Leonard not only eliminates the need for the "intrusive author" but also characterizes both individuals at once. From beginning to end, he never stops characterizing. He also achieves a strong sense that his characters are actually interrelating, because each is seen in turn through the eyes of someone else. That is why Leonard's writing is so much more effective than most category fiction and why he has transcended his genre.

In *Fifty-two Pickup*, Leonard was only partially successful in telling his story through the viewpoints of his characters. The "good guys," a middle-class husband and wife who are being victimized by blackmailers, come alive; however, the "bad guys" are two-dimensional characters exuding the all-too-familiar blend of sadism, cynical humor, and innuendo. Leonard knew that he needed to humanize his villains in order to give his novels balance. In his next novel, *Swag*, he tells the story from the points of view of the "bad guys," two likable young men who take up armed robbery for fun and profit.

Swag may be the best novel Leonard has written, although it is far from being his best known. Held in the robbers' viewpoints like a fly in amber, the reader is helplessly but deliciously dragged into one holdup after another and lives out his own secret fantasies about walking into a store with a big Colt .45 automatic and walking out with a bag of cash. The reader experiences all the dangers of the profession and ponders all the intangibles: "What if the clerk dives for a gun?" "What if a customer starts screaming?" "What if an alarm goes off?" "What if a cop drives up?" Here, to quote horror-writer Stephen King, is "the kind of book that if you get up to see if there are any chocolate chip cookies left, you take it with you so you won't miss anything."

This kind of story has drawbacks. For one thing, the reader is willing to identify with the "bad guys" only as long as they refrain from killing innocent people. Also, stories such as this one usually end with the protagonists being shot or sent to prison—as in the films *Bonnie and Clyde* (1967) and *Butch Cassidy and the Sundance Kid* (1969). In *Swag*, the antiheroes inevitably become overconfident and walk into disaster. Finally, the viewpoint characters in *Swag* seem less like real criminals than like middle-class young men who are playing at being criminals. Such a "Robin Hood" plot might serve for a single novel but could not be extended to a career technique. Leonard realized that he needed to learn more about the criminal mentality.

In 1978, Leonard spent two and a half months haunting police headquarters in downtown Detroit, soaking up the atmosphere and listening to the way detectives, criminals, lawyers, and witnesses really talked. He also established contacts with working detectives, contacts that have continued to prove useful to him. His later novels show a much better balance between protagonists and antagonists.

Leonard's highly successful *Freaky Deaky* is an example of his mature technique. A detective who specializes in bomb disposal is pitted against a beautiful but treacherous former convict plotting to extort a fortune from a pair of multimillionaire brothers, whom she suspects of informing on her back in the 1960's when they were antiwar activists together. The chapters alternate between the mind of the detective and that of the female extortionist, until all the principals are brought together at the end. The reader sees the world through the bomber's jaundiced eyes and sympathizes with her; however, the reader also sees the world through the detective's eyes and sympathizes with him a bit more. Leonard has become expert at manipulating the sympathies of his reader, which enables him to create more realistic characters. Like people in the real world, the characters in his best novels are not all good or all bad, but mixtures of both.

Leonard follows the same blueprint in *Killshot*. The main villain, a halfbreed Indian, is a cold-blooded professional killer; however, the reader achieves a strong identification with and even affection for this lonely, unhappy individual, because the reader spends so much time in the killer's point of view. Leonard seems to understand the criminal mentality so well that many people have labored under the erroneous impression that he must have an unsavory past. Whereas he once had trouble making his villains seem credible, his problem later in his career has been making his law-abiding characters seem equally credible. In his next novel, *Get Shorty*, he did away with "good guys" altogether.

In *Get Shorty*, for the first time in his career, Leonard sets a novel in Hollywood, California. Here he reaps a rich harvest from his many years of experience as an author of original scripts, adaptations of other authors' novels, and adaptations of his own novels, and as an author of works that have been adapted by others. Among all of his novels, *Get Shorty* most clearly reveals his intention of making his fiction read like motion pictures. He even incorporates some pages of a screenplay that his sleazy characters are trying to peddle. Some of his Hollywood characters are so hopelessly immersed in the fantasy world of filmmaking that they see everyone as an actor and every event as a sequence of medium shots, closeups, and other types of camera shots with varied lighting effects—even when that other character might be coming to shoot them or throw them off a cliff. Leonard is suggesting that Americans are so brainwashed by films and television images that it is becoming impossible to distinguish between fantasy and reality.

Like pop artist Andy Warhol, Elmore Leonard does not merely flirt with commercialism: he dives headfirst into the deep end and turns "schlock" into art. He shows that the line between category fiction and the highbrow commodity called "mainstream" or "serious" fiction is like some imaginary barrier created by a hypnotist. His mature technique offers fascinating tools for novelists to play with and is sure to be widely imitated. In fact, it makes the old-style third-person narrative with straight dialogue seem ossified. Reading the latest Leonard novel is like watching an exciting film—which is exactly what he has been aiming at all along. It is the fruition of his long association with Hollywood and the consummation of the illicit romance that has been going on between the amoral but enticing young film genre and the aristocratic but impecunious old novel genre ever since motion pictures were old enough to talk.

Bill Delaney

Other major works

SCREENPLAYS: *The Moonshine War*, 1970; *Joe Kidd*, 1972; *Mr. Majestyk*, 1974; *High Noon Part 2: The Return of Will Kane*, 1980; *Stick*, 1985; *Fifty-two Pickup*, 1986; *The Rosary Murders*, 1987; *Desperado*, 1987.

Bibliography

Geherin, David. *Elmore Leonard*. New York: Continuum, 1989. The first book-length study of Leonard, this volume provides a brief biography and then a critical evaluation of Leonard's works, beginning with his early Western short stories and concluding with more detailed discussions of his novels of the 1980's. Also includes a chronology, notes, a selected bibliography, and an index.

Most, Glenn. "Elmore Leonard: Splitting Images." *Western Humanities Review* 41 (Spring, 1987): 78-86. This in-depth scholarly analysis of *Split Images* suggests some of the hidden psychological and sociological implications of Leonard's apparently simple writing. It also exemplifies the serious critical attention that Leonard's work has begun to receive.

Sutter, Gregg. "Advance Man: Researching Elmore Leonard's Novels, Part 2." *The Armchair Detective* 19 (Spring, 1986): 160-172. This continuation of Sutter's article (see above) completes the picture of Leonard as an unusually painstaking and conscientious writer of category fiction. It is especially interesting to see how factual details are transformed and integrated by Leonard's creative imagination.

_____. "Getting It Right: Researching Elmore Leonard's Novels, Part 1." *The Armchair Detective* 19 (Winter, 1986): 4-19. Sutter became Leonard's research assistant in 1981 and has worked closely with him ever since. He offers a wealth of information about Leonard's novels since 1981 as well as a description of Leonard's approach to fiction writing, which relies heavily on research, interviews, and direct observation.

Wholey, Dennis, ed. "Elmore Leonard." In *The Courage to Change: Personal Conversations About Alcohol with Dennis Wholey*. New York: Warner Books, 1986. This interview provides the best available information about Elmore Leonard as a human being. He describes his growing problem with alcohol over two decades and the psychological insights that enabled him to stop drinking. Leonard's hard-won victory over alcoholism has had an important influence on his writing technique and choice of subjects.

Yagoda, Ben. "Elmore Leonard's Rogues' Gallery." *The New York Times Magazine*, December 30, 1984, 20-29. An excellent profile piece based on interviews with Leonard, full of revealing, often amusing direct quotations. A good source of information about Leonard's personal life and his philosophy, writing habits, and business dealings with book publishers and film producers.

DORIS LESSING

Born: Kermanshah, Persia; October 22, 1919

Principal long fiction

The Grass Is Singing, 1950; *Martha Quest*, 1952; *A Proper Marriage*, 1954; *Retreat to Innocence*, 1956; *A Ripple from the Storm*, 1958; *The Golden Notebook*, 1962; *Landlocked*, 1965; *The Four-Gated City*, 1969; *Briefing for a Descent into Hell*, 1971; *The Summer Before the Dark*, 1973; *The Memoirs of a Survivor*, 1974; *Shikasta*, 1979; *The Marriages Between Zones Three, Four, and Five*, 1980; *The Sirian Experiments*, 1981; *The Making of the Representative for Planet 8*, 1982; *Documents Relating to the Sentimental Agents in the Volyen Empire*, 1983; *The Diary of a Good Neighbour*, 1983 (as Jane Somers); *If the Old Could . . .* , 1984 (as Jane Somers); *The Diaries of Jane Somers*, 1984 (includes *The Diary of a Good Neighbour* and *If the Old Could . . .*); *The Good Terrorist*, 1985; *The Fifth Child*, 1988.

Other literary forms

Doris Lessing has published numerous volumes of short stories. She has also written memoirs, documentaries, essays, plays, reviews, and a book of poems.

Achievements

Lessing has been one of the most widely read and influential British novelists of the second half of the twentieth century. Her works have been translated into many languages and have inspired critical attention around the globe. Generally serious and didactic, Lessing's fiction repeatedly urges the human race to develop a wider consciousness that would allow for greater harmony and less violence. Although known particularly as a master of realism, Lessing is often experimental or deliberately fantastic, as shown in her science-fiction novels. Her interests are far-ranging, from Marxism and global politics to the mystical teachings of Sufism to the small personal voice of the individual. Her awards include the Somerset Maugham Award, the German Shakespeare Prize, the Austrian Prize for European Literature, and the French Prix Médicis for Foreigners.

Biography

Doris May Lessing was born in Kermanshah, Persia (later Iran), in 1919, the first child of Alfred Cook Tayler and Emily Maude McVeagh Tayler, who had emigrated from England to Persia shortly after World War I. A brother, Harry, was born two years later, and in 1925 the family moved to a farm in Southern Rhodesia (later Zimbabwe). Her parents were never financially successful. Her father was a dreamer who became a cynic; her mother was domineering but ineffective. Despite Lessing's love of the African landscape and the isolated veld, she was eager to leave her family behind. She attended a Catholic convent school in Salisbury (now Harare) but left when she was fourteen, saying that she had eye problems, though she continued her voracious reading.

In 1938 Lessing moved to Salisbury to work in various jobs, mostly clerical, and began writing fiction. She was married to Frank Charles Wisdom, a minor civil servant, in 1939, and had a son, John, and a daughter, Jean. Divorced in 1943, she was remarried two years later to a German-Jewish refugee, Gottfried Lessing. They had a son, Peter, in 1947. She divorced Gottfried Lessing in 1949 and that same year moved to England, settling in London; in 1950 she published her first novel. Since then she has continued to live in London and to make her living as a professional writer, writing reviews, media scripts, and nonfiction in addition to her novels, short stories, drama, and poetry.

Lessing's interest in politics began with a Marxist group in Rhodesia, and in England she was briefly a member of the Communist Party, leaving it officially in 1956. In the late 1950's she participated in mass demonstrations for nuclear disarmament and was a speaker at the first Aldermaston March in 1958. During the early 1960's she worked in the theater, helping to establish Centre 42, a populist art program, and writing her own plays. In the late 1960's Lessing's thinking began to be heavily influenced by the mystical teachings of Indries Shah and Sufism, which emphasizes conscious evolution of the mind in harmony with self and others. Although for many years Lessing resisted the role of public persona, since the mid-1980's she has made numerous public appearances in many countries.

Analysis

Doris Lessing is a powerful writer committed to the lofty goal of changing human consciousness itself. The narrative voice that weaves throughout her prolific fiction is that of an intense thinker who observes, explores, and describes the contemporary world but whose ultimate sense of human life is that the individual, and indeed the human race, is meant to go beyond mere recognition of perceived reality and to struggle with visions of the possible. Her novels repeatedly suggest that changes in the way humans view themselves, their world, and their relationships with others are imperative if life on this planet is to survive.

Lessing's scope is wide. Her creative imagination is able to provide a close analysis of a character—with all that individual's fears, longings, and contradictions—and to relate that individual not only to his or her circle of acquaintances but to patterns of global economics and politics as well, and then to sweep beyond even this planet to the cosmos and a perspective that encompasses the metaphysical questions of existence. Her fictional explorations are multiple, multidimensional, and overlapping, suggesting that no one viewpoint is adequate or complete. This range is also reflected in her varied narrative forms, which include realism, naturalism, science fiction, utopian and dystopian, fantasy, fable, transcultural postmodernism, and experimental combinations of these. This heterogeneity of themes, techniques, and perspectives illustrates Lessing's overriding premise that truth and substance cannot easily be compartmentalized or assigned fixed labels: existence is always process, always in flux.

Lessing's position as an exile is a prominent aspect of her work, both in content and in theme. Born in the Middle East of English parents, she spent her adolescence in Southern Rhodesia, first with her family on an isolated and impoverished farm whose workers were all native black Africans, and then on her own in Salisbury. In the city she became involved with a group interested in international politics whose most specific focus was increased rights for black Rhodesians. Her experiences there in the 1940's, including two marriages and three children, became material for nearly all of her novels for the first twenty years of her writing career.

In 1949 Lessing arrived in London with her youngest son and the manuscript of *The Grass Is Singing*. In many ways this first book established a pattern for subsequent novels. Her manuscript was accepted for publication within three days of her submitting it to a publisher. The novel was well received and went through seven reprintings within five months. The title comes from part 5 of T. S. Eliot's *The Waste Land* (1922); Lessing's wide reading included the twentieth century writers as well as the great British, French, and Russian novelists of the nineteenth century. She most admired those writers with a sense of moral purpose, a sense of commitment to all humanity. *The Grass Is Singing* clearly shows the horrific effects of apartheid and racial prejudice on both the white colonial rulers and the black people who make up the overwhelming majority of the populations of southern Africa.

In a stylistic technique directly opposite to that of a stereotypical detective story, the third-person narrator reveals at the outset of *The Grass Is Singing* that Mary Turner, the wife of a poor farmer, has been killed by a houseboy, Moses, who confessed to the crime. The opening chapter shows the confusion and emotional collapse of Mary's husband, Dick Turner, and the reactions of Charlie Slatter, a neighbor, and Tony Marston, a young recent immigrant from England. The plot then becomes straightforward as it gives the background and chronology of events that led to the murder.

Mary grew up in the city and had established a pleasant though rather meaningless life after the death of her parents. At age thirty she begins to overhear acquaintances' disparaging remarks about the fact that she has never married. Suddenly seeing herself as a failure, she agrees to marry virtually the first man available, an impractical farmer who comes to town for supplies. Dick Turner immediately takes her to his isolated shack, where they are surrounded by black workers; the nearest white neighbor is many miles away. Mary is unprepared for marriage and totally inept at dealing with the series of houseboys Dick brings from the field to do cooking and housework. In exile from her city life, Mary is further hampered by the typical white Southern Rhodesian belief that natives are basically nonhuman, or at least subhuman and destined to inferiority. She cannot handle the intimate day-by-day contact with the native houseboys who seem so alien to her, and with the advent of the arrogant Moses, the many psychological strains lead inexorably to her almost invited death. Mary and all of white culture are guilty, but it is the black Moses who will be hanged.

Mary's failures are also a result of her inability to understand herself. She is not a reader. She has dreams and nightmares but makes no exploration of their possible significance. She has never examined social and political realities and has no one with whom to discuss her problems. She is unable to adjust to her current reality and unable to create any alternative reality.

Martha Quest, *A Proper Marriage*, *A Ripple from the Storm*, *Landlocked*, and *The Four-Gated City* trace in detail the growth and development of Martha Quest, an autobiographical character who, unlike Mary Turner, is intensely interested in knowing herself and making sense of the world. Together these novels make up the Children of Violence series. The first four are set in Africa, while *The Four-Gated City*, which nearly equals in length the preceding four, is set in London and traces Martha Quest from her arrival there around 1949 to the late 1990's. The novels set in Africa are categorized as social realism, while *The Four-Gated City* moves beyond that to discuss what are often considered paranormal capacities, and the work concludes after some unspecified disaster has destroyed much of life on earth. The futurist world Lessing depicts here is neither entirely utopian nor dystopian, and despite forces beyond the control of the individual, Martha Quest and some of the other inhabitants of the postcatastrophic world epitomize the continuing need for individual responsibility and commitment to a more harmonious world.

Martha Quest, as her surname suggests, is a quintessential Lessing heroine, always examining the human condition and searching for a higher consciousness to change herself and her world. The characterization is detailed and frank, including descriptions of Martha's sexual relationships and, in *A Proper Marriage*, a lengthy and explicit description of childbirth. Yet Martha's perceptions and innermost thoughts also provide a historical overview of an entire era and a challenge to the status quo. Central to all Martha's struggles is her determination to grow and to envision a freer and more responsible world.

It is well to note that Lessing interrupted the writing of the Children of

Violence series to work on *The Golden Notebook*, published in 1962 and generally acknowledged as her most impressive and influential novel. "The two women were alone in the London flat," begins the long novel, and from this simple statement Lessing creates a fascinating portrait of the modern world. The protagonist is Anna Wulf, a writer who says that she is suffering from writer's block after a successful first novel about racial problems in Africa. Anna's friend Molly is a divorced mother trying to make a life for herself. Through them Lessing perceptively examines the problems of the intelligent and disillusioned modern woman. Anna tries to create order out of chaos by keeping a diary, which she divides into four notebooks: a black notebook recounting her experiences as a young woman in Africa; a red notebook for her Communist and political activities; a yellow notebook, which includes her fictional attempts to understand herself, including the creation of an autobiographical character named Ella who is also writing a novel; and a blue notebook to record the factual details of her daily life and her relationships with men. Sections of these notebooks are repeated sequentially four times and are finally superseded by another notebook, the golden one of the novel's title, in which Anna attempts to integrate these compartmentalized and often-conflicting aspects of her life. In the golden notebook section, influenced by the mental breakdown of one of her lovers, Saul Green, Anna goes through layers of madness in herself and questions the idea of reality itself.

The shape of this pivotal metafictional novel is further complicated by sections called "Free Women," which open and close the book as well as separating the repeated sections of the black, red, yellow, and blue notebooks. The five "Free Women" sections together form a conventional novel about sixty thousand words long. Although it deals with the same characters and events recounted in the various notebook sections, it does so in a reductive and more structured way. It is as though the "Free Women" novel were what Anna is able to produce to end her writer's block, but a novel that shows that fiction is unable to capture the intricacies and complexities of actual existence. Since the sections of this conventional novel frame and appear throughout the larger work, the contrasts and variations with the notebook sections make *The Golden Notebook* as a whole a complex structural and stylistic achievement.

While *The Golden Notebook* elaborates Lessing's attitudes toward racism, sexism, and the interconnections between the personal and the political, it also shows the development of Lessing's thinking to include the benefits of the irrational and the necessity of exploring areas beyond the layers of social pretense and conventionality. These areas are further addressed in *The Four-Gated City* and in three subsequent novels, *Briefing for a Descent into Hell*, *The Summer Before the Dark*, and *The Memoirs of a Survivor*. Each of these novels breaks from traditional versions of realism and insists upon a wider definition of the possible.

Briefing for a Descent into Hell, one of the very few Lessing novels with a male as the central character, presents Charles Watkins, a classics professor at the University of Cambridge, who is found wandering incoherently in the streets and is hospitalized for treatment of a mental breakdown. While in the hospital, Watkins, who has forgotten even his name, imagines himself taken away in a spaceship, and most of the book relates his various encounters with unfamiliar creatures and situations that seem almost mythological. Many of these experiences are painful or frightening. Often he is alone, yet he feels a sense of urgency and intense anxiety: he must accomplish certain tasks or risk total failure for himself and others. He also has times of exceptional joy, as he sees the beauty of creation and has revelations of a harmony that could prevail if each creature accepted its part in the scheme of things and made its responsible contribution. In the final pages of the book, Watkins is given electroshock treatment and yanked back into his old life, but both he and the reader are left with the sense that compared to his previous insights he has been forced back to a shallow and hollow "normalcy."

In *The Summer Before the Dark,* Kate Brown, a woman in her early forties, also goes through a period of "madness," which reveals the extent to which she has previously succumbed to the pressures to become only roles: wife, mother, sex object, efficient organizer, selfless care-giver. During the summer that is the time frame of the novel, Kate's husband and grown children are away from home; at loose ends, Kate accepts a position as translator for an international food organization. She soon finds herself traveling and organizing global conferences. She spends some time in Spain with Jeffrey Merton, a young man whose psychosomatic and psychological illnesses spill over into her own life, and she returns to London to deal with her doubts and confusions. She stays for a while in a flat with Maureen, a twenty-two-year-old who is establishing her own identity. Through her reactions to Maureen, Kate comes to understand much about herself and her own family, and she finally grasps the relevance of a recurring dream about a seal. The seal dream appears fifteen times in the novel, and the basic image is of Kate struggling to return an abandoned seal to the ocean. When Kate is finally able to finish the dream and return the seal to water, she realizes that what she has been burdened with is her own ego and that she must fight against the power of repressive institutions and roles.

Lessing again shows the conjunction between the individual and the larger society, including the importance of responsibility and direction, in *The Memoirs of a Survivor* in this dystopian rendering of the "near future," the unnamed first-person narrator records her observations of a world in a state of cultural and social decline following an unexplained catastrophe. A stranger consigns into the narrator's care a girl of about twelve, Emily, who has with her Hugo, an ugly cat/dog creature. Much of the novel describes Emily's accelerated development through puberty and her association with Gerald, a young gang leader who, with Emily's help, tries to rebuild some semblance of order or at least some system of survival in a degenerated and nonfunctional society. From the window of her flat the narrator watches groups abandon the city, never to be heard of again, and she witnesses the collapse of civilization, demonstrated particularly in the very young children who fend for themselves and who have only fleeting connections to others for immediate gain. In these children, not only respect for others but also language itself has broken down, and they attack their victims or one another with barbaric yaps.

In the midst of all this collapse, the narrator has become aware of another layer of reality in and through the walls of her flat. When she enters this space, she is confronted with a variety of scenes from the past, not necessarily her own past, and usually she sees something that she must do. On one journey through the walls she glimpses a figure of a woman, perhaps a goddess or some aspect of herself, who fills her with a sense of hope. Surrounded by despair in the present world, the narrator constructs an alternative visionary world, and at the end of the novel, when even the air is unbreathable, the collapsed world is left behind as the narrator steps through the wall through both a willed and a magical transformation. She takes with her Emily and Gerald and their group of youngsters as well as Hugo, transformed from an ugly beast into something shining with hope and promise.

After a rare gap of five years without a novel, Doris Lessing burst forth with *Shikasta*, which she announced was the first in a series called Canopus in Argos: Archives, and in the next four years she published the other four books in the series. A number of loyal readers were disappointed with what Lessing called her "space fiction," with its undeveloped, stylized characters and strangely unexciting interplanetary rivalries. Yet the series attracted a new audience of science-fiction readers, and taken as a whole the series continues Lessing's themes: the individual versus the collective, political systems and their interference with racial and sexual equality, the interconnectedness of all life, and the need for a more enlightened consciousness.

Some of the terms used to describe the varied genres in the Canopus in Argos novels—outer space fiction, science fiction, fantasy, psychomyth, allegory, utopian—indicate the variety within and among these books. They do not even comfortably fit the classification of series, or *roman fleuve*, since traditionally a series centers on a single character, as Lessing had done with Martha Quest in *Children of Violence*. *Shikasta* is filled with reports, journals, and interviews by aliens who discuss the fate of Earth, or Shikasta. *The Marriages Between Zones Three, Four, and Five* does not seem to be set on another planet so much as in the realm of myth and legend as Al·Ith moves between the zones in search of her destiny. *The Sirian Experiments* is told by a woman named Ambien II, who is a leading administrator in the Sirian Colonial Service. She discovers that the rival Canopean Empire is actually in advance of Sirius in every way and more deserving of conducting experiments on Shikasta than is her own empire, though the Sirians certainly do not want to hear this. *The Making of the Representative for Planet 8* is the story of a small planet whose inhabitants live comfortably until the time of The Ice begins, with ice and snow covering most of the globe. The inhabitants are unable to emigrate, but a few of them survive in some nonphysical but essential existence. *Documents Relating to the Sentimental Agents in the Volyen Empire* uses testimonies and histories to show that the Volyen Empire has failed to keep its promises to its inhabitants and to the cosmos. The empire suffers a rhetoric-induced downfall, as its leaders had become enamored with the sound of their grand ideas rather than performing the actions that should have accompanied them.

None of the narrators and voices in the Canopus in Argos series is entirely reliable, and many questions are left unanswered. Perhaps this confusion is itself Lessing's goal: to make her readers question and reconsider ideas and actions. As Johor, an emissary to Shikasta, comments on the very first page of the series: "Things change. That is all we may be sure of. . . . This is a catastrophic universe, always; and subject to sudden reversals, upheavals, changes, cataclysms, with joy never anything but the song of substance under pressure forced into new forms and shapes."

The same year the final volume of Canopus in Argos was published, another novel appeared titled *The Diary of a Good Neighbour*, purportedly by a new British writer, Jane Somers. It was not until the following year, and after the publication of another Jane Somers novel, *If the Old Could . . .* , that Lessing publicly revealed her authorship with the publication of the two novels together as *The Diaries of Jane Somers*. In her introduction to the book Lessing discusses some of her reasons for having used a pseudonym. One was to create a new persona as the narrator: how would a real Jane Somers write? Another was to show the difficulties unestablished writers have in getting published, and indeed the first manuscript was rejected by several publishers before it was printed by Michael Joseph in London, the same firm that had accepted the unknown Doris Lessing's *The Grass Is Singing* nearly four decades earlier. Lessing also says that she wanted the novels to be judged on their own merit, apart from the Lessing canon. When the Jane Somers novels first appeared, they sold in only modest numbers and received favorable but very limited attention from reviewers. Lessing notes that the modern publishing business markets high-volume, high-profile authors with the planned expectation that the novels will have a short shelf life—big sellers for a few weeks but soon replaced and out of print; such policies do not favor new and experimental novelists.

The Diaries of Jane Somers focuses on old age, especially the relationship that develops between the middle-aged Jane Somers, head of a high-fashion magazine, and Maudie Fowler, a poor but proud woman in her nineties. Set in a realistic London, the novels, particularly *The Diary of a Good Neighbour,* give an insightful analysis of contemporary health-care services and again show the impact of social attitudes and governmental policies on the individual. The social realism of the novel, with its discussions of aging and dying, is given contrast by the summaries of novels Jane writes about Maudie's life. Maudie tells stories of her long, hard life, and Jane transforms them into successful romanticized fictions, which Maudie then enjoys hearing. Jane, whose friends call her Janna, is repeatedly mistaken for a "Good Neighbour," a social worker, as though there could be no other explanation for her friendship with Maudie. The layers of illusion and reality, fictions and lives, add to the emotional power of the novel and make it an important addition to Lessing's later works.

The Good Terrorist shows rather stupid and totally unsympathetic would-be revolutionaries who move from city to city in England planning random bombings. Contrary to the title, there is no good terrorist in the novel, and it is just as well that these characters have a tendency to blow up themselves accidentally rather than killing others. A much more interesting novel is *The Fifth Child*, which can be read as an accurate and realistic account of an unfortunate English family, but which to other readers is a science-fiction fantasy, a tale of an alien being born into a human family. The novel hovers on some point that embraces both readings. The setting is England in the 1960's. Harriet and David Lovatt want a big family and a settled home life. Everything seems to be working according to their plan until the birth of their fifth child. Ben has nothing childlike about him: he is gruesome in appearance, insatiably hungry, abnormally strong, demanding and violent. In no way does he fit into the happy home. Yet Harriet, steeped in the idea of motherhood, cannot bear to abandon him in some mental institution and insists on keeping him with her. As the years pass, the older children escape though already harmed by Ben's weirdness and violence, and even David finally recognizes he cannot continue to live with such a creature. The novel ends in despair, the problems unresolved. Ben is well on his way to becoming a fully grown criminal, a rapist and murderer, with no one able to subdue him. The story of the Lovatts becomes a parable of the modern world, the vision of a simple and happy existence shattered within the family itself and a society unwilling to confront and unable to control its own most brutal aspects.

Lessing has had a wide readership. For years she has been on best-seller lists, and her novels have been translated into many languages. Her work is widely anthologized and has been closely read by many contemporary authors, particularly women writers. The number of critical articles, books, and sections of books about her work is enormous and international in scope, reflecting the wide diversity of readers and the serious attention her work has commanded throughout her writing career.

Lessing's novels, far-ranging in scope and treatment, resist any easy labels.

Still, her major themes, though presented in a variety of ways, have been remarkably consistent. The individual has responsibilities, Lessing always shows, not only to achieve self-knowledge and inner harmony but to contribute to the greater harmony of society as well. Human consciousness must expand and people's attitudes and actions must change if human life is to survive.

Lois A. Marchino

Other major works

SHORT FICTION: *This Was the Old Chief's Country*, 1951; *Five: Short Novels*, 1953; *The Habit of Loving*, 1957; *A Man and Two Women*, 1963; *African Stories*, 1964; *The Temptation of Jack Orkney and Other Stories*, 1972 (also known as *The Story of a Non-Marrying Man and Other Stories*); *This Was the Old Chief's Country: Volume 1 of Doris Lessing's Collected African Stories*, 1973; *The Sun Between Their Feet: Volume 2 of Doris Lessing's Collected African Stories*, 1973; *Sunrise on the Veld*, 1975; *A Mild Attack of Locusts*, 1977; *To Room Nineteen/Her Collected Stories*, 1978; *The Temptation of Jack Orkney/Her Collected Stories*, 1978; *Stories*, 1978.

PLAYS: *Each His Own Wilderness*, 1958; *Play with a Tiger*, 1962.

POETRY: *Fourteen Poems*, 1959.

NONFICTION: *Going Home*, 1957; *In Pursuit of the English: A Documentary*, 1960; *Particularly Cats*, 1967; *A Small Personal Voice*, 1974; *Prisons We Choose to Live Inside*, 1987; *The Wind Blows Away Our Words*, 1987.

Bibliography
Draine, Betsy. *Substance Under Pressure: Artistic Coherence and Evolving Form in the Novels of Doris Lessing*. Madison: University of Wisconsin Press, 1983. Draine traces Lessing's themes and their relationship to Lessing's narrative strategies, the evolution of form as an imperative pressure on content, and the historical influences on Lessing's formal choices. The book covers Lessing's novels through the Canopus in Argos series.

Fishburn, Katherine. *The Unexpected Universe of Doris Lessing: A Study in Narrative Technique*. Westport, Conn.: Greenwood Press, 1985. This study considers Lessing's science fiction from *Briefing for a Descent into Hell* through the Canopus in Argos series. It argues that the science fiction has the purpose of transforming reality and involving the reader in ideas and the intricacies of the texts rather than in characterization. Fishburn also published *Doris Lessing: Life, Work, and Criticism* (Fredericton, New Brunswick, Canada: York Press, 1987), which provides a brief overview of Lessing's life and works, including literary biography, critical response, and an annotated bibliography.

Rose, Ellen Cronan. *The Tree Outside the Window: Doris Lessing's Children of Violence*. Hanover, N.H.: University Press of New England, 1976. Rose applies Erik Erikson's theory of ego development to Lessing's *Bildungsroman* Children of Violence series to show the metaphoric progression of Martha Quest from the shell of childhood to "the tree outside the window" in creating herself.

Rubenstein, Roberta. *The Novelistic Vision of Doris Lessing: Breaking the Forms of Consciousness*. Urbana: University of Illinois Press, 1979. This volume shows the cyclic design in Lessing's repeated themes, particularly the mind discovering, interpreting, and ultimately shaping its own reality. In a comprehensive chronological approach through 1978, it examines the relationship between fictional structure and meaning, the purpose of doubling, and the relationship between fiction and reality.

Schlueter, Paul. *The Novels of Doris Lessing*. Carbondale: Southern Illinois University Press, 1973. Schlueter provides a thematic approach to Lessing's novels through 1972, focusing particularly on the appeal of communism to Lessing's liberal mind, the racial problems of southern Africa, the role of liberated women in a patriarchal society, and writing as an aspect of self-examination.

Seligman, Dee. *Doris Lessing: An Annotated Bibliography of Criticism*. Westport, Conn.: Greenwood Press, 1981. Seligman incorporates earlier checklists and bibliographies and provides a comprehensive annotated bibliography through 1978. She includes a bibliography of research and teaching suggestions, interviews with Lessing, and book reviews. Marshall Tymn draws on Seligman's bibliography and updates it to 1988 in the *Journal of the Fantastic in the Arts* special issue on Doris Lessing edited by Nicholas Ruddick (volume 2, no. 3, 1990).

Sprague, Claire, and Virginia Tiger, eds. *Critical Essays on Doris Lessing*. Boston: G. K. Hall, 1986. This collection includes review essays and various other articles plus a general introduction to Lessing and a chronology of her works. It is divided into sections entitled "Politics and Patterns," "Female (Other) Space," "Inner and Outer Space," and "Reception and Reputation."

C. S. LEWIS

Born: Belfast, Northern Ireland; November 29, 1898
Died: Oxford, England; November 22, 1963

Principal long fiction

Out of the Silent Planet, 1938; *Perelandra*, 1943; *That Hideous Strength: A Modern Fairy Tale for Grownups*, 1945; *The Lion, the Witch, and the Wardrobe*, 1950; *Prince Caspian*, 1951; *The Voyage of the Dawn Treader*, 1952; *The Silver Chair*, 1953; *The Horse and His Boy*, 1954; *The Magician's Nephew*, 1955; *The Last Battle*, 1956; *Till We Have Faces: A Myth Retold*, 1956.

Other literary forms

Though his novels for adults and children continue to be widely read and admired, C. S. Lewis is also well known as a religious essayist and literary scholar-critic. His religious writings of three decades include autobiography (*The Pilgrim's Regress*, 1933; *Surprised by Joy: The Shape of My Early Life*, 1955; *A Grief Observed*, 1961) and essays in varying lengths and forms. Some of his essays include *The Personal Heresy* (1939, with E. M. W. Tillyard), *Rehabilitations* (1939), *The Problem of Pain* (1940), *The Screwtape Letters* (1942), *The Abolition of Man* (1943), *Miracles: A Preliminary Study* (1947), *Mere Christianity* (1952), *Reflections on the Psalms* (1958), and *The Four Loves* (1960). Posthumous works of a religious nature include *Letters to Malcolm: Chiefly on Prayer* (1964), *Letters to an American Lady* (1967), *God in the Dock* (1970), and *The Joyful Christian: 127 Readings from C. S. Lewis* (1977).

Lewis' criticism, focused primarily on medieval and Renaissance studies, includes *The Allegory of Love* (1936), *A Preface to "Paradise Lost"* (1942), *English Literature in the Sixteenth Century, Excluding Drama* (1954), *Studies in Words* (1960), *An Experiment in Criticism* (1961), and *The Discarded Image* (1963). Several posthumous volumes of criticism appeared, including *Spenser's Images of Life* (1967), *Selected Literary Essays* (1969), and *Present Concerns* (1986).

Less widely known are Lewis' early volumes of poetry, *Spirits in Bondage* (1919), a collection of lyrics; and *Dymer* (1926), a narrative. The posthumous *The Dark Tower and Other Stories* (1977) includes an unpublished fragment of a novel. This collection and one other, *Of Other Worlds: Essays and Stories* (1966), contain the only extant fictional pieces not printed during Lewis' lifetime. The Wade Collection at Wheaton College (Illinois) and the Bodleian Library, Oxford, hold many volumes of Lewis papers, including eleven volumes of Lewis family letters written from 1850 to 1930.

Achievements

Lewis' achievements as a novelist are hard to separate from his role as a

Christian apologist and from his impeccable literary scholarship. Many of Lewis' readers believe that his greatness lies in the unusually wide scope of his work: he wrote so much so well in so many forms. His *Mere Christianity*, for example, is a superb primer on Christian ideas, while *The Four Loves* and *A Grief Observed* are powerful explorations of the endurance of love despite doubt and deep pain. *The Screwtape Letters*, Lewis' most popular book in America, still enthralls new readers with its witty, yet serious study of the war between good and evil in the contemporary world. Among his critical writings, *The Allegory of Love* remains a classic study of medieval literature and society, while *The Discarded Image* is one of the very best discussions of the contrast between the medieval world view and the modern mind.

The popularity of Lewis' novels for adults (*Out of the Silent Planet*, *Perelandra*, and *That Hideous Strength*—known as the "space trilogy"—and *Till We Have Faces*) owes more perhaps to their treatment of themes also developed in his nonfiction than to their literary excellence, although the space trilogy is widely read among devotees of fantasy and science fiction who have little acquaintance with Lewis' other works. The extraordinary appeal of Lewis' fiction for children, the Narnia books, is undisputed. Each year, these seven novels gain thousands of new readers of all ages and are, for many, the introduction to Lewis which inspires them to delve into his other works. Indeed, had Lewis never published another word, the Narnia books would have ensured his reputation with both critics and the public.

Biography

Born in Belfast in 1898, the son of Albert Lewis, a successful lawyer, and Flora Hamilton Lewis, a writer and mathematician, Clive Staples Lewis spent his early childhood in an atmosphere of learning and imagination. His mother tutored him in French and Latin before he was seven; his nurse, Lizzie Endicott, taught him the folktales of Ireland. Clive and his brother, Warren, devoted long, often rainy afternoons to exploring the book-lined corridors of Little Lea, their home. As small children, the brothers invented their own country, Boxen, for which they wrote a four-hundred-year chronicle and which they peopled with animal characters who became subjects of individual stories. These early childhood adventures were of incalculable influence on Lewis' long fiction, written almost a half century later.

With his mother's death from cancer in 1908, Lewis' life changed drastically and irrevocably. A disconsolate, bewildered Albert Lewis sent his sons to boarding school in England, the first of several cruel experiences before age sixteen that nurtured in Lewis a hatred for public school education. At last persuading his father to place him with the demanding but kind tutor W. T. Kirkpatrick in 1914, Lewis developed his great scholarly talents and won a scholarship to University College, Oxford, two years later. Before taking his entrance exams, however, Lewis was recruited into the Army and served as a second lieutenant on the front lines in France.

Surviving a wound and the mental shocks of war, Lewis happily entered Oxford life in 1919, his education financed by his father—whose support in other ways would always be lacking. Perhaps to compensate for this lack of parental affection, Lewis developed a steadfast friendship with a Mrs. Moore, the mother of a friend who had died fighting in France. With Mrs. Moore and her young daughter, Maureen, Lewis set up housekeeping, this arrangement continuing thirty years, until Mrs. Moore's death in 1951. Lewis' tenure at Oxford, as student, tutor, and fellow of Magdalen College, lasted even longer, ending in 1954 with his acceptance of the chair of Medieval and Renaissance Literature at Magdalene College, Cambridge. During the Oxford years, he wrote and published most of his fifty-eight books of adult and children's fiction, literary criticism, essays, Christian apologetics, and poetry. It was there also that Lewis, influenced by such close friends as J. R. R. Tolkien, underwent his conversion to Christianity.

Lewis' Christian fervor led to widely read publications and to a long series of radio talks before and during World War II. His faith also inspired fictions, including his space trilogy, written during the war, and his Narnia books for children. Many of his Oxford colleagues, however, were offended by his overt religiousness—and his popularity. Through these years, they thus denied Lewis the Magdalen professorship that his eminence as a literary scholar warranted.

With his rise to a more esteemed position in the more congenial atmosphere of Cambridge, Lewis completed, among other projects, the books of Narnia, the first of which had been published in 1950, and wrote perhaps his finest novel, *Till We Have Faces*. This last work of fiction was dedicated to Joy Davidman Gresham, an American admirer with whom he had corresponded for several years and who came to England to join him in 1955. They were married in 1956, and, according to Lewis, "feasted on love" for the four years they shared before Joy's death from bone cancer in 1960. Despite his own worsening health, Lewis continued to produce autobiographical and critical works until suffering a heart attack in 1963. He died on November 22, the date of John F. Kennedy's assassination and of the death of Aldous Huxley.

Analysis

The happy fact of C. S. Lewis' creation of long fictions is that the more of them he wrote the better he became as a novelist. This is not to say that with each book from *Out of the Silent Planet* to *Till We Have Faces* he measurably improved, but from the early space trilogy (1938-1945) through the Narnia tales (1950-1956) to his last novel, there is a clear change in Lewis' conception of fiction. In the early books, characters exemplify definite sides in an ethical debate, and plot is the working out of victory for Lewis' side. In the later books, however, character becomes the battleground of ambiguous values, and plot takes place more and more within the minds of the characters.

The hero of the space trilogy, Oxford don Elwin Ransom, is often less the protagonist of novels than an embodiment of the Christian and intellectual virtues that Lewis recommended in his essays. Throughout the trilogy, Ransom represents Lewis' ideal of the relentless intellectual, his learning solidly founded on respect for great ideas from earlier ages, who valiantly maintains his integrity despite the powerful temptations posed by modern materialism. In both *Out of the Silent Planet* and *Perelandra*, Ransom's journeys to Mars (Malacandra) and Venus (Perelandra), respectively, Ransom's adversary is as clearly villainous as Ransom himself is heroic. The antagonist is Edward Weston, a brilliant physicist, who represents for Lewis that most insidious modern outgrowth of Renaissance humanism: the belief that the highest goal of humankind is to establish its dominance over all forms of life in as many worlds as it can conquer. This view, which Lewis saw as the root of the boundless ambition of Adolf Hitler, Joseph Stalin, and Benito Mussolini, is exemplified in Weston's misuse of technology to build a spacecraft that enables him to reach other planets, so that he might make them colonies of Earth.

By moving the scene of this attempt away from Earth, Lewis can manipulate material reality so that the limitations of Weston's philosophy become obvious and his actions ludicrous. Assuming the innate superiority of man over all other forms, and thus a perpetual state of war between man and nature, Weston fails to see the simplest, most significant facts of the new worlds he intends to conquer. As Ransom, the Christian student of myths and languages, easily perceives, the forces that rule Mars and Venus are both fully hospitable to humankind and infinitely more powerful. Thus, Weston shoots gentle creatures because they appear strange and, in a parody of the European explorers, tries to bribe with shiny trinkets the "Oyarsa" of Malacandra, who, as Ransom learns, is second only in power and wisdom to "Maleldil," ruler of the universe. In contrast to Weston, Ransom—a far truer scientist than his opponent—befriends and learns the language of these extraterrestrials; hence, mysteries are opened to him. In *Out of the Silent Planet*, he learns that only Earth (Thulcandra), long under the dominance of the "bent eldil," is deprived of clear knowledge of the Oyarsa and Maleldil; Thulcandrans believe themselves enlightened above all others, when in reality they are the most benighted. He learns also that the universe is in a state of becoming: that the creatures of old worlds, such as Malacandra, can no longer be endangered by such forces as those which guide Weston, but that newer worlds, such as Thulcandra, are still theaters of contending principles, while the youngest worlds, such as Perelandra, have yet to achieve spiritual identity.

This is vital knowledge for Ransom, who realizes, in the second book, that he has been given wisdom because he has also been given the responsibility of helping to bring about Maleldil's reign on Perelandra, which places him in open confrontation with Weston, now clearly the mere instrument of the bent eldil. In a probing recapitulation of the temptation of Eve, Lewis has Ransom and Weston contend, somewhat in the mode of the medieval *psychomachia*, for the mind of Tinidril, the first woman of Perelandra. As the confoundingly subtle arguments of the "Unman" (the spirit which controls Weston) begin to conquer Tinidril, Ransom at last understands that he must physically fight, to the death, with his adversary. Despite his slim chance of survival, Ransom attacks the Unman; he ultimately defeats him, though suffering wounds, incredible fatigue, and near despair. It is an epic battle, reminiscent of the Pearl-Poet's fourteenth century manuscript *Sir Gawain and the Green Knight* and Edmund Spenser's *The Faerie Queene* (1590, 1596); Ransom's faith and courage in the fight prepare the reader for his apotheosis in the final chapters, wherein Lewis' paradisiacally lush description of Perelandra takes on an almost beatific vividness and illumination.

In novelistic terms, *Perelandra* surpasses *Out of the Silent Planet* in its attention to the development of Ransom's awareness of his role and his struggle to maintain his integrity in the face of fears and misleading appearances. Nevertheless, its extraterrestrial setting and its clearly demarcated hero and villain make *Perelandra* more an epic romance than a novel. This is not to prefer one book to the other, but it is to distinguish them both from the third part of the trilogy, *That Hideous Strength*, which may be Lewis' most interesting fiction, although not his most consistent. *That Hideous Strength* tries to harmonize heterogeneous elements of romance, epic, and novel. Following the novelist's impulse, Lewis brings his setting back to earth and localizes it in the sort of place he knew best, a venerable English college town, which he calls Edgestow. He also centers the reader's interest on two authentic protagonists, Jane and Mark Studdock, whose story is their painful, humiliating, sometimes dangerous progress toward faith and self-awareness. They act bravely in the ultimate crisis, both risking torture and death, but they engage in nothing like the epic struggle of Ransom and the Unman.

Still, the events in which they engage are of epic magnitude, and in this thrust of the book Lewis returns to familiar fictional territory. The plot concerns a powerful conspiracy to turn Britain into a totalitarian state. This conspiracy is opposed most strenuously by a small underground directed by Elwin Ransom, now a heroic, almost godlike leader, whose powers are spiritual rather than physical. His main adversaries are men who, like Weston, call themselves scientists, but whose distinguishing traits are lust for power, deviousness, and cruelty. Having established a research institute called the National Institute of Co-ordinated Experiments (N.I.C.E.), these men use the press, political infiltrators, and their own "police" to avoid, placate, or squash opposition to their Nazi-like program of "social planning." Mark Studdock is one of the bright but indecisive minds easily coopted by the N.I.C.E. Lewis shows convincingly how the leaders play on his ego and his fears of rejection in order to exploit his talent as a journalist. Conversely, Jane Studdock falls in with the resistance group; she weighs its values against those of her husband, and gradually comes to see that whichever road she chooses will mean great danger for both of them. She chooses the resistance.

Had Lewis limited the book to the clash between political philosophies and its impact on two ordinary people, he would have had a conventional novel, but he wanted to portray this clash as occurring on a cosmic level, as a war between pure good and pure evil. Since the combatants in this novel are the human representatives of these supernatural forces, the reader necessarily finds himself once more in the realm of romance. Aware of his mixing of genres in *That Hideous Strength*, Lewis called the amalgamation a fairy tale, arguing that his work fell into that long tradition in which supernatural events subsume the ordinary activities of realistic characters. What fairy tale means here is that when the N.I.C.E. performs such blatant works as the turning of rivers from their courses, the trapping of huge numbers of animals for vivisection, and the deforestation of ancient preserves, they call down on themselves the wrath of nature, personified in a resurrected Merlin, who pledges allegiance to Ransom as the spiritual successor of Arthur. His obedience allows Ransom to reinvest him with eldilic power, which enables him singlehandedly to destroy the N.I.C.E. Add to the appearance of Merlin such important romantic elements as Jane Studdock's clairvoyance and the veneration of a talking head by the N.I.C.E., and *That Hideous Strength* seems almost more romance than novel.

The book should be judged as a fairy tale. Lewis warns the reader in his Preface not to be deceived by the "hum-drum scenes and persons" into thinking this a realistic fiction. He merely intends the familiar names and places to heighten the reader's appreciation of the importance of the spiritual battles occurring around and within each individual. Indeed, one explicit purpose of the book is to warn England—here Lewis was prophetic—that radical social evil would not be eradicated with Hitler's defeat. The formal problem, however, is that a bit of realism begets the expectation of total realism, and so readers accustomed to novels will naturally look askance at Merlin's return and the survival of the severed head, while they will accept the generic consistency of the floating islands in *Perelandra*. Even if Lewis had deleted these effects from the third book, however, he would have had to substitute other supernatural manifestations in order to be consistent not only with the pattern of the first two books but also, more important, with his religious conviction of the imminence of the supernatural in everyday life. Viewing the book as a fairy tale, Lewis felt, would allow the reader sufficient suspension of disbelief to become involved with the characters. Nevertheless, the reader would still face, as in all of Lewis' other works, the challenge of accepting or rejecting Lewis' position on God, nature, and humanity.

Lewis actually began the first book of the Narnia series, *The Lion, the Witch, and the Wardrobe*, in 1939, when four children, inspiration for the Pevensie children in the stories, were evacuated to his home at the start of the war. Returning ten years and many books later to the idea of writing for children, Lewis found the fictional form perhaps best suited to his genius. These tales of ordinary boys and girls transported to another world allowed Lewis to relive in some sense the childhood idyll at Little Lea that had been cut short by his mother's death; moreover, they let him put directly into prose the fantastic images—fauns, castles, golden lions—that came to him, without his having to adapt them, as he had in the space trilogy, to the narrower tastes of adult readers. The fairy-tale form restricted him to simpler vocabulary and syntax, as well as to a more exclusively narrative and descriptive mode, but these restrictions freed him to do what he did best in fiction: dialogue, action narrative, and vivid description of select detail. More than anything else, however, the form let him depict given characters as essentially good or evil, though careful readers will observe that these qualities are consistently dramatized in action, not merely posited by authorial fiat. One of the many virtues of these stories is that appearance never defines character; the reader likes or dislikes persons or animals in these books only when he has come to know them.

The seven books traverse some sixty years of English time, roughly between 1895 and 1955, and more than a thousand years of time in Narnia, a land which is the home of Aslan, the Golden Lion, as well as talking animals, dwarves, fauns, satyrs, witches, men and women, boys and girls. The chronicle begins with *The Magician's Nephew* (the sequence of publication differs from the internal chronology of the series), in which young Digory Kirke and Polly Plummer magically enter Narnia at the time of its creation by Aslan. Unfortunately, the curious Digory inadvertently breaks the spell which has bound Jadis, the White Witch, who becomes the main enemy of the Narnians. In *The Lion, the Witch, and the Wardrobe*, almost fifty English years have passed, but an untold number in Narnia. The visitors are now the four Pevensie children, who enter Narnia through a magical wardrobe in the spacious country home of an old friend of their parents—Professor Digory Kirke. They find a cold world in terror of the Witch. The children eventually join those who are still rebelling against her, and their faith is rewarded when Aslan returns. His conquest is not complete, however, until he has been ritually murdered by the Witch, only to be reborn in far greater splendor. The four children are crowned kings and queens of Narnia.

The Horse and His Boy occurs during the reign of Peter Pevensie as High King of Narnia. It concerns Shasta, a boy of neighboring Calormen, who through various adventures is revealed to be the true prince of Archenland, another Narnian neighbor. The fourth part of the chronicle, *Prince Caspian*, takes place a thousand years forward in Narnian time, but only two or three years after the adventure through the wardrobe. The four children are transported to Narnia from a railway bench, only to find all record of their reign obliterated by time and by the purposeful lies told by invaders. The children's arrival, however, coincides with another coming of Aslan, who, aided by an alliance of all the creatures of Narnia, restores to the throne the true heir, Caspian. He is still king of Narnia when the fifth adventure, *The Voyage of the Dawn Treader*, occurs. This time, the two younger Pevensies, Edmund and Lucy, accompanied by a recalcitrant friend, Eustace Scrubb, reenter Narnia to help Caspian sail the farthest seas to find seven Narnian lords banished by the invaders. On their voyage, they discover lands beyond imagining, including Aslan's country itself. The sixth chronicle, *The Silver Chair*, is another story of a search, this time by Eustace and a friend, Jill Pole, who are called to Narnia to find the dying Caspian's long-lost son, Rilian. Despite many deceptions and dangers, the children eventually discover the prince, by then the rightful king of Narnia.

The chronicles end with *The Last Battle*, the apocalypse of Narnia. King Tirian, Rilian's descendant, is joined by Eustace and Jill in a final battle to save Narnia from invading hordes of hostile neighbors. As they go to certain death, they are suddenly greeted by Aslan, who ushers them into the real Narnia, of which the mere parody is now disappearing as quickly as it had been born centuries before. There they are joined by all the friends of Narnia, including three of the four Pevensies, who, with their parents, have come to the real Narnia thanks to a railway accident in "their" world. Aslan tells them that this Narnia is forever, and that they need never leave: "The term is over; the holidays have begun. The dream is ended; this is the morning."

Almost nothing of the style of the space trilogy is recognizable in *Till We Have Faces*, Lewis' first novel for adults after 1945, and the last of his career. Though Lewis here was reworking an ancient myth, that of Cupid and Psyche, this book can be unambiguously called a novel, in the full modern sense of that word. It begins and ends in the spiritual turmoil of the mind of the narrator, Orual, Queen of Glome, a tiny state somewhere north of Greece, sometime in the centuries just preceding the birth of Christ. The novel is the story of her life, told in two parts. The first, much the longer, is Orual's complaint against the gods for their hatred of humankind, hatred shown most obviously in their failure ever to make themselves clearly known. The second part, a few brief chapters hastily penned by the dying queen and ended in mid-sentence by her death, repents for the slanders of Part One and tells of a few pivotal encounters and an extraordinary dream that have resolved her anger.

Part One recalls a lifelong source of her rage, her ugliness, which has made Orual hated by her father, the king, and shunned by most others. A far greater injury, however, is the sacrifice of her wonderfully beautiful sister, Psyche, whom the head priest of Glome offers to the god of the Grey Mountain in hopes of ending a drought. Orual cannot forgive the gods for taking the only joy of her life. What irritates her most, however, is her discovery that Psyche has not been devoured by the god of the mountain, as most people believe, but that he has wedded her. Moreover, Psyche is happy. Convincing herself that her sister's happiness can only be a fatal delusion, Orual persuades Psyche, with a threat of suicide, to disobey her lord's one command: that she never look at him. The result is that Psyche is banished and forced to undergo ordeals. Orual is also punished: the god tells her, cryptically, "You also will be Psyche." Never fully comprehending this sentence, and enraged by the ambiguity of the portent, Orual passes the years, eventually succeeding her father and distracting her thoughts by careful attention to government of her people. Orual becomes a wise and masterful ruler, but her mind remains troubled. When, by chance, she discovers that the story of Psyche has given rise to a cult of worshipers, she decides finally to spill her anger and doubt onto paper. The story the sect tells is false, she feels: in it, Psyche's sister is accused of deliberately plotting her fall. She feels that she must write to clear the record, to exonerate herself.

In Part Two, she repents. She admits that the very writing of Part One has brought back disquieting memories: perhaps she had been jealous of Psyche. Her self-awareness grows when two meetings with longtime observers of her life convince her that her perspective on people and events has always been narrow and selfish. Finally, two terrible dreams—visions, she realizes—bring her crime before her eyes; she understands the sentence of the god. She has indeed been Psyche, in that while her sister has performed the ordeals assigned her, Orual, in her years of suffering, has borne all the anguish of them. Thus, she has both committed the crime and expiated the guilt. Her confession in Part Two gives way to thanksgiving, as she discovers that, washed clear of her guilt, she is as beautiful as the sister whom she is at last free to love.

The richness of Orual's character has been likened by critics to the increasing depth of compassion in Lewis' essays of these later years. The striking resonance of these works has been attributed, at least in part, to the influence on Lewis' life at this time of Joy Davidman, to whom he dedicated *Till We Have Faces*. That Lewis' renunciation of bachelorhood late in his life signaled an opening of himself, and his prose, to emotions and ways of seeing that he had not before allowed himself seems plausible; nevertheless, the simple design and straightforward nature of this last novel can as easily be explained as further developments of Lewis' style in the direction taken by the Narnia books. Perhaps the exploration of his own childhood necessitated by writing these books taught him lessons about his writing as profound as those Orual learned in trying to recapture her past. Perhaps he learned that he was truly happy as a writer when he could explore the curious corridors of his personality, just as he had loved to explore the rooms and passages of his boyhood home. It is surely no coincidence that the first part of his autobiography, *Surprised by Joy*, was published in 1955, while he was at work not only on *Till We Have Faces* but also on *The Last Battle*. All three books reveal an exquisite sensitivity which can be attributed to his deep introspection at this time. This sensitivity, this honesty, makes these books far more memorable in themselves than his more clever experiments in less traditional forms.

Christopher J. Thaiss

Other major works

SHORT FICTION: *The Dark Tower and Other Stories*, 1977.

POETRY: *Spirits in Bondage*, 1919; *Dymer*, 1926; *Poems*, 1964; *Narrative Poems*, 1969.

NONFICTION: *The Pilgrim's Regress*, 1933; *The Allegory of Love*, 1936; *A Preface to "Paradise Lost,"* 1942; *Hamlet: The Prince or the Poem*, 1942; *Beyond Personality*, 1944; *Arthurian Torso*, 1948; *English Literature in the Sixteenth Century, Excluding Drama*, 1954; *Surprised by Joy: The Shape of My Early Life*, 1955; *Studies in Words*, 1960; *An Experiment in Criticism*, 1961; *A Grief Observed*, 1961; *The Discarded Image*, 1964; *Studies in Medieval and Renaissance Literature*, 1966; *Letters of C. S. Lewis*, 1966; *Letters to an American Lady*, 1967; *Spenser's Images of Life*, 1967; *Selected Literary Essays*, 1969; *They Stand Together: The Letters of C. S. Lewis to Arthur Greeves, 1914-1963*, 1979; *On Stories, and Other Essays on Literature*, 1982; *C. S. Lewis: Letters to Children*, 1985; *Present Concerns*, 1986; *Letters: C. S. Lewis and Don Giovanni Calabria, a Study in Friendship*, 1988.

RELIGIOUS WRITINGS: *The Personal Heresy*, 1939 (with E. M. W. Tillyard); *Rehabilitations*, 1939; *The Problem of Pain*, 1940; *The Screwtape Letters*, 1942; *Broadcast Talks*, 1942; *Christian Behaviour*, 1943; *The Abolition of Man*, 1943; *The Great Divorce*, 1945; *Miracles: A Preliminary Study*, 1947; *The Weight of Glory, and Other Addresses*, 1949; *Mere Christianity*, 1952; *Reflections on the Psalms*, 1958; *The Four Loves*, 1960; *The World's Last Night, and Other Essays*, 1960; *Letters to Malcolm: Chiefly on Prayer*, 1964; *Christian Reflections*, 1967; *God in the Dock*, 1970; *The Joyful Christian: 127 Readings from C. S. Lewis*, 1977.

MISCELLANEOUS: *Of Other Worlds: Essays and Stories*, 1966; *The Business of Heaven*, 1984; *Boxen: The Imaginary World of the Young C. S. Lewis*, 1985.

Bibliography

Carpenter, Humphrey. *The Inklings: C. S. Lewis, J. R. R. Tolkien, Charles Williams, and Their Friends*. Boston: Houghton Mifflin, 1979. A major study of the lives and works of the "Inklings," a name first applied by Lewis, perhaps as early as 1933, to a group of literary friends who met regularly together at Oxford University. Capsule biographies of the Inklings, bibliographies of their major works, a section of photographs, extensive notes and an index enhance an illuminating exploration of Lewis' literary milieu.

Como, James T. *C. S. Lewis at the Breakfast Table and Other Reminiscences*.

New York: Macmillan, 1979. Brief memoirs of Lewis from former students and lifelong friends, including Walter Hooper, trustee of the Lewis estate, who provides an account of Lewis' spirited debates at the Oxford Socratic Club from 1942 to 1954. Twenty-four chapters offer anecdotes ranging from Lewis' taste in food to his thoughts on sex. Contains twenty-seven-page bibliography, including published letters, book reviews, and poetry, as well as an alphabetical index of Lewis' writings.

Gilbert, Douglas, and Clyde S. Kilby. *C. S. Lewis: Images of His World*. Grand Rapids, Mich.: Wm. B. Eerdmans, 1973. Photographer Gilbert's several hundred color and black-and-white portraits of friends of Lewis, as well as the British countryside that was his continual inspiration, are coupled with excerpts of Lewis' published and unpublished writings. Kilby, curator of the Lewis collection at Wheaton College in Illinois, has added a chronology of Lewis' life. Lewis family pictures and photographs of his juvenilia complement this visually impressive volume.

Manlove, C. N. *C. S. Lewis: His Literary Achievement*. New York: St. Martin's Press, 1987. An explication of Lewis' major works of fiction, from *The Pilgrim's Regress* (1933) to *Till We Have Faces: A Myth Retold* (1956), including an analysis of each of the Narnia books (published between 1950 and 1956). Representative of a subgenre of Lewis studies and easily accessible is its consideration of narrative, structure, and theme in Lewis' stories. Finds Lewis' use of imagery and analogy a potent means of giving literary vitality to traditional Christian doctrines, though his complexly patterned works raise him above a facile religious apologist.

Sayer, George. *Jack: C. S. Lewis and His Times*. San Francisco: Harper & Row, 1988. An intimate biography by a former pupil and lifelong friend of Lewis. Assesses Lewis' experience of grade-school life as less abnormal than that portrayed in his own autobiography, suggests that Lewis and Mrs. Moore were not lovers, and provides a personal account of the last years of Lewis' life. Lewis emerges a gifted and sincere nonsectarian Christian. A section of black-and-white photographs, a classified bibliography, and an extensive index are included.

Smith, Robert Houston. *Patches of Godlight: The Pattern of Thought of C. S. Lewis*. Athens: University of Georgia Press, 1981. A scholarly but accessible analysis of Lewis' philosophy of religion, linking what is dubbed his Christian "Objectivism" to the profound influence of Platonism on his views of the nature, of man, and of God. A sympathetic treatment which nevertheless finds Lewis to have been flawed as a philosopher, a rational mystic torn between a romantic vision of the absolute and the boundaries of a reasoned faith. Extensive notes, a bibliography, and an index add to the worth of the study.

Wilson, A. N. *C. S. Lewis: A Biography*. New York: W. W. Norton, 1990. An important interpretation of Lewis and his work from a Freudian perspective. Paints Lewis as neither a saint nor a full-time Christian apologist but as a man of real passions and a contradictory nature unbefitting the cult following that developed after his death. The chronological biography traces many of his adult preoccupations to the sometimes traumatic experiences of his early childhood and comes to some controversial conclusions regarding several of Lewis' relationships (especially regarding Mrs. Moore). Black-and-white photographs, a select bibliography, and an index complete what turns out to be an iconoclastic portrait of the creator of Narnia.

MATTHEW GREGORY LEWIS

Born: London, England; July 9, 1775
Died: At sea, near Jamaica; May 14, 1818

Principal long fiction

The Monk: A Romance, 1796 (originally published as *Ambrosio: Or, The Monk*).

Other literary forms

Matthew Gregory Lewis' work in genres other than fiction deserves more critical attention than it has generally received. In his own day, his reputation as a dramatist almost equaled his fame as the author of *Ambrosio: Or, The Monk*, commonly referred to simply as *The Monk*. *The Castle Spectre* (1798), a Gothic drama, was a major success. Clearly the work of the author of *The Monk*, the drama is populated by stock characters who move through an intricate plot decorated with ghosts and spectacle. *The Castle Spectre* allowed Lewis to show what *The Monk* would only let him describe. *Alfonso* (1801), a tragedy, was much hailed by critics and helped establish Lewis' reputation as a major figure in the literary world of the early nineteenth century.

Lewis also wrote poetry. Some of his finer pieces appear in the text of *The Monk*. One, "Alonzo the Brave and the Fair Imogine," is still read as an excellent example of the then popular Gothic ballad and is included in *The Oxford Book of Eighteenth Century Verse* (1926). Lewis is also highly respected as a writer of nonfiction. *Journal of a West India Proprietor* (1834) is a detailed and vivid account of Jamaica in the days of slavery and of the reactions of a genuinely humane person to this environment.

Achievements

Lewis' outstanding achievement is his famous novel, *The Monk*. Often mentioned but seldom read today, this work helped to define a particular type of Gothic novel that is still popular today. Rather than merely suggesting a dangerous supernatural presence by the careful use of tone, *The Monk* relies upon graphic description and bold action. Lewis' imagination worked with clear visual images rather than with hints and elusive impressions. Indeed, he has contributed more to the Gothic conventions of stage and cinema than he has to later horror fiction. The great Gothic writers of the nineteenth century—Nathaniel Hawthorne, Edgar Allan Poe, Emily Brontë—relied more on psychological effects and less on graphic horror than did Lewis. Lewis' true successors are contemporary novelists such as Stephen King and Peter Straub, who have taken the graphic depiction of horror to new extremes.

Among the countless readers of *The Monk*, perhaps none has enjoyed the book so thoroughly as Lewis did himself. In September, 1794, he announced in a letter to his mother that he had produced "a romance of between three and four hundred pages octavo" in a mere ten weeks. With the outrageous immodesty of youth, he proclaimed, "I am myself so pleased with it, that, if the Booksellers will not buy it, I shall publish it myself." Two years later, the novel was published with a preface in imitation of Horace: "Now, then, your venturous course pursue,/ Go, my delight! dear book, adieu!" *The Monk*'s course has been "venturous" indeed. An immediate success, it went into a second edition the same year it was published, and by 1800, readers were buying the fifth edition. The first edition had been published anonymously; the second, however, not only bore the proud author's name but also his title of MP (Member of Parliament).

While the earliest reviews of *The Monk* had been generally favorable—the book was deemed artful, skillful, interesting—the second wave of criticism brought judgments less kind. *The Monk* was "a poison for youth, and a provocative for the debauchee," said Samuel Taylor Coleridge in the *Critical Review* for February, 1797. Moreover, the poison had been brewed by a Member of Parliament, the critics were fond of noting. Such criticism did no harm to the sale of the book, but an embarrassed Lewis expurgated later editions of *The Monk*.

Biography

Matthew Gregory Lewis was the oldest of four children born to Matthew Lewis and Frances Maria Sewell. Both families were quite prominent: Frances was the daughter of Sir Thomas Sewell, Master of the Rolls, and Matthew, born in Jamaica to a landed family, was Deputy-Secretary at War. They were an ill-matched pair, the elder Matthew being distant and austere, his wife delighting in gay times and the company of musical and literary people. The marriage failed, and the Lewises separated. While loyal to both parents, young Lewis was his mother's favorite, and he returned her affection in full.

From an early age, Lewis showed a great love for music and drama. At fifteen, he submitted a farce to the Drury Lane Theatre; it was rejected, but this did nothing to curb his industry. He sent his mother numerous songs and poems and outlined his plan to write a two-volume novel, burlesquing popular novels of sensibility. His father intended him for a diplomatic career, and in preparation, Lewis spent school vacations in Europe, where he soon mastered German. Through his father, he received a position as an attaché to the British embassy in Holland. While at The Hague, he completed *The Monk*. Lewis returned to England, and his novel was published in March, 1796.

Still in his early twenties, "Monk" Lewis became one of the most popular writers in England. In the following few years, this popularity was reinforced by some noteworthy successes on the stage. *The Castle Spectre* enjoyed a long run at Drury Lane; *Alfonso* played to enthusiastic audiences at Covent Garden. In the later years of his short life, Lewis turned away from literary effort. Having achieved great prominence at an early age, he seems to have found little reason to continue in an activity which could bring him no greater fame and which he did not need to pursue for a livelihood. "The act of composing has ceased to amuse me," he wrote in the Preface to *Venoni* (1808).

Lewis' father provided more than adequate support, and after his death in 1812, the son inherited substantial fortune and property. Modest in his own needs and habits, he was known to his friends (who included Percy Bysshe Shelley, Lord Byron, and Sir Walter Scott) as a man of generosity and deep concern for the oppressed. In 1815, he sailed for Jamaica to do all he could to improve the conditions of the slaves on his estates. He was responsible for important reforms and improvements, including a hospital and a humane code regulating punishments for crimes. After a brief return to England and then to Italy to visit Shelley and Byron, Lewis sailed again for Jamaica. During a five-month stay, he continued to work for better conditions for slaves. He left the island on May 4, 1818. Already sick with yellow fever, his health declined over the next several days. He died on shipboard, on May 16, and was buried at sea. According to witnesses, the coffin was wrapped in a sheet with sufficient ballast to make it sink. The plunge caused the weights to fall out, however, and the loose sheet caught the wind. The body of "Monk" Lewis, the author of one of the most fantastic books in the English language, was last seen in a sailing coffin headed for Jamaica.

Analysis

While *The Monk* is seldom read today, few students of English literature have not heard of this scandalous example of the Gothic novel. While the modern devotee of popular Gothic literature and film whose sensitivity has long since been dulled by graphic, technicolor horrors may find *The Monk* mild stuff indeed, the novel is not without excitement, and its relation to modern Gothic cinema is closer than that of most other classic Gothic novels, especially those of Mrs. Ann Radcliffe. Radcliffe would not allow her imagination to break free from eighteenth century rationalism; the supernatural, in the end, had to be given a natural explanation. Matthew Gregory Lewis' Gothic vision looked toward nineteenth century romanticism. He endowed certain characters with total confidence in tangible reality only to deflate their skepticism with head-on encounters with the supernatural that defy reason's best efforts to explain. Magic works in *The Monk*; the ghosts are real and interfere with human destiny; demons interact with men, and Satan himself, as a *deus ex machina*, finally resolves the plot.

The plot of *The Monk*, like the plot of most classic Gothic novels, is not easily summarized. Father Ambrosio, a renowned priest and orator of Madrid who symbolizes all that is chaste and holy, falls in love with an innocent girl in his congregation, Antonia. He is, at the same time, pursued by the bolder

Matilda, who enters the order disguised as a novice in order to be near Ambrosio. She and Ambrosio become passionate lovers, and Matilda, seeing that Ambrosio still pines for the young Antonia, promises to grant her to him by the aid of magic. Ambrosio bungles the staged seduction, kills Antonia's mother Elvira by mistake, and is forced to abduct Antonia to the dungeon of the monastery, where he drugs and rapes her. Seized with remorse and fear of exposure, he drives a knife in her heart when she returns to consciousness and begins to cry out. Imprisoned and faced with an Inquisitional investigation, he yields to Matilda's entreaties to sell his soul to the Devil in exchange for release from prison. He soon bitterly realizes that he faces far worse punishment at the Devil's hands than he would have had he faced the Inquisitioners, who were preparing to pardon him.

A subplot of the novel involves Agnes, a youthful nun who has given birth to the child of her lover, Raymond. She and the child are condemned to languish without food or water in the deepest part of the dungeon. In the final chapters of the book, she is discovered, half dead, and restored to Raymond.

Perhaps the most important thing to remember about Lewis the novelist is that he was also a successful playwright for the popular stage. Readers of *The Monk* do not have to concern themselves with questions of interpretation; they need not be bothered with understanding complex characters and subtle motivations. Lewis has made all the important decisions, principally that the supernatural is not only real but also a controlling force in human affairs, and with that decision, complex characterization becomes impossible and unnecessary. While Lewis denied his creation some of the elements that make a novel great, he added enough action to produce a good story.

Critics in Lewis' time generally agreed that the disreputable member of Parliament who authored *The Monk* had indiscriminately heaped immoral action upon blasphemous action to create a plot utterly devoid of moral purpose. Such a charge is not entirely fair, for *The Monk* obviously teaches a number of moral lessons. Antonia demonstrates that innocence alone is no defense against evil. The adventures of Agnes could hardly be said to promote promiscuity, and the decline and fall of Ambrosio, the monk, provides the major theme: pride is a vice that can pervert all virtues, even religious piety.

Nevertheless, those early critics were not altogether unfair in their severe judgment, for Lewis' morality is only shallowly rooted in his plot. Antonia, a model of virtue, is forcibly raped and then stabbed to death by the panic-stricken monk. Agnes, in the heat of passion, gives herself to Raymond; her reward, after suffering the loss of her child and imprisonment in a subterranean crypt, is finally to be united in matrimony with her dashing and well-to-do lover. Ambrosio is proud of the spirituality and dedication to priestly celibacy that sets him above men bound to the flesh. A truly tragic Ambrosio would finally come to understand that his pride was misplaced, for, indeed, he is a man like his fellows. In fact, the events of the book viewed in the light of the revelations at the conclusion may even support Ambrosio's original pride. The monk is enticed to damnation by the personal attention of the Devil himself, who is apparently unwilling to trust this prize to the temptations that are sufficient to damn normal men.

Until the final two or three pages of the novel, Ambrosio seems quite capable of damning himself with no outside help, and more than one sentence would be helpful in understanding why this particular monk is deserving of such special demoniac effort. Lust, perfidy, rape, and murder so much direct his actions that the reader is at a loss to understand how Ambrosio has ever been considered virtuous. Those last pages, however, cast the preceding four-hundred in a quite different light. After revealing that Elvira and Antonia (the murdered mother and daughter) were, in fact, Ambrosio's own mother and sister, the Devil goes on to brag,

> "It was I who threw Matilda in your way; it was I who gave you entrance to Antonia's chamber; it was I who caused the dagger to be given you which pierced your sister's bosom; and it was I who warned Elvira in dreams of your designs upon her daughter, and thus, by preventing your profiting by her sleep, compelled you to add rape as well as incest to the catalogue of your crimes."

The prior existence of that virtue is suddenly given credibility by this surprise revelation of the total manipulation that was necessary for its destruction.

These concluding revelations come as such a surprise that some critics regard them as merely tacked on to the action of the novel. In particular, the revelation of Matilda's true nature suggests that the conclusion was a kind of afterthought. Early in the novel, disguised as a young monk, she wins the friendship of Ambrosio. When she reveals her true sex, friendship turns to lustful love, and when Ambrosio's lust cools, her love becomes utter dedication to satisfying his every desire, even his desire for Antonia. Matilda is, in some ways, the most interesting and complex character in the novel. In the conclusion, however, Lewis does his readers the dubious favor of unraveling her complexity by having the Devil finally announce that she is not a woman at all but a lesser demon in human form, whose every action has followed the Devil's own blueprint for Ambrosio's destruction. This is especially puzzling for the careful reader who remembers that in earlier pages, Matilda professed love for Ambrosio while thinking him asleep, and that on more than one occasion, even the narrator presented her affection as sincere.

The Monk's conclusion, then, both damages the credibility of the narrator and clouds whatever moral might be found in the fall of Ambrosio. More accurately, he does not fall; he is pushed. Those late eighteenth and early nineteenth century critics for whom morality was a measure of artistic accomplishment had some cause for their attack on *The Monk*. A more generous interpretation will allow that Lewis did not construct his plot or characters to illustrate morals; he only tried to salvage what morality he could from a plot that was allowed to go its own way in search of excitement and adventure.

While there was much in *The Monk* to surprise and shock readers of the day, the novel was, in many ways, highly conventional. For example, the death of Antonia was demanded by convention. Once deflowered, an unmarried female character was useless as a symbol of virtue. Although the woman was raped against her will, her very participation in an extramarital sex act destroyed her aura of purity for eighteenth century audiences. If the association of purity with that particular character was still needed to move the plot or motivate other characters, as Antonia's purity is clearly still needed as a contrast to Ambrosio's final sin, the selling of his soul, then something must be done to remove the taint of sex and reestablish the woman in her former symbolic role. She must pay for her unintentional sin through sacrifice, and Lewis' audience expected the ultimate sacrifice: death. After her rape, Antonia, alive, is of no use to the novel; her marriage to her sweetheart, Lorenzo, a man of wealth and breeding, would be unthinkable. Dead, however, her purity is restored and can effectively serve as a foil to Ambrosio's depravity. Antonia's fate could not have been otherwise.

Romantic conventions also demanded a happy ending for the characters left alive. Lorenzo's all too rapid recovery from the loss of his beloved Antonia and his speedy attachment to Virginia, a minor character introduced late in the plot as an obvious replacement, is perhaps Lewis' most awkward attempt to satisfy convention.

His handling of Agnes, the other major female character, is considerably nonskillful. In a cast of one-dimensional characters, Agnes stands out, if only as a slightly more believable human being. She displays moral frailty without becoming a caricature of lust; she is possessed of a sense of humor and at least enough intelligence to remind the reader that the quality is generally lacking among the other characters. Agnes, like Antonia, loses her virginity. That she does so with her own true love, Raymond, whom she hopes to marry, helps only a little. Lewis recognized that it would be awkward indeed to kill off Agnes in addition to Antonia. He would then be forced to end his story with a miserable Raymond or to find some way to kill him as well. Either solution would detract from the utter misery of the monk, whose fate is seen as all the more wretched in contrast to the final happiness of the other characters. Another Virginia created in the last pages to help Raymond forget his lost love would be more than even a reader of romances could accept. Forced by his plot to allow Agnes to live, Lewis at least attempted to satisfy his audience's predictable indignation at her indiscretion by bringing her as close to death as possible.

Before her happy reunion with Raymond, Agnes passes through a purgatory as horrible as any in literature. Thought dead by all but a very few, the pregnant Agnes is imprisoned by the evil prioress in a hidden dungeon under the convent's crypt. There, alone, with barely enough bread and water to sustain her, she gives birth. The child soon dies, and the nearly insane Agnes is left to lavish a mother's love on its putrefying corpse until her rescue by Lorenzo. Lewis was certainly aware that here he was walking a fine line between pity and disgust. If the audience reacts with repugnance, Agnes would acquire a new taint that would make her happy union with Raymond unacceptable. To avoid this, Lewis carefully chooses his words when Lorenzo comes upon the despairing Agnes. The dead baby is only a "bundle" with which Agnes refuses to part, and while the bundle's contents is obvious, Lewis wisely—and uncharacteristically—renders the scene vague and withholds description. Several pages later, a fully recovered and quite sane Agnes is allowed to tell her own story, and she tells it with such sensitivity and self-understanding as to convince the audience that she has passed through the fire, learned from the experience, and is now a proper wife for Raymond.

The destinies of the individual characters—Antonia, Lorenzo, Agnes, the monk himself—show that Lewis was not naïve. He knew what his readers demanded to satisfy their moral expectations and sense of justice, and as far as was convenient, he was willing to comply, but if popular expectation conflicted with his own sense of what made a good story—adventure, graphic detail, action rather than characterization, and no rationalization of the fantastic—then he was committed to disappointing expectation.

William J. Heim

Other major works

PLAYS: *The Castle Spectre: A Drama*, 1797; *The East Indian: A Comedy*, 1799; *Adelmorn the Outlaw: A Romantic Drama*, 1801; *Alfonso, King of Castile: A Tragedy*, 1801; *Adelgitha: Or, The Fruits of a Single Error, a Tragedy*, 1806.

POETRY: *The Love of Gain: A Poem Initiated from Juvenal*, 1799; *Tales of Wonder*, 1801 (with Sir Walter Scott, Robert Southey, and John Leyden); *Poems*, 1812.

NONFICTION: *Journal of a West India Proprietor, Kept During a Residence in the Island of Jamaica*, 1834.

TRANSLATIONS: *The Bravo of Venice: A Romance*, 1805; *Feudal Tyrants: Or, The Counts of Carlsheim and Sargans, A Romance*, 1806.

Bibliography

Irwin, Joseph James. *M. G. "Monk" Lewis.* Boston: Twayne, 1976. Presents the life and writings of Lewis, with a concluding overview of his achievements. Discusses his family background, the beginning of his literary career in Paris, and the consequences of his second journey to Jamaica. Concentrates on *The Monk*, which brought Lewis fame and notoriety and set the standard for tales of terror. Also surveys his success and failure in the theater, with attention to his non-Gothic plays, such as *The East Indian*, and his poetry, praised by Sir Walter Scott and Samuel Taylor Coleridge. One chapter argues that *Journal of a West India Proprietor* is about self-discovery and has humanitarian and social importance, anticipating critical study of slavery. Includes notes, an annotated bibliography, and an index.

Kiely, Robert. *The Romantic Novel in England*. Cambridge, Mass.: Harvard University Press, 1972. An important book on Romantic prose fiction, including Lewis' Gothic romances, which analyzes in depth twelve Romantic novels to define the intellectual context of the era. Notes that concepts of reality were tested and changed by Romantic novels and Edmund Burke's ideas of the sublime modified aesthetic forms. Lewis is given a prominent place in this general thesis, and *The Monk* is analyzed in detail as the focus of his chapter. Proposes that Ambrosio is a symbol of the artist and concludes that the novel is a nightmare vision of the chaos beneath the appearance of order. Finds a common drift toward death in most novels of this genre. Includes notes and an index.

Parreaux, André. *The Publication of "The Monk": A Literary Event, 1796-1798*. Paris: Librairie Marcel Didier, 1960. A study of *The Monk*'s impact on Lewis' contemporaries, in light of the historical and literary background of 1796-1798. Examines the immediate effects of the novel's publication, explaining the basis for burlesque ballads, a parodic novel, stage adaptations, and chapbook publication, and also analyzes the public's taste for horror and the book's critical reception. Details the moral and religious controversy raised by the novel's supposed blasphemy, which caused legal and political reactions. Concludes with a brief review of Lewis' career after the novel's publication, proposing that public persecution prevented him from becoming a better writer. Provides a select, annotated bibliography and indexes of names and titles.

Peck, Louis F. *A Life of Matthew G. Lewis*. Cambridge, Mass.: Harvard University Press, 1961. This first modern full-length biography of Lewis uses materials not available to earlier biographers, such as diaries, memoirs, and the correspondence of Lewis' contemporaries. Chapter 1 details his background and early life up to 1796 and devotes attention to *The Monk*, arguing that it was published in 1796 rather than 1795. Follows Lewis from his membership in Parliament in 1796 to the beginning of the Kelly affair in 1810, and also examines his dramas and his other prose and verse. Narrates Lewis' affairs in Jamaica and his death on board the ship returning him to England. Contains a collection of selected letters, a list of his principal works, a bibliography of works cited, notes, and an index.

Summers, Montague. *The Gothic Quest: A History of the Gothic Novel*. 1938. Reprint. New York: Russell & Russell, 1964. A pioneer study, placing Gothic in the Romantic movement and examining its popularity from the success of publishers and circulating libraries. After cataloging the influences of Continental literature on English Gothic writers, examines novels in the mode of the historical Gothic. Gives sustained attention to Lewis' career, sketching his life, summarizing his plots, describing the public's response to each novel, and suggesting various works directly influenced by his novels and dramas. Lewis is also cited throughout the book as a major contributor to the Gothic tradition. Contains sixteen illustrations, including a portrait of Lewis as a frontispiece, end notes for each chapter, and two indexes, one general and one for novels.

Varma, Devendra P. *The Gothic Flame*. London: Arthur Barker, 1957. A classic historical study of the Gothic novel in England, which examines the origins of the Gothic and analyzes Horace Walpole's *The Castle of Otranto* as the first novel in the genre. The study of Lewis is focused on, though not limited to, *The Monk*, showing how it derives from the taste for horror and how his writings influenced authors after him, including twentieth century American writers. Lewis was one of the earliest authors in the school of horror, emphasizing psychology, which combined with Sir Walter Scott's historical school and Ann Radcliffe's school of terror to produce Charles Robert Maturin and others. Includes three appendices, a bibliography, and an index.

SINCLAIR LEWIS

Born: Sauk Centre, Minnesota; February 7, 1885
Died: Rome, Italy; January 10, 1951

Principal long fiction

Our Mr. Wrenn: The Romantic Adventures of a Gentle Man, 1914; *The Trail of the Hawk: A Comedy of the Seriousness of Life*, 1915; *The Innocents: A Story for Lovers*, 1917; *The Job: An American Novel*, 1917; *Free Air*, 1919; *Main Street: The Story of Carol Kennicott*, 1920; *Babbitt*, 1922; *Arrowsmith*, 1925; *Mantrap*, 1926; *Elmer Gantry*, 1927; *The Man Who Knew Coolidge: Being the Soul of Lowell Schmaltz, Constructive and Nordic Citizen*, 1928; *Dodsworth*, 1929; *Ann Vickers*, 1933; *Work of Art*, 1934; *It Can't Happen Here*, 1935; *The Prodigal Parents*, 1938; *Bethel Merriday*, 1940; *Gideon Planish*, 1943; *Cass Timberlane: A Novel of Husbands and Wives*, 1945; *Kingsblood Royal*, 1947; *The God-Seeker*, 1949; *World So Wide*, 1951.

Other literary forms

Sinclair Lewis started writing regularly during his freshman year at Yale. His stories and poems imitating the manner of Alfred, Lord Tennyson and A. C. Swinburne appeared in the *Yale Literary Magazine*. His short stories began to appear in 1915 in the *Saturday Evening Post*. In 1935, Harcourt, Brace and Co. published his *Selected Short Stories* and *Jayhawker: A Play in Three Acts*. During his lifetime, there were numerous stage and screen adaptations of many of his novels. The year after Lewis' death, Harcourt, Brace and Co. published *From Main Street to Stockholm: Letters of Sinclair Lewis, 1919-1930*, containing the novelist's correspondence with that publisher. In 1953, his miscellaneous writings appeared under the title: *The Man from Main Street: Selected Essays and Other Writings, 1904-1950*.

Achievements

In 1930, Lewis received the Nobel Prize in Literature, the first American so honored. He acknowledged in his acceptance address that the Swedish Academy honored American literature with this prize. By awarding it to the novelist who not only added "Babbitt" to the American language but also enriched the European vocabulary with his "Main Street," Europe acknowledged America's coming of age. There may have been a touch of condescension in the Academy's choice; the image of America which Lewis projected seemed to reinforce the European perception of the United States as a dollar-hunting, materialistic country, alien to cultural refinement.

Lewis' road to fame was stormy. He wrote five novels before he achieved his first big success with *Main Street* in 1920. Critics were divided: *The Dial* neglected his books, and academic critics Fred L. Pattee and Irving Babbitt rejected him, but, at the peak of Lewis' career, V. F. Parrington, T. K. Whipple, Constance Rourke, Walter Lippman, and Lewis Mumford acknowledged his strengths as a writer despite some reservations; H. L. Mencken enthusiastically supported him. English writers paid him tribute; among them were E. M. Forster, Rebecca West, Hugh Walpole, and John Galsworthy. They were joined by such fellow American writers as F. Scott Fitzgerald and Vachel Lindsay. Lewis himself was generous with others; he helped young writers such as Thomas Wolfe and was quick to praise novelists of his own generation. In his Nobel Prize acceptance speech, which came to be called "The American Fear of Literature," he repudiated the genteel tradition, in which he included William Dean Howells, and praised Theodore Dreiser, Sherwood Anderson, and a score of younger writers. Like all his writings, this speech was regarded as controversial.

Each novel renewed the controversy; some considered him unworthy of the attention and overrated; others denounced his aggressive criticism of American life, but after *Arrowsmith* he received favorable recognition even in *The Atlantic*, *The Nation*, *The New Republic*, *The New York Times*, the New York *Herald Tribune* and the *Literary Review*. Indeed, his popularity in America reached unprecedented levels. In one decade, with the help of Harcourt, Brace and Co., he became the most widely known novelist in the country. An authentic interpreter of American life, he created self-awareness among the American people, yet this role was short-lived. In 1927, Walter Lippman called him a national figure, but by 1942, as Alfred Kazin pointed out, his importance was over. The short period of fame, preceded by long years of preparation, was followed by a painful period of decline marked by ten weak novels.

Biography

Harry Sinclair Lewis was born in Sauk Centre, Minnesota, on February 7, 1885. His father, Edwin J. Lewis, and his mother, Emma F. Kermorr, were both schoolteachers, but Edwin Lewis took a two-year medical course in Chicago and practiced as a country doctor, first in Wisconsin and later in Sauk Centre, a small Minnesota town with a population of 2,500. Harry Sinclair, nicknamed "Red" because of the color of his hair, was the third of three sons. His mother died of tuberculosis when he was three. Edwin Lewis remarried shortly after her death. The future novelist was an awkward, rather ugly, lonely child with little aptitude for sports or any type of physical exercise. He soon became an ardent reader; at an early age, he also started a diary and tried his hand at creative writing.

After a short preparation in the Oberlin Academy, Lewis became a freshman at Yale at the age of seventeen. There, too, he was a loner, even after he became a regular contributor of poems and short stories to the *Yale Literary Magazine*. In the summers of 1904 and 1906, he participated in cattle-boat trips to London, and in his senior year he left Yale. For a month, he worked as a janitor in Upton Sinclair's New Jersey commune, Helicon Hall. Since he had no financial support from his father at that time, he tried to make money, first in New York with his writing and then in Panama with work on the canal construction. Unsuccessful in both attempts, he returned to Yale and was graduated in 1908.

Between 1908 and 1915, Lewis traveled from New York to California in search of employment; he also sold story plots to other writers. From 1910 to 1915, he worked in New York for commercial publishers. In 1914, his first novel, *Our Mr. Wrenn*, was published, and on April 15, he married Grace Livingston Hegger. The couple settled in Long Island. In 1915, the *Saturday Evening Post* accepted one of Lewis' short stories for publication, the first of many to be published there. With some money at his disposal, he traveled around the country with Grace, publishing short stories and writing more novels.

The five novels following *Our Mr. Wrenn*, all published under pseudonyms, were unsuccessful, but *Main Street*, Lewis' first novel to be published by Harcourt, Brace and Co., suddenly made him famous. Never again did Lewis worry about money. With *Babbitt* his fame was firmly established. He went on a Caribbean tour in preparation for *Arrowsmith*, and from 1923 to 1925 he traveled with Grace in Europe. It is interesting to note that Lewis loved publicity. In 1925, while working on *Elmer Gantry*, he defied God from a pulpit in Kansas City, giving God fifteen minutes to strike him down. His refusal of the Pulitzer Prize in 1926—an obvious act of anger over a previous disappointment—became an internationally broadcasted event.

In 1927, Lewis separated from Grace and spent much of the next year in Europe. After Grace had obtained a Reno divorce, Lewis married Dorothy Thompson, whom he had met in Berlin, on May 14, 1928. At that time, Thompson was the best-known American newspaperwoman in Europe; she also became the first American journalist to be expelled from Nazi Germany. *It Can't Happen Here*, Lewis' novel about the possibility of Fascism in America, was written under Thompson's influence. In 1929, Lewis published *Dodsworth*, a product of his long stay in Europe, which dealt with the American-in-Europe theme. In 1930, Lewis received the Nobel Prize and reached the peak of his fame.

After this period of renown, Lewis' life and career declined. A long-time drinking problem grew worse and his health rapidly deteriorated. One sign of his restlessness was his break with Harcourt, Brace and Co.; he switched to Doubleday and Co. The world around him was changing rapidly; he became increasingly confused, unhappy, and lonely. In 1937, he separated from his second wife, and they were divorced in 1942. Lewis attempted to find a new career in acting and simultaneously had an affair with a young actress. His obsession with the theater is documented in *Bethel Merriday*. With *Kingsblood*

Royal, a novel about racism, he once more tried his hand at an urgent contemporary issue but his energy was decreasing. After World War II, he spent most of his time in Europe. He died in Rome, Italy, on January 10, 1951. His last novel, *World So Wide*, dedicated to "memories in Italy," was published posthumously in 1951.

Analysis

Early reviews praised or condemned Sinclair Lewis for a blend of realism and optimism; indeed, a curious mixture of almost naturalistic realism and a kind of romance characterized Lewis' fiction throughout his career. He failed to solve the dichotomy in his novels nor did he ever solve it for himself. If his characters sometimes behave as romantic rebels, so did Lewis, rebelling against a philistine life-style in which he was deeply rooted and to which he remained attached all his life. The five novels which made him famous, *Main Street*, *Babbitt*, *Arrowsmith*, *Elmer Gantry*, and *Dodsworth*, can be read as a series of variations on the same theme. Lewis exposed an America dominated by business and petty bourgeois mentality. His characters, still full of nostalgia for the excitement of the frontier, persuade themselves that what they have at the present represents the zenith, the summit of human potential. Descendants of pious pioneer Puritans, Lewis' wealthy Americans of the 1920's are in desperate need of a civilization they can call their own. This transitory stage of the American experience becomes the theme of Lewis' writings.

As Van Wyck Brooks described it, America's coming of age in the decade before World War I paved the way for a cultural and moral revolution, heralded by works such as Edgar Lee Masters' *Spoon River Anthology* (1915), Sherwood Anderson's *Winesburg, Ohio* (1919), and Lewis' *Main Street* (1920) and *Babbitt* (1922), with its bitter attacks on "boobus Americanus." *Civilization in the U.S.* (1921), edited by Harold Stearns, gave a rather bleak picture of the average American in the 1920's—materialistic, hypocritical, and suffering from emotional and aesthetic starvation. At his best, Lewis portrayed this same world and became himself part of "the revolt from the village."

There were three distinct stages in Lewis' career. As a young novelist, he published five novels between 1914 and 1918, probing the problem of escape or the contradiction between Easterners and Midwesterners, favoring Midwestern sincerity to Eastern refinement. The 1920's were highlighted by five novels, extremely successful and ultimately winning Lewis the Nobel Prize in Literature. This glorious decade, however, was followed by a twenty-year period of decline during which he published ten inferior novels. With the passage of time, Lewis became increasingly out of touch with a rapidly changing world. While Lewis was still writing about the period of transition from exciting frontier life to small-town boredom, America rapidly proceeded to new phases, to radically different and exciting experiences.

The influences on him were many; he acknowledged a debt to Henry Thoreau, and among his contemporaries had much in common with G. B. Shaw and H. G. Wells. His ability for mimicry and for detailed observation made him a true "photographer" of life. Indeed, his novels are almost historical documents. He documented a fixed period in the American development, the frustrations and disillusionments of one generation. Unfortunately, Lewis never went beyond documentation; he re-created the symptoms but never analyzed them, never provided any formula for a meaningful life. The pattern in his books is always similar: there is a central character who—at any given moment—realizes the emptiness of his or her life and tries to break out of the mechanical boredom of the suffocating environment. The revolt is short-lived and leads nowhere. The escape ends in an impasse because Lewis himself could never solve the strange paradox of his own dislike of and attachment to Sauk Center. If he was a loner in his native village, he remained lonely at Yale and in Europe as well. Unlike Mencken, who praised and encouraged him, Lewis was not a true iconoclast; deep down he remained attached to the values he exposed.

Lewis was an extremely hard worker; he did extensive research for each novel, carrying notebooks and drawing plans of streets, houses, furniture. All this made it possible for him to evoke a concrete world. This attention to realistic detail extended to the speech of his characters. More than any novelist of his time, Lewis made a systematic effort to record American speech from all levels of society, collecting examples of usage as if he were a student of linguistics. It is no surprise that Virginia Woolf claimed to have discovered the American language in Lewis' works. Lewis' creativity was that of a photographer with an admirable instinct for selecting his subjects but an inability to give a comprehensive evaluation of what he so diligently observed.

In his best novels, Lewis selected the most important issues of American life—village/small town in *Main Street*, business in *Babbitt*, science in *Arrowsmith*, religion in *Elmer Gantry*, politics in *It Can't Happen Here*, and finally, after World War II, racism in *Kingsblood Royal*—yet despite these successes, Lewis was not a great writer. As Lewis Mumford has pointed out, he was well aware of the limitations of his environment, of the life-style he depicted, but he lacked the strength and the imagination to overcome those very limitations in himself. The revolt in his fiction is always unsuccessful because it never presents any viable alternatives to the life Lewis opposed; he stopped at faithfully and photographically reproducing spiritual poverty.

In the year when Warren Harding was successfully campaigning for the presidency with the pledge of a "return to normalcy," Lewis captured the reading public with his *Main Street*. Stuart Sherman compared the book to Gustave Flaubert's *Madame Bovary*, and Mencken praised the central characters, Carol Milford-Kennicott and her husband Dr. Will Kennicott as "triumphs of normalcy." While there are surface similarities between the plight of Emma Bovary and that of Carol Kennicott, the two are very different characters and the novels even more so. In Flaubert's novel, the emphasis is on the personal tragedy of the heroine; Lewis, on the other hand, as always deals with a theme: the "village virus." In fact, Lewis had originally intended to give this title to the book. The village-virus syndrome was a characteristic of a certain period of American life. Describing it with photographic accuracy, Lewis preserved the atmosphere of a short historical stage in the American development. Village novels were no rarity in literature before Lewis, but Lewis' sharp satirical approach marks a radical departure from that tradition.

Main Street, the most popular book of 1920, is deeply rooted in the author's life. Gopher Prairie, population three thousand, is modeled on Sauk Center, Lewis' birthplace. Dr. William Kennicott is based in part on Lewis' father and on his brother Claude, who also became a doctor. Carol is partly Lewis himself, the romantic side of him. Born in Minnesota, she is not exactly a village girl when she first appears in the novel. It is 1906 and she is a student at Blodgett College near Minneapolis. Her studies in professional library work take her to Chicago, the center of a poetic revival in the twentieth century. There she is exposed to the benefits of America's coming of age: the Art Institute, classical music, intellectual discussions on Sigmund Freud, Romain Rolland, syndicates, feminism, radically new thinking in philosophy, politics, and art. She has a job at St. Paul's public library when she meets Dr. Kennicott. The bulk of the novel is about their married life in Gopher Prairie, where Will works as a country doctor; it covers the years 1912 to 1920, from World War I and the American participation in the war to 1920, the cynical decade of the Jazz Age. America was passing on to a new period in which the political and economic fiber of the country came to be shaped and determined in cities rather than rural communities. *Main Street* is not so much a chronicle of Carol Kennicott's life between 1912 and 1920 as it is a documentation of the national phenomenon of the village virus.

The village virus is best described by Gopher Prairie's frustrated liberal, Guy Pollock. He defines it as a vicious disease menacing ambitious people who stay too long in places such as Gopher Prairie. The small-town atmosphere breeds boredom, dullness, stupidity, complacency, and vulgarity, causing the inhabitants to wither away spiritually and become living dead men. Only a few of the inhabitants see Gopher Prairie as a menace. All the "important" people of the community—Ole Jensen, the grocer; Ezra Stowbody, the banker; Sam Clark, owner of a hardware store—take pride in Main Street. When she first sees Main Street, Carol is terrified by its repulsive ugliness, but to the others it constitutes the "climax of civilization."

All the people to whom Carol is drawn are outsiders in the community. Except for the resigned Guy Pollock, they all leave, disappointed and frustrated, or else die. Village atheist and political radical Miles Bjornstrom, leaves after his wife and child die of typhoid. Before her death, his wife Bea, formerly Carol's maid, is Carol's only confidante in Gopher Prairie. The young, idealistic teacher Fern Mullins is cruelly driven out of town by Mrs. Bogart, the hypocritical watchdog of Puritan morality, and her son Cy Bogart, the village bully. Erik Valborg, an artistically minded eccentric with whom Carol almost engages in a love affair, leaves because of gossip. Those who always triumph are the Bogarts and Stowbodys; they succeed in slowly killing all of Carol's romantic ambitions.

When Carol arrives in Gopher Prairie, she is determined to bring about changes for the better. Much of the novel is about her frustrated reform efforts. Again and again she tries to initiate new and fresh ideas and plans, but all of them fail because of the all-pervasive spiritual emptiness of Gopher Prairie. People there are not interested in poetry nor in theater nor in intellecutal discussions. Will Kennicott proves to be the gentle husband through all of his wife's efforts and failures. Though he does not understand Carol's frustration, he not only stands by her but also tries to help in every way he can.

Carol leaves Gopher Prairie with their son just as the war is ending. Will is there to wave good-bye as the train taking her to Washington, D.C., pulls out of the station. In the nation's capitol, Carol is on her own; she tries to find her identity, tries to become a whole person, not simply a wife. She succeeds and enjoys the opportunity of a new life in which she can be active and in which she can use her brain once again, as she did in her girlhood, but she learns something else too: the radical changes in the behavior and attitudes of the young girls around her shock her as much as her behavior once had shocked a sleepy Gopher Prairie. In the end, she returns with Will to their home and settles down in Gopher Prairie, this time permanently. She still has dreams for her baby girl and likes to picture her as a future feminist or scientist; to the end, Carol remains a dreamer rather than a doer.

The last word in the novel belongs to the pragmatic Will Kennicott. He is Lewis' real favorite—the simple country doctor who performs acts of quiet heroism and worries about matters such as putting up storm windows. Lewis is unquestionably drawn to this stable, dependable, and reliable man, representing in his view the best of middle-class America. Lewis only half-heartedly endorses Carol's romantic attempts at beautifying Gopher Prairie because he himself was of divided mind whom to prefer: the artistically minded Carol or the always commonsensical though unsophisticated Will. If the cigarette-smoking modern young girls of the 1920's shocked Carol, Lewis, too, was unable to catch up with new trends. In this sense, *Main Street*, a novel about the village virus, is also an autobiography of Sinclair Lewis' spiritual development or, rather, spiritual stagnation.

The year 1921 was highlighted by an outburst of favorable and unfavorable reactions to this novel. First, there emerged a series of Main Street literature, attacking, burlesquing, and imitating the original, among them Carolyn Wells's

Ptomaine Street, Meredith Nicholson's *Let Main Street Alone*, and Donald Ogden Stewart's *A Parody Outline of History*. At the same time, dramatized by Harving O'Higgins and Harrier Ford, *Main Street* was performed at New York's National Theater.

Even before he finished *Main Street*, Lewis had started work on *Babbitt*, a novel about a land speculator. From Main Street, U.S.A., "the climax of civilization," the novelist moved to an imaginary city in the Middle West, satirically named Zenith, symbolizing the average American city and its status symbol oriented population. Set in the boom-decade of the 1920's, the novel concentrates on the new national disease, which came to be called "Babbittry," after the book's protagonist. Webster's dictionary now defines a Babbitt as "a seemingly self-satisfied businessman who readily conforms to the norms and ideas of middle-class society." The term "seemingly" is important; it indicates that even in this realistic, satirical presentation of middle-class America and its business culture, Lewis' romantic side is present; it finds outlet in Babbitt's dissatisfaction with his life. Predominantly, though, the almost photographic portrayal of Zenith prevails. While President Harding was hoping to plant a Rotary Club in every city and village in the country to insure the propagation of American ideals, Lewis was provoking the anger of those very Rotary Clubs by holding up a mirror to their Tartuffe-like hypocrisy and their materialistic culture.

Just as *Main Street* killed the friendly village novel by concentrating on the village virus, so *Babbitt* undercut the traditional business novel. With *Babbitt*, Lewis demonstrated that the era of the independent, creative tycoon was over. The tycoon gave way to the joiner, the conformist relying on status symbols and good public relations rather than daring and creative initiative. Babbitt, positively no giant, is almost a pathetic figure in his desperate need for approval. Far from being a tycoon, he lacks any individual ideas. He is a Booster, an Elk, a Presbyterian, a member of the chamber of commerce, a family man—nothing more. Senators of the Republican Party prescribe his political beliefs; national advertisers dictate his preferences in consumer goods. Without all these accessories, he is nobody; Babbitt is spiritually empty. While he relies on the sham values that make him a "solid citizen," he becomes a pitiful victim of mechanical gadgets; his identity depends on having a car, the newest device alarm clock, and a royal bathroom.

Lewis worked very hard on this novel, which some critics consider his best. He prepared detailed maps of Zenith, plans of the decoration and furniture of Babbitt's house. The mimicry of language is superb, culminating in Babbitt's famous address at the meeting of the Zenith Real Estate Board. In his speech, Babbitt pours scorn on moth-eaten, old-fashioned Europe and glorifies the city of Success, known "wherever condensed milk and paste-board cartons are known." The pitiful, empty world of Zenith is presented in loosely connected episodes, the sequence of which could almost be changed, and which are held together only by the presence of Babbitt. They take the reader through the most important aspects of middle-class life: politics, leisure, clubs, class, labor, religion, and family.

This apparent contentment, however, is one side of the novel; Babbitt is only "seemingly" satisfied. In reality, this prosperous real estate agent passionately desires something more and different from mere material success. This desire leads to his unsuccessful, vague, romantic rebellion against the Zenith world. Closely linked to his desire for escape is his longstanding friendship with Paul Riesling. Paul is one of those lonely, out-of-the-ordinary characters who emerge in all Lewis novels—creative, individualistic, nonconformist. With Paul, Babbitt escapes to Maine, but the escape does not help; his frustration remains.

Amid this frustration, crisis enters Babbitt's life. Paul is condemned to three years in prison for shooting his wife in what is described as temporary insanity. Without Paul, life seems impossible for Babbitt to bear; he tries to leave Zenith again but very soon returns. Zenith is the only thing in the world he knows; without it he is empty, a nobody. Like Lewis, who could never get rid of Sauk Center, Babbitt takes Zenith with him wherever he goes. For a while, he tries to outrage Zenith society by drinking heavily and by associating with the wrong people—with the adventuress Tanis Judique and her bohemian friends, called the Bunch. At the same time, Vergil Gunch, one of the exemplary solid citizens, is organizing the Good Citizens' League. Babbitt shocks all his former friends and associates by defying Vergil's request to join their antilabor vigilante organization.

In *Main Street*, Lewis made Carol Kennicott return to Gopher Prairie. In a similar spirit of compromise, he finds a convenient way for Babbitt to give up his empty rebellion. His wife Myra has to undergo emergency surgery; her hospitalization pulls Babbitt back to his duties as a solid citizen. To seal his return to normalcy, he joins the Good Citizens' League. At the end of the novel, he is taken by surprise by his younger son; Ted drops out of school and elopes. In a private, man-to-man talk with his son, Babbitt acknowledges that he admires him for doing what he wants. He, Babbitt, never did that all his life. In *Main Street*, Carol Kennicott's rebellion dwindles to romantic dreams for her daughter; all that remains of Babbitt's rebellion is his pleasure in his son's defiance and an encouragement not to let himself be bullied by Zenith. At the moment, however, Ted does not hold out much promise; rather than going to college he wants to be a mechanic at a factory.

Although *Babbitt* outraged certain sectors of the business community, the novel became an international success. Europeans loved it even more than *Main Street*. They enjoyed seeing America portrayed as they believed it was: materialistic, vulgar, standardized, and hopelessly without culture. They enjoyed the language; the British edition even added a glossary of 125 "American" terms. It is interesting to note that even while the novel was being angrily attacked, a number of Midwestern cities claimed to have been the model for Zenith. Without offering any cure, simply by diagnosing and photographically reproducing symptoms of a national phenomenon, Lewis promoted self-awareness among his many readers.

Critics who wondered whether Lewis himself was Babbitt, lacking all spiritual ideals, were surprised by *Arrowsmith* (1925), which featured an idealistic hero with spiritual values. In 1922, while gathering material in Chicago for a labor novel Lewis met Paul de Kruif, a teacher of bacteriology at the University of Michigan and experienced in immunology research. They became friends and Lewis changed his plans; assisted by Paul de Kruif's expertise, he decided to write a novel on the medical profession. Lewis had some personal experience on which to draw; his father, his brother Claude, an uncle, and a grandfather were doctors. He needed help, however, in the field of scientific research; that is what de Kruif provided him. Because a plague in the West Indies was to be an important part of the novel, they took a tour in the Caribbean together. De Kruif stayed with Lewis in England while he was working on *Arrowsmith*, a well-researched novel and his best-plotted one.

Arrowsmith was an instant success, being the first American novel about a medical researcher. The central character, Martin Arrowsmith, is a real hero with a purpose: he is wholly dedicated to pure science. The plot develops around the dramatic conflict between Martin, a few others of the same mind, and a society based on profit. Arrowsmith, Gottlieb, Sondelius, and Terry Wickett are akin to earlier idealists in Lewis' fiction, to Eric Valborg in *Main Street* and Paul Riesling in *Babbitt*, but there is a significant difference. Eric and Paul are lonely figures; Martin and his associates are not alone and they do not give up; they put up a fight against the commercial standards of a society that does not understand their ideals.

Martin Arrowsmith is introduced on the first page of the novel as a fourteen-year-old boy sitting in a country doctor's office. From his hometown of Elk Mills, the hero moves on to college to pursue his dreams; he regards himself as a "seeker of truth." At the University of Winnemac, young Martin associates with two kinds of people who symbolize the opposing forces of material versus purely scientific values. On the one hand, there are the people involved in fraternity life; on the other, there is the German-born biologist, Max Gottlieb, modeled on Jacques Loeb, who allows Martin to work in his lab. Two events disrupt the smooth course of young Martin's drive to achieve his goal. First, he meets a nurse, Leora Tozer, and they fall in love; then, an irritable Gottlieb dismisses him from the laboratory. Martin and Leora marry, and, after an internship in Zenith General Hospital, they settle down in Wheatsylvania, Dakota, responding to pressure from Leora's family.

As a country practitioner, Martin finds himself in a situation well-known to Lewis. The young idealist who hopes to become another Robert Koch is increasingly in the position of a businessman in rivalry with other country doctors. At the same time, Martin's idol Gottlieb is undergoing a similar experience. After his defeat at Winnemac, he is faced with a new crisis in Pittsburgh when he refuses the request of a large pharmaceutical firm to have his antitoxin patented. Finally, a frustrated Martin escapes to Nautilus, Iowa, another Zenith, and then to the Rouncefield Clinic in Chicago. One of his articles catches the attention of Gottlieb, now associated with the McGurk Institute of Biology in New York, and the two are reunited. Martin even finds a new kindred spirit in Terry Wickett. Life at the Rouncefield Clinic and then at the McGurk Institute provides ample occasion for Lewis to describe the internal rivalry in such institutions, the pressures from outside and the search for power and fame.

When a severe plague erupts in the West Indies, Martin's recent discovery catches the attention of the outside world; this is the most dramatic part of the novel. Gottlieb's approach is not philanthropic but scientific. He wants Martin to use the antitoxin only with half of the patients so that its true value can be tested, but on the islands Martin is faced with real people. His faithful assistant Sondelius dies and so does Leora. He initially intends to be a scientist and not a sentimentalist, but in the end he gives in, hoping to save more lives. On his return to New York, he finds changes at the Institute; Gottlieb is pensioned and the new director is all for "practicalness." The frustrated Martin marries a wealthy socialite, Joyce Lanyon, and they have a baby; but Martin and his friend Terry find themselves out of place in the Institute under the new direction and Martin does not find in Joyce the companion he had in Leora. The two friends escape to Vermont to fish and to pursue their drive for pure science. While commercial society in Washington and elsewhere continues in its Babbitt-Zenith ways, Martin and Terry discuss quinine research in their boat.

The conclusion is rather romantic, sentimental, and unsatisfactory, but despite this flaw and some misgivings on the part of the medical community, *Arrowsmith* was universally acclaimed. Even the Pulitzer Prize, so far denied Lewis, was his, but he refused to accept it at that time. The retreat to Vermont in *Arrowsmith* was no real solution to the dilemma, but once again Lewis had presented, and called attention to, a genuine problem in American society. *Arrowsmith* celebrates an unwillingness to compromise and a dedication to ideals which give this novel a heroic dimension missing in all other Lewis novels.

Lewis dedicated *Elmer Gantry* (1927) "with profound admiration" to Mencken, and rightly so, because in this novel the romantic side of the novelist is overshadowed by a brutal, iconoclastic, almost fanatical satire. From his idealistic excursion in *Arrowsmith*, Lewis returned to his former mood, except that this time he created in the central character a complete villain. Elmer Gantry is the American Tartuffe. The reader can feel compassion for Carol Kennicott and pity toward Babbitt but there is absolutely no saving grace for

Elmer Gantry, the fundamentalist preacher in Lewis' novel.

Elmer Gantry was probably Lewis' most thoroughly researched novel. In 1922, a preacher named William Stidger suggested to Lewis that he write a novel on the subject of religion. In the anti-Puritan 1920's, religious life was in a disarray in America. When Lewis finally decided to write a novel on the topic, he went to Kansas City in search of Stidger, living there for a considerable time in order to prepare material for *Elmer Gantry*. In Kansas City, he visited churches, preached himself, and investigated and worked with a group of fifteen clergymen of various denominations in what he called "Sinclair Lewis's Sunday Work Class." There were tragic events in his own life while he was working on the novel: his father died, his marriage with Grace broke up, and he was literally drunk when writing the final pages in New York.

The most obvious characteristic of the novel is its brutality; there is no trace of that sympathy which mitigated the dark picture in *Main Street* or *Babbitt*; there is no trace of a love/hate relationship with Elmer Gantry. He as well as the novel's other major characters have few redeeming qualities. The novel, indeed, is an uncompromising indictment of American religious practices in the early century. This most devastating of Lewis' satires is similar to *Babbitt*, in that it is loosely structured and episodic. Its three main parts concern Elmer Gantry's involvement with three different women. In no other Lewis novel is the sexual element as important as in this one; it is Gantry's sexual desire that threatens his rise in religious circles.

The young Elmer Gantry attends a Baptist College and is ordained a minister. As soon as he receives his first pulpit, he becomes sexually involved with a young girl. He gets rid of Lulu by casting doubt on her character, revealing the depths of falsehood and villainy of which he is capable. In the second phase of his religious career, he becomes an evangelist, the partner (religious and sexual) of the female evangelist Sharon Falcon. They are two of a kind who never consider "their converts as human beings"; they regard them as a surgeon regards his patients or as a fisherman regards trout. Sharon dies in a fire, and Elmer Gantry's adventures take him to the Methodist denomination. There, he rises fast and is promoted to pastorates in larger and larger communities. He is made a Doctor of Divinity, marries, becomes the first preacher whose sermons are broadcast, and tours Europe. Suddenly his fame and position are almost destroyed by a new love affair. Hettie and her convict husband try to outwit Gantry; they set a trap for him. For a short time he is frightened, but influential and clever friends come to his rescue and he bounces back again. At the end of the novel, he is leading his congregation in prayer, determined "to make these United States a moral nation." Like all true hypocrites, Gantry convinces himself of his sincerity.

Understandably, the novel outraged churches all over America. Some clergy even called Lewis "Satan's cohort," but the book sold 175,000 copies in less than six weeks, and a motion picture was made of the novel in 1960.

With *Dodsworth* (1929), Lewis returned to Zenith. At the beginning of the novel, Sam Dodsworth, a successful businessman in his forties, undergoes a crisis similar to Babbitt's but there the similarities end. Sam, a Yale graduate, is much better-educated than Babbitt and is receptive to the arts. A self-made man, he built his own company, but, following the prevailing trend in America, his small business is bought by a conglomerate. This causes the active, enterprising Sam to believe himself to be a useless part of a big bureaucratic machine, and provides an opportunity for his snobbish wife Fran to persuade him to go with her on a long European tour. This trip takes up the major part of the novel, which is a rather shallow treatment of Henry James's "international theme."

Sam Dodsworth does not know how to spend his wealth or his leisure time meaningfully; also, he is painfully gauche. In spite of these flaws, the author's sympathies are with him. Sam is trying hard to please his empty-headed wife. In her utter stupidity, Fran tries to imitate the worst symptoms of the decaying European aristocracy. At the end, she takes a lover and proposes divorce to Sam in the hope of an exciting marriage. These plans fail, and Sam is there to rescue her, but their marriage cannot be saved. Lewis condemns the superficiality of European high society, but he is far from criticizing European culture; his satire is concentrated on Fran. Finally, Sam finds an understanding companion in a widow, Edith Cortright, who appreciates his qualities, his honesty and integrity, likes him for what he his, and does not want to change him into something else. At the end of the novel, they are in Paris discussing marriage, but they are planning to return to America, where they know they belong.

Significantly, Lewis always turned back to the middle class for his subject matter. In *It Can't Happen Here* (1935) inspired by Dorothy Thompson's anti-Fascist stand, Lewis exposed the danger inherent in right-wing extremism in America; but at the end of the 1930's, when the new left-wing writers hoped to see him write a proletarian novel, the essentially middle-class Lewis could not accommodate them.

During the long and painful years of his decline Lewis tried to continue to focus on issues of importance—the career woman (*Ann Vickers*, 1933); organized philanthropy (*Gideon Planish*, 1943); American marriage (*Cass Timberlane*, 1945). American life was changing too rapidly for Lewis, however; he was never able to catch up with the changes. He did hit upon an important theme in *Kingsblood Royal* (1947), but by that time his greatest ability—to re-create the world around him in photographic detail—seemed to have abandoned him.

Lewis' aesthetic shortcomings are obvious, but so are his merits. A writer of international reputation, he made American literature acceptable in Europe, becoming the first American winner of the Nobel Prize for Literature. His

Main Street was one of the most sensational successes in American publishing history. His biographer, Mark Schorer, describes him as a major force in the liberating of twentieth century American literature. Yet, at present, he is virtually ignored by critics. A well-balanced, objective evaluation of this controversial novelist is long overdue; the necessary distance in time should make it soon possible.

Anna B. Katona

Other major works
SHORT FICTION: *Selected Short Stories of Sinclair Lewis*, 1935.
PLAY: *Jayhawker: A Play in Three Acts*, 1934 (with Lloyd Lewis).
NONFICTION: *From Main Street to Stockholm: Letters of Sinclair Lewis, 1919-1930*, 1952 (Harrison Smith, editor); *The Man from Main Street: Selected Essays and Other Writings, 1904-1950*, 1953 (Harry E. Maule and Melville H. Crane, editors).

Bibliography
Bloom, Harold, ed. *Modern Critical Views: Sinclair Lewis*. New York: Chelsea House, 1987. Bloom has gathered together an excellent spread of criticism on Lewis. Essays range from an analysis of *Arrowsmith* to discussion on the tension between romanticism and realism in his work. Bloom's introduction comments on the irony that the satirist Lewis should be remembered for the "idealizing romance" of *Arrowsmith*.

Derleth, August. *Three Literary Men: A Memoir of Sinclair Lewis, Sherwood Anderson, Edgar Lee Masters*. New York: Candlelight Press, 1963. A personal account of Derleth's meetings and correspondence with Lewis. A lively piece, but somewhat marred by Derleth's promoting of his own work.

Koblas, John J. *Sinclair Lewis: Home at Last*. Bloomington, Minn.: Voyageur Press, 1981. A look at Lewis' life and his Midwestern roots, from which he tried to remove himself but to which he continually returned in his fiction. A valuable study, with much insight into the author and the places that were meaningful to him.

Light, Martin. *The Quixotic Vision of Sinclair Lewis*. West Lafayette, Ind.: Purdue University Press, 1975. A respected critic of Lewis, Light examines the conflict of realism and romance in Lewis' work, which he terms the quixotic element. An invaluable and perceptive critical study of Lewis.

Parrington, Vernon Louis. *Sinclair Lewis: Our Own Diogenes*. Seattle: University of Washington Press, 1927. Reprint. New York: Haskell House, 1973. An essay on Lewis which discusses his role as the "bad boy of letters." Looks at Lewis' disillusionment through his novels *Babbitt* and *Arrowsmith*. A good example of critical thinking of the 1920's.

Schorer, Mark, ed. *Sinclair Lewis: A Collection of Critical Essays*. Englewood Cliffs, N.J.: Prentice-Hall, 1962. A compilation of criticism from H. L. Mencken's "Consolation" (1922) to Geoffrey Moore's "Sinclair Lewis: A Lost Romantic" (1959). A useful complement to the more current criticism available in Bloom's volume.

WYNDHAM LEWIS

Born: Amherst, Canada; November 18, 1882
Died: London, England; March 7, 1957

Principal long fiction

Tarr, 1918, 1928; *The Childermass*, 1928; *The Apes of God*, 1930; *Snooty Baronet*, 1932; *The Revenge for Love*, 1937; *The Vulgar Streak*, 1941; *Self Condemned*, 1954; *The Human Age: Monstre Gai* and *Malign Fiesta*, 1955; *The Red Priest*, 1956; *The Roaring Queen*, 1973 (written in 1936); *Mrs. Dukes' Million*, 1977.

Other literary forms

In addition to ten book-length works of fiction (including the trilogy *The Human Age*), Wyndham Lewis published more than thirty other books in his lifetime; two novels, a volume of letters, and numerous collections of previously unpublished or uncollected material have appeared since his death. This mass of material is awesome in its diversity as well as in its bulk. It includes three volumes of short stories (*The Wild Body*, 1927; *Rotting Hill*, 1951; *Unlucky for Pringle*, 1973); two plays and a book of poems (*The Ideal Giant*, 1917; *Enemy of the Stars*, 1914, 1932; *One-Way Song*, 1933; these have been brought together in *Collected Poems and Plays*, 1979); and two autobiographies (*Blasting and Bombardiering*, 1937; *Rude Assignment: A Narrative of My Career Up-to-Date*, 1950). The bulk of Lewis' writing, however, is not fictional nor, strictly speaking, literary, He wrote enough art criticism to fill one volume (*Wyndham Lewis on Art*, 1969) and enough literary criticism to fill several (*Men Without Art*, 1934; *The Writer and the Absolute*, 1952; *Enemy Salvos*, 1976), but even while writing such criticism he always focused on the political, cultural, and philosophical implications of the works of art. In keeping with this, Lewis wrote extensively on politics and philosophy, and his work of this kind should probably be called political, cultural, and philosophical criticism, as in these books he was always on the attack. Far and away the best known and most important of these works is *Time and Western Man* (1927); E. W. F. Tomlin's fine anthology, *Wyndham Lewis: An Anthology of His Prose* (1969), provides an excellent selection from the rest. A new collection of essays, *Creatures of Habit, Creatures of Change*, appeared in 1989.

Achievements

It is often, and probably correctly, said that Lewis' actual achievements fell far short of what he should have achieved, given his immense talents. Those talents were widely recognized by some of his most eminent contemporaries: T. S. Eliot called him "the most fascinating personality of our time" and "the greatest prose master of style of my generation—perhaps the only one to have invented a new style"; W. B. Yeats read his philosophical work "with evergrowing admiration and envy"; Ezra Pound thought that he should have won the Nobel Prize for his late novel, *Self Condemned*. Yet he did not win and, unlike these friends and admirers, he never became a household name. Lewis continues to appeal only to a small—if devoted—audience.

In a sense, Lewis had too much talent. Both painter and writer, novelist and critic, philosopher and political thinker, he tried to do everything. He simply wrote too much and did too many different kinds of writing to achieve perfection in any one thing. In this, he is more like Ford Madox Ford or D. H. Lawrence than Eliot or James Joyce, who wrote little and therefore had time to perfect everything. Lewis' achievement is scattered across forty or fifty books, which makes it difficult to see his work as a whole or to find the right place to start. Each book has its interest; none is perfect.

Each book *does* have its interest, however, which is no mean achievement considering the size of Lewis' oeuvre. A constant source of interest is the personal nature of Lewis' work. No advocate of impersonality, in the manner of Gustave Flaubert, Henry James, or James Joyce, Lewis is on constant display in his work. More like a Victorian than a modern, in the tradition of, for example, Thomas Carlyle, he also resembles Carlyle in that the personality displayed is partisan, contentious, opinionated, domineering, and eccentric. This is probably why Lewis, virtually alone among modern British novelists, managed to write intellectually rich fiction. Ideas, far more than character or plot, are the fundamental material for Lewis' novels, which at times seem more like long arguments than narratives. Lewis wrote, of course, a great deal of nonfiction, and the fiction and the nonfiction interpenetrate. One finds in *The Childermass*, for example, essentially the same analysis of contemporary politics as that found in *The Art of Being Ruled* (1926).

Lewis' novels, however, are not simply romans à these, illustrations of points of view found in the nonfiction. In many cases, they are much more interesting and vital than the nonfiction. The reason for this is Lewis' unforgettable style, which Eliot rightly saw as strikingly original. The originality and achievement of his style also stem from his overwhelming presence in his works. Never striving for the objective representation of the familiar world which is the aim of the realistic novelist, Lewis through his style uncompromisingly creates a world of his own. Some of his novels are what would today be called science fiction; the majority, set in contemporary society, are not. Whatever the genre of Lewis' novels, however, he always keeps one aware that one is reading a novel written by Wyndham Lewis. Many readers may find this irritating, preferring the pretense of the conventional novel that it is not a fiction, that it is about something that really happened. Indeed, one aspect of Lewis' considerable achievement as a novelist is that he anticipated by a full generation the self-conscious fiction of Jorge Luis Borges, Flann O'Brien, Alain

Robbe-Grillet, John Barth, and others.

Lewis' achievement as a novelist, in short, is that, though he may not have written a single work of the stature of *Ulysses* (1922), he is always intelligent, always interesting; in the era of postmodernism, he is a contemporary to an extent that others of his generation such as Eliot or Joyce, let alone E. M. Forster or Lawrence, are not.

Biography

Percy Wyndham Lewis was born on his father's sailboat off Nova Scotia in 1882. His parents made an improbable couple, his father an independently wealthy American from Upstate New York, his mother an Englishwoman who returned to England with her child after the marriage collapsed when Lewis was ten. Lewis then attended a number of schools, including Rugby, without distinction and finally went to the Slade School of Art in London from 1898 to 1901. After that came an extended period of wandering through Europe, particularly Germany, France, and Spain. The ostensible purpose of these travels was to paint and to study painting, but Lewis also saw himself as a writer, and his first appearance in print, in *The English Review* in 1909, was with a sketch drawn from his travels.

By 1912, the family finances could no longer support such travels, and Lewis returned to London to make his mark in the art world. He founded an art movement, Vorticism, published a magazine, *Blast*, which caused a sensation though it only appeared twice, and created a distinctively Vorticist style in both painting and writing. By 1914, the year of the Vorticist move- ment, it looked as if he were on the verge of a brilliant career, but World War I interrupted these plans. Vorticism came to an end in the war, and Lewis fought in the trenches in France as a bombardier.

Keeping a much lower profile after the war, Lewis, though he continued to paint, saw himself and was seen more and more as a writer. He published twenty-six books between 1926 and the outbreak of World War II. These works aroused considerable controversy, both because of Lewis' satiric attacks on well-known literary figures and because of the often outrageous stands he took on political questions in the 1930's. This meant that he was increasingly isolated as a writer and painter, an isolation made absolute during World War II, when he and his wife, Anne, whom he had married in 1929, lived mostly in Canada.

This isolation lessened after World War II. Lewis became the regular art critic of *The Listener* until he went blind in 1951. He received various tributes, including an honorary D.Litt., a Civil List Pension, and a major Tate Gallery retrospective in 1956. In a final burst of energy, he published a book a year the last eight years of his life, some of his finest works among them, even though he was dying from the tumor which had first made him blind. Lewis died in March, 1957. It is reported that his last words, addressed to a nurse, were, appropriately enough for a man of his temperament, "Mind your own business."

Analysis

Wyndam Lewis published his first novel, *Tarr*, in 1918. *Tarr* began as two separate stories which grew and were fused together, somewhat awkwardly, to form the novel. The first, which can be called "Tarr," is about Frederick Tarr, a young English painter living in bohemian Paris and engaged to a German, Bertha Lunken. Tarr is full of opinions about everything, and his part of the book is mostly taken up by his disquisitions, primarily on aesthetics. The other story, "Kreisler," is about an impoverished German sculptor, Otto Kreisler. Kreisler, as contemptible a failure in life as in art, runs out of money, rapes Bertha, gets in a duel, kills his opponent before the duel can take place, and finally commits suicide. The basic split between Tarr and Kreisler runs throughout Lewis' fiction. Mind and body, intellect and emotion, art and life—these are some of the obvious terms for expressing this split. *Tarr*, *The Childermass*, and *The Apes of God*—Lewis' first novels—are essentially about this split, the satiric comment of someone committed to art and the intellect on the limitations of those committed to the values of life and the body.

The Childermass and *The Apes of God* are considerably more dense, difficult, and ambitious works than *Tarr*. *The Childermass*, first published in 1928, is the first book of *The Human Age*, Books II and III of which were not published until 1955, but it really stands on its own. Set in the life after death, it also divides into two parts. The first is about how James Pullman and Satterthwaite, a famous writer and his "fag" at school, make their way to the camp of the Bailiff outside what they take to be Heaven. The second half is a long debate, mostly between Hyperides, a Tarr-like figure who sounds remarkably like the Lewis who wrote *The Art of Being Ruled* and *Time and Western Man*, and the Bailiff, the political ruler of at least this corner of the afterlife, not Heaven at all, as Pullman slowly grasps.

The Apes of God is set in contemporary London. A vicious satire in which most of the targets of Lewis' satire are recognizable, it is a prolonged attack on Bloomsbury, which Lewis saw as full of people aping their God, the artist, and in the process making the life of the genuine artist impossible. Everyone here is a follower of the Bailiff, or his worldly equivalent; the only person in the novel who does not seem to be an ape, Pierpoint, remains offstage, only speaking through disciples who, the reader should soon see, are as apelike as the rest.

The Childermass and *The Apes of God* are both books which cannot be taken lightly. Either one takes their vision and judgment of contemporary society very seriously or one cannot take them at all. They have been praised very highly by Ezra Pound, I. A. Richards, and others, and they are probably Lewis' ultimate achievements in the sense of being the most unusual, the most personal, and the most Lewisian of his works. Nevertheless, most readers find them unreadable. They are, frankly, very difficult to read; W. B. Yeats, no stranger to difficult texts, called one passage in *The Childermass* "the most obscure piece of writing known to me." This difficulty is deliberate: Lewis is trying to defamiliarize the world for his readers, to present it, not as it is habitually seen, but as it should be seen. Lewis sees most people as little more than automata or machines, so he presents them in his fiction as such. This satiric strategy can have one of two effects on a reader; in neither case is Lewis left with much of an audience. Either the reader grasps the satiric point Lewis is trying to make, or he takes Lewis' novels as eccentric mythologies. Those who grasp the point are likely to feel insulted, for the reader is subsumed in Lewis' vision under the category of ape as well; those who appreciate mythological or fantastic fiction tend to prefer more genial mythologies.

Lewis himself must have sensed the problems inherent in *The Childermass* and *The Apes of God*, for the novels he wrote in the 1930's, *Snooty Baronet*, *The Roaring Queen*, and *Revenge for Love*, are very different. The first important difference is that in them Lewis abandons the attempt to write fiction as though no one else had written any before. There are no formal models for *Tarr*, *The Childermass*, and *The Apes of God*; they obey no generic laws of any kind, which is much of the reason why they seem so sprawling, so formless. Lewis' novels of the 1930's, by contrast, are generic parodies: *The Revenge for Love* is a political thriller, *Snooty Baronet* a travel book-cum-murder mystery, and *The Roaring Queen* a country house weekend novel, a parody of early Aldous Huxley and Evelyn Waugh. The second important difference is that none of these novels contains the all-knowing Lewis persona who comments on the action. They do express much the same vision of man: human desires seem just as bizarre, as animalistic, as trivial in *Snooty Baronet* as they do in *The Apes of God*. What is missing is the eternal comment on this vision: Lewis abandons the static novel of ideas and presents his vision far more through what happens than what is said. These two changes make his novels of the 1930's far less intense and far more enjoyable to read.

How Lewis could have written *Snooty Baronet* two years after writing *The Apes of God* has long mystified critics. In 1977, however, *Mrs. Dukes' Million*, a novel Lewis began in 1908, about when he began *Tarr*, was published and made this shift far more comprehensible, though it made Lewis' beginnings as a novelist look much more complicated. *Mrs. Dukes' Million* is a fascinating if bizarre attempt at a detective thriller. Lewis frankly wrote it for money, but he could not quite write a straight example of the genre, so *Mrs. Dukes' Million* ends up being the same kind of parodic genre novel as *Snooty Baronet*. Thus, Lewis' impulses as a novelist were divided from the beginning: on the one hand, he wanted to be a serious novelist of ideas and a modernist innovator, which led to difficult, static works such as *The Apes of God*; on the other hand, he had a tremendous talent for narration and for a subversive handling of genre.

In Lewis' greatest novel, *The Revenge for Love*, he manages to put these impulses together. *The Revenge for Love* is a satire on 1930's leftism, on the "parlour pinks" of London, and on the tremendous gap between the humanitarian idealism of these figures and the murderous nature of the ideology they espouse. It is as biting and incisive as *The Apes of God*, yet this commentary is embedded in a fast-moving thriller plot about smuggling arms into Republican Spain. Lewis' use of the thriller genre is perfectly opposite because *The Revenge for Love* is a meditation on the nature and value of action, and the thriller is the novel of action *par excellence*. Hence, the playful and the serious sides of Lewis' art come together perfectly in what is one of the most underrated novels of the twentieth century.

A new note is also struck in *The Revenge for Love*, a note which was to predominate in the major novels Lewis wrote after World War II, *Self Condemned* and Books II and III of *The Human Age*, *Monstre Gai* and *Malign Fiesta*. In the first part of his career, until *The Revenge for Love*, Lewis had been absolutely sure of his position, of his values, of his satirical critique of man. Lewis' role, as he saw it, was to castigate man for his lack of freedom and his deadness. In this role, he called himself the "Enemy" and set out to oppose virtually everything in the name of art, the intellect, and detachment. In *The Revenge for Love*, Lewis continues to attack most of what he portrays. The two major male characters are Percy Hardcaster, a professional Communist who holds the intellectual fellow-travelers around him in contempt, and Victor Stamp, a hapless artist who gets drawn into the same gunrunning scheme as Hardcaster. These characters are not grotesques such as those in *The Apes of God*, but neither are they figures with whom the reader identifies. The third major character, however, is Victor's wife, Margot. Initially an object of caricature, a young devotee of Virginia Woolf, Margot grows in stature as the novel progresses. She stands in opposition to the world of action, politics, and men, portrayed in the rest of the novel, and stands for the bonds of love and human affection. In earlier Lewis novels, her feminine values, as Lewis labels them, would have been lumped in with the male values of activity and attacked from Lewis' detached, intellectual perspective. Here, though, Margot becomes a moral authority, and Lewis begins—tentatively, one must admit—to criticize his earlier position as excessively harsh and arid. Margot's death at the end is a real tragedy, inducing even in the tough Percy Hardcaster a tear that rolls down his cheek at the very end of the novel.

Self Condemned continues this process of self-criticism, as should be obvious from the title. It is, obliquely, about Lewis' experiences during World War II in Canada, which he hated. René Harding, a distinguished English historian, and his wife, Hester, leave England for Canada, where they gradually deteriorate. Hester commits suicide rather than remain in Canada as René wishes, and at the end René has become "a glacial shell of a man." Hester, like Margot, is the moral center of the novel, and her suicide is an eloquent condemnation of René and his arid intellectualism. René may in part be Lewis' own sense of what he might have become had he similarly turned away from his wife; in any case, in *Self Condemned*, as in *The Revenge for Love*, women characters are the vehicles for an implicit critique of Lewis' earlier values.

The Human Age covers the same ground, in a sense, but from a more profound and developed perspective. Male and female in *The Revenge for Love* and *Self Condemned* serve as a kind of shorthand for the values of selfish indifference and unselfish compassion, respectively. In *The Human Age*, this sexual symbolism is replaced by a religious perspective, and Lewis' art takes an explicitly theological turn. *The Human Age* is a continuation, after twenty-five years, of *The Childermass*, though written in the restrained style of his later years, not with the modernist pyrotechnics of *The Childermass*. In Book II, *Monstre Gai*, Pullman and Satterthwaite have entered Third City, which is neither Heaven nor Hell, but a bland third state reminiscent of the postwar Britain of the Welfare State. Pullman, who as *The Human Age* develops, grows to resemble Lewis more and more, does not dislike this state of affairs but, flattered by the Bailiff's attention and desirous of obtaining power, becomes a close ally of the Bailiff. *Monstre Gai* ends when the Bailiff has to flee Third City and goes to Hell, taking Pullman and Satterthwaite with him.

Malign Fiesta, Book III of *The Human Age*, Lewis' most striking work of fiction after *The Revenge for Love*, is set in Hell. The Bailiff is rather a minor personage there, and Pullman soon becomes an important adviser to Sammael, Satan himself. Much of the artistic power of *The Human Age* stems from Lewis' ability to use the traditional conceptions of the afterlife to create his own special universe. The plot of *Malign Fiesta* centers on Pullman's and Sammael's plans to found a new human age. They want to humanize the angels in order to subvert the stark opposition between the human and the Divine and between good and evil which, Sammael concludes, have always served God's aims. In order to do this, Pullman, the specialist in Man, draws on all the resources of modern publicity to set in motion a gigantic party for the angels, the malign fiesta which gives the book its title, the purpose of which is to interest the angels in such human activities as drunkenness and lechery. God does not like this at all, and after warning Pullman repeatedly, He invades Hell. The book ends as Pullman is carried off to Heaven by some of God's soldiers.

There was to be a fourth book which Lewis never finished, which would have concerned Pullman's turn to and acceptance of the Divine. This had already begun in *Malign Fiesta*, as Pullman was becoming more and more convinced of the wickedness of what he was doing, even though he continued to work with Sammael. What links this to Lewis' other novels is that Pullman's self-critique is Lewis': from the theological standpoint of *The Human Age*, Lewis criticizes the indifference and lack of compassion of his earlier work. He, too, has done the Devil's work and now wishes to turn to the Divine.

This shift toward the end of Lewis' life and career can, however, be overstated. Lewis did not go on to write the fourth volume of *The Human Age* set in Heaven. Instead, he completed *The Red Priest*, a minor if entertaining novel satirizing a Communist priest, and started on another novel, *Twentieth Century Palette*, about a young painter early in the century. The novel was unfinished at Lewis' death. A thoroughly affirmative Lewis, in any case, would have been a Lewis deprived of much of his interest. *The Revenge for Love*, *Self Condemned*, and Books II and III of *The Human Age* are Lewis' greatest novels precisely because they continue the attack on the modern world begun in *The Childermass* and *The Apes of God* while qualifying and criticizing that attack as they articulate it. The resulting ambivalence is fascinating, far richer than the more single-minded earlier work. They also carry forward what was begun in *Snooty Baronet* and the other 1930's novels, as they are written in a more conventional and readable style and conform somewhat to generic expectations. The later Lewis, in short, writes in a way that acknowledges that others have written, which makes his work much more accessible, yet his work remains completely his own.

Lewis' novels form one of the most fascinating bodies of work written in this century. A less sympathetic account of his work could have pointed out many flaws not discussed here; nevertheless, the universe created in his oeuvre is a capacious if demanding one, a realm that many more readers should discover and explore.

Reed Way Dasenbrock

Other major works

SHORT FICTION: *The Wild Body*, 1927; *Rotting Hill*, 1951; *Unlucky for Pringle*, 1973.

PLAYS: *Enemy of the Stars*, 1914, 1932; *The Ideal Giant*, 1917.

POETRY: *One-Way Song*, 1933.

NONFICTION: *The Art of Being Ruled*, 1926; *The Lion and the Fox: The Role of the Hero in Shakespeare's Plays*, 1927; *Time and Western Man*, 1927; *Paleface: The Philosophy of the Melting Pot*, 1929; *Satire and Fiction*, 1930; *The Diabolical Principle and the Dithyrambic Spectator*, 1931; *Hitler*, 1931; *The Doom of Youth*, 1932; *Filibusters in Barbary*, 1932; *The Old Gang and the New Gang*, 1933; *Men Without Art*, 1934; *Left Wings over Europe*, 1936; *Count Your Dead, They Are Alive*, 1937; *Blasting and Bombardiering*, 1937; *Wyndham Lewis: The Artist from "Blast" to Burlington House*, 1939; *The*

Hitler Cult, 1939; *The Jews, Are They Human?*, 1939; *America, I Presume*, 1940; *America and Cosmic Man*, 1948; *Rude Assignment: A Narrative of My Career Up-to-Date*, 1950; *The Writer and the Absolute*, 1952; *Letters of Wyndham Lewis*, 1963 (W. K. Rose, editor); *Wyndham Lewis on Art*, 1969; *Hitler, the Germans, and the Jews*, 1973 (5 volumes); *Enemy Salvos*, 1976; *Creatures of Habit, Creatures of Change*, 1989.

Bibliography

Campbell, SueEllen. *The Enemy Opposite*. Athens: Ohio University Press, 1988. Concentrates on Lewis' critical work during the decade 1924-1934, when he was most productive. Lewis saw the world in sharply dualistic terms and tended to view ideological opponents as personal enemies. He was a shrewd judge of hidden themes in the work of others and thus may be considered a precursor of postmodernist criticism.

Jameson, Fredric. *Fables of Aggression*. Berkeley: University of California Press, 1979. An analysis of Lewis' novels by a leading Marxist critic, this book has aroused great controversy. Regards Lewis as a populist radical rather than a conservative. He had a sensitive perception of the dominant social movements of his time and wished to create new forms of literature in reaction to them. In doing so, he became a leading modernist. At times Jameson's own political agenda intrudes on his discussion.

Kenner, Hugh. *Wyndham Lewis*. Norfolk, Conn.: New Directions, 1954. Although relatively short, Kenner's work remains the standard account of Lewis. Stresses Lewis' opposition to the emphasis on time and change characteristic of most twentieth century thinkers, who instead believed in order and permanence. Rates Lewis' exposition of his views, *Time and Western Man*, as one of the key works of the twentieth century. Kenner's careful discussion of Lewis' work is based in part on his personal friendship with him.

Meyers, Jeffrey. *The Enemy*. London: Routledge & Kegan Paul, 1980. This long book is the standard biography, giving a full picture of Lewis' life and his work: fiction, painting, and criticism. Includes new information based on his access to Lewis' papers: for example, Lewis' activities in trying to secure Ezra Pound's release from prison. Contends that *Self Condemned* is Lewis' greatest novel.

Meyers, Jeffrey, ed. *Wyndham Lewis: A Revaluation*. London: Athlone Press, 1980. Contains articles by leading authorities on Lewis on all aspects of his work. Among the essays are John Holloway's "Machine and Puppet: A Comparative View," which analyzes the theme of man's transformation into machinery and his reanimation. Marshall McLuhan discusses Lewis' prose style and Alistair Davies claims that *Tarr* is a Nietzschean novel.

DAVID LODGE

Born: London, England; January 28, 1935

Principal long fiction

The Picturegoers, 1960; *Ginger, You're Barmy*, 1962; *The British Museum Is Falling Down*, 1965; *Out of the Shelter*, 1970; *Changing Places: A Tale of Two Campuses*, 1975; *How Far Can You Go?*, 1980 (also known as *Souls and Bodies*); *Small World*, 1984; *Nice Work*, 1988.

Other literary forms

Mediating between theory and practice, David Lodge has proved himself one of England's ablest and most interesting literary critics. In addition to his novels and criticism, he has written short stories, television screenplays of his novels *Out of the Shelter* (not produced) and *Nice Work*, and (in collaboration with Malcolm Bradbury and Jim Duckett) several satirical revues.

Achievements

As a novelist Lodge has made his mark in three seemingly distinct yet, in Lodge's case, surprisingly congruent areas: as a writer of Catholic novels, of "campus fiction," and of works that somehow manage to be at once realist and postmodern. The publication of *Changing Places* in 1975 and *Small World* nine years later brought Lodge to the attention of a much larger (especially American) audience. *Changing Places* won both the Yorkshire Post and Hawthornden prizes, *How Far Can You Go?* received the Whitbread Award, and *Nice Work* was shortlisted for Great Britain's prestigious Booker Prize.

Biography

David John Lodge was born on January 28, 1935, in London's lower-middle-class East End, the only son of a musician father and a staunchly Catholic mother. The family's straitened economic situation, his conservative Catholic upbringing, and the dangers of wartime London left their mark on young David. He began his first novel (unpublished) at eighteen while still a student at University College, London, where he received his B.A. in English (with his first honors) in 1955 and an M.A. in 1959. Betweentimes Lodge performed what was then an obligatory National Service (1955-1957). Although the two years were in a sense wasted, his stint in the army did give him time to complete his first published novel, *The Picturegoers*, and material for his second, *Ginger, You're Barmy*, as well as the impetus to continue his studies. In 1959 he was married to Mary Frances Jacob; they were to have three children. After a year working as an assistant at the British Council, Lodge joined the faculty at the University of Birmingham, where he completed his Ph.D. in 1969; he eventually attained the position of full professor of modern English literature in 1976.

The mid-1960's proved an especially important period in Lodge's personal and professional life. He became close friends with fellow critic and novelist Malcolm Bradbury (then also at Birmingham), under whose influence Lodge wrote his first comic novel, *The British Museum Is Falling Down*, for which the publisher, not so comically, forgot to distribute review copies; he was awarded a Harkness Commonwealth Fellowship to study and travel in the United States for a year (1964-1965); he published his first critical study, the influential *The Language of Fiction* (1966); and he learned that his third child, Christopher, suffered from Down's syndrome (a biographical fact that manifests itself obliquely at the end of *Out of the Shelter* and more overtly in one of the plots of *How Far Can You Go?*). Lodge's second trip to the United States, this time as visiting professor of English at the University of California at Berkeley in 1969, during the height of the Free Speech Movement and political unrest, played its part in the conceiving and writing of his second comic novel, *Changing Places*, as did the critical essays he was then writing and would later collect in *The Novelist at the Crossroads* (1971) and *Working with Structuralism* (1981). The cash award that went along with the Whitbread Prize for his next novel, *How Far Can You Go?*, enabled Lodge to reduce his teaching duties to half-year and to devote himself more fully to his writing. He transformed his participation in the Modern Language Association's 1978 conference in New York, the 1979 James Joyce Symposium in Zurich, and a three-week world tour of conferences and British Council speaking engagements into his most commercially successful book, *Small World*, later adapted for British television.

His reputation growing and his financial situation brightening, Lodge donated all royalties from his next book, *Write On: Occasional Essays, '65-'85* (1986), to CARE (Cottage and Rural Enterprises), which maintains communities for mentally handicapped adults. Taking advantage of early retirement (part of Prime Minister Margaret Thatcher's austerity plan for British universities) in 1987, Lodge continued to write fiction, plays, and literary criticism.

Analysis

In order to understand David Lodge's novels, it is necessary to place them in the context of postwar British literature; the "Movement" writers and "Angry Young Men" of the 1950's, whose attacks on the English class system had an obvious appeal to the author of *The Picturegoers*, the English Catholic novel and the "campus novel" traditions, and finally the postmodernism to which British fiction (it is often claimed) has proved especially resistant. In addition, Lodge's novels are significantly and doubly autobiographical. They draw not only on important events in the author's life, but also on his work as a literary critic. In *The Language of Fiction* Lodge defends the aesthetic validity and continuing viability of realist writing on the basis of linguistic mastery rather than fidelity to life, and in *The Novelist at the Crossroads* he rejects Robert Scholes's bifurcation of the contemporary fiction into fabulistic and journalistic modes, positing the "problematic novel" in which the novelist innovatively builds his hesitation as to which mode to adopt into the novel. Lodge's own novels are profoundly pluralistic yet manifest the author's clear sense of aesthetic, social, and personal limitations, and his awareness of working within as well as against certain traditions and forms.

Set in a lower-middle-class area of London much like the one in which Lodge grew up, *The Picturegoers* is an interesting and even ambitious work marred by melodramatic excesses. As the plural of its title implies, *The Picturegoers* deals with a fairly large number of more or less main characters. Lodge's title also is indicative of his narrative method: abrupt cinematic shifts between the different plots, use of a similarly shifting focalizing technique, and a stylizing of the narrative discourse in order to reflect features of an individual character's verbal thought patterns. Of the seven main characters, Mark Underwood is the most important. A lapsed Catholic and aspiring writer, he arrives in London, rents a room in the home of a conservative Catholic family, the Mallorys, and falls in love with the daughter, Clare, formerly a Catholic novitiate. The affair will change them: Clare will become sexually awakened and then skeptical when Mark abandons her for the Catholicism from which she has begun to distance herself. Interestingly, his return to the church seems selfish and insincere, an ironic sign not of his redemption but of his bad faith.

Dismissed by its author as a work of "missed possibilities" and an "act of revenge" against Great Britain's National Service, *Ginger, You're Barmy* continues Lodge's dual exploration of narrative technique and moral matters and largely succeeds on the basis of the solution Lodge found for the technical problem which the writing of the novel posed: how to write a novel about the tedium of military life without making the novel itself tedious to read. Lodge solved the problem by choosing to concentrate the action and double his narrator-protagonist Jonathan Browne's story. Lodge focuses the story on the first few weeks of basic training, particularly Jonathan's relationship with the altruistic and highly, though conservatively, principled Mike Brady, a poorly educated Irish Catholic, who soon runs afoul of the military authorities; on the accidental death or perhaps suicide of Percy Higgins; and on Jonathan's last days before being mustered out two years later. Lodge then frames this already-doubled story with the tale of Jonathan's telling, or writing, of these events three years later, with Jonathan now married (to Mike's former girlfriend), having spent the past three years awaiting Mike's release from prison. The novel's frame structure suggests that Jonathan has improved morally from the self-centered agnostic he was to the selfless friend he has become, but his telling problematizes the issue of his development. Between Mike's naïve faith and Jonathan's intellectual self-consciousness and perhaps self-serving confession there opens up an abyss of uncertainty for the reader.

This moral questioning takes a very different form in Lodge's next novel. *The British Musuem Is Falling Down* is a parodic pastiche about a day in the highly literary and (sexually) very Catholic life of Adam Appleby, a twenty-five-year-old graduate student trying to complete his dissertation before his stipend is depleted and his growing family overwhelms his slender financial resources. Desperate but by no means in despair, Adam begins to confuse literature and life as each event in the wildly improbable series that makes up his day unfolds in its own uniquely parodied style. The parodies are fun but also have a semiserious purpose, the undermining of all forms of authority, religious as well as literary. Parodic in form, *The British Museum Is Falling Down* is comic in intent in that Lodge wrote it in the expectation of change in the church's position on birth control. The failure of this expectation would lead Lodge fifteen years later to turn the comedy inside out in his darker novel, *How Far Can You Go?*

Published after *The British Museum Is Falling Down* but conceived earlier, *Out of the Shelter* is a more serious but also less successful novel. Modeled on a trip Lodge made to Germany when he was sixteen, *Out of the Shelter* attempts to combine the *Bildungsroman* and the Jamesian international novel. In three parts of increasing length, the novel traces the life of Timothy Young from his earliest years in the London blitz to the four weeks he spends in Heidelberg in the early 1950's with his sister, who works for the American army of occupation. With the help of those he meets, Timothy begins the process of coming out of the shelter of home, conservative Catholicism, unambitious lower-middle-class parents, provincial, impoverished England, and sexual immaturity into a world of abundance as well as ambiguity. Lodge's Joycean stylization of Timothy's maturing outlook proves much less successful than his portrayal of Timothy's life as a series of transitions in which the desire for freedom is offset by a desire for shelter, the desire to participate by the desire to observe. Even in the epilogue, Timothy, now thirty, married, and in the United States on a study grant, finds himself dissatisfied (even though he has clearly done better than any of the novel's other characters) and afraid of the future.

Lodge translates that fear into a quite different key in *Changing Places*. Here Lodge's genius for combining opposites becomes fully evident as the serious Timothy Young gives way to the hapless English liberal-humanist Philip Swallow, who leaves the shelter of the University of Rummidge for the expansive pleasures of the State University of Euphoria in Plotinus (Berkeley). Swallow is half of Lodge's faculty and narrative exchange program; the other is Morris Zapp, also forty, an academic Norman Mailer, arrogant and ambitious. Cartoonish as his characters—or rather caricatures—may be, Lodge makes them and their complementary as well as parallel misadventures in foreign parts humanly interesting. The real energy of *Changing Places* lies, however, in the intersecting plots and styles of this "duplex" novel. The first two chapters, "Flying" and "Settling," get the novel off to a self-consciously omniscient but otherwise conventional start. "Corresponding," however, switches to the epistolary mode, and "Reading" furthers the action (and the virtuosic display) by offering a series of newspaper items, press releases, flysheets, and the like. "Changing" reverts to conventional narration (but in a highly stylized way), and "Ending" takes the form of a filmscript. Set at a time of political activism and literary innovation, *Changing Places* is clearly a "problematic novel" written by a "novelist at the crossroads," aware of the means at his disposal but unwilling to privilege any one over any or all of the others.

Lodge puts the postmodern plays of *Changing Places* to a more overtly serious purpose in *How Far Can You Go?* It is a work more insistently referential than any of Lodge's other novels but also paradoxically more self-questioning: a fiction about the verifiably real world that nevertheless radically insists upon its own status as fiction. The novel switches back and forth between the sometimes discrete, yet always ultimately related stories of its ten main characters as freely as it does between the mimetic and diegetic levels of the story and its narration. The parts make up an interconnected yet highly discontinuous whole, tracing the lives of its ten characters from 1952 (when nine are university students and members of a Catholic study group led by the tenth, Father Brierly) through the religious, sexual, and sociopolitical changes of the 1960's and 1970's to the deaths of two popes, the installation of the conservative John Paul II, and the writing of the novel *How Far Can You Go?* in 1978.

The authorial narrator's attitude toward his characters is at once distant and familiar, condescending and compassionate. Their religious doubts and moral questions strike the reader as quaintly naïve, the result of a narrowly Catholic upbringing. Yet the lives of reader and characters as well as authorial narrator are also strangely parallel in that (to borrow Lodge's own metaphor) each is involved in a game of Snakes and Ladders, moving narratively, psychologically, socially, and religiously ahead one moment, only to fall suddenly behind the next. The characters stumble into sexual maturity, marry, have children, have affairs, get divorced, declare their homosexuality, suffer illnesses, breakdowns, and crises of faith, convert to other religions, and join to form Catholics for an Open Church. All the while the authorial narrator of this most postmodern of post-Vatican II novels proceeds with self-conscious caution, possessed of his own set of doubts, as he moves toward the open novel. Exploring various lives, plots, voices, and styles, Lodge's artfully wrought yet ultimately provisional narrative keeps circling back to the question that troubles his characters: "how far can you go?" in the search for what is vital in the living of a life and the writing (or reading) of a novel.

Lodge goes still further, geographically as well as narratively speaking, in his next novel. A campus fiction for the age of the "global campus," *Small*

World begins at a decidedly provincial meeting in Rummidge in 1978 and ends at a mammoth Modern Language Association conference in New York one year later, with numerous international stops in between as Lodge recycles characters and invents a host of intersecting stories (or narrative flight paths). The pace is frenetic and thematically exhaustive but, for the delighted reader, never exhausting. The basic plot upon which Lodge plays his add-on variations begins when Persse McGarrigle—poet and "conference virgin"— meets the elusive Angelica Pabst. As Angelica pursues literary theory at a number of international conferences, Persse pursues her, occasionally glimpsing her sister, a pornographic actress, Lily Papps, whom he mistakes for Angelica. Meanwhile, characters from earlier Lodge novels reappear to engage in affairs and rivalries, all in the international academic milieu. A parody of (among other things) the medieval quest, Lodge's highly allusive novel proves at once entertaining and instructive as it combines literary modes, transforms the traditional novel's world of characters into semiotics' world of signs, and turns the tables on contemporary literary theory's celebrated demystifications by demystifying it. At novel's end, Lodge makes a guest appearance, and Persse makes an exit, in pursuit of another object of his chaste desire. The quest continues, but that narrative fact does not mean that the novel necessarily endorses the kind of extreme open-endedness or inconclusiveness that characterizes certain contemporary literary theories. Rather, the novel seems to side with the reconstructed Morris Zapp, who has lost his faith in deconstruction, claiming that although the deferral of meaning may be endless, the individual is not: "Death is the one concept you can't deconstruct. Work back from there and you end up with the old idea of an autonomous self."

Zapp's reduced expectations typify Lodge's eighth novel, *Nice Work*, set almost entirely in Rummidge but also, as in *How Far Can You Go?*, evidencing his interest in bringing purely literary and academic matters to bear on larger social issues. The essential doubleness of this geographically circumscribed novel manifests itself in a series of contrasts: between the nineteenth and twentieth centuries, literature and life, the Industrial Midlands and Margaret Thatcher's economically thriving (but morally bankrupt) London, male and female, and the novel's two main characters. Vic Wilcox, age forty-six, managing director of a family-named but conglomerate-owned foundry, rather ironically embodies the male qualities his name implies. Robyn Penrose is everything Vic Wilcox is not: young, attractive, intellectual, cosmopolitan, idealistic, politically aware, sexually liberated, as androgynous as her name, and, as temporary lecturer in women's studies and the nineteenth century novel, ill-paid. The differences between the two are evident even in the narrative language, as Lodge takes pains to unobtrusively adjust discourse to character. The sections devoted to Vic, "a phallic sort of bloke," are appropriately straightforward, whereas those dealing with Robyn, a character who "doesn't believe in character," reflect her high degree of self-awareness. In order to bring the two characters and their quite different worlds together, Lodge invents an Industry Year Shadow Scheme that involves Robyn's following Vic around one workday per week for a semester. Both are at first reluctant participants. Displeasure slowly turns into dialogue, and dialogue eventually leads to bed, with sexual roles reversed. Along the way Lodge smuggles in a considerable amount of literary theory as Vic and Robyn enter each other's worlds and words: the phallo and logocentric literalmindedness of the one coming up against the feminist-semiotic awareness of the other. Each comes to understand, even appreciate, the other.

Lodge does not stop there. His ending is implausible, in fact flatly unconvincing, but deliberately so—a parody of the only solutions that, as Robyn points out to her students, the Victorian novelists were able or willing to offer to "the problems of industrial capitalism: a legacy, a marriage, emigration or death." Robyn will receive two proposals of marriage, a lucrative job offer, and an inheritance that will enable her to finance the small company Vic, recently fired, will found and direct and also enable her to stay on at Rummidge to try to make her utopian dream of an educated, classless English society a reality. The impossibly happy ending suggests just how slim her chances for success are, but the very existence of Lodge's novel seems to undermine this irony, leaving *Nice Work* and its reader on the border between aspiration and limitation, belief and skepticism, the romance of how things should be and the reality, or realism, of how things are—a border area that is one of the hallmarks of Lodge's fiction.

Robert A. Morace

Other major works

PLAYS: *Between These Four Walls*, 1963 (with Malcolm Bradbury and James Duckett); *Slap in the Middle*, 1965 (with Duckett and David Turner).

NONFICTION: *Graham Greene*, 1966; *The Language of Fiction*, 1966; *Jane Austen: "Emma," a Casebook*, 1968 (edited); *Evelyn Waugh*, 1971; *The Novelist at the Crossroads*, 1971; *Twentieth Century Literary Criticism: A Reader*, 1972 (edited); *Scenes of Clerical Life*, by George Eliot, 1971 (edited); *The Woodlanders*, by Thomas Hardy, 1974 (edited); *Modes of Modern Writing: Metaphor and Metonymy and the Typology of Modern Literature*, 1977; *Working with Structuralism*, 1981; *The Best of Ring Lardner*, 1984 (edited); *Write On: Occasional Essays, '65-'85*, 1986; *Modern Criticism and Theory: A Reader*, 1988 (edited); *After Bakhtin*, 1990.

Bibliography
Bergonzi, Bernard. "A Conspicuous Absentee: The Decline and Fall of the Catholic Novel." *Encounter* 55 (August/September, 1980): 44-56. Dis-

cusses the twentieth century Catholic novel tradition in England, with particular emphasis on Graham Greene and Evelyn Waugh, and then places Lodge's three "Catholic" novels within that tradition. *How Far Can You Go?* depicts changes in contemporary Catholicism but fails to consider "what motivates the religious life."

Honan, Park. "David Lodge and the Cinematic Novel in England." *Novel: A Forum on Fiction* 5 (Winter, 1982): 167-173. Placing Lodge at one pole of avant-garde English writing (the new realist) and B. S. Johnson at the other, Honan analyzes Lodge's use of impressionistic-cinematic techniques, especially the limiting of dialogue and the cinematizing of "the language of fiction so that varied 'styles' cling completely to the thing represented."

Jackson, Dennis. "David Lodge." In *British Novelists Since 1960*, edited by Jay L. Halio. Vol. 14 in *Dictionary of Literary Biography*. Detroit: Gale Research, 1983. Provides a brief yet thorough and certainly informed and insightful overview of Lodge's life and writing. Jackson reads Lodge as a realist working within the tradition of the English comic novels of Evelyn Waugh and Kingsley Amis.

Mews, Siegfried. "The Professor's Novel: David Lodge's *Small World*." *Modern Language Notes* 104 (April, 1989): 713-726. Mews begins by placing *Small World* within the context of American, British, Canadian, and German campus fiction. He then analyzes specific features of Lodge's novel that support his conclusion that despite its playful surface, *Small World* presents a serious questioning of contemporary literary theories from an essentially Arnoldian point of view.

Morace, Robert A. *The Dialogical Novels of Malcolm Bradbury and David Lodge*. Carbondale: Southern Illinois University Press, 1989. Provides chapter-length readings of all Lodge's novels through *Small World* in terms of Mikhail Bakhtin's theory of the dialogical novel. As a novelist, Lodge (like Bradbury) works simultaneously within and against the English novel tradition, as he seeks neither to perpetuate old forms and their ideological assumptions nor to surrender to the new (particularly American postmodernism and Continental poststructualist theories) but instead to renegotiate the terms upon which the English novel can remain viable.

Widdowson, Peter. "The Anti-History Men: Malcolm Bradbury and David Lodge." *Critical Quarterly* 26 (1984): 5-32. Argues that the progressive postmodern surface of Lodge's and Bradbury's fiction serves to mask a reactionary ideology and to protect "English culture against charges of provincialism." In support of his position, Widdowson discusses the vague values Lodge espouses, Lodge's typically liberal fear of history and politics, and the willed closure of his novels in which the return to home and family and the liberal freedom of having it both ways often play especially important parts.

JACK LONDON

Born: San Francisco, California; January 12, 1876
Died: Glen Ellen, California; November 22, 1916

Principal long fiction

A Daughter of the Snows, 1902; *The Call of the Wild*, 1903; *The Sea-Wolf*, 1904, *The Game*, 1905; *White Fang*, 1906; *Before Adam*, 1906; *The Iron Heel*, 1907; *Martin Eden*, 1909; *Burning Daylight*, 1910; *Adventure*, 1911; *The Abysmal Brute*, 1913; *The Valley of the Moon*, 1913; *The Mutiny of the Elsinore*, 1914; *The Scarlet Plague*, 1915; *The Star Rover*, 1915; *The Little Lady of the Big House*, 1916; *Jerry of the Islands*, 1917; *Michael, Brother of Jerry*, 1917; *Hearts of Three*, 1920; *The Assassination Bureau, Ltd.*, 1963 (completed by Robert L. Fish).

Other literary forms

Jack London's fifty-nine published works include plays, children's fiction, sociological studies, essays, short stories, and novels. Although generally known as a writer of short fiction, London is also remembered for his pioneering work in tramp fiction (*The Road*, 1907), screenwriting (*Hearts of Three*, 1920), and the science-fiction novel (*The Star Rover*). London was also a journalist, serving as a newspaper correspondent for the San Francisco *Examiner* during the Russo-Japanese War in 1904 and, later, during the Mexican conflict in Vera Cruz in 1915. His accounts of these wars were published in 1970 under the title *Jack London Reports*. London's correspondence, first published in one volume in 1965, will soon be available in a multivolume, greatly expanded edition.

Achievements

Called at one time the "Kipling of the Klondike," London was in the forefront of the move toward naturalistic fiction and realism. His social fiction, which included the first sympathetic and realistic treatment of the convict and the tramp, gave him credence as a spokesman for the working class. As a folk hero, London has achieved a popularity which, along with Mark Twain, may make him a permanent figure in American mythology. London is also extremely popular abroad—especially in Europe and the Soviet Union. His work has been translated into more than fifty languages, and his stories appear in countless anthologies of short fiction. Complete editions of London's work have recently been published in French, German, and Russian, and a complete edition of his work in English is now planned. London's novels, especially *The Sea-Wolf* and *The Call of the Wild*, are taught each year in high school and college English courses; a number of his books remain in print year after year. London's reputation as a solid craftsman—especially of short stories—has now been established firmly, even among literary critics. His novels, still regarded by many as weak and unpolished, have gained in stature in the last decade as more and more critics find London's work a subject worthy of discussion.

Biography

A sometime tramp, oyster pirate, seaman, Socialist, laundryman, and miner, Jack (John Griffith) London is as famous for the life he lived and the myths he wove around it as he is for the short stories and novels he wrote. Largely self-educated, London was the product of California ranches and the working-class neighborhoods of Oakland. His rise to literary fame came as a result of the Klondike gold rush. Unsuccessful in his attempt to break into the magazine market, London joined the flood of men rushing toward instant riches in the Yukon. He found little gold, but returned after the winter of 1897 with a wealth of memories and notes of the Northland, the gold rush, and the hardships of the trail. By 1900, London had firmly established himself as a major American writer.

Also in 1897, London married Elizabeth May Maddern. The couple settled in Oakland, soon adding two daughters to their family. In 1904, seeking new material for his stories and escape from his marriage, which by this time had gone sour, London signed with William Randolph Hearst to cover the impending Russo-Japanese War for Hearst's newspaper the San Francisco *Examiner*. His photographs and accounts of that war were among the first to be published, and he returned to California in triumph, only to face a divorce action.

London's next years were marked by further adventures and travels. In 1905, he journeyed across the United States, lecturing on the need for a socialist revolution. He married Clara Charmian Kittredge that same year, and together they planned a seven-year voyage around the world on a yacht they named *Snark* after Lewis Carroll's mock epic. Ill-health forced abandonment of the adventure after only two years, however, and London returned once more to California, this time to create a large ranch complex in Sonoma County.

To support his travels and building program, as well as an extravagant lifestyle, London wrote at a furious pace, publishing fifty books by his fortieth year. His body could not withstand the brutal treatment it received, however, and shortly before his forty-first birthday, Jack London died. His death, officially labeled uremic poisoning and renal colic, was widely rumored to have been suicide. The mysterious circumstances surrounding it have never been explained satisfactorily.

Analysis

Jack London's fame as a writer came about largely through his ability to interpret realistically man's struggle in a hostile environment. Early in his career, London realized that he had no talent for invention, that in his writing he would have to be an interpreter of the things which are, rather than a creator of the things which might be. Accordingly, he drew his plots, characters, themes, and settings from real-life experiences and published accounts.

London's career as a novelist began shortly after the turn of the century with the publication of *A Daughter of the Snows*. It ended nineteen novels later with the posthumous publication of *The Assassination Bureau, Ltd.* (1963). The novels vary widely in length, subject matter, and (especially) artistic quality, for while London could write bold, violent, and sometimes primitive short stories of immense power, depicting the frontier environment and man's struggle within it in memorable fashion, his novels oftentimes suffered from weakness of structure and excessive didacticism. London's failure of invention, never a significant problem in his short stories, all too often surfaced in his longer works. Some critics have complained that a few of his novels (such as *Burning Daylight*, for example) are not novels at all, but merely strings of short stories hung together by the merest contrivance.

London's novels characteristically contain at least one of three different settings: the Canadian Northland, where he began his literary apprenticeship; the primitive South Seas and Hawaii, where his career began anew following a short decline; and the California wilderness—particularly the Sonoma Valley—where London retreated during the last years of his life.

Each novel also generally contains a philosophical focus. Popular at the time were Charles Darwin's theory of evolution, as interpreted by Herbert Spencer; Friedrich Nietzsche's version of the superman, and, much later, the new psychology of Sigmund Freud and Carl Jung, as well as Karl Marx's theories of a new social order. All fired London's imagination and provided fuel for his characters and plots, and their presence—particularly London's version of the Darwinian "survival of the fittest" motif—lends credence to London's claim for membership in the naturalistic school of fiction.

London was at the height of his powers when he wrote *The Call of the Wild*. He was dealing with the kind of subject matter, theme, and setting with which he was most comfortable. Written with vigor and intensity, the novel was intended originally only as a companion story to "Batard," an earlier short story. The story literally "got away from him," as he explained in a letter to a friend, and he was forced to expand it to its present length. The book was written shortly after his return from the slums of London. Wanting to escape the degradation and poverty he had witnessed there, London returned to the clean, frozen, beautiful world of the North, where the struggle for survival was elemental, uncomplicated, and fierce. The story is that of a dog, Buck, who is kidnaped from his home on a California ranch and taken to the Yukon, where he is forced to pull heavily laden sleds for inhuman masters. In order to survive, Buck must adapt, falling back on primitive instincts. With domesticity stripped from him, Buck learns the ways of his ancestors; he learns the law of the club: that he will be beaten, but will survive. Gradually, as he completes his initiation into the primitive, Buck learns to respond; he learns the law of the fang: that he must be quick to use his own fangs, before others use theirs on him. By adapting to his new environment, Buck survives, learns the instincts of his forebears, and finally, hears the true call of the wild.

Incredibly, London's most successful novel was the one least understood by its author. He did not foresee its popularity, and sold it outright to his publisher for two thousand dollars. He did not like its title, which now has become a recognizable phrase in the English language, nor did he understand the most powerful element in the book—the human allegory.

In *The Call of the Wild*, London was able to incorporate to good advantage the popular notion of the fierce Darwinian struggle for survival of the fittest. Curiously, he modified the Darwinian theme slightly. Buck must struggle to survive, but his survival is not predicated upon ultimate triumph. He must learn how to use his instincts, he must learn to be a good sled dog, but he need not become the team leader in order to survive. Struggle for its own sake also appears in *The Call of the Wild* and in other London novels. The team does not have to kill the snowshoe rabbit: at the time they are sleek and well-fed. Yet, they chase after the animal anyway for the sheer sport of the kill. Struggle for its own sake reappears in *The Iron Heel*, *Martin Eden*, and *The Valley of the Moon*.

London's tenth book, *The Sea-Wolf*, drew on his youthful adventures in the sealing grounds off Japan. The novel concerns the survival of upper-class Humphrey Van Weyden, a man who finds himself, through means beyond his control, aboard *The Ghost*, a sealing schooner on its way to Japan. Van Weyden soon finds that the captain of the schooner, Wolf Larsen, has created a hell-ship, filled with brutality and sordidness, where even the ship's practical purpose—to hunt seals—is lost in the misery of mere survival. Van Weyden survives this environment because, like Buck, he is able to adapt to it, learning new codes of survival, drawing upon unknown instincts, and using to best advantage all the benefits of his upbringing and status: intelligence, optimism, and a capacity to love. Van Weyden's growth is the focus of the novel.

If Van Weyden survives because he, too, has learned the law of the club and the fang, the ship's captain, Wolf Larsen, dies precisely because he cannot adapt. At least, that was London's intention, but it was lost upon many early-day critics. "I attacked Nietzsche and his super-man idea," London wrote to Mary Austin. "Lots of people read *The Sea-Wolf*, [but] no one discovered that it was an attack upon the super-man philosophy."

The Sea-Wolf is a fine example of literary naturalism. Larsen, a sensitive, intelligent, domineering man, treats his crew with arrogance. He has no inhibitions and also no friends. Alone, his life lacks purpose and direction, and his aloneness and alienation from nature and from man, and, in fact, from himself, lead to his inevitable destruction. Without Van Weyden's ability to adapt, Larsen dies.

If London fails to convince his reader that Larsen died because he was a superman, perhaps it is because London did not fully subscribe to the idea himself. The world is full of supermen—London fancied himself one in many ways—and the Socialist alternative which London supported intellectually was one he could not accept emotionally. This conflict between the superman idea and socialism erupts full-scale in *Martin Eden*, when London again takes Nietzsche to task.

While *The Sea-Wolf* may have failed to convey its point to the critics, it did not fail to capture the fancy of the reading public. Next to *The Call of the Wild*, it was (and is) London's most popular book, and it gave the author the financial security he so desperately needed.

The last third of the book is concerned not only with the powerful element of Larsen's degeneration (which Ambrose Bierce called "unforgettable") but also the introduction of Maud Brewster. London generally had trouble with female characters in his fiction—his editors demanded strict Victorian morals, and London was happy to oblige—and following Maud's introduction, the book is reduced to a sentimental shambles. While the love story, in great part, insured the critical failure of the book, it also insured the book's popular success. As soon as Maud steps aboard, Van Weyden reverts to his earlier stature, as if wholly unaffected by the events that have thus transpired: his growth and adaptation are cast aside. The contradictions of *The Sea-Wolf* mirror the contradictions of London's own times. The novel is successful in depicting the turn-of-the-century society in which London lived, which was shaking off the morals and ways of the last century, yet still was holding on to vestiges and customs of the earlier time.

If *The Call of the Wild* is a novel about a dog who reacquaints himself with his ancestral instincts and learns survival by adaptation, *White Fang* is both its sequel and reverse. *White Fang* is the story of a wolfdog brought from the Alaskan wilderness to Californian civilization. Just as Buck used his civilized intelligence to survive, so White Fang uses his primitive strength and endurance to survive in a new environment—the world of civilized man. Environment is London's primary focus in this novel, as he traces the changes in the animal's behavior as it moves first from the wolf pack to an Indian village, then to the white settler, and, finally, to the Santa Clara Valley in California. White Fang is tamed by love, and successfully makes the transition from savage wolf to loving house pet. While the book does not have the power of *The Call of the Wild*, it does show White Fang's struggle with nature as represented by Indians, dogs, white men, and finally, after critical injuries suffered while defending his new benevolent master, death itself.

London was interested intensely in sociology and sociological studies. He wrote one himself, *The People of the Abyss*, and planned another one about the slums of New York City. Much of his interest in the subject can be explained by his belief in socialism, an answer to the problems many sociologists revealed. Thus it is not surprising that he would write *The Iron Heel*, a novel espousing a Marxist solution.

Like *The Valley of the Moon*, *The Iron Heel* is a novel set in the California wilderness. The similarities end there, however, for while London would later see his agrarian vision as a solution to the economic troubles of his time, in 1905, he still believed that a socialist revolution was necessary and inevitable. He documented it in this futuristic novel of social science fiction—a twentieth century vision of blood, fire, and destruction.

Basing his story on a small book by W. J. Ghent entitled *Our Benevolent Feudalism* (1902), London poured out his private dreams of revolution and glory. If Martin Eden would later die because he was Jack London without socialist fervor, Ernest Everhard, the hero of *The Iron Heel*, cannot live because he lacks the depth and conviction of his own cause. London preaches in *The Iron Heel* without dramatizing his beliefs in convincing action. Indeed, he tried to convince his audience of the righteousness of a cause in which he did not fully believe. Everhard is too superhuman to be credible; Avis Everhard, the widow of the leader of the revolt, is disembodied. Not until the struggle in the book reaches a climax and the battle in the street begins does the novel start to take life.

London used a number of complicated plot structures to convey his point in *The Iron Heel*, and, as usual when dealing with fiction of greater length, he was not entirely successful in sustaining the plot or action. *The Iron Heel* is supposed to be a copy of the Everhard manuscript, a fragment of a paper hidden away by Avis Everhard. This paper was supposed to have been found, some seven centuries later, edited by Anthony Meredith, and then brought to publication as *The Iron Heel*. Covering the period 1912-1913 when the oligarchy rises to power and destroys all forms of free speech and opposition, the paper tells of Everhard's struggle against the oppression, and his final flight underground, where he continues the fight, sometimes, as in *The Call of the Wild*, for the sheer sport of it. The novel reaches a bloody climax in Chicago when the mob is slaughtered by the Iron Heel mercenaries.

As might be expected, London's novel was not particularly popular with the reading public. His vision was not accepted by the Socialists, either, perhaps because they sensed that the book was written as a half-hearted attempt at reaffirmation. The struggle between man and nature, so convincingly portrayed in *The Call of the Wild*, becomes a struggle between man and man, oppressed and oppressor, and even London was unsure who would really win the battle.

While sailing around the world on his yacht *Snark*, London attempted a novel to bolster his career, which, in 1907, was sagging badly. The result, *Martin Eden*, was a profoundly moving novel, but also, as literary critic

Franklin Walker would later note, a most puzzling work. Called alternately London's finest and his worst novel, *Martin Eden* was meant as another attack on individualism and the Nietzschean superhero. As in *The Sea-Wolf*, London was only partially able to convey this intention. The rags-to-riches motif runs so strongly through the book that the reader is compelled to identify and sympathize with Martin, a lowly seaman, who without education or culture is thrown into the world of the educated and cultured. His introduction to their world fires his mind, and he yearns for their sophisticated ways, their knowledge, and the woman who brings it to him. Like London himself, Martin decides that the path to social betterment lies through his writing talent, and the novel masterfully describes Martin's (and London's) literary apprenticeship, early failure, and final success.

Martin Eden is a *Bildungsroman*—a novel of education. It employs the potent cultural myth of rags-to-riches, and masterfully depicts Martin's painful transition from the innocence of unknowing to the power of knowledge. As Martin grows and learns, he finds himself embroiled in the battle of the Iron Heel, pitting man against man, oppressed against oppressor. London offers Martin the key to salvation through the poet Brissenden—socialism—but Martin rejects it, and in so doing seals his fate. By the time Martin's road to success ends, it is too late. Without a reason for living, Martin rejects all that he has sought, and, finally, takes his own life.

Martin Eden was written aboard ship and is about a sailor. It is therefore not surprising that the paramount symbol in the novel is water. Beginning life as a sailor, coming from the ocean, Martin must return to his beginnings, and he does so by booking passage on an ocean liner and then committing suicide by drowning in the sea.

London returns to the theme of *The Call of the Wild* in *Martin Eden*, with one peculiar twist. Like Buck, Martin begins life unconscious of himself. He does not know that his grammar is imperfect, that his dress is slovenly, or that his manners are uncouth until Ruth Morse educates him. As he learns about himself, he becomes self-conscious. No longer do the instincts which Buck uses to adapt and survive work for Martin. Unable to adapt to his new environment, Martin returns to the only thing he knows best—the sea—and, fulfilling the paradox of knowing and unknowing, dies.

Martin Eden is a profoundly moving work of imaginative realism, but, like much of London's longer work, it suffers from an uneven structure and sometimes clumsy expression. The major flaw of the book, however, is London's failure to convey his point. The reader is so caught by the potent myth, so sympathetic toward Martin and his fight to the top, that he cannot understand Martin's inevitable death and feels cheated by it. There is too much of Jack London in Martin Eden, too much of London's own confusion over individualism versus Marxism, to carry the novel, and so it fails, as London did, in the attempt.

In a May, 1911, letter to editor Roland Phillips, London outlined his plan for *The Valley of the Moon*: the theme of the book would be back-to-the-land, a likely motif, for it paralleled London's own life-story. The agrarian vision, London wrote, would be accomplished by a man and a woman, both wage earners, who meet and grow to love each other in the confines of a big city. Hard times befall them, and the woman, in an attempt to regain the good times they had had together, leads them both on a pilgrimage through California which ends, finally, in Jack London's own valley, the Valley of the Moon.

As London matured, he saw a return to the soil as the solution to the great economic problems of the age. He used this agrarian vision to advantage in his writings and also on the acres of his own expanding ranch. The theme runs through much of his work, including not only *The Valley of the Moon* but also *Burning Daylight* and *The Little Lady of the Big House*.

To solve the problems of the city, Saxon and Billy, the two characters in *The Valley of the Moon*, flee, as they must. London saw the strikes, the fierce struggles for economic and human survival, as symptomatic of the greater problem of man out of touch with himself. To return to the soil, to gain salvation, man must restore rural America. Billy and Saxon set out to do this, but first they must be reborn; London did not advocate an escape to the wilderness, but a return to the goodness of nature. To return to Eden, Billy and Saxon must first gain salvation so that they do not spoil Eden as their ancestors once did.

Eden, of course, is London's own ranch, and once Billy and Saxon arrive they begin applying the principles of agrarian success London fancied himself to be applying. They bring with them the good intentions, motivation, good character, and knowledge necessary to treat the land gently. They do not make the same mistakes the old-style American farmer made; they do not use the land up, or wear it out; they apply new methods they have learned from foreigners, Portuguese farmers, to restore the land to its former richness. London realized there was no longer a vast American West. The land beyond the horizon had long been conquered and ruined. It was up to enlightened men and women to restore the land for the reruralization of America that was to come.

Although much more successful as a short-story writer than as a novelist, London's best novels remain alive and vibrant even to this day. His longer fiction was often episodic, disjointed, and loosely structured; his plots were often weak, and many times he let his characters preach rather than act out their philosophy. Nevertheless, London offered a compelling vision of the human condition. The Darwinian struggle for survival was at the forefront of American thought at the turn of the twentieth century; London's fiction mirrored his society, including its contradictions, and led his readers to the primitive arenas where the struggle for survival is best laid bare. London's contribution to the naturalistic tradition and his raw power as a storyteller insure his continued place in the American literary heritage.

David Mike Hamilton

Other major works

SHORT FICTION: *The Son of the Wolf*, 1900; *The God of His Fathers and Other Stories*, 1901; *Children of the Frost*, 1902; *The Faith of Men and Other Stories*, 1904; *Moon-Face and Other Stories*, 1906; *Love of Life and Other Stories*, 1906; *Lost Face*, 1910; *When God Laughs and Other Stories*, 1911; *South Sea Tales*, 1911; *The House of Pride and Other Tales of Hawaii*, 1912; *Smoke Bellew Tales*, 1912; *A Son of the Sun*, 1912; *The Night-Born*, 1913; *The Strength of the Strong*, 1914; *The Turtles of Tasman*, 1916; *The Human Drift*, 1917; *The Red One*, 1918; *On the Makaloa Mat*, 1919; *Dutch Courage and Other Stories*, 1922.

PLAYS: *Scorn of Women*, 1906; *Theft*, 1910; *The Acorn-Planter*, 1916.

NONFICTION: *The Kempton-Wace Letters*, 1903 (with Anna Strunsky); *The People of the Abyss*, 1903; *The War of the Classes* (1905); *The Road*, 1907; *Revolution and Other Essays*, 1910; *The Cruise of the Snark*, 1911; *John Barleycorn*, 1913; *Letters from Jack London*, 1965 (King Hendricks and Irving Shepard, editors).

CHILDREN'S LITERATURE: *The Cruise of the Dazzler*, 1902; *Tales of the Fish Patrol*, 1905.

Bibliography

Hamilton, David Mike. *The Tools of My Trade: The Annotated Books in Jack London's Library*. Seattle: University of Washington Press, 1987. An exceptionally valuable tool for the London scholar. Hamilton spent ten years going through London's personal library, cataloging his collection, and noting the annotations he wrote in his books. Hamilton gives the impression that London was as much influenced by the books in his library, especially by the writings of the psychologist Carl Jung, as he was by his real-life experiences.

Hedrick, Joan D. *Solitary Comrade: Jack London and His Work*. Chapel Hill: University of North Carolina Press, 1982. A Marxist-feminist interpretation of London's life and work. An interesting book with a distinct point of view: that London used his writing to search for "selfhood."

Labor, Earle. *Jack London*. New York: Twayne, 1974. Presents the story of London's life, mixed with critical analysis of his major works. Provides an annotated bibliography. A good introduction to London for all students.

Stasz, Clarice. *American Dreamers: The Story of Charmain and Jack London*. New York: St. Martin's Press, 1988. Jack London and his wife, Charmain—his "mate-woman," as he called her—were married for eleven years. This study, largely based on forty years of Charmain's unpublished diaries, focuses on their relationship.

Watson, Charles N. *The Novels of Jack London: A Reappraisal*. Madison: University of Wisconsin Press, 1982. A very good critical overview of London's fiction. Highly readable and accessible to students of all levels.

EARL LOVELACE

Born: Toco, Trinidad; July 13, 1935

Principal long fiction
While Gods Are Falling, 1965; *The Schoolmaster*, 1968; *The Dragon Can't Dance*, 1979; *The Wine of Astonishment*, 1982.

Other literary forms
While Earl Lovelace is primarily a novelist, he also writes poetry, short stories, and plays. He has published in *Voices* and *Tempo*, West Indian magazines. Beginning with *New Boss* (1964), he has had seven plays produced: *House of Flowers* (screenplay, 1971), *Wine of Astonishment* (screenplay, 1974), *The Schoolmaster* (screenplay, 1975), *Jestina's Calypso* (1976), *My Name Is Village* (musical drama, 1977), and *The New Hardware Store* (1980). His short stories were collected in 1988, in *A Brief Conversion*. He lectures frequently on such topics as the contributions of Creole, black, and East Indian communities to West Indian culture.

Achievements
The honors that have been awarded to Lovelace as a writer and teacher are particularly impressive when it is noted that his formal educational training was in agriculture and forestry. His first novel, *While Gods Are Falling*, received the British Petroleum Independence Literary Award (1964). His skills as a teacher led to a creative writing post at Federal City College, Washington, D.C., from 1971 to 1973, and to the position of visiting novelist at The Johns Hopkins University from 1973 to 1974. In 1980, he was named a Guggenheim Fellow.

First and foremost, Lovelace explores the character of his native countrymen in the rural and urban areas of Trinidad. While it would be easy to dwell upon the obvious difficulties of life in an out-of-the-way, developing country that has only recently emerged from colonial rule, Lovelace chooses to focus on the possibilities for growth within the spirit of his people. In pursuit of this aim, he captures the physical environment, the social turmoil, the dreams, and the very language of his island. Because of his ability to engage the reader in the struggles of his characters, he is a powerful storyteller.

Biography
Earl Wilbert Lovelace was born on July 13, 1935, in Trinidad. After receiving a basic education at a number of schools in Port-of-Spain, he was graduated from Ideal High School with his Cambridge School certificate in 1953. In 1962, he attained a diploma with specialized agricultural training from the Eastern Caribbean Farm Institute in Centeno, Trinidad. At the age

of eighteen, he was appointed a forest ranger in the Department of Forestry. After six years as a ranger, he transferred to the Ministry of Agriculture in 1959, where he remained an agricultural assistant from 1959 to 1966.

Encouraged in part by the favorable reception and the British Petroleum Independence Literary Award that attended publication of his first novel, *While Gods Are Falling*, he resigned from the civil service to undertake studies that would be more closely related to his writing. He spent the 1966-1967 academic year at Howard University in Washington, D.C., and then returned to Port-of-Spain as a journalist for the *Express* newspaper.

Beginning in the early 1970's, he served as a teacher and lecturer in a number of schools while pursuing his writing career. He taught at Federal City College, Washington, D.C., from 1971 to 1973, at The Johns Hopkins University from 1973 to 1974, and at the University of the West Indies, St. Augustine, from 1979 to 1980. He made his home at Francis Trace, Matura, Trinidad.

Analysis

No travel book, no matter how copious its factual data, could match the four published novels of Earl Lovelace in their depiction of the living reality of his native Trinidad. Since the central settings vary—urban apartment dwellings in Port-of-Spain for *While Gods Are Falling*, a remote mountain settlement for *The Schoolmaster*, a hillside slum yard for *The Dragon Can't Dance*—Lovelace touches nearly every segment of the population as widely different individuals confront the shifting problems of modern life. Complicating the plot of each novel are the problems of characters adjusting to societies in transition.

True to his name, Walter Castle, the protagonist of *While Gods Are Falling*, is engaged in preserving the security of his home. As Lovelace makes abundantly clear, Walter is threatened not so much by the restless young men who turn streets into battlegrounds as by a pervasive sense of life's aimlessness. With no more gods to claim meaningful authority, the younger generation has no guiding purpose. Fearful for his family because of the random violence and discouraged by his slow advancement at work, Walter's first impulse is to escape to peaceful farm life.

Stephanie Castle's reluctance to follow her husband's rash decision provides subtle motivation for the narrative's ebb and flow. In the intervals between their arguments, Walter reminisces about his childhood and his growth through a series of jobs into adulthood and marriage. Lovelace uses such flashbacks to indulge his love of Trinidad's lush forests and colorful rural folkways. The contrast with the city's hectic turmoil is quite effective. In the end, however, Stephanie aids Walter as he discovers the necessity of choosing a more responsible course.

At this point, Lovelace expands his message to encompass the larger community. As Walter assists a desperate mother to reclaim her wayward son, he enlists the support of prominent neighbors. Just enough realistic obstacles exist to prevent the solution from appearing facile. Walter and his friends eventually accept the fact that individual members of a community must not rely on institutions of state or religion for social progress. In the void left by the withdrawal of colonial rule, personal integrity and values reside more than ever in the hands of the citizenry.

While messages are available in *The Schoolmaster*, this second novel avoids didacticism by refusing to offer a final solution. The central conflict arises when a pastoral village decides to open a local school and end its isolation. Despite the dire predictions of their priest, the peasants of Kumaca have to accept exposure to civilization's corruptions as the price for giving their children a chance in the modern world. Ironically, corruption takes the form of the schoolmaster who is responsible for preparing the children for the future. When he rapes his assistant, he sows the seed of destruction for an innocent way of life. The pregnant girl commits suicide, the villagers conspire to hide the circumstances of the schoolmaster's violent death, and the inevitable transformation of a rustic society takes its toll.

The West Indian poet, Edward Brathwaite argues that the question of faith is central to the plot of *The Schoolmaster* and that the priest and the old mule-driver, Benn, should have carried more of the story. Father Vincent, whose faith depends upon church doctrine, is unable to protect his flock from evil, and in the end, his weakness allows him to accept the schoolmaster's ill-fated scheme to marry the girl he has violated. Going against his knowledge of human nature, he hopes for a miracle. Old Benn, who believes only in the rigors of a hard life, is able to instruct the priest in the lessons of experience. Their first serious dialogue leads the priest to recognize that, like Christ and Peter, men today must face temptation. The old mule-driver's philosophy is couched in terms of the agonizing choices and the defeats he has survived, leaving him with more questions than answers. Rather than allow an employer to take from him a beautiful colt that he loved like a son, Benn simply made a gift of the horse. Prevented in this way from exercising his power, the white man showed his spite by killing the animal. Benn's strength is in his having learned to live with bitter despair.

Benn's peasant knowledge bears witness to the earthy resilience of his people, while the priest appears anemic by comparison. On the final page, when Father Vincent accepts the mule-driver's invitation to visit his home, there is the suggestion that spirit and flesh may accommodate each other to mutual advantage. Their intermittent debates, Catholic against existentialist, do provide broad exposition for the issues that arise, but the drama belongs to the village itself. Lovelace's manipulation of the peasants' natural speaking voices brings their agony—of love, petty jealousy, greed, and vengeance— to full life.

Lovelace's third novel, *The Dragon Can't Dance*, is more completely integrated than his previous works; the narrative burden rests primarily with Aldrick Prospect but passes smoothly to several other characters who extend the application of the central theme. Each carnival season, Aldrick takes on the costume of the dragon—virile, fierce, the emblem of the individual's right to assert his spiritual independence. The problem that evolves in the novel is the insufficiency of his kind of freedom.

Two factors force the issue. For Aldrick personally, there is growing love for Sylvia; he cannot hope to have her as long as he disregards the basic provisions of food, clothing, and shelter. On a larger scale, for the yardlife on the hill overlooking modern Port-of-Spain, there are the encroachments of civil government; Aldrick, Fisheye, Pariag, Philo, and the others must compromise or be left behind. Pariag, the only East Indian in the yard, and Philo, a rising calypsonian, accept what must be done and thrive. Pariag learns that the blacks and Creoles will never become his friends, but his industry leads to ownership of his own shop. Philo discovers that sex and socially acceptable satire open the way to fame and fortune, while serious protest is counterproductive.

Given the choice between abrasive traditional Kaiso (guaranteeing continued obscurity) and popular homogenized calypsos for a more settled audience, Philo bows to popularity. Fisheye and his "bad Johns" of the street corner openly reject Philo's success; by contrast, they succumb to the futile "dragon dance" gestures of violence. Philo must then reach through the superficial paraphernalia of fame to reestablish his friendship with Aldrick and his long-standing love for Cleothilda.

Aldrick is slower to learn than Philo, and Fisheye exemplifies the fate of the incorrigible misfit. Through most of the novel, Aldrick regrets the loss of pride and strength, the growing anonymity of Trinidad's postcolonial society. Gradually, he comes to the realization that his self-assertion and Fisheye's outlaw behavior are no longer appropriate. What once was useful to survival under colonial domination is now irresponsible behavior within a society whose members need to be encouraged to work together for the common good. While serving his sentence in prison for disturbance, Aldrick matures quickly. When released, he reminds Sylvia that she has valid choices beyond the material blandishments of middle-class conformity. For his own future, he ignores organized politics, places his faith in community responsibility, and takes a steady job. Lovelace's final pronouncement is Sylvia's choice: she breaks her ill-advised engagement to seek out Aldrick. Thus, in his third novel, Lovelace returns to the theme of individuals growing into members of a larger community.

In his fourth novel, *The Wine of Astonishment*, Lovelace dramatizes the historical conflict between Trinidad's spiritual Baptists (Shouters) and a repressive colonial government. By his own account, Lovelace experiments in

The Wine of Astonishment with a language close to that spoken by his countrymen—to decrease the distance between the novel and the people who inspire its pages.

As he delves into the complications of people trying to live according to their faith under a ban that denies their religious liberty, he focuses on Bolo, a renegade stickfighter. The story is of the Baptists' and Bolo's struggle to accommodate the contradictions of colonial existence. Against the backdrop of tropical vegetation and the surrounding sea, these children of Africa must adjust to the conflicts between their old heritage and the New World's colonial values. There are the contending attractions of country and city life and the transition from familiar ways to the political realities of the twentieth century.

The historical basis of the novel is in the various attempts by colonial governments to suppress native forms of expression. Along with the Baptists, such practices as stickfighting and African drumming have been confronted with bans. There is thus, in *The Wine of Astonishment*, at least the suggestion of a parallel with the theme of *While Gods Are Falling*. The dignity that Walter Castle desires is similar to the dignity inherent in the freedom of religious worship and cultural self-determination.

From the beginning, there is a clarity of purpose and design in Lovelace that makes his work available, on the level of storytelling, to almost any reader. Deeper within the action, however, are authentic revelations which demand serious consideration. According to Edward Braithwaite, Lovelace's importance is in the quality of faith he projects. He offers no easy solutions but rather, he demonstrates the possibilities of working within a community which he accepts, with all its attendant challenges.

Robert D. Hamner

Other major works
SHORT FICTION: *A Brief Conversion*, 1988.

PLAYS: *New Boss*, 1964; *House of Flowers*, 1971; *Wine of Astonishment*, 1974; *The Schoolmaster*, 1975; *Jestina's Calypso*, 1976; *My Name Is Village*, 1977; *The New Hardware Store*, 1980; *Jestina's Calypso and Other Plays*, 1984 (includes *The New Hardware Store* and *My Name is Village*).

Bibliography
Barratt, Harold. "Metaphor and Symbol in *The Dragon Can't Dance*." *World Literature Written in English* 23 (1984): 405-413. Describes Lovelace's novel, *The Dragon Can't Dance*, as a parody of the crucifixion and redemption and its characters as "wrongsided" saints. The comparison between the events in the novels and the rites of Roman Catholicism suggests that the story is conceived as a kind of reverse "sacred liturgy," which helps to capture the essence of the lost society about which Lovelace is writing.

Cary, Norman Reed. "Salvation, Self, and Solidarity in the Work of Earl Lovelace." *World Literature Written in English* 28 (1988): 103-114. Noting that little criticism is available on what is considered a major West Indian writer, this essay sets out to address Lovelace's novels and plays as significant postcolonial writings. Examines what is called "their quest," which is often expressed in religious terms. Yet this quest does not lead to spiritual salvation but to a secular affirmation that decolonizes Caribbean society and provides it with an identity apart from that bestowed by the former colonial powers, Great Britain and the United States.

Gowda, H. H. Anniah. "A Brief Note on the Dialect Novels of Sam Selvon and Earl Lovelace." *The Literary Half-Yearly* 27, no. 2 (1986): 98-103. Draws comparisons between Lovelace's use of dialect and that of Samuel Selvon, another West Indian novelist. In the process, offers insights into how the Third World writer rebels against standard English and creates authenticity by attempting to record the actual speech of the people.

Reyes, Angelita. "Carnival: Ritual Dance of the Past and Present in Earl Lovelace's *The Dragon Can't Dance*." *World Literature Written in English* 24 (Summer, 1984): 107-120. Shows how the novel *The Dragon Can't Dance* makes symbolic use of the traditions surrounding the idea of Carnival and how, in this indirect way, Lovelace conveys social change and history in the Caribbean. Analyzes the way the narrative shapes itself around the Carnival seasons, concluding that Carnival exemplifies a form of Third World resistance against past colonialism and neocolonialism.

Thorpe, Marjorie. "In Search of the West Indian Hero: A Study of Earl Lovelace's Fiction." In *Critical Issues in West Indian Literature*, edited by Erika Sollish Smilowitz and Roberta Quarles Knowles. Parkersburg, Iowa: Caribbean Books, 1984. Examines Lovelace's search for a hero figure and considers the quest as central to the theme of his four novels. Depicts the kinds of heroes that appear in his fiction: the false ones whose only interest is materialism, the failures who become isolated, and the true heroes who express their Caribbean identity.

MALCOLM LOWRY

Born: Liscard, England; July 28, 1909
Died: Ripe, England; June 27, 1957

Principal long fiction

Ultramarine, 1933, revised 1962; *Under the Volcano*, 1947; *Lunar Caustic*, 1968; *Dark as the Grave Wherein My Friend Is Laid*, 1968; *October Ferry to Gabriola*, 1970.

Other literary forms

All but two of the volumes now attributed to Malcolm Lowry were published after his death at the age of forty-seven. During the last decade of his life, after the publication of *Under the Volcano*, Lowry worked more or less concurrently on numerous projects but was unable to finish any of them before his death. The one closest to completion when he died was *Hear Us O Lord from Heaven Thy Dwelling Place* (1961), a collection of seven interrelated tales. Additional short fiction has been collected in *Malcolm Lowry: Psalms and Songs* (1975), edited by Margerie Bonner Lowry. A selection of poems, edited by Earle Birney, appeared in 1962. *Lunar Caustic*, a novella edited from two earlier versions by Birney and Margerie Bonner Lowry, was published in 1968. Throughout his career, Lowry elaborated and reelaborated a massive scheme of interlocking narratives called, collectively, "The Voyage That Never Ends," which, had he lived to complete it, would have included all of his longer works, with *Under the Volcano* at the center of the "bolus," as he called it. The *Selected Letters of Malcolm Lowry*, edited by Harvey Breit and Margerie Bonner Lowry, appeared in 1965 and played a large part in the revival of interest in Lowry during the 1960's and 1970's. Lowry was also much interested in the cinema and, in collaboration with his second wife Margerie Bonner (herself a published novelist), prepared a screenplay for an adaptation of F. Scott Fitzgerald's *Tender Is the Night* (1934); the film was never produced, but the Lowrys' notes for the film script were published in 1976. Malcolm Lowry's life is the subject of the film *Volcano: An Inquiry into the Life and Death of Malcolm Lowry* (1977), directed by Donald Brittain.

Since so many of Lowry's works were left unfinished at his death, and since even the works published posthumously are selections from numerous versions Lowry left behind, selections made and pieced together by editors, the authenticity of the texts published after 1957 is at least questionable. The special collection of Lowry manuscripts housed at the University of British Columbia Library in Vancouver is, therefore, very important.

Achievements

The only Lowry novel to attract any notable attention during his lifetime was *Under the Volcano*, which was in general very warmly received (in France and the United States at any rate, though curiously it was all but ignored in England) upon its appearance in 1947. During the ten years following, however, no extended works of fiction by Lowry appeared in English, and by the time of his death, even *Under the Volcano* was out of print. Nevertheless, an underground following quietly persisted in its admiration for what must then have seemed, to most, a cometlike blaze of genius revealed in that one novel, appearing out of nowhere and as suddenly disappearing from sight.

The situation altered with the posthumous publication of other Lowry works in the 1960's, beginning with *Hear Us O Lord from Heaven Thy Dwelling Place*. By 1965, a selection of poems had appeared, *Ultramarine* and *Under the Volcano* had been reissued, the *Paris Review* offered a new edition (the first to appear in English) of *Lunar Caustic*, and *Selected Letters of Malcolm Lowry* was published to largely favorable reviews. Lowry was belatedly "discovered" in England, and *Under the Volcano* was hailed as "one of the great English novels of this century" (Philip Toynbee). With the appearance at the end of the decade of the heavily edited, fragmentary novels *Dark as the Grave Wherein My Friend Is Laid* and *October Ferry to Gabriola*, however, a reaction set in. Both books were widely regarded as failures, and Lowry's tendency toward solipsism was judged to have gotten the better of him in his abortive later works. This view probably does an injustice to Lowry. First, works never brought to completion by Lowry cannot be justly measured against a fully realized work on which the author lavished almost ten years of concerted labor. Even so, Douglas Day's long-awaited authorized biography, published to nearly universal acclaim in 1973, seemed to legitimize the view of Lowry as an artist *manqué* whose single triumph amounted to a kind of fluke accomplished despite its author's compulsive tendencies to self-destruction and willed failure. More recently, there have been salutary signs of a reassessment of the Lowry canon as a whole, with such critics as Muriel C. Bradbrook, Ronald Binns, and Sherrill Grace arguing persuasively against the distortions of the "one-book author" label.

Biography

The youngest of four brothers, Clarence Malcolm Lowry was born at Warren Crest, North Drive, Liscard, Cheshire, England, on July 28, 1909. His father, Arthur O. Lowry, was a wealthy cotton-broker of sturdy Victorian probity; his mother, Evelyn Boden, was the daughter of Captain Lyon Boden of Liverpool. A prominent shipowner and mariner, Captain Boden had died of cholera while homeward bound from Calcutta in 1880. This part of the family legacy, so unlike that of the paternal side, would provide Malcolm Lowry with the doom-tinged romantic yearning for the sea much in evidence in his fiction.

At fourteen, Lowry was sent to a public school, The Leys, from which he was expected to proceed to Cambridge University, as his brothers had done.

It was during his four years at The Leys, however, that he began to engage in what amounted to a subtle subterfuge of the respectable middle-class life that his father had prescribed for him. He became infatuated with jazz and took up playing the "taropatch" or tenor ukulele. Enthusiastic readings of Herman Melville, Joseph Conrad, Jack London, and the early Eugene O'Neill fed his dreams of adventure at sea. Meanwhile, encouraged by one of his schoolmasters (the model for James Hilton's "Mr. Chips"), he began to write his own stories for the school's literary magazine. At this time, too, he began, surreptitiously at first, what would become another of his lifelong infatuations: alcohol.

By 1927, the conflict with his father had become overt, but Lowry finally agreed to go to Cambridge—after going to sea. In May, he shipped as deckboy aboard the *S.S. Pyrrhus*, outward bound for the Far East. This experience, which lasted about six months and was to provide the raw material for *Ultramarine*, punctured at least some of his youthful illusions about the sea. It was followed, in the summer of 1928, by another pilgrimage, this time to New England, where he went to pay homage to Conrad Aiken. The American writer's experimental novel of the sea, *Blue Voyage* (1927), was the catalyst of a kind of private tutorial (Lowry being already engaged in the writing of *Ultramarine*). The two got on famously, beginning a literary kinship—and, later a competition—as of father and son, which would last in one form or another for thirty years.

At Cambridge, Lowry scarcely applied himself to his formal studies. Instead, he plumped the role of the loutish yet brilliant sailor, took up jazz again, became a connoisseur of avant-garde German silent films, drank, ran with an "advanced" circle of friends, and continued to work on *Ultramarine*. In November, 1929, one of his friends, Paul Fitte, committed suicide. The circumstances remain uncertain, but it is clear from the obsessive references to this event in his later fiction that Lowry felt partly responsible for it. The other significant occurrence of this time came in the summer of 1930, when Lowry again shipped out, this time as fireman on a Norwegian tramp steamer bound for Archangel in the White Sea. His purpose was to pay a visit to Norwegian author Nordahl Grieg, whose novel *The Ship Sails On* (translated in 1927) seemed to Lowry as important a precursor as Aiken's *Blue Voyage*. This journey and the eventual meeting between the two men gave Lowry the idea for another novel, *In Ballast to the White Sea*, on which he worked intermittently for the next fourteen years until the manuscript (running to some one thousand pages) was destroyed in a fire at his home in Canada in 1944.

After graduating with third-class honors in English, Lowry traveled on the Continent, meeting Aiken in Spain in the spring of 1933. There he also met and soon married Jan Gabrial, formerly a stunt woman in Hollywood films. It was an unhappy match, and Jan left him only a few weeks after their marriage in January, 1934. She returned to the United States, Lowry following her by ship the next autumn. In June, 1935, after a particularly severe bout of drinking, he was admitted to the psychiatric ward of Bellevue Hospital in New York. Upon his release ten days later, he began, between further drinking marathons, to write the first draft of *Lunar Caustic*. When an attempt to find a job in Hollywood proved fruitless, Jan and Lowry sailed to Mexico in November, 1936, settling soon after in Cuernavaca, where he began to write *Under the Volcano*. In December of the following year, Jan, who had never been faithful to the unstable Lowry, left him permanently. He drifted south to Oaxaca, where he spent some days in jail and formed an important friendship with a Mexican named Juan Fernando Márquez. Almost continually drunk, Lowry, with the assistance of "agents" sent by his father, was at length put on a train out of the country in July, 1938.

Back in California, Lowry met and fell in love with another American, Margerie Bonner. By the end of 1940, divorced from Jan and remarried to Margerie, Lowry had moved with Margerie into a squatter's shack in Dollarton, on Burrard Inlet, British Columbia. Here they would remain, with occasional trips to Mexico, Haiti, and Europe, for the next fourteen years. It was by far the happiest, most sober (comparatively speaking), and most productive period of Lowry's life. By December, 1944, he had completed the fourth and final version of *Under the Volcano*. A five-month return visit to Mexico between 1944 and 1945 had nearly disastrous consequences—a suicide attempt, more drinking, the discovery that his Mexican friend, Juan Fernando Márquez, had been killed, trouble with the Mexican authorities, and finally deportation—but from these experiences Lowry gained most of the materials for *Dark as the Grave Wherein My Friend Is Laid* and the unpublished fragment *La Mordida*. By 1950, he was working as it were simultaneously on these novels, the stories to be collected in *Hear Us O Lord from Heaven Thy Dwelling Place*, the film script for *Tender Is the Night*, his poems, and *October Ferry to Gabriola*.

This period of intense creative effort came to an end in 1954, when Lowry's American publisher, out of patience with his proliferating but seemingly unproductive schemes for his "bolus," severed their contract. Another severance occurred when the Lowry's left their "northern paradise" in Dollarton. After a final, brief reunion with Aiken in New York, they sailed for Italy. In late 1955, Lowry was admitted to a hospital in London for psychiatric treatment. Released in February, 1956, he settled with Margerie in the village of Ripe, Sussex, where he resumed his work. His sudden death, on June 27, 1957, caused by a fatal combination of alcohol and barbiturates, was officially termed "death by misadventure." Not surprisingly, Lowry had long since arrived at his own verdict:

> Malcolm Lowry
> Late of the Bowery

His prose was flowery
And often glowery
He lived, nightly, and drank, daily,
And died playing the ukulele.

Analysis

Like most artists, Malcolm Lowry was always fascinated by the mystery of the creative process. Unlike many other modern writers, however, he was little inclined to the explicit formulation of aesthetic theories. Still, his attitudes toward art, particularly his own art, are frequently embodied in his fiction. In the opening chapter of *Under the Volcano*, for example, one of the main characters, a film director named Jacques Laruelle, sees a drunken horseman "sprawling all over his mount, his stirrups lost, . . . barely managing to hold on by the reins, though not once . . . [grasping] the pommel to steady himself." Hurtling at breakneck speed through the narrow, winding streets of a Mexican village, the rider slips to one side, nearly falls, rights himself, almost slides off backward, and barely regains his balance, "just saving himself each time, but always with the reins, never the pommel." A closer look reveals a machete in one of the rider's hands, used to beat the horse's flanks furiously. It is, as M. Laruelle reflects, a "maniacal vision of senseless frenzy, but controlled, not quite uncontrolled, somehow almost admirable." This image serves, *mutatis mutandis*, as an epitome of Lowry's art: full of high risk, willfully unstable, disdainful of conventional controls, precariously balanced—but balanced all the same.

Obviously, such balance is achieved, when it is achieved, with great difficulty. This was particularly true for Lowry, whose inclination was always to follow the minutest divagations of the mind. His is an art of excess, in several senses. The composition of a novel, for him, meant continual amplification and expansion, patiently adding layer after layer of meaningful reference and telling detail, until the structure of the whole fairly exploded with a rich profusion of reverberating meanings. Such "overloading," to use Lowry's own word describing his technique, is felt at every level. His prose style, for example, is characterized by wheeling complex sentences, rife with qualifications, suspensions, and parentheses. Brian O'Kill has aptly described this style as "expansive" and "centrifugal," persistently "avoiding the closed unit of the periodic sentence in favor of an open form with an almost infinite capacity for addition and reduplication."

Lowry's range of tone is also unusually wide and varied. As Robert B. Heilman observed,

In recording a disaster of personality that is on the very edge of the tragic, [Lowry] has an extravagant comic sense that creates an almost unique tension among moods. Desperation, the ludicrous, nightmare, the vulgar, the appalling, the fantastic, the nonsensical, and the painfully pathetic coexist in an incongruous melange that is still a unity.

In a famous letter defending *Under the Volcano* against various suggestions for further revision, Lowry argued that the book could be regarded as a symphony, an opera, a jazz break, a poem, a tragedy, a comedy, a farce, a churrigueresque chathedral, a wheel, a cryptogram, a prophecy, a film, and a kind of machine. If this claim sounds extravagant, it should be remembered that Lowry believed, with Charles Baudelaire, that "life is a forest of symbols." Virtually everything in this novel—from a theater marquee to items on a menu, newspaper advertisements, an armadillo digging a hole, a cat chasing a dragonfly, amusement park rides, a travel brochure, a urinal—*everything* signifies. Appearing amid profuse allusions to the Bible, Christopher Marlowe, Dante, the Cabbala, John Bunyan, Sophocles, William Shakespeare, Herman Melville, and T. S. Eliot among many others, these "found objects" in the setting gradually develop into a vast network of the protagonist's plight, elevating it to the level of a modern myth, indeed a tragedy for modern times.

In these respects, as in many others, Lowry resembles no one so much as Melville. (Lowry once admitted, characteristically with irony at his own expense, that he identified himself with the American novelist for several reasons but "mostly because of his failure as a writer and his whole outlook generally." Both novelists were acutely aware of the monstrous potencies of the human imagination, which could envision—and proceed resolutely to enact—apocalyptic destruction as readily as it could create life-serving works of art. Both knew well the dangers involved in unleashing those potencies, particularly in the service of a narcissistic quest for what Melville's Ishmael calls "the ungraspable phantom of life," the self.

Such a view of the imagination, overtly Romantic and possessed by the seductive demoness of an artistic ego of leviathan, of volcanic, proportions, is clearly fraught with risk. Lowry, like Melville, accepted the risks involved, not the least of which was the gamble that the reader would go along, entertain the terms of the risk. There are times when, inevitably, the gamble fails. "Overloading"—the Melvillian tendency in Lowry to pile on six portents or allusions or symbols to evoke something that another writer would either summarize in a simple declarative sentence or else not attempt to say at all—sometimes threatens to sink the vessel. Reading the work of both men requires the granting of far more than the usual share of indulgences before the bountiful aesthetic rewards can be reaped.

Some readers, however, do not find such tolerance of unevenness to their taste, and *Under the Volcano* is on the way to becoming one of the least read of great novels, in company with *Moby Dick* (1851). Lowry's other works (like Melville's *Pierre*, 1852, and *The Confidence Man*, 1857) are so much the more neglected, despite the recent efforts of critics to call attention to their worth. One can only regret this aesthetic stinginess, along with the more commonplace preference for readily accessible, streamlined fictions. In Lowry's case, the reader who gives himself to the experience proffered, accepting the terms of risk including the excesses involved, and the occasional failings, is likely to find that the gamble more than justifies itself. For, as Matthew Corrigan has aptly observed, when such "writing works for us, it does so . . . because it entails a vision of a higher order of creative existence altogether than we ordinarily get in modern literature."

Under the Volcano is a book of wonders, a grand testament to the undiminished plentitude of the English language and the prodigious powers—both creative and destructive—of the human imagination. Not the least of its wonders is that Malcolm Lowry began writing it while he was in Mexico suffering through the personal anguish of a failed marriage, chronic alcoholism, and a terror of life so pervasive that it is a minor miracle he survived at all, much less that he was able to write. The novel went through at least four complete drafts in nine years (the third draft having been rejected by no fewer than thirteen publishers), and was finally completed in December, 1944. By that time, Lowry, from the far more stable perspective provided by living simply on the beach in Dollarton with his second wife Margerie, had succeeded in sufficiently harnessing his inner demons so as to transform his earlier sufferings into art. He described the work in an important letter to his British publisher, Jonathan Cape, as a "drama of . . . man's struggle between the powers of darkness and light," but it would be more precise to call it a "Bible of Hell" written by one who had been a member of the devil's party and knew it well.

One index of Lowry's ability to amplify his experience, transmuting it into a pattern with universal implications, is his management of setting. While the fictional village of Quauhnahuac is loosely modeled on Cuernavaca, where Lowry lived between 1936 and 1938, there is no attempt at documentary realism. To be sure, Lowry selects elements from the real town—the surrounding mountains dominated by the great volcano, Popocatepetl, the Cortes palace with its revolutionary frescoes, the Hotel Casino de la Selva, the dilapidated Borda Gardens of Maximilian and Carolotta, the winding cobbled streets, the quaintly named cantinas, the fetid barranca or ravine winding through the town—but his rendering of them emphasizes not mere "local color" but the power of the mind to metamorphosize external reality into an interlocking set of correspondences to the inner life of man. One of Lowry's strongest convictions was that life was, as Charles Baudelaire said, a forest of symbols. Thus, Hernando Cortes' palace and the Diego Rivera frescoes adorning it suggest the Spanish Conquest and the Mexican Revolution of 1910 to 1920, which in turn suggest both the endless internecine conflicts of history and the perpetual battle of the individual human soul against the powers of darkness. The Borda Gardens embody similar meanings, along with the aura of doomed love.

The volcano literally looms large over the entire novel, its snowy summit serving as a symbol of the characters' spiritual aspiration toward ascent, while at its base winds the ubiquitous barranca, suggestive of an alternative destination awaiting the wayward soul. The proximity of the barranca to the totemic volcano and to the many gardens in the novel (most of them, like the Borda Gardens, overgrown, untended, and ruined) calls attention to one of Lowry's central themes: the "infernal paradise" that is the essence of Mexico and, by extension, the modern world itself. This oxymoronic image owes something to D. H. Lawrence, whose novel *The Plumed Serpent* (1926) similarly links the contradictions endemic to revolutionary Mexico with the struggle of his protagonist to undergo a kind of rebirth of spirit. In Lowry, however, the allure of the infernal paradise does not liberate his protagonist from the despoiled garden of life and propel him toward redemption; rather, it arrests him in a state of prolonged inertia, a paralysis of will which renders him finally incapable of actively pursuing the spiritual ascent he so often imagines for himself. In Lowry's version of the myth, at least in *Under the Volcano*, man is condemned to inhabit a garden gone to seed, bereft of its creator: paradise, surviving only as an image of longing, is irretrievably lost. Solipsistic dreams of ascent succeed only in preventing the upward progress of the soul and, indeed, in promoting its gradual descent into the infernal abyss.

Lowry's narrative, like his setting, is designed to encourage the reader to view the events in broadly symbolic terms. Apart from the opening chapter, which is set one year to the day after the events recounted in the rest of the novel, the narrative's present action is confined to the events of a single day, November 2, 1938, the last day in the life of the protagonist Geoffrey Firmin, a British ex-Consul and an alcoholic's alcoholic. It is also the last day in the life of his wife, Yvonne. The Firmins have been divorced for nearly a year, but on this holiday, known to all in Mexico as the Day of the Dead (All Soul's Day), Yvonne has returned to try to reconcile with Geoffrey. He realizes, however, that such a reconciliation—which he himself has desperately longed for during her absence—would require that he give up drinking, and this he cannot bring himself to do. They quarrel, fail at making love, and part for a time, the Consul to the company of a bottle, Yvonne to that of Geoffrey's half brother Hugh, formerly her lover. Later, the threesome make a day-trip "downhill" by bus to Tomalín, where, as Hugh makes a spectacle of himself at an event called a "bull-throwing," Yvonne fervently proposes to Geoffrey that they leave Mexico and try to make a new life together in some "northern paradise" (clearly a reference to Dollarton).

At length, after more drinking and more quarreling, the Consul emphatically refuses and runs off alone, claiming that he prefers "hell" to her offer of a "sober" northern paradise. Pursuing Geoffrey in the darkness through the woods, Yvonne encounters a spooked horse and is trampled to death. The Consul, meanwhile, has gone to the lurid Farolito cantina in Parián, where, after a series of misunderstandings and mescal-inspired blunders— culminating in his freeing of a tethered horse (the same animal that tramples Yvonne in the forest), an act of fuddled yet genuine protest—he is accused of being a Communist spy and is shot to death by Fascist "irregular police." His body is thrown down into the barranca along with that of a dead dog. In the novel's opening chapter, these tragic events, along with many earlier incidents in the lives of the doomed Firmins, are recollected on the Day of the Dead one year later by Jacques Laruelle, a retired French film director who had once been the Consul's closest friend, as well as another of Yvonne's lovers.

Such a summary is inevitably misleading, for *Under the Volcano*, like most of Lowry's fiction, really offers little in the way of conventional plot. For one thing, the story is deliberately deprived of any ordinary sort of suspense by the disclosure of its tragic outcome in the first chapter. What this curiously epiloguelike prologue accomplishes, among other things, is a displacement of emphasis away from the sequence of events themselves to their causes and, in the grief of M. Laurelle, some of their effects. Other disruptions of the superficial story interest stem from the frequent use of flashbacks (although strictly speaking, the entire novel after the first chapter is a flashback), as the characters brood on their past lives leading up to this day of crisis; from ellipses caused by the Consul's passing out or hallucinating; and from the constantly shifting narrative viewpoint: five of the novel's twelve chapters are presented from the Consul's perspective, three from Yvonne's, three from Hugh's, and one from Laruelle's. The focus is thus chiefly inward, on the embattled consciousness of the characters.

Even the characters' surroundings in the external world—Laruelle's bizarre mosquelike house with the oracular inscription on one of the towers (*no se puede vivir sin amar*—"one cannot live without loving"); the municipal garden with its equally oracular warning sign (*¿Le gusta este jardín que es suyo? ¡Evite que sus hijos lo destruyan!*—"Do you like this garden that is yours? See that your children do not destroy it!"); the amusement park rides, including a loop-the-loop contraption called (after a play by Jean Cocteau) *La Máquina Infernal* and a "luminous wheel" that is as much time or fortune as a ferris wheel; the advertisements for a horror film, *The Hands of Orlac*, about an artist-turned-murderer; a cantina called *La Sepultura*, and another called *Salón Ofelia*; the forest around Quauhnahuac and Parián equated repeatedly with Dante's dark wood—all of these external places or objects (and there are many other examples) are essentially coordinates on the map of the mind that the novel traces. Indeed, so densely overgrown is Lowry's "forest of symbols" that one can sometimes lose sight of the immediate or human level of the story. At such junctures, time seems to be arrested or abolished by the "self-reflexive" play of images and motifs, just as it does in *The Waste Land* (1922) and other great "spatializing" works in the modernist tradition. Yet in *Under the Volcano*, the force of time is powerfully affirmed at the bottom of the reeking barranca.

Despite the novel's inward focus, Lowry manages to achieve an ironic detachment from his characters. This is no mean feat, not only because of the autobiographical origins of the story, but also because the Consul himself lays claim to ironic detachment even as he observes his own downfall. Lowry's detachment is achieved precisely through the form of the novel, an exceedingly complex design which includes but is finally larger than even the Consul and his remarkably resourceful capacity to transform his life into species of "quixotic oral fiction." Even though the Consul's tragedy in a moral sense is of his own making, it is made by Lowry to resonate like a central melodic pattern within an enormous surrounding symphonic structure. In part, this resonance derives from the novel's frequent echoing of its own infernal music—the *leitmotivs* mentioned previously. Equally important are the allusive echoes to literature, myth, and history.

The novel teems with allusions direct and implicit to the Bible, the Cabala, Sophocles, Ovid, Dante, Christopher Marlowe, William Shakespeare, Johann Wolfgang von Goethe, William Blake, Percy Bysshe Shelley, Edgar Allan Poe, Herman Melville, Joseph Conrad, and T. S. Eliot, among others. Persistently, the Consul's situation is compared (often by the Consul himself) with that of Oedipus, Prometheus, Adam, Christ, Judas, the Fisher King, Faust, and Hamlet. These allusions, moreover, are not gratuitous. Individually and collectively, they amount to a kind of running commentary on the pattern of heroism to which the Consul, and sometimes the other characters, aspire, and against which his downfall may be measured. What is one to make, for example, of a hero who, at one moment, proclaims in impressive Promethean tones that "the will of man is unconquerable. Even God cannot conquer it," and who collapses "with a crash," unconscious, the next?

Even more tellingly ironic are the historical analogues that Lowry draws between the Consul and such figures as Cortes, William Blackstone the explorer, Maximilian, and General Victoriano Huerta. All of the latter were men of action, which the Consul emphatically is not; yet, like him, they all became involved, sooner or later, in nefarious political intrigues whose result—sometimes unwittingly—was the exploitation of a subject people, usually of another nation or race. During World War I, Geoffrey, then lieutenant commander of a Q-boat, the *S.S. Samaritan*, was obscurely implicated in the murder of captured German officers; and as Lowry wrote to Cape, "you can even see the German submarine officers taking revenge on the Consul in the form of the *sinarquistas* and semi-fascist *brutos* at the end." However absurd on the face of it, the political pretexts for the murder of the Consul by the pro-Fascists carry a certain underlying truth.

In an important episode in Chapter VIII, a wounded Indian is found by the roadside. Because of a Mexican law prohibiting any interference in a crime, even after the fact, the Consul prevents Hugh from attempting to help the dying man. "*Compañero*," the Indian says, appealing to them, but all they can do is ruminate on the horror of it all, even as another traveler on the bus to Tomalín openly steals the dying man's money. Clearly, there is but a small difference between this sin of commission, the theft, and the Consul's sin of omission, so that in the last chapter, it is fitting that *he* should be "the one dying by the wayside and no good Samaritan would halt." "We evict those who destroy," warns the terrible sign in the garden (as meaningfully mistranslated by the Consul) and, like Cortes, Huerta, and no doubt every other man, in one diluted way or another, Geoffrey Firmin stands guilty at heart: "*No se puede vivir sin amar.*"

Yet while Lowry more than encourages the reader to see his characters against this elaborate backdrop of interrelated allusions, symbols, and motifs, it would be a mistake to overemphasize the backdrop at the expense of the foreground figures. The Consul, Hugh, Yvonne, and Laruelle are the cynosures through whose eyes the reader is allowed to glimpse the "massive interests" of a world sliding into the abyss beneath the volcano. At the same time, there is admittedly a deficiency in Lowry's portrayal of character, if by "portrayal" one has in mind the conventions of realistic characterization such as found in Henry James. Lowry was well aware of this deficiency. "The truth is," he wrote to Jonathan Cape, "that the character drawing [in *Under the Volcano*] is not only weak but virtually nonexistent, save with certain minor characters, the four main characters being intended, in one of the book's meanings, to be aspects of the same man, or of the human spirit." Lowry seems almost to be opting for a kind of allegorist's stance when he adds that there "are a thousand writers who can draw adequate characters till all is blue for one who can tell you something new about hell fire. And I am telling you something new about hell fire." This is, as it were, Lowry's *donnée*. He is not particularly interested in his characters as fully realized individuals whose development over the course of time is gradually presented.

The four main characters are all, as he said to Cape, "aspects of the same man." Hugh is "Everyman tightened up a screw . . . the youth of Everyman"; Yvonne is "the eternal women," the anima principle; Laruelle is the Consul's *Doppelgänger*, a surrogate for the artist/betrayer with blood on his hands. Although Lowry has provided glimpses into these characters' past lives, his purpose is less to trace the etiology of, for example, the Consul's alcoholism, than it is to locate key moments which chime with the present situation or offer ironic contrast to it. As Terence Wright has noted, "Lowry is not concerned with the Consul's fall as a *process*, nor with the attempts to save him as a thing which may or may not be accomplished, but with the *contemplation* of a state of affairs—the state of affairs being that a man is in Hell."

Notwithstanding the Consul's grandiose gestures toward Promethean rebellion, what is really most remarkable about him is his readiness to embrace his own death and damnation. This is perhaps what Lowry was referring to when he claimed to be teaching the world "something new about hell fire." The Consul *knows*, as his very utterance indicates ("A corpse will be transported by express!"), that his "glorious" descent is nearing its conclusion and that death is imminent, just as the reader knows, from the opening chapter, that Geoffrey has *already* succeeded in finding the disaster he has so ardently courted. This curious sense that everything has already happened conditions the whole feeling of the book and makes possible a range of effects—including moments of wild comedy and soaring lyricism—that one would not ordinarily expect to find in a tragic tale. It is as if the Consul, having resigned himself to the inevitability of his downfall, having indeed long since chosen the "hell" of addiction, solipsism, and despair represented for him by the Farolito, can undergo his descent and simultaneously observe himself descending, even deriving a certain amusement from the spectacle. The Consul's semi-detachment from his own suffering derives in part from his very awareness of the paradigms of tragic downfall in literature, above all Marlowe's Doctor Faustus, whose despairing quest for forbidden knowledge he deliberately emulates. At the same time, indulging in this "heroic" despair, he seems to harbor the illusion (derived this time from Blake) that "right through hell there is a path" leading to a "new life" beyond: by sinking as low as it is possible for a man to sink, giving himself over to complete damnation, he will somehow be saved in the end.

Salvation, however, will come, if it comes, not in the form of a loving union with Yvonne in some sober northern paradise but in the form of mystical vision—a state of mind for which, he believes, alcohol is *"absolutamente necesario."* The Consul regards his drinking as a religious exercise comparable to the partaking of an eternal sacrament. His determination to resist the meddling "salvage operations" of Hugh and Yvonne takes on the significance of a kind of holy war, an anticrusade, so to speak. As he tells Jacques Laruelle, he is fighting for nothing less than "the survival of the human consciousness." The fact that these are, on one level, an alcoholic's rationalizations, does not alter the issue. Drink, as the principal means of access to the visionary state, has become an integral part of his quest for occult knowledge and as such is immutably associated with a peculiar kind of fulfillment that the Consul has actually known, " . . . how, unless you drink as I do, can you hope to understand the beauty of an old woman from Tarasco who plays dominoes [in the cantina] at seven o'clock in the morning?"

This mixture of attitudes accounts for the "tragic joy" that, for a time, mitigates the gathering darkness of *Under the Volcano*. The Consul's vision at such moments is of genuinely heroic proportions, for he succeeds not merely in embracing Faustian despair but in transcending it, albeit fleetingly. The

Consul is a man of awesome imaginative energies and tremendous resources of humor and intelligence, so that when he dies, the reader experiences that sense of immense waste that accompanies the deaths of great tragic heroes such as Doctor Faustus. Yet the very qualities that set him apart contribute directly to his downfall. The ultimate irony here is that even though he succeeds in finding at the Farolito the "hell" he has sought all along, he succeeds "in a manner somewhat outside his calculations." He finds that damnation is not so ennobling—much less is it an amusing object for detached contemplation—after all. Knocked flat on his face by the shots of a Chief of Rostrums (of all people), the Consul is disappointed, as he was bound to be: "Christ . . . this is a dingy way to die," he tells himself. At this point, the Consul in effect sloughs off the trappings of a borrowed literary heroism and achieves his own "autochthonous" stature as a hero. He dies not as a modern-day Faustus but as Geoffrey Firmin, self-evicted from the potential satisfaction of living in even an infernal paradise. Nevertheless, as he lies dying, shorn of all vestiges of grandiosity, he recognizes what, in his solipsism, he has become. He acknowledges the tragic error of attempting to live without loving—faces, that is, his own essential humanity—though, as his final vision of climbing the volcano only to find himself hurtling down into it makes clear, it is too late for him to act on this new awareness. Moreover, even if he could somehow act, Yvonne is no longer attainable, thanks to his last defiant gesture of releasing the horse.

The novel closes with the Consul's final vision (chorically echoed by the oracular warning sign in the ruined garden), at once the culminating comment on his life of solipsistic denial and a vision of apocalyptic destruction:

> The world itself was bursting, bursting into black spouts of villages catapulted into space, with himself falling through it all, through the inconceivable pandemonium of a million tanks, through the blazing of ten million burning bodies, falling, into a forest, falling.

Although *Under the Volcano* is Lowry's best and most highly regarded work, his other pieces have received recently more sympathetic treatment. Muriel C. Bradbrook was the first to call attention to Lowry's early experiences on the Wirral Peninsula, in public school, and at Cambridge as in many ways the crucial source of his mature vision, an emphasis that nicely balances Douglas Day's excessive dwelling on the last, doom-haunted years. Ronald Binns is one of several critics to examine Lowry's fiction after *Under the Volcano* both seriously and sympathetically, finding in it evidence of a new direction toward the "metafictional" mode of such postmodernists as Samuel Beckett, Vladimir Nabokov, and Jorge Luis Borges, rather than mere failed attempts to repeat the "high modernist" performance that links *Under the Volcano* with the older tradition of James Joyce and Marcel Proust. For her part, Sherrill Grace maintains that *Under the Volcano* is "best viewed as the magnificent Popocatepetl among lesser, but by no means uninteresting, peaks." In short, although *Under the Volcano* still stands as Lowry's undisputed masterpiece, an adequate appreciation of his complex achievement finally depends on a firm understanding of his "bolus" as a whole. When this understanding occurs, there is reason to believe that Lowry will be recognized as one of the greatest of modern visionary artists.

Ronald G. Walker

Other major works

SHORT FICTION: *Hear Us O Lord from Heaven Thy Dwelling Place*, 1961; *Malcolm Lowry: Psalms and Songs*, 1975 (Margerie Bonner Lowry, editor).

POETRY: *Selected Poems*, 1962 (Earle Birney, editor).

NONFICTION: *Selected Letters of Malcolm Lowry*, 1965 (Harvey Breit and Margerie Bonner Lowry, editors).

MISCELLANEOUS: *Notes on a Screenplay for F. Scott Fitzgerald's "Tender Is the Night,"* 1976 (with Margerie Bonner Lowry).

Bibliography

Barnes, Jim. *Fiction of Malcolm Lowry and Thomas Mann*. Kirksville, Miss.: The Thomas Jefferson University Press, 1990. Barnes contrasts and compares these two authors who both "trace a protagonist's journey into the lower depths of the self." Examines the mythical patterns of the two writers and the structures they employ to give their works unity and universal truth. An important contribution to the criticism on Lowry.

Binns, Ronald. *Contemporary Writers: Malcolm Lowry*. London: Methuen, 1984. Discusses the Lowry "myth," with emphasis given to *Under the Volcano* and the autobiographical elements in his writing. The chapter on "metafictions" is a particularly useful survey of Lowry's late experimental novels and stories. A valuable guide for the beginning reader of Lowry.

Bowker, Gordon. *Malcolm Lowry Remembered*. London: British Broadcasting Corp., 1985. A readable collection of reminiscences that attempt to "penetrate the myth and reach the man." Some of the essays are published here for the first time. Also includes interviews with Lowry's two wives and many of his friends and admirers.

Costa, Richard Hauer. *Malcolm Lowry*. New York: Twayne, 1972. The second half of this study deals with Lowry's work during his fifteen years in Canada. Costa approaches his study of Lowry from a Jungian perspective and looks at this author's "mystical-messianic aspects."

Kilgallin, Tony. *Lowry*. Erin, Ontario: Press Porcepic, 1973. Good criticism on *Ultramarine* and on Lowry's response to film. The analysis of *Under the Volcano*, however, is uneven and fragmented.

Markson, David. *Malcolm Lowry's Volcano: Myth, Symbol, Meaning*. New York: Times Books, 1978. An in-depth critical study of Lowry's *Under the Volcano*, considered his masterpiece and recognized by many critics as a major novel of this century. Indispensable to the serious scholar of Lowry.

ALISON LURIE

Born: Chicago, Illinois; September 3, 1926

Principal long fiction

Love and Friendship, 1962; *The Nowhere City*, 1965; *Imaginary Friends*, 1967; *Real People*, 1969; *The War Between the Tates*, 1974; *Only Children*, 1979; *Foreign Affairs*, 1984; *The Truth About Lorin Jones*, 1988.

Other literary forms

Besides writing fiction, Alison Lurie has distinguished herself in two other areas, children's literature and the semiotics of dress, and her novels reflect both concerns as well. Her interest in children's literature is reflected in *Only Children*, in which two little girls pose their fantasies against the shocking reality exposed to them by their parents, and in *Foreign Affairs*, in which one of the two central characters, Vinnie Miner, spends her sabbatical in England collecting playground rhymes. Real children's rhymes, Lurie has observed, are surprisingly subversive, not like the "safe" literature written for children by adults. She developed this insight in a nonfiction work, *Don't Tell the Grown-ups: Subversive Children's Literature* (1990). Lurie's fascination with the semiotics of clothing (*The Language of Clothes*, 1981) is reflected frequently in the novels, where she pursues the relationship between clothing and personal identity. An especially provocative example can be found in *Imaginary Friends*, where Roger Zimmern, forced by a strange religious group to abandon his normal academic dress in favor of cheap suits, loses his sense of identity.

Achievements

Lurie's fiction has received much praise from critics, and her work has been very popular with the broader reading public. Her first novel, *Love and Friendship*, appeared in 1962 and was followed by several prestigious grants and fellowships: Yaddo Foundation fellowships in 1963, 1964, and 1966; a Guggenheim grant in 1965-1966; a Rockefeller Foundation grant in 1967-1968; a New York State Cultural Council Foundation Grant in 1972-1973. *The War Between the Tates* in 1974 brought Lurie a popular audience and more critical acclaim. An American Academy of Arts and Letters award followed in 1978, and for *Foreign Affairs* she was awarded a Pulitzer Prize in 1985. All of Lurie's fiction displays a remarkable control of language, a style which surprises and amuses. Both for her wit and for her sharp-edged, satiric depiction of human follies, she has often been compared to Jane Austen.

Biography

Alison Lurie was born September 3, 1926, in Chicago, Illinois, but grew up in White Plains, New York. An avid reader as a child, she began at about the age of thirteen or fourteen to read such authors as Charles Dickens, George Bernard Shaw, and Jane Austen. In 1947, she was graduated from Radcliffe, where she had met many people who later became important literary figures—Barbara Epstein, for example, later an editor of *The New York Review of Books*, and Jonathon Peale Bishop, a teacher, critic, and essayist whom she married in 1948. Lurie is a professor of children's literature at Cornell University in Ithaca, New York, where she has taught since 1969.

Analysis

Alison Lurie's novels are known for their comedy and satire, and her acute observation is most often trained on the complications of love, marriage, and friendship as they affect the lives of the upper classes, the educated, the academic. Many of her novels take place at the fictional Convers College in New England or at Corinth University in upstate New York (based on Cornell University, where Lurie has taught for many years) or concern characters who teach at or have been associated with Corinth. These novels are not, however, all academic satire; the academics often travel to other places or become involved in issues beyond the campus.

Lurie's style is most often detached and ironic, a treatment that has won for her both blame and praise. Her novels, except for *Only Children*, explore the time in which they are written and reflect the events and culture of Lurie's own adult years. The novels typically cover a short space of time, a crisis point in the lives of the characters, but several of the characters are seen at different points in their lives because of Lurie's use of the same characters in different novels, sometimes as major, sometimes as minor characters. Lurie works successfully with a variety of narrative points of view: omniscient narration in *The War Between the Tates*, first-person narration in *Real People*, third-person focus narration in *Imaginary Friends* (expanded to include two focus characters in *Foreign Affairs*). She shows no penchant for either the happy or the unhappy ending, realistically leaving her characters to continue to work out their lives as best they can.

At the heart of Lurie's first two novels are couples trying to work out their relationship. Her first novel, *Love and Friendship* (a title taken from Jane Austen), draws out the main lines of the issue. What is love and what is friendship? Are they different in what is best and most enduring? In this novel, the main character, Emmy Turner, "loves" her lover more than she does her husband. In the end, however, she chooses her husband over her lover because he needs her and to him she can be a friend. Indeed, what first led her to enter into a love affair was a frustration with her husband's failure to make a friend of her, to discuss with her his work and his concerns. Ultimately, Lurie suggests, friendship is more satisfying and lasting than love; indeed, love at its best is friendship at its best. In her second novel, *The No-where City*, the ending is the opposite, but the implication seems the same. Paul Cattleman rediscovers his wife at the end after much neglect and many adulteries. It is too late, however: Friendship is lost, and with it love; she tells him that she is not angry with him, but she just does not know him anymore.

While the love and friendship theme becomes a secondary issue in *Imaginary Friends*, she made it once again the central focus of *Real People*. In this novel, Janet Belle Spencer, a writer, has taken up residence at Illyria, a haven for writers and artists. She has gone there primarily to work, since she cannot seem to write at home, but she is also drawn there by her love for an artist, Ken, with whom she believes she has much more in common than with her insurance-executive husband. The artists' colony of Illyria is an unreal world, however, and Janet discovers that she and Ken are not really friends; she learns much about her writing that she resolves to change. It is at home with her husband, Clark, not at Illyria, she finally realizes, that she will be able to put to work her new understandings.

Love and friendship in marriage are explored most intensively in Lurie's next and most celebrated novel, *The War Between the Tates*. Erica and Brian Tate, a young academic couple, are in their own eyes and the eyes of their friends the perfect couple, but as middle age looms, Brian becomes increasingly frustrated at not being famous, while the children become rebellious teenagers. True love and friendship appear to be lacking. Finally, Brian has an affair with a student whom he makes pregnant, Erica befriends the student, and both Brian and Erica, but especially Erica, wander through a bewildering maze of events that leave their earlier sense of themselves and their marriage damaged. As the novel ends, they drift back together, confused, "out of love," but basically seeking a peace they can find only with each other.

Love and friendship in marriage is the topic once again of *Only Children*, but this time the actions of the adults are seen through the eyes of two little girls, Lolly and Mary Ann, who respond to what they see in the behavior of their elders, especially their parents. In each set of parents there is one serious, deeply dedicated person (Lolly's mother, Mary Ann's father) and one shallow, egotistic, flamboyant hunter of the other sex. The two sets of parents ultimately stay together, but, lacking a love based on friendship, they are merely maintaining a façade, and their example will cripple their children's ability to love.

The love and friendship theme appears again in *Foreign Affairs*, which juxtaposes two main characters, one married and one not. Vinnie Miner, a middle-aged professor, finds love surprisingly where she had least expected it, in a friendship with a man totally unlike her, a retired sanitary engineer. The other main character, a handsome young man in Vinnie's academic department, begins the novel estranged from his wife, is temporarily dazzled and infatuated by a far more glamorous Englishwoman, but returns to his wife at the end, finding her superior in trust, honesty, and common decency.

Lurie's novels concern themselves with relationships between people, and these relationships are at the center of all of her work. Yet the lives of Lurie's characters are affected by more than personal forces alone. Context, temporal and physical alike, is also central to these novels, and the direction of the lives of Lurie's characters is profoundly affected by the times and the places in which they live. The most persistent context, moreover, is academic, since many of these characters, like Lurie herself, are university professors or members of their families. In this case again, *Love and Friendship* sets a pattern which other novels will follow. Emmy Turner's husband, Holman Turner, is a young instructor at Convers, a small, exclusive liberal arts college in New England. Emmy wants to share her husband's academic interests but he shuts her out, treasuring her as an ideal wife and mother but bored by her attempts to enter into his intellectual concerns. Ironically, Emmy should be more at home at Convers (her wealthy father is a trustee, and two brothers are alumni), while Holman has come from a very different background, yet it is he, not Emmy, who seems the "Convers type." Emmy's love affair flaunts the Convers traditions, while Holman seems the perfect instructor. In the end, however, he falls afoul of those same Convers traditions, and it is Emmy who must stay to save him.

The academic world is also a factor in *The Nowhere City*, although the story takes place in a Los Angeles setting which dominates the novel. Paul, in the end, will retreat to the Eastern academic world that he knows (remaking his relationships with his old Harvard friends and taking a teaching post at Convers College), while Katherine, who had initially seemed the more Eastern academic of the two, refuses to return with him there and seems to find a new self in Los Angeles.

The War Between the Tates again makes the academy not only strong backdrop but also actor in the events. Brian Tate is a highly successful sociology professor at Corinth University in upstate New York; his wife, Erica, a faculty wife. Their two closest friends, who divorce in the novel, are Leonard Zimmern, an English professor, and Danielle Zimmern, Erica's closest female friend, a part-time faculty member in the French department. The convulsions of American academe in the late 1960's interfere directly in Brian's and Erica's lives. Brian, though very successful academically, has always dreamed of fame as an adviser to governments and presidents, and his middle-aged frustration makes him susceptible to trying to recover his lost youth by mixing socially with his graduate students, increasingly adapting his clothing and other styles to theirs, finally indulging in his affair with Wendy. Erica, like Katherine Cattleman in *The Nowhere City*, attempts to preserve her traditional moral values in the face of all this upheaval and tries not only to adapt herself to these values but also to give direction to Brian and Wendy, even to the point of insisting that Brian divorce her and marry Wendy. She becomes peripherally involved, through her friend Danielle, in the Hens, a local feminist group, and finding the local Hare Krishna guru of the students to be an old school friend, under his guidance has her own adventure with LSD. Brian and Erica, then, experience their marital troubles amid the student rebellions of the 1960's. Though the novel does not probe as deeply as *Imaginary Friends* into the political and intellectual doubts and troubles of academe, these influences are present, shaping their reaction.

In *Foreign Affairs*, the two main characters are again college professors, both from the English department at Corinth University: the middle-aged, internationally famous expert in children's literature, Vinnie Miner, and the young specialist in the eighteenth century, Fred Turner, both on leave to do scholarly work in London. The novel for the most part tells their stories separately, their paths crossing significantly only twice. While their common background does make their lives cross in significant ways, and while both their lives are shaped by their academic backgrounds, the primary focus of the novel is on other aspects of their lives, which will be discussed below.

The university campus, then, demonstrates the importance of time and place in Lurie's novels. This is also true in a larger sense, since American culture itself, with its regional and sociological tensions, plays just as important a role as the characters do. If *Love and Friendship*, the first novel, works off a Jane Austen theme, it also echoes a peculiarly American, Fitzgeraldian theme in which the different regions and classes of America become important players in the conflicts of the novel. Emmy is New Jersey rich, her lover Will Thomas Southern shabby genteel, and her husband Holman Chicago shabby but respectable poor. As the marital couple work out their conflicts with traditions of Convers College playing an important role, these different regional and class conflicts do much to shape their actions and reactions. In *The Nowhere City*, 1960's America, with its new and strange customs and dress, almost overpowers its characters' ability to work out their human problems. Here, Los Angeles is the city in which "nowhere" comes to mean "present but lacking history and future." Strange and mixed new forms of architecture in both house and public building design, styles of hair and dress, sexual life-styles, artistic forms, even subjects being studied in the universities are all strange, macabre, and new, dividing Katherine and Paul Cattleman as they respond to them so differently. Setting plays just as important a role in *Imaginary Friends*, which brings two very traditional strongholds, the enclosed small town and the principles of academic inquiry, together with the strains of the world without.

Real People, again, though it removes its main characters to an isolated, protected, ideal world of the artists' colony, nevertheless shows that the best work cannot be done in an artificial atmosphere but only when the artists are living and writing truthfully about the world in which they are "real people."

Again, too, despite all the 1960's campus shenanigans of *The War Between the Tates* (drugs; strange new life-styles, clothes, and hairstyles) the novel presents a strong sense that the campus is only reflecting all the major movements, confusions, and displacements of the society at large. In *Only Children*, which is set during the Great Depression, the characters reflect the concerns of that time, including its powerful economic and political conflicts. Bill Hubbard, for example, is an example of the FDR-type liberal democrat, dedicated to social reforms which will lift the poor, while Dan Zimmern represents the nascent Madison Avenue type, flamboyant and driven to succeed. *Foreign Affairs*, in the experiences of both Vinnie Miner and Fred Turner, discloses the tensions of many cultural mores, especially different class and sexual expectations, complicated further by differences between Great Britain and the United States.

The lives of the individual characters are additionally set against the backdrop of the world of literature itself. In *Real People*, Janet Belle Spencer images Ken as the ideal reader of her fiction, largely because he recognizes every literary reference—which in turn is reminiscent of Lurie's own rich texture of literary reference. In this regard, as already observed, she uses the "love and friendship" theme from Jane Austen. Another novelist to whom Lurie is greatly indebted is Henry James, especially in *Imaginary Friends* and *Foreign Affairs*. Indeed, *Imaginary Friends* in many ways duplicates the plot of James's *The Bostonians* (1886), in which a young woman named Verena leads a band of truth-seekers, by an extraordinary gift of public speaking, which seems to proceed from a trancelike ability to contact higher powers. Lurie's Verena, like James's heroine is torn between her group and her believers there, and a young man in love with her who wishes to carry her away. This role, taken by Basil Ransome in James's novel, is split in *Imaginary Friends* between the narrator, Roger, and the young man Ted, who does finally marry Verena and carry her off to the University of Arizona, where they are last seen as student agitators.

Foreign Affairs enlarges on the Jamesian theme not only by explicitly introducing James's work by name but also by exploring one of his most insistent themes: what happens when basically good, decent Americans encounter a far more culturally sophisticated European society. In James's novels of this type, the balance is struck in favor finally of the basic, honest decency of Americans against the more sophisticated but possibly corrupt world of the Europeans, and Lurie's novel arrives at the same resolution. This exploration is complicated by the fact that, of the two Americans, Vinnie Miner is very sophisticated in the ways of the English, knowing their ways and customs so well that she really feels more culturally at home there than in the United States. Fred Turner, on the other hand, despite his great physical charms and handsomeness and his knowledge of eighteenth century literature, is basically a raw recruit to European culture. Both, however, have "foreign affairs":

Vinnie, with an almost illiterate Oklahoman whom she meets on the plane on the way over, so embarrassingly crude that she dreads presenting him to her friends; Fred, with an English aristocrat and actress so elegant and sophisticated that his American life appears crude by comparison. Despite this structural converse, in which Vinnie loves an American far less presentable than her European friends, and in which Fred loves an Englishwoman far more sophisticated than his American wife and friends, both find, despite all of their differences, their American loves superior after all, and their European friends, for all of their sophistication, less satisfying morally as friends and lovers than their American friends. Thus, the pattern of James's international novels in which superior American decency confronts and ultimately wins out over superior European elegance and sophistication, is repeated here in Lurie's fiction.

If Lurie's readers often spot resonances from other fiction, they also have the pleasure of recognizing characters they have met in other Lurie novels, for Lurie frequently works with recurring characters. Emmy Turner's four-year-old boy Freddy from *Love and Friendship* is one of the grown-up main characters in *Foreign Affairs*, while Fred's wife Roo in that same novel appeared as a child in the earlier *The War Between the Tates*. Sometimes Lurie will in a later novel go back to an earlier period in a character's life: Miranda, the grown-up, married mother of three children in *Love and Friendship*, is seen as a child in the later novel *Only Children*. Of all the characters that recur, the most persistent one is Leonard Zimmern, first seen in *Real People* as a middle-aged, distinguished critic of American literature living in New York; later, in *The War Between the Tates*, as a friend of Brian and Erica. He is also the father of Roo, a child here but an adult in *Foreign Affairs*. In *Only Children*, the Depression-era story, Zimmern is a teenager, and in *Foreign Affairs* he is the father of a grown-up Roo, the famous critic whose harsh article on Vinnie Miner's work in children's literature haunts Vinnie as she goes to England. Roger Zimmern of *Imaginary Friends* is mentioned briefly in *The War Between the Tates* as Leonard Zimmern's cousin. This remarkable amount of recurrence suggests Lurie's strong interest in understanding how her characters came to be who they are, despite her novels' time frames. Her novels, as noted before, cover only short periods of time—one, *Only Children*, takes place in a single weekend. In order to continue her characters' development, then, Lurie often spreads out their lives over several novels, the recurrence of her characters in different novels doing much to tie their lives together.

As in the other novels, all the themes discussed so far are treated as well in *Imaginary Friends*. Their treatment in that novel, however, represents perhaps Lurie's broadest and deepest effort, for the academic backdrop she uses so often elsewhere is broadened here to embrace the most fundamental of human questions, questions of knowledge, of identity, of sanity, and finally of madness. The main character in this novel, sociologist Roger Zimmern— a young, brand-new Ph.D. at a large, upstate New York university—goes to Sophis, a nearby small town, as the research assistant of Thomas McCann, a famous senior professor in his department whom Roger admires despite rumors he has heard about him from other young faculty members and despite the realization that McCann's form of empirical sociology (the case-study method) is passé. To investigate McCann's hypothesis that small groups can build so powerful a belief system that it can withstand, rationalize, and incorporate doubting attacks from within and without, Roger infiltrates, under the cover of a public opinion seeker, a group of religious fundamentalists called the Truth-seekers, whose young leader, Verena, leads and directs through automatic writing from superior beings on another planet, named Varna. McCann is introduced as a businessman friend, also interested in their theories. Roger's secure identity is overset by his mentor's unscientific attempt to control the experiment in the direction of this hypothesis rather than merely observe and record, by the degree to which he sees this tendency in his mentor, driven by academic rivalry and jealousy. Also tormented by his sexual attraction for Verena, he reaches a point where he no longer knows what he believes in, no longer knows who he is, no longer knows whether there is in his discipline any objective basis for scientific inquiry. He believes that he is going mad but decides that it is, rather, his mentor who is insane and becomes unwillingly the primary witness whose testimony results in McCann's being committed to an asylum. The novel ends with Roger maintaining tenuous but commonsensical hold on his own sanity. Here, Lurie has touched upon questions central not only to academic life but to the lives of everyone else as well: How can one truly observe and know? How real is our own sense of self?

Taken as a whole, Lurie's novels reveal a remarkable uniformity. Her own background in academe provides the most common setting for her novels, and frequently this setting is broadened to reflect the central questions with which Lurie is concerned. Her interest in clothing and identity, in the lives of children, indeed in the lives of all of her characters, is unusual. Her work is best considered not as a series of separate novels but as a continuity in which her characters' lives continue, not ceasing with the end of a particular novel but continuing as do all our lives: growing and changing through time.

June M. Frazer

Other major works

NONFICTION: *The Language of Clothes*, 1981; *Don't Tell the Grown-ups: Subversive Children's Literature*, 1990.

CHILDREN'S LITERATURE: *The Heavenly Zoo: Legends and Tales of the Stars*, 1979; *Clever Gretchen and Other Forgotten Folktales*, 1980; *Fabulous Beasts*, 1981.

Bibliography

Evory, Ann, ed. *Contemporary Authors*. Rev. series, Vol. 17. Detroit: Gale Research, 1981. Lists Lurie's work, with brief commentary on her novel *The War Between the Tates*. Notes her recurrent theme of satirizing the American wealthy and educated middle classes. Also lists biographical and critical sources.

Hall, Sharon K., ed. *Contemporary Literary Criticism*. Vol. 39. Detroit: Gale Research, 1986. Presents a short commentary on Lurie's work to date, with an overview of her novels, and notes her preoccupation with the American middle class. Includes review extracts on her novel *Foreign Affairs*, which received the Pulitzer Prize for Fiction. The reviews here reflect the critical acclaim this book received, with a few dissenters.

Helterman, Jeffrey, and Richard Layman, eds. *Dictionary of Literary Biography*. Vol. 2. Detroit: Gale Research, 1978. A short but appreciative piece on Lurie by Everett Wilkie and Josephine Helterman with some useful background information and discussion of her novels. Mentions the common theme of adultery in Lurie's work, as well as her "conservative, even pessimistic" view of nature. Examines the techniques Lurie uses to convey satire in her work.

Hite, Molly. *The Other Side of the Story: Structures and Strategies of Contemporary Feminist Literature*. Ithaca, N.Y.: Cornell University Press, 1989. A brief entry on Lurie with reference to her novel, *Foreign Affairs*. Places Lurie in the genre of women writing in the margins, the metaphor in their novels being minor characters playing major roles.

Riley, Carolyn, ed. *Contemporary Literary Criticism*. Vol. 4. Detroit: Gale Research, 1975. Presents a sampling of reviews on Lurie's novel *The War Between the Tates*. Reviews range from favorable (*The New York Times Book Review, Spectator, The Washington Post Book World*) to outspokenly negative (*New Leader*), with *The Village Voice* taking the middle ground.

ROSE MACAULAY

Born: Rugby, England; August 1, 1881
Died: London, England; October 30, 1958

Principal long fiction

Abbots Verney, 1906; *The Furnace*, 1907; *The Secret River*, 1909; *The Valley Captives*, 1911; *The Lee Shore*, 1912; *Views and Vagabonds*, 1912; *The Making of a Bigot*, 1914; *Non-Combatants and Others*, 1916; *What Not: A Prophetic Comedy*, 1918; *Potterism: A Tragi-farcical Tract*, 1920; *Dangerous Ages*, 1921; *Mystery at Geneva*, 1922; *Told by an Idiot*, 1923; *Orphan Island*, 1924; *Crewe Train*, 1926; *Keeping Up Appearances*, 1928 (U.S. edition, *Daisy and Daphne*, 1928); *Staying with Relations*, 1930; *They Were Defeated*, 1932 (U.S. edition, *The Shadow Flies*, 1932); *Going Abroad*, 1934; *I Would Be Private*, 1937; *And No Man's Wit*, 1940; *The World My Wilderness*, 1950; *The Towers of Trebizond*, 1956.

Other literary forms

Though principally a novelist, Rose Macaulay wrote prolifically in several genres. Early in her career, she published two slim volumes of verse, *The Two Blind Countries* (1914) and *Three Days* (1919), both of which earned favorable reviews in the British press. For many years, Macaulay contributed reviews and essays to such publications as *The Spectator*, *The Guardian*, and the *New Statesman*; she produced two generally well-received book-length critical studies, *Milton* (1934, revised 1957) and *The Writings of E. M. Forster* (1938). Some of Macaulay's best prose can be found in two of her widely acclaimed travel books, *Fabled Shore: From the Pyrenees to Portugal* (1949) and *Pleasure of Ruins* (1953).

Achievements

Throughout much of her lifetime, Macaulay was one of Great Britain's best-known authors. Many of her lighter sketches and essays appeared in the *Daily Mail*, the *Evening Standard*, and other newspapers and periodicals aimed at large, general audiences; some of her fiction appeared in serialized form in *Eve*, a popular English magazine aimed at women and filled mainly with froth. Yet Macaulay's more serious works consistently earned high praise in Great Britain's most respected literary publications; her twenty-third and final novel, *The Towers of Trebizond*, won the prestigious James Black Tait Memorial Prize. In 1951, Macaulay was awarded an honorary doctorate of letters from Cambridge University; in 1958, she was named a dame commander of the British Empire. Her death from heart seizure in 1958 brought forth warm and respectful tributes from many leading literary figures, including Harold Nicolson, Rosamond Lehmann, and Anthony Powell.

Biography

Emilie Rose Macaulay was born in Rugby, England, on August 1, 1881. Her father, George Macaulay, was a schoolmaster and Latin scholar; her mother, the former Grace Conybeare, was a bright, energetic, but rather severe woman who sought to impart to her children a High Church interpretation of Anglican Christianity. Rose Macaulay was related to a long line of ministers, teachers, and authors (the celebrated historian Thomas Babington Macaulay was her paternal grandfather's first cousin); not surprisingly, she was so well schooled by her parents that, by early adolescence, she was already on very familiar terms with, among other classics, Dante's *Inferno* (c.1320) and Shakespeare's plays. Because doctors prescribed warmth and sunshine as a means of treating her mother's tuberculosis, Macaulay spent the better part of her childhood in Varazzo, Italy—a place she would later recall with considerable fondness. In 1900, she entered Oxford's Somerville College, where she studied modern history and became—as her biographer Constance Babington Smith records—"a chatterbox who gabbled away so fast that at times she was hardly intelligible, a ready speaker who made lively contributions to undergraduate debates." Soon after completing her studies at Oxford, Macaulay—while living with her parents in Wales—began work on her first novel, *Abbots Verney*, which critics praised for its artistic promise. In 1915, Macaulay acquired a flat of her own in London, where she quickly developed friendships with such influential literary figures as Hugh Walpole, J. C. Squire, and Walter de la Mare, and where, in 1917, she entered into what became a twenty-five-year love affair with Gerald O'Donovan, a married man and a former Catholic priest who was himself well-known in London's literary circles as the author of the highly autobiographical and anticlerical novel *Father Ralph* (1913). Though she traveled frequently, widely, and often intrepidly to locations that saw little tourist activity, Macaulay continued to make her home in London, where even in old age she was seen—as one friend recalled—"at every party, every private view, protest meeting, cruise, literary luncheon, or ecclesiastical gathering." Macaulay began openly to identify herself as an agnostic during her university days; much of her fiction pokes generally gentle fun at organized religion. After O'Donovan's death in 1942, however, she experienced a renewed interest in orthodox Christianity, an interest much in evidence in her later novels.

Analysis

Over a writing career that spanned fifty years, Rose Macaulay produced twenty-three novels. She understandably came to regard the earliest of these—including *The Furnace*, *The Secret River*, and *The Valley Captives*—as immature and rather badly made, and she did nothing to encourage their republication. In her novels, Macaulay utilizes a wide variety of carefully rendered settings (some of which are quite exotic); her prose is beautifully cadenced and richly detailed. Occasionally, however, the exuberance and ornateness of Macaulay's prose can be distracting, and, occasionally, her plots bog down beneath the weight of the descriptive digressions and authorial intrusions that pepper her texts. Many of Macaulay's characters are both convincing and memorable. Some, however, are both stereotypical and stiff and appear to be exchanging speeches rather than engaging in spontaneous conversation. Macaulay recognized that, as a novelist, she was least skilled at characterization; indeed, she was sometimes urged by friends and critics to concentrate on the essay form. Yet Macaulay also recognized that her fiction had a large and rather devoted readership and that, moreover, fiction could provide her with an entertaining vehicle for disseminating, and dissecting, a wide range of stimulating ideas.

As a novelist, Macaulay returned again and again to the same provocative themes. It is plain that, on the whole, she very much liked human beings. Still, she was severely critical of the intellectual laziness that she found epidemic in the human race. Repeatedly, her novels mock and sometimes savage characters who unthinkingly digest easy answers to the questions of life and who are prone, then, to sentimentality and cant. Though she is not generally ranked among her generation's more overtly feminist authors, Macaulay frequently reveals in her work a deep disdain for a social system that continued to deny women equal access to education and adventure. She regularly features as central figures young women who are witty, well-read, and intellectually ambitious.

Many of Macaulay's recurring concerns are overtly stated in *Potterism*, one of her most enduring novels—and the first to sell impressively in the United States. *Potterism* is, in fact, dedicated to "the unsentimental precisians in thought, who have, on this confused, inaccurate, and emotional planet, no fit habitation." It features among its five epigraphs Dr. Johnson's injunction to "clear your mind of cant. . . . Don't *think* foolishly." At the core of *Potterism* is the abrupt death of a young newspaper editor recently wed to Jane Potter, whose father is the publisher of a string of superficial, cant-spewing newspapers, and whose mother, under the pseudonym of Leila Yorke, churns out foolish and schmaltzy novels that enjoy huge sales. In order to discuss and analyze this somewhat suspicious demise from varying perspectives, Macaulay presents "extracts" from the "private journals" of several characters who knew the young editor, including his novel-writing mother-in-law. Employing clichéd and rather empurpled prose, Mrs. Potter shows herself to be quite capable of the sort of overemotionalism and muddled thinking that Macaulay, throughout her career, so thoroughly disdained. The three authors of the other journal entries are the friends of the Potter twins, Johnny and Jane, who have sought to distance themselves from what they disparagingly refer to as the "Potterism" of their parents. Macaulay demonstrates that Johnny and

Jane and their university-trained friends are not without their own pretensions and illusions, but she makes it clear that their crusade against vulgarity and stupidity—though quite probably quixotic—is well worth the taking.

Macaulay's thirteenth novel, the highly praised *Told by an Idiot*, is set in England between 1879 and 1927 and takes its title, and its epigraph, from Macbeth's well-known observation that life is a "tale told by an idiot, full of sound and fury,/ Signifying nothing. . . ." In this work, Macaulay focuses on the family of Maurice Garden, whose continuing struggles with faith and doubt have made him at various times a Catholic, a Baptist, a Positivist, an Anglican, "a plain agnostic," and, when the novel opens, an enthusiastic member of the Ethical Society. Garden's theological gyrations are well tolerated by his calm wife and his bright children, whose ranks include lively daughters named Imogen, Stanley, and Rome. Through her portrait of Maurice, Macaulay not only conveys something of her sense of the futility of most conflicting "isms" but also provides an acute portrait of the mental landscape of Victorian England. Through her depiction of the Gardens' daughters, she is able to portray young women who, though by no means perfect, possess energy, perspicacity, and a desire for independence.

In *Orphan Island*, perhaps Macaulay's most satisfactorily plotted novel, she harshly satirizes the sort of narrow-minded smugness that was not uncommon among influential people in the Victorian age. In the novel's early chapters, Macaulay describes how in 1855 a ship carrying dozens of young English orphans is blown off its California-bound course during a violent storm and winds up wrecked along the coast of a small, uncharted island in the South Pacific. In succeeding chapters, she shows how the prim and proper Miss Charlotte Smith—the orphans' supervisor—gradually turns the island into a model of Victorian England and establishes herself as its stern and platitudinous queen. In the 1920's, Miss Smith's island is rediscovered by a team headed by Mr. Thinkwell, a Cambridge lecturer in sociology. Thinkwell is astonished to discover that, in the remotest part of the South Pacific, Victorian England—complete with pronounced social inequities and an obsession with propriety—is, in effect, frozen in time. Still, Thinkwell enjoys the island's remarkable beauty, which Macaulay effectively renders through frequent and detailed descriptions of its sunny skies, lush plant life, and exotic vegetation. He also becomes attached to his growing status as a man of great intelligence and learning. In fact, near the novel's close and soon after the ancient Miss Smith's long-expected death, he becomes the island's prime minister, bent on reforming the corrupt monarchy into a republic where freedom and social justice can thrive. Macaulay does not reveal whether Thinkwell succeeds, though she does point out that, in the end, human folly has a way of winning out, and that the island is "likely" to become "as tyrannous, as unfair, as oligarchic in constitution and economic condition" as it was during Miss Smith's curious reign.

Macaulay's sole historical novel is *They Were Defeated*, called *The Shadow Flies* in its American edition, which takes place in England and covers an eight-month period beginning in the fall of 1640. Essentially, the novel centers on the often bloody and self-defeating religious conflicts that were then taking place between Puritans, Anglicans, and Roman Catholics. Among its characters are several well-known historical and literary figures, including the poets Robert Herrick, John Cleveland, and John Suckling. The scholarly and highly analytical Dr. Conybeare, himself based on one of Macaulay's distant relations, is one of the many central characters in her fiction who finds himself struggling with religious doubts. Similarly, his daughter Julian is a recognizable Macaulay "type": She bears what is commonly regarded as a male name and desires for herself the male prerogative to ask questions and obtain knowledge. In a prefatory "Note" to this long, intricately plotted and largely convincing book, Macaulay explains,

> I have done my best to make no person in this novel use in conversation any words, phrases, or idioms that were not demonstrably used at the time in which they lived; though I am aware, for all the constant and stalwart aid of the Oxford Dictionary, and the wealth of literature, letters and journals of the period that we possess for our guidance, that any such attempt must be extremely inadequate; or, at least, that mine is so.

In fact, after the publication of *The Shadow Flies*, Macaulay received assurances from several students of the language that her errors in word usage were both minor and few.

Going Abroad, Macaulay's next novel, represents a decided change of pace. Dedicated to two friends "who desired a book of unredeemed levity," *Going Abroad* is set largely in Zarauz, a coastal resort town in the Basque country of Spain. It features a large cast of British eccentrics, including a Dante scholar, a young aesthete, a rigid colonel, and a woman schooled in the classics who seeks to relocate and re-create the Garden of Eden. Also featured in *Going Abroad* is a pair of vulgarians who run a string of beauty parlors and a group of hearty Oxford students who seek to spread goodness and religion through the Moral Re-armament Movement, and who are successfully portrayed by Macaulay as both foolish and, in their own sort of way, admirable. By focusing on the often strained interaction of these diverse types, Macaulay created a highly successful comic novel set in an appealingly sunny climate—one that deserves to be ranked among the most amusing of its time.

During the 1950's, Rose Macaulay produced two novels that are generally placed among her most accomplished. The first of these, *The World My Wilderness*, draws heavily upon the recent events of World War II. Its central figure, a seventeen-year-old girl named Barbary, spent the war years in France, where she witnessed or was touched by a host of brutalities, including her stepfather's murder by Resistance fighters who believed, wrongly, that he collaborated regularly with the Nazis. After the war, Barbary moves to London to live with her father, a wealthy barrister. She studies art and tries to start a more ordered life. As Macaulay repeatedly emphasizes, however, the ruins of war still dominate London: Blocks and blocks of buildings have been shattered, and so have innumerable lives. Thus, Barbary and her brother Raoul eventually fall in with a group of young Londoners who have been similarly affected by the recent violence and chaos and who spend their days wandering around in the city's many ruins, their energies focused on petty crime. During the war, Macaulay's small flat was itself destroyed by German bombs; she lost all of her letters, manuscripts, and books. Certainly, much of her sense of loss and despair informs *The World My Wilderness*.

The Towers of Trebizond, Macaulay's final novel, begins with the delightful and arresting words, "Take my camel, dear." This work—which is set principally in Turkey, along the Mediterranean coast—seems at first glance to be an outrageous and funny farce in the manner of *Going Abroad*. For example, one of its main characters, the camel-riding Aunt Dot, is immediately recognizable as yet another of Macaulay's eccentric—and harmless—fanatics. Her goal is to spread single-handedly the doctrine of female emancipation throughout Islamic Turkey, while along the way bringing wayward Moslems into the Anglican fold. She is accompanied on her trip by a priggish, relic-scavenging and very High Church priest, and by a niece, Laurie, who relates the novel's action.

Like many of Macaulay's earlier novels, *The Towers of Trebizond* pokes gentle, rather affectionate fun at zealous churchgoers. Like many of her novels, it displays a subtle, complex, and rhythmical prose style that sometimes dazes and more frequently dazzles. Laurie, its narrator, is certainly very much in keeping with Macaulay's earlier central figures. She is witty, intelligent, and widely read. In the final analysis, Laurie's observations on many serious matters give *The Towers of Trebizond* a far less farcical tone than *Going Abroad*. Indeed, Laurie—Macaulay's last heroine—is, perhaps appropriately, her most autobiographical. She not only freely expresses a mixture of guilt and joy at having maintained a long and intimate relationship with a married man, but—like Macaulay after Gerald O'Donovan's death—she repeatedly reveals a deep desire to return to the Church which she denied for so many years. Even more revealing, however, is her zest for life. Like Macaulay, Laurie has read and traveled and carefully observed because, as she points out,

> life, for all its agonies of despair and loss and guilt, is exciting and beautiful, amusing and artful and endearing, full of liking and of love, at times a poem and a high adventure, at times very gay; and whatever (if anything) is to come after it, we shall not have this life again.

Brian Murray

Other major works

POETRY: *The Two Blind Countries*, 1914; *Three Days*, 1919.

NONFICTION: *A Casual Commentary*, 1925; *Catchwords and Claptrap*, 1926; *Some Religious Elements in English Literature*, 1931; *Milton*, 1934, revised 1957; *Personal Pleasures*, 1935; *The Writings of E. M. Forster*, 1938; *Life Among the English*, 1942; *They Went to Portugal*, 1946; *Fabled Shore: From the Pyrenees to Portugal*, 1949; *Pleasure of Ruins*, 1953; *Letters to a Friend, 1950-1952*, 1961; *Last Letters to a Friend, 1952-1958*, 1962; *Letters to a Sister from Rose Macaulay*, 1964.

Bibliography

Bensen, Alice. *Rose Macaulay*. New York: Twayne, 1969. This standard account is especially valuable because there are few books devoted to Macaulay. Offers a survey of her widely varied output: novels, short stories, historical works, travel books, essays, and book reviews. Her tolerance for and sympathy with others are brought out. Macaulay belonged to the species of "gifted amateurs," and her carefully wrought style was sometimes too arch.

Fromm, Gloria G. "Re-inscribing *The Years*: Virginia Woolf, Rose Macaulay, and the Critics." *Journal of Modern Literature* 13 (July, 1986): 289-306. Argues that Macaulay had a strong influence on Virginia Woolf; in spite of her ridicule of Macaulay, Woolf found her essential. They knew each other for twenty years, and Macaulay makes frequent appearances in Woolf's diaries.

Passty, Jeanette. *Eros and Androgyny: The Legacy of Rose Macaulay*. London: Associated University Presses, 1988. Sees Macaulay as a feminist pioneer who repudiated the traditional pattern of the male-dominated family in favor of an androgynous ideal, arguing that people should pursue their aims in a gender-free way. Gives an account of Macaulay's work, the most comprehensive available, with the feminist theme always in the forefront. Her correspondence with Father Hamilton Johnston and its importance for her work receive detailed attention.

Smith, Constance Babington. *Rose Macaulay*. London: Collins, 1972. The standard (and only) biography of Macaulay. Presents a detailed account of her family background and sheds light on key episodes in her life, such as her unrequited love for Rupert Brooke. Gives synopses of most of her major works. A useful feature is an appendix that contains tributes to Macaulay from a number of her friends, including Harold Nicolson and Rosamond Lehmann.

Stewart, Douglas. *The Ark of God*. London: Kingsgate Press, 1961. Discusses Macaulay as one of a group of five novelists, stressing her Anglican background, which was influential in a number of her novels. She is portrayed as a deeply earnest writer and presented with unusual sympathy.

CORMAC McCARTHY

Born: Providence, Rhode Island; July 20, 1933

Principal long fiction
The Orchard Keeper, 1965; *Outer Dark*, 1968; *Child of God*, 1974; *Suttree*, 1979; *Blood Meridian: Or, The Evening Redness in the West*, 1985.

Other literary forms
Cormac McCarthy is almost exclusively a writer of novels. Short excerpts from his novels in progress have sometimes appeared in such literary magazines as *Yale Review*, *Sewanee Review*, and *TriQuarterly*. He also wrote the script for *The Gardener's Son*, a teleplay in the "Visions" series shown on national public television. First broadcast in January, 1977, the drama is based on an actual murder in 1876 in Graniteville, South Carolina. In a story full of dark implications, crippled Rob McEvoy, son of a poor working family, kills the son of the local textiles mill owner. The teleplay's director, Richard Pearce, recruited McCarthy to write the script.

Achievements
Few writers have received such critical acclaim as McCarthy without also gaining wide popularity. He has consistently been praised for his carefully crafted work, his unflinching, dark vision, his immense range of vocabulary, and his powers of observation and description. These qualities have also won for him rich recognition in the form of prizes and grants. *The Orchard Keeper* won the 1965 William Faulkner Foundation Award as the best first novel by an American writer and helped win for McCarthy an American Academy of Arts and Letters traveling fellowship to Europe in 1965-1966. The following years, as more of McCarthy's work appeared, brought him grants from the Rockefeller, Guggenheim, Lyndhurst, and MacArthur foundations. McCarthy has been compared to Faulkner, Edgar Allan Poe, and Mark Twain.

The same qualities in McCarthy that have been praised have also been the cause of criticism and help to explain why he has not been more popular. He writes slowly, having taken at least twenty years to produce his first five books; thus, McCarthy seems to fade from the public eye between books. His subjects—killings, incest, necrophilia, Knoxville lowlife, and scalp-hunting Western marauders—may repel some readers, and others may find his dark vision too unrelenting and morbid. Finally, his tendencies to ransack the dictionary for unusual words and to describe his dripping horrors in overwritten prose make him sound occasionally like gothic writer H. P. Lovecraft.

McCarthy has, however, continued to develop as a novelist. Despite the recognized high quality of his first three works, as exemplified by the praises and prizes given his very first novel, there is evidence that these works are derivative, that McCarthy was assimilating various influences as he wrote them. Although McCarthy continued to assimilate influences as he wrote *Suttree* and *Blood Meridian*, he also seemed to find his own voice in these novels, which are undoubtedly his best. McCarthy's control of his description has improved as his settings have widened, and his thematic perspective has widened with his settings. At first, pigeonholing critics thought McCarthy an East Tennessee regionalist, and then a Southern gothic, but *Blood Meridian* is a dark Western with hints about Western civilization itself. These terms illustrate the dangers of labeling a developing writer, but they also suggest the continuity, progression, and extent of McCarthy's development. His original gifts and his ability to grow make McCarthy a formidable writer who has yet to be fully recognized.

Biography

Cormac McCarthy is the product of a middle-class Catholic family—about as far as one can get from the background of most of his characters (with the notable exception of Suttree). He was born in Providence, Rhode Island, in 1933. When McCarthy was four, his family moved to the Knoxville, Tennessee, area, where his father was chief legal counsel to the Tennessee Valley Authority (TVA). There, McCarthy grew up, attending parochial school, Catholic High School, and the University of Tennessee. He dropped out of the university after one year, traveled for a year, and then joined the United States Air Force, in which he served for four years. Afterward, he attended the University of Tennessee for three more years but finally left in 1959 without getting a degree.

McCarthy did discover his writing vocation at the University of Tennessee, where he began work on a novel. After the publication of *The Orchard Keeper*, he traveled in Europe for three years, living in London, Paris, and on the Spanish island of Ibiza. While in Europe, he married Anne de Lisle of Hamble, England. Later, they lived on a small farm in Rockford, Tennessee, just outside Knoxville. McCarthy moved to El Paso, Texas, during the time he was writing *Blood Meridian*.

As *Blood Meridian* and his East Tennessee novels show, McCarthy is influenced by the landscape around him and is good at absorbing local talk, color, and tradition. Whether he was more directly influenced by his father's work with the TVA is an interesting question. For many families who had been living in the mountain valleys for generations, the TVA was their first contact with big government—a traumatic one that has still not been forgiven. The permanent flooding of their land by TVA projects, despite "compensation," resulted in massive dislocations within the traditional mountain culture. One of the more gruesome aspects was transferring the contents of cemeteries to higher ground—a scene of the restless dead that seems to be echoed repeatedly in McCarthy's work, as is the theme of the government's bringing of change.

Analysis

Like British Catholic writer Graham Greene, Cormac McCarthy is reluctant to develop any optimistic themes. He is also reluctant about stating his themes, although some of his titles offer strong hints. For the most part, he merely tells his stories and leaves it up to the reader to interpret their meanings. As a result, one critic has judged McCarthy to be nihilistic, but surely this judgment is incorrect. McCarthy's reluctance to preach about the good news masks a profoundly moral sensibility that is forced to face the worst in human nature and to recognize the power of evil. In this way, his novels are comparable to the medieval morality play or to such films by Ingmar Bergman as *Det sjunde inseglet* (1956; *The Seventh Seal*, 1958).

There is also a softer, more modern side to McCarthy's morality. Few writers identify so thoroughly with people beyond the pale—the poor, the homeless and dispossessed, the criminal and degenerate, the outcasts. He manages to find some humanity even in the worst of these and to ascribe their conditions partly to contingency, bad luck, or the operations of respectable society. Their nemesis (besides themselves) is often the law and its officers, who, for them, become additional embodiments of the death and destruction that pursue everyone. McCarthy's refusal to avert his sympathies from the outcasts thus raises some complex social and theological issues.

McCarthy's first novel, *The Orchard Keeper*, introduces the outcasts as members of the disappearing mountain culture of East Tennessee. Young Marion Sylder lives by bootlegging, and in self-defense he kills a man and disposes of the body in an abandoned peach orchard that symbolizes the dying culture. Old Arthur Ownby, who fondly watches over the orchard, finds the body, but he does not report it. He lets it rest in peace for seven years. The old man also believes in his own peace and privacy, and when these are disturbed by a government holding tank erected on a nearby hill, he shoots his X on the tank's side. Both the men live by old mountain codes which, by definition, are outside the law of the intruding modern world. Yet the enforcers of the law, who finally arrest and beat Sylder and send the old man to a mental institution, seem degenerate in comparison to them. The novel's theme is also represented in John Wesley Rattner (ironically, the son of the dead man), a boy who hunts and traps, is befriended by the two men, and comes of age in the novel. He decides to cast his loyalties with the old ways even if they have become anachronistic.

The episodic converging stories and italicized flashbacks of *The Orchard Keeper* recall Faulkner's narrative techniques, and McCarthy's second novel,

Outer Dark, also owes a debt to Faulkner. The novel takes place in some vaguely Deep South setting early in the twentieth century and deals with the horrible consequences of incest between Culla and Rinthy Holme, brother and sister. Rinthy delivers a baby boy, and Culla abandons it in the woods, where a passing tinker finds and takes it. Culla tells Rinthy that the baby died, but Rinthy digs up the shallow grave, discovers his lie, and intuitively goes in search of the tinker. Culla goes after Rinthy to bring her back. Their wanderings on the roads recall those of Lena Grove and Joe Christmas in Faulkner's *Light in August* (1932). Everyone she encounters befriends Rinthy, who moves along dripping mother's milk for over six months, but Culla meets nothing except suspicion and trouble. These episodes also recall the journey down the river in Mark Twain's *The Adventures of Huckleberry Finn* (1884), particularly a wild incident in which a loose ferry is swept down a raging river.

McCarthy's most original and unforgettable creation in *Outer Dark* is a set of three avenging angels, or devils, who rove about the landscape murdering people. On a realistic level, they are lawless, asocial drifters who have gone totally beyond the pale into the "outer dark." They have lost all caring. Appropriately, Culla meets this unholy trio of blood brothers near the novel's end. The three hang the tinker and dispose of the baby (now symbolically scarred as in a Nathaniel Hawthorne story) before Culla's eyes: One slits the baby's throat and another sucks its blood.

If *Outer Dark* does not contain horror enough, McCarthy followed it with *Child of God*, which returns to a rural East Tennessee setting. Here, mountain man Lester Ballard loses his farm for failure to pay taxes; embittered and alone, he sinks gradually into necrophilia and then murder. His degeneration is marked by movement from the farm to an abandoned shack that burns to a cave where he stores his supply of dead women. He is finally captured, dies in a state mental hospital, and is dissected in a medical laboratory. His neighbors, whose choruslike, folksy comments are interspersed throughout the story, always thought him a bit strange, with bad blood. McCarthy suggests that all Lester ever needed, however, was a home and love. Lester was only "a child of God much like yourself perhaps."

A short, tightly unified work, *Child of God* contrasts with McCarthy's next novel, *Suttree*, usually considered his masterpiece. *Suttree* displays the variety and range of McCarthy's talent. Set in Knoxville during the 1950's, the novel is a long, rambling work rich in incident, character, language, and mood, including some surprisingly amusing, bawdy humor. Yet *Suttree* has certain features in common with *Child of God*. Misery and unhappiness also predominate here, and instead of one child of God, *Suttree* has hundreds— drunks, prostitutes, perverts, petty criminals, and the poor generally, black and white—all dumped together in a slum known as McAnally Flats. The characters have such names as Gatemouth, Worm, Hoghead, and Trippin

Through The Dew, and their dialogue is spiced with slang and expletives.

The central character is Cornelius "Buddy" Suttree, scion of a prominent local family. He has deliberately chosen to live in this slum on a houseboat moored in the Tennessee River, from whose filthy waters he catches a few carp and catfish to sell. Why he has made this strange choice gradually becomes clear. On the one hand, he has made a mess of his life. He and his parents are no longer on speaking terms, and his wife left him long ago, taking their child (who dies in the novel). Suttree sank to drink and served a term in the prison workhouse. Now he lives in McAnally Flats because, on the other hand, he feels at home there. There, he can find the company of likeminded, fun-loving pals who can help him pass the time and avoid involvement in the pain of life. There he sits, the fisher king in his wasteland, and with dread and longing he awaits the oblivion of death.

A happy flaw in Suttree's character, however, prevents his nihilistic scheme from taking effect: compassion. He cannot avoid feeling compassion for the people around him, such as the ignorant but irrepressible Gene Harrogate, a country boy who serves a term in the workhouse for having sex with a farmer's watermelons and who dynamites the city's sewer system down on himself trying to rob a bank (the "country mouse," as he is first called, soon becomes the "city rat"). Further involvement with people leads to further pain for Suttree—a girl he falls in love with is killed, his long affair with a rich prostitute breaks up, and most of his pals are killed or imprisoned. Deeper emotional commitment on Suttree's part, however, might have saved both the girl and the affair with the prostitute. After a solitary retreat to the Great Smoky Mountains and a near-fatal illness, Suttree decides to embrace life—pain and all—and to leave Knoxville. He leaves just as the McAnally Flats are being torn down to make room for an expressway. His parting words of advice concern the hounds of death: "Fly them."

McCarthy's fifth book, *Blood Meridian*, is a historical novel set in the American Southwest and northern Mexico around the middle of the nineteenth century. The novel's protagonist is a nameless character known only as "the kid" (with suggested parallels perhaps to Billy the Kid), who runs away from his Tennessee home when he is fourteen and heads west. His story might be that of Huck Finn after Huck "lit out for the territory" and left civilization behind. After repeated scrapes, always moving west, the kid joins a band of scalping bounty hunters who hunt the Apaches when the Apaches are not hunting them. The massacres go on endlessly, all duly noted in the running summaries that head each chapter.

In some ways, *Blood Meridian* provides a useful retrospective view of McCarthy's work. It returns to the horrors of his earlier novels but seems to relate these to the social themes of *Suttree*. The scalp hunters are, after all, the advance guard of Western civilization. They suggest a terrible moral ambiguity at the heart of civilization, as in the hearts of individuals, that enables it to stamp out Apaches and backward mountaineers and to create such slums as McAnally Flats. Judge Holden, the repulsive and evil philosopher of *Blood Meridian*, argues that God made man thus, that morality is irrelevant, and that superior violence shall triumph. The naked judge finally embraces the kid with an apparent death hug inside a jakes behind a whorehouse in Fort Griffin, Texas. Readers can probably find a warning in this to flee such philosophers.

Harold Branam

Other major work
TELEPLAY: *The Gardener's Son*, 1977.

Bibliography
Bell, Vereen M. *The Achievement of Cormac McCarthy*. Baton Rouge: Louisiana State University Press, 1988. The first thorough critical study of McCarthy, in which Bell explains McCarthy's unconventional methods and his emphasis on language as responses to the fact that the real world is tainted by evil. The vivid description of that world can in some sense underline the value of life. Interestingly, Bell points out that McCarthy's literate readers would be better able to transcend reality through language than most of his characters. Contains a good bibliography and a full index.
_____. "The Ambiguous Nihilism of Cormac McCarthy." *Southern Literary Journal* 15 (Spring, 1983): 31-41. Focuses on what Bell sees as the central conflict in McCarthy's fiction: the impossibility of fitting the self, which yearns for purpose, into a world which is meaningless and miserable, filled with alienation, suffering, and violence.
Ditsky, John. "Further into Darkness: The Novels of Cormac McCarthy." *The Hollins Critic* 18 (April, 1981): 1-11. Ditsky argues that McCarthy carries grotesque action and obscure prose even further than William Faulkner did. Much of the essay describes what Ditsky sees as the gradual change in McCarthy's work, from the description of a barbaric but rich primitive world, which finds meaning in ritual or magic, to a more naturalistic view of life, without even the illusion of meaning.
Longley, John Lewis, Jr. "Suttree and the Metaphysics of Death." *The Southern Literary Journal* 17 (Spring, 1985): 79-90. Focuses on the protagonist in *Suttree*, a character who critics agree is more perceptive and more intelligent than the usual McCarthy characters. Although the work is set in the 1950's, Suttree is a 1960's-style dropout from a society which he believes to be corrupt. Explores Suttree's perception of the actual violence and death, as well as the death-in-life, of his world.
Schafer, William J. "Cormac McCarthy: The Hard Wages of Original Sin." *Appalachian Journal* 4 (Winter, 1977): 105-119. Even in what most critics

see as naturalistic or nihilistic fiction, one can see traces of the tradition of Southern Calvinism. This essay provides a difference of perspective and perhaps an alternate source for McCarthy's pessimism.

Sullivan, Walter. "Model Citizens and Marginal Cases: Heroes of the Day." *Sewanee Review* 87 (Spring, 1979): 337-344. Sullivan focuses on McCarthy's major characters, who like the author view the world with an impressive appetite for accurate detail but finally refuse to take responsibility for it. Because it emphasizes the relationship of character to theme, this fairly brief article would be a helpful introduction to McCarthy's complex fiction.

MARY McCARTHY

Born: Seattle, Washington; June 21, 1912
Died: New York, New York; October 25, 1989

Principal long fiction
The Oasis, 1949; *The Groves of Academe*, 1952; *A Charmed Life*, 1955; *The Group*, 1963; *Birds of America*, 1971; *Cannibals and Missionaries*, 1979.

Other literary forms
First known as a book reviewer, drama critic, and essayist, Mary McCarthy also wrote short stories, collected in *The Company She Keeps* (1942) and Cast a Cold Eye (1950). Her drama criticism is collected in *Sights and Spectacles: 1937-1956* (1956) and in *Mary McCarthy's Theatre Chronicles, 1937-1962* (1963). *Venice Observed* (1956) and *The Stones of Florence* (1959) are books of travel and art history. *The Writing on the Wall* (1970) and *Ideas and the Novel* (1980) are literary essays and lectures. *On the Contrary: Articles of Belief* (1961) contains autobiographical essays and literary criticism. *Memories of a Catholic Girlhood* (1957) and *How I Grew* (1987) are memoirs of her childhood and youth. Her books *Vietnam* (1967) and *Hanoi* (1968) oppose United States involvement in the Vietnam War, an interest which she continued in *Medina* (1972) and in *The Seventeenth Degree* (1974). *The Mask of State* (1974) presents impressions of the Watergate hearings.

Achievements
From the appearance of her first book reviews, when she was just out of college, to the time of her death, Mary McCarthy was one of the leading figures on the American literary scene. In her novels as much as in her essays and reviews, she was above all a critic, a sharp observer of contemporary society. For students of twentieth century American culture her work is indispensable.

Biography
Born into an affluent family of mixed Irish and Jewish heritage on June 21, 1912, in Seattle, Washington, Mary Therese McCarthy had a segmented childhood. After six years of what she called a "fairy-tale" existence of happiness, both parents died of influenza in 1918 during a move to Minneapolis. Mary and her three younger brothers, placed with their grandaunt and uncle, then entered a bleak phase of intense, strict Catholicism, which Mary described in *Memories of a Catholic Girlhood*. In 1923, Mary's grandparents moved her to a convent school in Seattle for the seventh and eighth grades; she spent her ninth grade year in a public school and then her remaining high school years at the Annie Wright Seminary in Tacoma, from which she was graduated

in 1929 at the top of her class. In the same year of her graduation as a Phi Beta Kappa from Vassar College in 1933, she married Harold Johnsrud, a marriage which lasted three years. She reviewed novels and biographies for *The New Republic* and *The Nation*, worked for the left-wing publishers Covici Friede, and, in 1937, involved herself in Trotskyite politics. In 1937, she became drama editor for the *Partisan Review*.

The next year, Mary McCarthy married Edmund Wilson and gave birth to a son, Reuel Wilson; also, at Wilson's urging, she wrote her first fiction, a short story. Thereafter, the stories she wrote for *Southern Review*, *Partisan Review*, and *Harper's Bazaar* were collected in 1942 in the book *The Company She Keeps*. She separated from Edmund Wilson in 1945, the same year that she was teaching literature at Bard College; and in 1946, she married Bowden Broadwater. In 1948, she taught one semester at Sarah Lawrence College and, in 1949, was a Guggenheim Fellow, an award which was repeated in 1959. Also in 1949, she received the *Horizon* literary prize from the publishers of her novel *The Oasis*. In 1961, she was divorced from Bowden Broadwater, married James Raymond West—a State Department official assigned to Paris—and went to live with him in France.

Two events dominated the 1960's for McCarthy. The first was the enormous popular success of her novel *The Group*, which became a number-one best-seller. The second was the Vietnam War; she was an outspoken critic of United States policy in Vietnam. In the 1970's she published two novels with social and political themes: *Birds of America* in 1971 and *Cannibals and Missionaries* in 1979; the latter, she said, would be her last novel.

In 1980, an offhand remark on "The Dick Cavett Show" embroiled McCarthy in a prolonged legal battle that became a *cause célèbre* in the literary community. McCarthy said of Lillian Hellman that "every word she writes is a lie, including 'and' and 'the.'" Hellman sued. The resulting legal maneuvering was costly for McCarthy (in contrast, the wealthy Hellman did not count the cost), ending only in 1984, when, after Hellman's death, the suit was dropped before going to trial. Meanwhile, legal issues aside, the controversy brought several of Hellman's autobiographical works under close scrutiny, and the consensus was that McCarthy's judgment, clearly stated in hyperbolic terms, was vindicated.

In 1987, McCarthy published *How I Grew*, the first installment in what was projected to be a multivolume intellectual autobiography. In general, critics found it inferior to *Memoirs of a Catholic Girlhood*, which had covered some of the same territory from a different perspective. McCarthy died in New York on October 25, 1989.

Analysis

Mary McCarthy's novels often feature herself, with an assumed name, as protagonist; she also exploited her husbands and other people close to her for fictional purposes. Her characters generally have a superior education and/or intellect so that citations and quotations from learned sources—mainly classical or artistic—spring into their conversations. This heightened discourse promotes compact paragraphs of dialogue, in which several persons speak to the same topic, in contrast with the usual fictional technique of a separate paragraph for each speaker. Yet, in the close conceptual unity of McCarthy's novels, lengthy paragraphs of extensive character analyses frequently fill several pages without interruption. As a result, the technique of several speakers in one paragraph seems to support the general schema. It supports, also, the paradigm of the group.

Structurally, the three novels preceding *The Group* develop around separate chapters, each presenting the viewpoints and the consciousness of the different characters; their point of unity is the common awareness of the social group. A protagonist, often a reflection of the author, generally emerges from among these peripheral persons, but the effect of each chapter remains that of the portrait or sketch.

Several factors of McCarthy's work can be inferred from this structure. As an orphan and a Catholic among Protestants, she no doubt had an early sensitivity to the significance of the group and the outsider. Furthermore, the intensely autobiographical nature of her work blurs the lines of genre, so that her essays read like short stories and her short stories like essays. Genre distinction, then, becomes a problem in any analysis of her work. An example is *The Company She Keeps*, short stories which are pulled into book form and revolve around a central theme—the quest—and parallel the structure of her novels. Furthermore, McCarthy did not term *The Oasis* a "novel" but called it a *conte philosophique*. Also, several chapters of her novels were published individually as short stories before being incorporated in the novels. The effect of this technique raises the question of whether she pushed the boundaries of the traditional novel outward or merely retreated to its earliest phases of development. She lamented the loss of a "sense of character" in modern novels, saying it began to fade with D. H. Lawrence. She admired Leo Tolstoy, Gustave Flaubert, George Eliot, Charles Dickens, and "all the Elizabethans."

The dominant quality of McCarthy's work is satire, and much of it is achieved by exaggeration and generalization. The dominant organization is the pairing of a separate character with each chapter, infused with an occasional chorus of viewpoints. McCarthy compared the technique to ventriloquism: the author throws her voice into various characters who speak for her. The long paragraphs of explication or character analysis tend to minimize plot; the concentration is on the psychological effects of what are frequently trivial incidents—as in *The Oasis*, when a couple illegally picking berries on the group's farm destroys the group.

The themes of McCarthy's novels generally concern the social failures of a group—of Utopian communities in *The Oasis*, of progressive education in *The Groves of Academe*, or of cultural progress in *The Group*. The interest in group attitudes can be best observed in the political content of McCarthy's novels, many of which feature a person who had some affiliation with the Communist party and defected or failed to become a member. Her work also shows a persistent aversion to the efforts of Senator Joseph McCarthy to eradicate Communists in the United States.

McCarthy's first novel, *The Oasis*, was published in *Horizon* under the title *A Source of Embarrassment* and puts into practice the theories of Arthur Koestler about "oases," small libertarian groups that would try, as McCarthy said, "to change the world on a small scale." Set at Pawlet, Vermont, at an abandoned hotel on an isolated mountain in 1946 or 1947, the novel brings together a group of about fifty people of varying backgrounds and motives. The characters seek to revive the concept of Utopian communities and welcome defectors from Europe. Their efforts, however, remain confined to the daily problems of food gathering and management and fall short of the larger goals.

First, the group fails to agree on its purpose. The purists aspire to a millennium but the realists seek only a vacation or a retreat from atomic warfare. They disagree, also, about who should be permitted to join the group, and some oppose the admission of businessman Joe Lockman. Next, they find that intellect, good intentions, and the simple life without electricity do not bring about moral reform: personal relationships and property ownership intrude. Joe Lockman leaves oil in the kitchen stove which singes the eyebrows of Katy Norell, and then, as a prank, he frightens Will Taub by pointing a gun at him. Later, when intruders pick their wild strawberries (the stolen fruit in their Eden), Katy is highly offended at the theft of *her* property, and Joe is indignant about the other colonists' attempts to drive away the berrypickers, until he realizes that it was his property, the gun, they used in the assault.

The first to defect from the community is Will Taub, in whom many readers recognized Philip Rahv; and Katy, who resembles Mary McCarthy, dreams of the dissolution of the community at the book's end. With Joe Lockman cast in the role of the outsider, with little plot and with incident minimized, and with much explication of philosophical theory and discussion of ideals and goals, the book sets the style for McCarthy's other novels.

Suspense is greatly improved in McCarthy's next novel, *The Groves of Academe*, set in a small Pennsylvania college called Jocelyn and resembling Bard College. Directing its satire at progressive education, this novel pits the progressive against the classical, satirizes the small college in general, and exposes the evils of McCarthyism, focused in Senator Joseph McCarthy's House UnAmerican Activities Committee. The group here is the English department faculty, from which Professor Henry Mulcahy finds himself dismissed. He rallies the faculty to his support, although he is a poor academician and deserves dismissal, and gains it through an appeal for sympathy for his wife and children. McCarthyism brought him to the position—the president hired him because he had been unjustly accused of being a Communist sympathizer—and, finally, it accounts for his retention. Mulcahy loses his chief faculty supporter when she discovers that he lied about his wife's illness, but he gains another weapon through a visiting poet who recognizes him from Communist party meetings. At the climax of the novel, the McCarthy scare is shown at its most evil: protecting the college, the well-meaning president conducts an interview into Mulcahy's past, which results in getting himself charged with libel. The unstable Mulcahy triumphs and secures his position at Jocelyn—certain to continue bullying students and colleagues alike—and the president resigns.

In *A Charmed Life*, Martha Sinnott returns to a group of artistic people at New Leeds, a small New England village based on Wellfleet, Cape Cod, where she had lived with her former husband (much like McCarthy had lived at Wellfleet and returned with a second husband). Martha returns determined to be different from and independent of the New Leedsians who live a charmed life of many accidents, none of which kills them. Here, time, which signifies the mortal, is askew and awry, as indicated by the many problems with clocks and calendars. Part of Martha's anxiety about her return to New Leeds is the possibility of meeting her former husband (based on Edmund Wilson) with his new wife and child and the fear that he will reestablish domination over her. When he seduces her and she later finds herself pregnant, she cannot remember the date well enough to determine whether her former or present husband is the father. Her moral decision to have an abortion because she cannot live a lie results in her death; returning from borrowing money for the abortion, she drives on the right side of the road, contrary to New Leeds custom, and meets another car head-on. The charmed life of New Leeds goes on, but Martha lives and dies an outsider.

McCarthy called this novel a fairy tale. Loosely analogous to "Sleeping Beauty," Martha Sinnott pricks her hand at the beginning of the novel, lives in self-doubt on the fringes of the immortality of New Leeds (the timelessness of a century of sleep), and is awakened to the new existence of pregnancy and decision. The prince who wakens her with a kiss (the seduction), however, is an evil prince.

With a theme of the failure of modern progress, *The Group* was published in November, 1963. At that time, Betty Friedan's *Feminine Mystique* (1962) and other feminist writings had focused on the problems of women, and the public was responsive to works focused on the problems of the emancipated woman. Although the novel is set in the seven years from 1933 to 1940, the progressiveness of the eight *cum* nine young Vassar women seemed to be the progress which was engulfing women of the 1960's. Like gleanings from an alumnae bulletin, the random appearances, different voices, and loose ends are not expected to be resolved. The undistinguished occupations of the group, also, confirm the alumnae magazine reports of most women graduates, but somehow more is expected of Vassar women. Not only the money but also increased competition for admission meant that, by 1963, most women could not get into Vassar. For the general public, there is some comfort in the failure of the culturally advantaged.

The novel begins with the wedding of Kay Strong in 1933 and ends with her death seven years later at the age of twenty-nine. Of the eight members of the group who had lived in the same dormitory, plus one outsider, Kay seemed to be most forward-looking and progressive. Like McCarthy, she comes from the West and, immediately upon graduation, she marries her lover of some time, a mostly unemployed playwright named Harald Petersen who resembles Harold Johnsrud. Part of McCarthy's personality is dispersed among the other characters, especially Libby MacAusland, a woman of formidable intellect who writes book reviews and becomes a literary agent.

The elegant, beautiful, and wealthy Elinor Eastlake disappears into Europe and reemerges a Lesbian prior to Kay's death. Polly Andrews becomes attached to a married man who is obviously well adjusted except that he pays twenty-five dollars a week for psychiatric counseling. Working in a hospital, Polly becomes engaged to another man, a psychiatrist who has defected from the profession and thus augments the satiric attack on psychiatry. Helena Davison, in Cleveland, remains the stable rich girl, highly intelligent and analytic. Priss Hartshorn marries a pediatrician, and, attempting to breast feed her son and train him by modern theories, provides the satire on this aspect of progressivism. Pokey Prothero, from a household organized and represented by an invaluable butler, plans to become a veterinarian.

Kay, during a fight with Harald, gets a black eye and finds herself committed to a mental hospital. Despite Harald's admission that she does not belong there, she decides to stay for a rest and then disappears from the story until she reemerges after a divorce and a year in the West. Back East, ready to start a career again, she falls to her death while spotting planes from her window and becomes the first casualty of the war.

Representing a culmination of the group philosophy and the disjointed voices of the earlier novels, *The Group* with its timely feminist content earned for McCarthy a great deal of money and many appearances on talk shows and in magazines. Some Vassar alumnae were recognizable in it, and the film version omitted naming the college. This novel established McCarthy as a popular writer, but she did not attempt to capitalize on it with a follow-up novel. Instead, eight years later, she brought out a novel of a different sort altogether.

Departing from the group structure, McCarthy's next novel, *Birds of America*, begins in 1964 with Peter Levi's return at age nineteen to Rocky Port, Maine, after an absence of five years. During his absence, his favorite horned owl died. With his divorced and remarried mother Rosamund, he searches for a waterfall that they cannot find: the victim of a highway project. In their respective ways, the village and the mother cling to fashions of the past but rapidly succumb to modernity.

Peter goes to the Sorbonne for his junior year in college but finds his ideals of French culture in conflict with the realities. His friends are American, he has a painful Thanksgiving dinner at an American general's home discussing vegetarianism and the war in Vietnam; he runs afoul of the French police while watching a demonstration; and he spends Christmas vacation in Rome where the masses of tourists interfere with his appreciation of the Sistine Chapel. Returned to Paris, he attempts in his Kantian way—"Behave as if thy maxim could be a universal law"—to help the street drunkards. Everywhere he goes, he tangles with human refuse, which is best revealed in a long letter home about the filth of Parisian toilets. Clinging to his preferences for nature, however, he grows vegetables and other plants in his apartment and joins a bird study group. At a zoo at the close of the novel, he is attacked by a swan while attempting to feed it from his hand. He wakens, later, in a hospital recovering from a reaction to a penicillin shot. At this point, Kant speaks to him, saying that "nature is dead, my child."

Peter (obviously modeled on Reul Wilson) calls his father "babbo," has prior Italian experience, speaks both French and Italian, and is an intellectual like his mother. This novel, much different from the other seven, is the only one with a clear and unmistakable protagonist. The group Peter satirizes are tourists as a group; but the group does not make up the novel's characters.

The group of *Cannibals and Missionaries*, originally formed as a committee of six to fly by Air France to Iran to investigate reports of the Shah's torturing of prisoners, expands, by the time the plane is hijacked to Holland, to twenty-four hostages and eight terrorists. Set during the administration of President Gerald Ford, the novel takes its title from the puzzle in which three cannibals and three missionaries must cross a river in a boat that will hold only two people, and if the cannibals outnumber the missionaries, they might eat the missionaries. In the novel, however, there is no clear indication as to which group represents the cannibals and which the missionaries.

In one passage of explication, McCarthy points out that the terrorists' demands accomplish nothing but the reabsorption into the dominant society of whatever they demanded; prisoners released, for example, are eventually returned to prison. Confined in a Dutch farmhouse, hostages learn of their terrorists' demands from television: one and a quarter million dollars, Holland's withdrawal from NATO, the breaking of relations with Israel, and the release of "class war" prisoners from Dutch jails. Like the other groups in McCarthy's fiction, the members of this group are pulled together in a common cause; even though divided between hostages and terrorists, the hostages willingly aid the terrorists in some efforts and feel triumphant in the successful completion of a task, such as hiding the helicopter that brought them to the farmhouse. At the novel's conclusion, however, all but four are killed, one of whom claims that she has not been changed by the experience.

The European settings of the last two novels reflect McCarthy's travel experiences and utilize her interest in art. In *Cannibals and Missionaries*, McCarthy returned to her early interest in Communism and to the group structure with separate narrative voices.

While *The Groves of Academe* is still highly esteemed as an example of the academic novel, and *The Group* is read by students of popular fiction and women's issues, McCarthy's novels considered by themselves do not make up a lasting body of work. Rather, they derive their lasting significance from their place in the life and work of an exemplary woman of letters.

Grace Eckley

Other major works

SHORT FICTION: *The Company She Keeps*, 1942; *Cast a Cold Eye*, 1950; *The Hounds of Summer and Other Stories*, 1981.

NONFICTION: *Sights and Spectacles: 1937-1956*, 1956; *Venice Observed*, 1956; *Memories of a Catholic Girlhood*, 1957; *The Stones of Florence*, 1959; *On the Contrary: Articles of Belief*, 1961; *Mary McCarthy's Theatre Chronicles, 1937-1962*, 1963; *Vietnam*, 1967; *Hanoi*, 1968; *The Writing on the Wall and Other Literary Essays*, 1970; *Medina*, 1972; *The Seventeenth Degree*, 1974; *The Mask of State*, 1974; *Ideas and the Novel*, 1980; *Occasional Prose*, 1985; *How I Grew*, 1987.

Bibliography

Auchincloss, Louis. *Pioneers and Caretakers: A Study of Nine American Novelists*. Minneapolis: University of Minnesota Press, 1961. Auchincloss regards McCarthy the novelist as a caretaker of American culture. Covers McCarthy's transition from novellas ("a perfect medium for [her]") to longer works such as *The Oasis*. Considers *The Groves of Academe* the apex of her satirical art. A valuable guide to McCarthy.

Gelderman, Carol W. *Mary McCarthy: A Life*. New York: St. Martin's Press, 1988. Probably the most thorough study available on McCarthy and a must for scholars of her work as well as fans of good biography. Essentially a biography, but includes much valuable criticism of her novels and extracts from her letters and other writings. The material is arranged chronologically and is well organized. No bibliography, but includes extensive notes.

Grumbach, Doris. *The Company She Kept*. New York: Coward, McCann, 1967. A full-length study of McCarthy with special emphasis on her Catholic upbringing. In a personal and accessible style, Grumbach skillfully interweaves biography with criticism of McCarthy's novels, stressing her profoundly feminine approach. Follows McCarthy's development as a writer, including her involvement with the *Partisan Review* circle in the late 1930's, her time in Europe, the elusiveness of critical acclaim for her work, and the popular success of *The Group*.

Munroe, Gretchen Himmele. "Mary McCarthy." In *American Novelists Since World War II*, edited by Jeffrey Helterman and Richard Layman. Vol. 2 in *Dictionary of Literary Biography*. Detroit: Gale Research, 1978. In addition to an overview of McCarthy's life, which in itself is of interest, there is a discussion of her writings to 1974, with special mention of *The Company She Keeps*, *A Charmed Life*, *The Group*, and *Birds of America*. Acknowledging that McCarthy has been received with mixed criticism, Munroe argues that "the brutal honesty of her confrontations places McCarthy clearly in the mainstream of modern American thinking."

Stock, Irvin. *Mary McCarthy*. Minneapolis: University of Minnesota Press, 1968. A pamphlet that offers accessible, readable criticism with insight into McCarthy's motives as a writer. Takes the point of view that McCarthy's work is loyal to the life that she lived—that the mind's accomplishments are worth little in the face of life's difficulties. Includes discussion of McCarthy's nonfiction as well as her novels, in particular her controversial piece *Vietnam*. Selected bibliography.

CARSON McCULLERS

Born: Columbus, Georgia; February 19, 1917
Died: Nyack, New York; September 29, 1967

Principal long fiction
The Heart Is a Lonely Hunter, 1940; *Reflections in a Golden Eye*, 1941; *The Member of the Wedding*, 1946; *The Ballad of the Sad Café*, 1951; *Clock Without Hands*, 1961.

Other literary forms
Carson McCullers published a number of short stories, some of which are included in the volume containing *The Ballad of the Sad Café*, and some in a collection of short works, *The Mortgaged Heart* (1971), edited by her sister, M. G. Smith. The latter also contains some magazine articles and notes of her writing. McCullers adapted *The Member of the Wedding* for the stage in 1950 (a film version appeared in 1952). She wrote two plays, including *The Square Root of Wonderful* (1957). McCullers' poetry is published in *The Mortgaged Heart* and in a children's book, *Sweet as a Pickle and Clean as a Pig* (1964).

Achievements
Like William Faulkner, McCullers has literary kinship with those older, midnight-haunted writers—Edgar Allan Poe, Nathanial Hawthorne, and Herman Melville among them—who projected in fable and with symbol the story of America's unquiet mind. Against her Southern background she created a world of symbolic violence and tragic reality, indirectly lighted by the cool Flaubertian purity of her style. Of the writers of her generation, none was more consistent or thorough in achieving a sustained body of work.

Several of McCullers' works received critical acclaim. "A Tree, a Rock, a Cloud," a short story sometimes compared in theme to Samuel Taylor Coleridge's "The Rime of the Ancient Mariner," was chosen for the O. Henry Memorial Prize in 1942. The dramatic version of *The Member of the Wedding* was extremely successful, running on Broadway continuously for nearly fifteen months, and it was named for both the Donaldson Award and the New York Drama Critics Circle Award in 1950. In addition, McCullers was a Guggenheim fellow in 1942 and 1946, and she received an award from the American Academy of Arts and Letters in 1943.

Biography
Carson McCullers was born Lula Carson Smith on February 19, 1917, in Columbus, Georgia. Marguarite Smith, McCullers' mother, was very early convinced that her daughter was an artistic genius and sacrificed herself and,

to some extent, McCullers' father, brother, and sister, to the welfare of her gifted child. McCullers grew up, therefore, with a peculiar kind of shyness and emotional dependence on her mother, combined with supreme self-confidence about her ability. McCullers announced early in life that she was going to be a concert pianist, and indeed displayed a precocious talent in that direction. Smith placed her daughter under the tutelage of Mary Tucker, a concert musician, who agreed that McCullers was talented.

McCullers came to love Mrs. Tucker and her family with an all-consuming passion, a pattern she was to follow with a number of other close friends during her life. Dr. Mary Mercer, a psychiatrist friend of McCullers' during her later years, suggested that the emotional devastation of the adolescent girl in *The Member of the Wedding*, when she was not allowed to accompany her beloved brother and his bride on their honeymoon, was an expression of McCullers' despair when the Tuckers moved away from her hometown. She seemed to experience every break in human contact as personal betrayal or tragedy.

Writing was also an early enthusiasm of McCullers. As a child, she created shows to be acted by herself and her siblings in the sitting room. Her mother would gather in neighbors or relatives for an appreciative audience. In an article entitled "How I Began to Write" (*Mademoiselle*, September, 1948), McCullers said that the shows, which she described as anything from "hashed-over movies to Shakespeare," stopped when she discovered Eugene O'Neill. She was soon writing a three-act play "about revenge and incest" calling for a cast of a "blind man, several idiots and a mean old woman of one hundred years." Her next opus was a play in rhymed verse called *The Fire of Life*, starring Jesus Christ and Friedrich Nietzsche. Soon after, she became enthralled by the great Russian writers, Fyodor Dostoevski, Anton Chekhov, and Leo Tolstoy—a fascination she never outgrew. Years later, she was to suggest, with considerable cogency, that modern Southern writing is most indebted to the Russian realists.

The Smith household, while never wealthy, was not so hard pressed for money as McCullers sometimes later pretended. Lamar Smith, her father, was a respected jeweler in Columbus, Georgia, and a skilled repairer of clocks and watches. There was enough money, at least, to send the seventeen-year-old McCullers to New York City to attend the famous Juilliard School of Music. There was not enough, however, to replace the tuition money she had lost in the subway. Perhaps she was too moritified to ask for help, foreseeing that her father would simply send her a ticket to return home.

Whether through carelessness or naïveté, McCullers found herself almost penniless in New York. Having already paid her tuition for night classes at Columbia University, however, she intended to survive as best she could with whatever odd jobs she could find. Her inexperience and ineptness led to her being fired repeatedly from whatever employment she could find. One way or another, McCullers managed to support herself through the school term. By the time she came home in the summer, she had begun to write in earnest, and the dream of being a concert pianist was entirely displaced by the vision of becoming a great writer. She had launched her publishing career by selling two short stories to *Story* magazine: "Wunderkind" and "Like That." Her first novel, *The Heart Is a Lonely Hunter*, was in its formative stages.

Back home, McCullers met a handsome young soldier Reeves McCullers, who shared both her ambitions of living in New York and of becoming a writer. In 1936, Reeves left the army and traveled to New York to attend Columbia University, as McCullers was doing. His college career lasted only a few weeks, however, before he withdrew entirely to escort McCullers back home to Georgia to recover from one of her many serious illnesses.

In 1937, Carson and Reeves were married, although Reeves was financially in no condition to support a wife. Though idyllically happy at the first, their marriage became increasingly troubled. While McCullers' first novel, published when she was twenty-two, brought her immediate recognition in the literary world of New York, her husband met with continual frustration in his own ambitions.

Their problems did not derive simply from the professional dominance of McCullers. Both she and her husband were sexually ambivalent. The repressed homosexuality and odd love triangles that are so characteristic of McCullers' fiction had some correlation to real-life situations. McCullers had a disconcerting tendency to fall in love with either men or women, and to suffer inordinately when such attentions were repulsed. As her fiction suggests, she believed that one of the central problems of living was to love and be loved in equal measure.

McCullers often left Reeves to his own devices when professional opportunities or invitations came her way. She was offered a fellowship, for example, in the prestigious Bread Loaf Writers Conference, where she consorted with such persons as Robert Frost, Louis Untermeyer, John Marquand, and Wallace Stegner. That same summer, she also met Erika and Klaus Mann, Thomas Mann's children, and Annemarie Clarac-Schwartzenbach, a prominent Swiss journalist and travel-writer. McCullers fell deeply in love with the stunning Annemarie. When Annemarie left the country, it was another terrible "desertion" for McCullers. *Reflections in a Golden Eye*, McCullers' second novel, was dedicated to Annemarie.

In 1940, McCullers and her husband separated, and McCullers moved into a two-room apartment in a large Victorian house in Brooklyn Heights, owned by George Davis, editor of *Harper's Bazaar*. The old house became the temporary home for a stimulating group of artists, including poets Wystan Auden and Louis MacNeice; the composer Benjamin Britten; Peter Pears, tenor; Gipsy Rose Lee, fan dancer and writer; and novelist Richard Wright. These were only the earlier residents. A group of musicians and composers, including Aaron Copland, Leonard Bernstein, and David Diamond, joined the ranks at one time or another. Diamond was to become another of those fateful friends who was emotionally involved with both McCullers and Reeves. Also temporarily in residence were Salvador Dali and his wife Gala, as well as other prominent surrealist painters.

A new and terrifying illness drove McCullers back to the South to her mother's care. She was afraid this time that she was going blind. Years later, doctors declared that this episode, when she was barely twenty-four years old, was her first cerebral stroke. There was no paralysis, but her recovery was slow.

McCullers and Reeves tried again to live together in New York and for a time took comfort in a new intimacy with their friend David Diamond. McCullers was invited to Yaddo, a retreat for resident artists situated a few miles from Saratoga Springs, New York. The motherly overseer of the colony, Elizabeth Ames, became almost a second mother to McCullers, who returned again and again to this peaceful setting, and considered it the place most conducive to writing.

McCullers eventually divorced Reeves; he went back into the service, became a much-decorated war hero, was wounded several times in action, and finally returned as an officer beloved by his men. McCullers was so admiring of his new role that they were remarried. As a civilian husband, however, Reeves could not maintain the independence and pride he had so hardily won as a soldier. He turned increasingly to drink and eventually expressed the desire to commit suicide. When, in Europe, he seemed determined that they should both hang themselves, McCullers fled from him in terror and returned home alone. Shortly thereafter, Reeves was found dead in a Paris hotel.

After McCullers finished *The Member of the Wedding*, which proved immensely popular, her friendship with dramatist Tennessee Williams encouraged her to attempt a stage adaptation of the work. After many trials in deciding on an agreeable version for the stage, the play finally was produced, starring Ethel Waters as the black maid and Julie Harris as the lonely adolescent. McCullers wrote one other play, *The Square Root of Wonderful*, which was not nearly so successful. *The Member of the Wedding* was eventually adapted into a motion picture with the original cast. John Huston produced a movie version of another of McCullers' works, *Reflections in a Golden Eye*, shortly before her death.

McCullers' last years were a nightmare of pain, though she continued to maintain a fairly cheerful social life while partially paralyzed and often bedridden. She had two strokes, underwent several operations on her paralyzed left arm, leg, and hand, had a cancerous breast removed, broke her hip and elbow in a fall, and finally died after another massive stroke. She was fifty years old.

Analysis

Carson McCullers' fiction has a childlike directness, a disconcerting exposure of unconscious impulses in conjunction with realistic detail. She is like
the candid child who announces that the emperor in his new clothes is really
naked. She sees the truth, or at least a partial truth of the human psyche,
then inflates or distorts that truth into a somewhat grotesque fable which is
sometimes funny, but always sad.

Such a tragicomic effect derives, apparently from an unusual openness to
subconscious direction, combined with conscious cultivation of a style that
best exploits such material, weaving into it just enough objectively observed
reality to achieve plausibility. McCullers herself explained the technique by
which she achieved the fusion of objective reality with symbolic, psychic
experience. In "The Russian Realists and Southern Literature," first published
in *Decision*, July, 1941 (now available in *The Mortgaged Heart*), she speaks
of the charge of cruelty which was brought against both Russian writers
(particularly Fyodor Dostoevski) and Southern writers such as William Faulkner and herself, though she does not refer to her own works.

> No single instance of "cruelty" in Russian or Southern writing could not be matched or
> outdone by the Greeks, the Elizabethans, or, for that matter, the creators of the Old
> Testament. Therefore it is not the specific "cruelty" itself that is shocking, but the manner
> in which it is presented. And it is in this approach to life and suffering that the Southerners
> are so indebted to the Russians. The technique briefly is this: a bold and outwardly callous
> juxtaposition of the tragic with the humorous, the immense with the trivial, the sacred
> with the bawdy, the whole soul of a man with a materialistic detail.

What is peculiar to the Russians and the Southerners is not the inclusion
of farce and tragedy in the same work, but the fusion of the two so that they
are experienced simultaneously. McCullers uses Faulkner's *As I Lay Dying*
(1930) as an example of this technique. She could as effectively have demonstrated it with her own *Ballad of the Sad Café*, which is a masterpiece of
tragicomedy. The relative lack of success of the earlier *Reflections in a Golden
Eye* results partly, perhaps, from her inability to balance the sadomasochistic
elements with elements of satire or farce. She reportedly claimed that incidents such as the rejected wife cutting off her nipples with garden shears were
"hilariously funny." This may demonstrate an oddly warped sense of humor,
a failure of craft, or simply ignorance about her own creative processes, or
it may simply be a way of shunting off rational explanations of a work of art,
a red herring to confuse critics. As a novelist, McCullers operates like a poet
or perhaps like a surrealist painter, who tells the truth but "tells it slant."

The thematic content of McCullers' works is consistent: All her stories deal
with the metaphysical isolation of individuals, and their desperate need to
transcend this isolation through love. Love is the key to a magnificent transformation of leaden existence into gold, but the exalted state is doomed

because love is so seldom reciprocated. Though this feeling (and it is more feeling than thought) may stem from McCullers' early fears and dependence on her mother, it strikes a universal chord. That McCullers projects this terrible sense of unrequited love into all kinds of human relationships except that between mother and daughter may be suggestive in itself. In an interview with Virginia Spencer Carr, Lamar Smith, Jr. said that his sister did not depict a meaningful mother-daughter relationship in her fiction because she did not want to strip herself bare and show the utter dependency that she felt for her mother.

Nevertheless, McCullers successfully universalizes the state of metaphysical isolation as a perennial human condition, not merely a neurotic regression to childhood. Her first novel, *The Heart Is a Lonely Hunter*, has as its child character, Mick Kelly, who clings to John Singer, the deaf-mute, who, she fancies, understands and sympathizes with her problems. McCullers' own definition of the character in "Author's Outline of 'The Mute'" (*The Mortgaged Heart*) reveals an almost transparent self-dramatization: "Her story is that of the violent struggle of a gifted child to get what she needs from an unyielding environment." Only metaphorically is Mick's struggle "violent," but even when McCullers presents physical violence in fiction it often seems to function as the objective correlative to mental anguish.

McCullers casts Jake Blount, the ineffectual social agitator, as a would-be Marxist revolutionary, but he may seem more like an overgrown frustrated child. Her outline says, "His deepest motive is to do all that he can to change the predatory, unnatural social conditions existing today. . . . He is fettered by abstractions and conflicting ideas. . . . His attitude vacillates between hate and the most unselfish love."

Dr. Benedict Copeland is the more believable character, representing the peculiar plight of the educated black in the South, who has internalized the white man's condemnation of black cultural traits. His daughter's black dialect and careless posture embarrass him, and he frowns on what he considers the irresponsible fecundity and emotionality of the black youth. What McCullers calls his "passionate asceticism" has driven away even his own family.

Biff Brannon, the proprietor of the local restaurant, is the dispassionate observer of men, sympathetic, in a distant way, with all human oddities. Like Mick, he seems almost a part of McCullers, a grown-up version of the child who sat silently in the corners of stores watching people, who loved to listen to the voices of blacks, and who paid her dimes repeatedly to see the freaks in the side shows. Brannon is also sexually impotent, with homosexual leanings. He is cold and withdrawn with his wife and has a repressed attraction for Mick in her tomboyish prepuberty—an impulse that fades as soon as she shows sexual development.

All of these characters pivot around the deaf-mute, John Singer, who is the central symbol of man's metaphysical isolation. They take his silence as wisdom and pour out their hearts to his patient, but unreceptive ears. He does lipread, so he knows what they are saying, but he has no way to communicate with them in reply. Moreover, the experiences they confide to him seem so alien to his own that he does not really understand. Mick talks about music, which he has never heard; Jake Blount rants about the downtrodden working classes; Dr. Copeland speaks of his frustrations as a racial leader without any followers; and Biff Brannon simply looks on with no project of his own.

Yet, John Singer shares their universal need to love and communicate with a kindred soul. The object of his adoration is another mute, a sloppy, retarded Greek named Antonopoulos, who loves nothing but the childish pleasure of a full stomach. When the Greek dies in an institution, Singer commits suicide. The whole pyramid of illusion collapses.

This bleak tale suggests that the beloved is created in the lover's mind out of the extremity of his need, and projected upon whomever is available. Singer drew the love of these desperate souls on account of his polite tolerance of their advances coupled with an essential blankness. They looked into his eyes and saw their own dreams reflected there, just as Singer himself read a secret sympathy and understanding in the blank round face of Antonopoulos, who was actually incapable of such sentiments.

The haunting quality of this story may derive partly from the impression of getting an inside look at a multiple personality. Eve may have revealed three faces to the psychologist, but the young McCullers displays more, with a curious ability to divide her ambivalent psyche to create new, somewhat lopsided beings. McCullers had never seen a deaf-mute, for example, and when Reeves wanted to take her to a convention of deaf-mutes, she declined, saying she already knew John Singer. Marxist political agitators may have been just as foreign to her actual experience, but she could create one from the jumble of liberal sentiment she acquired through educated friends and through reading. If the issues were not clear in her own mind, it did not really matter, because Jake was a confused and drunken loser. McCullers has been praised by black writers for her sensitive portrayal of blacks, yet the peculiar warmth of the relationship between Dr. Copeland's daughter Portia, her husband, and her brother suggests the triangular love affairs McCullers sometimes acted out in her own life and dramatized several times in other fiction.

McCullers wrote *Reflections in a Golden Eye* in a short period of time, "for fun," she said, after the long session with *The Heart Is a Lonely Hunter*. The idea for the story germinated when, as an adolescent, she first went to Fort Benning, but she also drew on her experience of Fayetteville, where she and Reeves lived for a while, and nearby Fort Bragg. The story caused considerable shock in conservative Southern communities. Americans generally were not prepared for a fictional treatment of homosexuality. A perceptive reader might suspect the latent homosexuality in Biff Brannon, but there is no doubt about Captain Penderton's sexual preferences. Moreover, the sado-masochism, the weird voyeurism, and the Freudian implications of horses and guns are unmistakable. If *The Heart Is a Lonely Hunter* is about love, *Reflections in a Golden Eye* is about sex and its various distortions. These characters are lonely, isolated people, driven by subconscious impulses. The story concerns two army couples, a houseboy, a rather primitive young man, all of them somewhat abnormal, and a horse. One suspects the horse is akin to a dream symbol for the ungovernable libido.

Captain Penderton is impotent with his beautiful wife Leonora but is drawn to her lover, Major Langdon. The major's wife is sickly and painfully aware of her husband's affair with Leonora. Mrs. Langdon is solicitously attended by a Filipino houseboy, who is also maladjusted. The other character is Private Williams, an inarticulate young man who seems to be a fugitive from some-body's unconscious (probably Captain Penderton's). He has a mystical affinity for nature, and he is the only person who can handle Leonora's high-spirited stallion, Firebird. Captain Penderton is afraid of the horse, and he both loves and hates Private Williams.

D. H. Lawrence's *The Prussian Officer* (1914) may have provided a model for Penderton's relationship to Private Williams, since McCullers was an admirer of Lawrence. Private Williams is quite different, however, from the perfectly normal, healthy orderly who is the innocent victim of the Prussian officer's obsession. The silent Private Williams enacts a psychodrama that repeats, in different terms, the sexual impotence of Penderton. Having seen Leonora naked through an open door, he creeps into the Penderton house each night to crouch silently by her bedside, watching her sleep. When Pen-derton discovers him there, he shoots him. The scene in the dark bedroom beside the sleeping woman is loaded with psychological overtones. Not a word is spoken by either man. In one sense, the phallic gun expresses the captain's love-hate attraction to the private; in another sense, Penderton is killing his impotent shadow-self.

Technically speaking, *Reflections in a Golden Eye* is superior to McCullers' first novel; at least, it has an admirable artistic unity. Its four-part structure has the precision of a tightly constructed musical composition. In content, the story line seems as Gothic as Edgar Allan Poe's "Fall of the House of Usher," yet the style is objective and nonjudgmental—like the impersonal eye of nature in which it is reflected. McCullers was perfecting the kind of perception and style she spoke of in her essay on the Russian realists, pre-senting human action starkly without editorial comment.

McCullers' next work, *The Ballad of the Sad Café*, was a more successful treatment of archetypal myth, with its psychodramatic overtones tempered this time by humor. Like the true folk ballad, it is a melancholy tale of love. The setting is an isolated Southern village—little more than a trading post with a few dreary, unpainted buildings. The most prominent citizen is known as Miss Emelia, a strong, mannish, cross-eyed woman with a sharp business sense. She runs the general store and operates a still that produces the best corn liquor for miles around. There is nothing to do for entertainment in town except drink her brew, follow the odd career of this sexless female, and listen to the melancholy singing of the chain gang, which suggests a universal entrapment in the dreary reality of one's life.

The story concerns a temporary hiatus from boredom when Miss Emelia and the observing townspeople become a real community. Love provides the means for a temporary transcendence of Miss Emelia's metaphysical isolation, and through her, sheds a reflected radiance on all. Like John Singer, Miss Emelia chooses an odd person to love, a homeless dwarf who straggles into town, claiming to be her cousin and hoping for a handout. Although Miss Emelia had thrown out the only man who had ever loved her because he expected sexual favors when they were married, she unaccountably falls in love with this pathetic wanderer. She takes "Cousin Lymon" in and, because he likes company, begins a restaurant, which becomes the social center of the entire community. All goes well until the despised husband, Marvin Macy, is released from the penitentiary and returns to his hometown, bent on revenge for the monstrous humiliation Miss Emelia had visited upon him.

Another unusual threesome develops when Cousin Lymon becomes infatuated with Marvin Macy. The competition between Macy and Miss Emelia for the attention of Cousin Lymon comes to a tragicomic climax in a fist fight between the rivals. Miss Emelia, who has been working out with a punching bag, is actually winning when the treacherous Cousin Lymon leaps on her back, and the two men give her a terrible drubbing. Macy and Cousin Lymon flee after they vandalize Miss Emelia's store and her still in the woods. Miss Emelia is left in a more desolate isolation than she has ever known and becomes a solitary recluse thereafter. The coda at the end recalls again the mournful song of the chain gang.

There is no more somber image of spiritual isolation than the glimpse of the reclusive Miss Emelia at the window of her boarded-up café: "It is a face like the terrible, dim faces known in dreams—sexless and white, with two gray crossed eyes which are turned inward so sharply that they seem to be exchanging with each other one long and secret gaze of grief." This story, written in a style that precludes sentimentality, is surely McCullers' most successful treatment of unrequited love and betrayal. The fight scene is a satire of all traditionally masculine brawls for the love of a woman, witnessed by the entire community as a battle larger than life, for a prize both morally and physically smaller than life. Besides the satire on all crude American substitutes for the duel of honor, this story may also call to mind Faulkner's famous Gothic tale, "A Rose for Emily," about the genteel aristocratic lady who murdered her lover to keep him in her bed. Miss Emelia is certainly the absolute opposite to all conventions about the beautiful but fragile Southern lady, who is entirely useless.

The Member of the Wedding is possibly the most popular of McCullers' novels, partly because it was converted into a successful Broadway play—in defiance of one critic's judgment that the novel is entirely static, totally lacking in drama. In fact, the story has a quality somewhat akin to closet drama, such as George Bernard Shaw's "Don Juan in Hell," which is performed by readers with no attempt at action. The endless conversation occurs in one spot, the kitchen of a lower-middle-class home in the South. There are occasional forays into the outer world, but always the principals return to the kitchen, where real experience and visionary ideals blend in an endless consideration of human possibilities.

The protagonist, a motherless adolescent girl named Frankie Addams, is the central quester for human happiness, foredoomed to disappointment. She is similar to Mick in *The Heart Is a Lonely Hunter*. It is no accident that both their names reflect the genderless state of prepuberty; moreover, neither has been indoctrinated into the attitudes and conventional expectations of little girls. In the isolation and boredom of Frankie's life, the only exciting event is the upcoming marriage of her older brother. Frankie conceives of the dream that will sustain her in the empty weeks of the long, hot summer: she will become a member of the wedding and join her brother and his bride on their honeymoon and new idyllic life of love and communion.

This impossible dream is the central issue of those long conversations in the kitchen where the girl is flanked by a younger cousin, John Henry, who represents the childhood from which Frankie is emerging, and the black maid, Berenice, who tries to reason with Frankie without stripping her of all solace. Ignorant as she is of the dynamics of sexual love, what Frankie aspires to is not a love so self-seeking as eros, nor quite so all-encompassing as agape. She envisions an ideal love which establishes a permanent and free-flowing communication among the members of a small, select group. This imagined communion seems to express an unvoiced dream of many, sometimes situated in a visionary future, or an equally visionary past. Berenice, for all her gentle earthiness, shows that her vision of a golden age is in the past, when she was married to her first husband. She admits that after that man died, her other two marriages were vain attempts to recapture the rapport she had known with her first husband.

A curious irony of the story is that Frankie, with her persistent goal of escaping her isolated personal identity in what she calls the "we of me," actually comes closest to that ideal in the course of these endless conversations with the child and the motherly black woman. This real communion also passes away, as surely as the imagined communion wih the wedded pair never materializes. John Henry dies before the end of the story, symbolic perhaps of the passing of Frankie's childhood. Reality and banality seem to have conquered in a world unsuited to the dreams of sensitive human beings.

McCullers' last novel, *Clock Without Hands*, written during a period of suffering and ill-health, moves beyond the not-quite-adult problems of adolescence at the cost of much of her lyricism. Perhaps the novel is a somewhat feeble attempt to emulate the moral power of Leo Tolstoy's *The Death of Ivan Ilyich* (1884). It concerns a very ordinary man who faces death from leukemia and suspects that he has never lived on his own terms. The theme is still loneliness and spiritual isolation, but it has taken on existential overtones. The protagonist, J. T. Malone, like Tolstoy's Ivan, discovers too late that moral dignity requires some kind of commitment to action. In his new and painful awareness of his own moral vacuity, there are few decisions left to make. He does make one small gesture, however, to redeem an otherwise meaningless life. He refuses to accept the community's order to bomb the home of a black who had dared to move into a white neighborhood. McCullers' description of Judge Clane, Malone's aging friend, reveals with precision the peculiar combination of sentimentality and cruelty that characterizes conventional white racism of the old Southern variety.

Although Carson McCullers will probably endure as a writer with a very special talent for describing the in-between world before a child becomes an adult, the no-man's land of repressed homosexuality, and the irrational demands of love in the absence of any suitable recipient of love, the range of her fiction is quite limited. Somehow, the "child genius" never quite achieved maturity. Nevertheless, all people are immature or maimed in some secret way; in that sense, every reader must admit kinship to Carson McCullers' warped and melancholy characters.

Katherine Snipes

Other major works
SHORT FICTION: *The Mortgaged Heart*, 1971 (M. G. Smith, editor).
PLAYS: *The Member of the Wedding*, 1950; *The Square Root of Wonderful*, 1957.
CHILDREN'S LITERATURE: *Sweet as a Pickle and Clean as a Pig*, 1964.

Bibliography
Bradbury, John M. *Renaissance in the South: A Critical History of the Literature, 1920-1960*. Chapel Hill: University of North Carolina Press, 1963. In his chapter "The Later Traditionalists," Bradbury compares McCullers to Katherine Anne Porter and Eudora Welty, particularly in her thematic emphasis on loneliness, alienation, and the failure of communication, as well as in her occasional use of the grotesque. Yet he also specifically defines her unique qualities.
Carr, Virginia Spencer. *The Lonely Hunter: A Biography of Carson McCullers*. Garden City, N.Y.: Anchor Press, 1975. The most complete bio-

graphical study of McCullers. An impressive volume, based on interviews and research into published and unpublished materials over a period of seven years. Includes a preface by Tennessee Williams. Also contains numerous illustrations, a complete list of sources, and a helpful index.

Evans, Oliver. *The Ballad of Carson McCullers: A Biography.* New York: Coward, McCann, 1966. Although this work is fairly short, it is particularly valuable for the critical analysis of McCullers' works. Along with his own thoughtful comments, Evans includes references to major critical studies. Contains illustrations, a good index, and a bibliography which is helpful, although dated.

_____. "The Theme of Spiritual Isolation in Carson McCullers." In *South: Modern Southern Literature in Its Cultural Setting*, edited by Louis D. Rubin, Jr. and Robert D. Jacobs. Westport, Conn.: Greenwood Press, 1961. Although one of the major themes in Southern literature, it is significant that spiritual isolation is the topic specifically illustrated by McCullers in this important collection. This essay, which is clearly written and carefully supported by specific references, would be an ideal starting point for any study of McCullers' works.

Graver, Lawrence. *Carson McCullers.* Minneapolis: University of Minnesota Press, 1969. This monograph is a good brief introduction to McCullers which integrates biographical details with excellent discussions of her major works. Contains a thorough bibliography.

McDowell, Margaret B. *Carson McCullers.* Boston: Twayne, 1980. This volume provides a sound biographical outline. Its chief value, however, is that it has a full, carefully balanced discussion of differing critical interpretations of specific works and of differing assessments by critics of the author's artistic intentions and accomplishments. The bibliography, which is partially annotated, is especially helpful.

ROSS MACDONALD
Kenneth Millar

Born: Los Gatos, California; December 13, 1915
Died: Santa Barbara, California; July 11, 1983

Principal long fiction

The Dark Tunnel, 1944 (as Kenneth Millar; British edition, *I Die Slowly*, 1955); *Trouble Follows Me*, 1946 (as Millar; British edition, *Night Train*, 1955); *Blue City*, 1947 (as Millar); *The Three Roads*, 1948 (as Millar); *The Moving Target*, 1949 (as John Ross Macdonald; reissued as *Harper*, 1966); *The Drowning Pool*, 1950 (as John Ross Macdonald); *The Way Some People Die*, 1951 (as John Ross Macdonald); *The Ivory Grin*, 1952 (as John Ross Macdonald; reissued as *Marked for Murder*, 1953); *Meet Me at the Morgue*, 1953 (as John Ross Macdonald; British edition, *Experience with Evil*, 1954); *Find a Victim*, 1954 (as John Ross Macdonald); *The Barbarous Coast*, 1956; *The Doomsters*, 1958; *The Galton Case*, 1959; *The Ferguson Affair*, 1960; *The Wycherly Woman*, 1961; *The Zebra-Striped Hearse*, 1962; *The Chill*, 1964; *The Far Side of the Dollar*, 1965; *Black Money*, 1966; *The Instant Enemy*, 1968; *The Goodbye Look*, 1969; *The Underground Man*, 1971; *Sleeping Beauty*, 1973; *The Blue Hammer*, 1976.

Other literary forms

Ross Macdonald's reputation is based primarily on his twenty-four published novels, particularly on the eighteen which feature private detective Lew Archer. He also published a collection of short stories, *Lew Archer, Private Investigator* (1977), which includes all the stories from an earlier collection, *The Name Is Archer* (1955). *Self-Portrait: Ceaselessly into the Past* (1981) gathers a selection of his essays, interviews, and lectures about his own work and about other writers, including two essays first published in his *On Crime Writing* (1973). Macdonald edited a collection of short stories, *Great Stories of Suspense* (1974). He also wrote dozens of book reviews and several articles on conservation and politics.

Achievements

Macdonald was recognized early in his career to be the successor to Dashiell Hammett and Raymond Chandler in the field of realistic crime fiction, and his detective, Lew Archer, was recognized to be the successor to Sam Spade and Philip Marlowe. Macdonald's advance over his predecessors was in the greater emphasis he placed on psychology and character, creating a more humane and complex detective and more intricate plotting. He is generally credited with raising the detective novel to the level of serious literature. The Mystery Writers of America awarded him Edgar Allan Poe scrolls in 1962 and 1963. In 1964, *The Chill* was awarded the Silver Dagger by the Crime Writers' Association of Great Britain. The same organization gave his next novel, *The Far Side of the Dollar*, the Golden Dagger as the best crime novel of the year. Macdonald served as president of the Mystery Writers of America in 1965 and was made a Grand Master of that organization in 1974. In a review of *The Goodbye Look* in *The New York Times Book Review*, William Goldman called the Lew Archer books "the finest series of detective novels ever written by an American." His work has gained popular as well as critical acclaim: *The Goodbye Look*, *The Underground Man*, *Sleeping Beauty*, and *The Blue Hammer* were all national best-sellers. Three of his books have been made into successful motion pictures, two starring Paul Newman as Lew Archer: *The Moving Target* was made into the film *Harper* (1966) and *The Drowning Pool* was filmed in 1975. *The Three Roads* was filmed as *Double Negative* in 1979.

Biography

Ross Macdonald, whose real name is Kenneth Millar, was born in Los Gatos, California, on December 13, 1915. He published his early novels as Kenneth Millar or as John (or John Ross) Macdonald, but settled on the pseudonym Ross Macdonald by the time he wrote *The Barbarous Coast*, in order to avoid being confused with two other famous mystery writers: his wife, Margaret Millar, whom he had married in 1938, and John D. Macdonald. His family moved to Vancouver, British Columbia, soon after he was born, and he was reared and educated in Canada. After he was graduated with honors from the University of Western Ontario in 1938, he taught English and history at a high school in Toronto and began graduate work at the University of Michigan in Ann Arbor during the summers. He returned to the United States permanently in 1941, when he began full-time graduate studies at Ann Arbor, receiving his M.A. in English in 1943. During World War II, he served as communications officer aboard an escort carrier in the Pacific and participated in the battle for Okinawa. In 1951, he was awarded a Ph.D. in English from the University of Michigan, writing his dissertation on the psychological criticism of Samuel Taylor Coleridge. Macdonald belonged to the American Civil Liberties Union and, a dedicated conservationist, was a member of the Sierra Club and helped found the Santa Barbara chapter of the National Audubon Society. He lived in Santa Barbara, California, from 1946 until his death there of Alzheimer's disease on July 11, 1983.

Analysis

Ross Macdonald's twenty-four novels fall fairly neatly into three groups: Those in which Lew Archer does not appear form a distinct group, and the Archer series itself may be separated into two periods. His first four books, *The Dark Tunnel*, *Trouble Follows Me*, *Blue City*, and *The Three Roads*, together with two later works, *Meet Me at the Morgue* and *The Ferguson Affair*, do not feature Lew Archer. These six novels, especially the first three, are rather typical treatments of wartime espionage or political corruption and are primarily of interest to the extent that they prefigure the concerns of later works: *The Three Roads*, for example, is Macdonald's first explicit use of the Oedipus myth as a plot structure and of California as a setting.

The first six Archer books, *The Moving Target*, *The Drowning Pool*, *The Way Some People Die*, *The Ivory Grin*, *Find a Victim*, and *The Barbarous Coast*, introduce and refine the character of Archer, build the society and geography of California into important thematic elements, and feature increasingly complex plots, with multiple murders and plot lines. Archer still shows traces of the influence of the hard-boiled detectives of Hammett and Chandler (he is named after Miles Archer, Sam Spade's partner in Hammett's *The Maltese Falcon*, 1930, but closely patterned after Philip Marlowe), but he also shows marks of the sensitivity and patience, the reliance on understanding and analysis, that separate him from his models. Even in these early books, Archer is more often a questioner than a doer.

The next twelve Archer novels constitute Macdonald's major achievement. Crimes in these books are not usually committed by professional criminals but rather by middle-class people going through emotional crises. They followed a period of personal crisis in Macdonald's own life, during which he underwent psychotherapy; all these novels deal more or less explicitly with psychological issues. *The Doomsters*, although begun before his psychoanalysis, presents his first extended treatment of the plot of intrafamilial relations that dominates all the later books. Carl Hallman, a psychologically disturbed young man, appears at Archer's door after escaping from the state mental hospital. He has been confined there as a murder suspect in the mysterious death of his father. Although he knows himself to be legally innocent, he feels guilty for having quarreled violently with his father on the night of his death. This Oedipal tension between father and son, following the pattern of Sigmund Freud's famous interpretation, often serves as the mainspring of the plot in Macdonald's later novels. After hiring Archer to investigate the death, Carl panics and escapes again as Archer is returning him to the hospital. Carl's brother, Jerry, and sister-in-law, Zinnie, are subsequently murdered under circumstances which appear to incriminate Carl.

As it turns out, the case really began three years earlier, with the death by drowning, apparently accidental, of Carl's mother, Alicia. She had forced Carl's wife, Mildred, to undergo an abortion at gunpoint at the hands of Dr. Grantland. Mildred hit Alicia over the head with a bottle when she came out of anesthesia and assumed that she had killed her. Dr. Grantland actually killed Alicia and made it look like drowning, but he conceals this fact and uses his power over Mildred, who is becoming psychologically unstable, to persuade her to kill Carl's father. He has designs on the family's money and

Mildred is greedy herself. She is also influenced, however, by her hatred of her own father, who deserted her mother, and by her desire to possess Carl entirely, to gain his love for herself by eliminating conflicting familial claims to it. She murders his brother and sister-in-law, his only remaining family, as she increasingly loses touch with sanity. Women are frequently the murderers in Macdonald's books, and he analyzed the reasons behind this in an interview. He considered that people who have been victims tend to victimize others in turn, and he regarded American society as one which systematically victimizes women. Mildred's difficult childhood and gunpoint abortion provide a clear illustration of this theme.

While the focus on family psychology constituted a clean break with the Hammett and Chandler school as well as with most of his own early work, the next Archer novel, *The Galton Case*, was of even greater importance for Macdonald's career. In *The Doomsters*, the case is rooted in a crime committed three years earlier; in *The Galton Case*, as in most of the novels to follow, the present crime is rooted deeper in the past, in the preceding generation. This gives Macdonald the means to show the long-term effects of the influence of the family upon each of its members. The elderly Maria Galton hires Archer to trace her son Anthony, who had stolen money from his father after a quarrel (reminiscent of that between Carl Hallman and his father) and run off to the San Francisco area with his pregnant wife, Teddy, twenty-three years before. Archer discovers that Anthony, calling himself John Brown, was murdered not long after his disappearance. He also finds a young man calling himself John Brown, Jr., who claims to be searching for his long-lost father. Events lead Archer to Canada, where he learns that the young man is Theo Fredericks, the son of Nelson Fredericks and his wife. Mrs. Galton's lawyer, Gordon Sable, has planned Theo's masquerade as her grandson to acquire her money when she dies. Yet a further plot twist reveals that Theo really is Anthony Galton's son. Fred Nelson had murdered Anthony twenty-three years before for the money he had stolen from his father and had taken Anthony's wife and son as his own under the name Fredericks.

This summary does not reflect the true complexity of the novel, which ties together a number of other elements, but does bring out the major theme of the son searching for his father, a theme which will recur in later works such as *The Far Side of the Dollar*, *The Instant Enemy*, *The Goodbye Look*, *The Underground Man*, and *The Blue Hammer*. As Macdonald explains in his essay "Writing *The Galton Case*" (1973), this plot is roughly shaped on his own life. His own father left him and his mother when he was three years old. Like Macdonald, John Brown, Jr., was born in California, grew up in Canada, and attended the University of Michigan before returning to California. It is interesting that each man assumed his lost father's name: Macdonald was Kenneth Millar's father's middle name. This transformation of personal family history into fiction seems to have facilitated the breakthrough that led him to write the rest of his novels about varying permutations of the relations between parents and children.

The exploration of the relations between three generations of fathers and sons in *The Galton Case* was followed by examinations of father and daughter relationships in *The Wycherly Woman* and *The Zebra-Striped Hearse*. Macdonald always counted the latter among his favorites for its intensity and range. In *The Zebra-Striped Hearse*, Archer is hired by Mark Blackwell to investigate his daughter Harriet's fiancé, Burke Damis, with a view to preventing their marriage. The implication is made that Mark sees Damis as a rival for his daughter's love. Archer discovers that Damis is really Bruce Campion and is suspected of having murdered his wife, Dolly, and another man, Quincy Ralph Simpson. Suspicion shifts to Mark when it is revealed that he is the father of Dolly's baby and then to Mark's wife, Isobel, who knew Dolly as a child. Harriet disappears and Mark confesses to murdering her, Dolly, and Simpson before committing suicide. Yet Archer believes that Harriet is still alive and tracks her down in Mexico. She had killed Dolly to clear the way for her marriage to Bruce and had also killed Simpson when he discovered her crime. Underlying her motive for Dolly's murder, however, is another Freudian pattern. The child of Mark and Dolly is Harriet's half brother, making Dolly a sort of mother figure and, by extension, making her husband, Bruce, a sort of father figure. Harriet thus symbolically kills her mother and marries her father.

The Chill features one of Macdonald's most complex plots, but at its center is another basic family relationship, this time between a mother and son. Archer is brought into the case by Alex Kincaid, who hires him to find his wife, Dolly, who has disappeared the day after their wedding after a visit from an unknown man. The visitor turns out to have been her father, Thomas McGee, who has just been released from prison after serving a ten-year sentence for the murder of his wife and Dolly's mother, Constance. Later it is revealed that he had convinced her of his innocence and told her that Constance was having an affair with Roy Bradshaw. To learn more about Roy, Dolly has left Alex to go to work for Roy's mother, Mrs. Bradshaw, as a driver and companion. Shortly thereafter, she is found, hysterical, at the Bradshaws', talking about the murder of her college counselor, Helen Haggerty. Helen is soon discovered murdered and the weapon used is found under Dolly's mattress, though under circumstances that suggest that it may have been planted there. Archer learns from Helen's mother that she had been deeply affected by a death that occurred twenty years before. Luke Deloney had been killed in a shooting that was ruled accidental on the basis of an investigation that was conducted by Helen's father, but Helen was convinced that the facts had been covered up. Luke's widow admits to Archer that there had been a cover-up, that her husband committed suicide. Archer later discovers another connection between the recent death and those of ten and twenty years ago: Roy Bradshaw was the elevator boy at the building in which Deloney died.

Investigation of Roy reveals that he has been secretly married to Laura Sutherland, having recently obtained a divorce from a woman named Letitia Macready. Archer confronts Mrs. Bradshaw with the latter fact (though not the former), and after an initial denial she confirms that twenty years ago Roy had briefly been married to a much older woman. Letitia turns out to have been the sister of Luke's wife, and it was rumored that she was having an affair with her sister's husband. Letitia apparently died in Europe during World War II, shortly after Luke's death. Archer eventually draws a fuller story out of Roy: Deloney, who was indeed Letitia's lover, found her in bed with Roy. There had been a violent struggle, during which Letitia accidentally shot and killed Luke. Roy married her and took her to Europe, later returning with her to America. He had been leading a secret double life ever since, concealing Letitia, now quite old and sick, from all of his friends as well as from the police and, especially, from his possessive mother. During this confession, Archer answers a telephone call and hears Laura, who believes that she is speaking to Roy, tell him that "she" has discovered their secret marriage. Roy attacks Archer at this news and escapes in his car to attempt to intercept the other woman, who had vowed to kill Laura. Roy is killed when Mrs. Bradshaw's car crashes into his. Archer knows by now that Mrs. Bradshaw is not Roy's mother, but his first wife: She is Letitia Macready. Roy has acted out the Oedipal drama of the death of a father figure, Letitia's lover Luke, and the marriage to a mother figure, the older woman who posed as his real mother. (Macdonald develops the obverse of this plot in *Black Money*, which pairs a young woman with a much older man.) Letitia murdered Constance McGee because Roy had been having an affair with her and murdered Helen Haggerty in the belief that it was she rather than Laura Sutherland whom Roy was currently seeing.

This unraveling of the plot has come a long way from Alex Kincaid's request that Archer find his wife, but one of the characteristics of Macdonald's later novels is the way in which seemingly unrelated events and characters come together. The deeper Archer goes into a set of circumstances involving people who know one another, the more connectedness he finds. These novels all have large casts of characters and a series of crimes, often occurring decades apart. Once the proper connections are made, however, there is usually only one murderer and one fundamental relationship at the center of the plot. All the disparate elements, past and present, hang together in one piece.

While Freudian themes continued to dominate Macdonald's work, he often combined them with elements adapted from other stories from classical mythology or the Bible. *The Far Side of the Dollar* has been seen as a modern, inverted version of the story of Ulysses and Penelope. Jasper Blevins, the fratricidal murderer of *The Instant Enemy*, explicitly draws the analogy between his story and that of Cain and Abel. He has also murdered one of his stepfathers, adding the Oedipal masterplot to the biblical plot, and murdered his own wife in one of the series' most violent books, perhaps reflecting the violence of the wartime period during which the book was written. The complex events of *The Goodbye Look* are catalyzed by the search for a gold box which is specifically compared to Pandora's box. Again the myth is combined with the primal story of the parricide, this time committed by a child. All three of these books also repeat the quintessential Macdonald plot of a young man's search for his missing father.

The search for the absent father also sets in motion the events of *The Underground Man*, probably the most admired of Macdonald's works. This novel, together with his next, *Sleeping Beauty*, also reflects its author's abiding concern with conservation. Each novel examines an ecological crime as well as a series of crimes committed against individuals. In *Sleeping Beauty*, Macdonald uses an offshore oil spill, inspired by the 1967 spill near his home in Santa Barbara, as a symbol of the moral life of the society responsible for it, in particular that of the Lennox family, which runs the oil corporation and is also the locus of the series of murders in the book. In *The Underground Man*, the disaster of a man-made forest fire serves similar ends. The story begins unexceptionally: Archer is taking a day off at home, feeding the birds in his yard. He strikes up an acquaintance with young Ronny Broadhurst and Ronny's mother, Jean, who are staying at the home of Archer's neighbors. The boy's father, Stanley, disrupts the meeting when he drives up with a young girl, later identified as Sue Crandall, and takes his son to visit Stanley's mother, Elizabeth Broadhurst. They never pay the planned visit, and when Jean hears that a fire has broken out in that area, she enlists Archer to help her look for them. On the way there, Jean explains that her husband has gradually become obsessed by his search for his father, Leo, who apparently ran away with Ellen Kilpatrick, the wife of a neighbor, Brian, some fifteen years ago. It turns out that Stanley, accompanied by Ronny and Sue, obtained a key from Elizabeth's gardener, Fritz Snow, and had gone up to her cabin on a mountain nearby. There, Archer finds Stanley, murdered and half-buried. The fire originated from a cigarillo Stanley dropped when he was killed, creating a causal as well as symbolic link between the personal and ecological disasters.

After an investigation that is complex even by Macdonald's standards, Archer is able to reconstruct the past events that explain those of the present. The seeds of the present crimes are found in the previous generation. Eighteen years ago, Leo Broadhurst got Martha Nickerson, an underage girl, pregnant. She ran away with Fritz Snow and Al Sweetner in a car they stole from Lester Crandall. The incident was planned by Leo and Martha to provide a scapegoat to assume the paternity of her coming child. When they were tracked down, Al went to jail for three years, Fritz was sentenced to work in a forestry camp for six months, and Martha married Lester Crandall. Three years later, Leo was having an affair with Ellen Kilpatrick. She went to Reno to obtain a divorce from her husband, Brian, and waited there for Leo to join her. While she was gone, however, Leo went up to the cabin with Martha and their child, Sue. Brian, who knew about his wife's affair with Leo and wanted revenge, discovered the renewal of this earlier affair and informed Leo's wife, Elizabeth. She went up to the mountain cabin and shot her husband, believing that she killed him. Stanley, who had followed his mother that night, was an aural witness to the shooting of his father, as was Susan, also Leo's child. Yet Leo had not been killed by the bullet. He was stabbed to death, as he lay unconscious, by Edna Snow, Fritz's mother, in revenge for the trouble that Leo and Martha's affair had caused her son and also as a self-appointed agent of judgment on Leo's adulteries. She forced Fritz and Al to bury Leo near the cabin. Fifteen years later, on almost the same spot, she murders Stanley, who is on the verge of discovering his father's body and Edna's crime. Life moves in a circle as Ronny witnesses Stanley's death in the same place that Stanley witnessed Leo's shooting. The connection is reinforced by Sue's presence at both events.

The last novel Macdonald wrote is *The Blue Hammer*, and whether he consciously intended it to be the last, it provides in certain ways an appropriate conclusion to the series. It is the first time, apart from a brief interlude in *The Goodbye Look*, that Archer has a romantic interest. The effects of a lack of love preoccupy all the Archer novels, and Archer recognizes in this book that the same lack has had its effects on him. He has been single since his divorce from his wife, Sue, which took place before the first book begins. In the last book, he meets and soon falls in love with Betty Jo Siddon, a young newspaper reporter. Yet Macdonald knew that Raymond Chandler was unable to continue the Philip Marlowe novels after marrying off his detective, and perhaps he intended to end his own series similarly. It seems that the genre requires a detective who is himself without personal ties, who is able to and perhaps driven to move freely into and then out of the lives of others. Indeed, the involvement of Betty in the case does create a tension between Archer's personal and professional interests. Another suggestion that *The Blue Hammer* may have been intended to be the last of the Archer novels lies in its symmetry with the first, *The Moving Target*. In the earlier book, Archer kills a man in a struggle in the ocean, the only such occurrence in the eighteen books and an indication of the extent to which the compassionate Archer differs from his more violent predecessors. In the last book, he finds himself in a similar struggle, but this time manages to save his adversary. Archer specifically parallels the two events and feels that he has balanced out his earlier sin, somehow completing a pattern.

The plot of *The Blue Hammer* is built around the Dostoevskian theme of the double, a theme that Macdonald treated before in *The Wycherly Woman*, in which Phoebe Wycherly assumes the identity of her murdered mother, and in *The Instant Enemy*, in which Jasper Blevins takes on the role of his murdered half brother. The motif is developed here in its most elaborate form and combined with the familiar themes of the crimes of the past shaping those of the present and of the son's search for his true father, forming an appropriate summation of the major themes of MacDonald's entire Archer series.

Thirty-two years ago, Richard Chantry stole the paintings of his supposed half brother, William Mead, then serving in the army, and married William's girlfriend Francine. William murdered Richard when he returned and assumed his identity as Francine's husband, though he had already married a woman named Sarah and had a son, Fred, by her. Seven years later, Gerard Johnson, a friend of William from the army, appears at William's door with Sarah and Fred, threatening to blackmail him. William kills Gerard and then takes his name, in a doubling of the theme of doubleness. He returns to live with Sarah and Fred and remains a recluse for twenty-five years to hide his crimes.

The case begins for Archer when he is called in to locate a painting which has been stolen from Jack Biemeyer. He learns that it was taken by Fred Johnson, who wanted to study it to determine whether it was a recent work by the famous artist Richard Chantry, who had mysteriously vanished twenty-five years before. If genuine, it would establish that the painter was still alive. Fred had seen similar pictures in the Johnson home and had formed the idea that Chantry might be his real father. William steals the painting, which is one of his own works, in a doubling of his earlier theft of his own paintings from Richard. The painting had been sold by Sarah to an art dealer, and William is forced to kill again to prevent the discovery of his true identity and his earlier murders. By the book's guardedly positive resolution, three generations of men—Fred Johnson; his father, William Mead; and Jack Biemeyer, who turns out to be William's father—have all come to the admission or recognition of their previously concealed identities and have come to a kind of redemption through their suffering.

Macdonald's work, in terms of quantity as well as quality, constitutes an unparalleled achievement in the detective genre. The twenty-four novels, particularly the eighteen which feature Lew Archer, form a remarkably coherent body of work both stylistically and thematically. The last twelve Archer books have received especially high critical as well as popular acclaim and have secured Macdonald's standing as the author of the finest series of detective novels ever written, perhaps the only such series to have bridged the gap between popular and serious literature.

William Nelles

Other major works

SHORT FICTION: *The Name Is Archer*, 1955; *Lew Archer, Private Investigator*, 1977.

NONFICTION: *On Crime Writing*, 1973; *Self-Portrait: Ceaselessly into the Past*, 1981.

Bibliography

Bruccoli, Matthew J. *Ross Macdonald*. San Diego: Harcourt Brace Jovanovich, 1984. Describes the development of Macdonald's popular reputation as a prolific author of detective fiction and his critical reputation as a writer of literary merit. Includes illustrations, an appendix with an abstract of his Ph.D. thesis, notes, a bibliography, and an index.

Delaney, Bill. "Ross Macdonald's Literary Offenses." *The Armchair Detective* 19 (Summer, 1986): 246-258. Notwithstanding trenchant criticism of Macdonald's style, "soft" heroes, and pretentious psychology, provides interesting insights into Macdonald's habits as a writer. Includes notes.

Sipper, Ralph B., ed. *Ross Macdonald: Inward Journey*. Santa Barbara, Calif.: Cordelia Editions, 1984. This collection of twenty-seven articles includes two by Macdonald, one a transcription of a speech about mystery fiction and the other a letter to a publisher which discusses Raymond Chandler's work in relation to his own. Contains photographs and notes on contributors.

Skinner, Robert E. *The Hard-Boiled Explicator: A Guide to the Study of Dashiell Hammett, Raymond Chandler, and Ross Macdonald*. Metuchen, N.J.: Scarecrow Press, 1985. An indispensable volume for the scholar interested in tracking down unpublished dissertations as well as mainstream criticism. Includes brief introductions to each author, followed by annotated bibliographies of books, articles, and reviews.

South Dakota Review 24 (Spring, 1986). This special issue devoted to Macdonald, including eight articles, an editor's note, photographs, and notes, is a valuable source of criticism.

Speir, Jerry. *Ross Macdonald*. New York: Frederick Ungar, 1978. Serves as a good introduction to Macdonald's work, with a brief biography and a discussion of the individual novels. Includes chapters on his character Lew Archer, on alienation and other themes, on Macdonald's style, and on the scholarly criticism available at the time. Contains a bibliography, notes, and an index.

Wolfe, Peter. *Dreamers Who Live Their Dreams: The World of Ross Macdonald's Novels*. Bowling Green, Ohio: Bowling Green University Press, 1976. This detailed study contains extensive discussions of the novels and a consideration of the ways in which Macdonald's life influenced his writing. Includes notes.

JOSEPH McELROY

Born: Brooklyn, New York; August 21, 1930

Principal long fiction

A Smuggler's Bible, 1966; *Hind's Kidnap: A Pastoral on Familiar Airs*, 1969; *Ancient History*, 1971; *Lookout Cartridge*, 1974; *Plus*, 1976; *Ship Rock, a Place: From "Women and Men," a Novel in Progress*, 1980; *Women and Men*, 1987; *The Letter Left to Me*, 1988.

Other literary forms

Joseph McElroy's reputation stands on his achievements as a novelist. A number of excerpts from his massive novel *Women and Men* first appeared in short-story form; the excellence of three of these pieces ("The Future," "The Message for What It Was Worth," and "Daughter of the Revolution") was acknowledged by their selection for the *O. Henry Prize Stories* and *Best American Short Stories*. In addition, McElroy has published a number of uncollected essays on topics as various as the Apollo 17 launch, the influence on his generation of Vladimir Nabokov's fiction, and autobiographical aspects of his own work. Between 1971 and 1976 he was also a regular reviewer for *The New York Times Book Review*.

Achievements

From the start, McElroy was received as one of the generation of American novelists that includes William Gaddis, Robert Coover, and Thomas Pynchon—writers of long and technically demanding fictions. Among them, McElroy remains the dark star, outshone by their well-publicized brilliance while being acknowledged among his peers as the writer's writer, one who is committed to giving fictional order to a complex "information society" by optimistically recognizing its possibilities for narrative art and human growth. In 1977, McElroy's writing was acclaimed by an Award in Literature from the American Academy of Arts and Letters. Still, the regard of critics has been slow in coming, and reviewers have argued that the complexity of internal reference and detail in McElroy's work is too demanding of the reader. In a 1979 interview, McElroy countered that he continues to "hope . . . for readers who would be willing to commit themselves to a strenuous, adventurous fiction." The reissue of several of McElroy's novels, in addition to blooming scholarly acclaim, suggests that this hope is well placed.

Biography

Joseph Prince McElroy was born in Brooklyn, New York, on August 21, 1930, and has lived near there for most of his life. He received a baccalaureate from Williams College in 1951 and a master of arts degree from Columbia University in 1952. After two years with the United States Coast Guard (1952-1954), he returned to graduate studies at Columbia, completing the Ph.D. in 1962 with a dissertation on seventeenth century poet Henry King. From 1956 to 1961, he held positions as instructor and assistant professor of English at the University of New Hampshire. Since 1964, he has been a full professor of English at Queens College, City University of New York. McElroy has been a visiting professor or a writer-in-residence at a number of major universities, has received a wide range of fellowships and awards, and has served editorial terms on several literary magazines. He continues to make his home in New York City.

Analysis

Joseph McElroy's novels unfold in the topographies of mind. He has called them "neural neighborhoods." Within those imaginary spaces, McElroy's fictions grow from a profound desire for order, for a meaningful landscape of human intentions and actions. Also, they grow from a profound recognition that such orders may be unobtainable amid the fragmenting stresses of advanced machine culture. The point, as his books illustrate, is not to kick against this crux but to set the mind in motion within it, thus to create form and meaning. This precept is the source of both difficulty and great achievement in McElroy's writing.

Not that McElroy's neural landscapes stand apart from ordinary surroundings. Quite the opposite: His novels are saturated with the stuff of contemporary society, with references to and metaphors from urban culture, and from such wide-ranging pursuits as cinematography, information processing, linguistics, and the space program. Richly detailed and technically specific, these familiar endeavors illustrate the fragmentary nature of human knowledge. At the same time they point out unsuspected possibilities for human growth. McElroy's narrator-protagonists are imbued with an almost claustrophobic variety of concise memories and everyday desires. Yet within these mental topographies they are driven to discover order, or "plot," for novels are also "plotted," and it is of the essence of McElroy's novels that the action, the narrators' attempted discoveries, be seen as contemporary variations on the detective plot. They solve no significant enigmas. Not "representations" of events that have been rarefied by memory, McElroy's fictions are instead "demonstrations" of the complexities involved in reconstructing any past event. Inevitably the character's memory involves his own categories of feeling and linguistic mapping, which themselves become objects of scrutiny. The best one can do, suggests McElroy, is to "smuggle" or "kidnap" a perception or idea over the received boundary of some other. By thus learning to manipulate them, one surmounts the inadequacies and paradoxes of human knowledge.

This brief sketch of McElroy's principal concerns will suggest the interests he shares with many modern and contemporary writers. With modernists such as Marcel Proust and André Gide, he is concerned to show both the complexity and the potential illicitness of narratively reconstructed events, which are "counterfeit" creations precisely to the degree that they recognize themselves as ordered rememberings of life's dismembered orderings. With contemporaries such as Michel Butor, William Gaddis, Nicholas Moseley, and Thomas Pynchon, he reflects on the linguistic nature of this narrative activity. Like them, he sees the ability to manipulate hypothetical, alternative structures—for example, the worlds of "stories"—as a condition of social existence, and he reflects on how we too hastily suppose that continuity and causality are absolute requirements of that structuring work.

A Smuggler's Bible was a brilliant first articulation of these themes. By McElroy's own account, this novel was not his first, but developed after several aborted attempts at a rather conventionally sequential, causal type of long narrative. Its title describes the book's main emblem: a "smuggler's Bible" is a hollowed-out volume designed for carrying contraband over borders. Similarly, McElroy's narrative develops by making illicit leaps. Even though its eight parts are essentially disconnected, the reader still "smuggles" bits of information across their boundaries to reconstruct a "story" about its narrator-protagonist, David Brooke. In fact, readers are encouraged in this by another, omniscient narrative voice, which appears in short interchapters. This voice advertises itself as David's "creator" and comments on his task, itself also the reader's, which is to "analyze, synthesize, [and] assimilate" details gleaned by "projecting" oneself into others' experience. This is the task framed by a conventional, "realistic" novel. Yet a smuggler's Bible is also a clever deception: an illegal, profane business tucked inside an authorized, holy cover. In similar ways, David's eightfold story, a kind of experimental writing, can be read as trying, and failing, to disguise itself as an artistically conventional novel replete with causal plot.

The essentials of that inner narrative are as follows. David and his wife, Ellen, are passengers aboard a ship, the *Arkadia*, bound for London. There he must deliver to a mysterious "Old Man" the manuscript of a book he has written, each of its eight parts the story of an event or of characters with special significance in his own life. The ship's passage takes eight days. During that time, at the rate of a story per day, David struggles to give the manuscript continuity. He provides narrative transitions and "smuggles" characters from one narrative into another. He even attempts to structure each story according to some mythic subtext, such as those of Oedipus, Midas, or the Golden Ass. This technique of highly self-conscious parody—what T. S. Eliot called the "mythic method" in reference to James Joyce's *Ulysses*—is revealed as yet another mode of smuggling, which has lost that sacred magic it once promised to modernist writers. Thus, while David may think of himself as "an epistemological reuniac" attempting an integral, totalizing reconstruction of the past, *A Smuggler's Bible*, especially in its interchapters, tends contrariwise toward disjunction and incompleteness. McElroy has said that it "was designed to fracture."

Throughout this long, stylistically brilliant performance, the image one gets (not a "picture" but an immanence or field theory) is of women and men existing in a grand relational network. Yet only David's acts of memory hold that web in balance. This field of charged particles did exist, and had "reality," but only when a single mind was composing it, and that mind is, in the best sense of the term, *trivial*: It finds pattern and meaning in the accidental minutiae of ordinary lives.

A few examples: In the fourth of his "principal parts," David recounts the story of his acquaintance, at the University of New Hampshire, with an intellectual con artist named Duke Amerchrome. An immensely popular historian and theorist of American culture, Duke engineered his fame on forged sources and blustering rhetoric. He is an exemplar of the literati who smuggle themselves into positions of "authority." Tony Tanner thinks that the character is patterned on Norman Mailer, yet almost any other (such as Marshall McLuhan) would do, and one could also point to the autobiographical aspects and note that McElroy may have been exorcising personal as well as professional demons. In any event, much of Duke's story is transmitted to David through his son Michael, who discloses the man's use of counterfeited trivia about the Battle of Ticonderoga. Michael, however, has selfish motives for these disclosures, such as coveting his father's nubile young wife (Duke's third). This Oedipal motif broadens; the idea of "shadowing" a (supposed) father, tracking him and absorbing the minutiae of his days until one knows enough to expose and supplant him, recurs in other chapters. The first memory concerns a bored rare-book dealer named Peter St. John who is being followed by a boy who thinks that the man resembles his father. In the second, David's association with a group of eccentric fellow boarders eventually centers on a rare-coin dealer named Pennitt, who may be a counterfeiter; whether he is is never certain, because the old man brushes David off before disclosing any conclusive evidence. In the final part, David's father spins through his last, trivial thoughts while dying of angina and rectal cancer. David *inhabits* these memories, seeking safe harbor between antinomies: the imploding heart of man, symbolizing powers of empathy and connection, versus the exploding rectum, David's symbol of dispersal and "apartness." The book ends there, with the mind shuttling in between, never resolving that antinomy but finding art in the act of composing.

Hind's Kidnap, McElroy's next novel, takes these ideas a step further. Once again the concern is with detection, with the mind moving inside a labyrinthine network of information that points equally to integral order and to zeros of disorder. Yet this novel falls short of its ambition. Critics have aptly noted that the book succeeds better in its idea than in its stylistic performance, which often becomes tiresome.

The reasons are several. One is that the narrator's attention to matters of trivial but feasibly significant detail achieves a still closer focus than in *A Smuggler's Bible*, but this attention must be borne by units of narrative (sentences on up to chapters) that strain from sheer length, and hence from the span of attention demanded of readers. Another reason, and doubtless an attempt to explain (that is, to naturalize) the first, is that in *Hind's Kidnap* the narrator-protagonist is virtually obsessed with the dialectic of detection.

The story is related by Jack Hind, a six-foot, seven-inch, lookout tower of a man who, for years, has been intermittently tracking his way back and forth through the same case. A four-year-old boy, Hershey Laurel, was kidnapped from his rural home, and for seven years there has been no trace of the boy. Desperate to solve the enigma, Hind tells and retells the known facts to everyone he knows; in time, his auditors become so knowledgeable as to seem implicated in the original crime. Hind's recollections thus become a labyrinth without boundaries, as if all were "suspicioned" into the plot, often on the slightest of linguistic associations, such as a name. Midway through the narrative, with the book's reader now equally knowledgeable of the main "facts," it becomes necessary for Hind to "de-kidnap" everyone, to extricate them from the paranoid plottings of his own mind. Thus, Hind, too, becomes implicated. In the novel's second part, he turns his detective skills onto his own past: the early deaths of both parents, his childhood with a guardian (a linguist, as it happens), and the question of his own paternity (the guardian appears to have been his actual father). These matters explain his obsession. Jack's quest for the boy is a means of asserting his own guardianship, and so of questing into the self, of separating illusion from reality and discovering how he was misled by language. As the novel's subtitle implies, Jack thereby seeks to become a truer shepherd of both memories and the discourses used to shape them.

Yet the discourse of *Hind's Kidnap* is often so meditative, so far removed from the pitch and flow of narrative as to read like a poetic anatomy. This tendency continues in *Ancient History*, McElroy's third (and least satisfying) novel, in which the narrator, Cy, searches to explain the evident suicide of his friend, Dom. Like Hind, he discovers that every force expended in the effort of detection tends to reverberate throughout the web of his friend's associations, and eventually through his own memories. Yet the stylistic and technical demands of this novel also bring diminishing returns to the reader. The book becomes, at the last, a poetic demonstration of the spatial possibilities in linguistically organized memory. It has little in it of narrative action.

Lookout Cartridge, arguably McElroy's best work, resolves these problems. The plot crackles with action and the style surges ahead in a more declarative mode, while never weakening the complex power of its main idea.

A further "demonstration" of the dynamics and the essential incompleteness of memory in an information society, *Lookout Cartridge* asks to be read as a mystery-thriller.

The narrator-protagonist, Cartwright, a filmmaker who has been collaborating with a director named Dagger DiGorro on a politically radical documentary project, is literally pushed into his detective research. The narrative opens with the momentary fall (as a result of mechanical failure) of a helicopter hovering over a terrorist explosion in New York, itself partly explained at the novel's end. This recollection spins Cartwright into another beginning: an unseen hand that pushed him violently down an escalator, a fall he transforms by half-coordinated steps into a self-preserving forward stagger. In the narrative order, Cartwright's second "fall" thus redeems the mindless near-accident of his first. It also eventually emblematizes the detective activity, as a type of half-random, half-volitional motion. For a novel preoccupied with kinds of drive (physical and cinematic, social and narrational, epistemological and historical), this paradox is crucial.

Persons unknown, for reasons never fully explained, want Cartwright and Dagger's film destroyed, along with Cartwright's shooting diary, Cartwright himself, and perhaps even members of Cartwright's family who have knowledge of the film at second hand. All of this is apparently necessary because the film may have inadvertently recorded minute details of "an international power struggle." It may have, but without replaying or at least mentally reconstructing the footage, Cartwright can never know for certain. Therefore he sets to work. Like McElroy's previous detectives, he takes up the fragmentary evidence: the remaining chunks of the diary, recollections (often prompted) of friends and associates, material objects, whatever comes to hand during his headlong plunge through England, where much of the footage was shot, and New York City.

This urgency of self-survival gives *Lookout Cartridge* a sense of immediate purpose missing from the more abstract plots of *Hind's Kidnap* and *Ancient History*, and is something McElroy would capitalize on again, in *Plus*. As Cartwright shuttles back and forth between London and New York, and between pieces of contrary evidence, his in-betweenness becomes the basis for an uncannily creative power. Though he imagines himself as a "lookout cartridge" of film inserted "in someone else's system," still Cartwright discovers how, "between blind coghood" (the camera as simple recording instrument) and "that sinister hint of godhead" (in the conspiracies of unknown others), he himself has the power—even by using purest accident—of pushing events toward disclosure. Indeed, Cartwright finally nails both his assailants and their banal secrets. This resolution is the result, equally, of his power to manipulate details of story and his power simply to act by lunging forward, by reacting. Through it all, readers "have" only this Cartwright-Cartridge: the mind as recording machine, the machine as uncanny intercessor for the mind. What the lens records will depend entirely on where one is, what one wants to see, how long one rolls the film, and, later, how it is spliced. The camera thus becomes, like the remembering human subject, part of a relational system or associational grid whose power is greater than its parts.

This idea underwrites the lexicons of cinematography and information processing evident on the novel's every page. There is much, much more. Cartwright's narrative also includes speculations on Mayan calendars, on Mercator maps, and on Stonehenge or the standing stones of Callanish as ancient data-processing systems; details about the topographies of Corsica, London, or New York; and countless oblique references to the conspiracy-racked politics of the 1960's and 1970's. Involving readers in this labyrinth of events, representation techniques, and forms of knowledge, *Lookout Cartridge* surpasses the excesses and the feigned completion of other contemporary encyclopedic novels, such as Pynchon's *Gravity's Rainbow* (1973) or Coover's *The Public Burning* (1977).

By comparison to these, *Lookout Cartridge* makes far more demands on the reader. As the title suggests, the reader is also inserted into this survival-experience and discovers that what matters is not a final why, but how one might manipulate the journey. Yet many of the novel's critics were so taken by its profusion of reference and detail that they missed commenting on one of its completed enigmas, a palpable bit of political absurdity worthy of Joseph Conrad's *The Secret Agent* (1907). That explosion in chapter 1 was set off by a faction of Cartwright's assailants, who were terrorizing the city for towing their illegally parked car. This detail points to a wry, detached satire of a contemporary society in which politics is managed as sequences of media events.

At first glance, that potential for satire would also seem to be the motive force of McElroy's fifth novel, *Plus*, one of his most accessible works of fiction. Given the novel's premise, the chances for targeting the absurdities of contemporary "information society" were numerous. Its story concerns a disembodied brain inserted, cartridgelike, in an orbiting space platform called Imp, whose computer he—or it—was programmed to be. The engineers dubbed the combination "Imp Plus." Relaying technical data, controlling Imp's self-sustaining internal environment, and with its glucose-producing algae—these are its simple programmed functions. Yet as a relational network, an ecosystem, Imp Plus is more than a mere machine. It has the power of self-induced growth. In sum, once more the narration unfolds in the topography, now absolute, of mind, and the primary action again involves the composition of self from fragments of memory.

In a reconstruction of its past and present states (made difficult by its linguistic limitations), Imp Plus forms a new identity. Looking backward from this perspective, its story is simple. Exposed to lethal doses of radiation, a space scientist donates his brain, and Imp Plus is launched as an experiment in photosynthesis and symbiosis—the algae providing necessary glucose for the brain, the brain respiring carbon dioxide necessary for the algae, the brain and its mechanical platform interpreting and relaying data. Then, however, the brain begins re-forming itself. Imp Plus expands inwardly by recovering discrete sensual memories and thereby reconstructing language. (In an elegantly structured argument, Brooke-Rose shows how this develops from a hypothetically "nonsensical" sentence by linguist Noam Chomsky: "Colorless green ideas sleep furiously.") Imp Plus also expands outwardly by linking the neural sites of previous sensory activity, such as vision, to the platform's circuitry. It thereby realizes the practical and virtual reciprocity of mind and matter, a discovery tantamount to the age-old philosopher's stone. It also begins disregarding and disobeying signals from Earth, and when Ground Control threatens fiery destruction, Imp Plus carries out a ploy which will carom the platform off Earth's atmosphere and into deep space. There Imp Plus envisions further growth—leaving matter behind to become pure light, the wholly disembodied "Plus" of McElroy's title.

Plus can be read as a recapitulation of the principal themes of McElroy's previous books—a work of summary and consolidation. With *Plus*, he had published five challenging novels in just over a decade; his sixth novel, *Women and Men*, was itself ten years in the writing.

Everything about *Women and Men* proclaims its enormous ambition. Its title has the immodest sweep of Fyodor Dostoevski's *Crime and Punishment* (1866) or Leo Tolstoy's *War and Peace* (1865-1869). In sheer bulk, nearly twelve hundred pages, it easily outweighs any of McElroy's earlier books. In the complexity of its structure, the density of information it conveys, it is even more daunting than *Lookout Cartridge*. Reviewing the novel in *The Washington Post Book World*, Tom LeClair suggested that *"Women and Men* is the single book—fiction or nonfiction—that best manifests what human beings can know and be and imagine now and, just as importantly, in the future."

Whether such claims will stand up is a matter for time to tell. A first reading of *Women and Men* is essentially a reconnaissance mission. The action of the novel is set primarily in the mid-1970's. The two central characters— James Mayn, a journalist specializing in science and technology and economic issues, and Grace Kimball, a radical feminist guru—live in the same apartment building in New York. They do not know each other, but they have mutual acquaintances, and they are connected in more subtle ways as well. This pattern of coincidence is a model for the novel as a whole, which traces a multitude of unexpected connections both in the private lives and family histories of the characters and in the life of the planet.

While the intertwining stories of Mayn and Kimball constitute a loose narrative line, many chapters are self-contained vignettes that illuminate, from diverse perspectives, the relation between women and men at a time of significant change: change in assumptions concerning sexual roles, but also more broadly change in the assumptions by which we organize our experience. "The ways in which we embrace the world and embrace other people," McElroy has said, "can be more precise and clear than we sometimes think." Weather patterns, body chemistry, economic cycles: These are not merely esoteric academic subjects but rather the stuff of everyday life. All that is required is attentiveness to available knowledge.

Much of the knowledge that informs *Women and Men* is scientific, but this is complemented by a strong emphasis on what has been called New Age spirituality. Native American lore plays an important role in the book; Grace Kimball frequently invokes the Goddess (the primeval Earth Mother who, many feminists contend, was universally worshipped by humankind before the onset of patriarchy); and there are hints of reincarnation throughout the novel.

Indeed, several long sections, set in the future, are given to a chorus of disembodied spirits who comment on the action and the characters of the main narrative. Here McElroy seems to suggest a collective consciousness in which individual identity is subsumed. It is not clear how literally this vision is to be taken; even readers who find it unpersuasive will be left with a vivid sense of intricate order within the dizzying multiplicity of things.

Steven Weisenburger

Bibliography
Campbell, Gregor. "Processing *Lookout Cartridge*." *The Review of Contemporary Fiction* (Spring, 1990): 112-118. Explores *Lookout Cartridge*'s closed fictional system, modeled on physics and cybernetics, and mentions McElroy's use of film technology. Notes his love of abstraction and the complexity of the plot. Campbell praises the novel as a "triumph of information-processing design and technology," and claims that it can be viewed as a 1960's novel concerned with historical change.
LeClair, Tom. "Opening Up Joseph McElroy's *The Letter Left to Me*." *The Review of Contemporary Fiction* (Spring, 1990): 258-267. Contains McElroy's statement on his use of the word "attention" in *The Letter Left to Me*. LeClair gives critical commentary on this novel, noting that McElroy's use of language has "opened up sensibility for anyone to read. Everyone who cares about mastery in American letters should." Also discusses *Women and Men* and its peeling away of layers and obstacles.
LeClair, Tom, and Larry McCaffrey. *Anything Can Happen: Interviews with Contemporary American Novelists*. Chicago: University of Illinois Press, 1983. A thoughtful interview with McElroy by LeClair that provides much valuable information and insight into McElroy's work and vision as a writer. Includes a brief introduction by LeClair which is helpful in sum-

ming up the main themes in McElroy's writing.

Mathews, Harry. "We for One: An Introduction to Joseph McElroy's *Women and Men.*" *The Review of Contemporary Fiction* 10 (Spring, 1990): 199-226. Examines the novel's interchange between men and women and vice versa, noting its use of language and double entendres. Mathews makes liberal use of extracts from the novel and diagrams to illustrate his commentary. A complex piece of criticism that probes the function of the narrative in McElroy's work.

The Review of Contemporary Fiction 10 (Spring, 1990). This special issue is devoted to the work of McElroy, with a collection of important critical essays and a bibliographical essay. Includes an introduction by Stanley Elkin and a piece by McElroy entitled "Midcourse Corrections," followed by an interview with McElroy conducted by John Graham. A valuable resource for McElroy scholars and readers alike.

PATRICK McGINLEY

Born: Killaned, County Donegal, Ireland; February 8, 1937

Principal long fiction
Bogmail, 1978; *Goosefoot*, 1982; *Foxprints*, 1983; *Foggage*, 1983; *The Trick of the Ga Bolga*, 1985; *The Red Men*, 1987; *The Devil's Diary*, 1988.

Other literary forms
Patrick McGinley's published works have been exclusively confined to the novel form.

Achievements
From the outset, McGinley's fiction has enjoyed an enthusiastic reception from reviewers, particularly in the United States, where critics, inadequately acquainted with some of his background material, have misleadingly drawn attention to the work's Irishness. Reviews in England and Ireland, though less generous, have generally been favorable, if somewhat resistant to McGinley's prolificity. Apart from such popular success, however, McGinley remains more or less unknown; indeed, at a time when Irish fiction is receiving an increasing amount of academic attention, this author stands an excellent chance of becoming the most anonymous Irish novelist of his generation.

Biography
Patrick Anthony McGinley was born to a farming family in a comparatively remote area of County Donegal, Ireland's northwesternmost county. He was educated locally and at University College, Galway, from which he was graduated with a bachelor's degree in commerce in 1957. For five years after his graduation he taught secondary school in Ireland before emigrating to England and entering the publishing profession. Apart from a year in Australia (1965-1966), he remained in publishing and became managing director of Europa Publications. Married with one son, McGinley and his family made their home in Kent, outside London.

Analysis
Although Patrick McGinley is usually classified as a crime novelist, to consider him one in the conventional sense is both accurate and misleading. While it is true that McGinley has not deviated from the path signposted in the opening paragraph of his first published novel, *Bogmail*, where poisonous toadstools are being introduced to a mushroom omelet, and while it is also true that his publishers have tended to emphasize the murderous mysteriousness of his plots, there is both more and less than meets the eye to the conve-

nient classification. This state of affairs is of significance because it draws attention to the fact that it is impossible to approach McGinley's work without drawing attention to its bifocal character. McGinley's fiction evinces more interest in mystery than in solution—his work has only one detective, McMyler in *Goosefoot*, and the few policemen who crop up in the other novels are somewhat less than a credit to the force and have thoroughly earned their status as minor characters. The works' focus is directed gently but ineluctably toward those areas of existence that may not be brought within stable frameworks of perception. In particular, the unreasonable fact of death is so much more to the fore than is any power to counteract it that it is tempting to attach to the whole of this author's output the quotation from Robert Southey that is the epigraph to *Foggage*: "My name is Death: the last best friend am I."

For the most part, McGinley's novels are set in the author's native County Donegal. An exception to this general rule is *Foxprints*, which is largely set in the suburban Home Counties of England, a context that the author fails to enliven, perhaps because of its excessively social character. Typically, McGinley feels at home in remoteness, and Donegal settings possess a variety of strategic advantages for a writer of his proclivities. In the first place, by selecting Donegal as the scene of the action, McGinley is clearly presenting settings that he can treat with authority. So faithful is he to the fastidious re-creation of locales clearly maintained in his mind's eye by a deep attachment to his native area that he establishes a very palpable sense of place, and in every McGinley novel there are quietly rapturous descriptive passages that seem to hymn the landscapes they depict.

Situating his plots so squarely in a felt environment—in which the play of light, natural features, the oscillations of the sea, the weather's vagaries, and the presence of wildlife continually recur—seems to enable McGinley virtually to dispense with time. The exigencies of plot naturally require that time passes, but generally speaking there is little specific sense of period. Long historical perspectives have little or no part to play in the assessing of the characters' problematic destinies. What exceptions there are to this rule—the setting of *The Trick of the Ga Bolga* in the early years of World War II, or the rather boldly stated observations on the spurious development of rural Ireland propounded by the protagonist of *The Devil's Diary*—seem rather to underline how watertight the rule is, since neither note of contemporaneity contributes significantly to the balance of forces at the center of either of these novels.

One effect of McGinley's obviation of cultural conceptions of time, and a general relaxation of time-consciousness, is that it assists in the creation of atmosphere but inhibits in the creation of thrills. Such a result accentuates the all-enveloping quality of the rural setting, while at the same time drawing both the characters' and the readers' attention from event to perception of event. The mystery deepens to the degree that it becomes as much part of the nature of things as the landscape in which it is situated. Any tension that results from the distressingly arbitrary and violent events of the plot—often as much the result of accidents as of articulated intentions—are to be found, unreleased, within the consciousness of McGinley's protagonists, and its psychological repercussions fail, with what the protagonists understandably find to be a maddening consistency, to have an objective correlative in the natural world around them. Remoteness of setting therefore, is not merely an occasion of picturesqueness for McGinley. On the contrary, it is one of his fundamental means of lending plausibility to the sense of the inscrutable and uncanny that bedevils the mental landscapes of his protagonists, the majority of whom traverse the dual terrains of these novels like lost souls.

By virtue of its very naturalness, setting is experienced by McGinley's protagonists as a primary instance of otherness, of a set of conditions that are not comprehensible, tractable, alterable, or humanly amenable in any partic-ular—conditions that are, strictly speaking, mysterious. Yet it is important to note that McGinley is sufficiently resourceful to prevent his approach from becoming too schematic. The rich farming country of County Tipperary, which provides the setting for *Foggage* and in which its main characters are ostensibly firmly established, engenders as much distress and destruction as County Donegal ever did, revealing unsuspected psychic remotenesses, while in *Goosefoot* ungenial Dublin exposes the unsuspecting and vital Patricia Teeling to malevolences that are the antithesis of her winning sense of life.

McGinley's protagonists, settled or unsettled, are peculiarly susceptible to the atmosphere of their environments. For the most part they are unsettled, and it is generally this condition that has brought them to the locale of the story. Once arrived, they seem to believe, however, that they have found a secure haven: to a degree, the enclosed and remote character of their land-fall—typified by the Glenkeel in *The Devil's Diary*, which has the same road into it as out—seduces them into thinking that now they are safe, they have come to the end of a particular phase of their lives and are permitted by their new circumstances to live lives that are at once both self-engrossed and detached. In a number of cases—*Foxprints* and *The Trick of the Ga Bolga* are the most significant—the progatonists are on the run from unsatisfactory marriages. The protagonists' status as outsiders, however, gives them novelty value to the locals, and before long they are involved in local affairs, often in a very literal sense, one of the principal means of involvement being that of sexual attraction. The inability to deny the presence of their sexuality has the effect of replicating in more intense form the substance of earlier distressing experiences, with the result that settings that seemed to be escapes end up as terminuses. Aiming for simplicity, McGinley's protagonists find it only to discover its essential mysteriousness.

The repetition and duplication of experience, the unforsakable and evi-dently unforgiving character of one's own nature, are particularly crucial in

The Devil's Diary and *The Trick of the Ga Bolga*. Yet more important than their presence, and raising their significance beyond that of mere plot devices, is the fact that the protagonists perceive their condition for what it is. The typical McGinley protagonist is well educated and sometimes dauntingly well read. The unwitting choice of a volume of the *Encyclopædia Britannica*, eleventh edition, as a murder weapon seems virtually natural in *Bogmail*, whereas in most murder mysteries it would seem at least eccentric. There seems nothing unusual in Father Jerry McSharry taking down a volume of patristic theology for a little bedtime reading in *The Devil's Diary*. In addition, circumstances generally conspire to aggravate what seems to be the protagonists' natural predilection for self-scrutiny. Discrepancies between self and world begin to proliferate, and the capacity for consciousness to keep pace with them is frequently stretched unreasonably. A quest for pattern, for coherence, for congruity and perception bedevils McGinley's characters, who, for all of their learning, persist in giving the impression of innocence. The evil that their presence inadvertently uncovers strikes them as a force that cannot be reasoned away, and they become embroiled in a double bind: the more they see, the less they are able to believe. No satisfactory denouement results from their existential and epistemological entanglements. McGinley's apparent indifference to a resonant denouement has the effect of rendering his protagonists as occasions of authorial game-playing rather than more familiar, "well-rounded" characters. This ostensible deficiency must be considered, however, in the context of the essentially experimental nature of McGinley's work.

Not only do repetition and replication feature to a significant degree within each of McGinley's novels, but they are also notably present in his output as a whole. As a result, while resourceful variations in setting and protagonist occur—a female protagonist in *Goosefoot*, three protagonists in *The Red Men*, a suburban never-never land as the setting for *Foxprints*—and while these changes effectively vary the angle of approach from novel to novel, each work's ultimate preoccupations remain essentially unchanged. McGinley's output has a consistency of focus and pliability of approach that are crucially denied its characters. It hardly seems to matter that the English engineer Potter in *Bogmail* is a prototype for Coote, the protagonist of *The Trick of the Ga Bolga*, or that Coote's mistress has a formidable avatar in the insistently incestuous Maureen Hurley of *Foggage*. Story line is more ornament than staple, and while McGinley's plots are richly woven and colorfully peopled, they seem to be considered as no more than edifices of superficial plausibility to an investigation of whose inscrutable foundations the protagonist is, through no fault of his own (McGinley's fiction is resolutely amoral), condemned.

McGinley's sense of setting draws heavily on the elements—the motion of the seasons, the cloudscapes of the often protean Irish sky, the world of crag, pool, bog, and seashore. His sense of protagonist reproduces this concentration on the elemental. These characters seldom have a specific social role, or if they do—as in the case of Father Jerry in *The Devil's Diary*—it produces rather than defends against existential dread. On the other hand, the protagonists, for all the author's concentration on them and his use of them as both embodiments and victims of a unique optic on themselves and their world, are not sufficiently well endowed to render considerations of social role superogatory by functioning in a recognizable manner. Deprived of the safeguards that social and literary convention provide, they appear to have no choice but to assume a more fundamental, vulnerable, and elementary condition of selfhood—or rather, the plot lines of McGinley's novels show that fall taking place. In addition, the creation of mysteries without solution and the commissioning of crime without reproducing the social machinery of incrimination that is its normal, or generic, accompaniment, take at face value the genre to which these novels superficially belong, and by doing so subvert it, reducing it to such a bare embodiment of its elements that it only nominally maintains its presence.

The unemphatic but omnipresent concentration on a sense of the elemental in McGinley's fiction is nowhere seen to better advantage than in the works' recurring themes. Having brought his unsuspecting protagonists, who without knowing it are at the end of their tether, to what seems like the end of the world, the author subjects them to other experiences of the terminal. The most obvious one of these is death. Yet although its literal presence is of prime importance to sustaining these works' fragmentary figment of plot, death is not merely present in a literal sense. It also exists as the pun for sexual climax familiar to students of English Renaissance poetry, where it helps to make a familiar and typically antithetical conjunction for McGinley (the fact of death is frequently deeply implicated in the act of love). In addition, its presence denotes a primary instance of the chaos and nullity to which a protagonist's perception of life may in any case be reduced—a state of perception that is frequently the aftermath of the violent and unexpected deaths that punctuate the duration of the McGinley protagonist's rustication. Rather than describe McGinley as a writer of mysteries, it seems more appropriate to consider his works as those of a parablist, who utters in story what cannot be otherwise so readily articulated. At least one McGinley novel, *The Red Men* (commonly taken as a retelling of the parable of the talents in the New Testament, seems to support such a view. More broadly, a strong case may be made for McGinley's novels to be considered as sophisticated romances of consciousness, in which the romantic quest, for all of its pastoral trappings, is ironized by succeeding in finding that with which it cannot live.

What the quest locates reveals the philosophical undertow of McGinley's fiction. It would be misleading to consider McGinley a philosophical novelist of the school of, for example, Albert Camus, as is implied by his works' pleasing lightness of tone and deftness of manner. Philosophical themes, however fundamental to the extreme conditions to which action and character are reduced, are treated with no more intensity or deliberation than is any other feature of McGinley's fictional universe, possibly as a result of his having no ideological ax to grind. At the same time, the clearly existentialist scenarios, the manner in which action preys on mind in order to elicit meaning, the emphasis on the mutability of fate as a standby of plot, the frequent epiphanic encounters between man and nature, the quietly satirical allusions to mind-body problems, and the impetus toward pattern forming and pattern recognition that initially stimulates and ultimately frustrates the inquirer all suggest works of a speculative, philosophizing, intellectual character.

This omnipresent preoccupation with perception, cognition, and the impossibility to stabilize or normalize them that bemuses McGinley's protagonists seems to amuse the author. Not only is his style, for the most part, wry, succinct, and supple, but its tone is also frequently one of comic detachment. A great strength of his work is his ability to create compelling minor characters, all of them gifted talkers, whose presence both diffuses and enhances the works' central preoccupations. In addition, McGinley is not averse to placing the reader in the lexical equivalent of his protagonists' opacity of perception by the inclusion of archaic and unfamiliar terminology. Here again, however, this tactic is employed in a spirit of play rather than one of dogmatism, just as his works as a whole resist to an exemplary degree didacticism and moralizing, preferring to articulate consciousness as a field of forces too vivid to be ignored and too broad to be disciplined. The greatest pleasure to be derived from McGinley's fiction, therefore, is not merely from its undoubtedly attractive and distracting stories, locales, and characters but also from the ruminative cast of mind that sets the various fictive effects in motion.

Because of lack of serious critical attention, it is difficult to assess McGinley's status as a contemporary Irish novelist. Since the early 1960's, Irish writing in all forms has been undergoing major self-interrogation, accompanied by the new thematic and formal considerations. While, unlike many Irish writers, McGinley has been anything but vocal in this sustained period of reappraisal, it is instructive to see his work in such a context. Its individuality is arguably its most significant feature and, by a paradox more apparent than real, is the attribute that makes his novels symptomatic of new departures in Irish writing. At the same time, the representations of nature, the sense of the uncanny, the choice of traditional and relatively unchanging rural communities as settings, the focus on death, and the use of the romance form all reveal McGinley as being interestingly related to a long tradition of such preoccupations in Irish writing, from the seventh century writings of Saint Columkille, for whom McGinley's native place is named, to the modern era. More particularly, this author's fascination with reason's frailty and the fact of death makes his work an intriguing pendant to that of one of the most important Irish novelists of the twentieth century, Flann O'Brien. Because of

McGinley's difficulty in expanding his repertoire and enlarging his vision, as well as his reluctance to dramatize his concerns rather than state them, it is likely that he will not achieve major status as an Irish novelist. Regardless of McGinley's place in literary history, however, *Bogmail*, *Foggage*, and particularly *The Trick of the Ga Bolga* will reward any reader's attention.

George O'Brien

Bibliography

Cahalan, James M. *The Irish Novel: A Critical History*. Boston: Twayne, 1988. The concluding chapter of this study is a survey of contemporary Irish fiction, which provides a good sense of McGinley's context. There are also stimulating, though necessarily brief, asides on McGinley's works up to and including *The Red Men*.

Clissmann, Anne. *Flann O'Brien: A Critical Introduction to His Writings*. New York: Barnes & Noble Books, 1975. Chapters 2 and 3 of this work offer a useful means of assessing the imaginative terrain upon which much of McGinley's fiction rests.

Kenner, Hugh. "A Deep and Lasting Mayonnaise." *The New York Times Book Review*, July 21, 1985, 20. A review of *The Trick of the Ga Bolga* by a very influential commentator on Irish literary themes. Many of McGinley's interests and orientations are succinctly brought to the fore.

McGinley, Patrick. Interview by Jean W. Ross. In *Contemporary Authors*, edited by Susan M. Trosky. Vol. 127. Detroit: Gale Research, 1989. A wide-ranging response by McGinley to questions concerning his background, life as a writer, and writing methods.

THOMAS McGUANE

Born: Wyandotte, Michigan; December 11, 1939

Principal long fiction

The Sporting Club, 1969; *The Bushwhacked Piano*, 1971; *Ninety-Two in the Shade*, 1973; *Panama*, 1978; *Nobody's Angel*, 1982; *Something to Be Desired*, 1984; *Keep the Change*, 1989.

Other literary forms

In addition to writing novels, Thomas McGuane has produced work for motion pictures and for popular magazines. He wrote the screenplay and directed the film version of *Ninety-Two in the Shade* (1975), wrote the scripts for *Rancho DeLuxe* (1973) and *The Missouri Breaks* (1975), and shared credit with Bud Shrake for *Tom Horn* (1980) and with Jim Harrison for *Cold Feet* (1989). *An Outside Chance: Essays on Sport* (1980, rev. ed. 1990) contains many of his magazine pieces, and *To Skin a Cat* (1986) is a collection of short fiction.

Achievements

Early in his career, McGuane was heralded as one of the most promising writers of his generation, one with a good chance to become a major American writer. He appeared on the cover of *The New York Times Book Review* and was compared favorably with Ernest Hemingway, William Faulkner, and Saul Bellow. *The Bushwhacked Piano* won the Rosenthal Award, and *Ninety-Two in the Shade* was nominated for a National Book Award. In the mid-1970's, however, when he began to devote the majority of his energies to writing for films, McGuane was dismissed as a sellout. In the late 1970's, his film career seemingly over, McGuane returned to publishing novels. Although Hollywood would continue to option screenplays written in the 1970's, McGuane maintains that novels are his true calling, and his goal is to be "a true man of literature, . . . a professional." *Something to Be Desired* and *Keep the Change* reaffirmed his position as a contender for inclusion in the American canon. In 1989, Thomas McGuane received the Montana Centennial Award for Literature.

Biography

Thomas McGuane was born in Wyandotte, Michigan, on December 11, 1939. He was graduated with honors from Michigan State University in 1962, took an M.F.A. from the Yale Drama School in 1965, and spent 1966-1967 at Stanford on a Wallace Stegner Fellowship. His parents were New England Irish who migrated to the Midwest, where his father became an auto-parts tycoon. He believes that he inherited his storytelling impulse from his mother's family, who loved verbal sparring and yarn-spinning. McGuane is a highly visible writer, articles about him appearing regularly in newspapers and slick magazines. These articles usually center on the manic behavior, heavy drinking, and drug use that marked his film years, and his eventual return to sobriety, family life, and hard work. McGuane has preferred to pursue a career as a writer apart from life in the academic world, believing that his chances of writing interesting novels would be diminished were he to confine himself to life in English departments.

Besides writing, McGuane supports himself by raising and training cutting horses. He is a champion horse cutter who competes regularly in rodeos, and an accomplished sailor and fisherman who spends a part of every year at fishing haunts in Florida and Georgia.

Analysis

Thomas McGuane's fictional universe is a "man's world." His protagonists appear to do whatever they do for sport and to escape ordinary reality. They seek a world where they can, without restraint, be whoever they choose to be. This goal puts them at odds with prevailing social customs and middle-class ideas of morality and achievement. Unfortunately, most of these quests end in frustration. Finding themselves quite apart from the normal flow of society, McGuane's protagonists must try all the harder to fulfill themselves. As a result, they easily become self-absorbed and further jeopardize whatever ties they might once have had to conventional life. Usually this tie is to a woman, who, for her own self-fulfillment, must forsake the protagonist in the end.

McGuane's first novel, *The Sporting Club*, concerns the adventures of well-to-do Michiganders who maintain the exclusive and grand Centennial Club, to which they repair to fish and hunt. The story is limited to the point of view of James Quinn, who has emerged from a protracted adolescence to take over the family's auto-parts factory. Quinn's friend Vernor Stanton, however, refuses to take up the ordinary life and spends his time in the pursuit of games. Stanton is bored by the elitist pretensions of the club members and the pride they take in its noble heritage, and he is frustrated with Quinn for outgrowing the need for freedom and frolic. Stanton engineers a series of adventures which ultimately result in the collapse of the club. The noble pretensions of the membership are exploded when Stanton unearths a photograph which shows their ancestors engaged in an outlandish "sexual circus at full progress." Once the current members see the photograph, the pretense upon which they build their lives collapses and they run rampant with, as Quinn puts it, "moral dubiousness" emulating the sexual circus of the forefathers. In this way, McGuane manages to show that the established social order is rotten at its foundation, and the only sensible thing to do is to quest for a life in which one determines one's own values. Exposing this truth does nothing, however, for the survival of the McGuane protagonists. By the end of the aftermath occasioned by the photograph, Stanton is living under the surveillance of mental health workers at what is left of the club, and Quinn returns to the family business. They are no longer freewheeling protagonists able to make "the world tense."

In *The Bushwhacked Piano*, Nicholas Payne is more fortunate. Even though his father has the finest law practice in Detroit, Payne has no intention of doing anything respectable. He wants no part of his father's "declining snivelization" and "the pismire futilities of moguls." Payne does, however, want Ann Fitzgerald, an aspiring poet and photographer, whom he sees as almost a goddess.

Ann's parents do not approve of Payne; appearances, hard work, and achievement mean everything to them. They take Ann from Michigan to their ranch in Montana, but Payne follows because movement appeals to him, as well as the romantic idea of an almost unworldly mate. Ann is also sleeping with an establishment boyfriend whom she will not give up completely because she knows that someday she will have to behave like a conventional adult. For now, however, camera in hand, she joins Payne on an expedition to Florida to sell fraudulent bat towers. She goes more for the experience than simply to be with Payne, and ultimately she leaves him.

Payne not only loses Ann but also is arrested for selling a useless bat tower. Still, breaking the law is not as serious as breaking conventions. Payne goes free when he agrees to reenact his trial for a television program. Life, McGuane seems to say, is indeed a bewildering proposition, and the only way to emerge victorious is to determine one's own goals and always keep them uppermost in mind. Indeed, neither the loss of Ann nor the scrape with the law has a lasting effect on Payne. Those who live the conventional life will never understand Payne, but he will not relent. The novel ends with Payne proclaiming: "I am at large," which is the same language used to describe an outlaw on the loose. Payne's movement outside conventional spheres will not stop. He is, for better or for worse, in charge of his own life, the artist of his own destiny.

In *Ninety-Two in the Shade*, Thomas Skelton attempts to engineer his own fate when he tries to become a fishing guide with his own skiff off Key West. Nicole Dance, an established guide and murderer, forbids him to do so. When Dance plays a joke on Skelton, the young man burns Dance's skiff in retaliation. Dance vows to kill Skelton if he guides, but Skelton guides anyway, his fulfillment depending on it. The situation here is much the same as in earlier McGuane fiction. The protagonist must assert himself against the normal flow of life. With his life in danger, Skelton ought not to guide, but he knows that "when what you ought to do [has] become less than a kind of absentee ballot you [are] always in danger of lending yourself to the deadly farce that surrounds us." Couched in McGuane's wisecracking language is the idea that the deadly farce occurs when one absents oneself from vital energies and capitulates to the flow of ordinary life. Skelton must stand up for the self he desires to be and attempt the life he wants.

Ninety-Two in the Shade could be considered McGuane's most optimistic book if it were not for the fact that when Skelton becomes a fishing guide, Dance kills him. Until the very end, Tom seems to have everything going his way. He has determined his own values and his own fulfillment. He has the support of family and a fulfilling love relationship with Miranda, a local schoolteacher. Yet he also has his feud with Nicole Dance, who shoots him "through the heart." In spite of the protagonist's courage to pursue goals and the conviction to stand up to adversity, life does not come equipped with happy endings.

McGuane's fourth novel, *Panama*, more clearly points up the frustrations of the unconventional life. Protagonist Chester Hunnicutt (Chet) Pomeroy has become an overnight sensation, performing all the loathsome acts of the imagination for audiences. He has, for example, crawled out of the anus of a frozen elephant and fought a duel in his underwear with a baseball batting practice machine. He also vomited on the mayor of New York, which ended his career. As the novel opens, Chet has returned to Key West, Florida, in the hope of putting his life back together by reconciling with his wife, Catherine, who stuck by him until he became a national disgrace.

Even though she still loves him, Catherine wants nothing to do with him because his behavior is still bizarre. At one point, he nails his hand to her door; at another, he snorts cocaine off the sidewalk. He has lost his memory and given up all hope. Catherine accepts the fact that she cannot change him and leaves him for good to the emptiness he calls home.

Chet combats this emptiness by evoking a transcendent presence of Jesse James, who has the power to inhabit his loved ones. He prefers that James inhabit his father, a snack-foods tycoon. A typical McGuane protagonist, Chet is bothered by the security and ordinariness of his background. He insists that his father is dead and claims James as an ancestor, suggesting that Chester Hunnicutt Pomeroy really wishes he were someone else. Since the glories of the Old West are not available to him, he creates the myth of himself through bizarre behavior.

Chet's outlaw myth leads him nowhere. At the novel's conclusion, his father forces a reconciliation. Chet knows that all his father wants is for Chet to say hello, to acknowledge him as his father. To admit that his father lives will be to agree that Jesse James is dead. Chet will have to accept himself for who he is: the son of an unillustrious packager of snack foods, the perfect symbol of conventional modern life.

Nobody's Angel is McGuane's first novel to be set entirely in the West, a West which McGuane characterizes as "wrecked." In Deadrock, Montana, farmers abuse the land, cowboys are lazy, and Indians are nowhere to be found. Returning to this damaged world is thirty-six-year-old Patrick Fitz-patrick. Patrick is as unconventional as earlier McGuane protagonists. As a whiskey addict and a professional soldier, he has been a tank captain in the army for all of his adult life, most recently in Europe, and the only place he feels secure is inside his womblike tank. Suffering from "sadness for no rea-son," he has returned to the family ranch, which he will someday own. He feels stranded on the ranch because becoming a property owner is not a meaningful achievement for him. Patrick appears to be in the worst shape of any McGuane protagonist. He is not only without goals but also without any sense of himself, conventional or unconventional.

The effect of the wrecked West is seen in the character of Patrick's grand-father. The old man has been a cowboy all of his life, has known real gunfighters, and has run the ranch like an old-time outfit. The West has changed, however, and everything from sonic booms to valleys cluttered with yard lights has got the old man down. The only things he feels good about are Australia, which he has heard is open country like Montana once was, and Western films. His one fit of excitement comes when he signs on to be an extra in a Western about to be filmed locally. Even that, however, is accom-panied by overtones of sadness and ends in disappointment. The film is *Hondo's Last Move*, evocative of a legendary but nonexistent West popular-ized by John Wayne and Louis L'Amour. Even then, the "last move" refers to the dying of the West and perhaps Hondo himself. To make matters worse, the project folds when the distributor forsakes Westerns for science fiction. In the end, the old man moves into town and takes an apartment from which he can see the local film theater, which plays old Westerns, and a little bar in which hangs the head of the best elk he ever shot. The open West has been reduced to one-bedroom apartments, yesterday's movies, and mounted animals, which serve only to remind him of a glorious past.

In *Nobody's Angel*, McGuane continued to work the theme of unfulfilled love. Patrick hopes to bring purpose into his life by means of a love affair with Claire Burnett. Claire and her husband, Tio, are second-generation nouveau-riche Oklahomans summering in Montana. Not a genuine stockman like Patrick's grandfather, Tio is mainly interested in oil, cattle futures, row crops, and running horses. Since Tio's main hobby is pretending to be a good old boy, Patrick sees him as a personification of the substanceless modern West.

Patrick believes that "Claire could change it all" and wishes theirs could be a sentimental love story, the kind found in romantic books. Claire, however, will not become a part of Patrick's dream. Her commitment to Tio goes beyond Patrick's understanding. Her family provided the money to support their life-style. Tio's people are poor Okies, and this discrepancy in their backgrounds has driven him to incurable delusions of grandeur, to the point that Claire has promised that she will not abandon him. Even though she tells Patrick that she loves him, she never stops loving Tio, and Patrick's dream of a storybook romance crumbles. Even when Tio dies, Claire will not marry Patrick. She makes love to him one last time, explaining that love is "nothing you can do anything with." Patrick is not able to cope with Claire's pragmatic attitude about love and their relationship. She gives him a picture of herself, but he does not keep it with him, because it reminds him of the frustrations of his romantic hopes.

In the end, Patrick survives, but not in the West. When he was a teenager, Patrick invented an imaginary girlfriend named Marion Easterly. Even though he was eventually discovered, the fantasy has remained a part of his consciousness. He had hoped that Claire would replace Marion, but a living woman will never become the woman of a man's imagination, and when Claire dismisses him, Patrick rejoins the army and finds fulfillment in his fantasy. Word filters back that he is now a blackout drinker in Madrid and that he is living with a woman named Marion Easterly. Patrick Fitzpatrick remains "at large"—in the sense that his heavy drinking and fantasy lover keep him outside the normal boundaries of life—but without the hope and energy of Nicholas Payne. The McGuane protagonist seemingly must find a way to accommodate himself, at least partially, to the concerns of conventional life.

In *Something to Be Desired*, the McGuane protagonist combines both unconventional and conventional goals. Lucien Taylor grows tired of normality and destroys his perfectly fine marriage with self-absorbed erratic behavior. Once his single life becomes empty, he, like Chet, tries to put it back together again by reuniting with his former wife, Suzanne, and their son, James. Lucien's plight is not entirely the result of his disenchantment with conformity; he is victimized by his capricious lust.

Lucien's sense of sexual discipline was broken in college by Emily, who slept with him on their first meeting. Emily was engaged to a medical student and continued to sleep with both young men at the same time. Ultimately, she is abused by her surgeon husband and becomes totally self-absorbed and manipulating. Emily is a woman as selfish as Claire, and she continues her self-absorbed actions throughout the novel, exploiting everyone, including Lucien. Lucien, however, married Suzanne, who "took the position that this was a decent world for an honest player." This basic decency is what Lucien eventually comes to value, but when he hears that Emily is free of her marriage, he thinks nothing of destroying his own and returning to Montana in quest of her. Lucien is troubled by the lack of romance in his life, an element that Suzanne and James cannot provide. Suzanne sums up Emily by calling her the queen of the whores, an assertion which is borne out when, on her penultimate appearance in the novel, she is seen sleeping naked next to her purse.

Such a portrayal of women who do not measure up to male ideals or fantasies is not rare in McGuane's fiction: Ann (*The Bushwhacked Piano*) and Claire (*Nobody's Angel*) are two other disappointing women. Lucien has dreamed of Emily since their first encounter. Not until he finally decides that he wants nothing more to do with her does she tell him that she regards his concern for her an infantile gesture, a thing she holds in contempt. Indeed, she does not even think enough of him to shoot him, which she has done to her husband and, by this time, another lover. Lucien, however, like Nicholas Payne in *The Bushwhacked Piano*, does not lose momentum. He pulls off a crackpot piece of venture capitalism. Through a series of exchanges, he comes to own Emily's ranch and develops its sulfur spring into a thriving health spa. In short, he becomes rich. In this way Lucien remains unconventional, at the same time—new for a McGuane protagonist—gaining that which is admired by conventional society. Even though McGuane still maneuvers his protagonist through some outlandish paces because of his peripatetic penis, McGuane at the same time imbues Lucien with a sense of purpose higher than sport or making the world tense. Lucien, once his new wealth requires him to bring a semblance of order into his life, begins to want to think of himself as a working man with a family to support.

When Suzanne and James come for a visit, Lucien first attempts to reach James from the security of his own masculine interests. He takes him out to band some hawks. He baits the trap with a live pigeon. When the hawk strikes the pigeon, James screams and crawls off. As Lucien bands the hawk, James shakes. While Lucien admires the hawk, James's natural inclination is to cradle the dead pigeon; he manifests a sense of compassion that his father lacks. The violent world of nature is awful to him. Lucien actually finds himself liking the fact that his son is timid and made of more delicate and sensitive stuff than his father. Still, McGuane is not becoming sentimental. Later, when he understands how nature works, James explains that killing pigeons is how hawks have to live, but the fact remains that James was terrified by the killing. His explanation is not so much an emulation of his father's more hard-boiled ways as it is an acceptance of them as his father's ways. James is actually reaching toward a relationship with his father.

What is important here is that Lucien is attempting to reestablish his family because such a reestablishment would be better for all of them, not only for him alone. Lucien's is one of the few nonselfish acts committed by a McGuane protagonist. He would like not to see the child become a "hostage to oblivion." He wonders how he could leave him unguarded. His reward is that James begins not to fear his father.

Winning back Suzanne, however, is not as easy. She is too skeptical to welcome the sadder-but-wiser protagonist back into her arms. She tells him the truth about himself: He is self-absorbed, insensitive to those who love him, and not worth the effort of reconciliation. Lucien is going to have to recognize her as an independent and worthy person. Before the novel's end, she works through her sense of him as a totally selfish person, but even though she admits to loving Lucien, she is not sure if she is ready to trust him. As she and James drive away from the ranch, she does not look back. She is charting her own course, which may or may not include Lucien.

What is important here is that the McGuane protagonist has progressed through the state of self-absorption with adventure and sport. He has begun to understand that what matters about life is not being "at large" to commit glorious exploits, but being a part of a larger whole that includes the other people in the world. The full life is not lived in furious battle with the forces of conventionality, but in achieving deep and lasting relationships with human beings.

In *Keep the Change*, Joe Starling, Jr., an artist of limited talent, must come to understand this same truth. Chained by the ghost of his father, an overachiever who ultimately dies a failure, the young Starling's life is empty for no reason. He is not satisfied with his various successes as an artist, craftperson, cowboy, or lover, because everything pales in comparison with his expectations for himself. He ricochets among Montana, Florida, and New York City without fully realizing that individual human meaning is something created rather than found.

Two of McGuane's most fully realized female characters offer Starling the possibility of a fully actualized life, but he is too full of himself to seize the opportunity. Ellen Overstreet, a rancher's daughter as wholesome as the new frontier, presents him with the vulnerability of awkward young love. The dynamic Cuban Astrid, whom Starling loves for her outlandishness, sticks by him until he is hopelessly lost in pointlessness. After she leaves him, Starling seems to be beginning to understand that sharing the routine concerns of daily life with Astrid may be the source of true meaning.

Keep the Change signals a new development in McGuane's perception of male competition. Games are no longer seen as means to make sport of conventionality. Joe Starling's rival here is Billy Kelton, an honest and simple, if luckless, cowboy, who marries Ellen Overstreet. Kelton is Starling's physical superior and twice humiliates him with beatings. Violence here is real, not comic, and because it is real, it is bewildering and confusing. Kelton understands that his physical prowess is dehumanizing, and, in facing the struggles of life with his wife and daughter, he shows Starling the importance of a deeper, if simpler, emotional life.

The key to the novel is found in a painting of Montana mountains, the white hills, which hangs in a decaying mansion that once belonged to the most powerful man in the territory. The work itself is indistinguishable: "It had seemed an unblemished canvas until the perplexity of shadows across its surface was seen to be part of the painting." Ultimately, Starling discovers that the shadows are in fact its only real feature. There is no painting; there never has been a painting. Yet "somewhere in the abyss something shone."

That "something" is the meaning Starling seeks. He is the one who determined meaning in the painting and, by extension, in the hills themselves. He must then act to create a life for himself; he must determine his own meaning.

In Thomas McGuane's contemporary West, life is what you make it, nothing more, nothing less. His protagonists must work to fulfill hopes not by going against the grain of the conventional life, but by partaking of its normal flow and by building useful foundations on its undramatic but real joys.

Dexter Westrum

Other major works
SHORT FICTION: *To Skin a Cat*, 1986.

SCREENPLAYS: *Rancho DeLuxe*, 1973; *Ninety-Two in the Shade*, 1975; *The Missouri Breaks*, 1975; *Tom Horn*, 1980 (with Bud Shrake).

NONFICTION: *An Outside Chance: Essays on Sport*, 1980.

Bibliography
Carter, Albert Howard, III. "Thomas McGuane's First Three Novels: Games, Fun, Nemesis." *Critique* 17 (August, 1975): 91-104. Although McGuane's use of the pathos and humor inherent in competition has become decidedly more sophisticated as he has matured, this article is essential for understanding the early novels.

Grant, Kerry. "On and Off the Main Line: The Failure of Compromise in the Fiction of Thomas McGuane." *Mid-American Review* 3 (Spring, 1983): 167-184. This article is a very good explanation of the McGuane protagonist's failure to compromise with reality without first attempting to change the world through the maintenance of a unique self.

McCaffery, Larry. "On Turning Nothing into Something." *Fiction International* 4-5 (Fall/Winter, 1975): 123-129. This accurate introduction to early McGuane argues that his protagonists are transcendent beings because they maintain their ideals—although somewhat absurdly—without succumbing to tedium or despair.

Masinton, Charles G. "*Nobody's Angel*: Thomas McGuane's Vision of the Contemporary West." *New Mexico Humanities Review* 6 (Fall, 1983): 49-55. This article analyzes *Rancho DeLuxe* and *Nobody's Angel* and insightfully concludes that McGuane finds the contemporary West absurd and without hope.

Wallace, Jon. "The Language Plot in Thomas McGuane's *Ninety-Two in the Shade*." *Critique* 29 (Winter, 1988): 111-120. This useful essay determines that the protagonist mixes language codes in order to understand life and self.

_____. "Speaking Against the Dark: Style as Theme in Thomas McGuane's *Nobody's Angel*." *Modern Fiction Studies* 33 (Summer, 1987):

289-298. Asserting that language is McGuane's real concern, the article contends that the narrator is himself a fictional character, who defines the self in a fragmented world through verbal style.

Welch, Dennis M. "Death and Fun in the Novels of Thomas McGuane." *Windsor Review* 14 (Fall/Winter, 1978): 14-20. Although limited to the first three novels, the article successfully argues that the McGuane protagonist maintains his sense of the possibility of life by confronting the world with a purposely playful attitude.

HUGH MACLENNAN

Born: Glace Bay, Nova Scotia, Canada; March 20, 1907
Died: Montreal, Canada; November 7, 1990

Principal long fiction

Barometer Rising, 1941; *Two Solitudes*, 1945; *The Precipice*, 1948; *Each Man's Son*, 1951; *The Watch That Ends the Night*, 1959; *Return of the Sphinx*, 1967; *Voices in Time*, 1980.

Other literary forms

Throughout his career, Hugh MacLennan was a prolific writer of nonfiction. Following his youthful attempts at poetry, and the publication of his dissertation on a Roman colonial settlement in Egypt, *Oxyrhynchus: An Economic and Social Study* (1935, 1968), MacLennan began writing articles, reviews, autobiographical pieces, travel notes, and essays, publishing in a variety of magazines, including *The Montrealer, Maclean's,* and *Holiday.* Journalism sometimes served as a necessary supplement to his income, and occasionally was used to try out material later incorporated into his novels. It has been claimed that his talent finds truer expression in his essays than in his novels; while this may be a questionable judgment, there is no denying the excellence of much of his nonfiction. Selections from the more than four hundred essays that he wrote have been collected in four books, the first two of which won Canada's Governor General Award: *Cross-Country* (1948), *Thirty and Three* (1954), *Scotchman's Return and Other Essays* (1960), and *The Other Side of Hugh MacLennan: Selected Essays Old and New* (1978, Elspeth Cameron, editor). Additionally, his concern for Canada's history and geography has found expression in his *Seven Rivers of Canada* (1961, revised as *Rivers of Canada*, 1974) and *The Colour of Canada* (1967). *Rivers of Canada*, in which MacLennan provided the text to accompany the beautiful photography of John DeVisser, contains some of his best writing.

Achievements

MacLennan, as his biographer, Elspeth Cameron, has observed, "set out to be a writer, not a 'Canadian' writer," yet it was as a Canadian "nationalist" that he was first recognized, and in spite of his intermittent attempts to renounce this label, it was as a distinctively Canadian writer that his career and his reputation developed. He held a solid place as something like the dean of Canadian letters; for many years he was a public figure in Canada, appearing on radio and television, frequently being asked to comment not only on Canadian writing but also on culture generally, and politics. He made continual attempts to tap the American market (with some success, especially with *The Watch That Ends the Night*); his works have been translated into many languages; his last novel, *Voices in Time*, is international in setting, yet MacLennan was thought of both in his own country and elsewhere, as a, perhaps *the*, Canadian novelist.

Having written two unpublished novels with international settings, MacLennan turned to his own Halifax, Nova Scotia, when writing *Barometer Rising*. This first published novel was immediately successful and was praised for its Canadian nationalism. His next novel, *Two Solitudes*, treated the divisions between the English and French cultures in Quebec; the book's title, taken from Rainer Maria Rilke, entered popular usage as a convenient phrase to sum up this cultural schism. MacLennan continued to be hailed for his contributions to defining a Canadian identity. When his third novel, *The Precipice*, attempted to develop an international theme, presenting the love between a Canadian woman and an American man, he met with less critical acceptance. He returned to writing about Nova Scotia in *Each Man's Son*, and followed this with a novel set primarily in Montreal, *The Watch That Ends the Night*. This work was both a critical success and a best-seller, not only in Canada, but also throughout the English-speaking world; it also sold well in translation. MacLennan's reputation as a major novelist was assured; it was bolstered by Edmund Wilson's lavish praise in *O Canada* (1965). Even the many unfavorable reviews of MacLennan's subsequent novel, *Return of the Sphinx*, which treated the Quebec independence movement, did not call into question his importance in Canadian writing. Those who thought this importance was only historical, and that his novelistic powers had passed their peak, were proven wrong by his subsequent and last novel, *Voices in Time*, which was well received even though it clearly transcended Canadian national issues.

As *Voices in Time* suggests, seeing MacLennan in the narrow focus of Canadian nationalism is too limiting. It is certainly true that his work was informed by his nationality, and that younger Canadian writers owe a debt to his pioneering treatment of Canadian themes. It is also true that his achievement must be primarily judged thematically. While he was competent in plotting and occasionally excellent in characterization, these were not his strong points. He was a conservative novelist in craft, contributing no new forms to the genre, although his own technique did develop, especially in his use of point of view and manipulation of time.

Granting that MacLennan emphasizes theme and wrote out of his Canadian experience, his relationship to Canada can be best understood, however, if he is seen not as a nationalist or a local colorist, but rather as a writer who used his Canadian background to put into perspective his political, social, and psychological ideas, and to reinforce his sense of history. It is essentially as a creator of novels of ideas that MacLennan bids fair to appeal to future generations of readers around the world.

Biography

John Hugh MacLennan was born in Glace Bay, Cape Breton, Nova Scotia, on March 20, 1907. He drew on his memories of this birthplace, a coalmining company town set at the edge of the Atlantic, explicitly in *Each Man's Son*, but his impressions of the seagirt land, a topography appropriate to the Scottish Highland character which was his heritage, entered, less directly, into much of his work. In this setting, his father practiced medicine among the miners. A dominating figure, "the Doctor" was to become the prototype of a number of characters in his son's novels.

In 1915, when MacLennan was eight, the family moved to Halifax, a venerable but lively port which fascinated the boy. The small city, with its sense of community, became a lifelong ideal for MacLennan, as did the contrasting beauty of the Cape Breton countryside where the family spent time in the summer, prefiguring the thematic retreat to the woods of many of MacLennan's fictional characters. As recounted in *Barometer Rising*, much of Halifax was destroyed by an explosion in 1917, but the city was rebuilt, and MacLennan was reared there, doing well in both studies and sports, and was graduated from Dalhousie University in 1928.

Later in that year, a Rhodes scholarship allowed him to attend Oxford. While there he played rugger and tennis; an excellent athlete, MacLennan, as a novelist, frequently used sports to reveal character. At Oxford, he also wrote poetry and traveled extensively, during vacations, on the Continent. These holidays, especially those to Germany, were drawn upon in his first two, unpublished, novels, and returned to in *Voices in Time*, and some of his own experiences from this time were used in creating those of his character, Paul, in *Two Solitudes*.

MacLennan also studied at Oxford, quite diligently in fact, and was graduated in 1932, proceeding to graduate studies at Princeton. Returning to England, he met, on the ship, an American, Dorothy Duncan, who was to become his first wife. His developing love and his new devotion to becoming a novelist absorbed more of his attention than did his studies. While he did not find Princeton congenial, he completed his Ph.D. in history, with a dissertation discussing the Roman colonial settlement at Oxyrhynchus in Egypt.

In 1935, in the midst of the Depression, MacLennan's degree was not able to secure for him the university teaching position he desired; he accepted a job teaching at Lower Canada College, a boys' school in Montreal. (He was to give a fictionalized satiric portrait of the school in *The Watch That Ends the Night*.) After a year at the school, he married Dorothy Duncan and settled into a life of working as a schoolmaster during the day and writing at night, sinking in roots as a Montrealer, which he has remained.

His first novel, "So All Their Praises," had been completed while MacLennan was at Princeton; it was accepted by a publisher that ceased operation before the book was published. His second novel, "A Man Should Rejoice," suffered a similar fate in 1938; its publication was postponed and finally dropped. These novels, the first owing a debt to Ernest Hemingway, the second to John Dos Passos, although never published, have their virtues. They both present comments on the political situation preceding World War II and employ international settings.

For his next novel, MacLennan turned, upon his wife's suggestion, to Canada. *Barometer Rising* is set in Halifax in 1917. It was an immediate success. MacLennan continued his teaching and writing career in Montreal; a problem with an ear kept him out of the war. After the success of his second published novel, *Two Solitudes*, and the establishment, additionally, of his wife's successful career as a writer (Dorothy Duncan published nonfiction; one of her books, *Partner in Three Worlds*, 1944, won the Governor General's Award for nonfiction), he resigned from Lower Canada College in 1945. Following a period of journalism and broadcasting and the publication of *The Precipice*, in 1951 he took a part-time position teaching in the English department at McGill University; he assumed a full-time post in 1964, becoming professor emeritus in 1979.

During the years in which he was establishing himself as a writer in Montreal, publishing *Cross-Country*, *Each Man's Son*, and *Thirty and Three* (a period described in *The Watch That Ends the Night*), his wife's declining health—she suffered a series of embolisms—added greatly to the pressures he experienced. Dorothy Duncan died in 1957. MacLennan dedicated *The Watch That Ends the Night* to her; the novel, originally entitled *Requiem*, has as its heroine a figure whose characterization owes much to Dorothy Duncan. MacLennan married Frances Walker in 1959, and after a period of producing nonfiction—*Scotchman's Return and Other Essays*, *McGill: The Story of a University* (1960, edited), *Seven Rivers of Canada*—wrote *Return of the Sphinx*. This novel was unfavorably reviewed by a number of Canadian critics, but MacLennan continued to receive numerous honorary degrees and public recognition. He began consideration of another novel, but interrupted work on it to write *Rivers of Canada*. His last novel, *Voices in Time*, appeared to favorable reviews in 1980. In 1982, MacLennan retired from McGill, after more than thirty years of teaching there. He died in Montreal on November 7, 1990, at the age of eighty-three.

Analysis

Hugh MacLennan began as a historian and throughout his long writing career he had, in a sense, remained one. His doctoral dissertation, *Oxyrhynchus*, discussing the history of an area in Egypt during the seven hundred years that it was subject to the Roman Empire, foreshadowed such major themes in his novels as colonialism, the wanderer, the town-country antithesis, and geographical determinism. Underlying both the dissertation and the novels is a view of historical causality.

As Erich Auerbach has remarked, "Basically, the way in which we view human life and society is the same whether we are concerned with things of the past or things of the present"; a corollary of this may be that when a writer is, like MacLennan, both a historian and a novelist, his narratives of individual human lives will be shaped by larger forces which transcend the concerns of the psychological novelist. In MacLennan's fiction, geography is preeminently such a force.

In both his fiction and his nonfiction, MacLennan had a continual concern for the impact of geography upon character, and thus, as people make history, upon action, fictive or historical. That a Canadian, living in a frequently harsh terrain and climate, would appreciate the significance of geography is hardly surprising, but MacLennan went further, adopting a geographical theory of history. His sense of geography's interaction with psychology and history provides the ideological framework that, more than any other single factor, gives his work its distinctive character. This framework is especially useful to MacLennan as a way of putting into perspective his personal experience, for he drew less upon "pure" invention than do many novelists. His method, in both his essays and his novels, was to use personal experience to support general and philosophical concepts.

This means that, fundamentally, MacLennan wrote novels of ideas; it does not mean, however, that his ideas were necessarily free from self-contradiction, or that they remained entirely consistent throughout his career. His ideology, complex but ultimately growing from a sense of the fundamental importance of geography, is most explicit in his first three published novels, in which he worked toward a definition of Canadian identity by first contrasting Canada to England (*Barometer Rising*), then dealing with the potentials of Canadian unity (*Two Solitudes*), and finally differentiating Canada from the United States (*The Precipice*). The next novel, *Each Man's Son*, is transitional in that it conveys a strong sense of the land, Cape Breton in this case, while anticipating the greater interest in psychology that characterized his subsequent novels. Even in these later novels, however, history as geography remains a basic concept. While psychological concepts became more important to Mac-Lennan, he employed topographical images to express this interest.

Character, then, in a MacLennan novel is closely related to theme, as is plot, and the theme is tied to setting. While he created a fairly wide range of characters, including some minor figures that are presented with Dickensian humor, the central focus in his characterization was either in the "love-interest" or in a conflict of generations. Both of these recurring motifs are normally subservient to theme, in that the characters, whether they come together in love, as, for example, Paul and Heather in *Two Solitudes*, or stand apart in years, as do Alan Ainslie and his son in *Return of the Sphinx*, represent different value-systems or cultures. Their psychology, which motivates their interactions, is seen in terms of their conditioning by history and, ultimately, by geography.

Admittedly, this emphasis is modified, especially in the later novels, by MacLennan's concern with various ideological factors, such as Calvinism in *Each Man's Son*, and by his interest in psychological theories, especially Freudianism, particularly notable in *Return of the Sphinx*. Nevertheless, similar imagery and recurring motifs, reflecting a sense of historical causation, run through both his earlier and later works. One finds, for example, the antithesis between the city and the country; the retreat into the woods; the theme of the wanderer, exiled from his roots; frequent references to weather; and imagery of trees, gardens, and water, in all of his novels.

MacLennan's novelistic techniques did change, however, as he developed his craft, as can be seen in his plotting, use of point of view, and style. In plotting, as in many aspects of his craft, MacLennan was old-fashioned; he kept the reader interested in how the story will come out. MacLennan was by nature given to relatively happy endings, but after the upbeat conclusions characterizing his first three novels, his optimism became tempered, appearing more as a coda following climatic elements of tragedy in *Each Man's Son*, *The Watch That Ends the Night*, and *Return of the Sphinx*. *Voices in Time* has a series of climaxes occurring at different points in the novel and producing different effects on the reader. That MacLennan was able to unify the various narratives included in this, the most complex of his works in its plotting, is an indication of the development of his craftsmanship.

His ability to manipulate increasingly complex narrative patterns is closely related to his mastery of point of view. Although none of MacLennan's novels approaches a Jamesian concern for this aspect of the art of fiction, with *The Watch That Ends the Night*, as he moved away from straightforward chronological sequences, he slipped skillfully between first- and third-person narration. *Return of the Sphinx* uses third-person narration but with a shifting between the viewpoints of different characters. This novel, however, lacks what Henry James called "a fine central intelligence." Alan Ainslie does not provide this unifying quality as effectively as does John Wellfleet in *Voices in Time*; Wellfleet's perspective gives coherence to the novel's varied narrative strands.

As MacLennan's ability to structure his novels developed, slowly and within a fairly conventional framework, yet with increasing skill in his craft, so did his style mature. His earlier novels exhibited some tendency toward overwriting. *Barometer Rising* has "set-pieces" that skirt the borders of sentimentality; *Two Solitudes* is sometimes verbose; *The Precipice* is not free from clichéd expression. In *Each Man's Son*, the style, reflecting the dramatic structure, is tightened. *The Watch That Ends the Night* contains superior passages of description, although the dialogue (never one of MacLennan's strengths) occasionally shows some of the stilted qualities of the earlier novels. *Return of the Sphinx* is notable for its economy of style, and in this respect prepares for *Voices in Time*, in which MacLennan's style is the most fully unself-conscious and "organic."

MacLennan, then, is a novelist who may be read for the pleasure to be found in an interesting story well told, but he remains a writer less likely to be remembered as a storyteller or fictional craftsman than as a man of ideas, a dramatizer of history.

When, following his wife's advice to write of that which he knew best, MacLennan turned to his hometown, Halifax, and he used it not only as the novel's setting but also as its subject. In *Barometer Rising*, he was also writing of Canada; Halifax, with its colonial attitudes overlaying social and ideological divisions, is a microcosm of a new Canada. The book's title is in large part explained in a subsequent essay, in which MacLennan describes Halifax as a barometer for the whole country.

Yet what goes up must have been down; if the barometer rises, if, by implication, Canada faces a halcyon future, it does so only after a great storm and a particularly violent stroke of lightning. The action of *Barometer Rising* is centered on an actual historical event, the blast that occurred when a munitions ship exploded in Halifax harbor on December 6, 1917. The largest single man-made explosion before Hiroshima, it destroyed a major portion of the town and killed some two thousand people.

A result of Halifax's role in World War I, the explosion is also symbolically related to Canada's involvement in that bloody conflict. While the concurrent destruction of life, property, and outworn colonial beliefs—the old world dying with a monstrous bang—constitutes the core of the book, a number of other motifs are woven into its thematic patterns. The conflict of generations, the return of the wanderer and the Odysseus theme, the psychological aspects of technological change—these are all important elements of the novel that continued to reverberate in MacLennan's subsequent work. Underlying all the thematic strands is the author's view of historical process, a view that puts a strong emphasis upon the conditioning significance of physical geography.

It is Halifax's geographical situation that underlies the book's basic contrast, that between old and new Canada, colony and country. The harbor gives the town its meaning; facing away from the rest of Canada, Halifax looks toward Britain and the Continent, both in a literal and a figurative sense. From the topographical facts, carefully elaborated at the beginning of the novel, derive the prevailing attitudes of the Haligonians: it is the preservation of England that motivates all of what happens in Halifax; the colonial mentality prevails. Had the geography been different, the town's development and activity would have been different, and, consequently, its people would have been different.

Yet if geography is destiny, there is no rigid determinism in MacLennan's view of that destiny. Halifax, although pointed toward Britain physically and thus psychologically as well, is part of the New World, and has, therefore, the potential for a different orientation. This reorientation follows from the book's central event, the explosion, an event which, while the result of accident, is influenced by topography, in both cause and effect. The explosion is a result of the collision, in Halifax harbor, of a munitions ship with a Norwegian freighter; the crash occurs because the physical nature of the harbor limits visibility. As a result of the destruction, new values arise from the rubble of the old; Halifax is no longer dominated by the rigid ideas of its old colonial aristocracy.

While the story has this allegorical quality, with a message made explicit in a concluding passage on what might be termed Canada's "manifest destiny," its allegory is fleshed out with particular, three-dimensional characters, conditioned by geography and history, but living out their private lives within the interstices of that conditioning framework.

Neil Macrae, the book's hero, is, like Odysseus, a soldier returned from the war, bearing an assumed identity acquired after he was falsely accused of disobeying an order during an attack in which he was thought to have been killed. His accuser is the novel's villain, Colonel Wain, representative of the old order, and father of Penelope—whose Homeric name is intentional—the heroine with whom Neil is in love. The cast is completed by a number of skillfully drawn secondary characters derived from MacLennan's memories, including Penny's younger brother Roddie, modeled on MacLennan himself, and Angus Murray, also in love with Penny, the first in a series of heroic doctors who appear in MacLennan's novels.

Following the explosion and the vindication of Neil's conduct during the attack in France (the outcome of the battle depending, just as does the collision in the harbor, on terrain), Neil and Penelope are finally united; the storm is over, and the future is bright. While the novel is marred by this rather facile happy ending and by its general didacticism, the basic interest in both action and character, reinforced with symbolism, makes *Barometer Rising* artistically satisfying. Although MacLennan was to write more subtly in future novels, *Barometer Rising*, representing clearly his basic approach, fiction as dramatized history, remains one of his best achievements.

MacLennan's next two novels also used a love story to express theme and continued to demonstrate his interest in the impact of geography upon the character of a people. *Two Solitudes*, centered upon the romance between Paul Tallard and Heather Methuen, begins with a description of the landscape of Quebec; throughout, the symbolism of the river, the forest, and the town reinforces the theme of the relationship of the English and French in Quebec. *The Precipice*, with its love affair between a Canadian woman and an American man, contrasts Canada and the United States by relating the character of the peoples to their respective terrains. Set primarily in Ontario, the novel uses Lake Ontario as a dominant symbol, reinforced by references to weather, gardens, the city, and other prevalent MacLennan imagery.

Similar imagery informs *Each Man's Son*; thematic conflicts are drawn between two sides of the Scottish Highland character, between religion as a sense of sin and religion as inspiration, and between science and superstition, particularly focused through the contrast between the mines and the sea of Cape Breton. A major turning point in the plot occurs when Dr. Ainslie (whose name is taken from a Cape Breton place-name) gives his to-be-adopted son, Alan, a lesson in history, followed by one in geography.

Arguably MacLennan's best novel, *The Watch That Ends the Night* demonstrates a significant advance in his technique. The didactic quality of his earlier novels is reduced; the imagery becomes more involved, as does the handling of time; characters take on more interest, not as symbols, but in their own right. Concurrently, the sense of the formative power of geography upon character is moved more to the background, as though Canada, having been conditioned by geography, is able to go beyond this conditioning. Nevertheless, in this, as in all his novels, MacLennan writes from essentially the same perspective on history and employs many of the same patterns in fictional construction.

Again, just as in the earlier novels, the book is based on a strong sense of place, in this case Montreal, described in memorable, often loving detail. Again, the plot centers upon a love interest, a triangle involving George Stewart, who has autobiographical connections with MacLennan; Jerome Martell, a doctor with mythic qualities; and Catherine Carey, a remarkable woman (who takes on, for Canada, some of the symbolism Kathleen ni Houlihan did for Ireland) whose portrait owes something to MacLennan's wife Dorothy. George loves Catherine, but she marries Martell. After Martell is thought to have been killed by the Nazis, Catherine and George eventually marry, but, much later, Martell reappears. (The story begins at this point, and is told primarily through flashbacks.) Although Catherine stays with George, suffering a heart condition, she has little time left to live.

Within this framework, MacLennan presents a rich picture, with numerous well realized minor characters, of Montreal during the Depression and during the time of the Korean War. For all his interest in psychology in this work, it is, as are all his novels, less a "novel of character" than a working out, through characters, of ideas, and a dramatization of social-historical processes. While the plot (except in the New Brunswick section) does not hinge on terrain, the imagery does. Images derived from nature control much of the book's tone, with references to rivers and oceans particularly important. In *The Watch That Ends the Night*, MacLennan moved beyond any mechanistic application of historical theory to the novel; he did not, however, change his fundamental view of the forces underlying human events.

His next novel, *Return of the Sphinx*, reintroduced Alan, from *Each Man's Son*, now a grown man with his own son. Dealing, on the surface, with events of the Quebec liberation movement in the 1960's, it is set mainly in Montreal and Ottawa, but contains a "retreat to the woods" section and begins with an explicit statement of the impact of geography and weather upon culture; it ends with images of the land. Beneath the political action lies a deeper psychological theme, in essence that of the Oedipus complex, as MacLennan extends in this novel his interest in psychological theory, begun in *Each Man's Son* and continued in *The Watch That Ends the Night*; he also extends his use of imagery derived from nature and geography to express psychological states.

In MacLennan's final novel, *Voices in Time*, his lifelong interest in the perspective provided by history is obvious and central to the book's structure. Indeed, the direct, albeit complicated manner in which this interest informs the novel may be a key to its success. MacLennan's focus on history was always essentially pragmatic—to use the past to understand the present and anticipate the future; this is what *Voices in Time* undertakes.

The book intertwines the story of three men from three different generations: Conrad Dehmel, born in Germany in 1910, a concentration-camp survivor; Timothy Wellfleet, a Canadian born in 1938 who becomes a television interviewer; and John Wellfleet, another Canadian, born in 1964. John Wellfleet is the central narrator. He is one of the few humans who has lived through the "Destructions" of atomic explosions, and when the novel opens in 2039, he is approached by the young André Gervais, who has found materials related to Wellfleet's family and wants the old man to use them to reconstruct the past that has, in effect, been destroyed for Gervais and his friends. Wellfleet works out Dehmel's story, involving opposition to Hitler and love for a Jewish woman, and finds it subsequently connecting to Dehmel's stepson Timothy, who interviews Dehmel on television in 1970. As a result of the interview, during which Timothy accuses Dehmel of having been a Nazi, Dehmel is assassinated.

Obviously, the presentation of this material, these voices from different times, calls for a complicated structure: Timothy's story is told by John Wellfleet; Dehmel's by both Wellfleet and, through diaries, by himself; and Wellfleet's own story is concluded by Gervais. The time scheme moves from 2039, to the late 1960's, to 1909, to 1918-1919, to 1932-1945, to a climax in 1970, and finally to 2044.

Like the time scheme, MacLennan's view of causation which underlies this historical presentation is intricate, especially as compared to *Barometer Rising* and his earlier novels. Nevertheless, his belief in the significance of geography, nature, and landscape in motivating character can still be seen, even though the landscape has become primarily urban, and character may be formed, or deformed, by *separation* from fundamental geography. Nature continues to provide MacLennan with a thematic contrast to the urban, technological environment and to be a source of much of his imagery. Timothy is cut off, in his technological world, from natural geography; at nineteen thousand feet, he flies over the woods his father's generation had known intimately. Dehmel finds a temporary salvation, in both the world wars, in Germany's Black

Forest. John Wellfleet lives on the outskirts of what was once Montreal, with trees, flowers, and birds. Drawing upon Walt Whitman, MacLennan uses lilacs and a star to make a contrast with urban technology and its sense of time; he has Wellfleet think of the "time-clocks" of plants and birds. In one key passage, civilization is compared to a garden. Most significantly, perhaps, when compared to the thoughts about civilization, its rise and fall, and time, which MacLennan presents in *Rivers of Canada*, is the mentioning of rivers, as when, for example, the cautious optimism that tempers the tragic events narrated in *Voices in Time* is symbolized by the return of salmon to the St. Lawrence River.

Voices in Time was MacLennan's final novel and was a fitting climax to a successful career. It indicated that although he assuredly has a major position in the history of Canadian letters, he was one of those novelists who, although solidly rooted in time and place, transcended both. His ability to dramatize his geographical sense of history suggests that MacLennan is a writer who will continue to speak to future generations, to be, himself, a voice not stilled by time.

William B. Stone

Other major works

NONFICTION: *Oxyrhynchus: An Economic and Social Study*, 1935, 1968; *Cross-Country*, 1948; *Thirty and Three*, 1954; *Scotchman's Return and Other Essays*, 1960; *McGill: The Story of a University*, 1960 (edited); *Seven Rivers of Canada*, 1961 (revised as *Rivers of Canada*, 1974); *The Colour of Canada*, 1967; *The Other Side of Hugh MacLennan: Selected Essays Old and New*, 1978 (Elspeth Cameron, editor); *On Being a Maritime Writer*, 1984.

Bibliography

Buitenhuis, Peter. *Hugh MacLennan*. Edited by William French. Toronto: Forum House, 1969. Contains a biography of MacLennan, critical analyses of his six novels and his nonfiction, and a bibliography. In general, Buitenhuis supports MacLennan's preoccupation with Canadian nationhood. The assessment of MacLennan's strengths and weaknesses as a writer is even-handed but somewhat too academic.

Cockburn, Robert. *The Novels of Hugh MacLennan*. Montreal: Harvest House, 1969. Contains an introduction, a chapter on each of MacLennan's six novels, and a conclusion. Cockburn takes MacLennan to task for subordinating character to theme (especially that of the search for a "Canadian" identity) and for allowing his didacticism to overwhelm his narrative. A bibliography of primary and secondary sources is included.

Lucas, Alec. *Hugh MacLennan*. Canadian Writers 8. Toronto: McClelland and Stewart, 1970. Each chapter addresses a different component of Mac-

Lennan's vision, in general, and social morality, in particular. The introduction, conclusion, and a bibliography comprise the rest of this clear assessment of MacLennan's fiction and essays.

Twigg, Alan. "Hugh MacLennan." In *Strong Voices: Conversations with Fifty Canadian Authors*. Madeira Park, British Columbia: Harbour, 1988. This absorbing 1979 interview focuses mainly on MacLennan's lifelong interest in Canadian nationhood and the influence of that interest on his writing.

Woodcock, George. *Hugh MacLennan's "Barometer Rising": A Reader's Guide by George Woodcock*. Canadian Fiction Studies 2. Toronto: ECW Press, 1989. This careful, instructive methodology for reading the novel also includes a chronology of MacLennan's life and publications, biographical details, an assessment of MacLennan's place in Canadian literature, and a partially annotated "Works Cited."

_____. "Surrogate Fathers and Orphan Sons: The Novels of Hugh MacLennan." In *Northern Spring: The Flowering of Canadian Literature*. Vancouver, British Columbia: Douglas & McIntyre, 1987. In this essay from his two-part book on Canadian prose writers and poets, Woodcock examines what he perceives in MacLennan's writing as a central metaphor for the definition of "Canadian" nation: a generational theme. Also discusses the strongly didactic element that pervades MacLennan's works.

LARRY McMURTRY

Born: Wichita Falls, Texas; June 3, 1936

Principal long fiction
Horseman, Pass By, 1961; *Leaving Cheyenne,* 1963; *The Last Picture Show,* 1966; *Moving On,* 1970; *All My Friends Are Going to Be Strangers,* 1972; *Terms of Endearment,* 1975; *Somebody's Darling,* 1978; *Cadillac Jack,* 1982; *The Desert Rose,* 1983; *Lonesome Dove,* 1985; *Texasville,* 1987; *Anything for Billy,* 1988; *Some Can Whistle,* 1989; *Buffalo Girls,* 1990.

Other literary forms
In a Narrow Grave (1968) is a collection of nine essays Larry McMurtry wrote for various periodicals, mostly concerning Texas. He collaborated on the script for the motion picture of his novel *The Last Picture Show* (1971) and has written other scripts. In 1975-1976 he wrote monthly articles for *American Film* magazine, some of which were collected in *Film Flam: Essays on Hollywood* (1987).

Achievements
McMurtry's early reputation was based on his depiction of hard modern times in North Texas. *Horseman, Pass By, Leaving Cheyenne,* and *The Last Picture Show* are all located in that area, where the frontier and the old ranching way of life were disappearing while McMurtry was growing up. The second group of three novels, *Moving On, All My Friends Are Going to Be Strangers,* and *Terms of Endearment,* concerns an interrelated group of characters in the Houston area and focuses primarily on failed marriages. McMurtry's Pulitzer Prize and his greatest public success, however, came with his first venture into the traditional Western, his novel of the frontier past, *Lonesome Dove,* considered by many critics to be his finest achievement and the finest novel ever written in that form.

Biography
Larry Jeff McMurtry was born in Wichita Falls, Texas, in 1936, grandson of a pioneer cattleman in North Texas and one of four children of a ranching family. McMurtry grew up on the ranch, was graduated from high school in Archer City, Texas, the locale of much of his early fiction, in 1954, and after one semester at Rice University attended North Texas State University, from which he was graduated in 1958. He was married to Josephine Ballard in 1959; the marriage, which produced one son, ended in divorce in 1966.

McMurtry went back to Rice as a graduate student in English in 1958, beginning work on his first two novels. *Horseman, Pass By* was accepted for publication while he was at Rice and was published while he was a writing student at Stanford University in 1961. Between 1961 and 1969 he taught off and on at Texas Christian University and at Rice, while two more novels were published and he worked on his first long novel, *Moving On*. He had worked occasionally as a book scout for California bookstores while at Stanford, and in 1969 McMurtry left Houston and moved to Washington, D.C., where he became a partner in a bookstore. Since then he has divided his time between the store and his writing.

Many of McMurtry's books have been made into motion pictures, most notably *Hud* (1963; the screen name of *Horseman, Pass By*), *The Last Picture Show*, which was filmed by Peter Bogdanovich in Archer City, and *Terms of Endearment* (1983). Actresses and actors in all these films (Patricia Neal, Cloris Leachman, Shirley MacLaine, and Jack Nicholson) won Oscars for their performances. *Lonesome Dove* was made into a major miniseries for television, with Robert Duval and Tommy Lee Jones in the major roles. A film version of *Texasville* was released in 1990. McMurtry has chosen to lead a quiet life, devoted mostly to his two professions and avoiding talk shows and gossip columns.

Analysis

Larry McMurtry's best fiction has used the Southwest as its location and the characters typical of that area for its subjects. In the early years of his career he dealt with life in the dying towns and decaying ranches of North and West Texas, often using boys on the brink of manhood to provide perspective on a way of life that had reached a stage of corruption and betrayal. His trilogy, following these early novels, dealt with the tangled relationships among somewhat older characters and reflected McMurtry's own move from Archer City to Houston. Later, he invested the Western novel with new vigor in two novels, his classic *Lonesome Dove* and the satiric *Anything for Billy*, which holds the legend of Billy the Kid up to ridicule.

McMurtry has used a variety of styles, from the elegiac to the rapid narrative, from the hilarious to the mournful. He has shown an unusual ability to depict interesting and sometimes outrageous characters, especially women. While his fictional locales moved away from Texas for a time, in his later works he has gone back to the settings and sometimes the characters of his earlier works. A regional writer, he has transcended the usual limitations of regional writers and attracted a broad audience.

McMurtry himself eventually said that *Horseman, Pass By*, published when he was only twenty-two, was an immature work. This first novel, a story of ranch life, narrated by a seventeen-year-old boy whose grandfather's livelihood and life are ended when his herd of cattle must be destroyed, sets many of McMurtry's themes: the ease with which people learn to betray others, in this case the old man's betrayal by Hud, his stepson; the mental and physical wear inflicted by the harsh Texas land; and the importance of the affection an older woman (in this case the Bannon family's black cook, Halmea) can give to a young man. This novel and McMurtry's next, *Leaving Cheyenne*, are clearly preparations for the success of *The Last Picture Show*.

McMurtry's third novel is set in the small, dying North Texas town of Thalia (there is a town with that name in Texas, but its geography does not fit the fictional town, which is clearly modeled on Archer City). Its central characters are Sonny Crawford and Duane Moore, two boys in their last year of high school. Neither is in fact an orphan, but neither lives with his surviving parent; they rent rooms in the town's rooming house, support themselves working in the oil fields, and hang out at the town's pool hall, run by their aging friend and mentor Sam the Lion. In the course of about six months, Duane and Sonny learn hard lessons about life and love.

Sonny is the more sensitive of the two. He falls into a passionate affair with Ruth Popper, the frustrated and lonely wife of the high school athletic coach, a stock figure whose latent homosexuality is masked by an aggressive masculinity in the presence of his athletes. Ruth begins the affair in desperation and is startled by the depth of her feeling for Sonny, while the boy is surprised and gratified by the experience. Both realize that the affair cannot last, but Ruth is devastated when Sonny leaves her at the invitation of the town's reigning beauty, Jacy Farrow.

Jacy has been Duane's girlfriend, a monster of selfishness who plays games with both Sonny and Duane, almost destroying their friendship. She keeps putting off Duane's demands that she marry him and insists on seeing another young man and going with him to wild parties in Wichita Falls. When Duane leaves town to work in the oil fields, Jacy decides to take Sonny away from Ruth Popper. Duane finds out, fights with Sonny, and blinds his friend in one eye by hitting him with a beer bottle. Jacy convinces Sonny to elope with her as an adventure, arranging matters so that her father will stop them before they are actually married. Jacy's wise and experienced mother, Lois, offers Sonny brief consolation and shows him that he must make peace with Ruth Popper.

The boys' adventures have been made possible by the wise counsel and care of Sam the Lion. He has taught them about life, given them parental refuge, and showed them the limits of behavior by closing them out when they are involved in the mistreatment of his retarded ward, Billy. The safety of their world is shattered when Sam dies suddenly, leaving his pool hall and restaurant in the care of Sonny. The young man is forced to face the cruelty of the world when Billy, sweeping the streets of Thalia in his customary way, is hit and killed by a passing truck. The boys are reconciled when Duane leaves to join the army and fight in Korea.

The Last Picture Show, named for the film theater that is forced to close, symbolizing the decay of Thalia, is a compound of nostalgia, harsh realism, and tragedy. It deals with the inevitable loss of innocence of its central characters and with the hard realities of injury, loss, and death. It is frank about sex (Australian authorities banned the novel at one time), but it makes clear the price Sonny and Ruth Popper pay for their affair. At the same time, its depiction of adolescence is often amusing and colorful; the boys take off on a wild adventure south through Texas and into Mexico, they enjoy playing bad basketball for an increasingly frustrated Coach Popper, they enjoy earning their own livings. With the exception of the incident involving the joke played on Billy, they do harm only to themselves.

The Last Picture Show shows the meanness of the people in a small town: Ruth Popper is scorned for loving a boy much younger than herself; the sheriff and other observers are callously indifferent when Billy is killed; Sam the Lion has had to live without the love of his life, Lois Farrow, because of the mores of the town; the coach, despite his poor teams and his general ignorance and stupidity, is looked up to and admired by most of the town. Duane, the more conventional of the two central figures, is sometimes a bully and sometimes a fool.

There is a kind of soft quality to the novel, nevertheless. Most of those the boys encounter are sympathetic to them, including the waitress in Sam's café, the woman who is forced to close the theater, Ruth Popper, and Sam himself. They have no parents, but there are plenty of surrogates to guide and care for them, and they seem always to be forgiven by those they have hurt. Billy carries no grudge against either of them, Sam eventually shows that Sonny has done his penance, and even Ruth forgives Sonny for leaving her. Duane is hard enough not to need forgiveness.

McMurtry revived Thalia, Sonny, and Duane in *Texasville*, a comic look at Thalia after it has experienced the boom of high oil prices and then been hit by the oil depression of the early 1980's. In *Texasville* Sonny recedes into the background, a forgetful and lonely middle-aged man who seems to suffer from something like premature Alzheimer's disease. The focus is on Duane, whose oil business has gone to pot, whose marriage to Karla (a new character) is in deep trouble, and whose love life and civic responsibilities provide material for comedy. His life is further complicated by the return to Thalia of Jacy, thrice-married film starlet, mother of three children, saddened and made more human by the death of her young son. *Texasville* is longer, more comic, and more complicated than *The Last Picture Show*, but it is less affecting. Only an episode in which Sonny wanders off and is found sitting in the wreckage of the old theater recalls the tone of the earlier novel.

The Last Picture Show was McMurtry's sometimes bitter, sometimes nostalgic farewell to the North Texas setting of his early work. The next stage in his career focused on young people in the Houston area, beginning with *Moving On*, a long depiction of the damage wrought by a marriage that is falling apart, and a sad picture of university life and the lives of traveling rodeo performers. This second phase of McMurtry's career ended with *Terms of Endearment*, the story of a lively widow and her troubled daughter, who eventually dies of cancer.

Typifying this stage is *All My Friends Are Going to Be Strangers*, a novel held together only by the central character and narrator, Danny Deck, who was introduced in *Moving On*. Danny's experience is to some extent based on that of his creator. Early in the book, while he is a graduate student at Rice, Danny's first novel is accepted for publication. In the euphoric mood that follows, he leaves Rice, marries Sally, a beautiful and sexy young woman who holds no other interest for Danny and who proves to be a monster. Her former lover accompanies them part of the way to California, leaving after they survive a flash flood in West Texas. Once the couple has moved to San Francisco and Sally has become pregnant, she relieves her boredom by engaging in an affair with a blind musician and pushes Danny out of her life. Danny goes downhill, lives in a rundown hotel, and finds himself unable to do satisfactory work on his second novel.

Jill, a brilliant film cartoonist he meets on a brief excursion to Hollywood, pulls Danny out of his slump and lives with him for a while, setting his life in order. Temporarily he thinks that he has found the love of his life, and his writing is stimulated by an idea she has provided. Jill, however, has lost interest in sex (which seems to be Danny's chief interest), and their relationship deteriorates until she leaves him to return to Hollywood and Danny sets out for Texas.

The episodic nature of *All My Friends Are Going to Be Strangers* continues when Danny returns to Texas. He pays a visit to his Uncle L, providing a satiric picture of an old-time cowboy gone eccentric; he returns to Houston and makes love to various women, including Emma, the wife of his best friend, and Jenny, who had been his landlady; he goes through a nightmarish experience signing copies of his book at a bookstore; he has a horrible, violent encounter with Sally's parents, who prevent him from seeing his newborn daughter; he is harassed and cruelly beaten by two Texas Rangers who take a dislike to his long hair. He goes for several days without any real sleep. In the end he walks into the Rio Grande, pushing the manuscript pages of his new novel under the water and possibly intending to commit suicide by drowning; that is never clear.

Danny's experiences are intended to show the dislocating effects of early success on a young man who has cut himself off from his roots and has become unable to establish real connections with any other human beings. He falls in love easily enough, but neither Sally nor Jill can return his love in the way he needs, and he has no way to extend his brief affair with Jenny. His encounter with Emma can lead only to guilty feelings for both of them.

Danny is just as much at sea in the other kinds of life he experiences. The editor of his publishing house takes him briefly into a world of authors and sophisticates in which he feels himself to be totally out of place. His brief experience in Hollywood exposes him to people who mystify and amaze him, but for whom he has no respect. He twice pays brief visits to the Stanford campus where McMurtry spent two years, but what he gets from those experiences is the knowledge that he enjoys taking drugs and that he is no scholar. Uncle L shows him that there is nothing for him in ranching life, and the professor from whom he took Sally in the beginning makes it clear that the professorial life is dull and unrewarding.

All My Friends Are Going to Be Strangers is a depressing book. Danny Deck is neither admirable nor particularly amusing. The book is saved by two things. One is McMurtry's undoubted skill as a writer, which enables him to describe scenes as disparate as the flash flood, Uncle L's encounter with his wife, and a literary party in a posh San Francisco suburb vividly and entertainingly. The other is the presence of several interesting minor characters, from Wu, the exiled Chinese writer who admires Danny's work and plays table tennis with him, to Mr. Stay, the former-Communist bookstore owner and sonnet writer who hosts the book-signing party. Several of the women, including Jill, Emma, and Jenny, are memorable and distinctive. The novel suggests, however, that his Houston years did not provide the material or the inspiration for McMurtry's best fiction.

In a much later work, Danny Deck proves not to have killed himself: McMurtry brings him back in *Some Can Whistle* as a successful middle-aged writer who has chosen to live in relative isolation. He finds the daughter he has never known, T. R., and brings her and her two children to live with him. She is lively, engaging, and interesting; for a while she seems to be able to revive Danny's wish to be in closer touch with other human beings, but in the end, when T. R. is suddenly killed, the habits of his lifetime are too strong. He has not changed enough from his earlier self.

McMurtry, in the group of novels which followed *All My Friends Are Going to Be Strangers*, seemed to be trying to demonstrate that he could write successful novels that had nothing to do with Texas or with the life of a writer. The brief satiric glimpse of Hollywood given in *All My Friends Are Going to Be Strangers* was expanded in *Somebody's Darling*, whose central character is a film director trying to cope with her early success and the demands of two men she loves. The world McMurtry entered as a bookstore owner is reflected obliquely in *Cadillac Jack*, whose protagonist is an itinerant antique dealer and whose chief setting is Washington, D.C. The entertainment industry comes under further examination in *The Desert Rose*, which has as its heroine an aging topless dancer in Las Vegas. Each of these novels is entertaining and well written, but none did much to enhance McMurtry's reputation.

That enhancement had to wait until McMurtry decided to write a novel in one of the oldest and most persistently popular of American fictional traditions, the Western. With rare exceptions, Western novels have not been treated by critics as serious literature, since they have tended to follow hackneyed patterns of characterization and action. Patterns established by such writers as Ned Buntline and Doc Holliday in the nineteenth century were passed on almost intact to more recent writers such as Zane Grey and Louis L'Amour. What McMurtry did in *Lonesome Dove* was to reinvent the Western novel by taking its basic elements and elevating them to the level of epic.

The characters in *Lonesome Dove* are familiar to readers of Western fiction, here given new names: the silent hero, Woodrow Call, who cares more for horses than for women, and who leads other men by example and by courage; the other hero, Gus McCrae, talkative and easygoing, always ready for emergencies; the prostitute with a heart of gold, Lorena (Lorie) Wood; the evil renegade half-breed, Blue Duck; the naïve but courageous boy, Newt; the strong almost-widow, Clara Allen; the handsome but weak gambler, destined to come to a bad end eventually, Jake Spoon; the unimaginative but dependable sheriff, July Johnson; the comic deputy, July's aide Roscoe; and a cast of thousands.

McMurtry's achievement in *Lonesome Dove* is twofold. First, he puts his huge cast of characters into motion. Beginning with a rundown livery stable and cattle-trading business in a tiny Texas town south of San Antonio called Lonesome Dove, the former Texas Rangers Call and Gus put together a herd by rustling from Mexican ranches across the Rio Grande, hire enough cowboys to run the drive, and set out for Montana, where Jake Spoon has told them there is a world of grass unclaimed by white men. Their journey is difficult and tragic, lightened at times by comedy, but it is never dull or ordinary. Lorie, whose beauty has been the only relief to the boredom of Lonesome Dove, makes Jake take her along, to the great disgust of Call, the former Ranger captain who can see no use for women anywhere, much less on a cattle drive. She and Jake are not part of the drive, but they stay close to it; many of the cowboys, in love with Lorie, are kept in a state of agitation—especially the top hand, Dish, who desperately wants to marry her.

McMurtry's approach to his material is leisurely. More than two hundred pages at the beginning, exceeding one-fourth of the long novel, are devoted to preliminary events in Lonesome Dove and the first stages of the drive: the arrival of Jake, a former Ranger on the run from a murder charge, with his news of Montana; Call's sudden and uncharacteristic decision to go, after ten years of relative inactivity; the raids into Mexico to steal horses and cattle; the gathering of an outfit to supplement Newt, Pea Eye, and Deets, the Hat Creek crew; Lorie's instant love for Jake, even though she quickly sees his weakness. Most of this material is humorous, largely because Gus is a man who refuses to take life seriously. The raid into Mexico is exciting and potentially dangerous, but even this adventure turns to comedy when the Hat Creek cowboys encounter two lost Irish brothers who left Ireland headed for

Galveston and wound up missing their target by several hundred miles. The Irish brothers, despite their unfamiliarity with horses and cattle, are hired on.

The second major factor in McMurtry's success in *Lonesome Dove* is his ability to take stock characters and humanize them by making them recognizable and distinctive human beings while at the same time elevating them to mythic proportions. Call is a projection of the strong but silent type of frontiersman, quiet, self-contained, but restless and capable of angry outbursts. Despite his abilities, he is emotionally strangled. Gus McCrae is almost superhuman. When necessary, he can fight more effectively than other men, but he is also warm and sympathetic to women and to young boys in trouble, such as Call's unacknowledged bastard son, Newt. He brings Lorie out of her catatonic state and wins her love, but he is human enough to wish that he could have Clara instead. Newt Dobbs is the typical young man; subjected again and again to grief and strain, he grows and matures. The black scout, Deets, is everything a scout should be.

The pace of the novel accelerates once the herd is on the trail. As soon as the drive begins, disaster strikes. Two days out, the herd is hit by a storm, and the riders must stay up all night to keep the cattle from dispersing. The next day, crossing a stream roiled by the storm, the younger and sadder of the Irish brothers stirs up a nest of cottonmouth snakes and is horribly killed. It is the first of several deaths the men will encounter on their long odyssey.

Only late in this initial section does McMurtry introduce another set of characters: July Johnson, the sheriff of Fort Smith, Arkansas; his unhappy pregnant wife, Elmira, a former prostitute; her son, Joe; and the deputy Roscoe. In Fort Smith, July's brother, the town mayor, has been accidentally killed by a shot fired by Jake Spoon, and the mayor's widow is urging July to track down Jake and bring him back to hang. July, recovering from jaundice and convinced that the shooting was an accident, is reluctant to go, but eventually he sets out, at Elmira's insistence taking Joe along. Shortly thereafter, Elmira, pregnant with July's child, leaves town on a riverboat to seek out her former lover, the gambler Dee Boot, and July's sister-in-law insists that Roscoe track down July to tell him that his wife is gone.

All these characters, and others, eventually meet on the plains. Jake leaves Lorie to go to town to gamble, and while he is gone the Comanchero Blue Duck, a bitter, crafty, and resourceful renegade, kidnaps the terrified Lorie, takes her north to the plains, and keeps her barely alive only to sell her body to Kiowas and buffalo hunters, an experience that robs her of speech and very nearly of her sanity. She is rescued by Gus, but the cost of the rescue is high: July Johnson, still looking for Elmira, insists on helping Gus, and while they are dispatching the six Kiowas and two buffalo hunters who hold Lorie, Blue Duck sneaks into their small camp and murders Roscoe, July's stepson Joe, and a young girl who has been traveling with Roscoe.

Jake, in the meantime, has found himself entangled with the three Suggs brothers, hard cases who are getting harder. Jake accidentally kills another man and goes along with the Suggses, who kill several more, including the rancher Wilbarger, who has earlier befriended Gus. Call and Gus track down the Suggses and hang all three brothers; reluctantly, they also hang Jake.

Many of the elements of the plot resolve themselves in the Nebraska frontier town of Ogallala. Clara Allen, the only woman Gus has loved and lost, lives there with her comatose husband and two daughters. Elmira arrives first, has her baby, and departs with her buffalo-hunter escort, both soon to be killed by Sioux. Her lover, Dee Boot, is hanged. July Johnson comes next, sees his son, whom Clara has kept, and stays on as a hand at Clara's ranch. Gus and Call arrive with the herd, and Clara and Gus have a happy reunion, but she makes it clear that she will never marry him, even when her husband dies. Lorie finds herself welcomed by Clara, and she stays on when the herd moves north to Montana. Newt and the other young cowboys go to Ogallala and have their first experience with whores, and Newt decides to become a ladies' man like Gus.

In the final section, the herd moves north to Montana and the encounters with still-violent Indians. Deets is killed by a desperate young warrior who fails to comprehend that Deets is not hostile. Gus and the cowboy Pea Eye, scouting ahead for a ranch site, are cut off by a roving band and attacked. Pea Eye gets away, but Gus is wounded. He escapes from the Indians but dies in Miles City after refusing to allow the doctor to amputate both of his gangrenous legs.

Call finds a spot for a ranch, and the men build a ranch house and corrals and spend a hard winter there. When spring comes, Call leaves Newt in charge of the remaining men and the cattle, tacitly acknowledging that he is Newt's father, but he cannot bring himself to call the boy his son. He fulfills his promise to take Gus's body and bury it in a Texas glen where Gus and Clara had picnicked years earlier. On his long and difficult journey, Call passes through Ogallala, where Clara's husband has died and she and Lorie are mourning for Gus. Later, he pauses long enough to witness Blue Duck's death. Call is shot and goes through numerous other trials, but he manages to bury Gus; at the end, he makes his way back to the deserted town of Lonesome Dove.

In *Lonesome Dove* McMurtry is at the height of his powers. The disparate strands of the plot are handled skillfully, as the story moves easily from the herd to July Johnson to Jake Spoon to Elmira and then back to the herd. McMurtry's ability to depict action comes into play often, in the violent scenes of the young Irishman's death, Gus's explosion into the Kiowa camp where Lorie is held, the sudden thunderstorms that batter the cowboys and scatter the herd, the sudden descent of a plague of grasshoppers, and many other scenes. He is equally skilled at depicting character, not only the major figures such as Call, Gus, Clara, and Lorie but also young Newt and such minor characters as the cook Po Campo, Roscoe, Wilbarger, and Elmira. There is a leavening of humor, some of it hilarious, not only in the early sections of the novel but also throughout. At the same time, there is no attempt to downplay the violence and hardship of the lives of these men and women; the long journey is marked by one violent death after another. The hard life of the frontier is represented not only by Lorie's terrible experience in the hands of Blue Duck and the sudden deaths among the cowboys but also by Clara's loss of three sons and a husband to the harsh conditions of life on the prairies.

It is entirely fitting that the ending is grim. The most powerful scene in the final section is Clara's condemnation of Call when he returns to Ogallala with Gus's body, bringing the final notes the dying Gus wrote to Clara and Lorie. Her scathing denunciation of his single-mindedness and the human sacrifice and misery the trip caused raises disturbing questions about the meaning of the heroic journey the men have accomplished. The surviving hands are left on the isolated ranch in Montana. Clara and Lorie remain on the ranch outside Ogallala, with July hoping to marry Clara and Dish hopelessly in love with Lorie. Call has no idea where to go after the trip back to Lonesome Dove is ended.

The tone of McMurtry's later novel about the frontier, *Anything for Billy,* is very different. This book is a satiric retelling of the story of Billy the Kid, seen from the perspective of an Easterner who has been addicted to dime novels of the West. The combination of humor and violent action that marked *Lonesome Dove* is present in the later novel, but without the tragic undertone that gives *Lonesome Dove* its special power.

Larry McMurtry is a highly prolific novelist who has shown the ability to change his locales and his subject matter when he feels the need for novelty, and he has been willing to revive characters from earlier novels to suit new purposes. He has been most successful in exploring the past and present of his native Texas, a state and a state of mind that provide seemingly inexhaustible material for his special blend of satire, romance, and tragedy. His most important achievement, *Lonesome Dove,* has already attained the status of a classic of Western fiction.

John M. Muste

Other major works

NONFICTION: *In a Narrow Grave: Essays on Texas,* 1968; *It's Always We Rambled: An Essay on Rodeo,* 1974; *Film Flam: Essays on Hollywood,* 1987.

Bibliography

Kingsolver, Barbara. "Across Texas by Non Sequitur." *The New York Times Book Review* 94 (October 22, 1989), p. 8. A witty and insightful review of

Some Can Whistle, focusing on the novel's problems with Danny Deck as a successful retired television entrepreneur who cannot deal with other people close at hand and whose attempt to connect with his daughter ends in tragedy.

Neinstein, Raymond L. *The Ghost Country: The Novels of Larry McMurtry.* Houston: Creative Arts Book Co., 1976.

_____. Afterword to *All My Friends Are Going to Be Strangers*, by Larry McMurtry. Albuquerque: University of New Mexico Press, 1982. Neinstein's brief book and the essay are sensitive and intelligent introductions to the first half dozen of McMurtry's novels.

Nelson, Jane. "Larry McMurtry." In *A Literary History of the American West*, edited by Max Westbrook and James H. Maguire. Fort Worth: Texas Christian University Press, 1987. A brief study placing McMurtry in the context of the modern Western novel and showing some of the ways in which he has reinvented the form and given it more tragic shadings.

Peavy, Charles D. *Larry McMurtry.* Boston: Twayne, 1977. Peavy's study deals with the earlier novels and follows the formula established for Twayne's United States Authors series, but it is by far the most intensive and thorough study available of McMurtry's fiction.

Reynolds, Clay. "Back Trailing to Glory: *Lonesome Dove* and the Novels of Larry McMurtry." *The Texas Review* 8 (Fall/Winter, 1987): 22-29. This essay discusses the ways in which McMurtry's earlier novels about Texas, especially *Horseman, Pass By* and *Leaving Cheyenne*, prepared the way for the reviving of the more traditional Western novel in *Lonesome Dove*.

Schmidt, Dorey, ed. *Larry McMurtry: Unredeemed Dreams.* Living Authors Series 1. Houston: Pan American Press, 1978. This is a collection of essays by various students of McMurtry's fiction, focusing on the earlier novels and the theme of disappointment and loss found in all those books.

DAVID MADDEN

Born: Knoxville, Tennessee; July 25, 1933

Principal long fiction
The Beautiful Greed, 1961; *Cassandra Singing*, 1969; *Brothers in Confidence*, 1972; *Bijou*, 1974; *The Suicide's Wife*, 1978; *Pleasure-Dome*, 1979; *On the Big Wind*, 1980.

Other literary forms
David Madden is a prolific writer who has worked in almost every literary genre. Besides his seven novels, he has published numerous essays, short stories, and poems in a range of journals and magazines; two short-story collections, *The Shadow Knows* (1970) and *The New Orleans of Possibilities* (1982); several plays, including both one-act and three-act versions of *Cassandra Singing* (1957); a number of book-length critical studies; as well as a film script for the television movie of *The Suicide's Wife*. Additionally, Madden has edited more than ten volumes on such diverse subjects as the proletarian and tough-guy writers of the 1930's, James Agee, Nathanael West, the short story, film and the commedia dell'arte, and the popular culture explosion.

Achievements
Madden's work has been unevenly recognized throughout his career. His early novels—*The Beautiful Greed*, an M.A. thesis project, and "Hair of the Dog," initially published in *Adam* but never reprinted as a book—received virtually no attention at the time of their publication. Although Harry T. Moore praised *Cassandra Singing*, *Brothers in Confidence*, and *Bijou* as "significant contributions to contemporary American fiction," other critics have not viewed Madden's work so favorably. While Walker Percy found *Bijou* "a triumphant, brutal story of growing up," some reviewers faulted it for lack of unity and excessive nostalgia. Mixed responses also greeted *Pleasure-Dome*. One critic praised it as a "lyrical, quite wonderful novel"; another found it too "demanding and sometimes a bore."

Madden's short stories, however, have received more consistent recognition. Two have appeared in *Best American Short Stories*, for 1969 and 1971, respectively, and *The Shadow Knows*, Madden's first collection of short fiction, was the National Arts Council selection for 1970. In 1969, Madden was also the recipient of a Rockefeller grant for fiction.

Madden's achievement in the novel form rests in his exploration of the oral storytelling tradition and his evocation of east Tennessee and Kentucky landscapes and experiences, especially those of his youth. He often reworks autobiographical material—the major exception is *The Suicide's Wife*—much of it found in earlier novels or stories. Characters and situations recur; earlier stories reappear as segments of a later novel. Though redundant and at times tedious for the reader engaged in surveying all of Madden's novels, the retelling of this material in different forms allows the novelist to experiment with narrative voice and to explore in depth the relationship between the storyteller and his listener, a subject that has fascinated Madden since his youth.

Biography

Jerry David Madden was born July 25, 1933, in Knoxville, Tennessee, to James Helvy and Emile Merrit, unquestionably models for the parents of Lucius Hutchfield in *Bijou* and *Pleasure-Dome*. Madden has two brothers, both of whom figure in his fiction. As a child, Madden worked as a newsboy and a theater usher, two jobs also held by the autobiographical Lucius. Madden was also an avid storyteller, a trait inherited from his grandmother. "Telling stories as a child," he comments in *The Poetic Image in Six Genres* (1969), "acting out all the parts, doing all the voices, I was an actor on a stage, my spectators within reach. When I wasn't telling stories, I was daydreaming them." Like the characters in his novels—Lucius, Hollis Weaver in *Brothers in Confidence*, Big Bob Travis in *On the Big Wind*—Madden "wanted to be able to affect people" with his stories: his "two brothers, curled under quilts . . . neighborhood kids, huddled on our high front steps, and later . . . classmates during recess in grammar school." Inspired by the motion pictures he saw as an usher at the Bijou, Madden wrote his first story at age ten and thus discovered "the private, lonely thrill of affecting individual, absent readers—a relationship remote from the public, communal transaction of movies." With Thomas Wolfe as his "romantic," "nonliterary" model and Ernest Hemingway as the literary one, Madden launched himself in high school on a writing career that included sharing with Wolfe a nostalgic response to hometown and family and acquiring the same literary agent as Raymond Chandler.

During high school, Madden worked as a radio announcer—an experience that figures in the Big Bob stories and *On the Big Wind*. He also wrote, acted in, and directed a number of radio plays, feeding his interest in narrative voice and the teller-listener relationship. "Radio drama," after all, as Madden has acknowledged, "demands that listeners see through their ears" and grants thereby enormous evocative power and control to the actors.

By the time he was graduated from Knox High School in 1951, Madden had already won a state play contest that included having the award-winning play produced at the University of Tennessee. Madden enrolled for a time at the University of Tennessee, but he interrupted his education for the sake of adventure: travel, work in New York, and a stint as a messman on a United States merchant marine ship, an experience that provided the basis for *The Beautiful Greed*. From 1955 to 1956, Madden also served in the Army in

Alaska. He reenrolled in college in 1956, first at Iowa State Teachers College, then once again at the University of Tennessee, where he received a B.S. degree in 1957. In 1956, he married Roberta Margaret Young, whom he had met while working at a radio station in Iowa. During this period Madden continued to write, working on and off again on *Cassandra Singing* as a radio drama, a stage play, and a novel—a fourteen-year project. Indeed, the first one-act version of *Cassandra Singing* won third place in a contest at the University of Tennessee as early as 1954, and the planning of the novel was already under way in 1955 while Madden was stationed in Alaska.

In the fall of 1957, following completion of his undergraduate work at the University of Tennessee, Madden enrolled at San Francisco State College, where he continued to work on *Cassandra Singing* and completed the M.A. in creative writing. He then taught at Appalachian State Teachers College in Boone, North Carolina, for one year. From 1959 to 1960, he attended the Yale Drama School as a John Golden fellow in playwriting. After 1960, Madden taught in colleges and universities throughout the central, eastern, and southern United States: from 1960 to 1962 at Centre College in Danville, Kentucky; from 1962 to 1964 at the University of Louisville; from 1964 to 1966 at Kenyon College in Gambier, Ohio, where he was also assistant editor of the *Kenyon Review*; in 1966 at Ohio University in Athens; and in 1967 at the University of North Carolina at Chapel Hill. In 1968, Madden became writer-in-residence at Louisiana State University. He was named distinguished visiting professor of English at the University of Delaware in the spring of 1980.

Analysis

In *The Poetic Imagic in Six Genres*, David Madden acknowledges two principal influences on his work, both explored in the autobiographical novel *Bijou*: his grandmother's storytelling and Hollywood films. He considers both to be "extremes." Nevertheless, from his grandmother he learned the impact of the storyteller on his listeners and from motion pictures he learned the techniques for making his own "stories more vivid, the action more immediate." These two extremes or opposite forces—the oral storytelling tradition in the South and the visual realm of popular-culture films—combine in Madden's novels to produce an abiding fascination with the role of the narrator-performer and the contrast between the life of action, that of the speaker or storyteller, and the life of the imagination, that of the listener or audience. To some extent, most of Madden's novels explore this duality while also drawing on a nostalgia for old films and film heroes.

Because he comes out of the Southern oral storytelling tradition, Madden, like William Faulkner, relies heavily on a fairly fixed source of raw material that he reworks in various forms. Thus, characters from one novel may reappear, sometimes under different names; situations may recur as well, in stories retold from a different point of view or stitched into a novel. All of *Brothers in Confidence*, for example, reappears as part of *Pleasure-Dome*, a much later work, with changes in the principal characters' names. Most notably, Hollis Weaver, the narrator in *Brothers in Confidence*, is replaced by Lucius Hutchfield, who narrates both *Pleasure-Dome* and the earlier work, *Bijou*. Retelling the material from *Brothers in Confidence* allows Madden to reshape this material into a sequel for *Bijou*. On the Big Wind, which appeared in 1980, combines stories appearing in magazines as early as 1966, including "The Singer," a variation on the *Cassandra Singing* material which Madden reworked for fourteen years. Madden's justification for this reworking of material rests in his interest in the storytelling tradition, where repetition of a favorite story only enhances the storyteller-listener relationship, and in his interest in experimenting with point of view. "In this shifting from one perspective to another on the same material," he comments in *The Poetic Image in Six Genres*, "I have learned more about . . . my own interests, and about the teller-listener relationship."

One corollary of this fascination with the teller-listener relationship is Madden's concept of the artist-storyteller as "con man," an idea the novelist claims to have borrowed from Thomas Mann. In his 1980 essay, "Let Me Tell You the Story," Madden speaks of this metaphor as one way of focusing his interest. "The relationship between the storyteller and the listener," he adds,

> is like that between the con man and his mark, who charge each other through phantom circuits of the imagination; the storyteller uses many of the same techniques for capturing attention, holding it, and projecting the reader into a totally different world from the one he is living in.

Such creation Madden calls the "pleasure-dome," the concept explored in his sixth novel. Not surprisingly, most of Madden's novels involve some form of storytelling by central characters with listeners swayed or held captive by the magical words of the speakers. Often it is the con man, such as Travern Weaver in *Brothers in Confidence* or Lucius Hutchfield's corrupt older brother, Earl, who weaves these tales; often it is the artist-hero himself, Lucius in *Pleasure-Dome* or Hollis Weaver in *Brothers in Confidence*. Even a minor work such as "Hair of the Dog," a detective story showing the influence of the "tough-guy" writers of the 1930's on Madden's fiction, involves a story told in prison, as do *Brothers in Confidence* and *Pleasure-Dome*.

The two novels which do not explicitly explore this teller-listener relationship are *The Beautiful Greed* and *The Suicide's Wife*. Although both employ storytelling in at least one episode as a means of revealing character, even to some extent altering a relationship between the speaker and the listener, in neither novel is storytelling the focus of the book. Alvin Henderlight in *The Beautiful Greed* has shared a cabin for months with the mysterious Franco before Franco tells his story; in *The Suicide's Wife*, Ann Harrington's lack of inhibition in bed with her husband's colleague serves as a device for altering her life, not that of the listener.

Of these two novels, only *The Suicide's Wife* is not autobiographical. While it grew from a dramatic monologue concerning a suicide that happened on "the periphery" of Madden's life, it does not concern the writer or a writer-hero, the autobiographical hero in most of Madden's novels. Incidents from *The Beautiful Greed*, perhaps because they are largely autobiographical, do appear elsewhere, notably in Lucius' artist-con-man scheme in *Pleasure-Dome*. Only *The Suicide's Wife* remains outside of this storytelling context, unique also in its treatment of the duality of passivity and action within one central character, Ann Harrington, the suicide's wife.

Madden's first novel, *The Beautiful Greed*, was published by Random House in 1961 as part of the publisher's "First Novel" series. The book was Madden's M.A. thesis project at San Francisco State College and drew heavily on his stint as a crewman aboard a United States merchant marine ship scheduled for Brazil but, in the novel at least, destined for Taltal, Chile, on a mercy mission to aid Chilean earthquake victims. The novel's protagonist, Alvin Henderlight, is clearly autobiographical. Besides sharing with the novelist his merchant marine experience, Alvin is also from Knoxville, has motion-picture ideas about going to sea, reads voraciously (particularly Joseph Conrad and Herman Melville), and bears a physical resemblance to the novelist with his short stature and balding head. He also has a family much like Madden's own and that of other autobiographical heroes in Madden's novels: a father who drinks, a mother who works, most often as a maid or in a factory, and two vagabond brothers.

The Beautiful Greed is also a very conscious literary work strongly influenced by Joseph Conrad's sea fiction. The title comes from a passage from *Lord Jim* (1900) referring to the insatiable hunger of the seaman for experience and adventure, a passage that serves as the Epigraph for Madden's book. Like Conrad's novel, *The Beautiful Greed* takes illusion and reality as its central theme, particularly Alvin's gradual disillusionment. As the novel progresses, so does Alvin's awakening to the brute reality of life. His spiritual and psychological journey parallels the ship's slow progress south, through the Panama Canal, and eventually on to Chile and, for Alvin, true knowledge and experience.

The ship is, of course, another conscious literary device, a microcosm of the world's society. Young, old, bestial, intelligent, all different nationalities and human types are represented on board. Using these varieties of human beings, Madden explores the conflict between intellect—Alvin is dubbed the "professor" for his reading habits—and brute, insensitive action. Alvin and his cabin mate—the mysterious, remote Franco—are pitted against a crew of men whose brutal jokes include pitilessly trapping a sea bird and mercilessly using Franco as a scapegoat. For the most part, the novel follows the pattern of the *Bildungsroman*, but its message is clearly existential. When the enigmatic, falsely dignified Franco reveals the truth about himself in a compelling story, he also leaves Alvin to face the consequences of his choices and actions aboard ship. Once committed to staying on board the *Polestar*, Alvin must face the brutish men whom Franco escapes by returning to his home in Taltal. Alvin has passed the opportunity to leave with Franco; his change of mind comes too late to alter the implied course of events with which the novel ends: Alvin's own torture at the hands of the brutish crew. While relying excessively on conscious literary devices and on the author's own experiences, *The Beautiful Greed* is nevertheless noteworthy as a first novel for the author's attempt to deal with important issues about man's relationship with himself and his fellowmen and the meaning of his actions.

In *Cassandra Singing*, Madden turned away from predominantly autobiographical material to work with a story originating in a conversation with a messman aboard the novelist's merchant marine ship—a tale of a girl who joined a motorcycle gang after "her brother was killed in a smashup." Analogies exist in several forms, including various play versions and at least two short stories, "The Singer" and "Lone Riding." Madden acknowledges being obsessed with the story for more than fourteen years.

Set in eastern Kentucky rather than the Knoxville of the novelist's childhood, the story revolves around what Madden has described in *The Poetic Image in Six Genres* as "the strange relationship between a motorcyclist named Lone and his invalid sister Cassie. . . ." Besides this nearly incestuous relationship, Madden also attempts to capture the life of the mountain people and the threat to their folk existence posed by progress represented in the novel by the steady encroachment of bulldozers that will raze Lone and Cassie's home. His efforts are successful, for he is able to depict in detail the violence and deceptive simplicity of the mountain people, particularly through their dialect and mannerisms.

Perhaps because the story existed in dramatic form first, the novel relies heavily on dialogue, making immediate the conflict between Lone, who represents action, and his sister Cassie, who represents imagination. Through Lone's vivid retelling of his motorcycle adventures with his companion Boyd, Cassie, bedridden for years with rheumatic fever, is able to envision the life of action she has longed for but never had. Thus, she becomes one of the earliest of Madden's characters enchanted by the storyteller's art and imaginatively transported into a "pleasure-dome" of his own making. Lone likewise becomes one of the first of Madden's storytellers to dramatize the oral storytelling tradition prevalent among mountain and Southern people.

Despite its successes, *Cassandra Singing* moves too slowly at times. It represents a testament to Madden's love of words, an essential trait in any writer, and his skill in capturing the speech of mountain people, yet the conversations become too repetitious, the action too prolonged. Like *The*

Beautiful Greed, moreover, the novel draws heavily on other literary works and motifs. Cassie and Lone's relationship, as Madden has acknowledged in *The Poetic Image in Six Genres*, is "partly inspired" by the "brother-sister relationship in the *Oresteia* [458 B.C.], O'Neill's *Mourning Becomes Electra* [1931], Sartre's *The Flies* [1942], and Cocteau's *L'Enfant Terrible* [1929]," and Cassie herself by Frankie in Carson McCullers' *The Member of the Wedding* (1950) and Cassandra, "the Greek prophetess of doom, who was condemned never to be believed." Coupled with the biblical allusions that accompany Boyd's attempted crucifixion and threatened castration of Lone near the end of the novel, these powerful literary antecedents overtake the meaning of Madden's tale, leaving it wanting for power and impact.

Brothers in Confidence, which appeared in part in the *Southern Review* four years before its publication as an Avon paperback—the book has not been published in a hardbound edition—returns to largely autobiographical material. It is also one of the most playful and humorous of Madden's novels and the first to explore in depth the concept of the artist as con man. The first-person narrator, Hollis Weaver, is that artist. His goal is to save his younger brother, Cody, from serving a sentence on a chain gang for forgery. Like his brothers—Cody and the older Travern, also a criminal and forger—Hollis, though a writer and teacher by profession, must act the con man to persuade several good citizens of east Tennessee to accept a token payment as promise that Cody will make retribution and to agree to drop all charges against him. To do this, Hollis must travel the countryside weaving tales of Cody's neglected childhood—his parents resemble Lone and Cassie's as well as Lucius Hutchfield's—and ensnaring his audience with his storytelling art. His success depends on his skill in playacting, manipulating his audience, and vividly dramatizing Cody's life in order to win pity—all talents which the oral storyteller must possess. Only Travern's pose as a fancy lawyer, Mr. French, outshines Hollis' art. Travern, a genuine rogue since his youth and a thief who steals from his own family, goes directly to the judge and, by using a soapy story about holding the judge's only son as he dies in combat, convinces the old man to release Cody and accept several bogus checks as payment for court costs and ready cash so the Weaver brothers can leave town.

Brothers in Confidence is a lively, quick-paced, humorous portrait of three witty con artists caught in the act of writing bad checks and weaving outrageous tales. Like Madden, they delight in holding their audiences, both listeners and readers, with the magic of their stories. Episodic in structure, the novel follows the exploits of the narrator-hero as he travels the countryside, attempting to stay out of jail while trying also to free his brother. In these two respects, *Brothers in Confidence* is a picaresque novel, though sexual adventures are noticeably absent, having been saved for abundant use in *Bijou*. Also noteworthy is Madden's reliance on Hollis' storytelling to handle exposition and family history—a dramatic device from oral storytelling—and his use of motion pictures as a means of enhancing action and character. Hollis, like the later Madden hero Lucius Hutchfield and the novelist himself, has worked as an usher in a movie theater and served in the merchant marines. He envisions himself a romantic hero, an Alan Ladd figure acting out various roles assigned to him. Like Madden, he also has two brothers who have served time in prison.

In 1969, Madden received a Rockefeller grant in fiction to work on his fourth novel, *Bijou*. He wrote part of the novel in Yugoslavia, part in Venice— an "ideal place," he told Ruth Laney in an interview for the *Southern Review*. "When I got the grant," Madden continued, "I thought the best place to go to begin the book would be to a city that paralleled the exotic quality of the Bijou, both in the movies and in real life." In effect, through its focus on the aging theater at which its hero works, the novel duplicates the author's own nostalgia for the past. Its purpose is to capture the "seediness" of that theater, once a site for legitimate stage productions, now a place where pornographic films are shown.

Set in Cherokee, Tennessee, *Bijou* is another largely autobiographical *Bildungsroman*, tracing the life and adventures of thirteen-year-old Lucius Hutchfield during one turbulent and painful year. The period is immediately after World War II, and the romantic Lucius is infatuated with film stars and the memorable and not so memorable motion pictures of Hollywood's golden era. Like Madden, Lucius grows as an artist through two principal sources, both dramatized in the novel: his grandmother's storytelling and the movies.

Because the novel has little plot other than Lucius' growth over one year and his emergence as a young writer, it is highly episodic. *Bijou*, one critic complained, is "so long" (five hundred pages), "so unresponsive, and even irresponsible about itself" that the reader becomes bored and repulsed. Madden records virtually every intimate detail and every event, including bowel movements, every day of Lucius' life for a year. Some of the details are successful in capturing the formative factors in Lucius' growth; others are not. There is humor but also vulgarity and tedium.

Defending the novel, Madden told Ruth Laney that he had wanted "a concentration of effect, a sort of captivity in the Bijou" paralleling the enchantment the storyteller weaves through his words and movements, here created by a place. The problem is that the book lacks the "unity of place [which] would have enabled [the author] to shorten the novel and to realize [his] original purpose." To accomplish his task, Madden dramatizes his own adolescence and growth as a writer, filtering every detail through Lucius' consciousness, yet Lucius is incapable of distinguishing the valuable from the useless in his experience.

Madden also experiments with several narrative patterns. Some work, others do not. Film sequences and bits of movie dialogue blend with Lucius' thoughts and imaginings, successfully dramatizing the creative process and the impact of what Madden calls the "charged image" on the creative consciousness. Segments of night reveries in which Lucius nostalgically reviews his life, sections of the hero's diary, letters between him and his girl friend Raine—including one borrowed from a Joseph Cotton film—even whole stories written by the young Lucius appear as sections of narrative. Many of these bog down, particularly Lucius' and Raine's letters, which are often adolescent professions of love. The stories, though demonstrating the hero's early attempts at fiction-writing, mirror the artist's growth only part of the time. Finally, *Bijou* is not a successful novel; Madden's long autobiographical piece testifies, as does *Cassandra Singing*, to his love of literature, but it is also an instance of the novelist's having been caught in his own storytelling trance and nostalgia for the past.

The Suicide's Wife, which was made into a television film for which Madden wrote the script, is in many ways the novelist's most unusual—some might say successful and original—novel. It is unusual among his novels in focusing solely on a female character—*Cassandra Singing* does so only partially. Aside from a dramatic monologue by the wife, the novel has no predecessors in Madden's oeuvre, an unusual feature. It is also, in Madden's own words, "a very short novel inspired by something that happened" not in his own life, but "on the periphery, a suicide." The novel is also unique in that it does not dramatize the oral storytelling tradition, as do Madden's other works, and is crisp and Hemingwayesque in style. Filtered through the intelligence of the suicide's wife, Ann Harrington, the wife of an English teacher at a West Virginia university, the novel studies the struggle of "the wife" to acquire an identity of her own following her husband's apparent suicide. Her lack of knowledge about her husband and about herself is her source of motivation after her husband's death thrusts her into a world she is unprepared to confront. Set against the backdrop of the student riots and civil rights movement of the late 1960's, Ann's story becomes a parable for the women's movement, a tale of progression from passivity and emptiness toward action and self-fulfillment.

At the outset of the novel, Ann defines herself almost solely in terms of her vagina, an emptiness to be filled by her husband. Madden skillfully does not give his heroine a name in this opening section. Her identity is not yet established, either with the reader, or, more important, with herself. As the book progresses, however, Ann's painful growth is recorded increasingly in terms of herself with the narrative moving in and out of her thoughts, at times allowing Ann to think in first person as she develops some identity through action. The wife who is "still a wife" at the beginning of the novel "even though she doesn't have a husband" eventually realizes that the man to whom she felt inferior for years was in fact a nobody, as vague as she, as passive and purposeless and lost.

With *Pleasure-Dome*, Madden returned to the comic tone and first-person narrative voice he used in *Brothers in Confidence*, part of which is reworked here with Travern, Hollis, and Cody becoming Lucius Hutchfield of *Bijou* and his two brothers, Earl and Bucky. Like that earlier work, the novel is autobiographical and retells stories found in other forms and books. *Pleasure-Dome* is also a sequel to *Bijou*, with Lucius seven years older and experienced through travel and the merchant marines. At twenty, Lucius is also seeking more than his own past, though he must deal with his troublesome family members who are frequently in trouble with the law.

Pleasure-Dome is an interesting novel for what James Park Sloan in *The New York Times Book Review* cited as its combination of "profligate story-telling with reflections on the storytelling process. . . ." The narrator's consciousness—seen to a lesser degree but very evident nevertheless in *Brothers in Confidence*—emerges on the first page when he invites the reader into his tale with the traditional storyteller's line, "Did I ever tell you about the time. . . ?" In this first half of the novel, Lucius adopts what he calls his Mark Twain persona, retelling, as he must to save Bucky, sad stories about his childhood in Tennessee, while at the same time he is reporting to the reader-listener the chronicle of his adventures in conning those citizens pressing charges against Bucky.

Pleasure-Dome also moves beyond *Brothers in Confidence* and *Bijou* by adding a segment on Lucius' quest for a past other than his own, that of the legendary Jesse and Frank James. His search involves the attempt to learn the tale of Zara Ransom, an old woman who reportedly had a brief romance with Jesse James when she was a girl. To get her story, Lucius must once again successfully con his audience, here by using Zara herself; one of the fascinating complications is that it is Zara who enchants Lucius by telling her own story. *Pleasure-Dome* then contains two or more stories: the autobiographical one concerning the Hutchfields, and another, a second tale, of Zara Ransom and her relationship with a figure from America's legendary past. Both stories concern the past; both are narrated by oral storytellers. Both create a pleasure-dome for the reader-listener.

Pleasure-Dome is clearly a more sophisticated work than Madden's earlier novels which experimented with point of view and narrative art. By adding Zara Ransom's story and having her tell that story as Lucius writes it, Madden captures the storytelling process and the transmission of a dying art to the writer. As in *Cassandra Singing*, progress in the form of razing bulldozers is threatening the folkways of which the oral storytelling tradition is a part. Without Lucius' written record of Zara's story, handled with what he calls his Henry James persona, and his interpretation of the ending, the tale would be lost. Zara may or may not have been Jesse James's lover, but she is a legend that reminds people, Lucius thinks, "that those who do not remember the past are doomed never to relive it in the imagination." Significantly, at the end of the novel, Zara is destroyed, and Lucius is moved to guilt and deep feelings of "something . . . for the first time besides nostalgia."

With *Pleasure-Dome, On the Big Wind* dramatizes more successfully than any other Madden novel what the writer has described in *The Poetic Image in Six Genres* as "the teller's compulsion to tell a story," "the oral tradition" and the process by which it depicts, renders, and stimulates the art of oral storytelling. The book consists of seven episodes, most of which were originally published as short stories in a variety of magazines. The tone is clearly comic, as the subtitle indicates: "Seven Comic Episodes in the Fitful Life of Big Bob Travis." What is especially fascinating here is that each episode explores a different dramatic relationship between the storyteller and his audience. Thus, Madden's major theme of the power of storytelling gains power itself through the variety of ways in which the narrative voice of radio announcer Big Bob manipulates his audience. As the novel's epigraph, taken from Charlotte Brontë's *Jane Eyre* (1847), observes: "The eagerness of a listener quickens the tongue of a narrator."

In the opening episode, Big Bob is a night-owl country music disc jockey in Nashville given to having affairs with the women who call him. The "magic" in his voice enthralls countless women, but Big Bob, married to a meek housewife, is honest enough to have only one affair at a time. Problems occur when his wife, Laura, masks her voice and calls and seduces him as the deep-throated Morina. When Bob cannot resist a rendezvous with the mythical Morina, the result of the confrontation is divorce.

In later episodes, Big Bob's status in the radio business declines, then rises again. In each episode he plays a different role, sometimes with a different professional name, including a Jewish one. As David Epstein, he becomes a spokesman for environmental and social causes. As a rock-music disc jockey, he must fend off the attack of a menacing motorcycle gang by telling a story that mesmerizes the group. In another episode, he draws a huge crowd of people to a sleazy mobile-home sales park by narrating the activities of a van of hippies. In that scene, Big Bob, in the tradition of the oral storyteller, both creates and "narrates the news."

As in his other novels, Madden's concern in *On the Big Wind* is with narrative techniques more than with originality in character creation or invention in plot. Like the oral storyteller who draws on a seldomly changed repertoire, Madden is content to repeat a story if the retelling draws another member of the audience into his pleasure-dome.

Stella A. Nesanovich

Other major works

SHORT FICTION: *The Shadow Knows*, 1970; *The New Orleans of Possibilities*, 1982.

PLAYS: *Cassandra Singing*, 1955; *From Rome to Damascus*, 1959; *Casina*,

1960; *Fugitive Masks*, 1966; *The Day the Flowers Came*, 1975; *Three Mean Fairy Tales*, 1979.

NONFICTION: *Wright Morris*, 1964; *Tough Guy Writers of the Thirties*, 1968 (edited); *Proletarian Writers of the Thirties*, 1968 (edited); *The Poetic Image in Six Genres*, 1969; *James M. Cain*, 1970; *American Dreams, American Nightmares*, 1970 (edited); *Rediscoveries: Informal Essays in Which Well-Known Novelists Rediscover Neglected Works of Fiction by One of Their Favorite Authors*, 1971 (edited); *The Popular Cultural Explosion: Experiencing Mass Media*, 1972 (edited with Ray B. Browne); *Nathanael West: The Cheaters and the Cheated*, 1973 (edited); *Remembering James Agee*, 1974 (edited); *Creative Choices: A Spectrum of Quality and Technique in Fiction*, 1975 (edited); *Studies in the Short Story*, 1975 (edited with Virgil Scott); *Harlequin's Stick, Charlie's Cane*, 1975; *A Primer of the Novel: For Readers and Writers*, 1980; *Writer's Revisions*, 1980 (with Richard Powers); *Cain's Craft*, 1985; *The Works of Carson McCullers*, 1988; *Rediscoveries II*, 1988 (edited, with Peggy Bach).

Bibliography

Madden, David. Interview by Ruth Laney. *Southern Review* 11 (Winter, 1975): 167-180. This lengthy discussion with Madden during the second decade of his literary career explains much about his sources of inspiration, particularly his debt to folk tradition and popular culture.

_____. "Let Me Tell You the Story: Transforming Oral Tradition." *Appalachian Journal* 7 (1980): 210-229. Madden describes the influence of the Southern tradition of storytelling on his own developing imagination during his childhood years and explains how oral anecdotes develop into the written works of a conscious artist.

_____. "True Believers, Atheists, and Agnostics." Introduction to *American Dreams, American Nightmares*, edited by David Madden. Carbondale: Southern Illinois University Press, 1970. Madden explains his own analysis of American literature, which like American life itself he sees as strongly influenced by the ideal called the "American Dream." In addition to those who embrace the dream and those who bitterly reject it, there are some who are preoccupied with the ironic difference beween the ideal and the reality. The ideas expressed in this critical work are evident in Madden's own fiction.

Morrow, Mark. "David Madden." In *Images of the Southern Writer*. Athens: University of Georgia Press, 1985. Morrow's one-page report of his visit with Madden at his Baton Rouge home includes Madden's own comments on the influences which shaped his work, both events in his life and his historical and literary heroes. Opposite the interview is a full-page portrait of Madden in his library.

Pinsker, Sanford. "The Mixed Chords of David Madden's *Cassandra Singing.*" *Critique* 15 (1973): 15-26. In this interesting essay, Pinsker deals with the common perception of Madden as a brilliant writer who is, however, too undisciplined to produce the effects of which he is capable. Pinsker points out the ironic meanings which have been deliberately achieved in *Cassandra Singing*.

Schott, Webster. "Stories Within Stories." *The Washington Post Book World* (January 6, 1980): 9. Schott suggests that Madden's novel *Pleasure-Dome* suffers from his preoccupation with the subject of his own craft, which causes him to digress, seemingly to admire his own art. Despite the defects in plotting, however, Schott finds the work intellectually stimulating.

NORMAN MAILER

Born: Long Branch, New Jersey; January 31, 1923

Principal long fiction

The Naked and the Dead, 1948; *Barbary Shore*, 1951; *The Deer Park*, 1955; *An American Dream*, 1965; *Why Are We in Vietnam?*, 1967; *The Armies of the Night: History as a Novel, the Novel as History*, 1968; *Marilyn*, 1973; *The Executioner's Song*, 1979; *Of Women and Their Elegance*, 1980; *Ancient Evenings*, 1983; *Tough Guys Don't Dance*, 1984.

Other literary forms

Beginning with *The Armies of the Night*, Norman Mailer has published several works that cross the conventional boundaries of fiction and nonfiction: a "novel biography," *Marilyn*; a "true life novel," *The Executioner's Song*; and an "imaginary memoir," *Of Women and Their Elegance*. Because of his sophisticated handling of style, structure, point of view, and characterization, much of Mailer's journalism and reportage approaches the novel's complexity of language and form: *Miami and the Siege of Chicago: An Informal History of the Republican and Democratic Conventions of 1968* (1969); *Of a Fire on the Moon* (1970); *The Prisoner of Sex* (1971); *St. George and the Godfather* (1972); and *The Fight* (1975). His essays, interviews, short stories, and poems have been collected in *Advertisements for Myself* (1959); *Deaths for the Ladies and Other Disasters* (1962); *The Presidential Papers* (1963); *Cannibals and Christians* (1966); *The Short Fiction of Norman Mailer* (1967); *The Idol and the Octopus: Political Writings on the Kennedy and Johnson Administrations* (1968); *Existential Errands* (1972); and *Pieces and Pontifications* (1982). His work in drama and literary criticism appears in *The Deer Park: A Play* (1967) and *Genius and Lust: A Journey Through the Major Writings of Henry Miller* (1976).

Achievements

With the appearance of *The Naked and the Dead* in 1948, Mailer was hailed by many critics as one of the most promising writers of the postwar generation. Since his early acclaim, Mailer's reputation has risen and fallen repeatedly—in part because of the unevenness of his writing, and in part because of his intense participation in the causes and quarrels of his age. More important, however, his work has often been misunderstood because of its remarkably changing character and its innovative procedures, for Mailer has been restlessly searching throughout his career for the style and structure that would most effectively express his ambition to make "a revolution in the consciousness of our time."

By whatever standard Mailer is judged, it is already clear that several of his books have a secure place not only in postwar literary history, but also in the canon of significant American literary achievements. *The Naked and the Dead* and *The Armies of the Night* continue to receive attention as masterpieces, and in recent years his other novels have begun to benefit from the serious exploration accorded to the finest works of fiction. *The Executioner's Song*—very favorably reviewed when it first appeared—may eventually rank with Mailer's greatest writing because it contains a complexity of point of view and characterization rivaled only by *The Naked and the Dead*, *An American Dream*, and *Why Are We in Vietnam?*

In addition to receiving several literary honors and distinctions—including the National Book Award, the Pulitzer Prize, and election to the National Institute of Arts and Letters—Mailer has been the subject of more than a dozen book-length studies and hundreds of articles. His work is an essential part of college syllabi in contemporary literature, not only because he has addressed crucial events, concerns, and institutions such as World War II, the Cold War, Hollywood, Vietnam, the Pentagon, and capital punishment, but also because he has treated all of his important themes in the light of a deeply imaginative conception of literary form. As Robert Merrill notes, far too many critics have treated Mailer's writing as simply a record of his opinions. They have taken his musings for assertions, and they have failed to see that he aims at conveying the "meaning" of characters and events with the fluidity of metaphor. What Mailer *imagines* rather than what he *believes* is important in assessing all of his prose—and what he imagines consists of entertaining several possible selves, and several sides of issues and events, simultaneously. In other words, he rejects fixity of thought in favor of the play of prose, which in turn parallels the complex play of characters and events.

Biography

Norman Mailer grew up in Brooklyn, New York, and attended Harvard University (1939-1943), where he studied aeronautical engineering and became interested in writing. After he was graduated from Harvard, he married Beatrice Silverman and was inducted into the U.S. Army, serving with the 112th Cavalry out of San Antonio, Texas. He was overseas for eighteen months in Leyte, Luzon, and with occupation forces in Japan. His varied experience as a Field Artillery surveyor, clerk, interpreter of aerial photographs, rifleman, and cook undoubtedly contributed to the comprehensive portrayal of the military in *The Naked and the Dead*.

After his discharge from the army in May, 1946, Mailer immediately began work on *The Naked and the Dead* and completed it within fifteen months. In the next two years (1948-1950), he traveled in Europe, studied at the Sorbonne, wrote articles and delivered speeches, campaigned for the election of

Henry Wallace, worked briefly as a screenwriter in Hollywood, and finished his second novel, *Barbary Shore*, which was poorly received—in part because of his sympatheic engagement with Marxist ideas and his aggressive exploration of shifting political attitudes in the postwar years.

For the next ten years, Mailer was beset by various personal and professional traumas which he slowly surmounted. He divorced his first wife—they had one daughter—in 1952. He married Adele Morales in 1954; he stabbed her with a penknife on November 19, 1960, after a party organized to launch his New York City mayoral campaign. The couple was divorced in 1962. During this period, Mailer had difficulty getting his third novel, *The Deer Park*, published, while he simultaneously struggled to complete another novel. At the same time, his second and third daughters were born, and he married Lady Jeanne Campbell, who gave birth to his fourth daughter in 1962. With the publication of *Advertisements for Myself* he began to find a way of rescuing the fragments and dead-ends of his career, and with his essay, "Superman Comes to the Supermarket" (1960), he evolved a supple way of dramatizing and musing on social and political issues that freed him from the constraints of his not entirely successful first-person narrators in *Barbary Shore* and *The Deer Park*.

In many ways, the 1960's were Mailer's most productive years. Not only did he publish his two most sophisticated novels, *An American Dream* and *Why Are We in Vietnam?* and adapt *The Deer Park* for the stage, but also he directed and acted in three films—*Wild 90* (January, 1968), *Beyond the Law* (October, 1968), and *Maidstone* (1971)—which provoked him to write important essays on the nature of film and prepared him for his innovative "novel biography," *Marilyn*. He was an active journalist during this period, covering political conventions and the moon shot, and out of his reportage he created a book, *The Armies of the Night*, that transcends the immediate occasion of its conception—a protest march on the Pentagon—in order to probe the shaping processes of history and fiction and their mutuality as human constructs. In 1963, Mailer divorced Lady Jeanne Campbell and married the actress Beverly Bentley, who bore him two sons. He campaigned unsuccessfully for mayor of New York City in 1969, and fathered a fifth daughter by Carol Stevens in 1971. He has subsequently married and divorced her. His sixth wife is Norris Church.

In the 1970's and 1980's, Mailer continued to write nonfiction while working on his Egyptian novel, *Ancient Evenings*. Although he began in the mid-1970's to withdraw from public attention, his appearance in the film *Ragtime* and his defense of Jack Abbott, a writer-convict who committed a murder shortly after his release from prison, revived the image of a controversial, embattled author. As several reviewers pointed out, both *Ancient Evenings* (1983) and *Tough Guys Don't Dance* (1984) have first-person narrators who bear considerable resemblance to Mailer. His controversial tenure as president of the U.S. chapter of PEN (Poets, Playwrights, Editers, Essayists, and Novelists), along with the film of *Tough Guys Don't Dance*, which Mailer wrote and directed, once again focused public attention on him. An excerpt from a forthcoming novel, *Harlot's Ghost*, appeared in a 1990 issue of Esquire.

Analysis

Some of Norman Mailer's earliest writing, including "The Greatest Thing in the World," a prizewinner in a 1941 *Story* magazine contest, reveals that even at a very early age he could write accomplished, imitative apprentice fiction in the modes of Ernest Hemingway and John Dos Passos. Before his own service, Mailer was exploring the experience of war in "A Calculus at Heaven" (1942), which suggests his ambition to portray the sweep of his time, to show the psychological and sociological preconditions of war and the existential choices it demands.

Mailer advanced with astonishing rapidity from his first attempts at fiction, to his own war experience, to the writing of *The Naked and the Dead*. Although it is a very long novel, its coverage of so many diverse elements in remarkably fluid prose and in a compact four-part structure conveys a sense of a single complex concert of human motives and the vagaries of existence. *The Naked and the Dead* is far more than a war novel, more than a political novel, for it examines the way human experience is shaped and interpreted, and it establishes the ground out of which human character and belief arise.

Part One, "Wave," concerns preparations for the invasion of Anopopei, an island held by the Japanese. The first wave of troops will assault the beaches by riding through the surf and charging ashore. One wave against another, man against the nature of his own enterprise, is one of the dominant themes of the novel, as its second paragraph indicates by describing an anonymous soldier who "lies flat on his bunk, closes his eyes, and remains wide-awake. All about him, like the soughing of surf, he hears the murmurs of men dozing fitfully." The poker game the soldiers play, like the war itself, has its meaning in "the margin of chance," in the calculation and skill that is nevertheless vulnerable to luck, good or bad. Much of what makes the novel fascinating is its persistent aligning of the interface between planning and probability; each soldier tries to gauge what his chances are of surviving, or—in Sergeant Croft's and General Cummings' cases—dominating the war, although almost every man, like Martinez, has at least one moment of fear, of total vulnerability, when he feels "naked" and almost certainly dead under fire.

Part Two, "Argil and Mold," shifts from the reactions of the combat soldiers to war to the grand strategy of General Cummings, who plans on shaping his army to fit his master design. For Cummings, the war—like history itself—must have a pattern, one that he can follow and channel in his direction. He disclaims the operations of chance; seeming accidents, he contends, are actually a result of a person's failure to capitalize on the opportunities life affords. If Cummings does not yet know the precise trajectory of history, he is confident that he will be percipient enough to discover it eventually. His game is not cards; it is chess. "The trick is to make yourself an instrument of your own policy," Cummings advises his resistant subordinate, Lieutenant Hearn, who refuses to credit the General's command not only over the forces of history but also over Hearn himself.

In the course of his conflict with Hearn, Cummings reveals his disdain for the liberal's "exaggerated idea of the rights due" to persons as individuals. In the General's reading of history, it is not the development of individuality but of power concentrations that counts in evaluating the causes of the war. As a result, he violates the integrity of much of the experience that is portrayed in the novel, for each character—including the General—is given a unique biography, a singularity of purpose that defies the notion that individuals can be permanently fashioned as part of a power bloc. After the initial success of his landing on Anopopei, Cummings is thwarted: "The campaign had gone sour. . . . [H]is tactics were as well conceived as they had ever been, his staff performances as thorough, his patrols as carefully planned, but nothing happened. . . . A deep unshakable lethargy settled over the front-line troops." Like Hearn, Cummings finds he cannot argue his army into action for an indefinite period of time.

Each of the principal characters in the novel behaves not only in terms of his background (the "Time Machine" sections delineate prewar experiences) and his participation in a platoon (the "Chorus" sections suggest the extent to which individual experience can be collectivized), but also in terms of the power argument between Cummings and Hearn. That is why it is inevitable that Hearn will ultimately be placed at the head of Sergeant Croft's platoon, for Croft has often kept his men together by the force of his own will, by an invincible belief in the rightness of his position that is virtually identical to Cummings' self-assurance.

Like Cummings, Croft contends with a geographical and ethnic cross section of soldiers: Red Valsen, "the wandering minstrel" from Montana, who distrusts all permanent relationships; Gallagher, "the revolutionary reversed," an Irish Catholic from Boston who seems perpetually angry at the way the more privileged or the more conniving have deprived men of their dignity but who is also profoundly prejudiced against other groups, especially the Jews; Julio Martinez, the Mexican-American, who desperately asserts his loyalty, his integrity, by taking pride in courageously executing Croft's dangerous orders; Joey Goldstein, who from his "cove in Brooklyn" tries to ingratiate himself in a world inhospitable to Jews; and Wilson, the affable Southerner who traffics easily with women and the world, and who is without much sense of life's disparities and of how he has hurt as well as charmed others with his "fun." These characters and others are meant to convey the multiplicity of experience that Croft crushes in disciplining his platoon.

In one of the most telling scenes in the novel, Croft allows a captured Japanese soldier time to recover his composure, to express his humanity, to plead for his life, and to sense that he is in the presence of other compassionate human beings, before brutally shooting him in the very moment of his happiness. Croft's cruelty is the most extreme extension of Cummings' declaration that individuals do not count, that single lives are valued too highly. Ultimately, this kind of merciless wiping out of opposition does not make Croft a better solider; his attempt to scale Mount Anaka has been futile from the beginning, and the Japanese are defeated without the imposition of either Croft's of Cummings' will. Just as Croft's men accidently blunder into the hornets that drive them back down the mountain, so in Part Three, Major Dalleson, a mediocre, timid officer, blunders into easy and rapid victory over the Japanese while Cummings is away from the campaign seeking naval support for an elaborate plan that in the end proves superfluous in the defeat of a Japanese army almost disintegrating by itself for lack of food and military supplies.

Part Three, "Plant and Phantom," prepares for the novel's abrupt denouement by exploring Friedrich Nietzsche's troubling premise that "even the wisest among you is only a disharmony and hybrid of plant and phantom. But do I bid you become phantoms or plants?" The question of human nature is unanswerable; human beings are divided creatures, both body and mind, and neither side of that nature can entirely suppress the other even in the shrewdest of individuals. In the novel, men live and die as plants and phantoms, as thinking and feeling beings who are bound by the conditions of nature and by the consequences of their own actions, over which they often have surprisingly little control. Men are truncated, their lives are suddenly cut off, even as their thoughts appear to extend their hold over events. Thus, Hearn drives his men to the other side of the island, so that they can reconnoiter the possibility of an invasion behind Japanese battle lines. He suffers from weariness, from the men's resistance, from his own self-doubt, but he reasserts himself:

> As they moved along out of the hollow he felt good; it was a new morning, and it was impossible not to feel hopeful. The dejection, the decisions of the previous night seemed unimportant. He was enjoying this, but if he was, so much the better.
>
> A half hour later, Lieutenant Hearn was killed by a machine gun bullet which passed through his chest.

Hearn dies as swiftly as the Japanese defense crumbles, and in both cases the dissolution is all the more devastating when one considers their determination to survive.

Part Four, "Wake," is retrospective, a brief review of the invasion wave of Part One. The reality of the invasion has not conformed to expectations.

Even after the fact, Major Dalleson deludes himself about the significance of the campaign, supposing that the forces Cummings finally deployed with naval support behind Japanese lines were decisive. Dalleson's self-deception is just like Martinez's delusion that Hearn did not heed reports of Japanese in the pass where he died. Martinez forgets that Croft had cautioned him not to mention the Japanese to Hearn. In taking a superior attitude to Brown, Stanley forgets, or never actually realizes, his former sycophancy that ensured, with Brown's help, his promotion to corporal. Wilson muddles his trickery of his buddies—getting them to pay more for their liquor so he can have an extra bottle—into a belief in his generous provision for them. Even more self-conscious characters such as Hearn and Cummings catch themselves in self-deceptions. Hearn believes that he is rebelling against Cummings by crushing a cigarette on the General's immaculate floor when in fact he is playing his superior officer's game, getting himself into a position where Cummings is able to employ Hearn as just another pawn in his military strategy. Cummings, in turn, bitterly admits to himself that Hearn has a way of depriving him of his sense of command, for Hearn (who is something like a wayward son) represents the intractability of the fighting force Cummings wants to regard as an extension of himself. Mailer brilliantly reveals the ironies of Cummings' command in the General's discovery of the cigarette butt "mashed into the duckboards in a tangled ugly excrement of black ash, soiled paper, and brown tobacco." Cummings has been having bouts of diarrhea; what he sees on the floor is a manifestation of his lack of control, his inability to make his body, like his men, obey his rigorous schedule. In this encyclopedic novel—Mailer's attempt to write the equivalent of Leo Tolstoy's *War and Peace* (1865-1869) in his generation, to show that, like Napoleon, Cummings fails to reduce history to the curve of his desire—no character can claim mastery over himself or the world, for the interplay between individuals and events is too complex, too contingent, to be predictable, even though characters such as Cummings and Croft pursue their careers with the monomania of Herman Melville's Ahab in *Moby Dick* (1851).

The Naked and the Dead almost seemed to write itself, Mailer comments in *Advertisements for Myself*. In retrospect, Mailer felt he could not go on repeating a best-seller formula based on a skillful melding of Hemingway and Dos Passos. Given Mailer's ambition to be a great writer, it is not surprising that his obsession with style prompted him to devalue his first novel. If *The Naked and the Dead* is derived from the styles of other writers, it also conveys a sense of history that is almost entirely lacking in Hemingway and is diminished in Dos Passos by rather crude melodrama and determinism. In Mailer, there is no clear division of historical villains and heroes; on the contrary, he develops a dramatic dialogue of ideas that arise persuasively out of carefully delineated personalities. He did not equal this achievement for some time, perhaps because he had to go through various attempts at finding a style, a singular—even quirky—manner that is as individual as Dos Passos' "Camera Eye" sections in *U.S.A.* (1937) or the radically charged prose of William Faulkner's best work.

Mailer's next novel, *Barbary Shore*, was a disappointment to critics and to Mailer himself, even though he suggests in *Advertisements for Myself* that the novel helped to prepare him for becoming the kind of writer he would remain for the rest of his career. *Barbary Shore* seems detached from many of the basic assumptions of *The Naked and the Dead*, which has a naive confidence when viewed from the perspective of its successor. Although history is not controllable in *The Naked and the Dead*, it is not even certain that history is knowable in *Barbary Shore*, where several characters and events have a phantasmagoric quality. Characters often speak in an allegorical dialogue, so that the Soviet Union, for example, is referred to as "the land beyond the sea." One of the main characters, McLeod, has had a variety of identities, and it is never entirely clear what the truth of his life has been—not even to himself. The first-person narrator, Mike Lovett, is an amnesiac who vaguely recalls fragments of his past—most of them are memories of war—but is not sure that they are, in fact, his own. McLeod, at one time a foreign agent for the Communist Party, is pursued by Hollingsworth, who is some kind of government operative, an agent of the American status quo, on a mission to recover a "little object" (which is never identified) that McLeod is presumed to have stolen while working for what was probably a government agency—perhaps the same agency for which Hollingsworth works. The novel is further complicated by the presence of Guinevere, an apolitical sexual provocateur, who is discovered to be McLeod's wife. She attracts the amorous attentions not only of Lovett, Hollingsworth, and McLeod but also of Lannie, a bizarre, troubled woman who aligns herself first with Lovett, who befriends McLeod, and then with Hollingsworth. Hollingsworth alternately disputes and accedes to McLeod's hold over Lovett, for Lovett, with his lack of a past, represents the pure present over which conflicting personalities and ideologies contend.

Presumably, Mailer abandoned the realistic mode and third-person narration of *The Naked and the Dead* in favor of the ambiguities of *Barbary Shore* in order not only to suggest the Cold War period of shifting loyalties and competing ideologies but also to probe the divisions within his characters who suffer from crises of conviction. McLeod, for example, has tried but failed to follow the course of history, to remake the world into the fulfillment of revolutionary socialism. *Barbary Shore*, however, is unable to take the measure of McLeod in the way the *The Naked and the Dead* judges Cummings, for McLeod's dialogue with others, in which the weaknesses of his position are diagnosed, becomes a monologue that upsets the balance of the novel and makes it seem as if McLeod has somehow rescued himself from his defeat. Lovett is unwilling to abandon him even though he is fairly sure that McLeod has murderously attempted to enforce his revolutionary purpose on others.

It is true that his passing on of "the little object" to Lovett represents his final refusal to capitulate to the status quo, to the "two different exploitative systems," but his gesture to ameliorate "mankind in barbary," in a world where there is "war and preparation for new war" must be balanced by the novel's first historical parable.

Lovett describes his fantasy of a plump, complacent, middle-aged traveler who is anxious to get home. He is tired and "unaccountably depressed" after a long trip and suddenly shocked to find that while he recognizes the city in which he travels as his home, "the architecture is strange, and the people are dressed in unfamiliar clothing," and he cannot read the alphabet on the street sign. He tries to calm himself in the belief that he is dreaming, but Lovett shouts "this city is the real city, the material city, and your vehicle is history." The fantasy aptly conveys the novel's contention that man thinks he knows the course of his life, thinks that he can read the signs of history, when in fact what he has taken to be so familiar, so easily apprehended, is elusive, strange, and terrifying.

It is not difficult to regard Mailer's third novel, *The Deer Park*, as a mature rewriting of *Barbary Shore*. Once again, there is a first-person narrator, Sergius O'Shaugnessy, who, like Lovett, is a writer. Although Sergius knows his past, he is an orphan who shares Lovett's sense of uncertainty: "I was never sure of myself. I never felt as if I came from any particular place, or that I was like other people." His feeling of being like a "spy or a fake" recalls Lovett's adamant refusal to become a spy for Guinevere. Sergius, however, is more self-aware, more active as a writer in this novel than Lovett is in *Barbary Shore*, where his writing is a given but is not really explored. *The Deer Park*, on the other hand, is the product of Sergius' imagination; it represents his coming to terms with himself and the world. Although his friendship with Charles Eitel, a blacklisted Hollywood scriptwriter and director, is reminiscent of Lovett's friendship with McLeod, Eitel's story is framed in Sergius' words; Sergius contrasts Eitel's defeat with his victory.

Cold War politics play just as important a part in *The Deer Park* as in *Barbary Shore*, but the former eschews the strained allegorical rhetoric of the latter. Some of *The Deer Park*'s finest passages are the dialogues of Hollywood studio executives and politicians, in which the exploitative aspects of capitalist culture and government become apparent in the language, even in the physical gestures and tones of voice the characters employ, so that Mailer avoids merely talking *about* political issues by demonstrating how they arise in careers such as Eitel's. He has been a Communist sympathizer, a fellow traveler, whose presence embarrasses his motion-picture bosses. He then alienates them by refusing to cooperate with a congressional committee investigating subversives. Eitel turns from Hollywood with the hope that he can recover his talent honestly as an artist but finds that the great film he had always dreamed of creating has been corrupted by his absorption of the cheap techniques of commercial filmmaking. Eventually, he capitulates by agreeing to testify about his Communist past, and to construct his film according to Hollywood conventions.

At the same time, Sergius' own life-story—from orphan to war hero— draws Hollywood interest, and he is sorely tempted to sell his biography— sell himself, in effect—to the studio, where he may also become a film star. What prevents him from doing so is Eitel's example, or rather Sergius' interpretation of Eitel's biography, for at the end of the novel it is Sergius who has made some meaning out of Eitel's career:

> "For you see," [Eitel] confessed in his mind, "I have lost the final desire of the artist, the desire which tells us that when all else is lost, when love is lost and adventure, pride of self, and pity, there still remains that world we may create, more real to us, more real to others, then the mummery of what happens, passes, and is gone."

Sergius goes on to imagine that Eitel equates the creative act with Sergius' rebellion, with "the small trumpet of your defiance."

Sergius invents an Eitel from whom he can learn, and his lessons are facilitated by his relationships with many of Eitel's friends and lovers. Lulu Meyers, for example, has been married to Eitel but now is free to engage in an affair with Sergius, which she eventually terminates much to his despair. Sergius, however, avoids the extremes of self-pity and self-aggrandizement by reconstructing the affair between Elena Esposito and Eitel that is taking place during his pursuit of Lulu. Eitel's coldness, arrogance, and self-deceptiveness come through in Sergius' version of the affair, but, like McLeod, Eitel is essentially a sympathetic figure, and more believably so than McLeod, since Eitel's tragic realization of his limitations is not muffled by the slightest self-justification at the end of the novel.

If the novel's Hollywood milieu is like Louis XV's Deer Park, that gorge in which innocents like Sergius are engulfed, Sergius barely escapes the gorge by imagining for himself the lives of its victims, of its pimps and prostitutes, of its sultans and sycophants. If *Barbary Shore* begins to put the first-person narrator, the writer as actor, in a paramount position, then *The Deer Park* examines the drama of that position, which Mailer directly comments on in *Advertisements for Myself*, where he acknowledges the increasingly autobiographical nature of his narrators. Not that Sergius is in any simple way Mailer— in fact, he is far less self-conscious about his style than Mailer usually is— but Sergius' quest as a writer who needs to find his words, his style, through direct involvement that tests him against his characters' actions, provided Mailer with the conception of himself and the process of literary creation that has become central to nearly all of his work. Indeed, the process of literary creation itself becomes his theme. In other words, the writer himself becomes his subject.

An American Dream, by its very title, points to Mailer's fascination with the notion that America is a complex fiction, a drama of reality that is captured in the dynamic language of its narrator, Steven Rojack, Mailer's hipster hero *par excellence*, a war hero, a college chum of John Kennedy, a congressman, college professor, psychologist, television personality, and actor resembling the Sergius O'Shaugnessy who was supposed to be the major figure in Mailer's uncompleted novel, delivered in the form of "Advertisement for Myself on the Way Out" at the conclusion of *Advertisements for Myself*.

Rojack is also the first Mailer narrator to have an intellect, a vocabulary, and a multiplicity of roles that are commensurate with his author's own activities as soldier, writer, politician, film director, actor, and television personality. As a result, Rojack, like Mailer, registers and revalues his experience. Like his creator, he is never content with a single formulation of reality; on the contrary, he is a complex of shifting moods in response to the modulations of his environment. As Jennifer Bailey phrases it, in Mailer's mature work "identity is always a fiction insofar as it depends upon a constantly changing milieu for its definition."

All of Rojack's actions have to be viewed within the existential requirements of reality in the novel rather than within rigid moral codes applied by readers who want to keep "concepts firmly in category." For some readers, the novel's sense of absolute relativity, of moral fluidity, is repugnant, and *An American Dream* has been rejected out of hand as Mailer's most disturbing work, since Rojack as hipster does not merely live close to violence: he purges and cleanses himself through murdering his wife, Deborah.

In conventional fiction, Rojack's murder might be taken as the surest sign that he has lost control of himself. Yet, quite the contrary is true in Mailer's daring fiction, for Rojack regains possession of himself in committing his crime. In some of his most sharply driven, economical prose, Mailer has Rojack explain in the first chapter that he doubts his perception of the world in terms of a rational paradigm. He notes that "the real difference between the President and myself may be that I ended with too large an appreciation of the moon, for I looked down the abyss of the first night I killed: four men, four very separate Germans, dead under a full moon—whereas Jack, for all I know, never saw the abyss." In other words, Rojack senses the occult nature of reality, of forces that terrorize him until he has the courage to act in harmony with them.

Until he reached a point of self-identification, Rojack "remained an actor. My personality was built upon a void." He quit politics "before I was separated from myself forever by the distance between my public appearance which had become vital on television, indeed nearly robust, and my secret frightened romance with the phases of the moon." Virtually the entire novel is written in a style that dramatizes Rojack's search for a new basis on which to live. After considering suicide, after literally expelling from his system the rotting, half-digested food and drink that signify a life he cannot ingest, he confronts his estranged wife, "an artist with the needle," a woman from an influential family who has represented his "leverage" on life. Doing away with Deborah means confronting his case by himself, and he has never had "the strength to stand alone."

Rojack begins to stand alone by following the hipster's course set out in *The White Negro* (1957). He recognizes, in the words of that essay, that "one must grow or else pay more for remaining the same (pay in sickness, or depression, or anguish for the lost opportunity), but pay or grow. . . . What he must do . . . is find his courage at the moment of violence, or equally make it in the act of love." Rojack finds his lover, Cherry, a blonde with various qualities that remind him of Grace Kelly and Marilyn Monroe. More than that, however, is his sense that Cherry has "studied blondes," as if she has absorbed all of their styles. The multiplicity of her appeal is like the manifold manifestations of life that he intuits rather than grasps logically. Cherry, and many of the other characters in the novel, are viewed in a world of heightened senses, particularly the sense of smell. Rojack is constantly getting whiffs of things, of moods, of symbolic correspondences between people and ideas: "One kiss of flesh, one whiff of sweet was loose, sending life to the charnel house of my balls." The incredible number of smells that assault him prevent the novel from becoming mystical and abstract. Rather, the intangible linkages are permeated with the corporeality of bodies and beings. In this way, the world becomes an integral function in his psychic economy, and he is even able to face his wife's formidable father, Oswald Kelly, who would just as soon push Rojack to his death as to make him observe the proprieties of the funeral ceremony, where he expects Rojack's presence will help to subdue Kelly's embarrassment over the suspicious circumstances of Deborah's death.

Rojack's tie to Kelly becomes stronger when he discovers that Cherry has been Kelly's mistress—just one of those "coincidences" that rule Rojack's uncanny sense of the connections between lives. As he tries to save his integrity by confronting Kelly, he loses Cherry, who is murdered. He has been divided between returning to her (he senses her danger) and once again challenging the abyss, the drop from Kelly's high-rise apartment to the street, which represents the void Rojack must fill with his self-definition. At the end of the novel, in Las Vegas, he realizes that he has gambled for his life, that life is a gamble. If he has not been "good enough" to get it all, to have Cherry, he becomes "something like sane again," and departs for a "long trip to Guatemala and Yucatan," just two places, perhaps, on the itinerary of his voyage to selfhood.

If the examples of Hemingway and Dos Passos prevail over *The Naked and the Dead* and Mailer's other early fiction, and if F. Scott Fitzgerald figures largely in the composition of *The Deer Park*, then the measure of Mailer's progress as a writer can be taken in *Why Are We in Vietnam?*, a novel that invites deliberate comparision with Faulkner. Mailer deftly describes a bear hunt, as does Faulkner in "The Bear," that explores the fundamental meanings of American identity inherent in the conquest of animals and environment. Men must prove themselves no matter how much they override the intimate connections between humankind and nature. Rusty, the narrator D. J.'s father, "is fucked unless he gets that bear, for if he don't, white men are fucked more and they can take no more." This kind of reasoning leads to Vietnam, Mailer implies, just as the hunting of bear leads to slavery and other forms of subjugation in Faulkner. Both D. J. and Faulkner's Ike McCaslin come to identify with the animals whose lives they take and with the nature they usurp, so that they must also commune with their feeling of solidarity with life itself, as D. J. does in his remembrance of the mountain goat he has killed:

> It hit D. J. with a second blow on his heart from the exploding heart of the goat and he sat up in bed, in the bunk, listening to the snores, stole out to the night, got one breath of the sense of that *force* up in the North, of land North North above him and dived back to the bed, his sixteen-year-old heart racing through the first spooks of an encounter with Herr Dread.

However close Mailer comes to Faulkner in terms of style and theme, *Why Are We in Vietnam?* is still an insistently original novel. In the passage quoted above, for example, the point of view is wholly that of D. J., of the Texan teenager who has never encountered the raw elements of life, who is a disc jockey in his ventriloquizing of many voices in the manner of a radio rock-music personality. Although the prose has Faulkner's relentless flow, its flippant and frenetic beat suggests the repetitive rhythms of technology that heat up D. J.'s talk.

Even more striking is Mailer's playful sport with his narrator's identity. Is D. J. "a Texas youth for sure or is he a genius of a crippled Spade up in Harlem making all this shit up?" Or is D. J. imitating a "high I.Q. Harlem Nigger"? "There is no security in this consciousness," he maintains, since much of what one takes to be reality is an American dream, or rather a "dream field," a "part of a circuit" with "you swinging on the inside of the deep mystery." Inevitably, one is reminded of Ralph Ellison's *Invisible Man* (1952) narrated by a shifting persona, a man of many guises who impersonates others, who like D. J. follows many channels, as if he is broadcasting to the world at large, a world he has somehow subsumed in his supple prose. D. J. brashly appropriates and transforms the styles of others; whereas Ellison's narrator mellowly hints that on the "lower frequencies" he speaks for "you," D. J. commands: "Goose your frequency"—in other words, rev up your sensibility, your reception of the totality D. J. imagines.

As in *An American Dream*, the tendency for the language to turn mystical is checked, even substantiated, by scatological images and metaphors. Some readers find the style offensive, but it is absolutely at the heart of Mailer's vision, since he wants to show on a visceral level how the ideology of consumption works. Because he believes that "the secrets of existence, or some of them anyway, are to be found in the constructions of language" ("The Metaphysics of the Belly"), his style must go to the scatological site of those secrets. To extend D. J.'s remark, the world is "shit" made up by human beings, and in America such "shit" prevails because of the incredible amount of resources that are used, turned into waste products, into refuse which Americans refuse to see; as Mailer sums it up in "The Metaphysics of the Belly": "Ambitious societies loathe scatological themes and are obsessed with them." The last words of the novel, "Vietnam, hot dam," reflect D. J.'s anticipation; here is still another frontier on which to test himself, another territory for him to explore like Huckleberry Finn, to whom he compares himself at the beginning of the novel. D. J., "disc jockey to America," echoes the country's heated urge to dominate, to damn itself. Or is the minority voice mimicking the majority's will? "Which D. J. white or black would possibly be worse of a genius if Harlem or Dallas is guiding the other, and who knows which?" All the jive talk keeps the channels of possibility open at the end of *Why Are We in Vietnam?*, so that the question of the title has been answered in some ways but is still open-ended, like the identity of the narrator. The reader is left perfectly pitched between alternative readings, once again in the grip of the existential reality that Mailer has faultlessly articulated.

The Armies of the Night climaxed a period of impressive creativity for Mailer in the mid-1960's. A culmination of the self-review he began in *Advertisements for Myself* and *Cannibals and Christians*, it is a definitive portrait of himself as writer and actor, a discovery of his nonfiction aesthetic, and a subtle amalgam of documentary notation and novelistic interpretation that convincingly captures the complexity and ambiguity of the march on the Pentagon. The book's authority is established by its point of view: Mailer's assessment of himself in the third person, sticking close to his own consciousness in the same way that Henry James sidles along Strether in *The Ambassadors* (1903). Thus, Mailer is able to preserve the spontaneity of historic moments in which he is free to act like a fool or a philosopher while reserving the right as an aloof narrator to judge himself and others with the benefit of hindsight and later research. Futhermore, as Richard Poirier observes, Mailer "manages to be a witness of the present as if it were already the past. He experiences it from the perspective of his future talk and writing about it." The Mailer of the march is at various times "the Beast," "the Historian," "the Participant," "the Novelist," and "the Ruminant," all of which emphasize the many different guises he assumes depending upon the evolving context of his actions.

As rich as a novel in its use of dialogue and characterization, *The Armies of the Night* humorously pursues the contentions of competing personalities— of the poet Robert Lowell and Mailer himself in this example:

"I don't know, Cal, your speech really had a most amazing impact on me." Mailer drawled the last few words to drain any excessive sentimental infection, but Lowell seemed hardly to mind.

"Well, Norman, I'm delighted," he said, taking Mailer's arm for a moment as if, God and kingdom willing, Mailer had finally become a Harvard dean and could be addressed by the appropriate limb. "I'm delighted because I liked *your* speech so much."

By using circular dialogue, the search for an agreeable exchange between very different personalities—Lowell, "at once virile and patrician," and Mailer, "the younger, presumptive, and self-elected prince"—they have made a story of their relationship which they can share and repeat. The fictive quality of real events—one of Mailer's major points—is ably demonstrated by his own style. As Mailer says before this dialogue, "the clue to discovery was not in the substance of one's idea, but in what was learned from the style of one's attack."

The book shuttles from such intimate dialogue and precise character delineation to panoramic sweeps of the crowds of the Pentagon march. Book One, "History as a Novel," portrays Mailer as actor in order to show that history is understood only through a deep appreciation of the intersection of very personal feelings and public affairs. No episode, no idea, no impression remains unqualified by the circumstances out of which it arises, and chapter titles constantly emphasize the way in which the literary imagination shapes historical experience.

Book Two, "The Novel as History," goes even further than Book One in suggesting that history as a whole can make sense only when the interpreter employs all the "instincts of the novelist," for the record of the march is contradictory, fragmentary, and skewed by various viewpoints. Only an act of profound imagination, a reading of the significance of the event itself, can possibly make its constituent parts coalesce, and Mailer convincingly shows that he has studied the record and found it wanting. History is essentially interior and intuitive, he avers. He then proceeds to elaborate a complex re-creation of events that concretely exposes the factitiousness of newspaper accounts.

Beyond the immediate causes and consequences of the march on the Pentagon, Mailer sees the event as a rite of passage for the young marchers, expecially the ones who refuse to flee when their fellows are brutally beaten into submission in one of the most riveting and frightening pages in all of Mailer's writing. The coming of knowledge, of a historical fatalism, creeps into both Mailer's prose and his characters' weary postures as he recites events from America's past which reveal that it was founded on a rite of passage. It is as if these young people are suddenly imbued with historical consciousness, although Mailer's ruminations and their agony are kept separate on the page. Nevertheless, in his coda he suggests that if the march's end took place in the "isolation in which these last pacifists suffered naked in freezing cells, and gave up prayers for penance, then who was to say they were not saints? And who to say that the sins of America were not by their witness a tithe remitted?" His final words balance an earlier passage where he describes the marchers' opponents, "the gang of Marshals" who in their "collective spirit" emit "little which was good," and one of whom "paid tithe to ten parallel deep lines rising in ridges above his eye brows." Mailer achieves a harmony of form and an equilibrium of language that make the novel's ending seem as complex as the history it imagines, and as moving in its depiction of ignorance and confusion as the Matthew Arnold poem, "Dover Beach," from which Mailer's title is taken.

While they are satisfactory in sections, *Of a Fire on the Moon, The Fight,* and Mailer's other writings from the late 1960's to the mid-1970's do not equal *Marilyn,* his follow-up study of the ambiguities of fiction and history so magnificently explored in *The Armies of the Night. Marilyn* has a twofold purpose: to measure faithfully and evaluate the obstacles that bar the biographer's way to a full understanding of his subject's life, and to suggest tentatively a biographical method which will aim at re-creating the whole person even though conceding that the search for wholeness is elusive and problematical.

Furthermore, Monroe ranks with Mailer's other major characters, such as General Cummings. Just as Cummings works to make himself an instrument of his own policy, so Monroe paints herself into the camera lens as an instrument of her own will. She is Napoleonic and yet divided against herself, a Dreiserian character who traverses the continent in quest of her true self in much the same way as Lovett, O'Shaugnessy, and Rojack do, detecting voids in themselves and voyaging to find their genuine identities. Much of Mailer's work in film, and his discussions of film in "Some Dirt in the Talk" and "A Course in Film-Making" (both collected in *Existential Errands*), lead directly to his perception of Monroe's disrupted sense of self. Although his more recent "imaginary memoir," *Of Women and Their Elegance,* in which Monroe recalls her last years, seems less substantial than *Marilyn,* he carries his concern with "twin personalities" a step further by integrating his narrative with Milton Greene's provocative photographs, which are studies in the doubling of personality in a divided world.

Set against the background of his reflexive writing of the 1960's and 1970's, *The Executioner's Song,* Mailer's next major work of fiction, is a startling book. Its sentences are simple and clear, with an occasionally striking but not elaborate metaphor. Absent from the narrative is Mailer's characteristic sentence or paragraph, which is long and comprehensive—an encyclopedic attempt to gather all of reality in one magnificent statement. There is no intrusive voice to sum up the life of Gary Gilmore, a convicted and executed murderer, and the age in which Gilmore grows to kill. Mailer does not explicitly explore a theory of biography, and does not comment, except in his Afterword, on his interaction with the life he has written. His book seems keyed to a new aesthetic.

In spite of its 1,056 pages, *The Executioner's Song* is not a garrulous work; it is a quiet book punctuated by myriad silences. There is a double space following nearly every paragraph of the book, indicating the gap between events, the momentary pause that intervenes even in events that seemingly follow one another swiftly and smoothly. Reality is defined by these frequent intervals of silence, periods of stillness that intimate how much is left unsaid and how many characters fail to connect with one another. Gilmore is the most solitary character of all, cut off in large part from humanity and therefore able to murder.

A great deal of the book is dialogue or paraphrase of dialogue, which enhances the dramatic clash of details and conflicting points of view. Even the long descriptive passages and the evocations of characters' thoughts consist only of the results of the reporter who has interviewed these characters for their thoughts and who conveys what he has heard and observed. Hence, there is no privileged retrospective narrator to unify the book's disparate materials.

Mailer has called *The Executioner's Song* a "true life novel." By "novel" he seems to mean something somewhat different from his use of the term in *The Armies of the Night* and *Marilyn*, in which he employs a novelistic narrator to probe the unspoken motivations of his characters and to organize reality in creative metaphors. Of his unusual departure from past practice he remarks in *The New York Times Magazine* (September 9, 1979):

> I was convinced from the start that the materials were exceptional; it had the structure of a novel. Whenever I needed a character for esthetic balance—a new character of imposing dimensions—one just appeared out of nowhere. If I had conceived *The Executioner's Song* as a novel entirely drawn from my own imagination, I doubt I could have improved on those characters.

Mailer conceives of the characters as revealing themselves to him, so that he does not have to serve as a mediating voice. Instead, he orchestrates their disclosures by surrounding them with a quiet space and spare style that preserves their individual integrity.

Reading such sparely created scenes, one is tempted to comb through the details over and over again in order to search for the pertinent clue that will point to the meaning of Gilmore's story, but as Joan Didion points out in her review in *The New York Times Book Review* (October 7, 1979), "the very subject of *The Executioner's Song* is that vast emptiness at the center of the Western experience, a nihilism antithetical not only to literature but to most other forms of human endeavor, a dread so close to zero that human voices fade out, trail off, like skywriting." Mailer has chosen, this time, to make a literature that is articulately mute, almost muzzled in its restrained revelations of actions which remain voiceless, dumb, and frighteningly uncommunicative:

"Why'd you do it, Gary?" Nielsen asked again quietly.

"I don't know," Gary said.

"Are you sure?"

"I'm not going to talk about that," Gilmore said. He shook his head delicately, and looked at Nielsen, and said, "I can't keep up with life."

For Mailer, *The Executioner's Song* is biography in a new key, since he attends to the integrity of individual lives without quickly elevating those lives into symbolic significance. At the same time, the continuity of his concerns is apparent in his ambitious desire to show that true life must be mediated through the imaginative power of a singular intelligence. He understood that *The Executioner's Song* required a voice, flexible and comprehensive, in order to embody the myriad voices that make up reality. There are patterns that can be perceived on rereading the book, yet no single pattern is definitive. Gilmore seems to reach some genuine self-understanding and consistency, but his behavior is still sometimes contradictory and enigmatic. He approaches his execution wanting to die, and yet he searches for every possible means of escape. *The Executioner's Song* remains faithful to the elusiveness of self, to both the revelation and the inscrutability of identity.

Beginning with the first sentence—"Crude thoughts and fierce forces are my state"—*Ancient Evenings* embarks on a style that is new to Mailer and to his readers who have been accustomed to an active voice transforming everything it articulates. Something very strange is happening to the passive voice of the novel's first narrator-protagonist, the ka (spiritual emanation) of Menenhetet II, who is undergoing the process of rebirth. The first book of the novel is awesome and quite wonderful in its depiction of a consciousness trying to differentiate itself from all that surrounds it.

After the first book, much of the novel is narrated by Menenhetet I, the great-grandfather of Menenhetet II. Menenhetet I is the great ancestor who has been able to live four lives (1290-1100 B.C.) by learning how to ejaculate into a woman at the very moment of his death, thereby conceiving himself anew in a lover who becomes his mother. Menenhetet I aspires in his first life to supplant his Pharaoh as ruler of Egypt and dies in the act of sexual intercourse with the Pharaoh's queen. Menenhetet I carries Mailer's conception of himself and of the hero in his fiction to the farthest extreme: he is a man of many ages, the self-invented avatar of Menenhetet II's quest for distinction. Menenhetet I has been a warrior and high priest, a scholar and man of action, a great lover of queens and yet a farmer of peasant origin. In his fourth life, Menenhetet I would like to be the vizier of Ramses IX (Ptah-nem-hotep). In the very act of telling his four life histories to Ramses IX, however, Menenhetet I reveals an overweening ambition and fatal attraction to magical practices (including the repulsive eating of bat dung) that disqualify him for the role of Pharaonic confidant.

Ancient Evenings is embedded in the lush details of ancient Egypt, in the rhythms of an alien time. Even sympathetic readers have noted a numbing sameness in the prose that suggests that the author has striven too hard for unity, for the merging of the opposites that create so much exciting tension in *The Naked and the Dead*, *The Armies of the Night*, and *The Executioner's Song*. *Ancient Evenings* is Norman Mailer at his neatest, with the loose ends of his philosophy and his prose knit together rather impressively. Nevertheless, it seems static and too thoroughly thought-out; absent from it is the rough-edged stimulation of a writer on the make, who is best when he is suggestive rather than explicit, when he is promising to complete the circle and join the halves without ever quite doing so.

Like Mikey Lovett in *Barbary Shore*, Tim Madden in *Tough Guys Don't Dance* is an amnesiac: he cannot remember what happened the night before, and he cannot account for the large amount of blood on his car seat. He is clearly kin to Stephen Rojack. More or less kept by his prized wife, the wealthy Patty Lareine, Madden, a writer, finds that he cannot work when she deserts him.

As her name suggests, Lareine has been Madden's imperious queen, and he seems at a loss when he is not in the service of his "medieval lady." At the same time, he has clearly chafed under her rule, for he regrets having broken his code of male self-sufficiency. As a result, the couple's marriage has been turbulent, and in its later stages, husband and wife seem most alike in their murderous inclinations. The novel begins with Madden wondering whether the severed head he discovers in his marijuana hideaway is the result of a drunken evening's debauchery with another woman, which turned violent when Patty Lareine returned home.

The characters in *Tough Guys Don't Dance* relate to one another as in an Arthurian romance. Madden discovers that his wife has had another lover, the Deputy Police Chief, Alvin Luther Regency, a powerfully built, maniacal rival, who is part of the plot to set up Madden (who has already served a short term for possession of cocaine). Complicating matters further for Madden is the lurking presence of his envious former schoolmate, Meeks Wardly Hilby III, who was once married to Patty Lareine, and from whom Madden stole her. If Madden can make sense of the two murders, he can also begin to put his life back together—including his failed relationship with Madeleine Falco, his witty, tough counterpart, who left him when he took up with Patty Lareine and who now finds herself mired in a bad marriage to the dangerous Regency.

Readers who prefer murder mysteries with taut, spare plots and prose may bristle at the complications of Mailer's syntax and philosophizing. The heads and bodies buried in different locations are indicative of the splits in the human psyche that Mailer has pursued in much of his writing. Usually Mailer is able to finesse the shifts between the novel's ideas and events, and his delineation of characters through clipped dialogue is convincing. At a few points, his narrative flags, perhaps because he has tried to do too much, to integrate characters, ideas, and plot simultaneously in a single narrative voice.

Carl E. Rollyson, Jr.

Other major works

SHORT FICTION: *New Short Novels 2*, 1956; *The Short Fiction of Norman Mailer*, 1967.

PLAY: *The Deer Park: A Play*, 1967.

POETRY: *Deaths for the Ladies and Other Disasters*, 1962.

NONFICTION: *The White Negro*, 1957; *The Presidential Papers*, 1963; *Cannibals and Christians*, 1966; *The Bullfight*, 1967; *The Idol and the Octopus: Political Writings on the Kennedy and Johnson Administrations*, 1968; *Miami and the Siege of Chicago: An Informal History of the Republican and Democratic Conventions of 1968*, 1969; *Of a Fire on the Moon*, 1970; *The Prisoner of Sex*, 1971; *The Long Patrol: 25 Years of Writing from the Work of Norman Mailer*, 1971 (Robert Lucid, editor); *Existential Errands*, 1972; *St. George and the Godfather*, 1972; *The Faith of Graffiti*, 1974 (with Mervyn Kurlansky and Jon Naar); *The Fight*, 1975; *Some Honorable Men: Political Conventions 1960-1972*, 1975; *Genius and Lust: A Journey Through the Major Writings of Henry Miller*, 1976; *Pieces and Pontifications*, 1982.

MISCELLANEOUS: *Advertisements for Myself*, 1959.

Bibliography

Adams, Laura, ed. *Will the Real Norman Mailer Please Stand Up?* Port Washington, N.Y.: Kennikat Press, 1974. A valuable collection of reviews and essays on Mailer's life and work, which is arranged in strict chronological order to resemble a composite biography.

Braudy, Leo, ed. *Norman Mailer: A Collection of Critical Essays*. Englewood Cliffs, N.J.: Prentice-Hall, 1972. Contains an excellent introduction by Braudy surveying Mailer's career, providing thoughtful criticism on individual works and themes, and a bibliography.

Bufithis, Philip H. *Norman Mailer*. New York: Ungar, 1978. A succinct and perceptive study of Mailer's life and work.

Gordon, Andrew. *An American Dreamer: A Psychoanalytic Study of the Fiction of Norman Mailer*. Rutherford, N.J.: Fairleigh Dickenson University Press, 1980. One of the most penetrating studies of Mailer's fiction and nonfiction, which shows how deeply rooted in his work are aspects of his biography.

Lennon, J. Michael, ed. *Conversations with Norman Mailer*. Jackson: University Press of Mississippi, 1988. A collection of the most important interviews with Mailer, which reveals his developing and changing attitudes toward his work.

_____. *Critical Essays on Norman Mailer*. Boston: G. K. Hall, 1986. The most up-to-date collection of criticism on Mailer's work, important reviews, and an extremely valuable overview by Lennon of Mailer's evolving reputation.

Lucid, Robert F., ed. *Norman Mailer: The Man and His Work*. Boston: Little, Brown, 1971. Should be read in conjunction with collections by Adams, Braudy, and Lennon. Lucid's essay is particularly important in establishing the reasons for Mailer's need to create a public persona of the writer.

Manso, Peter, ed. *Mailer: His Life and Times*. New York: Simon & Schuster, 1985. An edited collection of interviews with the important figures in Mailer's life, arranged in chronological order. Mailer is interviewed as well, and there are excerpts from his correspondence. A valuable source of biographical information.

Merrill, Robert. *Norman Mailer*. Boston: Twayne, 1978. A brief introduction to Mailer's career, with a short biography, sound readings of individual works, and an annotated bibliography.

Mills, Hilary. *Norman Mailer: A Biography*. New York: Empire Books, 1982. The first full-fledged biography of Mailer based on extensive interviews. Mills treats the reception of Mailer's work but does not provide a critical perspective.

Poirier, Richard. *Norman Mailer*. New York: Viking Books, 1972. A brief but provocative critical study, considered to be one of the most insightful examinations of Mailer's career.

Solotaroff, Robert. *Down Mailer's Way*. Urbana: University of Illinois Press, 1974. An astute, comprehensive examination of Mailer's life and work, often cited in other studies of Mailer.

Wenke, Joseph. *Mailer's America*. Hanover, N.H.: University Press of New England, 1987. Concentrates on Mailer's attitudes toward America in his major fiction and nonfiction, including *Ancient Evenings* and *Tough Guys Don't Dance*.

BERNARD MALAMUD

Born: Brooklyn, New York; April 26, 1914
Died: New York, New York; March 18, 1986

Principal long fiction

The Natural, 1952; *The Assistant*, 1957; *A New Life*, 1961; *The Fixer*, 1966; *The Tenants*, 1971; *Dubin's Lives*, 1979; *God's Grace*, 1982; *The People*, 1989.

Other literary forms

While acknowledging his significant achievements as a novelist, many critics believe that Bernard Malamud's most distinctive and enduring contributions to American fiction are to be found in his short stories, particularly those collected in *The Magic Barrel* (1958) and *Idiots First* (1963). Malamud published three more volumes of short fiction in his lifetime: *Picture of Fidelman: An Exhibition* (1969), a collection of six linked stories featuring the same protagonist; *Rembrandt's Hat* (1973); and *The Stories of Bernard Malamud* (1983), twenty-five stories largely drawn from previously published volumes. The posthumously published volume *The People and Uncollected Stories* (1989) gathers a number of previously uncollected stories, most of them early pieces from the 1940's but also including two from the 1980's.

Achievements

With novelists such as Saul Bellow and Philip Roth, Malamud is among the most distinguished of a number of Jewish writers who did much to set the tone of postwar American fiction. Malamud's singular achievement is to have captured the experience of Jews in America at a point of transition between cultures. His characters—not only the Jews but also their Gentile counterparts—are not yet quite a part of American culture, nor have they fully abandoned the old culture of which they are no longer members. Out of this sense of dislocation and the struggle to create a new life, Malamud created most of his early stories and novels. Although not all the novels have Jewish protagonists—the first two in fact do not—the dilemma is constant; the Gentile characters are as displaced and alienated as the Jewish ones.

Biography

Bernard Malamud was born in Brooklyn to Russian immigrant parents. His father, like Morris Bober in *The Assistant*, was a small grocer, the family moving around Brooklyn as business dictated. When Malamud was nine years old, he had pneumonia and began a period of intensive reading. Later, encouraged by his teachers, he also began writing short stories.

From 1932 to 1936, Malamud was a student at the City College of New York. He later began work on an M.A. at Columbia University, and, while teaching night school at Erasmus Hall, his own alma mater, he started writing in earnest. He married Ann de Chiara in 1945, and four years later, he and his family moved to Corvallis, Oregon, where for twelve years Malamud taught English at Oregon State. A son was born before he left for Corvallis, a daughter after he arrived. While there, he published his first four books; after leaving, he wrote his satire of academic life in an English department, *A New Life*. Returning to the East in 1961, Malamud taught for many years at Bennington College in Vermont. He received numerous awards for his fiction, including two National Book Awards and a Pulitzer Prize. Malamud died in New York on March 18, 1986.

Analysis

In *The Natural*, Iris Lemon tells the protagonist that all people have two lives, "the life we learn with and the life we live with after that. Suffering is what brings us toward happiness." Although her statement requires qualification, it is a suggestive summary of the major theme of Bernard Malamud's work: the journey toward a new life, a journey marked by suffering, which may or may not be redemptive. In fact, however, Malamud's characters usually have three lives: one from which they have not learned and which they are attempting to leave behind, a life the reader sees in flashbacks and confessions as well as in brief opening scenes; a middle life, the learning life, which is the substance of the books; and the new life promised to successful characters at the end. Malamud's novels, then, are in the tradition of the *Bildungsroman*, but they have older protagonists than do most American novels of education. What Malamud depicts in each of his novels is a renewed attempt to find new life and to convert suffering to meaning, a second journey toward knowledge.

Of the old life, Malamud usually shows his readers little. *The Natural* opens with a brief pregame sketch that quickly shows Roy Hobbs's past. In *The Assistant*, the reader sees the robbery for which Frankie Alpine will try to atone, and in *The Fixer*, there is a short portrait of Yakov Bok's past in his village. Malamud's characters are trying to forget the past, so even when it enters their minds, they try to shove it away. Moreover, Malamud's novels usually begin with a journey away from a past life. Whether European Jews coming to America or moving from their *shtetl* to Kiev, or whether American Jews traveling from New York to Oregon or baseball players leaving the country for the big city, Malamud's protagonists are always travelers, uneasy with their past, uncertain of their future. In fact, they often try to conceal their past: Alpine and Hobbs work conscientiously to obliterate the stories of their earlier lives. Yakov Bok drops his prayer things, a reminder of his old life and its ways, into a river. One of Malamud's most frequent devices is to have characters change their names in an attempt to escape their past identity. Bok, trying to pass as a Gentile, becomes Yakov Ivanovitch Dologushev, his initials ironically spelling "yid."

What all of Malamud's characters must learn, however, is that they have to accept responsibility for their past actions. Paradoxically, while the evil that his characters have done remains with them and so must be acknowledged, the good can be erased. At the end of *The Natural*, Roy Hobbs, a failure in his quest for a new life, discovers that for his part in throwing the league playoffs, all of his baseball records will be expunged from the record books.

The journey is always a quest, as the mythological base of *The Natural*, Malamud's first and prototypal novel, makes clear. The public part of the quest takes place in the world of men, and its lesson is that of law, of the inner check, of renunciation. Hobbs is a natural hitter, but he lacks good judgment, both on the field and off. Frankie Alpine in *The Assistant* continually steals from Morris Bober. Saving Bober's daughter Helen from being raped, he is unable to control his own sexual appetite and rapes her himself. "Why do Jews suffer so much?" he asks Morris Bober, and after replying that to live is to suffer, Morris adds, "I think if a Jew don't suffer for the Law, he will suffer for nothing." Although Alpine is not yet a Jew, he does suffer for nothing.

Acceptance of the law, curbing one's appetite, is the first lesson. As Levin thinks in *A New Life*, "Renunciation was what he was now engaged in. It was a beginning that created a beginning." Yet law alone is not enough, and Malamud's questers must pass a second test as well for their journeys to be successful: the test of love, of dream, of acceptance of life in its fullness and ambiguity. Helen Bober could marry Nat Pearl, studying to be a lawyer, but lacking dreams, or she could choose Louis Karp, pure appetite, lacking law. She chooses neither, and at the novel's conclusion a chance remains for Frankie Alpine, who is learning what W. H. Auden calls a "law like love." In *A New Life*, Levin first picks up Henry James's *The American* (1877), a book that makes a case for renunciation, but Pauline Gilley, another man's wife whom Levin first renounces but later accepts, moves the discussion to William Dean Howells, who, like Malamud, prefers the economy of pain.

Another qualification to Iris Lemon's statement is necessary: suffering is what *may* bring one toward happiness. The quest is not successful for all of Malamud's characters. Many of them, already displaced from their European homelands, refuse to undertake another journey. Others learn the wrong lesson from their old life. "*Rachmones*, we say in Hebrew," says Yakov Bok. "Mercy, one oughtn't to forget it." Many, particularly women (there are no Jewish mothers in Malamud), do forget it and harden their hearts. Still others, having undertaken the journey, are, like Roy Hobbs, too selfish ever to move beyond themselves.

Not only do Malamud's novels tell and retell the same story, but they do so with similar casts and with the same images. The protagonist is typically without a close family, sometimes orphaned. He is often a *schlemiel* or a *schlemazl*, always wanting to escape his past, but unlucky and clumsy in the attempt. He is likely to be self-deceived. Early in *The Assistant*, while still stealing, Alpine tells himself that he is "an honest guy." Later he says, "Even when I am bad I am good," inaccurately viewing himself as a man of stern morality.

Especially in the early novels and short stories, there is a father figure, and the learning relationship is dramatized in terms of an apprenticeship. These figures become less important in the later novels. By *A New Life*, a transitional book, both would-be father-figures, the inane Fairchild and the more scholarly but weak Fabrikant, are failures. After *A New Life*, the questers are orphaned even in this middle life.

Malamud also makes frequent use of the double, figures both actual and dreamed. Roy and Bump Baily, the player he replaces, are identified with each other: they share the same girl and the same fault. Frankie Alpine enacts in his dreams the crimes Ward Minogue, his darker opposite, actually commits. In *The Tenants*, Harry Lesser and Willie Spearmint (born Bill Spear—blacks also change names in Malamud) act out the common racial stereotypes, reverse them, and then destroy each other's work and life. An image from William Shakespeare's *King Lear* (1605), each as the other's shadow, dominates the book.

Women in Malamud's work are of two types: the dark ladies (Memo Paris, who betrays Roy Hobbs, and Harriet Bird, who shoots him; Avis Fliss, who spies on Levin; and Zenaida, who gives false testimony against Bok) and the potentially redemptive ladies of the lake (Iris Lemon, Helen Bober, Pauline Gilley, Fanny Bick in *Dubin's Lives*). The function of the good women is in part to hear the hero's confession, enabling him to acknowledge his past, but the women confess too, and, as in Nathaniel Hawthorne, an earlier fabulist, the protagonists have the obligation to accept the women's ambiguous moral nature, a test they often fail. Roy, for example, who wants Iris's sympathy, is disquieted when she tells him that at thirty-three she is a grandmother.

Malamud is also consistent in his metaphors. The journey is often from a prison to freedom. Stores are identified as prisons; Alpine feels both imprisoned and entombed in Bober's grocery. Bok exchanges a *shtetl* for a prison, but learns the meaning of freedom while he is confined. Levin says that if you make the wrong basis for your life, "you spend your whole life in jail," though he later realizes that the prison is himself.

Another metaphor involves moving from a mirror to a window—and beyond. Characters must not reject the mirror, refuse to see themselves as they truly are, as Irene Bell, *née* Belinsky, does when she refuses to look into a dropped mirror in *The Tenants*. Unfortunately, after they know themselves, the characters sometimes become so fascinated with their own image that they cannot move on. *The Natural* opens with Roy Hobbs on a train, striking a match to look out the window but seeing only his own reflection; throughout the novel, he never achieves any higher values than those centered on himself.

Progress, the attempt to make contact with another, is often symbolized by gazing through a window—transparent, but still dividing, the attempt finally a failure. A common example of this failure is voyeurism; Levin eyes Pauline Gilley's house and watches her through binoculars at a basketball game, while Gerald, her husband, watches several characters through the viewfinder of his camera. Lesser in *The Tenants* is watched through a keyhole. Frankie Alpine climbs an airshaft to watch through a window as Helen Bober showers, and William Dubin in *Dubin's Lives* sneaks to Fanny Bick's house to spy on her and her boyfriend through a window.

Consistent images are linked in Malamud's novels. They must have about them a touch of red or black, a reminder of their human imperfection. They are associated, often by their names, with flowers (Iris, though with Lemon), with birds (Harriet Bird, Avis Fliss), and with trees. The bad women have sore breasts (Memo, Avis) and are like trapped birds and twisted trees.

If there is a conversion—an acceptance of the old life and a promise of a new—it takes place in an isolated, natural spot, such as the park in the urban world of *The Assistant*, where Alpine tells Helen that the best part of Leo Tolstoy's *Anna Karenina* is Levin's conversion in the woods; the lake in *The Natural* (Memo, the bad woman, is, however, associated with polluted waters); the woods in *A New Life*, where Malamud's Levin is converted; and the artificial jungle of *The Tenants*, where the meeting of Lesser and Spearmint ends in death. In *Dubin's Lives*, Dubin is running through the countryside when he first meets Fanny, and it is there that they finally make love.

Despite this consistency of theme, character, and image, Malamud's fiction changed during his career. The early works, with their blend of romance and realism, represent Malamud's best writing. About midway through his career, however, he seemed to have tired of his form; his novels became more discursive, his protagonists more articulate. On the one hand, he moved toward experimentalism, on the other hand, toward the novel of ideas. Quoting Herman Melville that to have a mighty novel, one needs a mighty theme, suggesting that "the purpose of a writer is to keep civilization from destroying itself," Malamud in his later novels reached obtrusively for significance. The protagonists of these later works are frequently blocked artists: the writers in *The Tenants*, the biographer in *Dubin's Lives*.

Malamud's first novel, *The Natural*, is a fanciful combination of American baseball lore with the myth of the wasteland. Here, the wasteland is a New York baseball team, the Knights, whose coach, Pop Fisher, is the fisher king of the legend. The quester and protagonist of the novel is Roy Hobbs; his name meaning rustic king, Roy undergoes a double-edged test to see if he can bring life to the baseball team, but the center of the novel is what Roy himself does—or does not—learn from the tests, the chance of a new life for the quester. Though *The Natural* is in many ways the least Jewish of Malamud's novels, it is the prototype for the rest of his fiction; the story it tells and the patterns it uses are those that persist through Malamud's work.

The pregame section of the novel, the brief history of the past life in which Hobbs does not learn and which he will attempt to leave behind, opens with the image of Hobbs staring at his own reflection in the train window. This inability to look beyond himself, his egocentric view of the world, is Hobbs's undoing. Both parts of Roy's testing are also prefigured in this section, which is a microcosm of the novel as a whole. In the public test, Roy, a pitcher, is challenged by an established batting king, whom Roy strikes out as Malamud draws the mythic parallels. The cost of that success is that Roy slays his first father-figure, his mentor who catches the pitches without adequate chest protection, is injured, and dies.

If Roy is at least partially successful in his physical challenge, he is not at all so in the world of moral choice. In the pregame section, he is questioned by the first of the women in the novel, Harriet Bird. The episode is based on the real-life shooting of a ballplayer. Harriet invites Roy up to her hotel room. She tests him with a series of questions about the value of his ambitions, but when Roy's self-centered answers reveal the limits of his aspirations—he plays only for his own glory—his unalloyed confidence is rewarded with a bullet. The section ends with a fantastic tableau: Harriet Bird doing a grisly nude dance around the fallen body of Roy Hobbs.

The nine inning-like sections of the novel which follow repeat more spaciously the double test the quester has to undertake to revitalize the team and prove himself worthy of a new life. When Roy arrives, everything is dismal; the Knights are losing, the players are dispirited, Pop Fisher is ailing. Even the drinking fountain produces only rusty water. Once Roy begins to play, however, the team's luck changes. Armed with his mythic bat, Wonder Boy, Roy hits five home runs and energizes the team. Rain falls, and the process of restoring life-giving water to the land begins. Roy, however, gets his chance to play only when another player, Bump Baily, is injured. Again, Roy's success depends on the suffering of another, suffering on which Roy is too willing to capitalize. Roy and Bump are doubles, Bump a darker projection of many of Roy's faults. As the fans and team-members point out, they share a common limitation: they play for themselves rather than for the team. The high point of Roy's career is Roy Hobbs Day, an event which occurs in the middle of this symmetrical novel. He is given a white Mercedes, a symbolic lancer on which he proudly rides around the stadium.

Roy's acceptance speech has only one theme, his own greatness, and from this triumph, Roy's downward path, indicated by his batting slump, begins. Although there are short times of solid hitting, as when Roy agrees to play for another, the on-field slump is accompanied by Roy's involvement with the illegal off-the-field dealings of the team's owner, who is setting up the throwing of the league playoffs, a fictive event modeled on the notorious "Black Sox" scandal of the 1919 World Series. Roy is in a world beyond his experience. Baffled by the owner's oily, cliché-ridden speeches, Roy participates in the fix. Although at the end of the playoff game Roy tries to play well to reverse the evil he has already done, it is to late; he can no longer free himself and strikes out. The story which begins with Roy striking out an aging star comes full circle with a new young pitcher striking out Roy.

In the private half of the test, Roy once again fails. As he has earlier made the wrong choice with Harriet Bird, he once again makes the wrong moral choices in this section of the novel. He becomes involved with the dark lady, Memo Paris, and they drive off together to a beach, even though the sign cautions danger, warning them of polluted water. There can be no symbolic cleansing here. Memo tries to explain the values she has learned from the suffering in her past, but what she has learned is solely to look out for herself. Roy wants to say something comparable about his own life, but he can think of nothing except more boasting about his future. When he returns to the ballfield after this episode, his grim future is apparent and his lack of control is magnified. The mystic meal is transformed into a large banquet where Roy eats so much he becomes too sick to play.

Memo's counterpart, the redemptive lady of the lake, is Iris Lemon. Like Memo and Harriet, she is associated with birds, flowers, and water, and as with Memo, the key scene involves a journey to the lake; Iris's role, however, is as potential savior of Roy. They drive together to a lake sheltered from the outside world, and it is there that Iris, too, questions Roy about his values, but she tries to lead him beyond boasting. She begins a confession of her own life. Although she is a grandmother at thirty-three, she has learned from her suffering, has transformed it into meaning. Roy is thirty-four, but something about Iris's confession repels him. They make love and Iris becomes pregnant—she is the only fruitful woman in the novel—but Roy finally rejects her. In the last game of the playoffs, he sees her in the stands, but he is intent on trying to hit a dwarf who habitually heckles him from the bleachers. The ball instead hits Iris, who has stood to cheer for Roy. In the final scene between them, Iris tells Roy that she is pregnant, that he has created a new life for another at least, and she asks Roy to hit one for their child. It is too late, and Roy strikes out. He thinks of all the wrong choices he has made and wants to undo them, but he cannot.

In addition to the myth of the wasteland and the quest for new life, a central image of the novel occurs in a dream Roy frequently has. It involves Roy and his dog in a forest, a secluded place where he can follow his inmost thoughts without shame. Driving once with Memo, Roy thinks he sees a boy and a dog emerging from a woods, a boy whom Memo seems to hit. Whether she has or not, Memo speeds on—leaving behind her destruction of Roy's innocence and his illusions. In the forest he thinks he will lose his directions in order to find himself, lose his life in order to save it, but for Roy, whose middle life is marked with nothing but wrong choices, there is no salvation, no learning. The boy and his dog have vanished along with Roy's innocence, and he has rejected Iris, who could have saved him.

In Malamud's second novel, *The Assistant*, the surface of the myth is quite different. The pastoral world of baseball gives way to an urban business setting. The rustic king gives way to the petty thief, and the myth of heroic action on which the fate of many depends is replaced by the legend of a saint. Spaciousness is superseded by narrowness, movement by confinement. *The Natural* is often humorous and always marked by energy; even evil is active. In *The Assistant*, gloom and lethargy hang over every scene, and the despair is oppressive. The mythic parallels in *The Natural* are elaborate and schematic; in *The Assistant*, implicit and suggestive.

These differences sketched, however, *The Assistant* remains another telling of Malamud's basic myth. For most critics, it is his most successful; the fusion of romance and realism, of surface accuracy with poetic evocation, is seamless and compelling. Like Roy Hobbs, Frankie Alpine, the protagonist of *The Assistant*, is without parents. Both find older men from whom to learn, and both are partially responsible for their deaths. When the lessons they encounter involve renunciation, a check on their passions, they refuse to heed the wisdom. Both learn the wrong lessons from their suffering, at least for a time, and both cheat for financial gain. The two novels are stories of their protagonists' education, and they both open with a glimpse of the old life: Frankie Alpine and a friend rob Morris Bober, the Jewish shopkeeper to whom Alpine apprentices himself. That old life indicated, Malamud settles into the central concern of his books: the middle life, the learning life, where suffering may promise the characters a new and better future.

Frankie returns to the scene of his robbery and begins to help Morris Bober in the grocery store. The relationship between the two is one of father and son, typically cast as master-assistant, an educational apprenticeship. There are three pairs of natural fathers and sons in the novel, and they contrast with Frankie and Morris in their inadequacy. The most promising of these is that of Nat Pearl, one of Frankie's rivals for Helen Bober's affection, with his father. Nat becomes a lawyer, but although he rises financially, he is shallow compared to Alpine, and his treatment of Helen is unkind. Less successful is the relationship of the loutish Louis Karp with his father, who is trying to arrange a marriage between Louis and Helen. The worst is that between Detective Minogue, who investigates the burglary, and his son Ward, who, with Frankie, has perpetrated it.

What Frankie must learn from his surrogate father is stated in a crucial scene in which Frankie asks Morris why Jews suffer so much. Morris first answers that suffering is a part of man's existence: "If you live, you suffer." He goes on, though, to indicate that suffering can be meaningful if one suffers not only *from*, but also *for*: "I think if a Jew don't suffer for the Law, he will suffer for nothing." Frankie's question is ironically self-directed, for it is Alpine himself, the non-Jew, who is suffering more than he has to: he is suffering not only the existential guilt that comes with living, but the contingent guilt that comes from his own stealing. Like Roy Hobbs, Alpine cannot check his appetite, and he continues to steal from Morris even while trying to atone for the earlier robbery. Though he steals only small amounts, though he promises himself he will repay Bober, and though he assures himself that he is really a good man, Alpine continues to violate the law, and he suffers unnecessarily for this violation. At the end of the novel, Alpine becomes a Jew and replaces Bober in the store. This action is not, as some critics have suggested, the pessimistic acceptance of a Jew's suffering or a masochistic embracing of Morris's despair; it is rather an acknowledgement of guilt for the suffering Alpine has imposed on others and on himself and the resolve to be like a Jew in suffering *for* something, in making suffering meaningful.

Alpine must learn more than just law, however, for man's needs are more complex than that. When Helen Bober meets Nat Pearl on the subway, he is carrying a thick law book; her own book seems to her protection, and when he asks what it is, she replies, *Don Quixote* (Cervantes, 1605, 1616). Like Quixote, she is a dreamer, unsatisfied with her life as it is, and it is this quality that she will share with Frankie and which draws them together. The dialectic that informs Malamud's work is represented here: the law book, from a discipline that recognizes man's limitations and demands his attention to the responsibilities of this world, and *Don Quixote*, the book which allows one to look beyond these limits and provides a model for noble action. Helen rejects Nat Pearl because the law is insufficient by itself. Her action is not, of course, a rejection of the law, for she rejects Alpine too, when he lives in a world of dreams, unbound by law, for his dreams lead him into actions the law forbids. The generative force is a synthesis of the two.

Helen is, then, the other person from whom Frankie will learn. That he has the capacity for knowledge and for gentle action—as well as for the lawlessness that has marked his life—is shown by his constant identification with St. Francis. He is from San Francisco, and his name resembles that of the saint. He looks at pictures of and dreams about St. Francis, striving for his quality of goodness. With Helen, too, though, Frankie must learn to moderate his passions; with her, too, he violates the law. He climbs an airshaft to watch her showering, a voyeur, like so many Malamud characters. The mirror having been replaced by a glass, the glass remains itself a partition, separating the dreamer from the object of his desires. More serious is his rape of Helen in the park. It is the low point of the novel: Morris fires Frankie; his business is failing and Morris tries to commit suicide. Frankie looks at himself in the mirror, finds himself trapped inside a prisonlike circle, and hates himself for always having done the wrong thing. He returns to the store and resolves to bring it back to life for the hospitalized Morris. Although Helen and her mother do not like Frankie's return, they have little choice but to accept him, and although Frankie occasionally backslides, he makes firmer progress at controlling his passions.

Helen never finally accepts Frankie in the course of the novel, but she does reject her other suitors, and in a series of dreams, the reader discovers a tentative acceptance of Frankie: in his dreams, Frankie, like St. Francis, performs a miracle, turning a wooden rose he has carved and given to Helen into a real flower. In life, she has thrown the present away, but in the dream she accepts it. Helen, too, dreams of Frankie, out in the snow, making "a wife out of snowy moonlight."

Unlike *The Natural*, with its unambiguously pessimistic ending, *The Assistant* ends on a note of hope. Morris has died and Frankie has taken his place, and there is a suggestion that Frankie may be entrapped by the small grocery and the poverty of the Bobers' life, but there is also in his conversion to Judaism and in his gradual winning of Helen's trust, a more powerful suggestion that he has learned the lessons of love and law, of dream and check, and that this middle life, for all its suffering, may indeed bring him toward happiness and offer him the promise of new life.

The Fixer is Malamud's most ambitious novel, both because the reality he creates to embody his myth—the historical trial of a Russian Jew accused of murdering a Christian boy—is the most distant from his own experience and because the purpose of the tale, its philosophic underpinnings, are the most explicit and have the most scope.

As usual the novel opens with a journey. The main character, Yakov Bok, sees his travels, the leaving of his *shtetl* for a new life in Kiev, as an escape from his past. Bok attempts to strip away his Jewishness: he shaves his beard and cuts his earlocks; on the ferry across the river to his new hell, he drops his prayer things into the water. Like many of Malamud's characters, Bok is first adopted by an older man as an employee-foster son. This father figure, whom Yakov finds lying drunk in the snow, is without wisdom; indeed, he is a member of a militantly antisemitic organization. His daughter is the first woman with whom Bok becomes involved, but she also turns against Bok, accusing him of raping her. Because, however, she has written him letters avowing her love, even those who want to cannot believe her.

There are other dark women. On leaving the village, Bok is given a ride by a Jew-cursing Christian; he dreams of Lilith. The most powerful of these women is a member of a gang; she has killed her own son and accuses Bok of the deed and of a sexual assault on the boy. In this version of Malamud's story, not only does the father-figure fail, but there is no redemptive counterpart of these betraying women to offer Bok hope or love.

Most of the novel takes place after the discovery of the murdered child's body and the imprisonment of Bok. The prison is a consistent metaphor in

Malamud for the confined lives of his characters; Bok has left a figurative prison for a literal one. Malamud allows Bok escape through the agency of his mind, especially in his dreams. Like those of most of Malamud's characters, however, Yakov's are full of bitterness and terror. If they provide him with a vision and a remembrance of life beyond the prison, they also remind him of the limits of his existence.

A second relief for Bok is that one of the Russian prosecutors, Bibikov, knows of Bok's innocence, and they share a philosophical discussion, its base in Spinoza, throughout the novel. Bok emphasizes that Spinoza, although he is a philosopher who asserts man's freedom, recognizes that man is limited; his name for that restrictive force is Necessity. The accumulated suffering in *The Fixer* is a powerful documentation of Necessity, and forces outside man's control play a more significant role in this novel than in any other of Malamud's works.

If Necessity is so powerful, asks Bibikov, where does freedom enter? Bok replies that freedom lies within the mind: one rises to God when he can think himself into nature. Bok also learns from one sympathetic guard, who quotes to him from the Bible that he who endures to the end will be saved. Yakov learns to endure, and he does so through the freedom his mind creates. He learns also that thoughtful endurance is not enough, for neither Bibikov nor that guard Kogin is allowed even to survive: Bibikov takes his own life; Kogin is murdered.

Bibikov has explained to Bok that there is in Spinoza something Bok has missed, another kind of freedom, more limited, but nonetheless real: "a certain freedom of political choice, similar to the freedom of electing to think." It is this freedom that Bok finally affirms. He has undergone the extreme suffering that Necessity entails. For most of the novel there is hope that in his mind he is at least free and can create new worlds, and there is hope that he will endure. The novel ends with a more political hope. Bok, at least in his dreams, elects to shoot the Tsar. He has created political freedom by electing to think of himself as free. Again he cites Spinoza that if "the state acts in ways that are abhorrent to human nature, it's the lesser evil to destroy it."

Much of *The Fixer* is a moving dramatization of these ideas, and much of it as well conforms to the basic pattern of Malamud's myth, which he has developed so often and so well. Yet *The Fixer* is marred, and its faults suggest those that damage many of Malamud's later works. The philosophy seems too often grafted onto a rather static tale, the story itself an excuse for the ideas rather than the ideas a product of the story. The historical events have been distorted to fit the ideas. There is no reason Malamud should be bound by fidelity to historical truth, but all of his revisions seem to be in the direction of simplicity—not the simplicity that allows the novelist focus, but a simplicity that reduces moral complexity to schematism. All of the the intellectual weight of *The Fixer* is given to one set of people who hold one set of values; it is not simply that the novel presents good versus evil, but that it presents eloquent and intelligent good versus inarticulate and stupid evil.

In the novels that followed *The Fixer*, Malamud's problems with form and with integrating form and meaning became more noticeable. *The Tenants* suffers from inadequately worked-out ideas. *Dubin's Lives* is marred by structural redundancy and by a facile ending, although it features an articulate and convincing hero, a failed artist's search to find himself. Dubin's own life is finally one of promise, and that is the story Malamud knew to tell.

God's Grace is the story of Calvin Cohn, the only surviving human after mankind has destroyed itself in a nuclear war. The novel opens with Cohn aboard a ship, where he discovers another survivor, a chimpanzee. Most of the book is set on an island where they discover other chimps, a reclusive gorilla, and some baboons. Unlike *Dubin's Lives*, *God's Grace* returns to the playfully fantastic style of Malamud's early stories, but like all of his work, it is another accounting of the middle life. For Cohn, the old life is completely dead; this is his new chance to re-create a life for himself—and for all the world. In part resembling Robinson Crusoe and his story of survival, *God's Grace* is more centrally a fable about Cohn's attempt to maintain his faith in a God who has allowed this destruction and his faith that man can develop order among the creatures that remain. He plays a record of his father singing, "They that sow in tears shall reap in joy," and that becomes Cohn's rationalistic credo.

When the chimpanzees begin talking, Cohn has a chance to verbalize his thoughts, but though this development would seem promising, Cohn's thoughts are insistently didactic. He is intent on teaching the animals to act morally, but his attempt fails: the tone darkens and the animals begin destroying each other and finally Cohn himself. His faith in the efficacy of reason to tame nature's cruelty is naïve, and just as he underestimates the darker passions, he omits love entirely from his list of virtues. In an ending reminiscent of the close of "The Magic Barrel," another story about the relationship of law and love, the gorilla George, who has remained outside the group, attracted only when Cohn is playing records of his cantor father's chanting, begins a Kaddish for the dead Cohn and his vanished dreams. Malamud asks perhaps too much of this work: the realism of survivorship does not always blend with the fantasy of animal speech; the playful beginning gives way too abruptly to the brutal ending, yet much that is sustained recalls Malamud's work at its best.

At the time of his death, Malamud was working on a novel entitled *The People*, having completed the first draft of sixteen of a projected twenty-one chapters. This unfinished work, published posthumously, is the story of a Jewish refugee who, like Levin in *A New Life*, is an anomalous figure set down in the American West. In *The People*, however, the time frame is the late nineteenth century, not the 1950's, and Malamud's protagonist is captured by a group of Indians whose chief and advocate he eventually becomes. Like *God's Grace*, *The People* is a fable, a darkly comic tale marked by the bleakness faintly laced with hope that characterizes Malamud's last works.

Howard Faulkner

Other major works

SHORT FICTION: *The Magic Barrel*, 1958; *Idiots First*, 1963; *Pictures of Fidelman: An Exhibition*, 1969; *Rembrandt's Hat*, 1973; *The Stories of Bernard Malamud*, 1983; *The People and Uncollected Stories*, 1989.

Bibliography

Astro, Richard, and Jackson J. Benson, eds. *The Fiction of Bernard Malamud*. Corvallis: Oregon State University Press, 1977. Malamud was an instructor in English at Oregon State University from 1949 to 1961. This volume has been faithful to the papers as they were presented in a tribute to Malamud at a conference held at the university. Contains the opinions of several foremost American critics about Malamud's work, interspersed with stories and anecdotes which make for lively reading. An extensive secondary bibliography is also provided.

Ducharme, Robert. *Art and Idea in the Novels of Bernard Malamud: Toward "The Fixer."* The Hague: Mouton, 1974. Examines in depth the theme of self-transcendence in Malamud's writings up to and including *Pictures of Fidelman*. Draws on the psychological and anthropological perspectives of Sigmund Freud, Carl Jung, Sir James George Frazer, Géza Róheim, Joseph Campbell, and Otto Rank.

Field, Leslie A., and Joyce W. Field, eds. *Bernard Malamud: A Collection of Critical Essays*. 1970. Rev. ed. Englewood Cliffs, N.J.: Prentice-Hall, 1975. This nine-essay volume is the modest version of the original 1970 publication, which compiled twenty-one of the most important essays on Malamud's work in the 1960's and 1970's. Contains an interview with Malamud based on discussions he had with the authors in 1973. Places emphasis on Malamud's Jewish background in the context of Israel, with an essay by Sheldon Norman Grebstein entitled "Bernard Malamud and the Jewish Movement."

Richman, Sidney. *Bernard Malamud*. Boston: Twayne, 1966. Although limited in scope, this criticism is a valuable overview of Malamud's work to the mid-1960's. Gives a sensitive reading of the author's first three novels and his first two collections of stories.

Salzberg, Joel, ed. *Critical Essays on Bernard Malamud*. Boston: G. K. Hall, 1987. An excellent source for diverse material on Malamud's writing; a must for Malamud scholars. Provides a strong introduction by Salzberg with much insight into Malamud's work and his place in literature. The essays are well chosen; some are reprints, but there is a first printing of an essay by Sidney Richman entitled "Malamud's Quarrel with God."

SIR THOMAS MALORY

Born: Warwickshire (?), England; early fifteenth century
Died: London (?), England; March 14, 1471

Principal long fiction
Le Morte d'Arthur, 1485

Other literary forms

Le Morte d'Arthur is the only work attributed to Sir Thomas Malory. It was published in 1485 by William Caxton, England's first printer. The 1485 edition, for centuries the only source of Malory's tale, is a continuous narrative of twenty-one "books," though at the end of some books which clearly complete a larger grouping or "tale," Caxton included "explicits" (concluding comments) by the author. These explicits indicate that Malory may have intended the work to be organized in a fashion somewhat different from that of the published version. A manuscript of *Le Morte d'Arthur* discovered in 1934 at Winchester Cathedral indicates that Malory did not write it as a single long work, but rather as a series of eight separate tales, each of which deals with some aspect or character of the Arthurian legend.

Achievements

Any assessment of Malory's achievement as a literary artist is inevitably bound up with a judgment of the form of *Le Morte d'Arthur*: Is it a single story or eight separate tales? As critic Stephen Knight points out, this question of form is central to critical inquiry, for "if we are not clear whether we have before us one book or eight, or something in between, then our attitude towards the work or works must be obscure and tentative." That Malory's *Le Morte d'Arthur* should be considered a series of separate "works" is argued forcefully by Eugène Vinaver, editor of the modern standard edition, conspicuously entitled *The Works of Sir Thomas Malory* (1947, 3 volumes). Vinaver argues in the Introduction to his edition that the unity that scholars have found in *Le Morte d'Arthur* was imposed by Caxton, not intended by Malory, and his edited text, based on the Winchester manuscript, restores many passages excised by Caxton in the 1485 edition. Vinaver's opinion has been challenged by several critics, most notably by R. M. Lumiansky, who has argued that even in the Winchester manuscript one can see a unity of design and a progression from early to late tales, suggesting that Malory himself conceived of his eight tales as forming a single "work."

Unfortunately, although this issue has been debated at length, it has not been settled with any real certainty, and any final judgment of Malory's talents as an original artist may remain in abeyance for some time. Yet, whether one considers the Caxton edition of *Le Morte d'Arthur*, where a stronger sense of unity is prevalent, or the Winchester manuscript, from which the argument for eight separate tales can be made more forcefully, one can see an unmistakable unity imparted by the ordering of the tales. Malory's story moves progressively from the birth of Arthur to his assumption of kingship and defeat of all opposition, through the numerous stories depicting the adventures of knights in service to him, to his death at the hands of his traitorous, illegitimate son, Mordred. This kind of chronological progress is noticeably absent in the romances which Malory used as sources for his work. In the romances, especially that amorphous collection known as the French Vulgate Cycle, from which Malory borrowed much of his materials, there is often little sense of direction or completeness to the knights' adventures. From the modern reader's point of view, Malory deserves special credit for unifying these disparate tales, and arranging them in an order that lends motivation to certain characters' actions and—perhaps more important—gives the reader a sense of the cause-and-effect relationship between certain incidents that is lacking in the "French books" from which Malory says he has "drawn out" his tales.

Malory's achievement in condensing and organizing his sources has also been a matter of debate. Nineteenth century scholars, possessed of newly discovered Arthurian manuscripts of the twelfth through fifteenth centuries, were divided on the issue. Several noted medievalists branded Malory as a mere "compiler"; others, equally respected, praised him for his originality. Perhaps the most laudatory comment was offered by George Saintsbury, who claimed that in *Le Morte d'Arthur*, Malory made a significant advance over the romance tradition by developing a firm sense of narrative purpose, akin to that of the modern novelist. Saintsbury sees Malory exhibiting "the sense of *grasp*, the power to put his finger, and to keep it, on the central pulse and nerve of the story." Saintsbury and others, notably W. P. Ker, also praised Malory for his strong, original prose style. T. S. Eliot has called Malory "a kind of crude Northern Homer," a fine prose stylist.

Regardless of the criticisms leveled at Malory's tale as an artistic achievement in its own right, there can be little question about the importance of *Le Morte d'Arthur* in literary history. Since its publication, it has stood as the preeminent English-language document to which readers of succeeding centuries have turned to learn of the Arthurian legend. Caxton's edition was followed by two others early in the sixteenth century, attesting to Malory's immediate popularity. Intellectuals during the Renaissance may have agreed with Roger Ascham, who commented in *The Scholemaster* (1570) that the chief pleasure of *Le Morte d'Arthur* lay in two points, "open manslaughter and bold bawdy." Nevertheless, the appearance of still more editions of the work and the numerous references to the Arthurian legend in the literature of the period offers further proof of the influence of Malory's work long after its publication. When English society developed a renewed interest in chivalric materials and especially in the Arthurian legend, *Le Morte d'Arthur* was the work to which writers from Sir Walter Scott to Alfred, Lord Tennyson turned as the *locus classicus* of the legend. It was by comparison to Malory that Tennyson's *Idylls of the King* (1859-1885) and the Arthurian poems of A. C. Swinburne, William Morris, and Matthew Arnold were judged by their contemporaries, and all openly acknowledged their debt to the author of *Le Morte d'Arthur*.

In part, *Le Morte d'Arthur*'s influence as a source for Arthurian adventure and chivalric virtue may be attributed to the good fortune of its having been printed, while hundreds or even thousands of Arthurian tales existed only in manuscript until the late nineteenth or even the twentieth century. Nevertheless, even after scholarly and popular bookshelves began to be filled with other versions, Malory's work continued to be regarded as the premier English rendition of the Arthurian story. In the twentieth century, T. H. White, who had at his disposal both medieval and modern accounts of the legend numbering in the hundreds, turned to Malory for inspiration in writing what is no doubt the most important twentieth century Arthurian tale, *The Once and Future King*. John Steinbeck, whose accomplishments as a novelist earned him the Nobel Prize, began a modern adaptation of Malory because he wanted to bring to "impatient" modern readers the "wonder and magic" of *Le Morte d'Arthur*. While the literary purist may question the value of modernizing Malory, one cannot quarrel too much with Steinbeck's motive, for he speaks truly when he observes that these stories "are alive even in those of us who have not read them." To write a work that becomes a part of the cultural heritage of one's country, and a classic of one's language and literature, is an achievement few writers accomplish; Malory is one of the exceptions.

Biography

Though it is clear that "Sir Thomas Malory, knight prisoner," wrote *Le Morte d'Arthur*, there is serious debate about which Thomas Malory actually authored the work. Records of fifteenth century England contain references to more than a dozen Thomas Malorys. Most modern scholars believe that the author of *Le Morte d'Arthur* was Sir Thomas Malory of Newbold Revell, Warwickshire, in southern England, but there are other candidates, most notably Thomas Malory of Hutton and Studley, Yorkshire, in the north.

That Thomas Malory of Newbold Revell was the author of *Le Morte d'Arthur* was first proposed in 1894 by George L. Kittredge, who examined both the Caxton text and historical records and deduced that the Newbold Revell knight met all the necessary criteria for authorship. From the explicit at the end of Book XXI of *Le Morte d'Arthur*, Kittredge concluded that Thomas Malory was a knight; that he was in prison (he prays for "good delyveraunce"); and that the book was concluded in the ninth year of the reign of Edward IV, that is, March, 1469, to March, 1470. Extant records indicated that the

Malory from Newbold Revell was the son of a gentleman and therefore probably received the education requisite to produce the work. He had been exposed to knightly virtues while in service to Richard Beauchamp, Earl of Warwick, who was said to have embodied the knightly ideals of the age. He is reported to have died on March 14, 1471, after the *terminus ad quem* of the book's composition.

Kittredge's identification of Malory was reinforced when, in the early 1920's, Edward Cobb found an indictment consisting of eight charges against the Newbold Revell knight. Although it is not clear that Malory was ever found guilty on any of the charges, it is certain that he spent time in jail; in fact, it appears that between 1460 and 1471, the Newbold Revell knight spent most of his time at Newgate prison. His presence there would explain his having access to the books upon which he based *Le Morte d'Arthur*, because Newgate was situated near a monastery with an excellent library. Malory may well have bribed his keepers to allow him to borrow the books.

The Winchester manuscript, discovered in 1934, contains several new explicits that provide additional information about the author. For example, at the end of the "Tale of Sir Gareth," Malory petitions his readers to pray that God will send him "good delyveraunce sone [soon] and hastely." Even more clear is the explicit at the end of the "Tale of King Arthur," in which the author says that "this was drawyn by a knyght presoner sir Thomas Malleorre." On this evidence, the knight from Newbold Revell has emerged as the leading candidate for the authorship of *Le Morte d'Arthur*.

The primary arguments discrediting the Newbold Revell knight have been made by William Matthews in *The Ill-Framed Knight* (1965). According to Matthews, no evidence suggests that this Malory had any familiarity with northern poetry, yet the dialect of *Le Morte d'Arthur* and its English sources (especially the alliterative *Morte Arthure*) are clearly northern. Further, none of the references to real places (many are mentioned in the text) are to locations near Warwickshire. Matthews contends, too, that it is doubtful that a criminal would have had access under any circumstances to the library near Newgate; and that there is no evidence that the monastery's library had the books upon which *Le Morte d'Arthur* is based. At the time the work was completed, Thomas Malory of Newbold Revell could have been seventy-five years old, much too old to have completed such an arduous task. Finally, the Newbold Revell knight's political alliances were Yorkist, and *Le Morte d'Arthur* is distinctly Lancastrian in outlook. Kittredge had also cited two documents to support his claim, but this documentary evidence is discounted by Matthews. Matthews says that Kittredge's Malory was too old to have participated in a 1462 winter siege in which a Malory is recorded to have taken part. Similarly, the Newbold Revell knight could not have been the one named in the pardon made by Edward IV in 1468, since the pardon applied to political prisoners, and the Warwickshire man was a common criminal.

Matthews has proposed a second candidate, Thomas Malory of Hutton and Studley in Yorkshire. This Malory was a member of an eminent northern family; it is realistic to assume that he could read French, had access to the necessary source documents, was familiar with northern poetry and places, and spoke the northern dialect prominent in *Le Morte d'Arthur*. In addition, he supported the Lancastrian cause. The objections to his candidacy for authorship are that he is not described in family genealogies as a knight or chevalier, and there is no record of his ever being a prisoner. Matthews argues, however, that these are not serious discrepancies. Many men who could do so did not claim the title of knight. That there is no record of the Yorkshire Malory being a prisoner is also explainable. Although records abound detailing the imprisonment of criminals, it was not a fifteenth century custom to keep records of prisoners-of-war. These prisoners often had some measure of freedom, and several wrote books while in captivity. It seems more likely that a work the scope of *Le Morte d'Arthur* would be written under these conditions than under those imposed on criminals. Further, the expression "knight-prisoner," used by Malory to refer to himself in the explicits, is applied in *Le Morte d'Arthur* to Lionel, Lancelot, and Tristram when they become prisoners-of-war. Similarly, "good deliverance" is used when Malory speaks of Tristram's trials in prison. Thus, the term "knight-prisoner" is used in a somewhat complimentary fashion as the epithet of a prisoner-of-war, not a common criminal. The claim for Thomas Malory of Studley and Hutton rests on these grounds.

Other candidates have been proposed as the author of *Le Morte d'Arthur*, but few can be considered seriously. Thomas Malorys appear in the records of English court and parishes as laborers, armigers—and one as a member of parliament (though he is mentioned only once, and nothing else is known about him). What is known for certain about the author of *Le Morte d'Arthur* can only be gleaned from the text of the work itself, and then verified—with much conjecture—by searching the records of fifteenth century England.

Analysis

The modern reader approaching Sir Thomas Malory's *Le Morte d'Arthur* may be perplexed at first reading, for while the story of Arthur and his knights has the appearance of a novel, it is certainly far removed from representatives of the genre with which today's reader is more familiar. Though there is an overarching structure to the work, provided by the chronology of Arthur's reign, individual stories often seem mere appendages that add little to the major plot and seldom seem to have concrete beginnings or endings themselves. The "fault" for this apparent lapse into chaos lies not so much with Malory (though too close a reliance on his sources does tend to cause the story to branch off in several directions that lead nowhere), but rather with the reader who is not familiar with medieval techniques of storytelling. It is not uncommon to find medieval romances that simply begin *in medias res*, and seem to end there as well. That form of narrative technique has been supplanted in today's literary world by the "well-made story," whose beginning, middle, and end are clearly defined, and whose parts are clearly integrated into the whole. The medieval audience demanded neither tight concentration on a single story line nor analysis of cause-and-effect relationships; to appreciate Malory and his achievement in the chain of events leading to the modern novel one must first appreciate that for writers before him, and for Malory himself, emphasis on the event itself, rather than on its consequences or on the role of characters, was of primary importance. Malory, in fact, was one of the first writers to delve into the minds of his characters and achieve a certain degree of verisimilitude in presenting the people who appear in his story.

Malory lacks originality in the modern sense, since almost everything he recounts in *Le Morte d'Arthur* is taken from medieval romances popular for centuries before his. His accomplishments as a storyteller and his claim to literary greatness lie in the artistry with which he wove together the elements of the Arthurian legend and in the insight he presents into the meaning of the story both for his contemporaries and for readers throughout the centuries. Beneath the surface chaos of the tales that make up the work, Malory has presented a unified vision of a society in triumph and in decay; his is a complex work with a complex purpose. As D. S. Brewer explains in his Introduction to *Malory: The Morte Darthur* (1968), the work was "a part of the movement that transformed the medieval knight into the English gentleman." Through this story of the "ideal society," Malory presents the enduring dilemma of man's attempt to reconcile individual demands with those of the society in which he lives, and those of the God he worships.

Le Morte d'Arthur consists of eight tales which Caxton divided into twenty-one books in his edition. The story itself divides into three large sections. The first, consisting of Books I through V in the Caxton text, details the coming of Arthur and the establishment of the Round Table. It begins with the adulterous conception of the King, tells the now-popular story of the Sword in the Stone, and continues with an account of the early battles and adventures of Arthur and his knights in their effort to subdue external threats to the realm. Always the careful craftsman where larger issues of plot and motivation are concerned, Malory skillfully interweaves into this larger story details that become important in later episodes: the "dolorous stroke" wielded by Balin that initiates in a curious way the Holy Grail quest; the hatred felt by Morgan le Fay for her brother Arthur; the power of Excalibur and its symbolic significance. In the final book of this section, Arthur is hailed as the conqueror of Rome and welcomed into the city by the Pope himself; the last great external challenge to this new order of society has been met and overcome.

The central books of *Le Morte d'Arthur* (XI-XVII) deal with the adventures of Arthur's knights. Included are tales of the prowess of Sir Lancelot, the dedicated idealism of Sir Gareth ("Beaumains"), and the accomplishments and deceptions of Sir Tristram and his paramour, La Beal Isould. In these accounts, the Court of King Mark is established as a kind of counterculture to that of Arthur, and the reader is made to feel the imminent doom that awaits Arthur's kingdom should the knights falter in their loyalty to their leader and the virtues he upholds. The final books of this section recount the quest of the Sangrail (Holy Grail), a devastating undertaking that strips Arthur of many of his knights and exposes the shortcomings of many of those considered the best in the realm. The quest marks the beginning of the end of the Round Table, for through vain pursuit of this holy artifact, the knights reveal their spiritual imperfection and perhaps their inherent imperfectability.

The third and final section of the work tells of the decay of Arthur's kingdom, a process that begins when the knights return from the unsuccessful Grail quest. Lancelot, by his actions, reveals that his dedication to the Queen is greater than his devotion to God, his personal needs more important than his public duties. Arthur becomes unable to effect a suitable compromise between public and private life, and as incident after incident forces him to choose between his queen and his knights, he reluctantly is forced to opt for the latter. His sad statement after the civil war has begun in his kingdom reflects his inability to maintain a balance between his private and public lives: "Much more I am sorrier for my good knights' loss than for the loss of my fair queen; for queens I might have enough, but such a fellowship of good knights shall never be together in no company." This conflict between public and private virtues, a universal condition of mankind that Malory perceived at the heart of the Arthurian tale that he was transcribing, is the cause of the tragic development in the story.

The essence of the conflict Malory portrays in *Le Morte d'Arthur* has been described by D. S. Brewer as "the divergence of the values of honour and goodness from each other." The concept of honor is the paramount public virtue, informing the code of chivalry and motivating actions of those who were proponents of knighthood. Goodness, on the other hand, is a private virtue, and in *Le Morte d'Arthur* it is specifically identified as a Christian attribute. Hence, the conflict between honor and goodness is elevated beyond the level of individuals struggling within themselves to choose the proper path in life; it becomes, under Malory's skillful handling of individual tales from Arthurian romances, a larger conflict between two modes of living—the way of the good knight, and the way of the good Christian.

The public virtue of honor had been the hallmark of chivalry for centuries before Malory brought it under scrutiny in *Le Morte d'Arthur*, and his characters all place great emphasis on winning and maintaining it. The promise of honor brings the knights to court; the chance to increase one's honor motivates them to accept the most impossible quests and to battle against the most insurmountable odds. The preservation of honor demands strict obedience to one's lord, unswerving fidelity to one's lady, unshakable loyalty to one's brother knights. By striving for honor, the knights make the Round Table great, and paradoxically, by striving to maintain their honor, they destroy it.

In the society that Malory's Arthur imagines and attempts to build, honor and goodness are inseparable. In a passage not in any of Malory's sources, the King charges all his knights "never to do outrageousity nor murder, and always to flee treason [that is, to avoid committing it]; also, by no mean to be cruel, but to give mercy unto him that asketh mercy, upon pain of forfeiture of their worship . . . and always to do ladies, damosels, and gentlewomen succour, upon pain of death." By their honor, the knights are committed to doing good deeds. As the story progresses, however, the requirements of honor and goodness begin to diverge, and the inability of the knights and ladies to reconcile the two leads to the tragic demise of Arthur's society.

Malory highlights the growing divergence throughout a number of stories in *Le Morte d'Arthur*, but in none more clearly than "The Poisoned Apple" (Book XVIII, Ch. 1-7). In this vignette, Guinevere is accused by Sir Mador of poisoning Sir Patrice, his cousin. Mador demands justice: either the queen is to be executed, or her champion must defeat Mador in battle. Arthur cannot fight, as he is to sit in judgment of the case, and Lancelot is not at court. Clearly this is a matter of honor—the king's lady is to be shamed, bringing dishonor on the entire court—and yet all of the knights present at court suspect Guinevere and refuse to fight in her behalf. In desperation, Arthur and Guinevere send for Sir Bors. They appeal to him to champion the queen not because she is to be shamed, and through her the court, but rather because he has an obligation to uphold the honor of his kinsman Lancelot, who no doubt would fight for the queen were he at court. Bors tells Arthur he will fight "for my Lord Luancelot's sake, and for your sake." Bors then appeals to other knights, claiming that "it were great shame to us all" should the wife of Arthur be "shamed openly"; he is rebuked by many who, while acknowledging their respect for the king, have no love for Guinevere because she is a "destroyer of good knights." Though Lancelot eventually arrives in time to fight for Guinevere and save her from this charge, of which she is innocent, the implication here—borne out later in *Le Morte d'Arthur*—is that the prowess that wins honor may also allow one to win when the cause for which one is fighting is on the wrong side of justice; might may indeed prevail for evil instead of goodness.

This sad fact is brought home to the reader in Malory's account of Lancelot's battles for the queen when she is accused of adultery. Lancelot is forced to come to Guinevere's rescue, even at the expense of creating strife within Arthur's realm, because his honor is at stake. "Whether ye did right or wrong,"

Bors advises him, "it is now your part to hold with the queen, that she be not slain . . . for and she so die the shame shall be yours." In the final chapters of *Le Morte d'Arthur*, Malory presents Lancelot fighting reluctantly against truth to preserve his honor. Arthur, too, fights reluctantly, even though he is on the side of truth, for he would rather preserve his noble society of knights than save his queen, and he appears willing to be cuckolded rather than have the Round Table destroyed by internal strife.

The clear dichotomy between knightly and Christian virtues is made evident at several points in *Le Morte d'Arthur*, but Malory makes his most forceful statement about the problem in "The Maid of Astolat" (Book XVIII, Ch. 9-20). Lancelot, fighting in disguise against his own kinsmen and the other knights of the Round Table, is wounded and taken to a hermitage to heal. The hermit attending him asks who this knight is, and when he learns it is one who fought against Arthur, remarks: "I have seen the day . . . I would have loved him the worse because he was against my lord, King Arthur, for sometime I was one of the fellowship of the Round Table, but I thank God now I am otherwise disposed." The hermit has renounced his former calling, perhaps because he has seen where the path of honor leads, and has adopted a new path and a new Lord. Lancelot, who recovers from his wound while at the hermitage, comes to a momentary realization of his folly and bitterly acknowledges that his "pride" has led to his being thrown into this lowly condition. Only much later, however, does he abandon the pursuit of honor through the chivalric code, and by then Arthur is dead, Guinevere has entered a nunnery, and the kingdom is in ruins. The sense that one gets from reading Malory's account of the last days of Arthur's realm is that even the most chivalric society is doomed to failure, and that man's only hope lies in adopting values and goals that transcend worldly ideals.

What, then, has Malory accomplished in telling this tale? In the strife that tears Arthur's kingdom apart, fifteenth century readers saw mirrored their own griefs over the demise of feudal England, ravaged by the bloody struggle for the English throne that became known as the Wars of the Roses. *Le Morte d'Arthur* offered these readers faith, in a curious way, since in his work Malory has shown that, despite the collapse of an ideal society, lives and societies continue.

Even in their failures, the characters of *Le Morte d'Arthur* appear as larger-than-life personages that speak to the reader of the potential greatness of mankind. If honor can somehow be wedded to goodness, if the public virtues that gave the knights their sense of purpose can be married to the private virtues that cause man to rise above societal bonds when necessary, the ideal society can be created. To his contemporary readers, Malory's story no doubt offered this note of special hope. Thus, *Le Morte D'Arthur* not only speaks to its fifteenth century readers, but through the story of Arthur and his knights, Malory also speaks to all peoples of all nations and times of the possibility of greatness, the inevitability of failure, and the glory that mankind achieves by striving for the impossible.

Laurence W. Mazzeno
Sarah B. Kovel

Bibliography

Hicks, Edward. *Sir Thomas Malory: His Turbulent Career.* New York: Octagon Books, 1970. A thoroughly readable account of Malory, his life, and his imprisonment, during which he wrote *Le Morte d'Arthur.* Contains a wealth of pertinent information, historical and social.

Ihle, Sandra Ness. *Malory's Grail Quest: Invention and Adaptation in Medieval Prose Romance.* Madison: University of Wisconsin Press, 1983. Examines "The Tale of the Sangreal" from *Le Morte d'Arthur,* looking both to its thirteenth century French source and to Malory's own structural and thematic adaptation. Gives insight into medieval literary theory and the underlying intentions of Malory's distinctive Grail quest.

McCarthy, Terence. *Reading "The Morte Darthur."* Cambridge, England: D. S. Brewer, 1988. A study intended to assist the newcomer to Malory's work. Follows Eugène Vinaver's division of this work into eight books. Presents various contexts through which to view *Le Morte d'Arthur.* A useful and accessible reader.

Merrill, Robert. *Sir Thomas Malory and the Cultural Crisis of the Late Middle Ages.* New York: Peter Lang, 1987. An original inquiry into the psychology of the knights of Arthurian romance and the impact of the Round Table on their lives. Traces the formation of medieval institutions, and explores the personal and social tensions in the Middle Ages that led to the Protestant Reformation.

Parins, Marylyn Jackson. *Malory: The Critical Heritage.* New York: Routledge, 1988. An important collection of early criticism and commentary on Malory's *Le Morte d'Arthur* in chronological order, beginning with William Caxton's preface to the first edition and ending with remarks by influential literary critic George Saintsbury in 1912.

Riddy, Felicity. *Sir Thomas Malory.* New York: E. J. Brill, 1987. An excellent critical commentary that examines *Le Morte d'Arthur* from a number of perspectives. This scholarly work contains much useful information.

DAVID MALOUF

Born: Brisbane, Australia; March 20, 1934

Principal long fiction

Johnno, 1975; *An Imaginary Life*, 1978; *Child's Play*, 1981; *The Bread of Time to Come*, 1981 (also known as *Fly Away Peter*, 1982); *Harland's Half Acre*, 1984; *The Great World*, 1990.

Other literary forms

Because literary recognition came to him first for his verse collections, for quite some time David Malouf was regarded primarily as a poet. His first published writings were poetry, and in addition to contributions to works featuring several authors, efforts such as *Bicycle and Other Poems* (1970; also known as *The Year of the Foxes and Other Poems*, 1979), *Neighbours in a Thicket* (1974), *Wild Lemons* (1980), and *First Things Last* (1981) have sustained his reputation in this genre. Some critics have discerned varying levels of sophistication where his earlier is compared with his later verse. Moreover, in addition to novels of varying lengths, Malouf has experimented with the writing of short stories, an autobiographical narrative, and drama. His stories "Eustace" (1982) and "The Prowler" (1982) concern isolated and apparently unsociable characters who seem misplaced yet oddly adapted to Australian settings. The collection *Antipodes* (1985) comprises short stories which in the main deal with the troubles of immigrants and problems of adjustment in Australia as well as the culturally ambivalent situation of Australians in Europe. Malouf has set down some of the personal sources behind themes and images in his fiction with the publication of *12 Edmondstone Street* (1985), a memoir which deals in part with the writer's childhood years in Brisbane and in part, somewhat impressionistically, with work and travel during the 1980's. For that matter, he has also written an opera libretto, and another line of creative interest was explored in his play *Blood Relations* (1988). Interviews and other writings of his have been published in leading periodicals in Australia and abroad.

Achievements

Many of David Malouf's works have won awards in his native country. For the poetry collection *Neighbours in a Thicket*, he received the Grace Leven Prize and the Australian Literature Society's Gold Medal, as well as an award from the James Cook University of North Queensland. He held an Australian Council fellowship in 1978, and his novel *An Imaginary Life* (1978) won the New South Wales Premier's Fiction Award in 1979. The short novel *The Bread of Time to Come* (published in Great Britain as *Fly Away Peter*) won two awards offered by the publication *The Age* in 1982, and his fiction was again honored with the Australian Literature Society's Gold Medal in 1983. His short stories won the Victoria Premier's Award in 1985, and his play *Blood Relations* received the New South Wales Premier's Award for drama. In addition to honors of this sort, Malouf frequently has been considered an important literary spokesman for his country, and much of his writing has been regarded as significant in indicating new trends in creative work.

Biography

The name Malouf is Arabic and was handed on by the writer's paternal grandfather, who emigrated from Lebanon to Australia late in the nineteenth century; other relatives were from England and were of Portuguese Jewish ancestry. David Malouf, the son of George and Welcome Mendoza Malouf, was born in Brisbane on March 20, 1934. He was educated at Brisbane Grammar School and was graduated in 1950. He earned a bachelor's degree, with honors in English, from the University of Queensland in 1954. For two years he taught there, and evidently during that period he also began to write poetry. Along with the works of other writers, his verse was published as part of the collection *Four Poets* in 1962. He had previously spent some time in Europe; between 1962 and 1968 he was a schoolmaster in England at St. Anselm's College, Birkenhead, Cheshire. When he returned to Australia, he served as a lecturer in English at the University of Sydney; he was also a member of the Literature Board of the Australia Council for two years, beginning in 1972. The increasing recognition accorded his work encouraged him particularly to devote time to his writing, and in 1978 he began spending part of each year in Australia and part in Grosseto, Italy. Appropriately, much of his writing has tended to deal with cultural confluences and differences that are felt in lands on two sides of the world.

Analysis

Malouf's first novel, *Johnno*, is a haunting and evocative depiction of youth and friendship in Australia and abroad during World War II. The narrator, Dante, an outwardly decent and somewhat impressionable young man, has become intrigued with the wayward habits of a certain Johnno, a fatherless boy who possesses a strange, attractive charm. Although Johnno's propensity for drinking and revelry has a darkly appealing side to it, Dante is unable quite to enter into the spirit of his companion's conduct, and later he becomes somewhat more suspicious and withdrawn from his friend. After some travels which bring them together in Paris, Dante returns home and learns that Johnno has drowned under circumstances that suggest suicide. He learns later, from a note that his friend has written, that Johnno indeed intended to take his own life, partly because he came to regard Dante as unsympathetic and uncaring. This unsettling denouement suggests the trouble and havoc which may lie beneath the surface of adolescent relationships.

Although much of Malouf's writing has dealt with settings and historical periods that have had some significance in his own life, *An Imaginary Life* aroused interest precisely because it represents a venture into an area that is remote in time and is all but unknown to historians and literary scholars. The famous Roman poet Ovid was sent into exile to an isolated outpost on the Black Sea in the year A.D. 8; the reasons for his banishment remain somewhat unclear. Apart from what can be gathered from his epistles in verse, the *Tristia*, which pleaded for his release, essentially nothing is known about the last decade of his life. From this point of departure, Malouf commenced with his own version of Ovid's last years, into which he also incorporated material from an account of the eighteenth century wild child of Aveyron.

The story is told in stark, spare, measured prose, and indeed the setting in which the fictional Ovid finds himself seems gloomy and desolate. His existence among the people of a small, primitive village would appear at the outset to be drab and monotonous, but after a while he has come to regard his life in exile with something more than resignation. As Malouf has portrayed the classical poet, Ovid feels the stirrings of new life even as he has become accustomed to surroundings that have little in common with the metropolis of imperial Rome. He regards himself as thrown back upon the most elemental and rudimentary sensations, when the most ordinary objects of the natural world arouse in him a wonderment that he has not felt before. Time and change seem recast as they operate in a fashion much different from that he knew before; with only the most basic temporal points of reference, he finds it difficult to keep track of passing days, and only transitions in the seasons serve to remind him that years have passed during the period of his banishment. When the villagers, who are accustomed to hunting wild animals in the open fields, bring in a small boy they have captured, Ovid takes an immediate interest in the child's welfare and for that matter believes that, though the boy may appear backward and inarticulate, the poet himself still may learn from the gradual development of his speech and manual skills. His affection reflects in some form memories of his own childhood; indeed, so captivated has he become by the boy's companionship that he ceases hoping for a return to Rome, and he has become reconciled with his fate. Nevertheless, the villagers, who follow a form of shamanism and believe that malevolent spirits are constantly lurking about them, are not quite so tolerant of the boy from the wild; when it is thought that the child is responsible for a mysterious illness that afflicts the local headman, Ovid concludes that he and the boy must leave the family with which they have been staying and venture off into the trackless steppelands to the north. His story ends in the open spaces where, far from other human habitations but without regrets or unhappiness, he and the child have found safety. It should be added that *An Imaginary Life* attracted much favorable comment for its originality, in supplying what was possibly a plausible ending in fictional form to what otherwise was a sizable lacuna in the literary history of classical times. Some have objected, however, that Malouf's depiction of Ovid is at odds with what is actually known about the earlier life of the Roman poet; Ovid, after all, made a name for himself in Rome for the elegance, wit, and virtuosity of his verse works, and to portray him as accepting a simpler and more austere way of life arguably is out of character with the historical figure.

A contemporary Italian setting was utilized in Malouf's short novel *Child's Play*, which deals with a young man who believes that his chosen calling deserves a better term than what the newspapers call "terrorism." The work itself serves to reconstruct, ostensibly from the inside, a hired gunman's characteristic mode of operation, and indeed the narrator's story of preparations for a planned assassination is gripping and engrossing in an eerie, offbeat way. The narrator, who maintains that for security reasons he must be reticent about his own past life and identity, nevertheless is willing to provide some glimpses of the inner operations of his group. He is twenty-nine years old, has an appearance devoid of distinguishing marks, and lives in an apartment where he is unlikely to be noticed; he frequents restaurants, Laundromats, and film theaters where the clientele are not likely to be remembered. His accomplices are known only by given names, and he finds it diverting to try to infer something about their backgrounds from the little that he actually does know about them. His victim is a venerable literary man, about eighty years old. As part of his assignment, the narrator has learned much about the man's publications and other aspects of his life as well. The great man has nothing really villainous about him, apart from being recognized and successful; he was a political émigré during World War II, and his subsequent activities were hardly of a sort that would provoke social or ideological hatreds. Nevertheless, because he is well known, he has been considered a suitable target by the organization that has employed the narrator; and in the course of methodical planning, which requires him to know precisely certain details of the victim's daily habits, the narrator has come to regard the old man as somehow a necessary component of a task he must accomplish. This curiously sympathetic evocation of the mind of a terrorist, and moreover one who has taken a distinctly impersonal view of his work (the narrator is moved by no sense of political commitment), may be taken perhaps as an oblique commentary on violent acts that seemingly would defy specific explanation.

Much of Malouf's writing has a retrospective tendency, where events from earlier portions of the twentieth century are called back in an effort to delineate the effects of historical change and upheaval on Australia and its people. *The Bread of Time to Come* concerns two young men in their early twenties, Ashley Crowther and Jim Saddler, who are drawn together by a common interest in the birds that gather at a local refuge. Strange, exotic birds of every sort, from as far away as Siberia and Norway, put in an appearance in the course of their elongated migratory flights. Just as it has become a destination for such journeys from afar, the island continent seems isolated yet a part of the greater pattern of events in the world at large. The outbreak of World War I in Europe sets in motion a delayed reaction in Australia. The men are packed off to the Western front in France, feeling perhaps at first some tug of patriotism; but the harsh and unpredictable realities of trench warfare leave them troubled and hardened. After one soldier, as part of a foolish bet, shows himself to snipers and is shot down, and an enemy shell leaves others dead or maimed, the grim, mindless, and destructive underside of armed conflict becomes apparent to them. When it is learned finally that, in another engagement, Jim has been killed and Ashley wounded, the news, when it reaches Australia, brings home finally the senseless and brutal wastefulness the war has brought.

One of Malouf's most highly regarded works of fiction is *Harland's Half Acre*, which portrays the development of an Australian artist against a historical backdrop that embraces much of the twentieth century. The title character, Frank Harland, is a crotchety, reclusive sort of person who wears his aspirations lightly. During the earlier portions of his career, when he has been beset by economic hardships, he finds odd ways to support himself during the difficult years of the Great Depression; he also becomes acquainted with others who have become impoverished by the onset of hard times. Later, during World War II, he comes to know refugees who have left Europe and learns that older established nations have cultural traditions with historical dimensions that Australia cannot yet share; on the other hand, Europe is also subject to political turmoil and upheaval that has not affected the island continent. Subsequently, for commercial purposes, parts of the old city of Brisbane have been transformed, and the advent of modern business techniques brings change in many forms. Much of Harland's story is told indirectly, through the accounts of others who have known him. It would appear that he has remained fiercely independent and stubbornly dedicated to his efforts at painting, during bad times and good; much of his later work is done on a small plot of land where he can preserve some sense of solitude. He has, however, acquired land elsewhere, partly in an effort to regain holdings that one of his ancestors, during the nineteenth century, lost in a card game. At times some of Harland's paintings are sold for relatively little; even toward the end, when he has become well known and his works have become collector's items with some value to investors, he does little to exploit the reputation he has earned. Critics have taken his story as in some way symbolic of the problematical position of creative art in Australia, which began with little legacy of its own. It seems likely as well that Malouf intended his title character's situation in some sense to suggest the personal isolation that may accompany any creative quest.

The Great World takes up various themes again in depicting the response to historical change that is felt among Australian men who grew up before World War II. Their uncomplicated existence is abruptly altered when war with Japan brings the men to Malaya with other Australian fighting forces. After their units have surrendered, the men, who have been trained in combat, are ill prepared for captivity, and waves of memories from the past sweep over them during the difficult early days of their confinement. Their lot is hard but not quite unbearable, though there are numerous discomforts and indignities. One of them fights with a guard and a full-scale riot erupts; even then, they are not mistreated as seriously as they had feared. Even wearying labor in a work camp set up along the lines of a railway into Burma does not daunt them entirely, though others among them fall victim to any of a multitude of diseases. In time, however, exhaustion and fevers begin to tell on them, and their life seems reduced to a few relatively simple elements. The men feel a common bond with one another; they also cherish the few letters that have been received from the outside world. Toward the end of the war, weakened by privations and troubled that they have become little more than coolie labor for their captors, they have nearly lost track of the passage of time, and when peace comes, they are somewhat taken by surprise. Even after they have been repatriated, afterimages from their years of ordeal haunt them occasionally; they also marvel at the vast spaces and natural scenery that they had not known during their wartime confinement. Nevertheless, there is also a sense of tedium and sameness to the routine into which they are cast in their civilian work. Renewing old acquaintanceships with men and women holds some fascination for them, but even this becomes tiresome after a while. Settled patterns of doing things eventually become habits that are followed almost instinctively. After the war, time seems to pass quickly and stealthily, sometimes in leaps of years at a time, and change engulfs Australia in odd, ironic ways. The Japanese, once feared as enemies, have become known now for their commercial acumen; another war, in Vietnam, comes and goes; and business expansion takes hold for a while. Toward the end, the two men who began as friends some decades before can look back on a bewildering array of images from the past even as financial reverses seem to have laid them low.

Some final words remain to be said about common characteristics of Malouf's major fiction. Many reviewers have commented upon the finely honed use of language and the delicately etched descriptive passages that have distinguished his important works. Often, affinities have been found between his poetry and prose writing, which possess similar lyrical traits. Certain thematic concerns—such as the effects of history, time, and memory, and the distinctive cultural position of Australia with respect to other nations—have also received comment. On the other hand, some readers have regarded Malouf's prose as somewhat coy and elusive, as hinting at meanings that are sometimes obscure or incompletely developed; indeed, some of his narrative works have been told through highly oblique means and have finished on rather inconclusive notes. In this view, Malouf's achievements in long fiction must be weighed against structural problems to the extent that the manner of his narration at times has threatened to overshadow the stories he has chosen to recount.

J. R. Broadus

Other major works

SHORT FICTION: *Child's Play, with Eustace and the Prowler,* 1982; *Antipodes,* 1985.

POETRY: *Four Poets,* 1962 (with Don Maynard, Judith Green, and Rodney Hall); *Bicycle and Other Poems,* 1970 (also known as *The Year of the Foxes and Other Poems,* 1979); *Neighbours in a Thicket,* 1974; *Poems, 1975-1976,* 1976; *Wild Lemons,* 1980; *First Things Last,* 1981; *Selected Poems,* 1981.

PLAYS: *Voss,* 1986 (opera libretto); *Blood Relations,* 1988.

NONFICTION: *12 Edmonstone Street,* 1985 (autobiography).

EDITED TEXTS: *We Took Their Orders and Are Dead: An Anti-War Anthology,* 1971 (with Shirley Cass, Ros Cheney, and Michael Wilding); *Gesture of a Hand,* 1975; *New Currents in Australian Writing,* 1978 (with Katharine Brisbane and R. F. Birssenden).

Bibliography

Attar, Samar. "A Lost Dimension: The Immigrant's Experience in the Work of David Malouf." *Australian Literary Studies* 13 (1986): 308-321. The significance of Malouf's own background is considered in this discussion of the place that issues concerning immigration and cultural identification have held in his writings.

Buckridge, Patrick. "Colonial Strategies in the Writing of David Malouf." *Kunapipi,* no. 3 (1986): 48-58. The odd balance between poetry and prose in Malouf's work is considered in this essay, in which "colonial" is taken in a literary as much as a political sense.

Dever, Maryanne. "Secret Companions: The Continuity of David Malouf's Fiction." *World Literature Written in English* 26 (Spring, 1986): 62-74. Parallel developments in outwardly disparate works are explored in this discussion of several prose efforts.

Hergenhan, Laurie. "Discoveries and Transformations: Aspects of David Malouf's Work." *Australian Literary Studies* 11 (May, 1984): 328-341. This article maintains that motifs in Malouf's poetry have been carried forward into his narrative fiction, thus suggesting a unified vision and some elements of continuity among phases of his career.

Leer, Martin. "At the Edge: Geography and the Imagination in the Work of David Malouf." *Australian Literary Studies* 12 (May, 1985): 3-21. Malouf's conception of Australia's place in the larger cultural scheme of things is dealt with in this short study of several works.

Mansfield, Nick. "Body Talk: The Prose of David Malouf." *Southerly* 2 (June, 1989): 230-238. It is suggested in this article that there are similar qualities in the depiction of writers and artists in various of Malouf's efforts.

Pierce, Peter. "David Malouf's Fiction." *Meanjin* 41 (December, 1982): 526-534. This interesting essay on basic issues in Malouf's writing suggests comparisons with other Australian writers.

JOHN P. MARQUAND

Born: Wilmington, Delaware; November 10, 1893
Died: Newburyport, Massachusetts; July 16, 1960

Principal long fiction

The Unspeakable Gentleman, 1922; *The Black Cargo*, 1925; *Warning Hill*, 1930; *Ming Yellow*, 1935; *No Hero*, 1935; *Thank You, Mr. Moto*, 1936; *Think Fast, Mr. Moto*, 1937; *The Late George Apley*, 1937; *Mr. Moto Is So Sorry*, 1938; *Wickford Point*, 1939; *Don't Ask Questions*, 1941; *H. M. Pulham, Esquire*, 1941; *Last Laugh, Mr. Moto*, 1942; *So Little Time*, 1943; *Repent in Haste*, 1945; *B. F.'s Daughter*, 1946; *Point of No Return*, 1949; *It's Loaded, Mr. Bauer*, 1949; *Melville Goodwin, U.S.A.*, 1951; *Sincerely, Willis Wayde*, 1955; *North of Grand Central*, 1956; *Stopover: Tokyo*, 1957; *Women and Thomas Harrow*, 1958.

Other literary forms

John P. Marquand was a prolific writer of short stories, especially for such mass-circulation magazines as the *Ladies' Home Journal*, *Collier's*, *Sports Illustrated*, and the *Saturday Evening Post*, as well as novels, many of which were serialized in these same magazines before book publication. Two of the serials, *3-3-8* (1937) for the *Saturday Evening Post* and *Castle Sinister* (1938) for *Collier's*, never did appear between covers. Marquand reprinted some of his short stories in *Four of a Kind* (1923), *Haven's End* (1933), and *Life at Happy Knoll* (1957). In addition, a collection of sketches, travel pieces, lectures, and short stories, *Thirty Years*, was published in 1954. Several of Marquand's novels were dramatized; the most successful dramatization of his work was *The Late George Apley: A Play* (1946), the result of a collaboration between George S. Kaufman and Marquand. His one foray into biography, *Lord Timothy Dexter of Newburyport, Mass.*, was originally published in 1925 and reissued and much revised in 1960 as *Timothy Dexter, Revisited*. Finally, there is *Prince and Boatswain: Sea Tales from the Recollection of Rear-Admiral Charles E. Clark* (1915), a volume of nonfiction Marquand compiled with James Morris Morgan while in the Navy.

Several of Marquand's novels were scripted for Hollywood films, and the Moto books inspired an entire series, starring Peter Lorre, patterned after the popular Charlie Chan mysteries. Unlike other novelists who were lured to the West Coast, Marquand only worked on a few of the scripts. Marquand also occasionally wrote for magazines such as *Harper's Magazine*, *The Atlantic*, and *Saturday Review of Literature*, contributing fiction and essays.

Achievements

Marquand is known primarily as a writer of slick magazine fiction and long popular novels dealing with upper-middle-class life. His reputation as a magazine writer, not only of short stories but also of longer, serialized fiction, rests on his association with such middlebrow magazines as *Collier's, Sports Illustrated, Ladies' Home Journal*, and the *Saturday Evening Post*, journals that have come to represent the mainstream in American culture. It is all too often forgotten that Ernest Hemingway, F. Scott Fitzgerald, and William Faulkner, to name only a select few, also wrote for such mass-circulation periodicals. Although Marquand's prominence as a writer of serious fiction dates from the publication of *The Late George Apley*, the popularity of the Mr. Moto books, *No Hero* and *Thank You, Mr. Moto*, had already established him with a wide audience. Unfortunately, in spite of a sizable output of additional serious fiction, he has been unable to shake his early reputation as merely a writer of popular novels and short stories.

In spite of his lack of critical standing, however, Marquand's literary achievement was substantial. In 1949, near the beginning of the final phase of his career, he wrote that what he had been trying to do was to write a series of novels that would depict a "segment of America during the last fifty years." Scholars are now realizing how successful Marquand was in capturing that fifty-year segment of American life, and his reputation as a novelist of manners has risen dramatically. He is now considered among the finest social critics of his time, one to compare with Charles Dickens, William Makepeace Thackeray, and Anthony Trollope as an accurate recorder of manners and customs. The nine serious novels that he wrote between 1937 and 1960 have secured for Marquand an important place in contemporary American fiction.

In the two decades since his death, Marquand's work has undergone a steady reappraisal. Two scholarly monographs and two biographies have appeared as well as a flow of articles dealing with his role in American letters. This reexamination has resulted in a growing appreciation of Marquand's novels of manners. C. Hugh Holman and John J. Gross, in the two major critical works of the period, have called for a reassessment of Marquand's standing in American literary history, and the final judgment of Marquand's work has yet to be written.

Biography

John Phillips Marquand was born in Wilmington, Delaware, on November 10, 1893. The history of his family reaches back into the precolonial world of the Puritans: he was a descendant on his mother's side of Thomas and Joseph Dudley, early governors of the Massachusetts Bay Colony, and he was a grand-nephew of Margaret Fuller. The Marquands, of Norman-French ancestry, emigrated from the Guernsey islands to New England in 1732, where they settled in Newburyport, north of Boston. Marquand came from a long line of shipbuilders, mariners, and Harvard men. During his early years, he lived in New York City, where his father made a comfortable living as a stockbroker. The family went broke during the Panic of 1907, and young Marquand was sent to live with two aunts and a great-aunt at the family home at Curzon's Mill, Kent's Island, west of Newburyport; his parents moved to the Panama Canal when his father returned to a career in civil engineering. Although he was unable to attend preparatory school, because of a lack of funds, Marquand did receive a scholarship to attend Harvard after he completed public high school. He felt keenly the class differences at Harvard and passed rather lonely years there devoting himself to reading and writing. With the exception of the *Lampoon*, he did not join any clubs.

After his graduation in 1915, Marquand went to work for the *Boston Evening Transcript* at fifteen dollars per week. During this time, he enlisted in Battery A of the Massachusetts National Guard, which was soon mobilized and sent to El Paso, Texas, for duty on the Mexican border. Originally mustered in as a private, he was sent in April, 1917, to Officers' Training Camp at Plattsburg, New York, where he headed the class of candidates. After receiving his commission in August, Marquand was shipped overseas with the Fourth Army to join the Allied Expeditionary Force in France, where he fought with the 77th Field Artillery at Saint-Michel, at the Vesle River, and in the Argonne. He returned to the United States in November, 1918, and was demobilized as a captain. Marquand returned to journalism when he got a job with the magazine section of *The New York Herald Tribune*; he soon left, however, for a copywriting job in advertising with the J. Walter Thompson Agency. In 1921, with four hundred dollars saved from his job, Marquand moved back to Curzon's Mill to write a historical romance based on an early nineteenth century gentleman, Henry Shelton. Set in Newburyport, the novel, of little consequence now, was of considerable importance to Marquand. In the novel, he introduced a number of those large themes, such as the New England past and the protagonist as a member of the upper class brought low by changing social and/or economic circumstances, which later provided such strong bonds among his novels. The acceptance of the novel for serialization by the *Ladies' Home Journal* and its subsequent publication as a book by Scribner's launched Marquand as a professional writer. In the same year, he sold stories to George Horace Lorimer of the *Saturday Evening Post* and to Ray Long of *Cosmopolitan*, beginning a long and profitable association with both periodicals.

On the proceeds from his first novel, Marquand traveled to Europe, where he became engaged to Christina Sedgwick, whose uncle was editor of *The Atlantic* and one of the literary arbiters of Boston. The couple was married on September 8, 1922, and moved to an old house on Beacon Hill in Cambridge, where they joined the social set. A son, John, Jr., was born in 1923 and a daughter, Christine, in 1927. Between 1921 and 1931, Marquand published five serials and fifty-nine short stories in the "slicks." As he was to write later, it was a period of apprenticeship during which he learned the craft of writing fiction. His second book appeared in 1923; *Four of a Kind* collected three short stories and a short novel, *Only a Few of Us Left*. In 1925, Marquand published two books set at least in part in Newburyport. The first, *Black Cargo*, originally a serial, dealt with the romantic exploits of a Yankee clipper-ship captain and his adventures in the Pacific. The second was a historical biography of an eccentric New Englander, *Lord Timothy Dexter of Newburyport, Mass.*, and proved to be of lasting interest to Marquand; a revised version of it was the last thing he published before his death.

In addition to the historical books, Marquand was also beginning to move toward the themes of his later and more important works. In *Warning Hill*, another serial published as a book in 1930, Marquand introduced a protagonist who because of the financial failure of his father is denied his rightful position in the class structure of a New England town. The setting, attitude, and even the tone of this work are repeated in his later novels. The second of the books of this period was *Haven's End* (1933), which consists of fourteen stories, some of them revised from versions previously published in the *Saturday Evening Post*. These tales, which range in period from the seventeenth to the twentieth centuries, deal with the rising new fortunes of the Scarlet family poised against the decline of the Swales, who built the town in which they are set. Apparent in these stories is Marquand's growing interest in the processes of social change.

For a variety of reasons both personal and professional, Marquand left for China in 1934, where he remained for nearly a year. As a result of his travels, Marquand wrote a serial, *Ming Yellow*, in which he combined local color with the usual materials of a novel of manners, and introduced his readers into the Oriental world which would provide the background for perhaps Marquand's most famous creation, Mr. Moto. While on his tour, he was divorced by Christina. He met Adelaide Hooker, a wealthy woman related by marriage to the Rockefellers, who was on tour with her mother; they later married, in 1937. Marquand followed up the success of the first of his Oriental books with *No Hero*, which had been serialized in the *Saturday Evening Post* the spring following *Ming Yellow*. "Mr. Moto Takes a Hand" introduced the Japanese intelligence agent who was to figure in five additional adventure stories. The Moto novels were to prove extremely popular, and the serials and short stories generated a sizable income for Marquand and may have been partly responsible for the gamble in "serious" fiction which he took when he published *The Late George Apley* in 1937.

Marquand began the novel in 1934 but did not complete it until 1936. It was a breakthrough period for him: not only did he publish a portion of *The Late George Apley*, but also he serialized two of the Moto books and published five short stories. In addition, he married Adelaide Hooker. *The Late George Apley* not only won the Pulitzer Prize for 1938 but also won unprecedented praise for Marquand's work from the critics. Although the writing of *The*

Late George Apley marked a turning point in his career and would ultimately move him away from slick fiction, Marquand continued to write serials during the late 1930's. In 1937, *3-3-8* appeared in the *Saturday Evening Post*, the same journal that ran *Mr. Moto Is So Sorry* in 1938. *Castle Sinister* came out in *Collier's* in the same year. A version of *Wickford Point* was serialized in the *Saturday Evening Post* in 1939, as was the adventure tale, *Don't Ask Questions*. *Wickford Point*, which also appeared as a book in 1939, forms a trilogy with *H. M. Pulham, Esquire*, which was published in 1941, and *The Late George Apley*. All three novels are connected insofar as they provide Marquand's contrasting views of Boston.

In 1940, Marquand's second daughter, Blanch Ferry, was born. Timothy Fuller, his second son, was born in 1942. A third son, Elon Huntington Hooker, was born in 1943. Marquand joined army intelligence and traveled extensively in the Pacific war zones during 1941. In 1942, he went to Hollywood to work on the film version of *H. M. Pulham, Esquire*, directed by King Vidor. In addition, he collaborated with George S. Kaufman on a stage adaptation of *The Late George Apley*, which enjoyed a successful run for a year in 1946. In 1944, he accepted a position on the board of editors of the Book-of-the-Month-Club. Marquand became a special adviser to the secretary of war and spent the bulk of 1944 and 1945 in Washington. Finally, he traveled for a portion of 1945 as a war correspondent in the Pacific.

Marquand did not give up his writing during the war years. He rounded out his adventure stories with a rather average thriller, *It's Loaded, Mr. Bauer*, which ran as a serial in *Collier's* but never appeared as a book in the United States. The war years also produced another of Marquand's trilogies. Using his extensive traveling around the United States during the war, Marquand wrote three novels concerning the homeside reaction to the global conflict and the accelerated social change brought on by the war. *So Little Time* is set in Hollywood and deals with a playwright who is trying to write a successful drama and to come to grips with his fleeting life. *Repent in Haste* is a lesser work about Navy fliers in the Pacific, and *B. F.'s Daughter* is a Washington novel concerned with an industrialist and his daughter in an almost painful re-creation of wartime society. The novel pointed the way to the series of brilliant portraits of American life Marquand was to produce following the war.

In 1949, Marquand published *Point of No Return*, generally considered one of his best novels, which he adapted for the stage with Paul Osborne in 1951. With this novel, Marquand inaugurated a tetralogy of books each dealing with a central character set against an organization. *Melville Goodwin, U.S.A.* was the second of this loose series and is centered on Goodwin, a general in the United States Army, who is subjected to the "opinion molders" that make him into a hero. In 1952, Marquand was profiled in *The New Yorker* by Philip Hamburger. A collection of short fiction and nonfiction, *Thirty Years*, which was published in 1954, contains a summary of his reflections on his craft and provides the only statement of his theory of fiction. Marquand continued his analysis of the organization man in *Sincerely, Willis Wayde*, which contains a generally unsympathetic portrait of a lower-middle-class boy who becomes a successful and unscrupulous businessman. In 1956, *North of Grand Central*, an omnibus volume containing the first three New England books, appeared with notes on each of the novels by Marquand. *Stopover: Tokyo*, the last of the Moto books, was published in 1957, as was a collection of pieces from *Sports Illustrated* dealing with a country club and entitled *Life at Happy Knoll*. In 1958, Marquand divorced Adelaide and published his last novel, *Women and Thomas Harrow*, the story of a thrice-married playwright whose success and talent fail to provide him with a happy or fulfilled life.

During the last years of his life, Marquand enjoyed the comfort which his considerable income provided. It has been estimated that he made some ten million dollars during the 1950's. He lived and worked in the family home at Curzon's Mill and made trips to Bermuda and the Bahamas. In 1960, he published his last book, *Timothy Dexter, Revisited*, a revised version of the volume he had written thirty-five years earlier. Marquand died in his sleep at his home on Kent's Island on July 16, 1960.

Analysis

Although debate continues over the merits of John P. Marquand's writing, there is little question that collectively, his novels provide a comprehensive and accurate picture of the changes in American society from the end of World War I to the beginnings of the 1960's, a *comédie humaine* of modern American life. Marquand was a realist and was largely conservative in style; his accuracy of detail gives his best work an uncanny sense of reality. He was a transitional figure in postwar American letters, and his adherence to the novel of manners, never very central to the American literary experience, dates his fiction. Since his death, his type of realism, with its emphasis on the public scene, has been relegated to the writers of popular fiction.

The world depicted by Marquand's novels seems irretrievably gone. His characters' need for loyalty and decency and courage in everyday life, out of which they constructed standards capable of withstanding the flux of their lives, seems antiquated now. Perhaps even his accurate sense of the havoc wreaked by the rapid social change of his time will eventually lose its impact as the generations for which he wrote pass on. His novels will remain valuable, however, for the understanding with which Marquand portrayed the American male, with "accuracy, compassion, incisive perception, and wry love." As a recent critic of Marquand's work has written, Marquand's American male is "obsessed with the material trivia of his daily needs and confused personal diplomacy which his marriage demands, trying frantically to find something meaningful somewhere to fill the hollowness at the core of his life."

The Late George Apley was the first of Marquand's major novels, has remained his most famous, and is considered by many to be his finest. In it, he set the pattern for the major novels which followed over the next twenty years. Briefly, the point of the book is to show how even though the community of Boston dominates George Apley, it nevertheless provides a comfortable social code within which he finds a measure of security. The novel itself begins with a "Foreword and Apology" by Horatio Willing, who has been chosen by Apley's son to write a "Life in Letters" study of his father. Marquand's pen was never sharper than in this novel which parodies the honorific biography. The novel traces Apley's life from youth to old age and death, and is concerned with the individual's place within a society and the possibility of remaining organically connected to a community but not smothered by social conformity. Marquand described the novel as "a savage attack on the old water side of Beacon Street." In spite of the satire, the reader's attitude toward Apley is one of affection. Willing appears smug and the society itself is stifling, but Apley remains a deeply human figure wrestling with himself to accommodate his own desires and dreams with the values of the community to which he feels such loyalty. Although Apley's values are for the most part admirable (for example, the Puritan attitude of responsible stewardship with which he distributes the family money), it becomes increasingly clear that he is a man out of touch with the changing society around him. It is his simple adherence to his values which renders him both a commendable product of his commnunity and heritage and an increasingly embarrassing anachronism within that community.

The tenacity of the past, which molds and influences the current generation, provides one of the central themes for Marquand's next two Boston novels as well. If *The Late George Apley* deals with the Boston of the past, *Wickford Point* is concerned with a contemporary, decaying New England family once dimly connected with the tradition of transcendentalism through a minor nature poet. The traditions and values which often rendered Apley merely silly are carried in this novel to grotesqueness. The story, filtered through the consciousness of a popular magazine writer, describes the Brills, an old family once of some prominence, who now are reduced to a quirky eccentricity, and it deals in particular with the narrator's relationship, both past and present, with Bella Brill, Marquand's study of the consummate bitch. In her, Marquand introduces the first of many "old-money" women who are denied to his middle-class protagonists. The third of the "Boston" novels, *H. M. Pulham, Esquire*, records the ineffectual efforts of Pulham, a businessman of post-World War I Boston, to rebel against the customs and background of his youth. This is a novel, as one critic described it, of "inexorable time, of mutability, of the flood of the largely wasted years" which make up the lives of so many of Marquand's central characters. In spite of Pulham's insistence that he did the right thing by not marrying the "wrong" girl or digging up his cultural roots and moving to New York, the reader understands, as is so often true in Marquand's books, the depth of the emptiness of Pulham's life. It is a portrait done with understanding, however, for in spite of his social obtuseness, Pulham remains a sympathetic character, one who retains a sense of decency and tenacity in the face of a shifting social order.

These three books, later issued in a single volume entitled *North of Grand Central*, were a critical as well as popular success; two of the novels were made into movies and one became a long-running play, and they did much to dispel Marquand's standing as a writer of slick magazine fiction. The trilogy also did much to label Marquand as a New England writer, a tag that annoyed him almost as much as the earlier designation as simply a writer of popular fiction. His next series of novels was set in a variety of American locations, in part in an attempt to dislodge the notion that he had become "merely" a writer of satiric regional books.

The three Marquand novels to come out of World War II exhibit the variety of activities which occupied him during these years. *So Little Time* is set in the worlds of the theater and of Hollywood and focuses on a playwright, Jeff Wilson, who must grapple with his failure as a writer, a father, and a husband. The war provides the necessary pressure to motivate him to rethink his life. Ranging from Wilson's recollections of the small New England town of his boyhood, to his experiences as an American aviator in World War I, his various jobs as a newspaperman, play "doctor," and scriptwriter, and the story of his married life, the novel offers a panorama of American life between the wars. The second of Marquand's war novels, *Repent in Haste*, originally serialized in *Harper's Magazine*, is a short work about navy fliers in the Pacific. The theme of this novel is the inexorable passing of time and the uncertainty of the future. It is an attempt to portray a generation at war and its search for values amid the flux of the modern world. As in *So Little Time*, there is a tentativeness about the conclusions drawn in this novel that reflects Marquand's growing uncertainty about values which could provide a stay against the chaos which he saw as increasingly characteristic of modern life.

Marquand's last novel of the war period, *B. F.'s Daughter*, was more ambitious stylistically and contains Marquand's only female protagonist, Polly Fulton. The portrait of B. F. Fulton, Polly's father, provides a prologue for Marquand's full-scale exploration of the businessman in *Sincerely, Willis Wayde* and points to the attention he will pay to organizations in the novels of his last period. Although none of the war novels is entirely successful, as a group they do represent a transition between the New England novels of the 1930's, with their search for contemporary values in the past, and the nihilistic tone of the books of the 1950's, with their despair and emptiness. Whether the relative failure of these novels was caused by a lack of perspective, as some critics have argued, or merely a lack of commitment on Marquand's part, is of minor concern, because these works of fiction provide the background against which were written the last four major novels, books that are considered by some critics to be the best of his career.

Point of No Return was Marquand's first postwar novel, and it captures with all of his old assurance the spirit of the late 1940's. In fact, it is so accurate in its depiction of the postwar world that it provides a more satisfactory study of American society of that period than can be found in such later sociological classics as William H. Whyte's *The Organization Man* (1956) and David Riesman's *The Lonely Crowd* (1969). *Point of No Return*, borrowing an aviator's term from the war for its title, deals with Charles Gray, once a native of New England and now a banker who lives in New York City, as he sifts through his memories while waiting to learn whether he is to be promoted to the vice-presidency of his bank. It is the comprehensive sweep of the book, Marquand's broadest, and the thoroughness of the depiction of Gray's small hometown in Maine which give the book its sociological accuracy. Once again, Marquand's protagonist must wrestle with the humiliation of his past social failure and the emptiness of his present financial success. Security seems as illusory as the past, and in Marquand's fictional world, where there are no second chances, Nancy and Charles Gray can only wonder at their lack of triumph in the promotion that comes at last. There is no "out-of-breath feeling" in success, only a continuation of the anxiety that propelled the effort in the first place.

Although Marquand wrote about military types in some of his wartime pieces, *Melville Goodwin, U.S.A.* is his only full-length book about the Army. Written at the height of the cold war, it is a satiric look at the power of mass communications to elevate a rather ordinary professional soldier to the role of a demigod. Both the military and the world of journalism are treated ironically in this novel, which has been proclaimed as Marquand's greatest stylistic triumph. Unfortunately, the complexity of the work opened it up to misinterpretation, and the satiric point of the book eluded many readers. It is instructive that Marquand writes about a man who is bound by the traditions and social rigidity of the military in order to explore a civilian world which he characterizes as irresponsible, self-indulgent, and morally adrift. Although the military always provides General Goodwin with a code of behavior, if nothing else, even he wonders what it would be like to share in the postwar world of which he is not really a part. It is remarkable that Sid Skelton, the journalist, and Goodwin can live in such different worlds yet are nevertheless capable of coexisting in something approaching harmony, and that Marquand can capture both the differences and the harmony with a measure of sympathetic understanding for each.

Marquand's next novel, *Sincerely, Willis Wayde*, was a thoroughgoing "business novel," written in the mid-1950's when such novels were in vogue. Marquand's special gift for close social observation, however, elevates Willis Wayde far above the other "organization man" ventures of the period. This study of the struggles of a lower-middle-class boy to achieve financial success is harsh and unsympathetic. Marquand anatomizes the process by which Wayde, the son of an independent-minded factory worker, becomes, in the words of his father, "a son-of-a-bitch." The conflict, by now a familiar one in Marquand's fictional world, is between old and new money, with the successful protagonist denied the social acceptance he needs to marry the right girl. In this novel, however, the business competence of Willis Wayde allows him to usurp the power of the "old money" Harcourt family. Although he still pays lip service to their values of loyalty, family, and place, Wayde is easily capable of circumventing them in favor of a new set of ethics based on the business world, where everything is relative. The old Harcourts, incapacitated by their leisure, must rely for their very survival on a quintessential organization man, a representative of the modern business community who is responsible for destroying their world. There is a further irony in that while Wayde is betraying the old values of his past and the way of life most associated with those values, he is unaware of what he is doing. He simply feels that he is streamlining the old to fit in with the new. By the time of the writing of his last novels, Marquand could only look backward in his search for an explanation of the modern world; it was only in retrospect that he could find meaning.

Women and Thomas Harrow is Marquand's exit work from the world of letters. The novel was not only Marquand's last novel but also was a dark summary work, full of pessimism and regret. It is the story of Thomas Harrow, a successful playwright, and his three marriages. Harrow, fundamentally a decent man, finds himself at odds with the modern world, a world which through no fault or action of his own has become alien to him. No longer can Marquand's protagonist retrieve even the vestiges of a value-system from within the community; values are all past and unreachable. Thomas Harrow becomes the repository of all the doubts that plague contemporary man, who acknowledges the inaccessibility of the past and realizes that there is no buttress against the vulgarity of the present. Like many of Marquand's protagonists, Harrow discovers that success and money are ultimately not enough. In the absence of a meaningful relationship with place or community, there is no safe haven in contemporary society. What Thomas Harrow discovers about life might well be applied to the other central characters of Marquand's fiction: "There was no safety in living, and in the end, about all you got out of life was learning how to face truth without side-stepping to avoid it."

Marquand once wrote that the aspect that interested him most in the phenomena of human nature was the individual caught in a pattern of social change. The principal characters in his novels are caught in a world undergoing rapid alteration: moral securities erode before them; the social order collapses; moral commitments pale; religious sureties evaporate. Perhaps, as one critic has suggested, modern society can best be portrayed by examining what it stifles in able, good, but weak men. Marquand's protagonists become standards for measuring society, and, lacking direction, they search the past for a meaningful order, for standards of value against which to judge the highly relativistic American culture of the present. Marquand as a novelist provided his readers with an incisive examination of the modern world, exposing the hollowness of contemporary life, and dramatizing the spiritual search prompted by the recognition of that emptiness. Hugh Holman has summed up Marquand's place in contemporary American literature as follows: "To our age, at least, he speaks with ease and skill, with irony and wit, but above all with the authority of unsentimental knowledge."

Charles L. P. Silet

Other major works

SHORT FICTION: *Four of a Kind*, 1923; *Haven's End*, 1933; *Life at Happy Knoll*, 1957.

PLAY: *The Late George Apley: A Play*, 1946 (with George S. Kaufman).

NONFICTION: *Prince and Boatswain: Sea Tales from the Recollection of Rear-Admiral Charles E. Clark*, 1915 (with James Morris Morgan); *Lord Timothy Dexter of Newburyport, Mass.*, 1925 (revised as *Timothy Dexter Revisited*, 1960); *Thirty Years*, 1954.

Bibliography

Bell, Millicent. *J. P. Marquand: An American Life*. Boston: Little, Brown, 1979. A comprehensive account of Marquand's life, with a biographical rather than a critical emphasis. In the prologue Bell describes Marquand's work as belonging to "the novel of manners" genre and compares him to William Dean Howells, Edith Wharton, Sinclair Lewis, John Updike, and John O'Hara, among others.

Birmingham, Richard. *The Late John Marquand: A Biography*. Philadelphia: J. B. Lippincott, 1972. A sympathetic biography of Marquand, by a young writer who had frequent contact with him, which includes some review of Marquand's writing. Helpful in providing personal background for the Marquand scholar.

Gross, John J. *John P. Marquand*. New York: Twayne, 1963. This full-length study examines Marquand's success in his day and gives critical acknowledgement of his expertise as a social novelist. Discusses the action in his later novels, written in the last twenty-five years of his life. Deliberately omits review of Marquand's work in popular magazines, gives some background information, and relates Marquand to other writers of his time. Includes a useful but dated selected bibliography.

Gura, Philip P., and Joel Myerson. *Critical Essays on American Transcendentalism*. Boston: G. K. Hall, 1982. Briefly mentions Marquand and the hero of his novel *H. M. Pulham, Esquire*. Gura and Myerson see this character as embodying the "genteel tradition" of American humanism, which becomes reactionary only when it is divorced from renewal and change.

Hamburger, Philip. *J. P. Marquand, Esquire: A Portrait in the Form of a Novel*. Boston: Houghton Mifflin, 1952. An unusual approach in which Hamburger unfolds aspects of Marquand's life in the novel form. Contains very little critical reference to his writings.

Heiney, Donald. *Recent American Literature*. Great Neck, N.Y.: Barron's Educational Series, 1958. The entry on Marquand gives a brief overview of his literary career and lists his novels with scant criticism. Cites *Sincerely, Willis Wayde* as his most cutting satire on the American businessman and compares the central character to Sinclair Lewis' *Babbitt*.

Hoffman, Daniel, ed. *Harvard Guide to Contemporary Writing*. Cambridge, Mass.: Harvard University Press, 1979. Discusses Marquand in the context of novelists of manners. Provides commentary on his novels, which is appreciative but also faults Marquand for becoming an emblem of the "trap of popular success." Names Sinclair Lewis as Marquand's master, but claims that Marquand lacks the "feeling for the awkwardness of human connections," a hallmark of Lewis' work. Contains some astute observations of Marquand's writing.

PETER MATTHIESSEN

Born: New York, New York; May 22, 1927

Principal long fiction

Race Rock, 1954; *Partisans*, 1955; *Raditzer*, 1961; *At Play in the Fields of the Lord*, 1965; *Far Tortuga*, 1975; *Killing Mister Watson*, 1990.

Other literary forms

Peter Matthiessen is perhaps better known, and certainly far more prolific, as a writer of nonfiction than as a novelist. He has produced numerous volumes of nonfiction, beginning with *Wildlife in America* (1959). Many are chronicles of Matthiessen's trips to distant and barely accessible areas of the earth: *The Cloud Forest: A Chronicle of the South American Wilderness* (1961); *Under the Mountain Wall: A Chronicle of Two Seasons in the Stone Age* (1962); *Oomingmak: The Expedition to the Musk Ox Island in the Bering Sea* (1967); *Blue Meridian: The Search for the Great White Shark* (1971); *The Tree Where Man Was Born: The African Experience* (1972); *The Snow Leopard* (1978); and *Sand Rivers* (1981). *The Shorebirds of North America* (1967) is straight natural history, and *Sal Si Puedes: Cesar Chavez and the New American Revolution* (1970) is a biographical essay and political commentary on the California labor leader.

Among his other works of nonfiction are *In the Spirit of Crazy Horse* (1983), *Indian Country* (1984), *Nine-Headed Dragon River: Zen Journals 1969-1982* (1985), and *Men's Lives: Surfmen and Baymen of the South Fork* (1986). Matthiessen has published two volumes of short fiction: *Midnight Turning Gray* (1984) and *On the River Styx* (1989); the former is a small-press publication, the contents of which overlap with the latter.

Achievements

Matthiessen's achievements lie in two distinct but interrelated genres—that of the personal essay, similar in many respects to the writings of Henry David Thoreau, and that of the novel. His most distinguished works of fiction—*At Play in the Fields of the Lord* and *Far Tortuga*—both draw heavily on the author's evocation of the natural world, that of the Amazon rain forest in the first case and the open sea and Caribbean islands in the second. Both novels are extended studies of man's interrelation with these wild environments, and much of their effectiveness lies in Matthiessen's ability to place the reader within the primeval setting, projecting the smell, taste, and feel of the jungle and the sea. Similarly, Matthiessen's nonfiction relies for its power on his transporting of the reader to a remote natural world and, by making that world live, impressing indelibly its importance on him. Matthiessen stresses the value of nature to man, as a fountainhead of fundamental impulses and as an avenue of self-exploration, a means of cutting away the confusions of the "civilized" world and probing the essential elements of human nature. Matthiessen is not, however, a naïve romantic, finding in nature a Rousseauistic panacea for all the ills of society. His essays, whether book-length or merely brief sketches, have a gritty objectivity that precludes any superficial romanticizing of the natural world.

Biography

Peter Matthiessen was born in New York City on May 22, 1927, of a well-to-do, if not wealthy, family. His father, Erard A. Matthiessen, was a well-known architect and for many years a trustee of the National Audubon Society. His interest in nature and conservation was passed on to his son, and many of Peter Matthiessen's essays were eventually published in the Society's magazine, *Audubon*. From childhood, Matthiessen was exposed to the New York world of literature and the arts. By the time he was sixteen, he had decided to become a writer. Following the path of many boys from prominent families, he was first educated at the Hotchkiss School, then at Yale University. He spent many of his summers on the Connecticut shore in the relatively exclusive society of friends from the New York intellectual world. "My first story," he later said casually, "was published by my girl's father"— Cass Canfield, then editor of *Harper's Magazine*.

Late in World War II, Matthiessen interrupted his education to join the navy, an experience of mixed success, since he was demoted for disciplinary reasons, but one which gave him his first real experience of the life of common men. He returned to Yale in 1947, continued creative writing, and wrote about hunting and fishing for the Yale *Daily News*. He was graduated from Yale in 1950, spent a year there as an instructor in creative writing, and moved to Paris, by then married to Patsy Southgate, the daughter of a socially prominent diplomat. The Matthiessens soon became the center of a glittering crowd of American expatriate intellectuals, including William Styron, James Jones, George Plimpton, James Baldwin, and Irwin Shaw. With Harold L. Humes, Matthiessen founded the *Paris Review*, which became one of the most influential postwar literary magazines; from that time until quite recently, Matthiessen served as fiction editor.

Matthiessen's first novel, *Race Rock*, was written in Paris. It looks back to the world of Matthiessen's youth: the characters are a group of disillusioned, upper-middle-class young people living on the New England Coast. Aimless and confused by their meaningless lives, they stagnate, wallowing in their angst and neuroses. A reunion of childhood friends degenerates into an overflow of emotions and finally violence. Sadder but wiser, the survivors face an uncertain future, vowing to profit from their past mistakes and show maturity in the future.

In 1953, the Matthiessens returned to the United States and settled in East Hampton, Long Island, where Matthiessen divided his time between writing in bad weather and commercial fishing in good. His second novel, *Partisans*, appeared in 1955. It was an obvious product of Matthiessen's knowledge of the avant-garde left wing that infested expatriate intellectual circles in the 1950's. (Ironically, in the light of his later political commitments, it was rumored among the *Paris Review* crowd that Matthiessen was a CIA agent, which would hardly have been surprising, considering his background and contacts.) The protagonist of *Partisans* is Barney Sand, a young American journalist and son of a diplomat, searching for a cause to which he can commit himself. With the pure idealism of a grail knight, he scours the Paris slums seeking Jacobi, an old and deposed revolutionary who has been rejected by the Communist party, but who is the emblem of purity and integrity to Sand. Like *Race Rock*, *Partisans* is a kind of *Bildungsroman* in which a young man grows into maturity, in this case coming to realize that his naïve vision is unattainable.

The Matthiessens' marriage ended in divorce in 1957, but by that time, Matthiessen had already begun the series of "world wanderings" which would provide him with the subject of his major works. With no formal scientific training, he spent three years studying American animals and birds, with particular attention to endangered species. The result was *Wildlife of North America*, a book widely praised for showing, as one reviewer wrote, "the skill of a novelist and the accuracy of a zoologist." In 1959 and 1961, he made the two difficult journeys which eventually provided him with the setting for *At Play in the Fields of the Lord*, the first to South America and the second to New Guinea. On both expeditions, Matthiessen penetrated the wilderness as deeply and thoroughly as possible, at times at considerable personal risk, and lived with the native tribesmen in an effort to come to known them.

Between these travels, Matthiessen produced a third "conventional" novel, *Raditzer*, drawing this time on the navy experience of his young manhood for material. The novel is the study of a pariah, Raditzer, a sailor who embodies virtually every human vice. A product of the slums, Raditzer is dishonest, paranoid, sadisic, servile, and bullying by turns—a more unpleasant version of James Wait of Joseph Conrad's *The Nigger of the "Narcissus"* (1897, Matthiessen has pointed to Conrad and Fyodor Dostoevski as two important influences on his fiction). An instinctive parasite, Raditzer attaches himself to the hero, a young intellectual sailor of good family, who, like the protagonists of *Race Rock* and *Partisans*, bears considerable resemblance to the author as a young man. When Raditzer becomes such a Jonah that his shipmates plot to kill him, the sailor finds himself in the disagreeable position of having his courage tested in the defense of a man he loathes. He comes to realize—as Barney Sand did, despising the poor whose cause he championed—that moral action does not come in neat, sanitized packages, and that good and evil are peculiarly muddled in the real world. Unlike most of Matthiessen's works *Raditzer* does not concern itself integrally with nature, and it is particularly interesting for the success with which it explores the lives of common working men, a topic of increasing interest to the author.

At Play in the Fields of the Lord signaled Matthiessen's coming of age as a writer and a thinker. In it, and in the rest of his mature work, he was to fuse the speculative insight of a philosopher, the lyricism of a poet, and the scrupulous observation of a scientist to produce a broad statement about the relationship between man and the natural world as profound as any in Western literature. His fifth novel, *Far Tortuga*, published in 1975, is a stylistic and structural tour de force as well as a profoundly moving elegy for the doomed world of the Caribbean turtle fishers. It followed a remarkable book-length essay, *The Tree Where Man Was Born: The African Experience*, an extended philosophical commentary on life and death in East Africa that contains some of Matthiessen's finest and most thoughtful observations concerning man's place in the natural world.

Matthiessen remarried in 1963, but his second wife, Deborah Love Matthissen, died ten years later after a long struggle with cancer. At the end of her life, both she and her husband had been moving deeply into a study of Zen, convinced that it offered an alternative to the emptiness of the modern world. After his wife's death, Matthiessen undertook a difficult and dangerous trip on foot into the Asian depths of Nepal to visit the Crystal Monastery, a center of Zen meditation and reverence; his companion on the trip was the noted naturalist George Schaller, who was studying Nepalese blue sheep. Matthiessen was specifically hoping for a sight of the real but mystical snow leopard, an animal so rarely seen that is has become a Zen symbol for everything possible and unattainable. *The Snow Leopard*, based on his journey, was published in 1978. It is Matthiessen's very personal account of his spiritual pilgrimage in the Himalayas, and was awarded the National Book Award.

In the early 1980's, Matthiessen published two books dealing with the fate of the American Indian: *In the Spirit of Crazy Horse* and *Indian Country*. The former, which argues for the innocence of Leonard Peltier, a member of the American Indian Movement convicted of murdering two agents of the Federal Bureau of Investigation, embroiled Matthiessen and his publisher, Viking Press, in two libel suits that lasted for six years. The result was the virtual suppression of the book, despite the fact that the suits were ultimately found to be without merit.

In 1990, Matthiessen published his first novel in fifteen years, *Killing Mr. Watson*. He continues to live in Sagaponack, Long Island, with his third wife, Maria.

Analysis

Peter Matthiessen is America's modern Henry David Thoreau. There are other fine contemporary nature writers, such as Edward Hoagland and John McPhee, but there is no one else who brings to his observation of the natural world and man's place in it Matthiessen's philosophical depth and poetic command of the language. His two finest novels, *At Play in the Fields of the Lord* and *Far Tortuga*, combine his experience as a naturalist with the felt immediacy which only a deeply persuasive work of fiction can provide.

Matthiessen's first twenty years as a novelist must really be divided into two phases, one comprising his first three novels—*Race Rock*, *Partisans*, and *Raditzer*—and the other, his two major works, *At Play in the Fields of the Lord* and *Far Tortuga*. The first three are thoroughly competent novels, and they certainly show the promise of the writer Matthiessen became. All exhibit a young man's fascination with the maturing process and the loss of innocence—with "rites of passage." All center on protagonists obviously surrogates of the author himself, idealistic but troubled young men of good family, aimless and seeking direction and commitment in a world of inexplicable evil and suffering. Although *Race Rock* in particular is rather complex in its presentation of multiple levels of time, all three books are essentially traditional narratives, accomplished but unextraordinary in any way.

Matthiessen's next two novels, however, are fundamentally philosophical meditations on the human condition. As such, they join the company of Herman Melville's *Moby Dick* (1851), Joseph Conrad's *Heart of Darkness* (1902), and Stendhal's *The Red and the Black* (1830), all works in which the narrative impulse, however strong, is essentially a vehicle for metaphysical statement; Matthiessen is concerned with *things*, but he is more concerned with the meaning of things. This is hardly to say that he is a didactic writer (although unequivocal pleas for environmentalism fill his nonfiction), but he is insistently an explorer of the meaning of life. In both *At Play in the Fields of the Lord* and *Far Tortuga*, that meaning is manifested in terms of man's place in the continuum of natural life on earth. In the former, Lewis Meriwether Moon deliberately and consciously projects himself into the world of the Niaruna, and his discovery of his identity as a natural man is the result of an act of will. In contrast, Raib Avers and the crew of the *Lillias Eden*, of *Far Tortuga* are in harmony with the sea and its creatures but have little opportunity to determine the lives they lead.

Unlike most philosophical writers, who persistently project man as a purely social or psychological being, Matthiessen insists that man is an animal, although not primarily in the naturalistic terms of Theodore Dreiser or Jack London, who write of man as a victim of fate, the pawn of uncontrollable chemical and biological impulses. Matthiessen's human beings, as animals, share a common heritage and destiny with all the living world. Both *At Play in the Fields of the Lord* and *Far Tortuga* do exhibit a fatalism, however, that suggests affinities with literary naturalism. An unavoidable destruction hangs over and overtakes the Niaruna, regardless of the efforts of the missionaries and Moon. Similarly in *Far Tortuga*, the last voyage of the *Lillias Eden* has a predestined quality about it, and the novel is full of omens and foreshadowings. There is, in Matthiessen's art, an ominous skepticism about the possibility of survival for traditional patterns of life. Men such as Moon and Avers, who cast their lot with the natural world, through choice or chance, are destined to go down with the ship; the smug, technocratic modern society has little place or tolerance for them. Still, there are survivors. These two novels are too open-ended to be tied up with certainties and happy endings, but both also hold out the possibility of hope. Moon soldiers on, "in celebration of the only man beneath the eye of Heaven," himself. Speedy, the most decent and heroic of the turtlers, survives the wreck, like Melville's Ishmael. The reader is unsure that he will live, but sure that the novel does not explicitly have him die with the rest of the crew.

Both *At Play in the Fields of the Lord* and *Far Tortuga* present the possibility of human fulfillment through the apprehension and acceptance of man's proper role in the natural world. That world is constantly threatened, however, by the values of "civilization." Still, Matthiessen believes, there is a chance of avoiding the spiritual damnation implicit in the destruction of the Niaruna and the turtlers. "I hope we'll be forced into a new value system," he said. "But I think we're going to be forced to the edge of the cliff first. It's going to be so close."

More than a decade after he published *At Play in the Fields of the Lord*, Matthiessen remarked that he thought of it as a "conventional novel . . . full of fine writing." The critics, however, saw the novel as extraordinary in theme, structure, and style, as well as in quality. "A most unusual novel," wrote Emile Capouya in *The New York Times*; Granville Hicks wrote of the book's "power over the imagination" and its "astonishing assortment of characters." More than any other work, *At Play in the Fields of the Lord* established Matthiessen, in fellow-novelist and poet Jim Harrison's words, as "our most eccentric major writer."

Superficially, the novel is an obvious outgrowth of Matthiessen's years as a wandering naturalist in obscure areas of the world. He had already produced two nonfiction studies of the tropical wilderness and its native inhabitants, both of which explored in depth the implications of the contact between the "civilized" world and the "primitive." *At Play in the Fields of the Lord* is set in the Amazon, and it is a study of the interpenetration, and ultimately the irreconcilability, of cultures.

At the center of the novel, more a presence than a group of characters, are the Niaruna, a tiny stone-age tribe precariously clinging to life on the banks of a jungle river. Matthiessen does not romanticize the Indians. They are crude, unthinking, dirty, and addicted to drugs and occasional violence, no noble savages. Still, there is a kind of purity and integrity in their lives which the more "civilized" characters lack. The greatest threat to the Indians' existence is the local governor, Guzman, "El Comandante," a petty dictator with a handful of bestial troops at his disposal. This vanguard of civilization is engaged in a "pacification" of the Niaruna bordering on genocide; only drinking and whoring in the squalid fleshpots of Madre de Dios, the little jungle town that provides much of the novel's early locale, and self-indulgent incompetence have kept these representatives of law and order from exterminating the Indians long since. A third cultural block is formed by an earnest pair of American missionary families, the Hubens and the Quarriers. Humorless hustlers for God's will as they see fit to interpret it, they seek to convert and uplift the Niaruna before El Comandante uses the tribe's savagery as an excuse for its liquidation or dispersal. For the missionaries, the salvation of the Niarunas' souls as well as their bodies is synonymous with the abandonment of their primitive, natural culture.

Caught between these groups, and emphatically not of any of them, are Lewis Meriwether Moon and his partner Wolfie. American soldiers of fortune on their uppers, they are stranded in the jungle after El Comandante has impounded their small plane, gaudily plastered with a sign reading "Wolfie and Moon, Inc.—Small Wars and Demolition." When Martin Quarrier sees it, he says, disbelieving, "It's a joke." So it is, and one of the aspects of *At Play in the Fields of the Lord* most frequently ignored is the pervasive comic irony of the novel. Wolfie is only a richly sketched bit player in the panorama of the novel, but Moon is the most thoroughly developed and complex character in all Matthiessen's fiction, and one of the most interesting in recent American writing; it is his novel. Part American Indian, something of a cynical philosopher, he masquerades as an amoral pragmatist. In fact, he is a closet mystic who practices introspection that borders on meditation (and which foreshadows Matthiessen's own developing interest in Zen which culminated in *The Snow Leopard*). El Comandante wants Moon and Wolfie to bomb the Indians for him, and at first, Moon is tempted. Gradually, though, circumstances and powerful but obscure forces in his own psychology impel him to cast himself in the role of a savior to the tribe. The native hallucinogen *ayahuasca* projects Moon into a weird and frightening drug-trip, an exploration into the depths of his psyche, rendered with astonishing effectiveness by Matthiessen's surrealistic prose. Moon goes to live among the Indians, his civilized persona dissolving as he adopts their simple ways. As he sheds his Western cultural skin and melds himself into the ethos of the tribe, Moon also discovers a new self lurking under his civilized mask—that of the Indian he comes to believe he truly has always been.

Walls of misunderstanding rise between the characters of this novel. Each group struggles against what it perceives to be the challenges of the others, crippled by a myopia that makes it impossible for any character but Moon to see beyond his own values. Doomed by their lack of knowledge and by the narrowness of their specialized world, the Niaruna tremble on the brink of extinction. Blinded to their own bigotry by their faith and by the arrogance of religious Babbittry, the missionaries seek to do everything for the Indians at Niaruna Station but understand and accept them for what they are. Les Huben is, in his own way, nearly as sinister an embodiment of progress as the soulless and corrupt representatives of the state who are more candid in acknowledging their desire to destroy the Indians.

Society, whether the elemental one of the Niaruna tribe or the neurotic and more complex one of the other characters, is only one pole of the action of *At Play in the Fields of the Lord*. The world of man is counterpointed throughout by the world of nature. The jungle hangs persistently about the characters, driving some to the verge of insanity, suffering every aspect of the book. The lushness of Matthiessen's rhetoric (which eventually led him to describe the novel as "ornate") complements the scrupulous accuracy of his observation, so that the forest is rendered with a rich immediacy unmatched in modern fiction. Matthiessen's jungle is *alive*, and the equal of the jungles of Conrad or of Melville in *Typee* (1846). So vividly is the natural world painted that it assumes a thematic weight and aesthetic value that makes it superior to its foil, the world of society and civilization. At the end of the novel, appropriately, the Niaruna are all killed or scattered, and Moon finds himself alone and naked in the jungle. Momentarily, at least, man and his societies have fallen away and the forest primeval has reassumed the land.

The jungle for Matthiessen is much more than simply a setting. So great is the power of his evocation of it that it becomes almost a character, and a character with a particular personality. It is schizophrenic—alternately rich and nurturing, then corrupt and threatening. The life with which it swarms is emblematic of degeneration and filth to Hazel Quarrier, but represents vitality and sustenance to the life-affirming Niaruna. As their chief says, "We have our river and our forest, we have fish and birds and animals to eat. . . . Surely we are living in a golden time!"

The jungle setting gradually absorbs, or rather subsumes, the other elements of the novel. The psychological, social, political, and religious forces that seethe through the early pages subside, replaced by an almost beatific peace that Moon finds withdrawing into the forest life of the Indians. Certainly, the threat of annihilation from outside society hangs over the book to the end, but it becomes a threat external to the organic integrity of the jungle life. By the time the Niaruna have been dispersed, all the characters have faded, and only the jungle earth remains.

The jungle earth remains, and Moon tenaciously endures. He finds himself with only his own soul for sustenance in the face of the awesomeness of nature. It is he alone, and not the Niaruna, who represents the force that counterpoints the rich, beautiful, but inhuman breadth of nature: the individual human mind. Matthiessen's fundamental apposition is not the traditional one between nature and society, but between the individual human consciousness and the great natural world within which it exists. Matthiessen maintains, in fact, that the true genesis of *At Play in the Fields of the Lord* was an image of isolation in nature: "I wanted to get at what I consider to be the essential human condition, which is solitude under a big sky. I think it's when we run away from that that we miss the whole reverberation of life."

This basic "reverberation of life" is the ultimate subject of the novel. In the end, Moon and the natural world vibrate to a common chord. Thematically, the civilized world falls away, and the individual human psychology forms a continuum with the natural world it inhabits. In this sense, *At Play in the Fields of the Lord* is a Romantic novel, with overtones of William Wordsworth and Percy Bysshe Shelley. Man for Matthiessen becomes something like the "mind that feeds upon infinity" of Wordsworth's *The Prelude* (1850), and nature assumes its traditional Romantic role as the path to transcendental experience.

In his developing power to interpret that experience, Moon becomes a priest of nature without portfolio, or, to use one of Matthiessen's favorite words, a shaman. Ultimately, *At Play in the Fields of the Lord* is a novel of religious conflict. On one side is the sterile and lifeless theology of the missionaries, on the other the natural celebration of life, biological and spiritual, practiced daily by the Niaruna. For the Indians, the jungle and their existence therein is truly sacramental—the external and visible manifestation of an inward and invisible state of grace. For the missionaries, God is extrinsic to the corrupt world of the tropical wilderness. Martin Quarrier, the most decent and conscientious of them, tries to come to grips with natural instinct as embodied both by the Indians and by his own lust for another missionary's wife, but he cannot bridge the gap between his rigid intellectualized Western mind and the elemental life of the jungle world. Only the part-Indian Moon can gain the natural world and not lose his individual soul in the process.

If Matthiessen could claim of *At Play in the Fields of the Lord* that it was a conventional novel, he could hardly say the same of the radical *Far Tortuga*, which James Dickey called a turning point in the evolution of the novel, "creating a new vision." *Far Tortuga* was widely hailed at its publication for its experimentalism in style and structure, reaping encomia even from the reclusive Thomas Pynchon. If not entirely unique, its departures from conventionality marked it as an impressionistic tour de force. Going beyond even the metaphor-free, plain style of writers such as Ernest Hemingway, Matthiessen trimmed his book of superfluities. Quotation marks, indicators such as "he said," and "there was," adjectives, and adverbs—all went out. Further, he used the physical form of the book itself and of words and sentences on the page to create a visual impression analogous to the typographic effects of E. E. Cummings. At times, the verbal yields to the ideographic in *Far Tortuga*: a black smudge represents the death of a man, a meandering line the horizon or the edge of the sea. Often, words or lines are accented by sweeps of empty white paper, and Matthiessen said that if he had the novel to do over, he would have written it even more like a musical score or an illuminated manuscript, with a much larger format and more dramatic utilization of space.

The form of the novel was an organic outgrowth of its subject, the dying world of a Caribbean turtle-fishing boat on its last voyage. The crew's world is a primitive one, like that of the Niaruna, an unintellectual existence of sea and sky, of superstitions, myths, and folktales, and of a rich cultural tradition succumbing to the modern world. The objective particulars of the turtlers' lives—the boat, the creatures of the sea, the shifting weather—parade through the novel without authorial comment, producing a stark, powerful texture that gives an impression of overwhelming physicality.

Like the cetology sections of *Moby Dick*, the action of *Far Tortuga* is rooted in a solidly constructed core of informational specifics delineating the turtlers' trade. The characters themselves, the doomed sailors of the decrepit boat *Lillias Eden*, live only in their speech and their actions, for Matthiessen never penetrates their minds. The novel's unique oral quality derives from its swell of dialect that seems increasingly natural as the book progresses. Rhythm is everything in *Far Tortuga*, rhythm and basic image (there is only a single simile in the entire work). As on the pages of Walt Whitman, Ezra Pound, or Charles Olsen, the basic elements of poetic evocation, words, raise up their images as *things*, hung together with a kind of narrative glue, the speech and stories of the turtlers. The dialogue is of a rich and variegated texture. As William Kennedy observed, the great strength of *Far Tortuga* is its use of detail, and both the dialogue and the narrative swarm with a wealth of objective particulars.

Like Matthiessen's Amazonian rain forest, this Caribbean setting is a singular one. Again, the book presents a simple people living close to nature and comfortable with it. Again, the protagonists' culture is threatened, on the brink of extinction. "The Modern World," as the turtlers bitterly call it, is a more distant enemy in this book, lurking outside the visual and verbal matrix which defines the narrative space of *Far Tortuga*, but the reader is well aware that it will soon bring the end of this culture. Modernity is distant only because, within the context of this novel, what is, and what is done, and what is said on the *Lillias Eden* is everything. On the one hand are the specific objects and actions which define activity on the boat. On the other hand, there is a kind of spirit-world bodied forth in the talk of the men. Legends, ghost stories, and most of all tales of the past, give the sense of an existence lived always in the shadow of the unseen. For these men, the sea turtle itself, like all of animate and inanimate nature, is imbued with a spiritual character, akin to a soul. The line, "Green turtle very mysterious, mon" runs through the novel like a chorus. Very mysterious, indeed: sacred, in fact.

The characterization in *Far Tortuga* is one of Matthiessen's most remarkable achievements. As the novel progresses, the reader is able to distinguish among the various speakers, and gradually, individual personalities emerge. The sailors are rendered only in terms of their verbal expression of the world in which they work and live. There are no narrative threads or subplots unrelated to the immediate action of the book. One character stands out, the captain of the *Lillias Eden*, "Copm" Raib Avers. He is a full-bodied creature, irascible, arrogant, and energetic. He is also the embodiment of the integrity of the turtlers' trade, for he is rightfully proud of his skill as a sailor and passionate in his desire to be as good as "de copms of old"—men to whom sailing and turtle fishing were a calling rather than a way of only getting by. Avers' character is totally a function of the sea-swept world in which he lives. He seems to be related to half the people in the story, and his speech is a continual tale of the folk. To listen to him is to hear a kind of cultural history of the Caribbean, in which the living and the dead, the real and the fanciful, the past and the present are interwoven to create a vivid tapestry. Avers is the voice of the *paideuma*, the wisdom, knowledge, and heritage of his people. "I really do know what working men talk like," Matthiessen said once. In *Far Tortuga*, he proves it.

If Avers is the mouthpiece of a communal voice, he is also, like Moon, an individual one. Doomed to defeat and death, each man on the *Lillias Eden* shares a common fate. If Avers' voice stands out, it is the choral effect that dominates the novel. The group of men moves as a unit toward its destiny, borne relentlessly by the tides and their own impulses, like the characters in a Greek tragedy. Avers repeatedly asserts his belief that he is the master of his fate and captain of his soul as well as of the ship. He is more aggressive and less introspective than Moon, more of an activist, and he sees his role in the natural world as confrontational, a constant struggle between himself and the sea. He accepts the struggle, even celebrates it in his rough way, but he does not dominate the novel. Ultimately, his life and death are merged into the total picture of the turtlers as a group.

Avers is not even the last to survive the wreck of the *Lillias Eden* after the ship strikes a reef and sinks. The last forty pages of the novel are a remarkable dying fall in which the turtlers, adrift and unprotected in catboats, die one by one. The furious, frenetic rush of sounds and images subsides as the life goes out of the men. Finally, only a few hesitant words scattered on otherwise empty pages remain, and finally only the last image—of a man, presumably Speedy, on a beach. One has escaped to tell the tale, to plunge again into the natural continuum of man and sea that is the turtler's life, the brilliant portrait of which is the ultimate achievement of this remarkable novel.

In the long hiatus between *Far Tortuga* and *Killing Mr. Watson*, Matthiessen was hardly idle, publishing a number of nonfiction works. Yet he has said "I have always considered myself primarily a novelist." In some ways,

Killing Mr. Watson strongly resembles *Far Tortuga*. Set in the Florida Everglades around the turn of the century, it centers on Edgar Watson, a brutal entrepreneur and murderer who, after years of unchecked rapacity, is killed by his neighbors in an act of collective justice. Rather than being presented head-on, Watson is seen from the diverse perspectives of many who knew him—or knew about him, or thought they did. Their sharply rendered and distinctive voices, like the voices of the fishermen in *Far Tortuga*, are the heart of the novel.

Like *Far Tortuga*, *Killing Mr. Watson* evokes the natural world in extraordinary detail and with a strong sense of loss brought about by the encroachment of human society. At the same time, *Killing Mr. Watson* relies more heavily on the adaptation to fiction of the techniques of nonfiction: the novel as research. With its documentary feel—Edgar Watson was a historical figure, and the structural frame of the novel is factual—*Killing Mr. Watson* departs from conventional fiction as radically in its own way as did *Far Tortuga*.

John L. Cobbs

Other major works
SHORT FICTION: *Midnight Turning Gray*, 1984; *On the River Styx*, 1989.
NONFICTION: *Wildlife in America*, 1959; *The Cloud Forest: A Chronicle of the South American Wilderness*, 1961; *Under the Mountain Wall: A Chronicle of Two Seasons in the Stone Age*, 1962; *The Shorebirds of North America*, 1967; *Oomingmak: The Expedition to the Musk Ox Island in the Bering Sea*, 1967; *Sal Si Puedes: Cesar Chavez and the New American Revolution*, 1970; *Blue Meridian: The Search for the Great White Shark*, 1971; *Everglades: Selections from the Writings of Peter Matthiessen*, 1971 (Paul Brooks, editor); *The Tree Where Man Was Born: The African Experience*, 1972; *The Wind Birds*, 1973; *The Snow Leopard*, 1978; *Sand Rivers*, 1981; *In the Spirit of Crazy Horse*, 1983; *Indian Country*, 1984; *Nine-Headed Dragon River: Zen Journals 1969-1982*, 1985; *Men's Lives: The Surfmen and Baymen of the South Fork*, 1986.
CHILDREN'S LITERATURE: *Seal Pool*, 1972.

Bibliography
Bishop, Peter. "The Geography of Hope and Despair: Peter Mathiessen's *The Snow Leopard*." *Critique: Studies in Modern Fiction* 26, no. 4 (1984): 203-216. Places Matthiessen alongside other literary travelers such as Graham Greene, Evelyn Waugh, and D. H. Lawrence. Discusses in-depth *The Snow Leopard* and compares it to *Far Tortuga* and *At Play in the Fields of the Lord*. Sees the book's lack of conclusion as its success. A thought-provoking article which presents psychological insights into Matthiessen.

Gabriel, Trip. "The Nature of Peter Matthiessen." *The New York Times Magazine*, June 10, 1990, 30. An insightful profile, based on interviews with Matthiessen and his circle. Gabriel focuses on *Killing Mr. Watson* but also provides an overview of Matthiessen's career. Neither sycophantic nor hostile, Gabriel presents a nuanced portrait of the man behind the books.

Grove, James P. "Pastoralism and Anti-Pastoralism in Peter Matthiessen's *Far Tortuga*." *Critique: Studies in Modern Fiction* 21, no. 2 (1979): 15-29. Discusses this highly praised novel and reflects on the influence of Zen on Matthiessen's views. An in-depth treatment of the content and intent of this novel within the theme of pastoralism.

Reilly, John M. "Peter Matthiessen." In *Contemporary Novelists*, edited by James Vinson. New York: St. Martin's Press, 1976. Makes very little distinction between Matthiessen's fiction and nonfiction. Only the novels are discussed, however: *Race Rock*, *Far Tortuga*, and *At Play in the Fields of the Lord*, the latter exceeding the form of the other novels. An altogether brief and rather spare chapter which consists mainly of overview but does contain some insights. A chronology, bibliographical information, and a list of published works and awards is provided.

CHARLES ROBERT MATURIN

Born: Dublin, Ireland; September 25, 1780
Died: Dublin, Ireland; October 30, 1824

Principal long fiction

Fatal Revenge: Or, The Family of Montorio, a Romance, 1807; *The Wild Irish Boy*, 1808; *The Milesian Chief: A Romance*, 1812; *Women: Or, Pour et Contre*, 1818; *Melmoth the Wanderer: A Tale*, 1820; *The Albigenses: A Romance*, 1824.

Other literary forms

In addition to his novels, Charles Robert Maturin also wrote plays, three of which were performed and published during his lifetime: *Bertram: Or, The Castle of St. Aldobrand, a Tragedy* (1816), *Manuel: A Tragedy* (1817), and *Fredolfo: A Tragedy* (1819). A fourth, *Osmyn, the Renegade: Or, The Siege of Salerno, a Tragedy*, written some time between 1817 and 1821, was produced in Dublin in 1830. It was never published in its entirety; excerpts were printed in *The Edinburgh Literary Journal* (April 24, 1830). Of these plays, only *Bertram* was financially successful. When it first appeared, it was one of the most talked about plays of the season, and today it is noted for being one of the first dramatic portrayals of the brooding, sinned against and sinning figure who has come to be called the Byronic hero.

In his role as a minister, Maturin published two volumes of sermons: *Sermons* (1819), a collection on various subjects; and *Five Sermons of the Errors of the Roman Catholic Church* (1824). Both these works are of interest for what they reveal of Maturin's mind and temperament. In them, he often concentrates on the fallen world and man's guilt, subjects similar to those in his novels. Two reviews published anonymously also offer some insight into Maturin's thoughts, especially his literary opinions. "*The Apostate*: A Tragedy in Five Acts, by Richard Sheil" appeared in *The Quarterly Review* (April, 1817), and "*Harrington and Ormond, Tales*" was printed in *The British Review, and London Critical Journal* (February, 1818).

Two short fictional pieces were published posthumously: "Leixlip Castle: An Irish Family Legend" appeared in *The Literary Souvenir: Or, Cabinet of Poetry and Romance* of 1825, and "The Sybil's Prophecy: A Dramatic Fragment" was printed in the 1826 edition of the same publication. Both these pieces are in the Gothic style.

Lastly, two poems are associated with Maturin's name: *Lines on the Battle of Waterloo*, which was the 1815 prize poem at Trinity College, and *The Universe: A Poem* (1821). The first appeared under the name of John Shee, a student of Maturin, but it is now believed to be Maturin's work. The second, although published with Maturin's name on the title page, is now believed to be the work of James Wills.

Achievements

Maturin is best known for the fifth of his six novels, *Melmoth the Wanderer*. Although, when it first appeared, many critics viewed it merely as an unfortunate attempt to revive the Gothic novel, a form earlier made popular by such authors as Ann Radcliffe and Matthew Gregory Lewis, scholars now consider *Melmoth the Wanderer* one of the finest examples of its genre. It is judged to be not only a culmination of the Gothic novel but also a forerunner of the psychological novels of such writers as Fyodor Dostoevski and Franz Kafka. Although Maturin's handling of narrative structure is often awkward and confusing, and although he borrowed so closely from the works of others that he can be accused of plagiarism, his novels are original in their depiction of extreme states of mind, especially those engendered by fear.

Maturin himself was aware of his major strength. In the prefatory pages of *The Milesian Chief*, he wrote: "If I possess any talent, it is that of darkening the gloomy, and of deepening the sad; of painting life in extremes, and representing those struggles of passion when the soul trembles on the verge of the unlawful and the unhallowed." His settings of mazelike madhouses and dungeons lead the reader into the dark places of the human soul. This particular aspect of his novels fascinated and influenced many other authors. Edgar Allan Poe, Robert Louis Stevenson, Oscar Wilde, Christina and Dante Gabriel Rossetti, Honoré de Balzac, and Charles Baudelaire were all impressed by Maturin's attempt to penetrate the mystery of evil. Recently, critical attention has been given to Maturin's role in Irish literary history. In such novels as *The Milesian Chief* and *The Wild Irish Boy*, descriptions of Irish settings and character play an important part. More study needs to be done to evaluate fully this contribution to the development of the Irish regional novel; whatever the outcome, Maturin's place among the significant writers of the English Gothic novel is assured.

Biography

Charles Robert Maturin was born in 1780, one of several children born to William Maturin and his wife, Fidelia Watson. The Maturin family was of French descent. One of their ancestors was a Huguenot priest who was forced to leave France because of religious persecution during the reign of Louis XIV. This aspect of his family history strongly impressed the young Maturin, and throughout his life he was fond of relating how his ancestors had suffered for their faith. He himself was strongly anti-Catholic, and especially opposed to the rule of monastic life, which he considered dangerously repressive. His novels contain many scenes and descriptions of monasteries as sadistic places where virtue turns to vice.

When in Ireland, Maturin's family became closely connected with the Anglican Church. Maturin's great-grandfather, Peter Maturin, was Dean of Killala from 1724 to 1741, and his grandfather, Gabriel James Maturin, succeeded Jonathan Swift as Dean of St. Patrick's in Dublin in 1745. Following this tradition, Maturin entered Trinity College in 1795 to study theology, and in 1803 took holy orders. In the same year, he married Henrietta Kingsbury, a daughter of the Archdeacon of Killala. From all reports, the couple were well suited and happily married. After ordination, Maturin served as curate in Loughrea, Galway for two years. He then returned to Dublin to become curate of St. Peter's, a position he held for the rest of his life. Unfortunately, his small income from this curacy was insufficient to support his family, especially after his father was accused of fraud and dismissed from his position with the Irish post office in 1809. Later, he was cleared and given another position, but for a time, the family struggled in severe poverty. In fact, Maturin was continually troubled by financial difficulties. To supplement his income, he ran a school to prepare boys for college, and later he turned to novel-writing.

The Prefaces of his novels and the styles of romance he chose to employ indicate that he wanted very much to become a popular writer. Because he realized that many of his parishioners and superiors might not approve of a minister writing novels, he used the pseudonym of Dennis Jasper Murphy, publishing three novels under that name. When it was discovered that he was the author of the play *Bertram*, a play involving adultery and an amoral hero, he was for a time in danger of losing his curacy. Apparently, friends intervened to soothe the necessary bishops. After this incident, since his identity was known, he published his next novels and plays under his own name. It is quite possible that his literary activities did prevent his advancement in the clerical profession. There were those who interpreted the beliefs of his characters, some of which were atheistic and heretical, as Maturin's own.

His novels did gain him one very influential friend, Sir Walter Scott. In 1810, Scott wrote a generally favorable review of *Fatal Revenge* for *The Quarterly Review*. Encouraged, Maturin wrote to him, and a correspondence was begun which lasted until Maturin's death. Although the two men never actually met, Scott did assist Maturin with encouragement and advice, and he was instrumental in Maturin's one financial success; he recommended *Bertram* to Lord Byron, who was then responsible for play selection at Drury Lane Theatre. Byron was favorably impressed, and the famous actor Edmund Kean agreed to play the lead. The play's success earned Maturin one thousand pounds, most of which paid a relative's debt. Earlier, Maturin had been able to sell the copyright of his third novel, *The Milesian Chief*, for eighty pounds (the first two novels he had printed at his own expense), and later he was advanced five hundred pounds for *Melmoth the Wanderer*, but his literary efforts never brought the long-sought and often desperately needed financial stability. Up until his death, he continually tried to write in a style that would sell. *The Albigenses* is a historical romance, a type Scott had established and made quite popular. This novel was the first in what was to be a trilogy depicting European manners in ancient, medieval, and modern times. Soon after *The Albigenses* was completed, Maturin died in his home on October 30, 1824, apparently after a long period of ill health. The exact cause of his death is not known. He left a wife and four children who were still in desperate need of financial assistance.

Analysis

In his Preface to *Fatal Revenge*, Charles Robert Maturin stresses the fear of the unknown as essential in man's emotional and spiritual life: "It is *not* the weak and trivial impulse of the nursery, to be forgotten and scorned by manhood. It is the aspiration of a spirit; 'it is the passion of immortals,' that dread and desire of their final habitation." In one of his sermons, he focuses on the same theme:

> The very first sounds of childhood are tales of another life—foolishly are they called tales of superstition; for, however disguised by the vulgarity of narration, and the distortion of fiction, they tell him of those whom he is hastening from the threshold of life to join, the inhabitants of the invisible world, with whom he must soon be, and be for ever.

These quotations indicate a major aspect of Maturin's perception of human existence; the haunted and the sacred are interwoven and share a common ground. Man's fascination with the supernatural, the world of demons and ghosts, springs from the same source as his desire to believe in salvation and a return to paradise. In fact, the road to salvation leads through the dark places of the soul where the individual must admit his fallen state, his own guilt. The theme of guilt is common in all of Maturin's novels. His major characters must struggle with the serpents in their own hearts, their own original sin. In keeping with this theme, the settings of his novels are generally those of a fallen world; dungeons and underground passages are common backgrounds for the action. Even in those novels which contain descriptions of more natural surroundings, storms and earthquakes are common occurrences, always reminding man that he has been exiled from paradise. Harmony with nature, with man, and with God has been lost.

Maturin develops this theme of guilt, which brings exile and separation, through his handling of character. Man's divided nature is represented by the pairing of characters, especially brothers: Ippolito and Annibal in *Fatal Revenge*, Connal and Desmond in *The Milesian Chief*, Paladour and Amirald in *The Albigenses*. These brothers are described in such a way as to suggest one identity fragmented into two opposing selves. Ippolito is passionate, Annibal rational; Desmond is the soft flower, Connal the proud oak. Often a character is torn in two opposing directions and does not know how to reconcile them: Connal between his Irish pride and his realization that the Irish peasants are not yet ready to govern themselves; Charles in *Women* is torn between his love for Eva, a shy quiet girl, and Zaira, a worldy and more accomplished woman. At times, a character seems pursued by a dark, sinister double: Montorio by Schemoli in *Fatal Revenge*; Alonzo by the parricide in *Melmoth the Wanderer*. By far the most striking and powerful example of this is the character of the wanderer himself. Melmoth represents the potential for evil which can be found in all men. In developing Melmoth's character, Maturin echoes the warning in Genesis against too much curiosity about the tree of knowledge of good and evil. Melmoth has sold his soul for increased knowledge; his sin is one of "pride and intellectual glorying," the sin of Lucifer and of the first mortals.

As Maturin's characters wander in a fallen world, little guidance is provided. Especially weak and ineffective are the parental figures. In fact, a distinguishing trait of this fallen world is the disintegration of the family. In all of Maturin's six novels, there are parents who are woefully irresponsible. They are often self-centered, putting their own greedy desires before their children's welfare, or they seek to expiate their own guilt by placing the burden of their sin upon their children. This selfish turning inward and transference of guilt to another is also found in Maturin's representations of larger structures of authority, especially the Catholic Church. As the divided soul wanders in a fallen world, parent and church offer little hope.

Maturin reserves the role of spiritual guide for the female characters who either love or are loved by the hero (such love is not always fulfilled or requited). Often his women are idealized creatures who can reconcile within themselves all conflicting opposites: in *Melmoth the Wanderer*, Immalee embodies passion and purity; in *The Albigenses*, Genevieve is a "mixture of strengh and purity that is never to be found but in woman." Even if a woman finds herself hurled into a world of experience and corruption, as Zaira is in *Women* her heart remains pure. At times, Maturin uses his female characters to symbolize self-sacrificing love which, although never placing the beloved before God, does place the beloved before the self. Despite Maturin's emphasis on such redeeming love, however, when domestic happiness is found by his characters it seems contrived and imposed upon them by others. Maturin is undoubtedly at his best when depicting man lost and searching for wholeness, not in actually finding it.

Maturin titled his first novel *The Family of Montorio*, but the publisher changed the title to *Fatal Revenge*, hoping to attract readers who would be interested in a Gothic tale. The novel is definitely written in the style of Ann Radcliffe—one of its central figures, a ghostlike monk who calls himself Schemoli, is clearly patterned after Radcliffe's Schedoni in *The Italian*—but Maturin uses what he borrows to develop his own characteristic theme with originality. Although he follows Radcliffe's technique of revealing the supernatural events as merely the result of disguise and charade, his descriptions of aberrant states of mind, to which all are subject, go beyond her handling of evil, and beyond the mere cataloging of grotesque horrors used by those writers who chose to imitate the more sensational style of Matthew Gregory Lewis. Annibal concludes after a brief period of solitary confinement that an "inward acquaintance" delights one not with tranquillity but, on the contrary, with "the grave of the mind." In describing the anguish of his guilt, Montorio cries, "the worm within me never dieth; and every thought and object it converts into its own morbid food." In Maturin, the evil within man is quite real.

The plot of this novel is complicated, and Maturin's narrative is at times twisted and confusing. The tale relates the vengeful machinations of Schemoli, the once noble Count Montorio. He is seeking revenge for the wrongs his younger brother committed against him by manipulating Ippolito and Annibal, two young men he believes are his brother's sons, into believing that they are fated to murder their father. In part, the novel's convoluted structure works to Maturin's advantage, for it helps create a nightmare quality which suits this theme of revenge and guilt. By the end of the novel, after several brutal crimes, it is clear that the words of Ippolito to the Inquisition accurately represent human nature as portrayed in the novel: "There is no human being fully known to another . . . [t]o his own consciousness and recollection, a man will not dare to reveal every thought that visits his mind; there are some which he almost hopes are concealed from the Deity."

Maturin's second novel, *The Wild Irish Boy*, although often following the style of the sentimental, regional novel, still has some of the same motifs and themes as those of the Gothic *Fatal Revenge*. The novel does have many flaws and is probably Maturin's poorest work: there are long pointless digressions, a decidedly awkward handling of point of view, and an ineffective mixture of literary techniques. Nevertheless, when Maturin touches upon those subjects which most fascinated him, he does so with some success. The novel's most interesting character is Lady Montrevor, a strong, compelling woman who through her own foolish vanity allows herself to be trapped into a loveless marriage, thus sacrificing the sincere love of a good man. She must bear the anguish of her loss and the knowledge of her guilt. She does so grandly, wanting no man's pity. Maturin often alludes to John Milton's fallen angel when describing her: she is "no less than archangel ruined." In many ways, she is a female Byronic hero who knows that evil is more than appearance. This type of female character clearly interested Maturin. Zaira in *Women* and Armida in *The Milesian Chief* are similarly delineated, and all three are quite unlike the sentimental heroines so typical of the other novelists of the day.

In Maturin's third novel, *The Milesian Chief*, his interest in the anguish of the proud heart reveals itself in his portrayal of the hero as well as of the heroine. Connal, the Irish rebel, is the once-great angelic chief fallen among lesser spirits, an appropriate male partner for the melancholy Armida, who is shaded by a "proud dejection, like that of an abdicated monarch." The novel is set in Ireland during an uprising against the British in 1798. As the plot unfolds, it becomes clear that Maturin is more successful in handling narrative structure and point of view than in his previous works, and although the final scene, in which the four major characters (Connal, Armida, Desmond, and Ines) all die more or less at the same time in the same place, seems contrived, it is psychologically appropriate. Throughout the novel, these four personalities have been interwoven. Connal and Desmond function as opposites linked in one identity, and each female character both mirrors and complements her male counterpart. Again, even when trying to write a regional novel, Maturin shows that his main interest lies in depicting the individual lost and searching for a way back to some longed-for paradise.

In his Preface to *Women: Or, Pour et Contre*, Maturin writes that he believes his previous novels failed to win popular approval because they lacked reality. He indicates that in this novel he has fashioned his characters to resemble those of "common life." This intention does not, however, cause any significant change in his major theme. Again, through his three central characters, Maturin depicts human nature as torn and guilt-ridden. Charles vacillates between his love for Eva, a shy innocent girl, and Zaira, the older more accomplished woman. He is never able to commit himself fully to loving one or the other until it is too late. Only when Eva is dying of consumption brought on by Charles' abandoning her for Zaira, does he desert Zaira to return to Eva. Throughout the novel, Eva has struggled with her love for Charles, for in her heart it conflicts with her love for God. On her deathbed, she rejects Charles completely, refusing even to see him, and she dies at peace with God. Zaira undergoes a similar ordeal after Charles abandons her. She turns to God, hoping for consolation; yet she continues to see Charles' image before her eyes. After Eva's death, Charles dies from fever and madness. As the novel closes, Zaira becomes the primary figure of guilt. She lives on, always holding her hand to her heart, accusing herself of having murdered her daughter. She has discovered that Eva was the child taken from her at birth, the child she has been trying to find. This discovery is not made until it is too late to remedy the painful consequences of the mother and daughter loving the same man. Maturin concludes the novel with an image typical of his style: "The serpents that devour us, are generated out of our own vitals."

Although Maturin's Preface to *Melmoth the Wanderer* suggests that what follows will show the reader the enemy of mankind in the form of Satan, the tales within tales which constitute the novel show instead that this enemy lies within each individual. By combining the qualities of Faust, Mephistopheles, and the Wandering Jew, Maturin fashioned a hero-villain suitable for leading the reader through the maze of tales which takes him into the obscure recesses of the human soul. Melmoth is Maturin's most compelling and powerful character; he is an embodiment of the dark side of each human being, the shadow that each man casts. Thus, it is particularly appropriate that in the narrative frame of these tales of man's malignity, John Melmoth, who bears the same name as the mysterious wanderer, inherits the task of dealing with the molding manuscript which will set him on his own journey into the mystery of evil. His withdrawal at midnight into a closed room, sealed off from society, to read the manuscript, disregarding his uncle's warning that perhaps he should destroy it unread, suggests a type of original sin. Indeed, as he pursues knowledge of the wanderer's life, he learns that all men are potential agents of Satan. After all, Melmoth the Wanderer did not spring from the fires of hell, but from his own family.

The hope which Maturin offers to man in his guilty state is to be found in self-sacrificing love; yet to love in this manner one must believe in the potential for goodness in mankind, the possibility of redemption. Melmoth is finally damned not because of his original bargain to sell his soul, but because of his own misanthropy. He believes in nothing but the hostility and evil of man's nature. Immalee, the island maiden who learns of suffering by loving him, was his hope. If he had chosen to trust in her love, seeing in it the essence of the greater self-sacrifing love of Christ, he might have been saved.

Maturin's last work, *The Albigenses*, is a historical novel which focuses on the crusade in 1208 against the Albigenses, a Manichaean sect declared heretical by the Catholic Church. Maturin, however, follows the historical facts only roughly, altering events and chronology to suit plot and character. Again, he portrays two brothers, Paladour and Amirald, and their two loves, Isebelle and Genevieve. Although the theme of the fragmented self is not as predominant as in his previous novels, it is present. Paladour and Amirald were separated at birth, and for most of the novel neither knows the other is his brother; they are characterized in such a way as to suggest differing aspects of one personality. Paladour is associated with iron, Amirald with flowers, yet they are bound together through suffering. In choosing their brides, they also reveal complementary personality traits: Paladour marries the noble Lady Isebelle, and Amirald chooses the simple peasant girl Genevieve. When the novel ends, the reader is left with the impression that all four live together in absolute harmony.

Such an easy resolution does seemed contrived, for *The Albigenses* begins with Paladour's sinister encounter with a seemingly demonic lady of the lake. He believes there is a curse upon him and that he is fated to murder his bride on their wedding night. When the effects of these dark tones are no longer wanted, Maturin quickly resolves all with rational explanations. Paladour is then free to live as a very natural husband. Part of the dissatisfaction the reader feels with this happy ending may be accounted for by the fact that the novel bristles with Gothic motifs which are not smoothly integrated into the historical aspects of the novel.

Despite Maturin's own belief that the day of the Gothic novel had already passed when he began writing, and his repeated attempts to use whatever narrative form might suit the reading public, he was continually drawn to the techniques of the Gothic tale. Whether it be a mysterious monk haunting underground passages or a madwoman raving prophetic truths, all his novels have Gothic elements. The Gothic novel provided him with a literary world suitable for the images of evil and suffering which populated his own mind, a mind repeatedly drawn to the problems of man's guilt and his divided soul. The body of Maturin's work, although uneven, offers ample proof of his ability to shape these dark themes with power and originality.

Diane D'Amico

Other major works

PLAYS: *Bertram: Or, The Castle of St. Aldobrand, a Tragedy*, 1816; *Manuel: A Tragedy*, 1817; *Fredolfo: A Tragedy*, 1819.

POETRY: *Lines on the Battle of Waterloo*, 1815 (as John Shee).

NONFICTION: *Sermons*, 1819; *Five Sermons of the Errors of the Roman Catholic Church*, 1824.

Bibliography

Bayer-Berenbaum, Linda. *The Gothic Imagination: Expansion in Gothic Literature and Art*. Rutherford, N.J.: Fairleigh Dickinson University Press, 1982. A sympathetic study of Gothicism, the essence of which is its confrontation with evil and feelings of doom. Contains chapters on literary Gothicism and Gothic art and its relationship to literature, as well as focused analyses of particular works of literature. As one of the central writers of Gothicism, Maturin is given considerable attention, including an extensive analysis of *Melmoth the Wanderer* which examines the novel as a pattern of expulsions and expansions. The conclusion sees a correlation between the Gothic urge for expansion and its style of intensification. Includes a bibliography and index.

Idman, Niilo. *Charles Robert Maturin: His Life and Works*. London: Constable, 1923. Although dated, this remains a valuable study. After offering a simplified view of Romanticism, briefly narrates Maturin's family background and early years. Sketches the Gothic tradition and reviews *Fatal Revenge*, *The Wild Irish Boy*, and *The Milesian Chief* with detailed paraphrases and summaries, comparing them to works by Ann Radcliffe and Sir Walter Scott. Also concentrates on his initial fame with *Bertram*, which he tried to sustain with *Women*, *Fredolfo*, and *Melmoth the Wanderer*, as well as Maturin's blank verse poem *The Universe* and his last novel, *The Albigenses*, published in 1824, the year of his death. Notes and an index are provided.

Kiely, Robert. *The Romantic Novel in England.* Cambridge, Mass.: Harvard University Press, 1972. An important book on Romantic prose fiction, including Maturin's Gothic romances, which analyzes in depth twelve Romantic novels to define the intellectual context of the era. Notes that concepts of reality were tested and changed by Romantic novels and Edmund Burke's ideas of the sublime modified aesthetic forms. Maturin has an important place in this general thesis, and *Melmoth the Wanderer* is analyzed in detail as the focus of his chapter. Finds this novel more emotionally involved with Roman Catholicism and rebellious against authoritarian political systems than other Gothic fiction, believing it to be a journey into the darkness of the mind. Finds a common drift toward death in most novels of this genre. Includes a set of notes and an index.

Kramer, Dale. *Charles Robert Maturin.* New York: Twayne, 1973. Analyzes Maturin's personality, describes the conditions of his life, and indicates his innovations in the Gothic tradition. Examines his early novels from *Fatal Revenge* to *The Wild Irish Boy*, then looks at Maturin's experiments on the stage, where he achieved popular success with *Bertram* but hardly any with *Manuel* and *Fredolfo*. Analyzes *Women*, Maturin's novel of "real life," and devotes a chapter to *Melmoth the Wanderer* as his most successful writing, favorably comparing it to Mary Shelley's *Frankenstein* and William Godwin's *Adventures of Caleb Williams.* Also examines *The Albigenses* as a descendant of Sir Walter Scott's historical romances and sketches Maturin's place in the history of literature. A chronology, notes and references, a selected annotated bibliography, and an index are included.

Lougy, Robert E. *Charles Robert Maturin.* Lewisburg, Pa.: Bucknell University Press, 1975. An insightful review of Maturin's life and writings, dividing his career into early, middle, and later years. *Fatal Revenge* is analyzed for his characteristic themes: fear and guilt. His other writings are placed in the context of his biography but also receive critical attention in comparison with one another, as well as with other works in the Gothic and Irish traditions. Focuses on *Bertram*, which benefited from the popularity of Lord Byron's *Childe Harold's Pilgrimage*, and concentrates on *Melmoth the Wanderer* as a unique adaptation, of the legends of the Wandering Jew and Faust. Although *The Milesian Chief* and *Women* deserve credit and Maturin's other writings are given some attention, his reputation rests on *Melmoth.* Includes a chronology and a selected bibliography of primary and secondary works.

W. SOMERSET MAUGHAM

Born: Paris, France; January 25, 1874
Died: Saint-Jean-Cap-Ferrat, France; December 16, 1965

Principal long fiction

Liza of Lambeth, 1897; *The Making of a Saint*, 1898; *The Hero*, 1901; *Mrs. Craddock*, 1902; *The Merry-Go-Round*, 1904; *The Bishop's Apron*, 1906; *The Explorer*, 1907; *The Magician*, 1908; *Of Human Bondage*, 1915; *The Moon and Sixpence*, 1919; *The Painted Veil*, 1925; *Cakes and Ale*, 1930; *The Narrow Corner*, 1932; *Theatre*, 1937; *Christmas Holiday*, 1939; *Up at the Villa*, 1941; *The Hour Before Dawn*, 1942; *The Razor's Edge*, 1944; *Then and Now*, 1946; *Catalina*, 1948; *Selected Novels*, 1953.

Other literary forms

A professional man of letters whose work spanned more than six decades, W. Somerset Maugham published in a wide range of literary forms, the significant exception being poetry. He first won success, fame, and wealth in the theater; his most acclaimed dramas were performed on the London stage during the first three decades of the twentieth century. He produced more than a hundred short stories, largely written during the period from 1921 to 1950; his collected short stories include four of the best-known stories of this century: "Rain," "The Outstation," "The Letter," and "The Colonel's Lady." Fifteen or more additional volumes are devoted to autobiography, literary and aesthetic criticism, and travel. Among these, the most useful for students are *The Summing Up* (1938), *Great Novelists and Their Novels* (1948), and *A Writer's Notebook* (1949).

Achievements

Maugham's twenty novels are exceptionally uneven; the first eight, though interesting, suggest the efforts of a young novelist to discover where his talent lies. From the publication of *Of Human Bondage* (1915) through *The Razor's Edge* (1944), he produced his most significant prose works. During this period, he was a world-famous man of letters with a following of many thousands who would buy and read anything he wrote; however, a few novels that he produced, such as *Then and Now* and *Up at the Villa*, were not in his best vein.

The novels brought Maugham acclaim and recognition both from a general audience and from the intelligentsia. Among common readers, he was perhaps the most successful English novelist of this century, and, as Samuel Johnson pointed out, the common reader is not often wrong. Yet, it must be admitted that Maugham's detractors, such as Edmund Wilson, present valid criticism: one expects a serious artist to exert an important influence, either thematic or formal, upon his medium. The symphony was forever altered by Ludwig van Beethoven; no similar statement can be made about Maugham and the novel. He sought to tell a story with clarity and grace, to embody a set of attitudes and values, and to entertain his readers with insights into character and life.

Biography

William Somerset Maugham, son of an English solicitor, was born in the British Embassy in Paris and spent his early childhood in France, learning French as his first language. Following the early death of both parents, Maugham went at age ten to England to live with his uncle, the Reverend Henry Maugham, Vicar of Whitstable, and his German-born wife. The rigid routine and disciplined family life of the Whitstable rectory contrasted with the casual, carefree existence and close warmth that Maugham had known in France. He was enrolled in the King's School, Canterbury, where he spent several unhappy years. A permanent stammer which developed during this period of his life destroyed any possibility of following the profession of his father and two of his brothers. Instead of enrolling in a university, Maugham chose to travel abroad to Germany, where at Heidelberg he saw Henrik Ibsen's dramas and attended lectures by Kuno Fischer on the philosophy of Arthur Schopenhauer. Returning to London, he enrolled in the medical school at St. Thomas' Hospital, where he received his M.D. in 1897.

Maugham's stronger interests, however, were literary and aesthetic, and when his first novel, *Liza of Lambeth*, achieved a modest success, he resolved to enter upon a career as a writer. None of the novels that Maugham wrote during the following decade repeated the success of *Liza of Lambeth*, yet he achieved sudden and unexpected acclaim through a series of plays, modern comedies of manners, beginning with *Lady Frederick* (1911). In 1908, four of his plays were running in London simultaneously. During World War I, Maugham served with British Intelligence in Switzerland and Russia. In 1915, he married Syrie Bernardo Wellcome, a marriage which ended in divorce in 1927. Following World War I, Maugham traveled to more remote areas of the world: the South Seas, Southeast Asia, and America, accompanied by his secretary, a gregarious American named Gerald Haxton, who aided the author in finding material for his fiction. Maugham acquired the Villa Maur-esque on the French Riviera in 1928, an estate which became his home for the remainder of his life, though he continued his frequent travels and spent several years during World War II living in the United States. Creative work during his later years centered principally upon short stories, novels, and autobiography.

Analysis

W. Somerset Maugham's novels are written in a style highly idiomatic and fluent, revealing the qualities of simplicity, lucidity, and euphony which the author sought to attain. Content to narrate an interesting story from his own unique angle of vision, he brought to the genre a gift for creating interesting characters who reflect life's ironies. In his later works, Maugham's narrative persona is a character interested in people, yet detached and somewhat clinical in his analysis of their actions and motives. The narrator demonstrates an unusual degree of tolerance for human peccadillos and incongruities and is reluctant to judge the actions of human beings. He writes primarily of adults in conflict with one another and with social mores. Frequently, his characters grow in tolerance and acceptance of human life, which is portrayed somewhat pessimistically. Maugham based his characters upon people whom he had known or whose lives he had somehow come to know; their actions are presented with consummate realism. They are motivated by their passions or emotions and by their attempts to control their destinies, not by an ideology or set of ideals. Though they may experience inner turmoil and conflict, they are seldom tormented by such emotions. Like their creator-narrator, the characters often have the ability to view themselves with clinical detachment and objectivity, to cast a cold eye on life.

Among the early novels of Maugham, *Liza of Lambeth*, published when the author was only twenty-three, is probably the best known. Set in the Lambeth slum along Vere Street, London, it depicts naturalistically the lives of people in a state of poverty, characters like those whom the author had come to know at firsthand as an obstetric clerk at St. Thomas' Hospital. In its depiction of character, *Liza of Lambeth* fits the tradition of the naturalistic novel, somewhat in the manner of George Gissing, whose work Maugham knew well. The Cockney dialogue which pervades the novel is accurately represented, both in its pronunciation and in its slang or colloquial expressions. As is typical of naturalistic fiction, the characters are generally without hope, yet even in a naturalistic tradition Maugham reveals an original perspective. Unlike much naturalism, *Liza of Lambeth* does not urge social reform; the characters exhibit more hostility toward one another than toward any system. They generally accept their lot, which would be bearable but for their own mistakes. Liza Kemp's friend Sally enters marriage with hope, only to find her chances for happiness shattered owing to her husband's bad temper following drinking bouts, a weakness he had previously concealed. Liza, brimming with life and energy, spurns the devotion of a staid suitor, Tom, and finds excitement in an affair with an older, married neighbor, Jim Blakeston. By allowing passion to dominate their lives, the characters create undue hardships for themselves. This theme is commonly found in Maugham's work.

Just as *Liza of Lambeth* represented an effort at producing a naturalistic novel, Maugham's other early novels give the impression of deliberate attempts at imitating well-established forms. In *The Making of a Saint*, he wrote a brief historical novel with a late fifteenth century Florentine setting. A story of intrigue, assassination, and revenge, it is derived from a brief passage in a work by Niccolò Machiavelli. *Mrs. Craddock* is set in rural England of the late nineteenth century, a novel of manners depicting provincial life, much in the manner of Arnold Bennett; *The Merry-Go-Round* belongs to a similar tradition. In *The Magician*, Maugham incorporates the conventions of the Gothic genre, though there is perhaps too much realism for this work to be designated a true Gothic novel.

In *Of Human Bondage*, Maugham's longest novel and his masterpiece, he turned to the well-known form of the *Bildungsroman*, the novel of a young person growing to maturity. *Of Human Bondage* is highly autobiographical, although it departs significantly from autobiographical accuracy in places. With the aid of an omniscient narrator, the reader follows the life of Philip Carey from his mother's death when he was only nine until he becomes a doctor and resolves to marry. Numerous characters in the novel are based upon people the author knew. The Reverend William Carey and his wife Louisa are based upon Maugham's uncle and aunt with whom he lived; Lawson is his friend Sir Gerald Kelly; Cronshaw derives from the eccentric poet Aleister Crowley, who had also been the model for Oliver Haddo in *The Magician*; Hayward is based upon Maugham's friend Ellington Brooks. In a similar manner, Maugham incorporates descriptions of places that he knew well, with names only slightly altered (Whitstable to Blackstable, Canterbury to Tercanbury) or not altered at all, as the countryside of Kent or the cities of London or Paris.

In *Of Human Bondage*, Maugham sees three forces impinging upon Philip, shaping and influencing his life, forces that the novel emphasizes strongly: passion, disillusionment, and the quest for purpose in life. Philip is ill-equipped to cope with passion. Having been born with a club foot, which becomes a source of ridicule among school boys, and having lost both parents in childhood, he becomes overly sensitive. He takes pleasure in the solitary pursuit of reading and is less in the company of others than most boys; as a result, he has little understanding of the world at large. He finds that women who adore him arouse in him no passion in return, whereas he falls irrationally and inexplicably in love with the common and venal Mildred Rogers. Only after a long period of bondage, humiliation, and pain can he free himself from this attachment, which he comes to regard as degrading. At the end of the novel, he proposes marriage to Sally Athelney, not because he feels passion for her but because he believes she will be a good wife. Maugham's view of romance in this work is consistent with the view presented in his other works and with Arthur Schopenhauer's pessimistic outlook—that romantic passion is a kind of trick played upon man by nature to foster procreation, that it does not last, that it is irrational, and that it represents a poor basis for marriage.

To express the necessity for disillusionment, Maugham depicts Philip as growing up in an atmosphere of illusion involving religious beliefs and assumptions about the code of an English gentleman. When Philip arrives in Germany, it becomes awkward to continue to maintain that a gentleman necessarily belongs to the Church of England. He encounters a diversity of religious beliefs, all sincerely held and advocated through conflicting arguments. The result is that he loses his religious faith, though he assumes that the actual cause of the loss is that he lacks the religious temperament. Losing a framework so basic, he experiences a sense of liberation, yet he finds his new freedom uncomfortable as well, lacking in certainties.

Philip clings to one certainty: he assumes without question that he must earn his living through some profession, and he begins to explore various unsuitable paths. He rejects the idea of becoming a clergyman, quits a career in accounting, abandons the struggle to become an artist after studying in Paris, and finally decides to pursue medicine. He does not escape hardship, for at one point he loses the money provided for his education and must work at a department store until his uncle's death brings a small inheritance.

Reflecting upon happiness, Philip is puzzled as to how this quality fits as a purpose in life, since his own is unhappy. He observes that happiness eludes people such as the dancers at the Bal Bullier in Paris who pursue it frenetically. Those who seek happiness through the enjoyment of art waste their lives, and those who struggle to create art seldom find happiness, even when they succeed. Yet, the paintings of El Greco suggest to Philip that the will of man is powerful, that life can be made meaningful through struggle. After this realization, Philip comes to understand the secret of a piece of Persian rug given him by an eccentric poet. The poet told him that the rug held the key to the meaning of life, but he refused to explain the puzzle to Philip. The solution becomes apparent to Philip years later, after much searching for it: Life has no meaning. There is no set of obligations by which a person must live, no certain path to follow. With this bleak conclusion, Philip comes to another realization: Like the weaver of the carpet, a man may choose the strands that please his aesthetic sense and make a pattern of his life satisfying to his own taste. Happiness and pain are important only as strands in the design. Though man is under no obligation to create a design, he is free to do so if he chooses; or, if he rejects freedom of the will, it may seem that he is free. Life for Philip, then, has purpose because he wills to endow it with purpose—a conclusion primarily existential but also in accord with Schopenhauer's view of man's will.

In *The Moon and Sixpence*, a novel which relies somewhat upon autobiographical materials used in *Of Human Bondage*, Maugham narrates a portion of the life of his hero Charles Strickland, a stockbroker turned artist whose character is based upon that of the artist Paul Gauguin. The narrator, or the Maugham persona, is a successful author who enjoys access to high society and like Maugham travels extensively around the world. He is detached and analytical in his attitudes, revealing a fondness for the maxims of Blaise Pascal and La Rochefoucauld. He prefers to permit the story to unfold in an episodic way by letting others whom he meets tell him what they know or think about Strickland. Maugham sees in Strickland the frustrated genius, a moderately successful businessman who, at age forty, decides to become an artist, ruthlessly throwing over everything to pursue his ambition, and succeeding.

The action occurs over a period of more than twenty years, with the setting shifting from London to Paris to Tahiti and back to London. As in the earlier *Of Human Bondage* and later in *Christmas Holiday*, art is an important theme, and allusions to paintings and painters are numerous. At the beginning of the novel, Maugham invents a "scholarly" tradition on Strickland, complete with footnotes, to enhance the realism. In the concluding segment set in Tahiti, he introduces characters who had known Strickland during his final years and who report on his decline and death. They are modeled after characters whom Maugham met in Tahiti, and who told him about Gauguin. With references to actual people whose identities the author does not very much bother to conceal, *The Moon and Sixpence*, then, is a *roman à clef*, as are its two most important successors, *Cakes and Ale* and *The Razor's Edge*.

In *Cakes and Ale*, the most "literary" of Maugham's novels, the narrator assumes the name Willie Ashenden, one that Maugham had used in his collection of short stories based upon his work as an intelligence agent (*Ashenden*, 1928). Ashenden is a novelist in his fifties who during the course of the narrative has several meetings with another novelist and critic, Alroy Kear. Kear, about the same age as Willie Ashenden, represents the Edwardian novelist Hugh Walpole. The unflattering portrait of Walpole, recognizable to many contemporaries and to Walpole himself, contributed to an attack on Maugham by Evelyn Wiehe in *Gin and Bitters* (1931), where he is given the name Leverson Hurle. Besides the narrator and Kear, another author plays a major role in the novel. Edward Driffield, the grand old man of Victorian literature, is based upon the character of Thomas Hardy. Rosie Gann, Driffield's first wife, is modeled after the actress Ethelwyn Sylvia Jones, to whom Maugham once proposed.

Alroy Kear, who is writing a biography of Driffield, discovers that Ashenden has been a longtime acquaintance of the Driffields. The Driffields once lived in Ashenden's village of Blackstable, where they were regarded with suspicion by the villagers, especially by Ashenden's uncle, the vicar, who represents the epitome of Victorian propriety and prudery. The villagers' suspicions are confirmed when the Driffields move to London, leaving behind debts to most of the merchants.

Later, Ashenden renews his acquaintance with the Driffields in London, gradually losing touch with them after Rosie leaves Driffield for a Blackstable coal merchant, Lord George Kemp. Ashenden's knowledge of all these details merges in flashbacks that go back as far as his childhood. Ashenden knows that a tactful biographer such as Kear, who has secured the approval of Driffield's second wife, cannot include such revealing recollections, and thus he tells them to the reader. He concludes his narrative with an account of meeting Rosie, then over seventy, in New York. She confesses to Ashenden that she ran off with Lord George because "He was always such a perfect gentleman," a judgment with which every other character in the novel would have disagreed.

Except for one brief episode that occurs in New York, the novel is set either in London or in the nearby villages and countryside. Maugham relies heavily on flashbacks ranging over a period of some forty years; *Cakes and Ale* is a novel cast in the form of reminiscences of a character, which assuredly would conflict with the "official" biography of Driffield as recorded by Alroy Kear. Its appeal lies primarily in its allusions to actual persons, its behind-the-scenes literary gossip, and the creation of Rosie Gann, probably the most appealing of Maugham's female characters—a wholesome, agreeable, and vivacious woman utterly lacking in pretense.

In *The Razor's Edge*, the narrator becomes "Mr. Maugham," a celebrated author and world traveler. With characters such as the urbane and aristocratic art agent, Elliott Templeton, he exchanges views and pleasantries in an attitude of amusement and tolerance. To younger characters such as Sophie Macdonald he offers sage advice. To readers he offers a variety of wry comments on the art and craft of the novel. He speculates as to why people whom he barely knows divulge their life-stories so readily to him. He admits the reader behind the scenes of the writer's study with such unguarded comments as the famous opening, "I have never begun a novel with more misgiving," and such wry asides as "I feel it right to warn the reader that he can very well skip this chapter without losing the thread of [the] . . . story. . . . I should add, however, that except for this conversation I should perhaps not have thought it worthwhile to write this book." Usually "Mr. Maugham" limits his involvement to conversation; his own actions, where they are noted (as when he withdraws to write a novel or takes his boat to Toulon), do not advance the plot. Occasionally, he does involve himself in the plot in some minor way. He contrives for the dying Elliott Templeton to receive an invitation to a party given by the Princess Novemali after she had deliberately snubbed Elliott; and he is on hand to identify the body of Sophie Macdonald.

"Mr. Maugham" reports the story as the major characters reveal it in their conversations. Isabel Bradley is in love with Larry Darrel but sensibly marries the successful Gray Maturin, only to find that after Gray loses his assets during the Depression, she and her husband and their two daughters must live on the generosity of her uncle Elliott. Larry, whose main interest in life is the study of philosophy and religion, attempts to marry Sophie Macdonald to save her from a dissolute life, an effort which Isabel shrewdly thwarts. Larry goes to a Benedictine monastery in France, later leaving it to study the

Hindu religion in India. Returning from India at the end of the novel, he gives up his independent income and resolves to find work in New York driving a taxi. The Maturins move from Paris to Dallas, where Gray has secured an executive position in an oil company. The plot ranges over more than a decade, with the settings in France, England, and America. Yet "Mr. Maugham," like the young Philip Carey, seeks a pattern in the lives of those he has met, and he finds that each life in *The Razor's Edge* has been a success. Even Sophie Macdonald, whose trauma caused her to seek death, found what she was seeking.

Maugham's three most significant novels following *Of Human Bondage* explore ideals which he considered in the final chapters of his autobiography, *The Summing Up* (1938)—truth, beauty, goodness. In *The Moon and Six-pence*, Charles Strickland represents the true genius whose work survives and speaks to posterity, even though his talent surfaced late in life and he violated accepted standards to advance it. In him, truth is neither obvious nor pleasant, but its existence can be confirmed by those who have felt the power of his work. Even the wife he abandoned displays reproductions of his paintings in her home and takes pride in his attainments. In *Cakes and Ale*, the ideal is beauty, which readers and critics find in the style, characters, and descriptions of Edward Driffield's novels. The narrator Willie Ashenden rejects this aesthetic beauty in favor of a more realistic beauty. He discovers the ideal in the warmth and charm of Rosie Gann, Driffield's first wife, who possessed neither fidelity nor business ethics but whose character brought others a wholesome sense of well-being. In *The Razor's Edge*, Larry Darrel reveals a basic goodness, a difficult quality to depict, partly because it may be attributed to the absence of either appetites or temptations. Though not an ascetic, Larry keeps passion and ambition in check and pursues his own spiritual development. He readily sacrifices himself for others, making a futile effort to save Sophie Macdonald from self-destruction through an offer of marriage, yet his sacrifices do not appear quixotic. A generous amount of modesty enables him to make the best of a life that reveals only goodness as an extraordinary element.

In each character, the ideal is neither obvious nor probable in the conventional sense. Its existence is ironic, and it might be overlooked were not the Maugham persona on hand to define it. Not even the narrator, however, can explain or account for it; the reader savors its presence without fully understanding its origin.

Among the remaining novels of Maugham, one finds works of literary merit and appeal, though they represent lesser achievements. A reader of Maugham would not want to miss novels such as *The Painted Veil* and *The Narrow Corner*, which narrate suspenseful and intense conflicts. Works such as these differ from the better-known novels in several important respects. First, the Maugham persona is either absent or less intrusive. In *The Narrow Corner*, for example, the author's viewpoint is usually expressed through Dr. Saunders, who lives on a Pacific island and has no literary interests or ambitions. Further, the settings are usually foreign or exotic—European or Oriental rather than American or English. Instead of spanning decades, the plots narrate events that occur during a few months; novels such as *Up at the Villa*, for example, differ little from some of Maugham's short stories.

Significantly, in Maugham's major novels, the important characters—Philip Carey, Larry Darrel, Rosie Gann, and Charles Strickland—either embody an ideal or achieve some measure of success in pursuit of an ideal, whereas idealism in the minor works is usually crushed and defeated. Fred Blake and Erik Christensen in *The Narrow Corner* find only disappointment, disillusionment, and early death, as does the unfortunate Karl Richter in *Up at the Villa*. Those who survive are worldly-wise and detached characters who can regard life as Maugham's spokesman Dr. Saunders does:

> Life is short, nature is hostile, and man is ridiculous but oddly enough most misfortunes have their compensations and with a certain humour and a good deal of horse-sense one can make a fairly good job of what is after all a matter of very small consequence.

The minor works reward the reader with their depiction of the ironies of human life, the eccentricities of human beings, the unusual settings and universal conflicts, yet, however rewarding, they lack the thematic richness and emotional concentration of Maugham's best novels.

Stanley Archer

Other major works
SHORT FICTION: *Orientations*, 1899; *The Trembling of a Leaf*, 1921; *The Casuarina Tree*, 1926; *Ashenden: Or, The British Agent*, 1928; *Six Stories Written in the First Person Singular*, 1931; *Ah King*, 1933; *East and West*, 1934; *Cosmopolitans*, 1936; *The Mixture as Before*, 1940; *Creatures of Circumstance*, 1947; *Here and There: Selected Short Stories*, 1948; *The Complete Short Stories of W. Somerset Maugham*, 1951; *The World Over*, 1952; *Seventeen Lost Stories*, 1969.

PLAYS: *A Man of Honour*, 1903; *Lady Frederick*, 1907; *The Explorer*, 1908; *Jack Straw*, 1908; *Mrs. Dot*, 1908; *The Noble Spaniard*, 1909; *Penelope,* 1909; *Smith*, 1909; *Loaves and Fishes*, 1911; *The Land of Promise*, 1913; *Landed Gentry*, 1913; *The Tenth Man*, 1913; *Caroline*, 1916 (as *The Unattainable*, 1923); *Our Betters*, 1917; *Caesar's Wife*, 1919; *Home and Beauty*, 1919 (also as *Too Many Husbands*); *The Unknown*, 1920; *The Circle*, 1921; *East of Suez*, 1922; *The Constant Wife*, 1926; *The Letter*, 1927; *The Sacred Flame*, 1928; *The Breadwinner*, 1930; *For Services Rendered*, 1932; *Sheppey*, 1933; *Collected Plays*, 1952 (3 volumes, including 18 plays).

NONFICTION: *The Land of the Blessed Virgin*, 1905 (also known as *Andalusia*,

1920); *On a Chinese Screen*, 1922; *The Gentleman in the Parlour*, 1930; *Don Fernando*, 1935; *The Summing Up*, 1938; *Books and You*, 1940; *France at War*, 1940; *Strictly Personal*, 1941; *Great Novelists and Their Novels*, 1948; *A Writer's Notebook*, 1949; *The Writer's Point of View*, 1951; *The Vagrant Mood*, 1952; *Ten Novels and Their Authors*, 1954; *The Travel Books*, 1955; *Points of View*, 1958; *Purely for My Pleasure*, 1962; *Selected Prefaces and Introductions*, 1963.

Bibliography

Cordell, Richard A. *Somerset Maugham, a Writer for All Seasons: A Biographical and Critical Study*. 2d ed. Bloomington: Indiana University Press, 1969. A valuable discussion of Maugham's philosophy, which Cordell finds in the "writings of wise men of all ages." Considers both sides— sympathetic and unsympathetic—to Maugham while focusing on his novels, short stories, plays, and nonfiction (briefly). The best of his work is *Of Human Bondage*, *The Moon and Sixpence*, and *Cakes and Ale*. Indexed.

McIver, Claude S. *William Somerset Maugham: A Study of Technique and Literary Sources*. Philadelphia: University of Pennsylvania Press, 1936. Well-documented study which looks for similarities and differences in method, material, and philosophy between Guy de Maupassant and Maugham. Maugham is a realist who draws from personal experience, a writer of common people whose lives are dramatic. McIver's analyses focus on satire and irony, sardonic humor, vividness and verisimilitude, economy of expression, and precision of form. Indexed.

Maugham, Robin. *Somerset and All the Maughams*. New York: New American Library, 1966. Maugham's complex personality is illuminated in this intriguing study of his ancestors and immediate family members. An index is included.

Morgan, Ted. *Maugham*. New York: Simon & Schuster, 1980. The first full-scale biography of Maugham and therefore an essential text in all studies of the man and his work. Unlike previous biographers, Morgan enjoyed the cooperation of Maugham's literary executor and, therefore, is able to correct many distortions in previous studies. Offers the most comprehensive account yet of the private man, including photographs, a complete primary bibliography, and an index.

Naik, M. K. *William Somerset Maugham*. Norman: University of Oklahoma Press, 1966. Argues that a conflic* between "cynicism" and "humanitarianism" kept Maugham from literary success. Only in *Cakes and Ale*, his short stories, and his travel books does he balance the two points of view.

Ward, Richard Heron. *William Somerset Maugham*. London: G. Bles, 1937. This balanced treatment finds in Maugham compassion, tolerance, and an absence of self-pity. Places the author between a totally "objective" writer and a "subjective" artist.

WILLIAM MAXWELL

Born: Lincoln, Illinois; August 16, 1908

Principal long fiction

Bright Center of Heaven, 1934; *They Came like Swallows*, 1937; *The Folded Leaf*, 1945; *Time Will Darken It*, 1948; *The Château*, 1961; *So Long, See You Tomorrow*, 1980.

Other literary forms

Ancestors (1971) is a history of William Maxwell's family, tracing his ancestry on both his mother's and father's sides to American pioneers and presenting much of the autobiographical material that is reflected in his fiction. *The Heavenly Tenants* (1946) is a fantasy for children. Maxwell is also well known for his short stories and reviews written during his long career (1936-1976) on the editorial staff of *The New Yorker*. Some of his stories have been collected in *The Old Man at the Railroad Crossing and Other Tales* (1966) and *Over by the River and Other Stories* (1977).

Achievements

William Maxwell is probably best known as a writer and fiction editor for *The New Yorker*, where he edited the works of John Cheever, Irwin Shaw, John O'Hara, and others. Although not well known among general readers, Maxwell has received much critical acclaim for his own fiction, earning many awards, including the Friends of American Writers Award in 1938 and the William Dean Howells Award for Fiction for *So Long, See You Tomorrow* in 1980. He received a grant from the National Institute of Arts and Letters in 1958 and served as that organization's president from 1969 to 1972. Maxwell has consistently been praised for the realism of his dialogue, his deep and sensitive insights into characters, especially children, and his depiction of the Midwest.

Biography

Born in the small Midwestern town of Lincoln, Illinois, in 1908, William Keepers Maxwell, Jr., was the second of three sons of William Keepers Maxwell, a traveling fire-insurance salesman, and Eva Blossom (Blinn) Maxwell. Maxwell examines his early family life in his only nonfiction work, *Ancestors*, and he remembers his parents' marriage and his childhood as being extremely happy. Maxwell was especially close to his mother, who died of Spanish influenza in 1918, only three days after giving birth to Maxwell's younger brother. This event, frequently recalled in Maxwell's novels, is a focal point in *They Came like Swallows* and *So Long, See You Tomorrow.* He recalls that his family never really discussed their grief with one another and therefore never fully recovered from the loss. His father's decision to remarry and move the family to Chicago four years later created more problems, for, although Maxwell's stepmother was pretty and kind, he resented her taking the place of his mother. The move to Chicago brought Maxwell, a small, bookish child who had no interest in sports, to the Nicholas Senn High School, where for the first time he was encouraged to study literature and music.

Maxwell received a B.A. from the University of Illinois in 1930 and an M.A. from Harvard University in 1931. He taught in the English department at the University of Illinois from 1931 to 1933. Shortly after the publication of his first novel, *Bright Center of Heaven*, Maxwell joined the editorial staff of *The New Yorker*, where he was fiction editor for forty years. Maxwell was married to Emily Gilman Noyes on May 17, 1945, and has two daughters.

Analysis

William Maxwell's fiction has a strong autobiographical basis. Especially noted for accurate and vivid depiction of small Midwestern towns in the first half of the twentieth century, Maxwell frequently draws from his early childhood in Lincoln, Illinois. Consequently, his novels deal with recurring themes and events that reflect his own experiences. The most common of these is the absence of one parent, stemming either from the death of Maxwell's mother or from estrangement from a father who never understood him, a condition that contributed to the loneliness of a child who had a reserved and intellectual temperament. Maxwell's sharp and insightful character delineations have consistently been praised by critics.

Maxwell's first novel, *Bright Center of Heaven*, is set on a farm called Meadowland near Thisbe, Wisconsin. The farm is run by Mrs. Susan West, a generous but absentminded and disorganized widow who, finding her husband's estate insufficient, takes in a number of boarders. Paul McKenzie is a former schoolteacher who is searching for meaningful work. His lover is actress Nigel Foley, who fears that she may be pregnant. Also staying at the house are a brokenhearted pianist, Josefa Marchand, and a depressed painter, Cynthia Damon. Mrs. West's two teenage sons, Thorn and Whitey, are of opposite temperaments. Thorn loves the farm and is very much like his father; he is also in love for the first time, with Nigel. Whitey spends most of his time running errands for his mother. Also living at Meadowland is Mrs. West's sister, Miss Ameilia Bascom, who has eaten nothing but cottage cheese and weak tea for three years and is easily upset and offended. Completing the family is nephew Bascom, who disturbs the tenants and talks incessantly. Most of the other characters suspect that Bascom is mentally unsound. The house is maintained by two servants: Johanna, the German cook, whose mother is dying overseas, and Gust, the old caretaker, who has worked for Mrs. West's family for many years and whose loyalty prevents him from retiring as soon as he would like. It is an eccentric household, and Maxwell moves among the points of view of all the characters, and then finally views the action through the eyes of Jefferson Carter, a Negro lecturer whom Mrs. West has invited to stay at the house—an act that almost guarantees a scandal. The novel runs through the course of one day, from breakfast to bedtime, and the simple, realistic dialogue, the ordinary daily tasks, and the exceptional circumstance of Carter's visit combine to permit great insight into the characters. Although the novel deals with subjects normally treated only in serious novels—subjects such as unwanted pregnancy, suicide, and racism—the novel is essentially a comic one and displays Maxwell's great potential as a novelist.

In *They Came like Swallows*, Maxwell again presents his story through various points of view. Beginning in November, 1918, and covering a period of about two months, Maxwell's second novel examines the effect that the death of Elizabeth Morison has on her husband and her two young sons. The novel is divided into three sections, each devoted to the point of view of one of these three characters. Eight-year-old Peter Morison, known as "Bunny" and clearly Maxwell's fictional alter ego, is exceptionally close to his mother and suffers his father's cold detachment, both common elements in Maxwell's novels. Bunny also experiences some sibling rivalry with his thirteen-year-old brother, Robert, who, despite having lost a leg in an accident, continues to participate actively in sports. In the beginning of the novel Bunny's mother is pregnant and reads the first newspaper reports on the mysterious Spanish influenza. World War I comes to an end and all seems well, but Bunny contracts the disease. When two sparrows accidentally become trapped in Bunny's room, his mother impetuously enters, although she has been banished from the room because of her pregnancy.

Because of complications with her first two pregnancies, Elizabeth goes to Decatur with her husband, James, to have the baby. Original plans to stay with their favorite Aunt Irene fall through, so the boys stay with their Aunt Clara; there Robert feels isolated and finally comes down with the flu as well. During their illness, the boys learn that both parents have also contracted the disease, and, shortly after the birth of a frail son, Robert and Bunny's mother dies. Each character has his own grief and feelings of guilt to confront. James fears that his rushing to get on a crowded train may have unnecessarily exposed his wife to the illness; Robert blames himself for allowing his mother into Bunny's room. James is completely helpless and considers sending the children permanently to Aunt Clara's. Yet through their shared grief, their reliance on one another, and the guidance of Elizabeth's sister Irene, who commits herself to helping James care for the three children, the Morison family will be able to survive their loss. The novel has been commended for its insights into children's perceptions and its avoidance of excessive sentimentality.

The child's loss of his mother and his subsequent loneliness, as well as the father's inability to deal with the loss, are also integral to the conflicts in *The Folded Leaf.* Lymie Peters is a small, nonathletic, lonely fifteen-year-old boy who, following his mother's death, has recently moved with his father to Chicago from a small town in Illinois. Lymie's father is neglectful, drinks excessively, and spends time with prostitutes. One day Lymie is rescued at the swimming pool by Spud Latham, who, despite his abilities in sports and making friends, also feels out of place, having just moved to Chicago from a small town in Wisconsin. The boys become goods friends. Craving the attention and warmth he receives from Spud's family, Lymie frequently stays at the Lathams' home, a tacky and cramped apartment. After the boys eventually go to college in Indiana, their relationship is strained when Spud joins a fraternity. Spud also finds a girlfriend, Sally Forbes, and Lymie is both attracted to Sally and resentful of the attention she gets from Spud. Feeling rejected, Lymie attempts suicide. In the hospital, he is visited by his father, whose main concern is why Lymie did not leave a note for him. The novel ends with Spud and Sally entertaining Lymie, but their childish games are stopped by a nurse. Lymie assures everyone that he has learned valuable lessons. Several critics have argued that this ending is unsatisfactory and Lymie's change unconvincing, as the reader is not presented with sufficient evidence of his maturity. Despite this criticism, *The Folded Leaf* is generally considered Maxwell's finest novel, and his portrayal of the Midwest in the 1920's is considered unparalleled.

Also an especially effective novel in terms of its nostalgic and accurate depiction of time and place is *Time Will Darken It*, set in 1912 in fictional Draperville, Illinois. Austin King, a lawyer in Draperville, and his wife, Martha, have one daughter and have just learned that they are to have another child. Austin has invited the Potter family from Mississippi to visit, honoring a family obligation (Austin's father was reared by Mr. Potter's grandfather). The invitation proves to have been a serious mistake, and the visit changes the lives of all concerned. The Potters and their grown children—Nora, intelligent and bored with Southern life, and Randolph, charming but cruel—stay for more than a month. The visit puts a great strain on the marriage of Austin and the beautiful Martha, who has never had a strong love for her husband and at times fantasizes about running away. Mr. Potter engages many of Austin's associates in a business scheme, which, when it later fails, causes some of the men to question Austin's honesty. When the Potters finally return home, Nora, who has fallen in love with Austin, decides to stay on with a nearby family, start a kindergarten, and read law in Austin's office. Flattered by Nora's devotion and stimulated by her intelligence, Austin irresponsibly encourages the girl. Not surprisingly, gossip runs rampant in the small town.

After Nora is horribly disfigured in a fire, she returns to Mississippi to be with her family. She is both physically and emotionally scarred. Martha King gives birth to her second child, but the labor is difficult, and she almost dies. Yet the King marriage, though strained, apparently will survive.

The Château again exposes Midwesterners to another culture but, unlike Maxwell's other novels, is set elsewhere. A young married American couple, Harold and Barbara Rhodes, are visiting Europe on a four-month holiday in 1948. They spend most of this time at the château of Madame Viénot. Though the Rhodeses know some French, they have considerable difficulty overcoming the linguistic and cultural barriers between themselves and the French. France still shows the ravages of World War II, and there are shortages of food and other supplies. The French also have considerable resentment toward American wealth and the country's involvement in the war. The Rhodeses fall in love with France, however, and despite the French people, whom they find moody—sometimes warm and generous, sometimes distant and rude—they form lasting friendships with members of Madame Viénot's household. Among those they meet are Eugène and Alix Boisgaillard, the son-in-law and daughter of Madame Cestre, Madame Viénot's sister. Eugène's moods alternate drastically, and Alix is similarly unpredictable. The Rhodeses also become quite fond of an old woman, Madame Straus, but as she often talks about associations with people who say that they have never heard of her, the Rhodeses wonder about her sanity and her integrity. When they return to the United States, however, Madame Straus continues to write them passionate letters, and they see her again when they return to France in 1953. Their closest alliance is formed, however, with Madame Viénot's daughter, Sabine, a kind and bright young woman who is isolated by her family's loss of wealth and status. The Viénot family has clearly experienced a dramatic and tragic change of fortune, and the Rhodeses view their French friends with a sense of mystery. How did the Viénots lose their money? Where is Monsieur Viénot? Why does Eugène's mood change so frequently and so abruptly? Is Madame Straus really who she says she is? In an unusual epilogue, Maxwell engages in a dialogue with an imaginary reader who asks these questions and demands answers. Maxwell obliges, but only after assuring the reader that the answers are unimportant and that all mysteries cannot be solved.

Maxwell's sixth novel, *So Long, See You Tomorrow*, is clearly based on events from the author's own life; in fact, the first half of the short novel reads more like autobiography than like fiction. Maxwell recalls a scandal in his hometown of Lincoln, Illinois, involving the family of his only boyhood friend, Cletus Smith. Maxwell was a frail child who would rather stay inside reading, close to his mother, than engage in sports. His father, who did not understand him, made him go outside to play; however, he had no friends, and the other boys teased him. He meets Cletus Smith, and they play together on the scaffolding of an unfinished house. Cletus' mother, Fern Smith, has been having an affair with Lloyd Wilson, who owns an adjacent farm and who is a good friend of the family. After she divorces her husband, Clarence, the truth of the affair comes out, and Clarence murders Lloyd and then kills himself. Maxwell does not see Cletus again until years later, after his mother's death, his father's remarriage, and his family's relocation to Chicago. Seeing Cletus in the hall of the high school, Maxwell snubs his friend rather than speaking to him. Nearly sixty years later, Maxwell still feels guilty and wishes to make amends.

In the first half of the novel Maxwell attempts to reconstruct the facts of the case, relying on the memory of witnesses and even obtaining information from court records. He digresses often to discuss his own early difficulties, including the loss of his mother and his general feelings of isolation. In the second half of the novel Maxwell attempts to reconstruct the scene by examining it through the varying points of view of the characters involved. Although *So Long, See You Tomorrow* contains the expected elements of Maxwell's fiction, critics have insisted that this novel represents a culmination rather than a rehashing of old ideas. Maxwell's careful honing has produced a work whose tight construction and poetic language reflect the author's development as one of the twentieth century's distinguished writers.

Lou Thompson

Other major works
SHORT FICTION: *The Old Man at the Railroad Crossing and Other Tales,* 1966; *Over by the River and Other Stories,* 1977.
NONFICTION: *Ancestors,* 1971.
CHILDREN'S LITERATURE: *The Heavenly Tenants,* 1946.

Bibliography
Maxfield, James F. "The Child, the Adolescent, and the Adult: Stages of Consciousness in Three Early Novels of William Maxwell." *Midwest Quarterly* 24 (1983): 315-335. Using primarily a psychoanalytic approach, Maxfield examines *They Came like Swallows, The Folded Leaf,* and *Time Will Darken It* as forming a trilogy that reflects the maturing of Maxwell as he confronts the loss of his mother and his father's remarriage. Chronologically, the three early novels represent the wish fulfillment of the author at three stages of life.

_____. "Memory and Imagination in William Maxwell's *So Long, See You Tomorrow.*" *Critique* 24 (1982): 21-37. Maxfield argues that in *So Long, See You Tomorrow* Maxwell combines factual and imagined elements to reconstruct the past in order to assuage his guilt for snubbing his friend Cletus and also to work out Oedipal conflicts with his father.

Maxwell, William. Interview. *Publishers Weekly* 216 (December 10, 1979): 8-9. In this interview published shortly before the release of *So Long, See You Tomorrow*, Maxwell discusses his career as fiction editor for *The New Yorker* and describes his own writing process. He explains that he is a slow writer and patient reviser, carefully cutting unnecessary detail and working hard to make the work appear effortless. Maxwell also discusses the importance of his Midwestern heritage in his writing.

Shereikis, Richard. "William Maxwell's Lincoln, Illinois." *Midamerica: The Yearbook of the Society for the Study of Midwestern Literature* 14 (1987): 101-112. Contrasting Maxwell to other Midwestern writers such as Sherwood Anderson and Edgar Lee Masters, Shereikis praises Maxwell's shunning extremes and portraying realistically the balance between the intolerance and generosity of the inhabitants of small Midwestern towns as well as Maxwell's ability to depict vividly this small, constricted world and still give it universal significance.

Wilson, Edmund. "Faintness of the *Age of Thunder* and Power of *The Folded Leaf*." *The New Yorker* 21 (March 31, 1945): 81-82. This review of Maxwell's best-known novel praises the authenticity of Maxwell's depiction of small-town life in the Midwest before World War II. Wilson notes, as have many critics, the simple but eloquent style of Maxwell's prose, and he stresses the distinctiveness of this novel when considered alongside the melodramatic works that grew out of the same period. Comparing Maxwell to the social realists of 1890-1920, Wilson observes that Maxwell lacks the bitterness of these other writers.

HERMAN MELVILLE

Born: New York, New York; August 1, 1819
Died: New York, New York; September 28, 1891

Principal long fiction

Typee: A Peep at Polynesian Life, 1846; *Omoo: A Narrative of Adventures in the South Seas,* 1847; *Mardi and a Voyage Thither,* 1849; *Redburn: His First Voyage,* 1849; *White-Jacket: Or, The World in a Man-of-War,* 1850; *Moby Dick: Or, The Whale,* 1851; *Pierre: Or, The Ambiguities,* 1852; *Israel Potter: His Fifty Years of Exile,* 1855; *The Confidence Man: His Masquerade,* 1857; *Billy Budd, Foretopman,* 1924.

Other literary forms

After the financial failure of *Moby Dick* and *Pierre*, Herman Melville, as if turning a new corner in his literary career, began a series of short stories. Published between 1853 and 1856, either in a collection (*The Piazza Tales,* 1856) or individually in journals such as *Putnam's Monthly Magazine* and *Harper's Monthly Magazine*, the tales present an enigmatic additon to Melville's artistry. Melville had difficulty with the short forms, and he seemed unable to work out the plot and characters in the space required. His best stories are novella length; and "Benito Cereno," "The Encantadas," and "Bartleby the Scrivener" are among the best stories in the language. With the publication of *The Apple-Tree Table and Other Sketches* (1922), all of Melville's stories became available in collection.

Melville also wrote poetry, which suffers from the same unevenness that plagues his short fiction. A handful of poems, gathered selectively from *Battle-Pieces and Aspects of the War* (1866), *John Marr and Other Sailors* (1888), and *Timoleon* (1891) are worthy of being anthologized with the best poetry of the nineteenth century. His worst poem, *Clarel: A Poem and Pilgrimage in the Holy Land,* (1876), a long, flawed reflection on Melville's travels in the Holy Land, continues to be of interest only for its revealing autobiographical and philosophical content. "Hawthorne and His Mosses," Melville's only serious attempt at criticism and analysis, is important as an assessment of Hawthorne's first important sketches.

Biography

Melville's achievements, before the discovery of *Billy Budd, Foretopman,* and the subsequent revival of Melville studies were viewed simply as writings from "a man who lived among the cannibals." He was remembered only for *Typee* and *Omoo,* his slight but extremely popular South Seas adventures. While important as the beginnings of the popular tradition of exotic romances, *Typee* and *Omoo* are not classics. Only with the publication of *Billy Budd,*

Foretopman, and the critical scrutiny that its publication encouraged, were *Moby Dick*, *Pierre*, and the rest reassessed, and Melville's reputation as a leader among giants affirmed.

Apart from introducing the South Seas tale to the American public, *Pierre* is arguably the first important work of psychological realism; and *Moby Dick* is a masterpiece of metaphysics, allegory, philosophy, and literary greatness which has never been surpassed in American fiction. The assessment of Melville's work was not realized until years after his death and almost seventy years after Melville had given up the novel form for the quick money of short stories, the personal introspection of poetry, and the security of a government post in the New York customs office. Melville was never psychologically or ideologically attuned to the demands of his public and, thus, popularity eluded him in his lifetime.

Biography

Herman Melville was born in New York City, August 1, 1819, the third child of a modestly wealthy family. His father, a successful merchant, traced his lineage back to Major Thomas Melville, one of the "Indians" at the Boston tea party. His mother, Maria Gansevoort Melville, was the only daughter of General Peter Gansevoort, also a revolutionary war hero. Melville had a happy childhood in a home where there was affluence and love. He had access to the arts and books, and he was educated in some of the city's finest private institutions. His father, however, considered young Melville to be somewhat backward, despite his early penchant for public speaking; and his father marked him for a trade rather than law or a similar professional pursuit.

The prosperity that the Melvilles enjoyed from before Herman's birth came to an end in the economic panic of 1830. Unable to meet creditors' demands, despite the financial aid of his family, Melville's father lost his business and was forced into bankruptcy. After attempts to save the business, he moved the family to Albany and assumed the management of a fur company's branch office. The move seemed to settle the Melville's financial problems until the cycle repeated itself in 1831. Melville's father, again, suffered a financial reversal, went into physical and mental decline, and died on January 28, 1832.

After his father's death, Melville became, successively, a bank clerk and accountant, a farm worker, a schoolteacher, and, after another economic failure—this time his brother Gansevoort's fur business—an unemployed, but genteel, young man seeking employment in New York City. With the aid of his brothers, Melville secured a berth on a Liverpool packet and thus launched his sea career, and indirectly, his literary fortunes. After one cruise, however, Melville returned to schoolteaching. When the school closed for lack of funds, he and a friend determined to go West to visit Melville's uncle in Illinois, hoping to find some type of financially satisfying arrangement there. Failing to find work, Melville returned to New York City and signed aboard the

Acushnet, a new whaler making her maiden voyage. From 1841 to 1844, Melville was to participate in seafaring adventures which would change American literature.

On his return to New York in 1844, he found his family's fortunes somewhat improved. He also found that the stories he had to tell of his travels were enthusiastically received by his friends and relatives. Finally persuaded to write them, he produced *Typee* and published it in 1846. The immediate success and acclaim which followed the publication assured Melville that he had finally found his place in life. He followed *Typee* with its sequel, *Omoo*, achieved a similar success, and resolutely set out to make his living by his pen. He found the financial return of two popular novels was not sufficient to support him, however, and he applied for a government position and was rejected. Melville married Elizabeth Shaw, moved to New York City with most of his family, and started a third novel which became *Mardi and a Voyage Thither*.

The visionary and allegorical structure of *Mardi and a Voyage Thither* did not appeal to the readers of his previous successes, and its failure frustrated Melville. In need of ready funds, he began two "potboilers" in order to produce those funds. After the publication and success of *Redburn* and *White-Jacket*, Melville moved his family to a farm in the Berkshires, which he dubbed "Arrowhead" because of Indian artifacts he found there, and assumed the life of a country gentleman and a member of the loosely knit literary society which included Oliver Wendell Holmes and Nathaniel Hawthorne and others living in the vicinity of Pittsfield, Massachusetts.

How Hawthorne and Melville met is not known, but that they met is witnessed by the production of *Moby Dick*. It was likely that Hawthorne encouraged Melville to write as he saw fit, not as the public demanded. Their correspondence reveals an intense, cordial friendship which was of immense value to Melville during this time of his greatest personal, emotional, and artistic development. Hawthorne was one of the first, not to mention the few, to praise Melville's whaling story. Despite Hawthorne's praise, *Moby Dick* was a financial and critical failure. *Pierre*, the "rural bowl of milk" which followed *Moby Dick*, defied Melville's predictions for its success and was also a failure. The dual failure caused Melville considerable pain and bitterness. As a result of the failures and the debt to his publishers, Melville turned away from the novel to the short-story form.

He was to publish two more novels in his lifetime, but neither was commercially successful. Melville began writing poetry in addition to the short story, but his poetry was even more introspective than his fiction and by the time he was appointed to the customs office of New York City in 1866, he had virtually stopped publishing for public consumption.

The security of the customs office eliminated Melville's need for the slim financial return of publication and he no longer felt compelled to write for an unwilling public. Yet, he continued to write. At his death, he left a box full of manuscripts of his unpublished work during the years from 1866 to his death (he had published some poetry). When the box was opened, it was found to contain one more novel. *Billy Budd, Foretopman*, published in 1924, was the final piece of Melville's frustration. He never finished it and never attempted to publish it, but since its discovery and publication it has been recognized as one of Melville's masterpieces. When Melville died in 1891, his obituaries recalled him not only as a man who wrote novels of adventure but also who had "fallen into a literary decline." It was left for another generation to appreciate and revere him.

Analysis

Herman Melville's career as a novelist breaks down, somewhat too neatly, into a three-part voyage of frustration and disappointment. The first part of his career is characterized by the heady successes of *Typee* and *Omoo*, the second by the frustrating failure of, among others, *Moby Dick*, and the third by his increasing withdrawal from publication and the final discovery of and acclaim for *Billy Budd, Foretopman*, thirty-two years after Melville's death. After the initial successes of *Typee* and *Omoo*, Melville never again achieved anything approaching popular success, but it was the acclaim over those two novels which assured Melville that he should attempt to make his way as a novelist. It probably did not occur to Melville at the time, but he was introducing a new genre into American literature.

Typee struck the American public like a ray of sunshine falling into a darkened room. The fresh descriptions and intriguing narrative of an American sailor trapped among the Rousseauvian natives of the Marquesas Islands were hailed on both sides of the Atlantic, and its sequel, *Omoo*, was received even more enthusiastically. The problems inherent in Melville's harsh treatment of missionaries and imperialism and the general disbelief of the veracity in the author's tale aside, the works satiated a public thirst for exotic places. That *Typee* and *Omoo* have survived in the estimation of critics is testimony to Melville's art even in those early stages of his development.

Whether it is the simple narrative or the dramatic suspense of impending doom which holds the reader, *Typee* offers a flowing romantic atmosphere of timeless days, pointless endeavor, and mindless existence. The Happy Valley in which Melville's Tommo finds himself trapped is an idyllic setting for the lovely Fayaway and Tommo to live and love. In *Typee* there is none of the agonizing speculation on life, man, philosophy, or the cosmos, which readers later came to expect of Melville. With only slight exaggeration and minimal research, Melville created the picture of a world beyond the ken of his readers but which would never die in his memories.

Omoo, a sequel to *Typee*, is only an extension of that idyll. There is a basic difference between *Typee* and *Omoo*, however; *Typee* is a tightly woven dramatic narrative, incorporating the day-to-day suspense of whether Tommo would be the Marquesan cannibals' next meal; *Omoo* is a more picaresque representation of the events, the charm in *Omoo* depends solely on the loosely tied chain of events encountered by the narrator and his companion, Dr. Long Ghost, among the natives of Tahiti. There is no threat hanging over them, as in *Typee*, and there is no necessity for escape. *Omoo* also differs in that it takes place in a tainted paradise. Tahiti has been, in *Omoo*, Christianized and settled and, thus, the natives are familiar with the white sailor and his games. This reduction of innocence colors *Omoo* in a way not reflected in *Typee*.

There is an inescapable glow of romance throughout Melville's two Polynesian novels. The record of missionary abuse and the encroachment of civilization does not make an overbearing appearance, but it does lay the groundwork for the reflections of Melville's despair and convoluted indictments of man and his world in later, more mature works.

Mardi, *Redburn*, and *White-Jacket* rapidly followed Melville's early successes. *Mardi*, opening like a continuation of *Typee* and *Omoo*, shocked readers when it lapsed into philosophical allegory. *Mardi*'s subsequent failure prompted Melville, in search of fame and funds, to return to sea-narrative in *Redburn* and *White-Jacket*, but despite their modest successes, Melville reviled them as hackwork.

In *Moby Dick*, there is evidence that Melville intended it to be little more than a factual account of the whale fisheries in the South Pacific detailed with firsthand tales of adventures on a whaler. When completed two years after its beginning, it was a puzzling, intricately devised literary work in which a white whale is the central character. Around this central figure, Melville weaves symbolism, speculation, philosophy, and allegory on life, God, man, and the human condition. In short, Melville had created an epic romance which stood at the brink of becoming mythology.

The plot of *Moby Dick*, when not interrupted by authorial asides and digressions, is relatively direct. A young man, Ishmael, comes to the sea seeking a berth on a whaling ship. He finds the *Pequod*; falls into a friendship with the cannibal harpooner Queequeg; discovers that the ship is captained by a madman, Ahab, who is driven to wreak vengeance on the white whale that took his leg off on a previous voyage; finds himself in a crew which is a microcosm of the world's peoples; watches as Ahab drives the ship and crew in pursuit of Moby Dick; and is the sole survivor when Ahab is killed in a direct confrontation with the whale. By itself, the plot is thrilling but does not have the ingredients of greatness. The layers of fiction—the levels that the reader must traverse in order to rend the novel for all its substance— make the work magnificent. To the surface adventure, Melville adds gleanings from volumes of cetological and marine lore, his own observations on the psychology of man, and, finally, his ultimate speculations on good and evil—

the basic morality of man and of man's place in the universe.

Melville's frequent displays of marine erudition are often cursed as flaws in an otherwise closely woven fabric. They seem to do little for the on-rushing spectacle of Ahab and his monomania, and they almost function as literary irritants designed to interrupt the reader's chain of thought. They are not intended to enhance the characterization of Ahab or his crew, nor are they an integral part of the narrative; they are, however, the essence of the novel's central character, the whale. Without Melville's lore, there is no reality to the ominously ethereal presence of Moby Dick. The periodic chapters of information and background are the author's reminders to the reader of the whale's presence and that the whale drives the story forward. The lore is also the foundation of belief in the whale. It promotes and maintains the physical presence of the whale by the sheer weight of scientific or pseudoscientific data. When the whale finally appears, the reader has been sufficiently educated and prepared. Melville creates the whale, vicariously, with his lore and trivia, and sets the stage for its appearance.

In describing Ahab, his ship and crew, Melville employs a nonnarrative form of characterization, where each individual is the subject of an inquiry or is an example of a human type. Of the major characters, Ahab is the most complex, but the others form a society in which that complexity can best be displayed. Starbuck, the first mate, Stubb, the second mate, and Flask, the third mate, are only the closest of several layers of the crew around Ahab. Queequeg, Tashtego, and Daggoo, the harpooners, form the next layer and the rest of the crew fill out Ahab's world, and, like Fleece, the ship's cook, and Pip, the mad cabin boy, they all perform vignettes which enlarge and enhance the magnitude of Ahab and his quest. For example, Ahab feels compelled to explain the real reasons behind his insane search for the white whale only to Starbuck, the conscientious, scrupulous first mate. Rather than simple revenge, as Starbuck supposes it to be, Ahab proposes to strike through the "pasteboard masks" of reality by striking at the whale. In his reasoning with Starbuck, Ahab demonstrates a side of himself which is otherwise hidden; there is purpose, calculation, and preparation in his madness. Ahab's insanity, thereby, becomes a divine sort of madness, and he transcends mere earthly logic to become an epic madman jousting with creation. It is through Starbuck and the others that the reader learns most about Ahab, and it is in such relationships that one sees the mastery of Melville's artistry.

Ahab becomes more than a simple villain when viewed against the backdrop of Starbuck and the other characters. He becomes a monolithic character testing a universe that he sees as perverse and unkind toward man's existence. He dares to confront nature itself and to challenge it to single combat. It is Queequeg who unwittingly provides the clues to the venture's outcome. He has a coffin built when he fears he will die of a fever, and when Moby Dick rams the *Pequod*, it is the coffin which supports Ishmael, the only survivor.

The coffin becomes the symbolic remainder of Ahab's world. Man and his science cannot stand against nature and hope to survive. It is Ahab's *hamartia* to believe that he can survive and his belief is the final sign of his ultimately evil nature.

Ahab would, he tells Starbuck, "strike the sun if he offended me," and he considers himself as the equal of any other force in nature. He forgets that he is limited by human frailty—or he believes he is no longer subject to the laws of temporal existence or his own physical shortcomings. He is, in one sense, a blighted Prometheus who can offer nothing but his vision to his fellow men, and they blindly accept it. Ahab's greatest evil is the corruption of his relatively innocent world, and its ultimate destruction is his sole responsibility.

Melville used many symbols and devices in *Moby Dick*, and they are important strands by which the story is held together. The names alone are important enough to demand attention. The biblical significance of Ishmael and Ahab, and of Jereboam and Rachel needs no explanation. Starbuck, Stubb, and Flask all have significance when examined symbolically. The mythical ramifications of a voyage beginning on Christmas night enlarge as the story unfolds. The ultimate device is Ishmael himself. Ostensibly the story's narrator, he only appears in about every fourth chapter after the first twenty-five. When he does appear, it is difficult to keep track of whether the narrator or author is speaking. Ishmael, however, is never used in an omnipotent, obtrusive manner which would belie his place on the *Pequod*, and, thus, the point of view remains clear. Ishmael opens the novel and Ishmael announces "and I only am escaped alone to tell thee," but he is there primarily to provide a frame for the story. This very flexible point-of-view is an adroit device by which the author can distance himself from the story, while still involving himself in a story as few authors have or will. When Melville finds Ishmael to be an encumbrance, he sheds him and speaks for himself. It remains an open question whether the story is Ishmael's, Ahab's, the whale's, or Melville's. It is not necessary, however, that the dilemma be resolved in order to appreciate and acknowledge the massive achievement in *Moby Dick*.

After the failure of *Moby Dick* to be a commercial success, Melville's increasingly sour approach to novel-writing produced *Pierre*, perhaps the first psychological novel in American literature but also a miserable failure; *Israel Potter*, a rewriting and fictionalizing of a Revolutionary War diary; *The Confidence Man*, a sardonic, rambling, loosely constructed allegory on American society; and *Billy Budd, Foretopman*. The last of Melville's attempts in the novel form *Billy Budd, Foretopman*, was never offered for publication by the author and was discovered and published in the mid-1920's. Despite its checkered publication history (it has appeared in any number of flawed or badly edited forms), *Billy Budd, Foretopman* has come to be recognized as Melville's final word on the great problems with which he first grappled in *Moby Dick*. Its form and simplicity make it the perfect companion for the epic proportions of *Moby Dick*. Its message is such that it seems Melville created it as a catharsis for the unanswered questions in the greater work.

Billy Budd, Foretopman, is a masterful twisting of historical event into fiction in order to maintain the tension of a gripping story. While so doing, Melville explores the stirring, but somewhat less exciting, problems of the conflict between man, good and evil, and the law. Melville uses a blend of the historically significant British mutinies of the *Nore* and at Spithead in 1797, and the 1842 execution of three alleged mutineers of the United States ship *Somers*, in which his cousin Guert Gansevoort played a significant part, to mold the setting and motive for his story leading to the trial and execution of the "handsome sailor." The events leading to the trial are relatively unadorned and there is little question prior to the trial where the reader's sympathies should be and which characters embody which attributes of human nature.

There is a slightly melodramatic air about the principal characters in *Billy Budd, Foretopman*. Claggart, by shrewd characterization and description, is the evil master-at-arms who is in direct conflict with the innocent, pure, guileless Billy Budd. Melville never makes clear why Claggart develops his seemingly perverse prejudice against Billy, but a definite line of good and evil is drawn between the two men. The evil is magnified by the mysterious impetus for Claggart's antipathy toward Billy; and the good is intensified by Billy's naïve ignorance of Claggart's malice, even though the entire crew seems to know of it and understand the reasons for it, and by his cheerful mien not only in the face of Claggart's bullying but also in spite of the circumstances which brought him to the *Indomitable*.

Billy is wronged from the beginning when he is impressed from the American *Rights of Man* to the British *Indomitable* (the names of the ships being a sly piece of Melville commentary on the British navy, the war of 1812, and Billy Budd's predicament, among other things). He is instantly recognized and accepted by his new mates on board the *Indomitable* and becomes a full and useful member of the crew and a good shipmate. Claggart, who has the unenviable job of policing a British man-of-war and administering the Queen's maritime justice, seems to extend himself to bring charges against the new man. When Billy is implicated in a mutiny rumor, Claggart seizes the opportunity to bring him before a drumhead courtmartial. At the hearing, Claggart concentrates all of his inexplicable venom against Billy Budd in false charges, innuendo, and lies calculated to ensure a guilty verdict for which Billy will be hanged.

The wonder of Billy Budd and Claggart is that Melville, while portraying the two extremes of human morality in human forms, avoids creating flat caricatures. Billy and Claggart seemingly are real people operating in a real world, and they develop in very believable ways, even given Claggart's behavior toward Billy. At the climax of the trial, perhaps the most fantastic moment in the novel, there is no appreciable relaxation of the verisimilitude Melville creates, even though Billy strikes Claggart dead with one crashing blow of his fist. The other major character of the novel fills the momentary gap in the credibility of the story after Claggart's death. Captain Vere commands not only the *Indomitable* but also the trial, and it is he who pushes the novel through its climactic scene and who, in essence, takes the message of the novel from Billy Budd and develops it to its fruition.

Edward Fairfax ("Starry") Vere appears at length only from the trial to the end of the novel, but, despite the title character and his antagonist, Vere is the heart of the novel. He is everything Billy and Claggart are not. He is a complex character—a philosophical ship's captain—and a man who is caught between many pressures as he decides the fate of a man whom he evidently likes. Faced with the precedent of the historical mutinies that Melville introduces into the novel's background, Vere feels the necessity of creating Billy Budd as an example to other prospective mutineers. Seeing Billy's innocence, and understanding at least part of Claggart's fulsome character, Vere is loathe to condemn a man who probably was within his moral right to strike his superior. Even so, the need for order and the maritime sense of justice force Vere to send Billy to the yardarm. Vere, more than anyone, recognizes that he is sacrificing an innocent man for the good of his ship, its crew, and, ultimately, for his society. He sentences Billy under the prescription of law, but he begs his forgiveness as a moral human being.

The sacrifice of the innocent is a theme which pervades Western literature, but in *Billy Budd, Foretopman*, Melville confronts the struggle between chaos and order, law and morality, man and his society. There is no clear decision as Vere dies in battle; Billy haunts him to his end. Yet, the society, the system for which Billy was sacrificed, survives and prevails. Vere remains incomprehensible except to the man he condemns. Billy Budd understands but does not have the capacity or the will to exert himself in order to save himself. He is reminiscent, in some respects, of the Christ-figure he has universally been called. In the final analysis, Vere, Claggart, and Billy are all sacrificed, and the initial skirmishes between good and evil become almost trivial when compared to the moral and philosophical riddles Melville poses.

From *Omoo* and *Typee* to *Moby Dick* and *Billy Budd, Foretopman*, Melville traverses the paths to maturity and complexity not only in prose fiction but in philosophical and spiritual understanding as well. Nevertheless, there is little difference between Tommo and Billy Budd, the two innocents of civilization. Ahab and "Starry" Vere are similar enough to be recognized as brothers of the quarterdeck and of mankind. While facing different problems and decisions, they both meet them and deal with them similarly—and both die for their causes. The thread of the sea is unmistakable in Melville, but he recognized the function of the ship at sea as a symbol or as an experimental station, isolated and representative of the world he examined. Melville had his causes and injected them into his stories, but he is primarily interested in the human condition. He inspects all facets of each character ruthlessly and meticulously, without judgment and without prejudice, and he allows the results of his inspection to speak for themselves without gratuitous commentary. Since the revival of Melville studies with the discovery of *Billy Budd, Foretopman*, Melville's reputation as one of America's most significant authors is secure.

Clarence O. Johnson

Other major works

SHORT FICTION: *The Piazza Tales*, 1856; *The Apple-Tree Table and Other Sketches*, 1922.

POETRY: *Battle-Pieces and Aspects of the War*, 1866; *Clarel: A Poem and Pilgrimage in the Holy Land*, 1876; *John Marr and Other Sailors*, 1888; *Timoleon*, 1891.

NONFICTION: *Journal Up the Straits*, 1935; *Journal of a Visit to London and the Continent*, 1948.

Bibliography

Berthoff, Warner. *The Example of Melville*. Princeton, N.J.: Princeton University Press, 1962. This well-written study presents Melville as a skilled artist who excels in his craft. Careful analyses of characters and conflicts, noticeably those of *Billy Budd, Foretopman*, are convincingly done. Writing from a humanist point of view, Berthoff does not hide his admiration for his subject.

Bryant, John, ed. *A Companion to Melville Studies*. Westport, Conn.: Greenwood Press, 1986. Excellent collection of twenty-five essays which together reflect contemporary trends in research. Divided into five parts which discuss Melville's life, give a summary and critical appraisal of his works, deal with thematic concepts, and evaluate the author's impact on twentieth century culture. Chapter bibliographies and a general index are included.

Dillingham, William D. *An Artist in the Rigging*. Athens: University of Georgia Press, 1972.

_____. *Melville's Short Fiction, 1853-1856*. Athens: University of Georgia Press, 1977.

_____. *Melville's Later Novels*. Athens: University of Georgia Press, 1986. Dillingham's full study successfully chronicles Melville's artistic development against the backdrop of nineteenth century America. Individual chapters read well and offer convincing close readings and original insights. Thanks to a well-developed index in each volume, the reader can easily access specific information.

Karcher, Carolyn L. *Shadow Over the Promised Land: Slavery, Race, and Violence in Melville's America*. Baton Rouge: Louisiana State University Press, 1980. This readable and important book shows Melville's deep resentment of slavery and oppression. Argues that, to convince his contemporaries, Melville uses a subversive strategy rather than direct accusation. The use of Marxist economic theory dates but does not derail some of Karcher's ideas. The bibliography and index are put together well.

Olson, Charles. *Call Me Ishmael*. San Francisco: City Lights Books, 1947. Witty and sparklingly irreverent, this slim but stimulating text combines postmodern stylistics and keen insights into the microcosm of the fictional whaling ship *Pequod* in Melville's *Moby Dick*. Somewhat of a "cult classic" of criticism, Olson's text has lost nothing of its poignancy.

Rosenberry, Edward H. *Melville*. Boston: Routledge & Kegan Paul, 1979. A richly illustrated, fine, and accessible introduction to Melville's life and career. This intellectually independent survey captures the reader's imagination and offers a fresh, contemporary overview of the artist's achievement without deterring jargon. Includes an index and bibliography to aid further study.

GEORGE MEREDITH

Born: Portsmouth, England; February 12, 1828
Died: Box Hill, England; May 18, 1909

Principal long fiction

The Shaving of Shagpat, 1855; *Farina*, 1857; *The Ordeal of Richard Feverel*, 1859; *Evan Harrington*, 1861; *Emilia in England*, 1864 (as *Sandra Belloni: Or, Emilia in England*, 1886); *Rhoda Fleming*, 1865; *Vittoria*, 1867; *The Adventures of Harry Richmond*, 1871; *Beauchamp's Career*, 1876; *The Egoist*, 1879; *The Tragic Comedians*, 1880; *Diana of the Crossways*, 1885; *One of Our Conquerors*, 1891; *Lord Ormont and His Aminta*, 1894; *The Amazing Marriage*, 1895; *Celt and Saxon*, 1910 (unfinished).

Other literary forms

Ironically, George Meredith, one of nineteenth century England's greatest novelists, actually considered himself a poet. Regrettably, the several volumes of poetry he published during his lifetime went largely unnoticed. Even though Alfred, Lord Tennyson, praised "Love in the Valley," published in his first volume, *Poems* (1851), dedicated to his then father-in-law, Thomas Love Peacock, it was as a novelist that Meredith achieved recognition in his own time. Undaunted, nevertheless, Meredith continued to write poems and, in keeping with his stated vocation and with his aspiration, both his first and his last published books were collections of poems.

Modern Love and Poems of the English Roadside (1862) represents Meredith's lyric and dramatic power at its height, especially in the sequence of fifty sixteen-line lyrics, *Modern Love*. In these poems, Meredith traces the dissolution of a marriage with an unrestrained candor which is more like the attitudes toward marital relationships of the 1980's than the straight-faced, closed-lipped Victorian notions. At the lowest point in the sequence, the persona exclaims, "In tragic life, God wot,/ No villain need be! Passions spin the plot;/ We are betrayed by what is false within." Herein Meredith seems to capture with great precision the essence of tragedy. Meredith's poetic vision is not always dark; light imagery, in fact, plays a significant role in his poetry.

The thinking man appears often in Meredith's works, but he is perhaps most prominent in the 1877 essay, "The Idea of Comedy and the Uses of the Comic Spirit." This essay is significant enough to be included in many contemporary collections of criticism, especially in those which pertain to drama. Acknowledging that the muse of comedy has never been "one of the most honored of the Muses," Meredith submits that it is the "Comic Spirit" that civilizes man. By means of thoughtful laughter, the Comic Spirit corrects and checks the foibles of all the men who exceed the bounds of temperance and indulge by excessive behavior. Although Meredith opened himself to censure in his own day, his ideas about women and their roles in comedy are particularly interesting to today's readers. Indeed, comedy, "the fountain of common sense," teaches that men and women are social equals and that women are often men's superiors.

Achievements

In the late nineteenth century, Meredith achieved the status of a literary dictator or arbiter of taste. The path toward this recognition was, however, a long and arduous one. For years, Meredith received little to no recognition, and he had to wait for the publication of *The Ordeal of Richard Feverel* before he enjoyed the limited appreciation of Algernon Charles Swinburne, Dante Gabriel Rossetti, and others among the pre-Raphaelites. Not until the appearance of *The Egoist* in 1879 did Meredith's literary reputation reach its zenith.

During his last years, Meredith received many awards and honors, including the succession of Alfred, Lord Tennyson, as the president of the Society of British Authors and election as one of the original members of the Order of Merit. Within twenty years after Meredith's death in 1909, nevertheless, his literary reputation began to suffer a partial eclipse, from which it has begun to recover in the 1970's. One explanation for Meredith's decline in reputation is simple: his turgid style and complex plots demand more from the average reader than he is often willing to give. C. L. Cline's three-volume edition of *The Letters of George Meredith* which appeared in 1970 and Phyllis B. Bartlett's two-volume, 1978 collection of *The Poems of George Meredith* have done much to reawaken interest in Meredith's work, particularly in his poetry, which seems to appeal to modern readers much more markedly than it had to those of his own time. Even so, the influence of Meredith the novelist on such younger writers as Thomas Hardy was decisive, and Meredith's theory of the Comic Spirit as the civilizing force of all thoughtful men speaks to all cultures of all times.

Biography

Born the son and grandson of tailors, George Meredith appears to have rejected his humble origins. Indeed, he once threatened that he would "most horribly haunt" any who attempted to reconstruct his biography. Despite his modest heritage, legacies from his mother and an aunt permitted him to attend private schools, St. Paul's Church School, Southsea, and the Moravian School of Neuwied, Germany. His objective in formal training was to become a lawyer, and he was apprenticed to a London solicitor in 1845. Young Meredith soon became dissatisfied with the legal profession, however, and began to seek a career as a journalist, a vocation which he pursued throughout most of his life, since he was never quite able to survive financially as an author of novels and poems.

From at least 1845 until his marriage in 1849 to Mary Ellen Nicolls, a widow and the daughter of Thomas Love Peacock, Meredith appears to have read widely and deeply in the literature of Greece, Rome, Germany, France, and England. The first few years of his marriage appear to have been ones of continued intellectual growth. The Merediths lived either with or near the aspiring young author's famous father-in-law. Meredith made good use of Peacock's extensive and often arcane library, whose shelves included volumes on such Near Eastern religions as Zoroastrianism, a faith that was later to have a profound influence on Meredith's novels and poems.

The first few years of apparent bliss were soon terminated, however, when Mary eloped in 1858 with the painter Henry Wallis to the isle of Capri. Meredith was consequently left alone to rear his son Arthur; the author later wrote about these unhappy times both in the novel *The Ordeal of Richard Feverel* and in the lyric sequence *Modern Love*. After Mary's death in 1861, Meredith married, within three years, Marie Vulliamy; this match proved to be both enduring and much happier. After serving as war correspondent, he and his new wife moved to Flint Cottage, Box Hill, Surrey, where he lived the remainder of his life. Box Hill is where admiring and enthusiastic young authors went to seek Meredith's sage counsel.

Analysis

Although George Meredith's works all emphasize the corrective, civilizing influences of the Comic Spirit, his novels, as well as his poems, forcefully work out a sort of theodicy which is consistently informed by the Near Eastern religion, Zoroastrianism. This philosophy that treats the being and government of God and the immortality of the soul displays the theme of the struggle between good and evil in the early work *Farina*. In the novel, surrounded by the trappings of medieval Germany, Farina, the hero of the tale, is left to contend with the evil effects of a bout between a monk and Satan. The monk represents the Zoroastrian god of light or good, Ormuzd, and Satan, the god of darkness or evil, Ahriman. In the later, much more successful novel *The Ordeal of Richard Feverel*, this dialectic is seen in the sixth chapter, "The Magian Conflict" (the magi were ancient priests of Zoroaster). In this case, Meredith assigns the roles of the two opposing parties of the struggle to a Tinker and a Yeoman; the witness to this debate is the adolescent Richard Feverel whose father, Sir Austin, has attempted unsuccessfully to shield him from any introduction to the world's forces of good and evil.

The Tinker, who appears to be a faithful follower of Zoroaster, the ancient prophet of the faith, asserts that the Good Spirit reigns supreme. The Yeoman, whom Meredith playfully calls Speed-the-Plough, protests, because of his recent misfortune of having lost several jobs, that the Evil Spirit dominates. The Yeoman is particularly hostile to Farmer Blaize, with whom Richard and a companion have also had an unpleasant encounter. Farmer Blaize is responsible for the beginning of the Yeoman's misfortunes. Tinker and Yeoman discuss the universal strife between good and evil in Zoroastrian terms, wherein the Good Spirit is supposed to hold dominion for a two-thousand-year period and the Evil Spirit is believed to assume dominion for a like period of two thousand years. Clearly, then, this debate challenges the young Richard to side with Ahriman (darkness) or to join the legions of Ormuzd (light).

Richard later relates the details of this encounter to Adrian Harley, a sort of tutor and confidant of the young Mr. Feverel, who is actually a disciple of the Comic Spirit and whom the narrator addresses as the Wise Youth. Adrian explains to Richard that "'I'm perfectly aware that Zoroaster is not dead. You have been listening to a common creed. Drink the Fire-worshippers, if you will.'" Adrian recognizes the nature of the timeless controversy and applies to it the synecdoche, "Zoroaster," to point out the age of the struggle. Adrian also emphasizes that this struggle is a universal one, the result of a "common creed," regardless of Sir Austin's refusal to acknowledge it.

Adrian's comic toast to the Fire-worshippers is also ironic in that Richard and Tom Bakewell, the ploughman, have plotted to burn Farmer Blaize's hayracks. That night, Richard and his friend Ripton Thompson watch the fiery destruction resulting from the match of Tom Bakewell, whose last name is comically appropriate to his role. This "Bakewell Comedy," however, has serious overtones when seen in the light of the Zoroastrian metaphor. The fire of the boys' vision is not a pure one, for there are "dense masses of smoke" amid the flames which leap into the darkness like "snakes of fire." In Zoroastrianism, Ahriman (Evil) is responsible for this corruption of the pure flame.

The chapter's title, "Arson," which initiates the Bakewell Comedy, effectively points out the boys' error. The boys are, like Tom Bakewell, not good Zoroastrians because the fire they are worshiping reflects the evil nature of their revenge. Adrian sees through their conspiracy; however, he does not expose the boys. Rather, in the true manner of the Zoroastrians, he believes that the most effective punishment would be a spiritual, inner conflict. "The farmer's whip had reduced them to bodily contortions; these were decorous compared with the spiritual writhings they had to perform under Adrian's skillful manipulation." Adrian knows the true value of fire to the Zoroastrians: it is a symbol of the inner light of the soul, which glows brightest when fired by Ormuzd. If the soul is possessed by the evil Ahriman, the spiritual light is contaminated and burns, if at all, with a dim, impure glimmer.

Richard's next crucial encounter intensifies the glow of the purer fire burning within him. He meets Lucy Desborough, destined to be his wife. The imagery used to describe this encounter is filled with references to light. Nature herself has provided "a Temple for the flame" of love. From a boat, Richard first sees Lucy pictured in an idyllic scene of radiant sunshine reflecting from the "green-flashing plunges of a weir." Lucy's face is shaded from the sun's illumination mysteriously but compellingly "by a broad straw hat with a flexible brim that left her lips and chin in the sun, and sometimes nodding, sent forth a light of promising eyes." Her hair was "golden where the ray touched" it. Even her name is derived from the Latin word for light: "Lux." Richard's soul is filled with the light of passionate love, but he has another journey to the vision of the celestial light of the Zoroastrians.

Other references to Zoroastrianism abound in the novel. For example, at a later point, Sir Austin yields to the dark force of Ahriman when he chooses to "do nothing" at a time when his son needs his counsel most. Consequently, he turns his son away from him, perhaps forever, thus proving that a father with a "system" for child-rearing cannot meet that system on its own terms.

Viewed within the bounds of the magian conflict, *The Ordeal of Richard Feverel* is seen as a novel about the inevitability of the human strife between good and evil, both of which are inextricably mixed within the souls of every human being. Some measure of hope is given to the novel, however, when the reader learns that, finally, Richard does view, if but for a moment, the celestial light of Ormuzd through the aid of a truly devoted wife.

It is this hope which raises *The Ordeal of Richard Feverel* to the level of true tragedy, which must in some measure be positive. Although Sir Austin falls victim to Ahriman, his son, Richard, has seen the vision of Ormuzd. By the use of Zoroastrian imagery, Meredith has greatly intensified his conviction that the ultimate destiny of mankind is unity with the light of the spirit or, more realistically for Meredith, unity with the great "Over Reason" of the universe. This unity directs man along the path of spiritual evolution and is the apex of Meredith's developing doctrine about man: blood (perfection of the body), brain (perfection of the mind), and spirit (perfection of the needs of man's spiritual consciousness by means of realizing his intrinsic independence and freedom).

The tone of the first half of *The Ordeal of Richard Feverel* is predominately one of comic irony; the latter half of the novel, however, assumes tragic dimensions. Meredith's later novels display a much greater reliance upon the comic mood. Even so, the essence of "The Magian Conflict" is never lost; rather, Meredith wields the forces of darkness against those of light to accentuate the balancing, equalizing role of his emerging Comic Spirit, whose seeds have been planted in the wise youth, Adrian Harley. The struggle to reach the evolutionary apex, the light of the spirit, assumes a background role in the novels following *The Ordeal of Richard Feverel* and is treated later most directly in the poetry. In his novels, Meredith becomes increasingly more concerned with the question of how one should meet the vicissitudes of everyday life.

Meredith published his essay "The Idea of Comedy and the Uses of the Comic Spirit" in 1877. *Beauchamp's Career* appeared the year before; quite naturally the novel portrays many of the theories Meredith proposed in his essay. In 1879, Meredith completed *The Egoist*, which the author named "a comedy in narrative." Meredith's last great achievement in the novel genre appeared in 1885 and was entitled *Diana of the Crossways*. The novels provide interesting examples of the working out of Meredith's theories centered in the Comic Spirit, and they demonstrate some degree of the use of Zoroastrian imagery. *Beauchamp's Career* employs the Zoroastrian contrast of light and dark to a much greater extent than the other two novels. Meredith draws from Zoroastrianism to a noticeable degree, however, in each of these three novels in order to make the instructive character of his Comic Spirit more emphatic.

Meredith makes repeated references to fire, sun, and light throughout *Beauchamp's Career*, which undoubtedly reflects his prior use of Zoroastrianism in *The Ordeal of Richard Feverel*. Meredith's dependence upon Zoroastrianism is most pronounced, however, in his characterization of Dr. Shrapnel. Nevil Beauchamp is ambitious and wants to be a politician; he plans to exercise his philanthropic desire to "save the world." He joins a radical political party in order to battle the more conservative Tory Party and to oppose the vehement objections of his Uncle Everard Romfrey, a hater of radicals. After Nevil loses an election for a seat in Parliament, he comes under the tutelage of Dr. Shrapnel, a professed Fire-worshipper.

Since "Fire-worshippers" is a name that Zoroastrians were often mistakenly called, when Dr. Shrapnel testifies "I am a Fire-worshipper," the reader perceives already an element of Meredith's comedy. Dr. Shrapnel, whose name calls to mind a number of images, all of which indicate either potential destruction or active destruction, has obviously become enamored of the mystic, esoteric nature of the religion and hence has adopted certain of its tenets to his own philosophy. Basically Shrapnel's personal doctrine is, in his own words: "That is our republic: each one to his work; all in union! There's the motto for us! *Then* you have music, harmony, the highest, fullest, finest!"

Admittedly, Shrapnel's philosophy is good, or superior in its idealism, and it represents a direct restatement of Meredith's own philosophy (expressed in many of his poems). At this point in the novel, however, the philosophy is stated by an extremist, hence there is a touch of the comic which becomes more apparent as the novel progresses. Meredith's infrequent use of the exclamation point and his almost negative use of italics make this particular passage stand out as the radical view of an extremist.

Rosamund Culling, the future wife of Nevil's uncle, thinks of Shrapnel as "a black malignant . . . with his . . . talk of flying to the sun." As may be expected from Rosamund's tone, Dr. Shrapnel has at some time in her company been overzealous in the expression of his republican sentiments. News of Dr. Shrapnel's inflammatory radicalism soon reaches Nevil's Uncle Romfrey, who proceeds to horsewhip Shrapnel to the point of severe injury. Lack of understanding by his fellowman appears to be Shrapnel's failing and provides the occasion for comment from the Comic Spirit, who judges that Shrapnel must suffer for his intemperance, for his imbalance. Compromise should be man's objective.

Both in *The Egoist* and in *Diana of the Crossways*, the part played by Zoroastrian imagery is greatly reduced from that which it played in *The Ordeal of Richard Feverel* and *Beauchamp's Career*. Meredith's Comic Spirit, however, comes to the front in full array; the increased subordination of Zoroastrian imagery to Meredith's portrayal of his Comic Spirit indicates that Meredith's theories and understanding of the purpose of his literary art were expanding and maturing. In the later novels, Meredith's Zoroastrian and classical images become frequently and inseparably fused, a combination which further exemplifies Meredith's artistry and more significantly indicates that Meredith's philosophy was progressively becoming more distinct. His thinking was beginning to become a cultivated doctrine.

The Egoist characterizes the egocentric element in Meredith's theory of high comedy. Sir Willoughby Patterne, who thinks himself to be the epitome of goodness and excellence in the world, surrounds himself with admirers and sycophants who satisfy his compulsion to be adored. In creating Patterne, Meredith has taken the next logical step from his production of Beauchamp. Patterne does not merely aspire to goodness and excellence; he actually believes himself to be the embodiment of these qualities.

Patterne attempts to satisfy his ego chiefly by involving himself with three women whom he manipulates with promises of marriage. His first "pretender," Constance Durham, sees through Patterne's facade of greatness with some degree of alacrity and leaves him. The lovely Clara Middleton, however, is not so insightful. She experiences a great deal of emotional turmoil, first in ascertaining the truth of Patterne's pose and then in distinguishing the light of "her sun" from that of Patterne's less self-assured cousin, Vernon Whitford, "a Phoebus Apollo turned Fasting Friar."

Here, Meredith gives more attention to extravagances so that he may better reveal the necessity for the corrective influence of his Comic Spirit. Sir Willoughby Patterne burns; he does not merely reflect. His fire is the product of his own egotism, which burns with an outer brilliance but promises no inner flame. Meredith may well be recalling satirically the Western world's traditional misconception of the importance of fire to the Zoroastrians, who do not worship fire for itself but only as a symbol of the light of the inner spirit.

The character of Vernon presents a striking contrast to that of Patterne. His light is the light of Apollo, who is not only the Greek god of poetry but is also the classical god of the sun. Meredith has fused classical allusion with the Zoroastrian importance placed upon fire. Vernon's flame is one of inner strength, for he burns with the light of poetic truth as well as with physical fire. He is also a Fasting Friar, however, a characteristic which raises doubt about the nature of his fire, since Meredith was not an ascetic. In effect, he has achieved in the characterization of Vernon the moderation that Dr. Shrapnel's explosive goals denied him, since Vernon's flame is tempered with some degree of asceticism. Vernon has measured life for what it is, but he has not given up the light of hope for what life can become. Meredith has achieved in his image of the contrast of the two fires the blending of Zoroastrian, classical, and Christian elements.

Laetitia Dale, the third of Patterne's "adorers," presents an interesting foil to Patterne's character. At the beginning of the novel, she is described as a delicate, misled woman, a "soft cherishable Parsee." The Zoroastrian connection is obvious: the Parsees are a modern sect of the Zoroastrians. Indeed, within Meredith's comic framework, Laetitia worships "her sun" much as the Parsees were reputed to worship a "god of fire."

Laetitia gradually becomes a strong, practical Parsee, however, as she, like the other two women in Patterne's egotistic design, begins to see that the source of Patterne's fire is not from within. Patterne is left in the end with Laetitia and is forced to accept her on her own terms. No reader of *The Egoist* can claim its conclusion as romantic or condemn it as pessimistic; rather, Meredith has achieved a noble expression of the corrective power of his Comic Spirit.

Meredith creates in *Diana of the Crossways* a character who faces decisions similar to those of the women in *The Egoist*. Even Diana's superior wit and intellect do not prevent her from battling the forces of darkness. Meredith prepares the reader for Diana's struggle in the introductory chapter of the novel. He develops a light image, "rose pink," which "is rebuked by hideous revelations of filthy foul," a likeness of darkness. Meredith opens this novel with a discussion of the same subject he had treated in his other novels. For man to think himself already a part of the celestial light at his present step on the evolutionary ladder is surreptitious folly. The future holds for him only "hideous revelations of filthy foul." The narrator further asserts that it is not within the capacity of man to suppress completely the evil forces of darkness. The duality of good and evil inevitably creeps into life.

Having established an atmosphere of foreboding, the narrator sets out to explore Diana's mental processes. Diana quickly becomes disillusioned by a mismatched marriage. Her husband, Warwick, is a man of limited intelligence. As a consequence, Diana becomes drawn to ideas outside the rigid, Victorian system of mores. Her desires strongly urge her to take leave of her witless, insensitive husband, who has accused her of infidelity. She experiences a night of conflict in which she fights like "the Diana of the pride in her power of fencing with evil."

Meredith's presentation of the strife between good and evil by his mixing of classical mythology with overtones of the Zoroastrian duality creates a sense of the universal nature of Diana's struggle. Diana must decide whether to remain loyal to her marriage vows or to strike out on her own and obey her inner compulsions. She finds the impetus for her escape in Dacier, a character who is associated with devil imagery. Indeed, Dacier is the embodiment of Meredith's assertion that there is "an active Devil about the world."

Dacier is a lure to Diana in her desire to escape. His devilish character, however, is ironically exposed by his sanctimonious friend, Sir Lukin. Lukin declares that no man should be fooled by masks of goodness which seem to cover the bad in the world. Dacier, who presents every indication of virtuous conduct, is compared to the old Jewish Prince of Devils, Asmodeus, who spurs on appetite and uproarious activities of all sorts. Although the name Asmodeus appears in the Apocrypha, it also bears connotations to *Eshina-Dewa*, a wicked spirit of ancient Persian mythology. This is one of Meredith's clearest fusions of Zoroastrianism with Christianity.

Dacier is thwarted in his evil intentions to seduce Diana. An acceptable guide appears for Diana in Thomas Redworth, a character capable of controlling Diana's energetic impulses. Dacier does obtain a prize, however, in the lovely but naïve Constance Asper. Constance is "all for symbols, harps, effigies, what not" and believes that brains in women are "devilish." Constance is perhaps the ideal mate for *The Egoist*'s Sir Willoughby Patterne, and she presents no problems for Dacier's devious motivations. Constance, along with Dr. Shrapnel and Patterne, has failed to see the smoke for the fire. All three are so enamored of the physical brilliance of the flames that they cannot see the subtle glow of spiritual truth within the heart of the blaze.

In *Diana of the Crossways*, Meredith suggests that the endurance of life is perhaps more replete with task than with play. The individual is forced to make a distinction between good and bad, which life seldom presents in a clear-cut fashion. Constance and Dacier somewhat ironically indulge each other in their ostensibly opposing forces. The subtle comment of the Comic Spirit is that both approach life with attitudes of excess; hence, both have lost contact with the steady movement toward self-improvement. Diana and Redworth offer hope to the reader, however, because they have accepted the moderation that the Comic Spirit has taught them and that is necessary for the future success of the human spirit.

These novels present Meredith's concern with the inevitability of "The Magian Conflict" in the life of each man. They also present Meredith's keen observation that this conflict is never one from which one emerges successfully with ease. The struggle makes man's attempt to choose an acceptable path— a way which is acceptable both to him and to his society—extremely difficult. The conflict is presented in terms of Zoroastrian, Christian, and classical myth; Meredith borrows from each in order to make his presentation of this undeniable, unavoidable battle assume universal dimensions. Meredith's Comic Spirit attempts to aid man in his struggle, but it is not always successful in exposing man's shortcomings, excesses, and his refusal to see himself in a true light. In the fullest meaning of Meredith's doctrine, however, the individual is also instrumental in the greater, universal struggle of mankind to move up the evolutionary ladder.

Meredith demonstrates in his attitude toward man and nature the belief that man can achieve his evolutionary destiny by conforming to the lessons and demands of nature. His philosophy is universal in scope and implies a comprehensive fusion of nearly all the ethical ideals which man has gathered from the beginning of time. Although Meredith does not discard all the dogma or the moral ideals of the many religious philosophies he studied, he does select with careful scrutiny those elements which he feels contribute to his own doctrines. Indeed, he demonstrates that he is vitally affected by all the religious thought known to him.

John C. Shields

Other major works
SHORT FICTION: *The Case of General Ople and Lady Camper*, 1890; *The Tale of Chloe*, 1890.

POETRY: *Poems*, 1851; *Modern Love and Poems of the English Roadside*, 1862; *Poems and Lyrics of the Joy of Earth,* 1883; *Ballads and Poems of Tragic Life*, 1887; *A Reading of Earth*, 1888; *Selected Poems*, 1897; *A Reading of Life, with Other Poems*, 1901; *Last Poems*, 1909; *The Poems of George Meredith*, 1978 (Phyllis B. Bartlett, editor, 2 volumes).

NONFICTION: *On the Idea of Comedy and the Uses of the Comic Spirit*, 1877; *The Letters of George Meredith*, 1970 (C. L. Cline, editor, 3 volumes).

Bibliography
Beer, Gillian. *Meredith: A Change of Masks*. London: Athlone Press, 1970. Attempts one of the first modern appraisals of Meredith's art, seeing him as a novelist anticipating twentieth century concerns and techniques, as well as questioning Victorian certitudes. Includes an index.

Pritchett, V. S. *George Meredith and English Comedy*. Toronto: Clarke, Irwin, 1970. A very readable introductory account of Meredith, constituting the five Clark lectures for 1969.

Shaheen, Mohammad. *George Meredith: A Re-appraisal of the Novels*. Totowa, N.J.: Barnes & Noble Books, 1981. Suggests that traditional Meredith criticism has viewed his fiction too much in the light of *The Egoist*. Concentrates on Meredith's other major works as more representative of his true independent mind and specifically explores how character expresses theme for Meredith. Contains selected bibliography.

Stevenson, Lionel. *The Ordeal of George Meredith*. London: Peter Owen, 1954. A straightforward, readable biography of Meredith. Includes a bibliography.

Williams, Ioan, ed. *Meredith: The Critical Heritage*. London: Routledge & Kegan Paul, 1971. A collection of reviews and essays showing the critical reception of Meredith's work from 1851 through 1911. Contains indexes of his work, periodicals, and newspapers.

JAMES A. MICHENER

Born: New York, New York?; February 3, 1907?

Principal long fiction

Tales of the South Pacific, 1947; *The Fires of Spring*, 1949; *The Bridges at Toko-Ri*, 1953; *Sayonara*, 1954; *The Bridge at Andau*, 1954; *Hawaii*, 1959; *Caravans*, 1963; *The Source*, 1965; *The Drifters*, 1971; *Centennial*, 1974; *Chesapeake*, 1978; *The Covenant*, 1980; *Space*, 1982; *Poland*, 1983; *Texas*, 1985; *Legacy*, 1987; *Alaska*, 1988; *Journey*, 1988; *Caribbean*, 1989; *The Novel*, 1991.

Other literary forms

Although James A. Michener considers himself primarily a novelist, he is also an accomplished short-story writer, essayist, art historian, and editor. Major themes in his nonfiction are travel and American politics. *The Voice of Asia* (1951) is in the same tradition, although it includes no fiction at all. *The Floating World* (1954) is a philosophical essay on Japanese art, a theme he treats in four other works, most notably in *Japanese Prints from the Early Masters to the Modern* (1959).

Achievements

In the early 1950's, Michener was heralded as the new voice in American fiction. Still basking in the considerable praise that followed his first book, *Tales of the South Pacific*, and the Pulitzer Prize that accompanied it, he shared the reflected glow of Richard Rodgers and Oscar Hammerstein's musical adaptation, *South Pacific* (1949). Although critics objected to the romantic cast of his early novels, they also found much to praise. Critical reaction to his later novels has also been mixed: While some consider them brilliant for their sweeping panoramic scope, others have condemned the novels for their mass of information, undeveloped characters, and lack of depth. Despite the doubts of literary critics as to the merits of Michener's novels, an eager public has responded to them enthusiastically.

In addition to the Pulitzer Prize, Michener's writing has earned for him a number of honorary degrees and awards, including the appointment to several government committees. His work on two of these committees—the Centennial Commission and the National Aeronautics and Space Administration (NASA) Advisory Council—contributed to research for his fiction.

Biography

Although standard references state that James Albert Michener was born on February 3, 1907, in New York City to Edwin and Mabel Michener, the facts of his birth are unknown; he was a foundling whom Mabel Michener reared from birth, moving at times to the county poorhouse to help the family through poverty and illness. On a scholarship, he attended Swarthmore College, from which he was graduated summa cum laude in 1929. For ten years, he taught at a variety of schools and universities, including the School of Education at Harvard, and in the early 1940's he became an editor at Macmillan. Although as a practicing member of the Society of Friends (Quakers) he might have been exempted from combat, in 1942 he volunteered for active duty in the United States Navy and was sent to the Pacific. Royalties and a small percentage of ownership in the musical *South Pacific*, which opened in April, 1949, assured him financial freedom to travel and write. Michener thus became an independent writer and scholar, publishing more than forty books, and an even greater number of articles, from his home base in Bucks County, Pennsylvania.

Overcoming serious heart problems in the 1980's, Michener has remained active in his ninth decade, writing and traveling. In addition, he has been generous in support of literature and the arts, endowing a fellowship for young writers and contributing in many other ways to the benefit of individual artists and arts institutions.

Analysis

In almost all of James A. Michener's novels, the story line is a loosely woven thread, a framework, a context in which to tell tales and provide geographic and historic detail. Although in his notes on *Centennial* Michener explains four different narrative devices he developed in the course of his writing career, each is still a framing device for a series of related events or information. Throughout all of his work Michener is the social science editor and teacher, using quantities of well-researched data and imaginative incidents to explain issues from his particular point of view. While each of his novels has a historical basis that covers hundreds or thousands of years, each is rooted in its own time as well.

Much of Michener's writing, both fiction and nonfiction, is journalistic in style, but his staccato rhythms are interrupted from time to time by florid descriptions and precise diversions, such as recipes and statistical contrasts. All of his writing is permeated by an unmistakable creed that affirms human values and a deep concern for America. The harsh facts of his early life shaped Michener's career, and his writing is that of a grateful man driven to repay society for the chances he was given in life. There is more to his writing, however, than a need to express gratitude: his broad panoramas are peopled with Dickensian characters from every part of society, although his sympathies remain with the sad and the unfortunate—even rogues such as Oliver Wendell in *Centennial* and Jake Turlock in *Chesapeake*—who can get by on their wits. Underscoring all of Michener's work is a strong statement of human courage and human tolerance, coupled with a driving concern for man's relationship with his environment. Many of his novels focus on racial discrimination of some kind, and each teaches the value of hard work and the necessity for change. As in his nonfiction, Michener does not hesitate to portray society's weaknesses. While critics have frequently panned both his style and the values it embodies, particularly in his later work, these same late novels have consistently been best-sellers.

Ironically, *Tales of the South Pacific* was not a best-seller, even though of all Michener's works it is perhaps the most familiar. Although it continues to sell as many copies today as when it was originally published and has won the Pulitzer Prize, the book was first printed on the cheapest paper with the poorest binding available—so little did the publisher think of its chances— and new chapters did not even begin at the tops of new pages. Even after its award, the novel would have continued to die a slow death were it not for the musical comedy based on it. Few successful writers have had a less auspicious beginning.

Tales of the South Pacific is a framing story that sets up many of Michener's themes; with it the author began a literary romance with the Pacific islands that would last for more than fifteen years and characterize much of his work. In this work, nineteen related episodes tell the story of America's commitment to the Pacific theater during World War II. The treatment of character as well as setting is significant to the body of Michener's work. No one character can be called the protagonist, although Tony Fry (a navy lieutenant) and the narrator are most central to the plot. By not having a protagonist, Michener implies that this is not the story of one man but rather the shared experience of all those who were in the Pacific during the war years. The narrator makes no moral judgments: Men and women are presented at their finest and their weakest moments; some die in war, but life somehow goes on.

With the exception of *The Fires of Spring*, a semiautobiographical novel that develops much of Michener's personal life through 1929, both the fiction and nonfiction which followed *Tales of the South Pacific* are steeped in Pacific history and his own war experience. All are connected as part of a cumulative statement; *Return to Paradise* (1951), for example, with its alternating essays and stories, begins with the description of islands emerging from the sea, the same technique Michener employs in the first of his "blockbuster" novels, *Hawaii*. Of these early works, *The Bridges at Toko-Ri* is particularly significant. The novel exemplifies Michener's typical blend of fact and fiction, as he exposes his reader to the Asian world and the Korean War experience. With the publication of the novel, the author observed that it was the "purest writing" he had done so far.

Although *The Bridges at Toko-Ri* is a short novel and neatly divided into sections—"Sea," "Land," and "Sky"—in it, Michener provides his strongest development of character. The protagonist is Harry Brubaker, a twenty-nine-year-old veteran of World War II and promising Denver lawyer, who resents fighting in Korea. In the first section, Brubaker is rescued from the frozen sea by another three-dimensional character, Mike Forney, a cocky Irishman from Chicago. Michener included an expanded version of both these characters in his later novel *Space*. The "Land" interlude takes place in Japan, a liberty stop, where Brubaker must rescue Forney and his friend from jail before he can visit with his family, who has come to see him there. In a human brotherhood scene typical of Michener, the Brubakers meet a Japanese family in a private pool at their hotel; paddling naked, the families intermingle and converse, resolving any conflict left over from the days before. At this point, the major conflict of the novel begins, however, as the carrier crew starts to plan its assault on four bridges across the canyon of the enemy center at Toko-Ri. Connected to the questions about the attack are more rhetorical ones, addressed to the reader: Will the flyers knock out the bridges? Will this make the Communists stop the war? Have Americans lost the strength to make this sacrifice? Where will America's last stand against the Communists come—in California, or Colorado, on the banks of the Mississippi?

The climax of the novel comes in "Sky," when the heroic Brubaker and Forney destroy the bridges but are killed in the aftermath of the attack. The action reaffirms that America has produced men who will always fly against bridges. The energy of this short section is powerful, deeply rooted in Michener's own naval air experience and the passion of his convictions.

Caravans is a transitional novel for Michener; while the setting is still Asia, it marks a western movement in both action and thought. Precursor to *The Drifters*, *The Source*, and to a lesser extent *Poland*, *Caravans* begins in 1946, in the aftermath of World War II. Here, the journalistic style that marks much of Michener's fiction is handled through a first-person narrator, Mark Miller, a junior-grade State Department officer stationed in Afghanistan. During the opening pages of the novel, Miller is sent on a mission to locate Ellen Jaspar, a high-spirited college girl from Dorset, Pennsylvania, who left Bryn Mawr College to marry an Afghan exchange student named Nazrullah. The plot is a series of adventures laced with romance, even after Ellen is found with a nomad caravan in the desert. The connecting link for the related incidents is the ancient route of the Kochis, whom Miller joins in the hope of convincing Ellen Jaspar to return to her parents. Again, in usual Michener fashion, the plot provides a context within which to describe geographic and historic detail and argue thematic questions.

In his excellent discussion of Michener's major works, George J. Becker points out that for more than twenty years the author was concerned with the "stresses and false values that beset American youth"; Becker applies his insight to *The Drifters*, but it is equally true of *Caravans*. Although the time of the story is 1946, Ellen Jaspar is almost a stereotype of college youth in the early 1960's, when the novel was written, in her dress, ideas, and life-style. For the last third of the book, she and Miller articulate the fiery rhetoric of campuses across America.

The thematic substance of *Caravans* goes further than any of Michener's previous work in its discussion of racial and religious prejudice. The dark-skinned Nazrullah explains his educational experience in Germany and America, infuriating Miller by comparing the American treatment of blacks to the German treatment of Jews. Although the reader's sympathy is with Miller, Nazrullah's point is well made. It is underscored in the climactic moment of the novel, when Miller—a Yale man, perhaps the most civilized member of the cast—announces that he is Jewish and nearly kills Dr. Stiglitz for his wartime Nazi efforts.

The majority of characters in the novel are Muslim, and a few are Christian. Repeatedly, however, the novel turns on a Jewish element, directly anticipating Michener's next major novel, *The Source*. Even Kabul, the Afghan capital, is used to show "what Palestine was like at the time of Jesus."

Chesapeake was the first of Michener's highly popular novels to deal with an indigenously American subject (one might take exception here with *Hawaii*, but that work seems clearly to belong to his earlier preoccupation with the Pacific). As in *Centennial* and later in *Texas*, Michener hoped to chronicle the making of America and to celebrate the courage of those who took part in that achievement. Spanning nearly four hundred years, the novel moves from the first Indians who settled the land to the funeral, in 1978, of one of the Quaker descendants of the earliest white men. In part, it is an instructive, political book, dealing with governments in Great Britain and France as well as the United States, culminating with Pusey Paxmore's suicide over his involvement in the Watergate scandal. For the most part, the focus is narrow—the Eastern Shore of Chesapeake Bay—despite the long roster of historical characters, from John Smith and George Washington to Daniel Webster and Henry Clay.

Here the episodes are organized in a fairly straightforward pattern—allowing for slight digression with a chapter devoted to a family of geese and another to a batch of crabs—and the third-person omniscient point of view does not shift. Four fictional families provide the substance of the book: the Catholic family of Edmund Steed who flees religious persecution in England and joins John Smith in exploring the land in 1607; the family of London thief and indentured servant Timothy Turlock, who arrives a generation later; the Quaker family of Edward Paxmore, who comes in search of religious freedom by way of Barbados and ironically receives the first slaves in the area; and the Caters, a family of former slaves, who build their contribution to the novel from the time just before the Civil War. Although there is great discussion of loyalties, each of the first three families fares well in the

Revolution: Steed is an interpreter for the French, Turlock a sharpshooter, Paxmore a builder of fine ships. The War of 1812 continues the tension that creates the climax of the novel, with the Emancipation Proclamation and the War Between the States. Certain characters are given focus—Rosalind Steed, for example—but Michener does not slow down to develop any of them fully; many are types used to maintain the human element while the narrative sweeps over succeeding generations. This large movement does not, however, mitigate the value of the novel.

From the outset, Michener's emphasis is on human courage and tolerance and man's relationship with his environment. Ample descriptions build a love for the land and for the watermen who work it; later chapters deal with ecological concerns—erosion, litter, and landfill. Early chapters ennoble the Indian and lament his passing. Perhaps the greatest weight throughout is given to the issues of racial and religious freedom. The suffering of both the Steeds and the Paxmores offers compelling insight into the theocracy of Puritan New England and those who came to America seeking religious freedom. In ironic contrast, both the Steeds and the Paxmores own slaves. The final struggle for black freedom comes at the start of the twentieth century, with an amendment to the Maryland constitution intended to disenfranchise blacks. Although the Steed and Turlock clans support it, Emily Paxmore champions the defeat of the bill by arguing that it can be applied equally to all European immigrants after 1869, and the campaign becomes her own personal Armageddon.

Chesapeake is a big novel, and it includes even a recipe for oyster stew; the fragments that fill the end are the unresolved conflicts of modern time— except for an account of the passing of Devon Island. As the scene of much of the action slips into the sea, Michener affirms that it will come again and again until at last the "great world-ocean" reclaims it.

Although his other novels touch on the twentieth century, *Space* is Michener's one piece of fiction that concentrates solely on life in twentieth century America. In it, he chronicles the space program from its inception in 1944 to an ebb in 1982 through a series of incidents that connect neatly to his work before and after it.

The novel begins on October 24, 1944, with scenes that introduce four major characters. The first is Stanley Mott, an American engineer, in London at the request of the American president, whose job it is to see that the German installation at Peenemunde is not bombed before three of the chief scientists can be captured alive. The second is Norman Grant, drawn much like Harry Brubaker, in the climactic naval battle of Leyte Gulf. The third is John Pope, a seventeen-year-old football hero from Grant's hometown of Clay. Finally, there is Dieter Kolff, one of the scientists whom Mott must rescue, who survives the bombing because he is with his girlfriend. The next part of the novel introduces the women who are loved by these men and advances the story through them. Because of the ingenuity of a Nazi officer who later becomes a leader of the American aerospace industry, Dieter Kolff and Leisl come to the United States, shepherded by Mott and his wife, Rachel. Pope gets appointed to Annapolis, on the recommendation of Grant, who has become senator from the state of Fremont; Pope's wife, Penny, earns a law degree and goes to work for Grant when he is appointed to the space committee; Grant's wife, Elinor, preoccupied with little green men, becomes the principal supporter of Leopold Strabismus and the Universal Space Associates.

These characters, and those who flesh out their stories, create the substance of the novel. While Michener's focus is on the space program, these people are among the most fully developed in all of his work. Systematically moving through the various stages of America's efforts in outer space, he keeps the weight of his research in careful balance with the stories of human lives. This is particularly true in the second half of the novel, which centers on six fictional astronauts (Pope among them). While the reader is drawn into the explorations (particularly the Gemini flight, which Pope shares with his likable opposite, Randy Claggett, and their adventures on the dark side of the moon), one's interest is held by the characters at least as much as by the technology. This is particularly true of the capable con man Strabismus.

At first Strabismus seems an unnecessary diversion—similar to the recipes Michener offers for Polish sausage or oyster stew—but as the story builds, he becomes an integral part of the work. Playing off the initials U.S.A., Strabismus moves through a series of lucrative rackets until he sets himself up as a preacher with the United Salvation Alliance. As he panders to the fears of the uneducated, he crusades against "atheistic humanism" and advocates a return to fundamentalism that will prohibit the teaching of evolution and forbid national park rangers from describing the geological history of their areas. He launches impassioned attacks on homosexuals and fosters a virulent anti-Semitism. Michener clarifies his point of view in the final confrontation between Strabismus and the "heroes" of his novel. Finally, Michener suggests, the conflict is part of the long march of history and will continue thousands of years hence.

Two massive novels are representative of Michener's later works: *Poland* and *Texas*. The first is a well-researched chronicle of Polish history that moves backward and forward, connecting the Communist country of modern time to the thirteenth century raids of Genghis Khan through the development of three fictional families. In the acknowledgments, in which the author explains his reasons for choosing this particular subject, he sounds very much as he did three decades before, when clarifying his interest in Asia. In both instances, the geographical and ideological positions of the areas indicate that they will become political focal points. Again, Michener is using his fiction to educate readers of his time, moving through history to explain the present.

Texas is perhaps Michener's largest novel: more than two hundred characters are involved in its story, a number of whom are historical figures, and
dialogue is the primary vehicle through which their story is told. With its
narrative framework and blending of fact and fiction, the novel compares
neatly with many of its predecessors. Despite its scope, however, one would
be hard-pressed to claim that *Texas* is among the finest of Michener's works.

Whatever the critical verdict on Michener the novelist, it is clear that Michener the educator-through-fiction has been a great success. To a popular
audience numbering in the millions, he has communicated the uniquely modern sense of the long view of history, and that is a considerable achievement.

Joan Corey Semonella

Other major works

SHORT FICTION: *Return to Paradise*, 1951.

NONFICTION: *Proposals for an Experimental Future of the Social Sciences:
Proposals for an Experimental Social Studies Curriculum*, 1939 (with Harold
Long); *The Unit in the Social Studies*, 1940; *The Voice of Asia*, 1951; *The
Floating World*, 1954; *Selected Writings*, 1957; *Rascals in Paradise*, 1957
(with A. Grove Day); *Japanese Prints from the Early Masters to the Modern*,
1959; *Report of the County Chairman*, 1961; *The Modern Japanese Print: An
Appreciation*, 1962; *Iberia: Spanish Travels and Reflections*, 1968; *Presiden-
tial Lottery: The Reckless Gamble in Our Electoral System*, 1969; *The Quality of Life*, 1970; *Facing East: The Art of Jack Levine*, 1970; *Kent State: What
Happened and Why*, 1971; *A Michener Miscellany, 1950-1970*, 1973; *About
"Centennial": Some Notes on the Novel*, 1974; *Sports in America*, 1976; *In
Search of Centennial: A Journey*, 1978; *Testimony*, 1983; *Collectors, Forgers,
and a Writer: A Memoir*, 1983; *Pilgrimage: A Memoir of Poland and Rome*,
1990.

ANTHOLOGY: *The Hokusai Sketchbooks: Selections from the Manga*, 1958.

Bibliography

Hayes, John P. *James A. Michener: A Biography*. New York: Bobbs-Merrill,
1984. Hayes conducted more than twenty-five interviews with Michener,
providing rich biographical material for this meticulous work that was ten
years in the making. Covers his prolific writings, from *Tales of the South
Pacific* to *Space*, and praises *Centennial*, even though it was rejected by the
literary community. Most useful for background information and anecdotes
on Michener.

Straub, Deborah A., ed. *Contemporary Authors*. New Revision Series 21.
Detroit: Gale Research, 1987. Chronicles the storytelling talents of Michener, the "master" reporter who has gone on to become a brand name
author of epic proportions, and mentions his major novels. An excellent
source for a variety of extracts of book reviews, many of which grudgingly
give praise to Michener's painstaking research. Includes a bibliography.

HENRY MILLER

Born: New York, New York; December 26, 1891
Died: Pacific Palisades, California; June 7, 1980

Principal long fiction

Tropic of Cancer, 1934; *Black Spring*, 1936; *Tropic of Capricorn*, 1939; *The Rosy Crucifixion* (includes *Sexus*, 1949, 2 volumes, *Plexus*, 1953, 2 volumes, *Nexus*, 1960); *Quiet Days in Clichy*, 1956.

Other literary forms

In an interview, Henry Miller once described himself as one part a writer of tales and one part a man electrified by ideas. This simple dichotomy provides a way to classify Miller's work, but, in truth, his whole canon is autobiographical. The many collections of his shorter pieces—portraits, essays, stories, travel sketches, reviews, letters—are all of value in ascertaining the truth of his life, his admitted literary goal. For example, *The Colossus of Maroussi: Or, The Spirit of Greece* (1941), Miller's first book about Greece, is ostensibly about George Katsimbalis, a leading figure in modern Greek letters. Katsimbalis, however, turns out to be Miller's alter ego, a fascinating monologist, and the book becomes the record of Miller's attaining peace of heart through the elemental beauty of Greece. *The Time of the Assassins: A Study of Rimbaud* (1956) is less about Arthur Rimbaud than about the romantic affinities between Miller's and Rimbaud's lives. In Miller's books, all things become translated into images of his own mental landscape.

Achievements

When Miller repatriated in 1940, only *The Cosmological Eye*, a collection of short pieces drawn from *Max and the White Phagocytes* (1938), had been published in the United States; all of his fiction was deemed too obscene for publication. In France, *Tropic of Cancer* and *Tropic of Capricorn* had been seized in 1946, and Miller was convicted as a pornographer. After an outcry of French writers, this conviction was reversed, but in 1950, *Sexus* was banned in France, and in 1957, it was condemned as obscene in Norway. When *Tropic of Cancer* was finally published in the United States, in 1961, by Barney Rosset of Grove Press, more than sixty suits were instituted against Miller and the book. Miller became the most litigated-against author in history, and the book was only allowed to circulate after a Supreme Court decision in 1965. The furor over his books' alleged obscenity prevented dispassionate evaluation of his literary merit for many years, and Miller feared that he would be dismissed as the "King of Smut." He was, however, inducted into the National Institute of Arts and Letters in 1957, and received a citation from the Formentor Prize Committee, in France, in 1961 and the French

Legion of Honor in 1975.

These memberships and citations, however, do not mark Miller's true achievement. His true quest and calling was to narrow the gap between art and life. That he—or his public persona of Paris expatriate, Big Sur prophet, desperado, clown, artist-hero, satyr—was the focus of critical attention throughout his life, rather than his books, testifies to the measure of success he achieved. Miller wanted to become free, as free as the young boy of the streets he had been in his childhood, in the face of a culture he saw as sterile, mechanical, and death-driven. He also wanted to discover and embody the truth of his life in art, in his "autobiographical romances." His defiant spit in the face of art in his first book *Tropic of Cancer* prompted critics to label his works as "antiliterature." Rather than deprecating literature, however, Miller saw art as a means to life more abundant. He conceived of his work as enlightening, as offering his vision of reality. Often described as a *roman-fleuve* of the life of Henry Miller, his fiction is neither strictly autobiographical nor realistic in method. As an artist, he notes in *The Wisdom of the Heart* (1941), he must give his reader "a vital, singing universe, alive in all its parts"; to accomplish this, he relied on the verbal pyrotechnics of surrealism and the temporal discontinuities of stream of consciousness. The result was a series of works full of contradictions, repetitions, incongruities, and rhetorical flights, all documenting his growth as a man and as an artist.

Biography

Henry Valentine Miller was born on December 26, 1891, in the Yorkville section of New York City. Both of his parents were of German stock: his father, a gentleman's tailor, came from jovial people; his mother and her family typified the austere, industrious, respectable bourgeois life against which Miller was to rebel so vehemently. For the first nine years of his life, the family lived in the Williamsburg section of Brooklyn, the Fourteenth Ward. For Miller, this was a child's paradise. When he was ten, his family moved to Decatur Street, the "Street of Early Sorrows," in Brooklyn's Bushwick section, His teenage experiences there helped form his attitudes on life, literature, and women. Miller was an affable young man; his special friends at this time were members of the Xerxes Society, a musical crowd. Male conviviality would be important to Miller throughout his life.

Miller was a model student, and was graduated as salutatorian from high school, but his formal education ended after a few months at the City College of New York. Always an avid reader—he had read through the Harvard Classics as well as many romantic and adventure tales—Miller became an autodidact. By the time he was twenty, he had devoured such diverse authors as Joseph Conrad, Madame Blavatsky, and François Rabelais, and had decided that he wanted to be a writer—about what, he did not know. Besides frequenting theaters in New York and Brooklyn, Miller was often to be seen at burlesque shows and in brothels. If his mother seemed cold and difficult to please, these women were open for sexual pleasure. Despite these experiences, Miller developed an intense idealism about love and the perfect woman, centering his longing on a school classmate, Cora Seward. At the same time, though, he began in 1910 an affair with a widow, Pauline Chouteau, closer to his mother's age.

In an effort to escape this passionate entanglement, Miller went to California in 1913, winding up miserable as a ranch hand near Chula Vista. Only hearing Emma Goldman in San Diego, extolling anarchism, redeemed the trip. The next year Miller was back in New York, working in his father's tailor shop (described in *Black Spring*) and reading omnivorously. He was attracted to universalizing ideas and grander interpretations of the meaning of life than those of his Brooklyn milieu. During the years 1914-1915, Miller began to practice piano seriously; through this enthusiam, he met Beatrice Sylvas Wickens, whom he married in 1917. Their stormy courtship and marriage is depicted graphically in *The World of Sex* (1940), *Tropic of Capricorn*, and *Sexus*. Drifting through many jobs, Miller found his way to the bottom— Western Union. His experience as a messenger employment manager opened his eyes to the underlying misery in America. His sympathy with these victims, adrift in a dehumanized urban landscape, was responsible for his unpublished first novel, *Clipped Wings*, dedicated to Horatio Alger. Miller's disillusionment with the American dream came at a time when his marriage was also foundering. His response, rather than despair or self-pity, was to begin keeping a journal and extensive files of material for later use. He was beginning to become a writer, establishing an aesthetic distance from life and from himself.

His delivery as a full-fledged artist was through the agency of June Edith Smith, the Mona, Mara, "She," or "Her" of his fiction, his second wife, whom he met at a Broadway dance hall in 1923 and married the next year. June was a creative artist—of herself and her life story—who showed Miller the bridge between life and the imagination. Convinced that he was a great writer, she made him quit his job and devote his life to his work. This metamorphosis is recorded in *Tropic of Capricorn* and *Plexus*. To relieve their desperate poverty, June began peddling a series of brief prose sketches Miller had written called "Mezzotints," signed "June E. Mansfield." Miller might have freed himself from a conventional American life, but June—her schemes, her stories, her lovers, herself—held him completely in thrall. When June eloped with her lover Jean Kronski to Paris in 1927, Miller began to record notes of his obsessional attachment to her. His life with June was to be the book he tried to write throughout his life, culminating in *The Rosy Crucifixion*. His second unpublished novel, *Moloch*, the story of Miller's experiences in the year 1923, was written under unique pressure: one of June's admirers promised her a year in Europe if she completed a book. *Moloch* was their ticket to Paris.

Their trip to Paris in 1928-1929 was unproductive; Miller painted watercolors instead of writing books. Only when he returned alone to Paris in 1930 and ran out of resources did he begin to live and write truly. Living a marginal life, he not only completed his novel about June and Jean, *Crazy Cock*, but also discovered "Henry Miller," the voice and main character of his "autobiographical romances." Alfred Perlès, "Joey," contributed his Bohemian lifestyle and epicureanism to Miller's new persona. The French surrealists gave artistic form to Miller's sense of incongruity. The photographer Brassai helped him see the poetry of the sordid side of Paris. Walter Lowenfels and Michael Fraenkel converted him to the "death school"—although Miller knew that he, for one, remained very much alive. Anaïs Nin became his ministering angel. Her love restored his faith in both himself and womankind. Her own journals confirmed him in the belief that his true subject was himself. Through her, he met the psychoanalyst Otto Rank: Miller's interest in psychology (and Nin) brought him back to New York for a brief period in 1936 to work as an analyst, but more important, it helped him understand his past and himself, which were to become the central concerns of his life. He kept a "dreambook" in this period, some of which reappears in his fiction. *Tropic of Cancer* and *Quiet Days in Clichy* draw on Miller's first two years in France. By 1936, Miller's apartment in Villa Seurat had become the center of an industrious artistic circle, which was joined in 1937 by Lawrence Durrell, Miller's first disciple. Far from Wambly Bald's Paris *Tribune* picture of the Great American Hobo Artist, Miller in his Paris years worked with Germanic regularity and thoroughness on his fiction and essays.

By 1939, Miller was able to finish *Tropic of Capricorn*. With its completion, Miller's furious literary activity abated. He began to lose interest in the narrative of his life and became engrossed in spiritual literature—astrology, Zen, Theosophy, Krishnamurti, the I Ching. When he left Paris in 1939, at the advent of World War II, to visit Durrell in Corfu, Greece, the stage was set for his third metamorphosis. He records in *The Colossus of Maroussi* that in Greece he discovered a new goal in life: not to be a writer, but simply to be. Images of simplicity—the land, sea, and silences of Greece—awakened in Miller, the city man, a response to the allure of nature.

Back in America in 1940, Miller continued his autobiographical saga, but his only major fictional endeavor in the next forty years was to be *The Rosy Crucifixion*, written between 1942 and 1959, in which he tried to capture the elusive truth of his relationship with June. Most of his writing during this period was nonfiction. On an advance from Doubleday, Miller and the painter Abraham Rattner went on a tour of the United States from 1940 to 1941. The resulting book, *The Air-Conditioned Nightmare*, turned out to be a jeremiad rather than a travelogue.

In 1942, Miller moved to California, settling into a cabin at Big Sur in 1944.

There, amid its natural splendor, he found his Walden. Miller was again the center of a circle of painters and writers, a group which came to national attention through a 1947 *Harper's Magazine* article, "Sex and Anarchy in Big Sur." Life, however, was not an orgy for Miller. He still remained in poverty, supporting himself by selling his watercolors and begging from his friends. In 1944, he married his third wife, Janina M. Lepska, who attempted to introduce domestic order into his life, but by 1948, she had left him. She and Conrad Moricand, an astrologer friend from his Paris days, were castigated as "devils" in his account of his life at Big Sur, *Big Sur and the Oranges of Hieronymous Bosch* (1957). In 1953, he married Eve McClure; their marriage was dissolved in 1962. In 1967, he married Hiroko "Hoki" Tokuda, a twenty-nine-year-old cabaret singer from Tokyo; that marriage ended in divorce in 1978. His later travails in love are described in *Insomnia: Or, The Devil at Large* (1971). Indeed, his later works seem to have been written to cleanse himself of the demons which possessed him. He finally came to terms with his mother, long dead, in *Mother, China, and the World Beyond* (1977), just a few years before his own death. His final days were spent in Pacific Palisades, California. The acclaimed father of the sexual revolution of the 1960's died on June 7, 1980. He was eighty-eight years old.

Analysis

Henry Miller's books, in their frank sexual description, pushed back the last frontier of American literary realism. Sex was, for Miller, a means by which to study the cosmos: he noted in *The World of Sex* that "to enter life by way of the vagina is as good a way as any. If you enter deep enough, remain long enough, you will find what you seek. But you've got to enter with your heart and soul—and check your belongings outside." Whatever he sought, women became his connection to the universal. Although women are often depicted as sexual objects in his fiction, sex, he insisted, is "an elemental force. It's just as mysterious and magical as talking about God or the nature of the universe." The way in which Miller used obscenity against the bourgeoisie is telling: that sex was considered "dirty" reflected the puritanical nature of the culture he was attacking.

Because of his use of the obscene, the world of Miller's books is often repulsive and degrading, filled with grotesque characters living on the margin of society. The harsh reality of life must be accepted, he felt, before it could be transcended. In *My Life and Times* (1973), he explained, "The only way you can prove you are not of it is by entering into it fully. . . . When you fully accept something, you are no longer victimized by it." Savoring the dregs of civilization, Miller castigated its pretensions with anarchic glee. Indeed, Miller's value lies not in a depiction of some salvific vision (reality always remains a bit hazy in his fiction), but in his searing indictment of the modern world's impoverishment of "soul life." Miller shared D. H. Lawrence's horror of the mechanical modern world and endorsed Lawrence's response—the instinctual life—yet for all his apocalyptic prophecies, Miller was no Lawrentian messiah. Indeed, the "Henry Miller" of the novels is a *flâneur*, an American picaro.

Ernest Hemingway's *The Sun Also Rises* (1926), Miller admitted in an interview at age eighty-four, was the impetus for his journey to Paris, the artists' mecca. What Miller found there in the 1930's forms the basis of his first and best novel, *Tropic of Cancer*: Paris provided both the impetus and the substance of his disjointed narrative. Paris, Miller writes, is like a whore, "ravishing" from a distance, but "five minutes later you feel empty, disgusted with yourself. You feel tricked." Whores—Germaine, Claude, Llona, and others—and their hangouts dominate Miller's Paris, suggesting the debunking of romantic ideals which was necessary for Miller before he could write. This is apparent in the evolving nature of his relationship to his wife Mona in the book. It begins with his anticipation of their reunion, which proves blissful but short-lived. Although he claims that "for seven years I went about, day and night, with only one thing in my mind—*her*," after she returns to America, her image—like all the rest of his old life—"seems to have fallen into the sea" until he can only wonder "in a vague way" at the novel's conclusion whatever happened to her. Paris has replaced her as the center of his attention, and Paris makes far fewer demands on his inner self. Like his superficial relationships with whores, his stay in Paris is a fruitful form of self-destruction out of which a new self emerges.

The predominant metaphor in *Tropic of Cancer* is that of the river, of all that flows, in contrast to the stultifying conceptions and conventions of modern civilization. Early in the book, the sight of the Seine, and the great unconscious life that it represents, is inspirational. He later learns to see the world without "boundaries" or preconceived notions and recognizes it "for the mad slaughterhouse it is." His two trips outside Paris demonstrate his acclimatization and the death of his illusions. Returning from Le Havre, he recognizes Paris' essential attraction for him, and he demonstrates in his outwitting of a whore his adjustment to the scene. Returning from Dijon, that bastion of medievalism which reminds him of the North (a bad place in Miller's geography, redolent of the coldness and sterility of his German ancestors), where everybody is constipated and even the toilet pipes freeze, he recognizes his previous dependency upon women, "a fear of living separate, of staying born." This realization enables him to free Fillmore from the clutches of the rapacious Ginette and himself from Mona. The climax of the episode, and of the book as well, takes him again to the River Seine. He has already announced his love for everything that flows—"rivers, sewers, lava, semen, blood, bile, words, sentences"—and in this climax, he surrenders himself with religious intensity to the flux of time and space: "I feel this river flowing through me—its past, its ancient soul, the changing climate."

While a parade of other displaced persons in Paris passes through the book, they are all, like Moldorf, a "sieve through which my anarchy strains, resolves itself into words." Unlike the Jews Boris and Moldorf, the reborn Miller enjoys his suffering, because it confirms his sense of this world as a "putrid sink." Van Norden exists as a foil to Miller, both in relation to women and to himself. Van Norden is a neurotic egotist who uses women to try to forget himself, personifying the lovelessness of the modern world where passion is removed from sex. As he watches Van Norden and his fifteen-franc whore grinding away, Miller compares him to a runaway machine or a maimed war hero: the human reality that gives meaning to the act is missing. Fillmore is another foil to Miller; like the typical American expatriate, he has come to France for wine, women, and song. Miller helps him escape Ginette and a marriage into the French bourgeoisie, and he returns to America disillusioned. Miller stays behind, his illusions gone, replaced by an appetite for life. The women characters of the book are negligible—with Mona's disappearance from his world, the woman has been replaced by her Pudendum.

Tropic of Cancer is Miller's gleeful song over the corpse of the twentieth century: "I will sing while you croak." The comedy, sexual and otherwise, is at the expense of everyone, himself included. The novel played a decisive role in Miller's career: in it, he found the distinctive voice which he never thereafter abandoned. In it Miller describes the realization of the insufficiency of all ideas and the justification for the abandonment of conventional beliefs: "I am only spiritually dead. Physically I am alive. Morally I am free. . . . The dawn is breaking on a new world." The book ends on this note of openness to a better life.

Tropic of Capricorn is Miller's *Künstlerroman*, depicting his own development as an artist. It records his struggle to achieve detachment from America and from his past life and become an angel, "pure and inhuman," in possession of his spiritual core. It is written from the perspective of one who has awakened from the "nightmare" of history, an achievement at first inspired by his friend Ulric and by the works of D. H. Lawrence and Fyodor Dostoevski, and later catalyzed by "Her," Mara.

The book opens "On the Ovarian Trolly," when the persona of Miller is still unclear, mired in the chaos of his surroundings. America is a "cesspool of the spirit," and its statistical wealth and happiness is a sham: everywhere, there is testimony to man's inhumanity to man. This inferno is revealed to him through his job as employment manager at a branch of the Cosmodemonic (or Cosmococcic) Telegraphic Company of North America. His own persona might still be gestating, but those of the messengers, Carnahan, Guptal, Dave Olinski, Clausen, Schuldig—with clipped wings all—are surely in focus. Their stories, as well as those of Miller's "merry crew," reveal the underside of America and constitute Miller's anti-Horatio Alger story. Determined to escape being a "failure or ridiculous," Miller sees art as a way out.

At the beginning of the second part, Miller's friend Kronski advises him that good writers must first really suffer. Miller scoffs at this "Jewish" advice, preferring the "terrific animal sense of adjustment" of his German milieu, but the experience with Mara that is to come—in this book only intimated surrealistically—will leave him a marked man. For the moment, eating is all, and his reminiscences of good food take him back to his "wonderful past" when his Aunt Caroline gave him a thick slice of sour rye bread. The bread, through the lenses of Miller's nostalgia, becomes transformed into the "communion loaf." Adulthood can only be a diminished realm: "The taste goes out of bread as it goes out of life. Getting the bread becomes more important than the eating of it."

The next section of the book, "An Interlude," depicts the "general sexual confusion" in "the Land of Fuck." It is clear that, in some sense, sex is the agent for Miller's regeneration—at least it provides him with an escape from the workaday world that is death-in-life. The Land of Fuck is ultimately disappointing to Miller, however, and his thinking "via the penis" leads absolutely nowhere. It only helps him to establish his first mask—that of Capricorn or the Goat—to deal with his life: "In this strange Capricornian condition of embryosis God the he-goat ruminates in stolid bliss among the mountain peaks." Moreover, sex puts Miller in touch with natural vitality.

The Land of Fuck is merely an interlude. What Miller really wants is love, the "Real Thing." From a wistful description of Una, his first love, Miller proceeds to the Amarillo Dance Hall: his encounter there with Mara is volcanic. Henceforth, he will be "Gottlieb Leberecht Müller," a man who has lost his identity. Mara, a fabulous creature whose life is a web of illusion, resembles a figure of mythology, a Juno or a Circe, or an archetype, a Terrible Mother.

Together with Mara in their Black Hole of Calcutta, Miller hibernates, "a blazing seed hidden in the heart of death." She is fascinating but terrible— "a dead black sun without aspect," a "great plunder-bird." In the coda, reflecting on this book as "a tomb in which to bury her—and the me which had belonged to her," Miller makes another attempt to explain how she became the Beatrice who led him to the Paradise of the imagination. The language he uses reveals that she might actually represent his unconscious life, the life whose very existence America denied. United with Mara, "the inner and the outer ego are in equilibrium. . . . Henceforth I take on two sexes. . . . I shall seek the end in myself."

As an artist, Miller achieves personal harmony and, more important, power. He feels a kinship with Knut Hamsun's Herr Nagel, the artist as unacknowledged saint, driven to art "because the world refuses to recognize his proper leadership." Like Abelard, like Christ, Miller sees his life as instructive, an object lesson in self-fulfillment: "All my Calvaries were rosy crucifixions, pseudo-tragedies to keep the fires of hell burning brightly for the real sinners who are in danger of being forgotten."

The value of Miller's work transcends the expression of his personality, however vital and unique that was. In the "Defense of the Freedom to Read" (1957), Miller notes, "Whatever I may say about my own life which is only a life, is merely a means of talking about life itself." Like Walt Whitman, Miller extended the literary terrain of American literature, democratizing it as well. Besides his direct influence on Lawrence Durrell and the Beat generation of the 1950's—Jack Kerouac, Allen Ginsberg, Lawrence Ferlinghetti, and Gregory Corso—Miller's influence can be detected in much postwar American fiction, with its blending of colloquial, surreal, obscene, fantastic, and desperate rhetoric. Miller's confessions provided a voice for the alienated individual who, against all odds, remains sure of his own humanity.

Honora Rankine Galloway

Other major works

PLAY: *Just Wild About Harry: A Melo-Melo in 7 Scenes*, 1963.

NONFICTION: *Aller Retour New York*, 1935; *What Are You Going to Do About Alf?*, 1935; *Max and the White Phagocytes*, 1938; *Money and How It Gets That Way*, 1938; *The Cosmological Eye*, 1939; *Hamlet*, 1939, 1941 (with Michael Fraenkel, 2 volumes); *The World of Sex*, 1940, 1957; *The Colossus of Maroussi: Or, The Spirit of Greece*, 1941; *The Wisdom of the Heart*, 1941; *The Angel Is My Watermark*, 1944 (originally published in *Black Spring*); *Murder the Murderer*, 1944; *The Plight of the Creative Artist in the United States of America*, 1944; *Semblance of a Devoted Past*, 1944; *The Air-Conditioned Nightmare*, 1945; *The Amazing and Invariable Beauford Delaney*, 1945; *Echolalia: Reproductions of Water Colors by Henry Miller*, 1945; *Henry Miller Miscellanea*, 1945; *Obscenity and the Law of Reflection*, 1945; *Why Abstract?*, 1945 (with Hilaire Hiler and William Saroyan); *Maurizius Forever*, 1946; *Patchen: Man of Anger and Light, with a Letter to God by Kenneth Patchen*, 1946; *Of, by and About Henry Miller: A Collection of Pieces by Miller, Herbert Read, and Others*, 1947; *Portrait of General Grant*, 1947; *Remember to Remember*, 1947; *Varda: The Master Builder*, 1947; *The Smile at the Foot of the Ladder*, 1948; *The Waters Reglitterized*, 1950; *The Books in My Life*, 1952; *Nights of Love and Laughter*, 1955 (Kenneth Rexroth, editor); *Argument About Astrology*, 1956; *A Devil in Paradise: The Story of Conrad Mourand, Born Paris, 7 or 7:15 p.m., January 17, 1887, Died Paris, 10:30 p.m., August 31, 1954*, 1956; *The Time of the Assassins: A Story of Rimbaud*, 1956; *Big Sur and the Oranges of Hieronymus Bosch*, 1957; *The Red Notebook*, 1958; *The Intimate Henry Miller*, 1959 (Lawrence Clark Powell, editor); *The Henry Miller Reader*, 1959 (Lawrence Durrell, editor); *Reunion in Barcelona: A Letter to Alfred Perlès*, 1959; *To Paint Is to Love Again*, 1960; *The Michael Fraenkel-Henry Miller Correspondence, Called*

Hamlet, 1962 (2 volumes); *Stand Still Like the Hummingbird*, 1962; *Watercolors, Drawings and His Essay "The Angel Is My Watermark,"* 1962; *Books Tangent to Circle: Reviews*, 1963; *Lawrence Durrell and Henry Miller: A Private Correspondence*, 1963 (George Wickes, editor); *Greece*, 1964; *Henry Miller on Writing*, 1964 (Thomas H. Moore, editor); *Letters to Anaïs Nin*, 1965; *Selected Prose*, 1965 (2 volumes); *Order and Chaos chez Hans Reichel*, 1966; *Writer and Critic: A Correspondence*, 1968 (with W. A. Gordon); *Collector's Quest: The Correspondence of Henry Miller and J. Rivers Childs, 1947-1965*, 1968; *Insomnia: Or, The Devil at Large*, 1970; *My Life and Times*, 1971 (Bradley Smith, editor); *Henry Miller in Conversation with Georges Belmont*, 1972; *Journey to an Unknown Land*, 1972; *On Turning Eighty*, 1972; *Reflections on the Death of Mishima*, 1972; *First Impressions of Greece*, 1973; *Reflections on the Maurizius Case*, 1974; *Letters of Henry Miller and Wallace Fowlie (1943-1972)*, 1975; *The Nightmare Notebook*, 1975; *Books of Friends: A Tribute to Friends of Long Ago*, 1976; *Four Visions of America*, 1977 (with others); *Gliding into the Everglades and Other Essays*, 1977; *Sextet*, 1977; *Henry Miller: Years of Trial and Triumph*, 1978; *My Bike and Other Friends*, 1978; *An Open Letter to Stoker!*, 1978 (Irving Stetner, editor); *Some Friends*, 1978; *Joey: A Loving Portrait of Alfred Perlès Together with Some Bizarre Episodes Relating to the Other Sex*, 1979; *Notes on "Aaron's Rod" and Other Notes on Lawrence from the Paris Notebooks of Henry Miller*, 1980 (Seamus Cooney, editor); *The World of Lawrence: A Passionate Appreciation*, 1980 (Evelyn J. Hinz and John J. Teumissen, editors); *Reflections*, 1981; *The Paintings of Henry Miller*, 1982; *From Your Capricorn Friend; Henry Miller and the "Stroker," 1978-80*, 1984; *Dear, Dear Brenda*, 1986; *Letters by Henry Miller to Hoki Tokuda Miller*, 1986; *A Literate Passion: Letters of Anaïs Nin and Henry Miller*, 1987; *The Durrell-Miller Letters, 1935-80*, 1988; *Hamlet Letters*, 1988.

Bibliography

Brown, J. D. *Henry Miller.* New York: Frederick Ungar, 1986. A concise assessment of Miller's work in relation to the events of his life, with a particularly good summary chapter entitled "Autobiography in America." Brown writes with clarity and knows the material well. Includes a chronology of the events of Miller's life, a bibliography of his writing through 1980, and useful sections listing interviews, bibliographical collections, biographies, and selected criticism.

Hassan, Ihab. *The Literature of Silence: Henry Miller and Samuel Beckett.* New York: Alfred A. Knopf, 1967. Although there is no real connection between the material on Miller and the material on Samuel Beckett, the explanations of Miller's main themes in terms of early postmodern thinking are very provocative and illuminating. Even when Hassan's thesis does not entirely apply, he has many perceptive observations to make, especially about some of Miller's subsidiary books of essays.

Lewis, Leon. *Henry Miller: The Major Writings*. New York: Schocken Books/ Random House, 1986. Concentrates on the seven books regarded as the heart of Miller's achievement as a writer, offering detailed critical analysis of each book as well as a comprehensive estimate of Miller's entire life as an artist. Relates Miller to the American writers he admired and to Albert Camus and the surrealists of the 1920's to locate him within literary and cultural traditions. Includes a bibliography and related criticism.

Mathieu, Bertrand. *Orpheus in Brooklyn: Orphism, Rimbaud, and Henry Miller*. Paris: Mouton, 1976. Mathieu is an expert on the work of Arthur Rimbaud, and his study focuses on the parallels between Miller and the French poet, particularly in regard to Miller's *The Colossus of Maroussi* (1941). Mathieu is very knowledgeable, writes with energy and insight, and offers the useful thesis that Miller's work is constructed on a plan similar to Dante's *The Divine Comedy*.

Mitchel, Edward, ed. *Henry Miller: Three Decades of Criticism*. New York: New York University Press, 1971. A representative compilation which indicates just how much controversy and personal response Miller's work elicited during the first three decades after *Tropic of Cancer* was published. A good companion volume is George Wickes's collection *Henry Miller and the Critics* (Carbondale: Southern Illinois University Press, 1963).

Nelson, Jane. *Form and Image in the Fiction of Henry Miller*. Detroit: Wayne State University Press, 1970. Nelson is extremely well versed in the theories of Carl Jung and Angus Fletcher and uses their ideas to write a detailed analysis of Miller's work. Nelson tends to rely too heavily on psychological jargon and forces some unwieldy material into the thesis, but her ideas are always intelligent and thought-provoking. The analysis of the feminine nature of Miller's writing is interesting in terms of Kate Millett's attack on Miller in *Sexual Politics* (Garden City, N.Y.: Doubleday, 1970).

BRIAN MOORE

Born: Belfast, Northern Ireland; August 25, 1921

Principal long fiction

Judith Hearne, 1955 (published in the United States as *The Lonely Passion of Judith Hearne*); *The Feast of Lupercal*, 1957; *The Luck of Ginger Coffey*, 1960; *An Answer from Limbo*, 1962; *The Emperor of Ice-Cream*, 1965; *I Am Mary Dunne*, 1968; *Fergus*, 1970; *Catholics*, 1972; *The Great Victorian Collection*, 1975; *The Doctor's Wife*, 1976; *The Mangan Inheritance*, 1979; *The Temptation of Eileen Hughes*, 1981; *Cold Heaven*, 1983; *Black Robe*, 1985; *The Color of Blood*, 1987; *Lies of Silence*, 1990.

Other literary forms

In addition to his novels, Brian Moore wrote a travel book, *Canada*, with the editors of *Life* in 1963. A number of his works are regarded by Moore himself as hackwork, written to support his serious fiction; these include romances and mysteries, some under the pseudonym "Michael Bryan." His dozens of short stories have appeared in a wide range of periodicals, from *Weekend Review* to *The Atlantic*, and in anthologies including *The Irish Genius*, edited by Devin A. Garrity (1960), *Canadian Writing Today*, edited by Mordecai Richler (1970), and *The Best American Short Stories, 1967*, edited by Martha Foley and David Burnett (1967). Throughout his writing career, he has published many articles and reviews. Several of Moore's books have been adapted for films and television, and he has written screenplays and teleplays produced in the United States, Canada, and Great Britain.

Achievements

Moore's first novel, published variously as *Judith Hearne* and as *The Lonely Passion of Judith Hearne*, established him as a contemporary novelist of the first order. He has appealed to many as a novelist who writes without embarrassment in the realistic tradition of the Victorians about distinctively modern topics: spiritual and erotic crises, the reality of the objective world, ethnic conflict, relationships between men and women, and the place of women in the societies of the old world and the new. Modern themes of alienation and estrangement are rooted firmly in Moore's work by a sense of place and of time. His evocation of Montreal in *The Luck of Ginger Coffey* has been compared to James Joyce's portrayal of Dublin on "Bloomsday." The bleak urban environment of Belfast of the earlier works and the windswept Irish coast of *The Mangan Inheritance* strike responsive chords in readers conditioned to the blank landscapes of much modernist literature. Just as Moore's geographical terrain changes, however, so do his characters and his stylistic formats. From the almost naturalistic treatment of the unfortunate Judith Hearne to the ghostly dialogues of Fergus and the magical creation of *The Great Victorian Collection*, from the Jesuit missionaries in *Black Robe* to the terrorists in *Lies of Silence*, Moore's unpredictable inventiveness and his sure hand in storytelling and character development have kept him in the forward ranks of living novelists.

Among the honors Moore has received are a Guggenheim Fellowship, an award from the American National Institute of Arts and Letters, a Canada Council Fellowship, the Author's Club of Great Britain First Novel Award, and the Governor-General Award of Canada for fiction. *Catholics* won the W. H. Smith Award in 1973, and *The Great Victorian Collection* was winner of the James Tait Black Memorial Prize in 1975.

Biography

The basic facts of Brian Moore's life are familiar to anyone who knows his work, for he has mined heavily his own experiences for his novels. Moore was born in Belfast, in 1921, to James Bernard Moore, a fellow of the Royal College of Surgeons, and Eileen McFadden Moore. His childhood was a stable and fundamentally happy one; the warm and well-ordered O'Neill family in *Judith Hearne* was in fact identified by Moore in an interview as "a sort of facsimile of my own." Although his work reveals a continuing ambivalence about the order and protection of the family, as about other highly ordered forms of community, he clearly finds much to admire in the sort of family structure that provided his early nurturing.

Moore was educated in Catholic schools, leaving St. Malachi's College, Belfast, in 1940 to join the Air Raid Precautions Unit in Belfast. He served with that unit until 1942, when he left Belfast to serve as a civilian employee of the British Ministry of War Transport in North Africa, Italy, and France. Immediately after the war, he served as a port officer in Warsaw, and then remained for some time in Scandinavia, where he was a free-lance reporter in Sweden, Finland, and Norway until he emigrated to Canada in 1948. From 1948 to 1952, he continued his career as a journalist in Montreal. His Canadian newspaper career began humbly; he was first a proofreader for the *Montreal Gazette*. He was promoted to reporter, an occupation he continued until he began writing pulp fiction to finance his serious work. Although some of his serious short fiction was published in the early 1950's, Moore was forced to continue to write pulp fiction until the appearance of *Judith Hearne* in 1955, and even after, under the pseudonym "Michael Bryan."

The early stages of Moore's life and work came essentially to a close only two years after the publication of *Judith Hearne* with the appearance of his second novel, *The Feast of Lupercal*. Shortly thereafter, he moved to the United States from Canada, and in 1959, received the Guggenheim Fellowship that allowed him to complete one of his most highly regarded works, *The*

Luck of Ginger Coffey (1960). Between 1960 and the publication of *The Emperor of Ice-Cream* in 1965, he published *An Answer from Limbo*. Moore has said, in an interview with Hallvard Dahlie, that a dramatic change in his life occurred in the years between the publication of the latter two novels: "I am much happier now than I was when I was thirty-five or forty. *Emperor* was written at a crucial time in my life—it was the first book after I changed." That change was demonstrated also in his personal life during the year of *The Emperor of Ice-Cream*'s publication. In 1966, Moore married his second wife, Jean Denny, his first marriage having been to Jacqueline Sirois.

Since 1966, Moore has continued to publish at the rate of a novel every one to three years. Although he has maintained Canadian citizenship, he continues to live in the United States, in a house overlooking the Pacific Ocean, near Oxnard, California.

Analysis

Although he has become increasingly cosmopolitan in his adult life, Brian Moore's work is very much rooted in the place of his origin—Northern Ireland—in his middle-class Irish Catholic upbringing, and in concerns readers have learned to recognize in the work of several generations of Irish writers, from J. M. Synge, W. B. Yeats, and James Joyce to the present. In his earlier work at least, Moore is fettered by the ghost of Evelyn Waugh's Irishman, "dragging everywhere with him his ancient rancours and the melancholy of the bogs." That Irishman, however, is transformed by the multiplicity of thematic and structural interests of the inventive Moore.

Beginning with *Judith Hearne*, the themes that have primarily occupied Moore throughout his literary career emerge. There is the struggle with the fathers—fathers embodied in the family, in the Church, in the community, and in Ireland itself which Moore portrays as a restrictively ordered world isolated from the freer West by Joyce's "dark, mutinous Shannon waves" ("The Dead"). Against the protective but stultifying structures that order life, the individual spirit struggles. On the one side is safety and security, but with the prospect of extended childhood, with its continuing demands for obedience and submission. On the other is adulthood, individual responsibility, the possibility of liberation through the imagination beyond the childish fantasizing that characterizes life within the restricted community—but also on that side is the threat of the void.

The tension between these conflicting choices provides both form and substance to nearly all of Moore's serious fiction. In the earlier works, the struggle is overt and played out in simple correspondences. Judith Hearne, middle-aged, unmarried, and without real personal attachments, except in fantasy, faces literal extinction in her crisis of faith. Diarmud Devine is left sexually and morally powerless as he submits to the hierarchy of the fathers at St. Michan's, and Ginger Coffey is a man without country or community as he severs all ties that bind him to his Irish past.

The tension that characterizes Moore's work is a familiar one, as is the resulting ironic tone that several generations of modern critics since Allen Tate have described. Perhaps in no literature, however, is either the tension or the ironic tone more pervasive than in the Irish tradition to which Moore so clearly belongs. Certainly, the conflict between the desire to identify with and belong to the community on the one hand, and the need, on the other hand, to define oneself as an individual is nearly universal in Irish literature. There is, moreover, as described by Andrew Carpenter (*Place, Personality and the Irish Writer*, 1977), a double vision possessed by Irish writers, which derives "from a view of life that is continually probing the different values which exist in Ireland and testing them one against the other," and from immersion in "interrelationships between values, philosophies and cultures antipathetic if not downright hostile to one another." The Irish writer thus comes naturally to multiple points of view, as well as to the idea that opposing points of view are equally acceptable. He "sees two things at once," but "with one eye at a time." This peculiar double vision is manifestly present in Moore's fiction.

Explaining the protagonist of the same name of his first novel, *Judith Hearne*, Moore told Hallvard Dahlie that "I wanted my major character to be someone who wasn't me—who could never be mistaken for me. . . . And yet, I was lonely for much of my life, and so I put something of myself into her." This lonely spinster on the brink of middle age with her "chances" all behind her is bedeviled by the same Irish ghosts that confront nearly all of Moore's protagonists, male and female. Judith Hearne is a true daughter of Catholic Ireland. The "real" world in which she lives is bounded by Church, family—or the idea of family—and sexual mores so restrictive that fantasy life becomes a compelling escape. In Moore's later novels, beginning with *Fergus*, this fantasy life imposed by the Irish past finds an outlet in art; Moore's protagonists become novelists, poets, and even, in *The Great Victorian Collection*, "necromancers." For Judith, however, there are only pitiful and predictable adolescent fantasies. Nearly forty, Judith has found herself penniless, without home or family or prospects for either. Wherever she wanders in her penury and displacement after her aunt's death, she anchors herself with two objects: a photograph of her aunt and a picture of the Sacred Heart. Like a child, she ritualistically bids good night to these images of the only protective forces she knows as she turns off the light in her latest bed-sitter, and is comforted by the knowledge that they are there for her in the darkness.

As her imaginary romance with Madden, the returned emigrant to America, unfolds, the childishness of Judith's fantasy life is revealed. Absorbed in personal ritual, she sits before her glass transforming through her imagination her plain, sallow face and angular figure into the "delightful illusion of beauty." Perhaps legitimately led to believe in Madden's interest in her—an interest later revealed to be motivated by a plan for a joint investment in a hamburger stand—Judith abandons herself to her fantasies. Her arrested sexual development and the debased view she, like nearly all of Moore's characters, has of the possibilities for relationships between men and women are demonstrated in a painful series of encounters with Madden, as in her daydreams about him: "He kissed her," she imagines, "Or, enraged about some silly thing she had done, he struck out with his great fist and sent her reeling, the brute. But, contrite afterwards, he sank to his knees and begged forgiveness."

Sexuality framed in violence, or tied to power struggles, is a hallmark of the identity crises that form the substance of so much of Moore's work. The submission and obedience demanded by religion and family preclude the assertiveness and self-confidence required for adult sexuality, or for any adult relationship. In the early novels, childish sexual fantasies, shaped by cheap romances and shadowed by disapproval of the fathers, are shattered in encounters with real men and women. Spiritual and erotic crises are thus established by Moore as essential to the search for identity in the restrictive world about which he writes.

Judith's passion is sexual, but it is the passion of religious suffering as well. When Judith's frantic search for meaning ends in her challenge to God in the tabernacle, even that door is locked against her. "In the old Irish choice between accepting actuality and retreating from it," Jeanne Flood observes, "the old Irish mistake is choosing the latter alternative" (*Brian Moore*, 1974). Judith's ultimate fiction at that moment of truth is to transform the scene into a pietà. Her imaginary salvation, like her crisis, is both religious and sexual: "His mother ran up the altar steps, her painted face still sadly smiling, lifted her as she lay broken on the steps. . . . And He, His fingers uplifted in blessing, bent over her, His bleeding heart held against His white tunic. Lifted her in His arms and His face was close to hers." In fantasy alone, Judith Hearne is able to have it all—the sheltering arms of family and religion, and the romantic encounter that can exist nowhere but in the adolescent imagination.

Although more obviously autobiographical, Moore's second novel, *The Feast of Lupercal*, is essentially a variation on the themes established in *Judith Hearne*. Set also in contemporary Belfast, the novel follows the ill-fated adventures of Diarmud Devine, a master at St. Michan's, the same Catholic school that Devine attended as a boy. Devine, now thirty-seven, has spent his entire life within the academic hierarchy of the Church. The family persists as a central force in his life as well, for Diarmud lives in a rented room furnished with the accoutrements of his parents' home. He sleeps in his boyhood bed and is watched over in his daily routines by his dead mother and father posed stiffly in their wedding picture.

The Feast of Lupercal, from which the novel takes its name, was a Roman festival celebrating the god of fertility. Against the ironic backdrop of a study of the festival with his sex-obsessed, leering, adolescent pupils, Diarmud is offered a chance at adult sexuality. The challenge is to abandon childish fantasy and to accept the demands of an adult relationship with its dimensions of sexuality, responsibility, and power. The nearly middle-aged man is unable, however, to bring the moment to its close. At the crucial moment, Dev sees the real Una not as a sinful temptress, but as a young girl in a white slip "so unlike his sinful imaginings . . . the sinful imagination which atrophied reality."

The repressive moral world from which Dev has been unable to manage even the slightest distance requires only the simple judgments of childhood, uncluttered by the ambiguities of adult life. So long as Una remained a "hot Protestant," a representative of the sex who were "mockers, character assassins, every single one of them," the simple equations upon which Moore's Catholic Ireland rests could be sustained. "Fancy putting yourself in a position where a woman could laugh at you. An intimate moment, a ridiculous posture—a declaration of love, for instance. Or on your wedding night, to hear a girl laugh at you." In the tradition of the early Church Fathers, man is the spirit and woman the body—the defiling physical presence. The sight of a real and vulnerable young woman, however, undoes the myth, and him, in a culturally caused sexual dysfunction suffered by heroes throughout Moore's work.

Dev makes the "Irish choice," retreating from actuality. Afraid of censure from the hierarchy of the fathers, who are embroiled in a power struggle of their own that threatens Dev, he abandons Una to the consequences of the morally compromising position in which he has placed her, and resigns himself to his narrow and deprived existence. The "boy who dreamed of marrying Madeleine Carroll, the film actress, and taking her to the Riviera where they would commit unknown flesh sins the priests warned about in sermons . . . [was] now a man of thirty-seven [who] had not lived a real life; he had been dreaming."

Moore's third novel, *The Luck of Ginger Coffey*, is set in Montreal, and its title character is a man who has nominally extricated himself from the ties of religion, family, and community that bind Judith Hearne and Dev. Still very much a son of Ireland, however, Ginger dreams of success in the New World, just as Judith dreams of love and marriage and Devine fantasizes sexual conquest. The affliction of the "Irish choice" makes Ginger a man for whom, as for Dev, real life is obscured by dreaming.

In Moore's later expatriate novels—and even at the end of *The Emperor of Ice-Cream*, when young Gavin Burke decides to leave Belfast—there is hope of fulfillment for his dreaming Irish men and women. Tierney in *An Answer from Limbo*, and the confused *poète maudit* of *The Mangan Inheritance*, Jamie Mangan, are endowed with the potentially transforming and liberating force of imagination. They are possessed of a creative power denied Ginger Coffey, as it had been denied to Judith and Dev.

Trapped in a series of cheap fictional images of success rooted in his Irish past, Ginger affects a Dublin squire look, and he thinks of himself as being in his soldierly prime, handsomely mustachioed and booted. A Canadian employer to whom he appeals sees him otherwise: "A limely type . . . with his tiny green hat, short bulky car coat and suede boots." Nor is he otherwise successful in adapting to his adopted country. The uniform of a diaper service delivery man is a mockery of his early dreams of military adventure. His dreams of an adventurous career as a journalist shrink in the cellar of the building where he works as a proofreader, and evaporate finally in the words of a dying co-worker: "Irish. An immigrant same as you," the dying man tells him. Nearly forty, he looks at his dying compatriot and realizes what he has abandoned, and how little he has gained. Will he so end his days, "his voice nasal and reedy, all accent gone"? Coffey denies such a fate: "Yes, I'm Irish. James Francis Coffey. Fine Irish name."

In the end, though, Coffey is a man without country or community, and a man nearly without family, as his wife and daughter yield to the attractions of the vulgar materialism of the country to which he has brought them, in which he has insisted they stay, and where at last he resigns himself to life with them in "humble circs." His marriage to Veronica, née Shannon, whom he calls by a name for Ireland, "Dark Rosaleen," is his only tie to his native land. He must pay a dear price to sustain that tie, his only protection from the chaos that threatened Judith Hearne, and that Dev could not even contemplate. The price is to be what he most feared—an Irish failure, living with a wife he no longer wants, and working at a job worse than the one he left behind in the scorned Ulster.

Ginger Coffey represents to Moore, as he told Robert Fulford, "what I was terrified would happen to me. I've always felt myself to be a misfit, I still do." By contrast, Brendan Tierney, the protagonist of *An Answer from Limbo*, is the first of Moore's protagonists to possess the creative power that seems to have been Moore's salvation. Curiously, however, Tierney is a less sympathetic character than any of the three doomed and powerless protagonists who precede him in Moore's work. The hapless Judith, who suffers a woman's fate along with the burden of the Irish cross; the tragicomic Dev; and the feckless Ginger, who befriends the lonely child of his landlady in the midst of his troubles—all are caught in the grip of social circumstances, and all struggle to maintain dignity and humanity in spite of those circumstances. That humanity is absent in Brendan Tierney. The theme of *An Answer from Limbo*, repeated in *Fergus* and in *I Am Mary Dunne*, is a problematic repudiation of the Irish past with its shackles of family, religion, and community in favor of a freer identity, shaped by the personal power of the imagination. Moore's disapproval of Tierney, as of later artist heroes, warns the reader, however, not to expect simple solutions to the conflict.

No childlike victim, no futile fantasizer, Brendan Tierney is a hard-eyed young writer who seems destined to achieve the success and fame for which he hungers. Replete with the self-confidence absent in Judith and Dev, and possessed of talent and purpose sadly lacking in Ginger, Brendan expects his future work to find a place among the ranks of "Kierkegaard and Camus, Dostoyevsky and Gide." As John Scanlan has observed, the theme here is Faustian. Tierney is the artist who sacrifices not only his own happiness for his art, but also the well-being of those who have loved him or depended upon him in the past. He drives his wife Jane into miserable infidelity; his rejected mother dies alone, waiting to return to Ireland. Mrs. Tierney is effectively "killed" by Brendan, who rejects her overtly and puts her out of his mind. In his single-minded devotion to his art, Brendan denies his past, the emotional solace and protection offered by Ireland, his family, and his religion. At the novel's end, he is overcome by the self-loathing that even Ginger Coffey was spared. Ginger was able to say at least, as he sought to reconcile himself to his failures, "Life itself is a victory." Brendan, even with the real prospect of attaining his dreams of success, is left with the knowledge that "I have altered beyond all self-recognition. I have lost and sacrificed myself."

I Am Mary Dunne marked a shift in direction for Moore. Having achieved a kind of resolution of his old material with the altered—and happier— perspective of *The Emperor of Ice-Cream*, Moore was ready in this sixth novel to move into new territory. It is significant that the protagonist of the first novel in this less traditional phase is, like that of his first novel, a woman. Just as he wanted to ensure that his first major character "wasn't me—could never be mistaken for me," so *I Am Mary Dunne* is determined to avoid the appearance of autobiography. Despite its innovative style, the novel takes up many of Moore's familiar themes. Mary is an artist—a failed one, perhaps— and an Irish expatriate whose haunted past is full of the old ghosts of religion, a troublesome father, and an identity and community that elude her in both Canada and New York.

Moore, whose insights into feminine psychology as well as sexual politics were demonstrated in *Judith Hearne*, makes clear the importance of Mary's sex in her search for identity. She has fitted herself to each of her husbands, adopting a new identity with each name-change. The novel's epigraph from Yeats is apt: it is no longer possible for Mary to tell the "dancer from the dance." She is threatened by the void that froze the earlier Moore characters into childhood, and drives the quest of the later characters for meaning through acts of the imagination. For Mary, though, the possibilities of the creative imagination have been discarded; her life as an actress is over, her potential as a writer and a painter lie fallow. Her current identity is defined by the successful playwright to whom she is now married. Thus, she tries to find herself by remembering who she once was—her mother's daughter, Mary Dunne.

In *Catholics*, Moore's eighth novel and one of his best, the religious commitment that was a major hedge against the void for the victimized early characters regains center stage. For the first time, however, the struggles are sexless. Neither the relationship between men and women nor the exercise of sexual power is at issue here. The confrontation with the empty tabernacle is drawn pure and simple. On a remote rocky island in Kerry, a priest's personal crisis of faith is played out against the clinical relativism of a twenty-first century world, represented by James Kinsella, a young priest sent by Rome to obliterate the last vestiges of the old order to which the priests and parishioners of Muck Abbey still cling.

Unlike Judith Hearne, whose ultimate capacity for childlike fantasy offered her protection against the void, the Abbott has no defenses. He had chosen long ago to forsake all else for his God, and now he has found that "there is no Father in Heaven." When he tries to pray, he "enters null." When the young priest, Kinsella, arrives, the Abbott has not prayed in years. He sees his role as a manager of the Abbey, and also as a human bulwark for others against the void he has confronted. The Abbott knows, just as the behaviorist friend of young Kinsella knows, that "People don't want truth or justice. They want certainties. The old parish priest promised them that." Thus, the Abbott tries to deliver certainty, although it is lost to him. The past, however, is irredeemable. Its loss began long ago with "that righteous prig at Wittenberg nailing his defiance to the church door." The Abbott's attempt to recall it is doomed, as is he.

While those last lines absolve Moore of any suspicion of romanticizing the past of which he once despaired, the earlier faith in the possibilities of the imagination to liberate and to create its own enduring reality seems all but lost here. *The Great Victorian Collection*, Moore's next novel, continues that dark view of the power of the individual spirit and the creative imagination.

Moore's increasingly pessimistic vision is expressed in the central conceit of *The Great Victorian Collection*: Anthony Maloney, an undistinguished young professor and student of Victorian life, dreams into existence an authentic and unprecedented collection of Victoriana, an opportunity for the creative synthesis of past and present, of tradition and the imagination, that would resolve the fundamental conflict Moore presents. Significantly, however, the Collection is dreamed into existence in California, a land of hollow dreams. Moreover, it appears in a motel parking lot in that precious California tourist mecca, Carmel-by-the-Sea, with its "galleries filled with local paintings, arcade shops selling homemade candles, and bookstores displaying the complete works of Kahil Gibran."

The California tourist town becomes, in this most imaginative of Moore's novels, a world that, however far in form and principle from Belfast, has an equivalent capacity to thwart the individual spirit and to stultify the creative process. Tony is trapped by the Collection, which begins to deteriorate as he allows his attention to waver from it. Trapped in the dilemma of the successful artist, he must involve other people in his work. Other people include, notably, a commercial agent whose efforts to "market" the Collection lead to great commercial success, but the real "success" is a facsimile of the Collection at a place and in a form more palatable to the public. Tony's own investment in his creation becomes increasingly detached, until the pieces of it become artificial, and his caretaking is mechanistic. His dreams are reduced to soul-deadening surveillance by a black-and-white television camera. Finally, he · tries to destroy his deteriorated creation, but it has assumed a life of its own and is indestructible.

This parable of the failure of the imagination to liberate or to sustain the spirit includes Moore's familiar erotic crisis. The creation of The Great Victorian Collection seems to be connected with Maloney's relationship with the beautiful young girl who comes into his life almost immediately after the Collection appears. A Dutch clairvoyant warns him that she is important to what has happened, and indeed, Mary Ann McKelvey soon emerges as Tony's anchor to reality in the feverish life of the imagination in which he finds himself. In a scene highly reminiscent of Moore's early works, their first and only sexual encounter ends in disaster, with Mary Ann thinking she has "failed" Tony. In fact, as with Dev, the apprehension of Mary Ann as a real woman "undid him." Tony "was, and always would be, a dreamer. . . . No longer a man and maid in those far-off wicked times, they were now equals, contestants, almost enemies." Unable to live with the human challenges of the real world or with women who are real people, and faced in his life as an artist with a choice between commercial exploitation of his gifts or the caretaking of deteriorating museum pieces, Maloney chooses to end his own life.

The connection between Moore's concern with a particular male inability to form adult sexual relationships and the failure of the imagination to craft a synthesis of tradition and the individual creative spirit is treated most directly in his two most recent novels. In *The Mangan Inheritance*, the connection, at least in outline, is simplistic. Jamie Mangan, failed poet, failed husband, perhaps even failed son, uses the windfall from his wife's sudden death to try to bury his failures in a return to a romanticized past. His search in the Irish village of his ancestors for confirmation of his relationship to the nineteenth century *poète maudit* James Clarence Mangan is a search for validation by the past, and is as doomed to failure as that of the Abbott in *Catholics*.

Unlike some of Moore's previous protagonists, however, Jamie is able to acknowledge his failures and learn from them. He refuses to succumb to the romantic fantasies that have spoiled the lives of past and present members of his Irish family. The excesses of the *poète maudit* are revealed to him in their sordid reality in the lives of his Irish cousins. He even comes to see his sexual infatuation with the beautiful but slovenly teenage Kathleen for the destructive fantasy it is in the light of the story of incest and sexual abuse he hears from his Irish *Doppelgänger*, Michael Mangan. In the end, Jamie is able to repudiate his fantasies, literary and sexual, and return to his dying father and to responsibility to a future generation. In the daguerrotype of James Clarence Mangan lying smashed beyond repair against the stones of ruined Irish castle, Jamie sees the features of his dying father and "wished that those features were his own." Implicit is the promise that his father's unborn child, whom he has promised to protect, will be welcomed into a family free of romantic illusion about itself, and that Jamie has a chance at fulfillment in the real world. The resolution is not unshadowed, however, for Jamie was a poet, and apparently will be no longer.

The note of guarded optimism on which *The Mangan Inheritance* ends is not repeated in Moore's next novel, *The Temptation of Eileen Hughes*. Bernard McAuley, the novel's "artist," is a strange admixture of Moore's earlier protagonists. Sexually paralyzed, though married to Mona, a beautiful woman who loves him, Bernard searches for identity and meaning in his life, ranging from "offering [himself] to God" as a priest and finding he "wasn't wanted," through studies of history, art, music, and business, and finally to his bizarre attempt to force his strangely celibate relationship with young Eileen Hughes into his sordid household.

The themes of sexual power and the act of the imagination attain a distorted unity in this novel. Bernard enacts an evolution into decadence, and in a confirmation of Moore's recurrent tendency to find healthy self-knowledge in women targeted as victims by male identity-seekers, Eileen ultimately understands the manipulative and powerful McAuleys: "It was not she who had been in their power but they in hers. She had escaped them. Would they escape her?" Like Mary Ann McKelvey, or Diarmud Devine's Una, Eileen is anchored in a reality to which men such as Bernard (and the women whose lives they steal) will be forever denied admission.

Moore's four novels since *The Temptation of Eileen Hughes* are diverse in setting and character, yet they are linked both stylistically and thematically; together they mark a new phase in Moore's work. In three of the four—*Cold Heaven*, *The Color of Blood*, and *Lies of Silence*—Moore has adopted the plot-scaffolding and many of the generic conventions of the thriller, while in *Black Robe*, set in the 1630's in the Canadian wilderness, he has adopted the conventions of the historical adventure novel.

Some reviewers have seen in this shift an attempt on Moore's part to win a larger audience. If that is the case, the attempt must be judged a failure, for while these works have been well received by critics, they have not made Moore a best-selling author. It seems just as likely, though, that Moore turned to the thriller for other reasons. In *Black Robe*, which centers on the physical hardships and spiritual conflicts of a Jesuit missionary to the Indians, in *The Color of Blood*, a pre-*glasnost* novel set in Eastern Europe and focusing on a Roman Catholic cardinal and the prime minister of an unnamed nation closely resembling Poland, and in *Lies of Silence*, about a man who is inadvertently drawn into a plot by Irish Republican Army terrorists, Moore grounds individual moral conflicts in the context of larger social and political struggles. The thriller (or the comparable historical adventure) has provided strong narrative drive, a structure in which to dramatize moral conflicts without excessive abstraction. Thus Moore's abiding concern with people in crisis has undergone yet another transformation.

Michele Wender Zak

Other major works

PLAYS: *The Luck of Ginger Coffey*, 1963; *Torn Curtain*, 1966; *The Slave*, 1967; *Catholics*, 1973.

NONFICTION: *Canada*, 1963; *The Revolution Script*, 1971.

Bibliography

Dahlie, Hallvard. *Brian Moore*. Boston: Twayne, 1981. A volume in the Twayne World Authors Series, this comprehensive study of Moore discusses his short stories and nonfiction as well as his novels. The study addresses the metaphysical dilemmas presented in those of Moore's characters who struggle for identity and meaning. No really original views on Moore here, but well worth reading for its comprehensive treatment and background. Selected bibliography and chronology.

Flood, Jeanne. *Brian Moore*. Lewisburg, Pa.: Bucknell University Press, 1974. Covers Moore's work until 1973, with some emphasis on *Catholics*. Each chapter looks at a different position the novelist takes. This slim volume is a solid if stolid piece of criticism and contains much insight into Moore's narrative technique and purpose. Chronology and bibliography.

Foster, John Wilson. "Passage Through Limbo: Brian Moore's North American Novels." *Critique: Studies in Modern Fiction* 13, no. 1 (1971): 5-18. Rejects the usual comparison of Moore to Joyce; instead, Foster sees Moore portraying age-old dilemmas instead of contemporary ones. Discusses *The Luck of Ginger Coffey* at length as well as *The Lonely Passion of Judith Hearne*, which Foster considers to be Moore's finest novel. Some refreshing views on Moore; all in all, a thoughtful critique.

Gindin, James. "Brian Moore." In *Contemporary Novelists*, edited by James Vinson. New York: St. Martin's Press, 1982. An overview of Moore's work that spans his first novel, *The Lonely Passion of Judith Hearne*, to *The Mangan Inheritance*, in 1979. Also discusses *The Luck of Ginger Coffey* in the light of popular genre of fiction. Gives insight into the plots of Moore's novels, which he applauds as "highly inventive."

Lanning, George. "Silver-Fish in the Plumbing." *The Kenyon Review* 23, no. 1 (Winter, 1961): 173-181. Lanning, the editor of *The Kenyon Review*, discusses four authors here—Muriel Spark, James Herlihy, Brian Moore, and Michael Campbell—and discusses how each portrays the human condition. Although Lanning gives a negative account of how Moore handles the theme of marital infidelity through his characterization, it is worth looking at the placement of Moore with these other authors.

GEORGE MOORE

Born: County Mayo, Ireland; February 24, 1852
Died: London, England; January 21, 1933

Principal long fiction

A Modern Lover, 1883; *A Mummer's Wife,* 1884; *A Drama in Muslin,* 1886; *A Mere Accident,* 1887; *Spring Days,* 1888; *Mike Fletcher,* 1889; *Vain Fortune,* 1891; *Esther Waters,* 1894; *Evelyn Innes,* 1898; *Sister Teresa,* 1901; *The Lake,* 1905; *Muslin,* 1915; *The Brook Kerith,* 1916; *Lewis Seymour and Some Women,* 1917; *Héloise and Abélard,* 1921; *Ulick and Soracha,* 1926; *Aphrodite in Aulis,* 1930.

Other literary forms

George Moore was man of letters rather than purely a novelist. He published seven collections of short fiction, and all but the first of his eight plays were produced in London or Dublin. He published two volumes of poetry in 1878 and 1881. Moore published numerous nonfictional works and more than a thousand of his periodical writings have been located in English, Irish, French, and American journals. In addition, he published a notable translation of Longus' *Daphnis and Chloë* in 1924.

Achievements

Moore's fiction was at all times innovative and influential. Amid much controversy in the early 1880's, he adapted the methods of French realism to the English novel. His earliest goals were to liberate the novel from Victorian conventions of subject and treatment and from commercial constraints imposed by a monopolistic book trade.

By the middle 1880's, he began to turn from realism to aestheticism. Under the influence of his friend Walter Pater and the rising symbolist poets of France, Moore anticipated the "decadence" of the 1890's by eschewing the conflict between realism and popular romanticism which had formerly absorbed him. He realized that these schools of writing were generally organized and evaluated on moral and social grounds. In regard to prose narrative, Moore's increasing and then sole preoccupation became literary art.

As an aesthete in the early 1890's, he composed his masterpiece *Esther Waters.* He also wrote some of the short stories that later contributed to his reputation as an inventor of modern Irish fiction. The large income generated by his books allowed him to quit his second career as one of England's leading art critics. He cofounded the Independent Theatre and Irish Literary Theatre and by the turn of the century he became a leading polemicist of the Irish revival.

The major achievement of Moore's Irish involvement was the composition of *Hail and Farewell: A Trilogy* (1911-1914). In the tradition of Laurence Sterne, Thomas De Quincey, and George Borrow, Moore wrote the story of his life using the conceptual framework of fiction rather than history. The trilogy contains an account of artistic movements of the late Victorian era, but attention is concentrated on the intellectual life of Dublin in the early years of the twentieth century.

During the 1910's and 1920's, Moore retreated from the popular literary market to the composition of prose epics. Biblical history in *The Brook Kerith*, medieval history in *Héloise and Abélard*, and classical history in *Aphrodite in Aulis* offered structural premises for a new exploration of human problems and for the development of a modern, rarefied aestheticism. Reviewers greeted the novels as exemplars of composition and elevated Moore to the status of England's senior man of letters.

Biography

The Moores of Moore Hall were a prominent Catholic family in the west of Ireland. Their home, a large gray stone mansion presiding over 12,500 acres, was built in 1795 by George Moore, the novelist's great-grandfather. The founder of Moore Hall was a businessman. His eldest son Peter was certified insane for most of his life; the second son John was martyred in the 1798 rebellion (see Thomas Flanagan's novel *The Year of the French*, 1979); the youngest son George, the novelist's grandfather, was a scholarly historian. George inherited the estate and through marriage established an intimate connection with the Brownes of Westport. His eldest son was George Henry Moore (1810-1870), a keeper of excellent racing stables and member of Parliament for the nationalist cause. In 1851, he married Mary Blake (1829-1895), daughter of a neighboring landlord.

George Augustus Moore, the eldest of G. H. Moore's five children, was born at Moore Hall on February 24, 1852. He was a robust but rather backward child: a late talker, then an endearing but poor pupil under a succession of governesses. Beginning in 1861, he attended Oscott College, Birmingham, a famous preparatory school designed as the Catholic complement of Eton or Harrow. He remained at Oscott until 1868, when his learning disabilities finally convinced the headmaster that further attempts at instruction would be futile.

After leaving Oscott, Moore lived with his parents in London while Parliament was in session. His time was divided between military tutors and amusements, including betting shops, music halls, and painting studios. When his father died suddenly in 1870, the quest for an army commission was dropped and soon Moore was devoting most of his energy to the study of painting.

From 1873 until 1879, he lived mostly in Paris, first as a student painter at the École des Beaux Arts and Académie Julian. Before setting aside his brushes in 1875, he had received instruction from James Whistler, John Millais, Alexandre Cabanel, and several less famous painters in France and England. Education did not make a painter of him, but it did help make him a sensitive art critic later in life. His first steps in literature during the later 1870's were likewise tentative. He was enraptured with French romantic drama and Parnassian poetry. By the time the income from his property suddenly failed and he was forced to leave France, he had published two volumes of exotic juvenile verse and a large romantic drama which was intended for but declined by Henry Irving.

Moore's literary career properly began in London in 1881. He was then settled in inexpensive rooms near The Strand and determined to make a living by his pen. While developing the plan of a naturalistic novel, he contributed paragraphs and reviews to the weekly press. Among his friends he numbered several poets and critics of the Pre-Raphaelite Circle, but these receded as his friendship with Émile Zola became a discipleship. "When I attacked the Philistine," A. C. Swinburne commented after reading *A Mummer's Wife*, "it was not with a chamber pot for a buckler and a dung fork for a spear." Moore's first two novels and his early journalism, though consonant with the ideals of the French avant-garde, drew charges of indecency from English readers. Though he moderated his style as his aestheticism changed, the reputation he got at the start of his career remained with him, and all of his fiction until the turn of the century was banned from the circulating libraries.

Moore continued to live in the vicinity of The Strand until 1886, when he moved to a village near Brighton and afterward to a house atop the Sussex downs. In the English countryside he found an almost idyllic refuge from the distractions of London. His fiction of the period shows an increasing tolerance of ordinary life, and his literary theories, which he collected for *Confessions of a Young Man* (1888), reveal a firmer, more self-reliant mind than was evident before. He returned to London in 1889, engaged to write art criticism for his brother's magazine *The Hawk* and, more important, with the plan for a novel which became *Esther Waters*.

From 1889 until 1895, Moore contributed columns of art criticism briefly to *The Hawk* and then to *The Speaker*, both weekly reviews of politics and the arts. He was the first Impressionist art critic in England. During this period he lived in The Temple, in a small bachelor's flat that was desirable because it was cheap. Aside from writing fiction and criticism, he became deeply involved in theater reform and in 1890 cofounded the Independent Theatre, where Henrik Ibsen and George Bernard Shaw got their London premieres. With the publication of *Esther Waters*, he was soon able to afford a more comfortable flat in Victoria Street and to leave the staff of *The Speaker*.

During the rest of the 1890's, Moore was prominent among the aesthetes and decadents generally associated with *The Yellow Book*. He also took a publicized interest in the revival of early music, begun by his friend Arnold

Dolmetsch, and in Wagnerism. His annual pilgrimage to Bayreuth began at this time, and his last novel of the century is permeated with musical theory. Drawn by the ideas of William Butler Yeats and others concerning the artistic possibilities of Gaelic, he also became involved in the Irish revival. With Yeats and Edward Martyn he founded the Irish Literary Theatre (precursor of the Abbey). In 1901, enamored of the "new Ireland" and bitterly depressed by British conduct of the Boer War, Moore sold his flat in Victoria Street and leased a house in Upper Ely Place, near St. Stephen's Green in Dublin. He remained there until 1911.

Owing mainly to aesthetic and religious convictions, Moore's return to Ireland was characterized more by frustration than success. Having learned his profession in Paris and London, he could feel little sympathy for the relatively parochial challenges that writers of the movement faced. His advocacy of intellectual freedom for the artist was inappropriate to prevailing ideology. Worse, his notion that a politically free Ireland was one that would disown both Westminster and the Vatican virtually exiled him from the cause he tried to embrace. Though he made several friends among literary Dubliners, wrote polemics in the Irish press, and published important fiction, his greatest achievement was the comic indictment of the movement which appeared, after he left Dublin, in *Hail and Farewell*.

From 1911 until his death, Moore lived in Ebury Street, London. For the first time he was associated with no movement, but instead practiced his art purely as an individual. His fiction and books of theory were welcomed by an elite readership of a few thousand. His best friends were the English Impressionist painters who lived in nearby Chelsea. Turning about face on the six-shilling format he had invented with publisher Henry Vizetelly in 1884, he issued his books in limited, sometimes elegantly illustrated editions that took him entirely out of the popular market. He died in his home on January 21, 1933, and was buried on an island in Lough Carra, in front of Moore Hall. Because the rites of burial were pagan, a police guard was called to protect the funeral. George Russell composed the oration and the epitaph of George Moore: "He forsook his family and friends for his art. But because he was faithful to his art his family and friends reclaimed his ashes for Ireland. VALE."

Analysis

Thirty of George Moore's fifty years as a novelist postdate the Victorian era, yet he is not generally remembered as a modern writer. To some extent this is because his aestheticism was the outcome of inspiration rather than experiment. "I desire above all things," he wrote in 1892, "to tell the story of life in grave simple phrases, so grave and simple that the method, the execution would disappear, and the reader, with bating breath, would remain a prey to an absorbing emotion."

Complexity and diversity are striking characteristics of the Moore corpus. He told "the story of life" ranging from classical Greece (*Aphrodite in Aulis*) to industrial England (*A Mummer's Wife*). His changing style reflected the influence of diverse writers, including Gustave Flaubert, Ivan Turgenev and Walter Pater. Confused by such diversity, Arthur Symons reached the conclusion that Moore had no style, and James Whistler believed that he had no conscience. In a curious way this is true. He achieved not style, but expression. As an artist he avoided moral judgments and ceased his endeavors after discovering the soul in the body, the idea in action. The nature of his critical theories and the evolution of his fiction confirm that he was not a modernist, but a classicist.

Moore's first novel, *A Modern Lover*, like his last, is a study of artistic temperament. The chief protagonist is Lewis Seymour, a young painter of middling talent whose problem is to advance his career. He is attracted to a fraternity of avant-garde artists called "the moderns," who advocate a radical departure from academic painting. On the other hand, he realizes that to achieve success in the sense of worldly recognition, he must be conventional and flatter the tastes of an ignorant public. The narrative traces Lewis' development as a painter with a "market" that expands in proportion to the distance between himself and personal integrity.

A Modern Lover represents the first conscious attempt to write a naturalistic novel in English. Reviewers noticed its power. In addition to its literary qualities, the novel offers an account of conflicting trends in art: "the moderns" are painters modeled after the French Impressionists; "the medievalists" are modeled after the Pre-Raphaelite Brotherhood; the Royal Academy appears as a copy of the original. Through the character of John Harding, Moore expounded his own views as a critic of Victorian culture and advocated reforms that prepared the way for a new definition of modern art.

Susan Mitchell noted in her study of Moore that he had an uncanny ability to understand women. *A Mummer's Wife* and *A Drama in Muslin* may be regarded as portraits of women: the first novel rather sinister and tragic, the second almost feminist and deeply encouraging.

Kate Ede is introduced in *A Mummer's Wife* as the wife of a shopkeeper living in the industrial town of Hanley. She is a young woman of sober character and dry religious convictions. Dick Lennox, the actor-manager of a touring company, rents lodgings in her house and seduces her. She is persuaded to leave her unhappy marriage and to accompany Dick on his travels. Among people of the theater, Kate's self-discipline gives way to a sensuous dreaminess. After becoming an actress, she marries Dick and has a baby by him, but her course runs steadily downward. As the moral underpinnings of her life are loosened, she slips almost unawares into depravity and dies in the end, an alcoholic among prostitutes.

Alice Barton, the heroine of *A Drama in Muslin*, is the daughter of an

Irish landlord. She is an intellectual girl and rather homely; consequently she is unfitted for the grotesque "marriage market" of the Castle season in Dublin. Her sister and acquaintances spend their energy and sometimes dignity in preparing for the most important event of their lives: the entrapment of a moneyed young man in matrimony. All the innocence, loveliness, and promise of girlhood are publicly and somewhat brutally bartered for the passing illusions of title and fortune. Alice remains aloof, quietly preparing herself for a literary career. In the end, because of her intelligence and self-reliance, she alone makes a happy marriage.

Apart from many distinguishing features, the one shared by Kate Ede and Alice Barton is a departure from the common rut of experience. When Kate becomes the mummer's mistress she breaks free from the paralyzing control of her husband and mother-in-law. During the months before conscience prods her to become the mummer's wife, she achieves sexual and emotional fulfillment and finds herself on the verge of a career and independence. Kate's is not a social tragedy: the opportunity to change her life was offered but for personal reasons she neglected it. Alice's success is likewise of her own making. The reader finds soon after beginning *A Drama in Muslin* that the heroine is set apart less by her lack of beauty than by her strength of character. By virtue of a correct perception of Vanity Fair, Alice disentangles herself from the fatal bonds of family, class, and background to secure a hopeful future.

Esther Waters, properly regarded as one of the greater novels in English literature, is also one of the least understood. From the year of its publication until the present, reviewers and scholars have persisted in classing it as a realistic novel, using "realism" to mean an imitation of nature. Moore explained in "Exteriority" (*The Speaker*, June 22, 1895) that though he deferred to realism in regard to subject matter, the book was formed on higher, more subjective principles. Returning to an argument published earlier in *The Speaker* (October 8, 1892), he observed that all art should contain truth and beauty, but these were separate attributes. Truth he associated with nature, so to be truthful the novelist chooses a realistic subject. Beauty he associated with imagination. To achieve beauty, the novelist permeates nature with his personal vision. Through the quality of expression, or literary form, he succeeds in conveying images to and from the soul and hallows nature with the spirit of art.

Esther Waters has been bound in its reputation of realism because Moore's choice of a subject from nature was powerful enough to be blinding. His protagonists were servants, characters whose place in English fiction had been confined to doing odd jobs and providing comic entertainment. Now they were comprehended as full human beings and their vast subculture moved from the periphery to the center of consciousness. The force of Moore's decision to write about servants was increased by the novel's central problem: the struggle of an unmarried mother to rear her child. By making Esther

Waters his heroine, Moore overturned an array of Victorian sexual mores and political assumptions.

It is not surprising that the controversy which greeted publication of the novel distracted readers from its artistic merits. It must be emphasized, however, that Moore was no champion of the working class; he was neither a sociologist nor a philanthropist. He was only what he claimed to be: an artist. Essentially, he was no more interested in servant girls than his friend Edgar Degas was interested in ballerinas: they merely represented new opportunities for artistic expression. To think otherwise is to obscure the development of Moore's fiction and to ignore his many explanations of his aestheticism.

The quality of beauty Moore captured in *Esther Waters* may be summarized in its theme: the drama of motherhood, the presence in human nature of maternal instincts that create and protect life in a threatening environment. Rising from numerous realistic scenes in mansion, tenement, hospital, and public house, at racecourses and in the streets of London, the ineffable mystery of human love and self-sacrifice irradiates the text. At the conclusion of the novel Esther does not inherit a fortune; her son does not grow up to be prime minister; the villains are not punished and the heroes are not rewarded. A life of dedicated struggle is simply allowed to come to rest with a mild sense of achievement. In so doing, this ordinary life becomes a thing of extraordinary beauty.

Evelyn Innes is another study of a woman seeking independence from stifling conventions and expectations. Evelyn, the daughter of a musicologist, carries on relationships with two men, each representing a principle of her life. Sir Owen Asher, the patron of her opera singing career, is the carnal. Ulick Dean, a musician and mystic, is the intellectual. The contradictory emotions these men inspire make her anxious about personal morality. The narrative traces her meditations until they reach a logical though drastic conclusion: religious vocation. Evelyn abandons love, career, and society, entering a convent in a desperate attempt to reconcile her life with her conscience. The novel concludes with a statement of her mature beliefs, which might be characterized as a somewhat secularized Christianity.

Moore did not explain why an author who cherished personal freedom, did not believe in God, and hated Catholicism should feel compelled to write the story of Evelyn Innes. Compelled by his imagination he certainly was, for he continued to revise the work for ten years until putting it aside, unsatisfied. It is possible that the trappings of Catholicism and musical theory were as incidental to his purpose as the kitchen and garret were in *Esther Waters*. He was essentially concerned about the problem posed by a woman's liberation from traditional restraint and the use to which she puts her freedom. Kate Ede in *A Mummer's Wife* shared Evelyn's dilemma, though in a different setting.

During the last twenty-five years of Moore's career, his longer fiction was historical. Ancient and medieval landscapes of Greece, Palestine, and France were more capable of supporting his literary ideas, though he continued to view the twentieth century in Great Britain through the media of essay and autobiography.

His turn from modern subjects was accompanied by a turn from modern spoken English. In regard to both subject and treatment, Moore wished to emulate Pater, whose pure literary English was free of associations carried over from worldly usage and whose setting, in the much admired *Marius the Epicurean* (1885), was remote enough from mundane reality to assume more easily the aura of myth.

The Brook Kerith retells the story of Christ in accordance with the Synoptic Gospels and later histories, but adds an enormous new dimension by allowing him to survive the crucifixion and live, in thoughtful retirement, at an Essene monastery. Christ in the Bible struck Moore as an unfinished man, a visionary glimpsed only in his immaturity. As Christ matures he develops a more generous and sympathetic morality as part of a better understanding of humanity. At the conclusion of the novel, St. Paul comes to the monastery. Messiah and apostle are brought face to face. When Christ hears about the founding of the bellicose Christian tradition, he is horrified. When Paul learns the identity of his auditor, he rages and strikes Christ to the ground. Their paths soon part, Paul to carry his dogma to Europe and Christ to carry the truth to Jerusalem.

The process of humanizing religious history and of faulting dogma in favor of free intelligence is continued in *Héloise and Abélard*. The figure of Abélard as perhaps the first Renaissance man was profoundly attractive to Moore, but he was equally moved by his conception of Héloise, who is his chief protagonist. The novel pits intellectual freedom and its complement, wholesome sexual love, against the rigors of doctrine and medieval customs of chastity and celibacy. In its blending of landscape and character, idea and expression, *Héloise and Abélard* might well be ranked the most nearly perfect "aesthetic novel" ever written.

In order to strengthen his sense of place in *The Brook Kerith* and *Héloise and Abélard*, Moore had traveled over Palestine and France and "assimilated" culture. By the time he had the plan for *Aphrodite in Aulis*, however, he was too old and frail to make a tour of Greece. Illness for the first time settled in his body, and, though his mind remained vigorous, he was forced to live with a great deal of pain. Despite these obstacles, he achieved a final novel of abundant mystery and flawed but engrossing beauty.

The story is set in Greece of the fifth century B.C. Kebren, a young Athenian actor and rhapsodist, settles in Aulis as the husband of Biote and business partner of her father Otanes. Biote gives birth to two sons, Rhesos the sculptor and Thrasillos the architect. After a period of training under Phidias in Athens, the brothers return to Aulis and marry their cousins Earine and Melissa. Earine is the inspiration for the figure of Aphrodite that Rhesos carves for a temple in Aulis. Following her role of inspiration, at the conclusion of the novel she embraces a new role as the mother of his children.

The book may be read as an act of devotion to art and thus a fitting conclusion to Moore's career. Throughout the narrative, art and life are almost hypnotically counterpointed. Each recovers the continuing theme from the other, seeming for a moment to frustrate the other's aims. In the end an exquisite harmony occurs: art is animated by life, while life is beautified and ennobled by art. That harmony characterizes the oeuvre of George Moore.

Robert Becker

Other major works

SHORT FICTION: *Parnell and His Island*, 1887; *Celibates*, 1895; *The Untilled Field*, 1903; *Memoirs of My Dead Life*, 1906; *A Story-Teller's Holiday*, 1918; *In Single Strictness*, 1922; *Peronnik the Fool*, 1924; *A Flood*, 1930.

PLAYS: *Martin Luther*, 1879; *The Strike at Arlingford*, 1893; *The Bending of the Bough*, 1900; *The Apostle*, 1911; *Esther Waters*, 1913; *Elizabeth Cooper*, 1913; *The Coming of Gabrielle*, 1920; *The Making of Immortal*, 1927; *The Passing of the Essenes*, 1930; *Diarmuid and Grania*, 1951 (with W. B. Yeats).

POETRY: *Flowers of Passion*, 1877; *Pagan Poems*, 1881.

NONFICTION: *Confessions of a Young Man*, 1888; *Impressions and Opinions*, 1891; *Modern Painting*, 1893; *Hail and Farewell: A Trilogy*, 1911-1914 (*Ave*, 1911, *Salve*, 1912; *Vale*, 1914); *Avowals*, 1919; *Conversations in Ebury Street*, 1924; *Letters from George Moore to Edouard Dujardin, 1886-1922*, 1929; *The Talking Pine*, 1931; *A Communication to My Friends*, 1933; *Letters of George Moore*, 1942; *Letters to Lady Cunard*, 1957 (Rupert Hart-Davis, editor); *George Moore in Transition: Letters to T. Fisher Unwin and Lena Milman, 1894-1910*, 1968 (Helmut E. Gerber, editor).

TRANSLATION: *Daphnis and Chloë*, 1924.

Bibliography

Cunard, Nancy. *GM: Memories of George Moore*. London: Rupert Hart-Davis, 1956. Personal reminiscences of Moore written with charm and frankness by the daughter of Lady Cunard, with whom Moore was closely associated. Includes extracts of some of the sixty-four letters Moore wrote to Nancy Cunard. Contains interesting background on Moore in a social context.

Dunleavy, Janet Egleson. *George Moore: The Artist's Vision, the Storyteller's Art*. Lewisburg, N.J.: Bucknell University Press, 1973. A review of Moore's work as an artist, presented in chronological form. Particularly useful commentary on his earlier novels.

_____, ed. *George Moore in Perspective*. Irish Literary Studies 16.

Totowa, N.J.: Barnes & Noble Books, 1983. A compilation of critical essays on Moore and his work from a variety of perspectives: his Irish background and the Irish Literary Renaissance, his connections with Samuel Beckett, and his relationship to James Joyce. The appendix includes a bibliographical essay by Edwin Gilcher. A valuable contribution to the criticism on Moore.

Farrow, Anthony. *George Moore*. Boston: Twayne, 1978. A helpful study of Moore for the beginning reader, but somewhat restricted in format. An appreciative approach to Moore that places him at a high level of literary distinction, despite the fact that his novels remain largely unread. Includes a selected bibliography.

Gilcher, Edwin. *A Bibliography of George Moore*. De Kalb: Northern Illinois Press, 1970. A valuable source of information on Moore, although Gilcher admits to omissions which he will include in an expanded and corrected edition of this bibliography. Some additions and corrections are mentioned in Gilcher's bibliographic essay in *George Moore in Perspective*.

Langenfeld, Robert. *An Annotated Bibliography*. New York: AMS Press, 1987. The most up-to-date and comprehensive bibliography on Moore. Gives credit to Gilcher's pioneering bibliography, and the introduction assesses Moore's reputation, past and present. An excellent resource.

Seinfelt, Frederick W. *George Moore: Ireland's Unconventional Realist*. Philadelphia: Dorrance, 1975. A full-length study that examines Moore's treatment of men and women in his novels. Seinfelt argues that Moore saw the two sexes as separate and incompatible, and that his works show "remarkable insight" into the state of marriage and male-female relationships. Includes an essay on the Wagnerian elements in Moore's writing, also referring to other influences on his work.

WRIGHT MORRIS

Born: Central City, Nebraska; January 6, 1910

Principal long fiction

My Uncle Dudley, 1942; *The Man Who Was There*, 1945; *The World in the Attic*, 1949; *Man and Boy*, 1951; *The Works of Love*, 1952; *The Deep Sleep*, 1953; *The Huge Season*, 1954; *The Field of Vision*, 1956; *Love Among the Cannibals*, 1957; *Ceremony in Lone Tree*, 1960; *What a Way to Go*, 1962; *Cause for Wonder*, 1963; *One Day*, 1965; *In Orbit*, 1967; *Fire Sermon*, 1971; *War Games*, 1972; *A Life*, 1973; *The Fork River Space Project*, 1977; *Plains Song, for Female Voices*, 1980.

Other literary forms

Several of Wright Morris' books, including *The Inhabitants* (1946), *The Home Place* (1948), *God's Country and My People* (1968), and *Love Affair: A Venetian Journal* (1972), are "photo-texts." In the first of these, Morris describes the "inhabitants" of America from coast to coast through photographs of their structures—buildings which have affected the "indwellers." Pictures of porch fronts in the West, for example, reveal New England influences, as do the inhabitants of the dwellings. The photographs, although not synchronized with the text, appear on facing pages and combine with it to make a larger statement than would be possible from either medium used alone—a statement about America and its people and their place in the changing world. Fences, privies, and churches are among the other artifacts pictured on unnumbered pages and bearing a poetic relationship to the human characters described in the text; it is up to the reader to determine the truths thereby conveyed.

In *The Home Place*, Morris uses a similar technique to explore further man's relationship with his home and its influence upon him. The protagonist Clyde Muncy, returning to the Nebraska of his childhood, discovers how crowded an empty house can be and moves on. The rural people who have never left Nebraska are a part of the surroundings, and the urbanized Muncy cannot insinuate himself comfortably into a changed landscape, worn, decaying, and void of certain landmarks present only in his memory. As in the earlier photo-text, however, people inhabit the artifacts, as the artifacts inhabit them.

God's Country and My People, more autobiographical yet less nostalgic than its predecessors, suggests present-day values and their usefulness to a later generation. *Love Affair*, utilizing color photographs taken in Venice in 1969, presents the problem of "shouting" that everything is of interest, while the black and white pictures of the photo-texts of the plains are more selective in their emphasis. Morris has also published several collections of photographs: *Wright Morris: Structures and Artifacts, Photographs 1933-1954* (1975), *Photographs and Words* (1982), and *Picture America* (1982). A meditation on photography and writing, *Timepieces: Word and Image*, appeared in 1989.

Morris' books of essays include *The Territory Ahead* (1963), a work of criticism expressing his admiration for the artistry of Henry James and the vitality of D. H. Lawrence, and his concern about the misuse of the past by sentimental illustrators or writers. *A Bill of Rites, a Bill of Wrongs, a Bill of Goods* (1968) contains more critical essays deploring the practices of professional reviewers, of speed readers, and of symbol-hunters, and the passing of the reader who simply wants to establish a dialogue with the writer. The writer's duty, says Morris, is to bring the real world into a field of vision that will give it meaning and to stir the readers' imagination. In this sometimes angry book, Morris also denounces advertising, which has created the consumer culture with its longing for possessions, and technological expertise, which allows humankind to explore space without at all improving life on Earth. In his third book of essays, *About Fiction* (1975), Morris describes the ideal reader, discusses point of view, and compares realism with "fabulation"—a more artistic, shapely, idea-filled narrative, exemplified by the works of John Barth, Thomas Pynchon, and Vladimir Nabokov. *Earthly Delights, Unearthly Adornments: American Writers as Image-Makers* (1978) surveys his own career and the course of American writing through quotations, recollections, and pictures. Perhaps the best summation of these books of essays is to be found in the subtitle of *About Fiction*, "Reverent Reflections on the Nature of Fiction with Irreverent Observations on Writers, Readers, and Other Abuses."

Morris' other works include a memoir, *Will's Boy* (1981), and an anthology, *Wright Morris: A Reader* (1970), which contains two short novels, *The Works of Love* and *The Field of Vision*, two short stories, and selections from eight other novels. *Real Losses, Imaginary Gains* (1976) is a collection of thirteen short stories; another volume of Morris' short fiction appeared in 1986, *Collected Stories, 1948-1986*. The autobiographical *Solo: An American Dreamer in Europe, 1933-1934* (1983) was followed by *A Cloak of Light: Writing My Life* (1985).

Achievements

While a few of Morris' books have European settings, he is most effective when writing about his native Nebraska and picaresque characters returning home to try to recapture memories or relive the past. That Morris is more concerned with his craft than are most modern writers is evidenced by his several books of essays on the writing of fiction and the readers thereof. A prolific writer, Morris is primarily a delineator of character, rather than a constructor of intricate plots. He pays considerable attention to the "arti-

facts" of his characters' worlds and to the workings of their minds, most particularly to the kinds of thoughts that are never expressed aloud.

Morris is inevitably compared to both James Agee and Walker Evans
because of his poetic, reflective prose about the dignity of rural life and
because his photography is reminiscent of Evans' in *Let Us Now Praise
Famous Men* (1960). Morris combines the talents of both men in his photo-
texts, conducting a search for the meaning of America through word and
picture.

Although Morris has always received critical acclaim, he has not enjoyed
a popular success. Robert Knoll has suggested that the reason may be his
failure to involve the reader in the exciting events of his fiction. He rather
invites the reader casually, as did Robert Frost, to come along and clear the
leaves away. His poetic style is as far removed as prose can be from the
popular journalistic narrative mode. Although Morris himself knows that
readers do not want fictive distance, he continues to create novels that create
rather than confess, that disturb rather than reassure.

Morris has received three Guggenheim awards, two of them for photography and the third for fiction (*The Deep Sleep*), the National Book Award
for *The Field of Vision* and *Plains Song, for Female Voices*, and the National
Institute for Arts and Letters Award for *Ceremony in Lone Tree*. He received
a National Institute Grant in 1960 and was fiction judge for the National
Book Award in 1969.

Biography

After his birth in Central City, Nebraska, Wright Morris lived with his
father in Schuyler, Kearney, and other small Nebraska towns along the Platte
River before moving to Omaha. He worked for two summers on his uncle
Harry's farm in Norfolk, Nebraska, but the move to Chicago in 1924 brought
him a different kind of employment at the YMCA. He attended Adventist
College in California for five weeks, then worked for several months on the
Texas ranch of his uncle Dwight Osborn. He entered Pomona College in
Claremont, California, but withdrew to spend a year in Austria, Italy, Ger-
many, and France. He had written some brief prose sketches while at Pomona,
and he returned to California to begin his first novel.

Morris married Mary Ellen Finfrock of Cleveland, Ohio, in 1934. Between
1935 and 1938, he wrote two novels and the sketches for *The Inhabitants* and
developed the interest in photography which flourished during two summers
at Wellfleet, Massachusetts. In 1940-1941, he toured the United States, taking
pictures to be used in *The Inhabitants*. He lived in California two more years
before moving to Haverford, Pennsylvania, in 1944. In 1954, he began spending more time in Venice, Italy, Mexico, and Greece, returning intermittently
to California. He has lectured at the University of Southern California and
at Amherst College and taught at the California State universities in Los

Angeles and San Francisco.

In 1961, he and his first wife were divorced, and Morris married Josephine Kantor. He was selected in 1983 to occupy the Visiting Writers' Chair at the University of Alabama.

Analysis

A novelist who has been read more—and surely appreciated more—in Europe than in his own country, Wright Morris has explored the legacies of heroism and nostalgia, the dreams and delusions examined by earlier twentieth century American writers. Another concern of Morris, whose novels seldom display violence, is the rise of violence in America. His narratives usually take place within a twenty-four-hour time period, suggesting the capture of a finite period of time as the photographer captures a finite space with his camera. This limitation of time unifies Morris' novels, which are more intimately related by the device of recurring characters. Indeed, David Madden and other critics have suggested that one must read Morris' entire canon in order to understand any one novel. Two books written in the 1970's, for example, retell the story of Uncle Dudley thirty years after his appearance as the protagonist of the first novel.

The spirit of place, whether it be the central plains, a California beach, a Philadelphia suburb, or an Alpine chateau, is central to Morris' novels, and the impingement of objects or places upon man a major facet of Morris' imagination, as they had been to Henry James, who believed that places gave out a "mystic meaning." Admittedly influenced by James and by D. H. Lawrence, Morris has been his own man for five prolific decades. Fortunate to have as his birthplace the "navel of the universe," the central United States, he has from that vantage point "salvaged" meaningful artifacts that represent an earlier American life and, concomitantly, the values of that life.

Accused by Alfred Kazin of overloading his fiction with symbols, Morris has disavowed any conscious symbolic creation, noting that symbols may appear without the author's deliberate intent in any good work of fiction. Obsessed by the cliché, which he considers a dead repository for something once alive, he peoples his fiction with stereotypes and challenges himself to bring them back to life. Wayne Booth describes Morris' transformation of clichés as "toying" with them. David Madden sees the characters' coming to terms with clichés as absolutely essential to their knowledge of the enjoyment of love, sex, their bodies—even of travel. He adds that after Morris, clichés are never the same, because they are killed and resurrected in the same moment, reappearing in an improved form.

It is not easy to generalize about an oeuvre as varied as Morris', but he does frequently disregard chronology, an attempt to possess time and understand it being one of his obsessions. A recurring relationship, as Madden points out, is that of the hero and his "witnesses"—the characters who are transformed because their lives have intersected his. The contact, strangely enough, is often more meaningful after the death of the hero. Wayne Booth notes that the novels of Morris begin with a problem or a misunderstanding and conclude with a solution or a clarification. While this statement could be made about most plots, it is not the beginnings and the endings that occupy Morris' inventive mind, but what is in between. The resolutions that he works toward require especially appropriate intervening incidents that require "a lot of doing." Morris, adds Booth, thinks of his introductions, not as promises to the reader, but as problems to be solved by the author himself. What is important in this kind of plot progression is the quality of the middle, and here Morris excels.

Believing that the fiction-writer must do more than reproduce facts, Morris transmutes his raw material, particularly his experience of the Midwest, through his imagination into something that he sees as more real than life itself.

My Uncle Dudley, Morris' somewhat autobiographical first novel, concerns an odyssey in an old Marmon touring car from California to the banks of the Mississippi. The central character, Uncle Dudley, a cross between a modern-day Odysseus and Don Quixote, describes himself as a "horseless knight." His impossible dream of committing one single audacious act is realized when he spits a stream of brown tobacco juice accurately into the eye of a sadistic, perverted policeman.

What is experimental about this novel is the use of the unnamed adolescent narrator, known only as the Kid, who records no emotion at all, thereby enabling the author himself to remain detached. As Madden has noted, the heroic act requires a witness. The Kid is Uncle Dudley's witness, through whose imagination the reader recognizes heroism and an unexpressed affection.

Morris acknowledges a debt to Mark Twain's *The Adventures of Huckleberry Finn* (1884), although he had not then read the Twain work "as a writer." The Kid is the Huck figure, Uncle Dudley the Jim-father, and the journey in the Marmon a flight from repressive civilization similar to the downriver trip of the raft. The unifying element in Morris' narrative is not the river or the road, however, but Uncle Dudley himself, whose final foolhardy act qualifies him as the first in a long line of heroes.

Agee Ward, the "protagonist" of *The Man Who Was There*, has gone to war and has been reported missing in action; he makes his presence felt through his absence, and is a hero not of action, as was Uncle Dudley, but of imagination. In the novel's first section, he is remembered at Grandmother Herkimer's funeral by Private Reagan, a boyhood friend, whose stare causes the minister to change his sermon subject to the desire for immortality. The middle section of the book, entitled "The Three Agee Wards," re-presents the hero through the media of family photographs, sketches, and letters, through knowledge about his ancestors, and through the mind of the village barber, who has seen him in the eyes of his now deceased mother. Her gravestone inscription announces, "She died that he might live."

The unity of the novel results from the hero's power to transform others. Agee has become a painter and a writer, whose notebooks contain drawings of such artifacts as a pump and a privy, his perspective faulty because his memory fails and because he cannot reconcile the real and the imaginary in his own mind.

The last witness to be transformed is his spinster landlady Gussie Newcomb, who becomes Agee's symbolic next-of-kin when she is notified by the War Department that he is missing. She barely remembers her lodger, but when the people who do remember him want to look at his belongings, Gussie moves into the apartment herself. Peter Spavic, who has kept up Agee's album, and who is obviously a witness, enables Gussie to absorb Agee's personality, the transformation assisted by her communion with the missing man's personal artifacts. Gussie begins to drink, to tell Agee jokes, to dress in some of his costumes, and to take the initiative in her relationship with her suitor, Mr. Bloom. She sits in the dark, as Agee had sat, and she agrees with Peter to name his first son Ward while she will name her first child Agee.

The book explores an idea which was then a cliché: the effect of a dead or missing-in-action soldier on those left at home. Agee, a hero in the literal sense because he actually wants to combat Fascism, transforms his witnesses by his very absence, at the same time suggesting the problems of an artist who tries to filter reality through his imagination.

The first few chapters of Morris' novel *Man and Boy* have been widely anthologized, with slight changes, as the short story "The Ram in the Thicket." The first of Morris' novels to depart from the plains tradition, *Man and Boy* takes place in Philadelphia and New York and describes a single day in the life of the remnants of a family. The Navy is to name a destroyer in honor of the Boy, who has died a hero. His father Warren recollects the day he gave the Boy an air rifle, a gift which caused his mother to abolish Christmas henceforth and the Boy to become a hunter, who perhaps wanted to die. Recalling the diverse impressions of Agee Ward in *The Man Who Was There*, the Boy Virgil appears to his two parents in different ways, transforming them both, but not improving their relationship.

Warren Ormsby, the Man, is a westerner who boasts that his pioneer grandfather used to eat three rabbits as a meal. He soon learns, however, that his wife Violet is not very "feminine." She has, in fact, appropriated to herself the virtues once attributed to pioneer men. Warren has to call her "Mother" and allows her to dominate the household. She rids the house of germs and bathroom sounds, and even of conversation. While Ormsby cares for the birds in a way that is to him a form of worship, a "Eucharist," Mother insists on calling them by their Latin names. After the Boy is dead, he appears to his father in a dream, wearing "bright, exotic plumage" and accompanied by a flock of birds. When the father tries to join the birds, they attack him. Even in his dream, he recognizes the Mother's effort to destroy the Boy's love for his father, who has been systematically unmanned by Mother.

Indirectly responsible for her son's death, Mother is selected to christen the boat named for her son; thus ironically ensuring the continuation of killing, to which she has been so opposed. The Boy lives on in the imagination of the Man, but Mother's power may extend over that realm eventually; it has embodied the sanitized house and defeated the United States Navy on the day of the ceremony.

Morris has admitted that he gave an inordinate amount of time to writing *The Works of Love*. In his first novel, he had set out to make a hero of a nonheroic figure, in the second to allow a man who was not present to dominate the action, and in the third, to allow a man to be dominated by a ruthless female, who finally won his grudging respect, if not admiration. In the fourth novel, the protagonist, Will Brady, learns to love in a prodigious, self-conscious, almost methodical manner, even though he has not himself been loved or found suitable recipients for his own works of love. The self-centered women in his life have not appreciated his fumbling, inarticulate efforts at communication. Two of them have been prostitutes, one of whom laughed when he proposed marriage; the other ran away and mailed him another man's baby son to adopt. After his marriage to the widow Ethel Bassett, who sleeps like a mummy tightly wrapped in a sheet, he lies beside her listing in his incipiently loving mind her reasons for doing so. The last woman to whom he tries to become a father-husband is a cigar-counter girl turned alcoholic streetwalker. In an effort to understand and grow closer to his adopted son Willy, Will searches the pages of *Penrod* and *The Adventures of Tom Sawyer* for enlightenment. His final role, that of a department store Santa Claus, allows him to touch and love little children, at the same time distributing some of the works of his abundant love.

Will handles the eggs that he sells with the same gentle touch that he reserves for women, sensing perhaps that both species contain the miracle of life. He is more at home, however, with the eggs than with the women, always a stranger in his own house. In his pursuit of love, he finally cuts himself off from all Midwestern, rural roots and heads for Chicago on a quest to fill his emotional void. His incapacity to receive love, his failure to understand himself, and especially his inability to communicate his feelings have set up an almost insurmountable barrier between Will and his love-objects. Significantly more at home in a hotel than in his house, he has, for most of his life, failed to connect with the rest of mankind.

In *The Deep Sleep*, Morris again presents a hero who has died, this time Judge Howard Porter. Porter's "witnesses" include the hired man Parson, who has worked for the Porter family for thirty years and loves the almost unlovable Mrs. Porter; the Judge's son-in-law Paul Webb, who gets to know him well just before the funeral, and the Judge's mother, who communicates by tapping her cane and never became acquainted with her son at all. Mrs. Porter had known her husband twice—once in the biblical sense, when their first child was conceived, and a second time just before the funeral, when she told their daughter Katherine that she missed him.

Paul Webb discovers that Mrs. Porter had not ruled her husband as iron-handedly as she had thought. Like Violet Ormsby's husband, the Judge had found a basement-toilet retreat where he stashed his whiskey. In addition, Paul discovers, Judge Porter had an attic hideout where he smoked cigars and admired his expensive Swiss watch, while he carried a cheap, loud, dollar watch in public. The artist Webb is objective enough to get a balanced picture of the Porter family as he studies the house, room by room. While his wife Katherine fears that he cannot show her mother the sympathy she deserves, the fact that the two finally arrive at the same conclusion about Judge and Mrs. Porter suggests that both are fair in their appraisal.

Like Gussie in *The Man Who Was There*, Webb takes on an additional characteristic of the dead man every time he gains a new insight. As Webb becomes the Judge's spiritual son, he reaches a better understanding of Mrs. Porter. The two watches become the artifacts that connect Webb and his mother-in-law, whose sense of order ("Never go to bed with dirty dishes in the house") leads to an understanding with daughter Katherine. Webb finds satisfaction in a compassionate act: he places the gold watch in the cabinet, where Mrs. Porter will have the pleasure of finding it herself.

David Madden explains that the novel's title refers to the deep sleep into which American males of the twentieth century have allowed themselves to fall. Like the sleep induced in Adam before God created Eve from his rib, it is so deep that the man never awakens. Woman is born; she dominates, and man sleeps on. That this is a twentieth century phenomenon is demonstrated in Morris' 1980 novel *Plains Song, for Female Voices*, whose character Cora carries out her wifely duties with such distaste that she bites herself on her wedding night. Her husband Emerson feels obliged to explain to the frontier doctor that Cora suffers from the bite of a horse; the uncomplaining Cora finds most of her life as a Nebraska farmwife distasteful, but rebellion never occurs to her.

Another novel with a dead hero, *The Huge Season* is different because it is told from the single viewpoint of Peter Foley, a professor of classics in a small Pennsylvania college and himself a fully developed character. Foley attempts to escape the bondage of two experiences from the past. The first took place at Colton College in California: Foley shared a suite with several other young men, among them Charles Lawrence, a would-be great tennis player who has since committed suicide. The second experience was a single day spent in New York after one of his other suitemates, Jesse Proctor, testified before the Senate Committee on UnAmerican Activities.

Lawrence, the hero who affects all the other men, is another Midwesterner with an audacious grandfather. Lawrence himself tries to be audacious, both in the bullring and on the tennis court. He succeeds at tennis, not because he plays well, but because he wills himself to win. As is to be expected, the hero strongly influences the lives of his witnesses—three of them actually write books about him.

Foley finally frees himself from captivity by re-creating the past in his mind while wearing his hero's jacket around the house. As he achieves his own freedom, Foley at the same time understands more about America. The title of the novel refers to the past—the youth—that Foley realizes is over when he is released into the present. Lawrence, however, continues to live in the imagination of his witness, who has also acquired the tennis player's audacity.

The past, so important in *The Huge Season*, is missing in *Love Among the Cannibals*. Macgregor and Horter, two middle-aged Hollywood songwriters, take two girls to Acapulco, one a Memphis "chick" who reads Norman Vincent Peale, the other Eva the Greek. The story is about people who live to the tune of "What Next?," a song in progress when Horter and Eva meet. Their car, a fire-engine red convertible with green leather upholstery, has a built-in record player. Macgregor, a true Hollywood cliché and composer of sentimental popular music, insists that what he is looking for in a woman is "the real thing." Horter, who writes cliché lyrics because that is what Hollywood demands, persuades Billie, Eva, and Mac that they can write a Mexican musical if they have the proper setting. Mac and Billie find romance in Acapulco and swear to be true to each other, but Eva leaves with a ladybug-shaped biologist, Dr. Leggett.

The Hollywood beach with its suntan oil and portable radios symbolizes the artificial present with no traditions or values, the Mexican beach the real present, unspoiled, honest, and authentic. The two "artists" deal in clichés of the kind demanded by mass culture, but Horter recognizes that even clichés can be powerful. He is transformed in Mexico by the natural, physical powers of the Greek, who is unabashedly tanned all over. As he appreciates her vitality and audacity, he even considers returning to the life of a serious poet. He has been stripped to essentials and returned to a wholeness and a recognition of his past that bring with them a hope for the future.

After several decades of novels about women who dominated their men, lured them into sex, and left them, or married them and honeymooned shrouded in a sheet, Morris' *Plains Song, for Female Voices* should perhaps have redressed some grievances. Madge, however, the only happy wife in the novel, is content with being a bearer of children and smelling Fels-Naptha soap. Cora, a plain Ohio girl, who marries Emerson to move to Nebraska, becomes Madge's mother. Cora's world is Emerson's farm, and although she finds enjoyment only with her chickens and her garden, she never considers widening her horizon. Sharon Rose, Madge's cousin, is the modern woman and artist who shuns men altogether, finding her happiness in fleeing Nebraska for Chicago and music study. Sharon cannot understand her past and cannot understand why her relatives are content with their bleak lives, but she does attain a certain amount of self-knowledge.

Like so many of Morris' protagonists, Sharon tries to go home again. What startles her memory is not the paint scaling off Emerson's house, but the absence of people. The dipper (a marvelous artifact) floats in a bucket of water, and Sharon smells scorched ironing. Displeased that Madge's husband Ned refers to his car as a "good girl," Sharon becomes ill when Avery, who plans to be a veterinarian, chips tartar off the teeth of a Maltese cat with his thumbnail while she is at the dinner table. On the train on the way back to Chicago, however, she is ashamed of disliking these friendly, decent people. She writes Madge's daughter to suggest that Blanche attend a private school for girls in Waukegan and spend her weekends in Chicago, because Sharon cannot bear the "thought of Blanche thick with child by some loutish youth."

When the pretty girl arrives, Sharon deliberately dresses her in a way to "emphasize her adolescence" so that the "idling males" will not be tempted to molest her. When she finds Blanche with a "beardless, oafish" young man, his arm about the girl's waist, she knows that her efforts to "citify" Blanche—actually to make her independent—have been in vain, and she allows her to return home to her daddy, whom she has missed a great deal.

Sharon finally teaches at Wellesley, more respected than liked by her students. On her last trip home for Cora's funeral, Madge's daughter Caroline assures Sharon that because of her example, the girls "don't get married anymore unless [they] want to." All that is left of her parents' farm is a pitted field of stumps. "There was nothing worth saving," says Caroline, who adds that she would never forgive Cora for her failure to complain about the hard farm life.

Funerals and eggs—an unlikely combination—continue to recur in Morris' fiction. Unlikely, until one realizes that, in a Morris novel, the dying will "connect" with and transform many characters, perhaps even achieving resurrection through them, and that eggs, important to Morris since his father sold them, represent not only a new and ongoing life, but also the rural Midwest to which he returns again and again for his fictional world.

The wasteland motif, actually verbalized in some of the novels, is to be found in a society without imagination, as on the Los Angeles beach where women wear bathing caps that look like fake hair. The one who can deliver others from such a wasteland is a man or woman with a creative heart—an audacious artist who dares to transform the clichés of the past into the wonders of the present and future, who can convert the raw material of America into values that enable man to endure.

Sue L. Kimball

Other major works

SHORT FICTION: *Green Grass, Blue Sky, White House*, 1970; *Here is Einbaum*, 1973; *Real Losses, Imaginary Gains*, 1976; *Collected Stories: 1948-1986*, 1986.

NONFICTION: *The Inhabitants*, 1946; *The Home Place*, 1948; *The Territory Ahead*, 1958, 1963; *A Bill of Rites, a Bill of Wrongs, a Bill of Goods*, 1968; *God's Country and My People*, 1968; *Love Affair: A Venetian Journal*, 1972; *Wright Morris: Structures and Artifacts, Photographs, 1933-1954*, 1975; *About Fiction: Reverent Reflections on the Nature of Fiction with Irreverent Observations on Writers, Readers, and Other Abuses*, 1975; *Earthly Delights, Unearthly Adornments*, 1978; *Will's Boy*, 1981; *Photographs and Words*, 1982; *Picture America*, 1982; *Solo: An American Dreamer in Europe, 1933-1934*, 1983; *A Cloak of Light: Writing My Life*, 1985.

MISCELLANEOUS: *Wright Morris: A Reader*, 1970; *Timepieces: Photographs, Writing, and Memory*, 1989.

Bibliography

Bird, Roy K. *Wright Morris: Memory and Imagination*. New York: Peter Lang, 1985. Makes the case that the most rewarding elements of Morris' works are his authorial intrusions and meditations on the status and meaning of fiction. Draws extensively from Morris' critical and autobiographical writings to illustrate his creation of self-conscious narratives, especially in *The Fork River Space Project* and *Plains Song, for Female Voices*. This perceptive study includes a bibliography and an index.

Crump, G. B. *The Novels of Wright Morris: A Critical Interpretation*. Lincoln: University of Nebraska Press, 1978. The most thorough consideration of Morris' art so far. Analyzes all of his works through *A Life*, shows the influence of such writers as Henry James, and places Morris in the context of contemporary American fiction. A bibliography and index are included.

Hicks, Granville. Introduction to *Wright Morris: A Reader*. New York: Harper & Row, 1970. A lengthy essay by a critic who followed Morris' career carefully from its beginning, praising both the uniqueness and universality of his characters and the originality of his style, particularly his manipulation of clichés.

Howard, Leon. *Wright Morris*. Minneapolis: University of Minnesota Press, 1968. This pamphlet-length study of Morris' works through *A Bill of Rites, a Bill of Wrongs, a Bill of Goods* argues that Morris is the most consistently original of contemporary American novelists. This excellent introduction to Morris illustrates how he uses the past to illuminate the present. A bibliography is included.

Knoll, Robert E., ed. *Conversations with Wright Morris: Critical Views and Responses*. Lincoln: University of Nebraska Press, 1977. This excellent collection contains three analyses of Morris' work, four interviews with

him, an essay by Morris, a selection of his photographs, the most extensive
bibliography available which includes reviews of his books, and an index.

Madden, David. *Wright Morris*. New York: Twayne, 1964. This first book-
length analysis of Morris is still the best and lays the groundwork for all
further study, examining his works through *Cause for Wonder*. Madden,
who has written several later essays about Morris, believes him to be the
most thoroughly American contemporary writer and shows how the brilliance of his style transforms the ordinary into art. Includes a lengthy annotated bibliography, a chronology, and an index.

Wydeven, Joseph J. "Images and Icons: The Fiction and Photography of
Wright Morris." In *Under the Sun: Myth and Realism in Western American
Literature*, edited by Barbara Howard Meldrum. Troy, N.Y.: Whitston,
1985. This lengthy essay is the best examination of the relation between
Morris' photography and his fiction. Shows how he explores the complex
relation between the reality and the myth of the American West. Six photographs are included.

TONI MORRISON

Born: Lorain, Ohio; February 18, 1931

Principal long fiction
The Bluest Eye, 1970; *Sula*, 1973; *Song of Solomon*, 1977; *Tar Baby*, 1981; *Beloved*, 1987.

Other literary forms
Toni Morrison is primarily a novelist. She has published a short story, "Big Box," in *Ms.* magazine (1980), and many essays, one of the most notable of which is "Unspeakable Things Unspoken: The Afro-American Presence in American Literature" (*Michigan Quarterly Review* 28, Winter, 1989: 1-34).

Achievements
Morrison is generally regarded as one of the most significant black American novelists to have emerged in the 1970's. Her novel *Sula* was nominated for the National Book Award in 1975. In 1977, *Song of Solomon* won the National Book Critics Circle Award. The former was a Book-of-the-Month Club alternate and the latter, a main selection. In 1988, *Beloved* was awarded the Pulitzer Prize.

Morrison's fiction, especially *Song of Solomon*, has been compared to Ralph Ellison's *Invisible Man* (1952) for its mixture of the literal and the fantastic, the real and the surreal. Morrison has been praised for her use of language and for the sense of voice that emerges not only in her dialogue but also in the movement of her narratives. Morrison's novels are also remarkable for their sense of place, for the detailed, coherent physical worlds she creates. Finally, her fiction is noteworthy for its depiction of the deep psychic realities of women's experience.

Biography
Toni Morrison, daughter of George and Ramah (Willis) Wofford, was born Chloe Anthony Wofford on February 18, 1931, in Lorain, Ohio. Her father, a laborer, simultaneously held three jobs to take care of his family. Morrison was graduated from high school with honors and entered Howard University in Washington, D.C., where she received a B.A. degree in 1953. In 1955, Morrison earned a master's degree at Cornell University. She subsequently taught undergraduate English at Texas Southern University, and in 1957, she joined the faculty of Howard University, her alma mater. While there, she married Harold Morrison, an architect originally from Jamaica. Morrison became the mother of two sons, Ford and Slade, before being divorced. While in Washington, Morrison joined a writer's group and began the story which became her first novel, *The Bluest Eye*. In 1965, Morrison became an editor

for Random House, first in Syracuse and later in Manhattan, where she became a senior editor. Beginning in 1967, she also taught as a visiting lecturer at Yale University and lectured at many other universities as well.

Analysis

In all of her fiction, Toni Morrison explores the conflict between society and the individual. She shows how the individual who defies social pressures can forge a self by drawing on the resources of the natural world, on a sense of continuity within the family and within the history of a people, and on dreams and other unaccountable sources of psychic power.

In *The Bluest Eye*, Morrison shows how society inflicts on its members an inappropriate standard of beauty and worth, a standard that mandates that to be loved one must meet the absolute "white" standard of blond hair and blue eyes. Morrison's narrator says that two of the most destructive ideas in history are the idea of romantic love (canceling both lust and caring) and the idea of an absolute, univocal standard of beauty.

In the novel, the most extreme victim of these destructive ideas is Pecola, who finds refuge in madness after she has been thoroughly convinced of her own ugliness (confirmed when she is raped by her own father, Cholly). Mrs. Breedlove, Pecola's mother, is another victim who gets her idea of an unvarying standard of beauty from romantic movies which glorify white movie stars. When she realizes the impassible gap between that ideal and her physical self (she has a deformed foot and two missing teeth), she also gives up any hope of maintaining a relationship with Cholly, her husband, except one of complete antagonism and opposition. Mrs. Breedlove even comes to prefer the little white girl she takes care of at work to her own daughter, Pecola, whom she has always perceived as ugly.

The ideal of unattainable physical beauty is reinforced by the sugary, unattainable world of the family depicted in the school readers—of Mother and Father and Dick and Jane and their middle-class, suburban existence. The contrast between that false standard of life and the reality lived by the children makes them ashamed of their reality, of the physical intimacy of families in which the children have seen their fathers naked.

Although Pecola is thoroughly victimized, Freida and Claudia MacTeer, schoolmates of Pecola, do survive with some integrity and richness. Freida seems to accept Shirley Temple as the ideal of cuteness, but her sister Claudia, a center of consciousness in the novel, responds with anger and defiance, dismembering the hard, cold, smirking baby dolls she receives at Christmas. What Claudia really desires at Christmas is simply an experience of family closeness in the kitchen, an experience of flowers, fruit, and music, of security.

Claudia's anger at the white baby dolls springs from a conviction of her own reality and her own worth. In defense of her own individuality, Claudia rejects Shirley Temple and "Meringue Pie," the high yellow princess, Maureen

Peal. It is that defense of her own reality that makes Claudia sympathize with Pecola and try to defend her, even to the point of sacrificing Freida's money and her own.

Claudia is especially puzzled and regretful that nobody says "poor baby" to the raped Pecola, that nobody wants to welcome her unborn baby into the world. It would be only natural, "human nature," it seems, for people to sympathize with a victim and rejoice at the creation of a human life. Instead, the springs of human sympathy have been dammed up by social disapproval. Suffering from the self-hatred they have absorbed from the society around them, the black community maintains inflexible social standards and achieves respectability by looking down on Pecola. The two MacTeer sisters appeal to nature to help Pecola and her unborn baby, but nature fails them just as prayer did: no marigolds sprout and grow that year. The earth is unyielding. The baby is born dead. Eventually, even the two girls become distanced from Pecola, whose only friend is an imaginary one, a part of herself who can see the blue eyes she was promised. Pecola functions as a scapegoat for the society around her, and Claudia's sympathy later grows into an understanding of how the community used Pecola to protect themselves from scorn and insult. What finally flowers in Claudia is insight and a more conscious respect for her own reality.

Sula also explores the oppressive nature of white society, evident in the very name of the "Bottom," a hillside community which had its origin in the duplicitous white treatment of an emancipated black slave who was promised fertile "bottom land" along with his freedom. In a bitterly ironic twist, the whites take over the hillside again when they want suburban houses that will catch the breeze. In taking back the Bottom, they destroy a place, a community with its own identity. In turn, the black community, corrupted by white society, rejects Sula for her experimenting with her life, for trying to live free like a man instead of accepting the restrictions of the traditional female role.

Sula provokes the reader to question socially accepted concepts of good and evil. As Sula is dying, she asks her girlhood friend Nel, "How do you know that you were the good one?" Although considered morally loose and a witch by the townspeople, the unconventional Sula cannot believe herself to be an inferior individual. Contrasting the traditional role of mother and church woman that Nel has embraced, Sula's individuality is refreshing and intriguing. Despite her death, Sula maintains an independence that ultimately stands in proud opposition to the established network of relationships that exist within conventional society.

The novel shows that the Bottom society encompasses both good and evil. The people are accustomed to suffering and enduring evil. In varying degrees, they accept Eva's murder of her drug-addict son, Plum, and Hannah's seduction of their husbands, one after another. The community, nevertheless, cannot encompass Sula, a woman who thinks for herself without conforming to their sensibilities. They have to turn her into a witch, so that they can mobilize themselves against her "evil" and cherish their goodness. Without the witch, their goodness grows faint again. Like Pecola, Sula is made a scapegoat.

Growing up in the Bottom, Sula creates an identity for herself, first from the reality of physical experience. When she sees her mother Hannah burning up in front of her eyes, she feels curiosity. Her curiosity is as honest as Hannah's admission that she loves her daughter Sula the way any mother would, but that she does not like her. Hearing her mother reject her individuality, Sula concludes that there is no one to count on except herself.

In forging a self, Sula also draws on sexual experience as a means of joy, as a means of feeling sadness, and as a means of feeling her own power. Sula does not substitute a romantic dream for the reality of that physical experience. She does finally desire a widening of that sexual experience into a continuing relationship with Ajax, but the role of nurturing and possession is fatal to her. Ajax leaves, and Sula sickens and dies.

A closeness to the elemental processes of nature gives a depth to the lives of the Bottom-dwellers, although nature does not act with benevolence or even with consistency. Plum and Hannah, two of Eva's children, die by fire, one sacrificed by Eva and one ignited by capricious accident. Chicken Little and several of those who follow Shadrack on National Suicide Day drown because acts of play go wrong and inexplicably lead to their destruction. Sula's supposed identity as a witch is connected to the plague of robins that coincides with her return to the Bottom. The people of the Bottom live within Nature and try to make some sense of it, even though their constructions are strained and self-serving.

On one level, Sula refuses any connection to history and family continuity. Her grandmother Eva says that Sula should get a man and make babies, but Sula says that she would rather make herself. On the other hand, Sula is a descendant of the independent women Eva and Hannah, both of whom did what they had to do. It is at least rumored that Eva let her leg be cut off by a train so that she could get insurance money to take care of her three children when BoyBoy, her husband, abandoned her. When her husband died, Hannah needed "manlove," and she got it from her neighbors' husbands, despite community disapproval. In their mold, Sula is independent enough to threaten Eva with fire and to assert her own right to live, even if her grandmother does not like Sula's way of living.

To flourish, Morrison suggests, conventional society needs an opposite pole. A richness comes from the opposition and the balance—from the difference— and an acceptance of that difference would make scapegoats unnecessary. The world of the Bottom is poorer with Sula dead and out of it.

In *Song of Solomon*, Morrison again traces the making of a self. The novel is a departure for Morrison in that the protagonist is not female, but a young man, Milkman Dead. Milkman grows up in a comfortable, insulated, middle-class family, the grandson of a doctor on his mother's side and the son of a businessman, whose father owned his own farm. Son of a doting mother, Milkman is nursed a long time, the reason for his nickname, and is sent to school in velvet knickers. Guitar Baines, a Southside black, becomes Milkman's friend and an ally against the other children's teasing.

As the novel progresses, though, and as Milkman discovers the reality of his family and friends as separate people with their own griefs and torments, Milkman comes to feel that everyone wants him dead. Ironically, Milkman's last name actually is "Dead," the result of a drunken clerk's error when Milkman's grandfather was registering with the Freedmen's Bureau.

Milkman learns that his mere existence is extraordinary, since even before his birth, his father tried to kill him. Milkman survived that threat through the intercession of his mother and, especially, of his aunt, Pilate, a woman with no navel. After having been conjured by Pilate into making love to his wife again, years after he had turned against her, Macon Dead wanted the resulting baby aborted. Ruth, the baby's mother, out of fear of her husband, took measures to bring about an abortion, but Pilate intervened again and helped Ruth to find the courage to save the child and bear him.

In the present action of the novel, Hagar, Milkman's cousin, his first love and his first lover, pursues him month after month with whatever weapon she can find to kill him. Hagar wants Milkman's living life, not his dead life, but Milkman has rejected her, out of boredom and fear that he will be maneuvered into marrying her. At this point, he does not want to be tied down: he wants freedom and escape.

Hagar, like Pecola of *The Bluest Eye*, feels unlovely and unloved, rejected because Milkman does not like her black, curly hair. Pilate says that Milkman cannot *not* love her hair without *not* loving himself because it is the same hair that grows from his own body. Hagar is another victim of an absolutely univocal standard of beauty, and she is a character who needs a supporting society, a chorus of aunts and cousins and sisters to surround her with advice and protection. Instead, she has only Pilate and Reba, grandmother and mother, two women so strong and independent that they do not understand her weakness. Unhinged by Milkman's rejection of her, Hagar chases Milkman with various weapons, is repeatedly disarmed, and finally dies in total discouragement.

Trying to find out about his family's past, Milkman travels to Virginia, to Shalimar, a black town, where the men in the general store challenge him to fight, and one attacks him with a knife. Milkman does not understand why these people want his life, but they think he has insulted and denied their masculinity with his powerful northern money and his brusque treatment of them, by not asking their names and not offering his own.

The most serious threat to Milkman's life, however, turns out to be Guitar,

Milkman's friend and spiritual brother. When Guitar tries to kill Milkman, he is betraying the reality of their friendship for the idea of revenge against whites and compensation for the personal deprivation he has suffered. Guitar thinks that Milkman has a cache of gold that he is not sharing with him, so he decides to kill him. Guitar rationalizes his decision by saying that the money is for the cause, for the work of the Seven Days, a group of seven black men sworn to avenge the deaths of innocent blacks at the hands of the whites.

Milkman's being alive at all, then, is a triumph, a victory that he slowly comes to appreciate after coming out of his comfortable shell of self-involvement. Unwillingly, Milkman comes to know the suffering and griefs of his mother and father and even his sisters Magdelene and Corinthians. The decisive experience in his self-making, however, is the quest for Pilate's gold on which his father sets him. In the first stage, the men are convinced that Pilate's gold hangs in a green sack from the ceiling of her house, and Guitar and Milkman attempt to steal it. The two friends succeed in taking the sack because the women in the house are simply puzzled, wondering why the men want a sack which is really full of old bones. In leaving the house, though, the two men are arrested, and Pilate must rescue them and the bones by doing an Aunt Jemima act for the white policemen. Milkman's father, Macon, is convinced that the gold still exists somewhere, and Milkman sets out to find it by going back to Pennsylvania, where Macon and Pilate grew up, and later to Virginia, where the previous generation lived.

Milkman's making of a self includes many of the archetypal adventures of the heroes of legend and myth. Like other heroes of legend, Milkman limps, with one leg shorter than the other, a mark of his specialness. Like Oedipus' parents, his parents try to kill him early in his life. There is a wise old lady who gives him help and advice. He goes on a quest for a treasure, and he hopes for gold and the hand of a beautiful princess. He solves a puzzle or riddle to achieve his quest and confirm his identity. He has a transcendent experience and reaches heights of prowess. (He can fly.) When his people turn against him, he gives his life for them.

Like Sula, too, Milkman creates a self from the reality of physical experience, the processes of nature, a connection to history and family continuity, and springs of human possibility through myth, dreams, legends, and other sources of psychic power. Milkman reaches an understanding of physical experience and the processes of nature in a struggle against the physical environment. As a rich city boy, Milkman was insulated from nature, but in his trip south to try to get the gold, he overcomes a series of physical obstacles to reach the cave where Macon and Pilate in their youth encountered the white man and the gold. Milkman gets there only after falling into the river and climbing up twenty feet of rock, splitting his shoes and the clothes that mark him as a city man. During the trip, Milkman loses his possessions—

trunk, clothes, and whiskey—and he makes it on his own, in a place where his father's name and father's money do not protect him. Milkman succeeds in finding Circe, who years ago sheltered Pilate and Macon when their father was killed, and he reaches the cave where there is no longer any gold.

Milkman also encounters nature as an obstacle to be overcome when, after the knife-fight in Shalimar, he is invited to go on a coon hunt into the woods with the older men of Shalimar. Again, Milkman undergoes a test, having to move through the woods in the dark, having to show the courage and physical endurance necessary to be one of the hunters. Milkman also experiences the music of the hunt, the communication between the men and the dogs, the language before language, of a time when men were so close to their physical reality that they were in harmony with all creatures.

Milkman also creates himself in searching for his origins. In searching for his fathers, he discovers himself; like Telemachus and Stephen Dedalus, Milkman must find the reality of his fathers to know his own potential. Milkman's original pursuit of the gold seems to be an impulse he gets from his father, the man of business, and even from his father's father, who was a lover of property. The quest, however, changes as Milkman pursues it, finding the thread of his family's history. Stopping in Pennsylvania, Milkman hears the stories of the men who knew his father and grandfather and who rejoice in their successes. The story of the Dead family dramatizes the dream and the failure of that dream for blacks in America. When the older Macon Dead was killed by white men for his flourishing farm, the possibilities of his neighbors were narrowed and their lives scarred. Seeing his father and grandfather through their former neighbor's eyes helps Milkman to understand better the pride that Macon had when he said that his father had let Macon work side by side with him and trusted him to share in his achievements.

In Shalimar, Milkman also learns about his great-grandfather by piecing together the memories of people there and by deciphering the children's game and song, a song about Solomon and Rynah that seems to be interspersed with nonsense words. Milkman matches this song to a song that he had heard Pilate sing about Sugarman. He solves the riddle of the song, and he even figures out what the ghost of Pilate's father meant when he said, "Sing," and when he told Pilate to go get the bones. Finally, he discovers that his grandmother was an American Indian, Singing Bird, and that his great-grandfather, Solomon, was one of the legendary flying Africans, the father of twenty-one sons, a slave who one day flew back to Africa. His grandfather Jake had fallen through the branches of a tree when Solomon dropped him, trying to take his last baby son back with him. Learning about that magic enables Milkman himself to fly when he surrenders to the air and lets himself be upheld.

Milkman creates a self so that he can share it and even sacrifice it for a friend. With Pilate, Milkman buries the bones of Jake, his grandfather, on

Solomon's Leap. Guitar, who has continued to stalk Milkman, shoots and kills Pilate, but Milkman, saying to Guitar, "Do you want my life? Take it if it is any good to you," leaps into the air and flies. Guitar is free to kill his friend, but Milkman soars.

The ending of the novel shows the transcendence of the spirit, as the hero achieves his destiny. The satisfaction of the ending, which also soars into legend, comes from the triumph of the human spirit, the triumph that even death cannot destroy. *Song of Solomon* is a beautiful, serious, funny novel that moves beyond the social to the mythic.

Tar Baby explores three kinds of relationships: the relationship between blacks and whites; the relationships within families, especially between parents and children; and the relationship between the American black man and black woman. In the epigraph to the novel, Saint Paul reproaches the Corinthians for allowing contentions to exist among their ranks; the quote serves to foreshadow the discord that abounds in the novel's relationships.

In *Tar Baby*, Morrison depicts not a self-contained black society, but an onstage interaction between blacks and whites. The novel juxtaposes two families, a white family of masters and a black family of servants. The white family includes a retired candy-maker, Valerian Street, and his wife Margaret, once the "Principal Beauty of Maine," who is now in her fifties. The couple's only son Michael lives abroad; his arrival for Christmas is expected and denied by various characters.

The black family consists of the husband, Sidney Childs, who is Valerian's valet and butler, and the wife, Ondine, who serves as cook and housekeeper. They are childless, but their orphan niece Jadine plays the role of their daughter. (Valerian has acted as Jadine's patron, paying for her education at the Sorbonne.)

The pivotal character, however, who enters and changes the balance of power and the habitual responses of the families, is a black man who rises out of the sea. His true name is Son, although he has gone by other aliases. The veneer of politeness and familiarity between the characters is shaken by Son's abrupt appearance. Uncomfortable racial and personal assumptions are put into words and cannot be retracted. The Principal Beauty is convinced that Son has come to rape her: What else would a black man want? (Jadine is convinced that if Son wants to rape anyone, it is she, not Margaret.) Sidney finds Son a threat to his respectability as a Philadelphia black because when Son appears, the white people lump all blacks together. Ondine seems less threatened, but most of her energy goes into her running battle with the Principal Beauty. Jadine is apprehensive at Son's wild appearance, and later she is affronted by his direct sexual approach. Only Valerian welcomes Son. He sees him as a vision of his absent son Michael, and he invites him to sit down at the dining table and be a guest.

Son's coming is the catalyst that causes time-worn relationships to explode when Michael does not come for Christmas. His failure to appear leads to the revelation that the Principal Beauty abused her son as a child, pricking him with pins and burning him with cigarettes. Ondine, the black woman, finally hurls this accusation at Margaret, the white, and makes explicit what the two women have known mutually since the beginning. Valerian, who has been haunted by the memory of Michael as a lonely child who would hide under the sink and sing to himself, is hit with a reality much harsher than he has known or admitted.

Structured as it is in terms of families, the whole novel revolves around family responsibilities, especially between parents and children. Michael Street does not come home for Christmas, but the abuse he suffered as a child seems to justify his absence. Thus, the undutiful mother Margaret has thrown the whole family off balance. In the black family, later in the novel, attention is drawn to the undutiful daughter Jadine, although it seems implied that she has learned this undutifulness, partly at least, from whites, wanting her individual success to be separate from family ties and responsibilities.

This undutifulness also springs from a question of identity. In Paris, even before she comes to Valerian's island, Jadine feels affronted by a beautiful, proud, contemptuous African woman in yellow, who buys three eggs and carries them on her head. She is herself and embodies her tradition consummately, exhibiting balance and physical grace which symbolize spiritual poise. Jadine feels diminished and threatened by the African woman, who spits at her. The scorn sends Jadine back to her family, Sydney and Ondine.

Jadine is similarly disturbed by her dream of the women with breasts, the mothers, who reproach her for not joining that chain of mothers and daughters who become mothers with daughters. Although Jadine herself is an orphan, reared by Ondine and Sydney and owing much to their care, she refuses to take the self-sacrificing role of the woman who cares for her family. Jadine wants money and the power it brings in the white world. After a little more modeling, she wants to run her own business, perhaps a boutique. Also, she may choose a white husband, like the man who bought her a seductive sealskin coat.

Jadine is the Tar Baby of the novel, and Son is Brer Rabbit from the Uncle Remus stories. As the Tar Baby, Jadine acts as a possible trap for Son set by his enemies, white society. Jadine, who has absorbed many white values, wants money and success. Son wants something purer, something associated with nature (he is associated with the sea and the beauty of the savannahs) and with family tradition. Nature, direct physical experience, and family traditions that are integral to personal identity are all important values in Son's existence. Son has a home—the completely black town of Eloe—and there he abides by the ideas of respectability held by his father and his Aunt Rosa. (He asks Jadine to sleep at Aunt Rosa's, apart from him, and he comes to her secretly only when she threatens to leave if he does not.) To amuse herself in the traditional town, in which she is uncomfortable, Jadine takes photographs of the people and steals their souls, stealing their individual beauty and grace. In the photographs, they seem graceless, poor, and stupid, even to Son, who usually sees them with loving eyes.

Individually, Son and Jadine love each other, but they seem unable to find a world in which they can both thrive. Yet Son is an undaunted lover, unwilling to let Jadine go, even when she flees from him. Son tries to return to Isle de Chevaliers, Valerian's island, to get news of Jadine, but the only way he can get there seems to be through the help of Thérèse, the half-blind, fifty-year-old black woman who says that her breasts still give milk. Thérèse takes him by boat to the island of the horsemen. Son has said that he cannot give up Jadine, but Thérèse tells him to join the fabled black horsemen who see with the mind. At the end of the novel, Son is running toward his destiny, whether that be Jadine and some way to make her part of his world or the black horsemen who ride free through the hills. The reader does not know what Son's fate is to be; he only knows that Son is running toward it, just as Brer Rabbit ran from his enemy Brer Fox and from the Tar Baby. Like Milkman Dead at the end of *Song of Solomon*, Son leaps into mythic possibility; like Brer Rabbit, Son, the black man, is a figure with the power to survive.

In her fifth novel, *Beloved*, Morrison confronts directly for the first time the institution of slavery. Morrison's intention is immediately apparent in the novel's dedication to the "Sixty Million and more" victims of slavery—a figure that is provocative not only in its sheer magnitude but also in its relation to the oft-cited "six million," that is, the number of Jews who perished in the Holocaust.

Spanning the period from 1855 to 1874, *Beloved* is at one level a powerful account of the slave experience, an intimate re-creation of suffering and struggle. Nevertheless, as readers of her previous novels might expect, to get at the deeper truth of her subject Morrison has created a lyrical, mythic narrative. At the heart of *Beloved* is a single terrible act: Sethe, a young slave, kills one of her children, a daughter not yet two years old. Much of the novel is devoted to making that act of murder comprehensible, not as an instance of insane cruelty but as an image of the legacy of slavery. That Morrison is thinking of that still-enduring legacy, a malign presence even in the late twentieth century, becomes clear when Sethe's murdered daughter, Beloved, appears as a young woman eighteen years after her death. A ghost story with echoes of Greek tragedy, an anguished, angry testament, *Beloved* is a significant addition to Morrison's body of work.

Kate Begnal

Bibliography

Bloom, Harold, ed. *Toni Morrison: Modern Critical Views*. New York: Chelsea House, 1990. A fine selection of criticism on Morrison, with an excellent introduction by Bloom and extensive bibliography. *Beloved*, Morrison's most recent novel for which she won the Pulitzer Prize, is discussed in three essays by Margaret Atwood, Margaret Sale, and M. S. Mobley. The real gem, however, is an essay by Morrison herself in which she argues for inclusion of black literature in the canon of American literature.

Bruck, Peter, and Wolfgange Karrer, eds. *The Afro-American Novel Since 1960*. Amsterdam, The Netherlands: B. R. Gruener, 1982. This compilation of essays on black authors includes a chapter on Morrison by Bruck, entitled "Returning to One's Roots: The Motif of Searching and Flying in Toni Morrison's *Song of Solomon*" (originally printed in 1977).

Davis, Thadious M., and Trudier Harris, eds. *Afro-American Fiction Writers After 1955*. Vol. 3 in *Dictionary of Literary Biography*. Detroit: Gale Research, 1984. The entry on Morrison by Susan Black chronicles Morrison's life as a writer and gives a brief synopsis of her four novels in the context of black culture. Black writes from the point of view that Morrison's novels are about self-knowledge and human relations. Useful secondary bibliography.

Holloway, Karen F. C., and Stephanie A. Demetrakopoulos. *New Dimensions of Spirituality: The Novels of Toni Morrison*. New York: Greenwood Press, 1987. In this study, each author contributes individually with a common theme of spiritual development in Morrison's four novels. Demetrakopoulos has a Jungian background and examines the archetypal feminine images of Morrison's heroines. The notes are themselves excellent secondary resources. The chapter "A Critical Perspective" provides valuable views on the criticism available on Morrison.

McKay, Nellie Y., ed. *Critical Essays on Toni Morrison*. Boston: G. K. Hall, 1988. This volume, which is part of a series on American literature, firmly places Morrison on the list as one of the "most important writers in America." A compilation of reprinted essays by various authors, nine of which are original and written specifically for this publication. Also includes reviews, interviews, and literary criticism of Morrison's first four novels. A diverse and comprehensive work on Morrison. No bibliography.

Middleton, David L. *Toni Morrison: An Annotated Bibliography*. New York: Garland, 1987. The articles and essays by Morrison and the interviews with her listed here are arranged chronologically to present clearly the evolution of her ideas. Includes critical reviews of her fiction and a listing of honors and awards. Subject index provided. An indispensable guide.

Otten, Terry. *The Crime of Innocence in the Fiction of Toni Morrison*. Columbia: University of Missouri Press, 1989. In this groundbreaking study of Morrison's five novels, Otten explores the mythic substance in her writings by tracing the motif of the biblical fall. Insightful readings and unflagging attention to the historical and literary backdrop. A valuable guide to the increasing scholarship on Morrison.

Samuels, Wilfred D., and Clenora Hudson-Weems. *Toni Morrison.* Boston: Twayne, 1990. This study analyzes all five of Morrison's novels, including *Beloved.* The authors explore common themes such as black folklore and mysticism in Morrison's writings. Contains excerpts from interviews.

IRIS MURDOCH

Born: Dublin, Ireland; July 15, 1919

Principal long fiction

Under the Net, 1954; *The Flight from the Enchanter*, 1956; *The Sandcastle*, 1957; *The Bell*, 1958; *A Severed Head*, 1961; *An Unofficial Rose*, 1962; *The Unicorn*, 1963; *The Italian Girl*, 1964; *The Red and the Green*, 1965; *The Time of the Angels*, 1966; *The Nice and the Good*, 1968; *Bruno's Dream*, 1969; *A Fairly Honourable Defeat*, 1970; *An Accidental Man*, 1971; *The Black Prince*, 1973; *The Sacred and Profane Love Machine*, 1974; *A Word Child*, 1975; *Henry and Cato*, 1976; *The Sea, the Sea*, 1978; *Nuns and Soldiers*, 1980; *The Philosopher's Pupil*, 1983; *The Good Apprentice*, 1986; *The Book and the Brotherhood*, 1988; *The Message to the Planet*, 1989.

Other literary forms

Iris Murdoch has produced a considerable amount of work in areas other than fiction, particularly in the areas of literary criticism, drama, and, most important, philosophy. Her first book, entitled *Sartre: Romantic Rationalist* (1953), was a critique of Jean-Paul Sartre's philosophy as it appears in his novels. She has written three plays for the theater and adapted several of her novels for the stage. *The Servants and the Snow* was first performed at the Greenwich Theatre in 1970, and *The Three Arrows* at the Arts Theatre, Cambridge, in 1972; the two plays were published together in 1973 as *The Three Arrows, and The Servants and the Snow: Two Plays*. Another play, *Art and Eros*, was performed at the National Theatre in 1980. Murdoch collaborated with J. B. Priestley to adapt her novel *A Severed Head* for the stage in 1963 (published in 1964), and with James Saunders to adapt *The Italian Girl* in 1967 (published in 1969). *The Black Prince* has also been adapted for the stage and was performed at the Aldwych Theatre in 1989. She has also produced two books on the subject of philosophy: *The Sovereignty of Good* (1970), which consists of three essays on moral philosophy, "The Idea of Perfection," "On 'God' and 'Good,'" and "The Sovereignty of Good Over Other Concepts"; and *The Fire and the Sun: Why Plato Banished the Artists* (1977), a study of Plato's objections to art and artists. In 1987 Murdoch added to her work on Plato in the form of two "platonic dialogues" entitled "Art and Eros: A Dialogue about Art" and "Above the Gods: A Dialogue about Religion" that she combined in a book entitled *Acastos: Two Platonic Dialogues*. She has also published several philosophical papers in the Proceedings of the Aristotelian Society and other important articles on philosophy and aesthetics, including "The Sublime and the Good" (*Chicago Review*) and "The Sublime and the Beautiful Revisited" (*Yale Review*). Her best-known essay, "Against Dryness: A Polemical Sketch," which appeared in the January, 1961, issue of *Encounter*, is a work of literary criticism which urges a return to the capacious realism of the great nineteenth century novelists.

Achievements

Murdoch, who is universally acknowledged as one of the most important novelists of postwar Britain, has combined a prolific output with a consistently high level of fictional achievement. From the beginning of her career as a novelist, she has been a critical and popular success in both Great Britain and the United States. In general, Murdoch is thought of as a "philosophical novelist"; and, despite her objections to this description, she has attempted a fusion of aesthetic and philosophical ideas in her fiction. Including her first novel, *Under the Net*, published in 1954, she has published twenty-four novels and has received a variety of literary awards and honors. In 1973, she was awarded the James Tait Black Memorial Prize for Fiction for *The Black Prince* and, in 1974, received the Whitbread Literary Award for Fiction for *The Sacred and Profane Love Machine*. *The Sea, the Sea* won the Booker Prize for Fiction in 1978. Murdoch became a member of the Irish Academy in 1970, an honorary member of the American Academy of Arts and Letters in 1975, and was awarded the honorary title of Commander of the British Empire in 1976. She was made a Dame of the Order of the British Empire in 1987, and in 1990 she received the Medal of Honor for Literature from the National Arts Club in New York.

Biography

Jean Iris Murdoch was born in Dublin, Ireland, on July 15, 1919, to Anglo-Irish parents, Wills John Hughes Murdoch and Irene Alice Richardson. The family later moved to London, where Murdoch attended the Froebel Education Institute; she finished her secondary education at the Badminton School, Bristol, in 1937. From 1938 to 1942, she attended Somerville College at Oxford University, studying classical literature, ancient history, and philosophy. After obtaining a first-class honors degree, she worked from 1942 to 1944 as the assistant principal in the British Treasury, and from 1944 to 1946 served as an administrative officer with the United Nations Relief and Rehabilitation Administration in England, Austria, and Belgium.

After the war, an interest in existentialism led Murdoch to turn her attention to philosophy. She was unable to accept a scholarship to study in the United States because she had become a member of the Communist Party while an undergraduate at Oxford, and instead attended Newnham College at Cambridge University from 1947 to 1948 after receiving the Sarah Smithson Studentship in philosophy. In 1948, she was made a fellow of St. Anne's College, Oxford, where she lectured in philosophy until 1963, when she was named an honorary fellow of the college. In 1956, she married John O. Bayley, and several other well-known critical books; Bayley is Thomas Warton Professor of English Literature at Oxford. From 1963 to 1967, Murdoch lectured at the Royal College of Art in London, after which she stopped teaching in order to devote her time to novel-writing, although she continues to do some work in philosophy. She lives with her husband in Oxford.

Analysis

A knowledge of Iris Murdoch's philosophical and critical essays is invaluable for the reader wishing to understand her fiction. Her moral philosophy, which entails a rejection of existentialism, behaviorism, and linguistic empiricism, informs her fiction throughout and provides a basis for an interpretation of both the content and the form of her work. Although early influenced by Sartrean existentialism, she has developed a radically different view of the human condition. The major disagreement she has with the existentialist position is its emphasis on choice, a belief Murdoch characterizes as "unrealistic, over-optimistic, romantic" because it fails to consider the true nature of human consciousness and what she calls "a sort of continuous background with a life of its own." Existentialism, which she calls "the last fling of liberal Romanticism in philosophy," presents man with "too grand" a conception of himself as isolated from his surroundings and capable of rational, free choice. She describes this picture of man as the "Kantian man-god" who is "free, independent, lonely, powerful, rational, responsible, and brave." Although she denies being a Freudian, Sigmund Freud's "realistic and detailed picture of the fallen man" is much closer to her own conception of human nature, and she agrees with what she calls Freud's "thoroughly pessimistic view" in which the psyche is described as an "egocentric system of quasi-mechanical energy" determined by its individual history; the natural attachments of this psyche are "sexual, ambiguous, and hard for the subject to control." The most important dimension of this description of the individual is his lack of rational free will, and Murdoch's statement in "Against Dryness" that "we are not isolated free choosers, monarchs of all we survey, but benighted creatures sunk in a reality whose nature we are constantly and overwhelmingly tempted to deform by fantasy" is perhaps her tersest summary of the human condition.

Murdoch's philosophical position is the basis for her choice of prose fiction as the most realistic literary genre. The novelist's advantage is his "blessed freedom from rationalism," and she sees the novel as the literary form which, because of its lack of formal restrictions, can best portray the "open world, a world of absurdity and loose ends and ignorance." Although she has reservations about modern literature and believes that the twentieth century novel tends either to be "crystalline" (self-contained, mythic, sometimes allegorical, and frequently neurotic) or "journalistic" (semidocumentary, descriptive, and factual), the nineteenth century novel as written by Leo Tolstoy,

Jane Austen, and George Eliot remains the best example of how fiction can create free, independent characters who are not "merely puppets in the exteriorization of some closely-locked psychological conflict" of the author. The nineteenth century novel, because it "throve upon a dynamic merging of the idea of person with the idea of class," was not simply a representation of the human condition but rather contained "real various individuals struggling in society"; in other words, it presented characters *and* the "continuous background with a life of its own."

Murdoch believes that the most important obligation for the novelist is the creation of particularized, unique, and ultimately indefinable human beings, characters who move outside the novelist's consciousness into an independent ontological status. This aesthetic theory has its corollary in Murdoch's moral philosophy, in which she stresses the need for the individual to recognize the "otherness" of other individuals. The great novelist, like the "good" person, has an "apprehension of the absurd irreducible uniqueness of people and of their relations with each other," an apprehension she castigates Sartre for lacking. Recognition of otherness is, to a degree, dependent upon the individual's ability to "attend" to other individuals, a concept Murdoch derives from the philosophy of Simone Weil. Murdoch describes attention as a "patient, loving regard, directed upon a person, a thing, a situation" and believes that we *"grow by looking"*; morality, both for the individual and the novelist who is attempting a realistic portrayal of human beings in the world, is an endless process of attending to a reality outside the individual consciousness. Attention is seeing, "a just and loving gaze directed upon an individual reality," and as such is an effort to counteract "states of illusion" brought about by selfish fantasy. For Murdoch, attention is also another name for love, and "the ability to direct attention is love." Imaginative prose literature, Murdoch believes, is the best medium in which to focus attention on the individual because it is *"par excellence* the form of art most concerned with the existence of other persons."

In "The Sublime and the Good," Murdoch defines love as "the perception of individuals. Love is the extremely difficult realization that something other than oneself is real. Love, and so art and morals, is the discovery of reality." She has also said that the main subject of her fiction is love, and her novels usually depict the difficulties involved in recognizing the uniqueness and independence of other human beings. In *The Bell*, the Abbess tells Michael Meade that "all of our failures are ultimately failures in love," a statement that neatly describes Murdoch's fictional world. The enemy of love in her novels is the propensity of the individual to fantasize and to create false pictures of reality, particularly distorted conceptions of other people. As a result, her novels frequently present situations in which characters are forced to confront the "otherness" of those around them, situations which often involve a realization of the past or present sexual involvements of other persons. The comfort and safety of the "old world," as it is called by many Murdoch characters, is destroyed by a discovery about the past or by characters suddenly falling passionately in love with each other. *A Severed Head*, in which Martin Lynch-Gibbon is shocked by a series of revelations about his wife and friends and falls precipitately and unpredictably in love with Honor Klein, is one of the best examples of this recurring pattern in Murdoch's work.

Murdoch believes that the experience of art can serve to shock the individual into an awareness of a reality outside the personal psyche, and her novels contain several scenes in which characters who gaze upon paintings are able to escape temporarily from solipsistic fantasy. Dora Greenfield in *The Bell*, Harriet Gavender in *The Sacred and Profane Love Machine*, and Tim Reede in *Nuns and Soldiers* each experience what Murdoch calls "unselfing" and Harriet Gavender describes as "not being myself any more"; in fact, Dora Greenfield notes that paintings give her "something which her consciousness could not wretchedly devour. . . . The pictures were something real outside herself." Murdoch, in "The Sublime and the Beautiful Revisited," calls art "spiritual experience" because it can bring out this radical change in perception, and in *The Fire and the Sun: Why Plato Banished the Artists*, she claims that in an unreligious age good art provides people with "their clearest experience of something grasped as separate and precious and beneficial and held quietly and unpossessively in the attention."

Murdoch's ambivalent attitudes about the role of art and artists are present in both her fiction and her philosophy. In an interview with Michael Bellamy, in *Contemporary Literature* (1977), she described art as a "temptation to impose form where perhaps it isn't always appropriate," and in the same discussion noted that "morality has to do with not imposing form, except appropriately and cautiously and carefully and with attention to appropriate detail." Murdoch has suggested to several interviewers that the basis of her novels is what she calls the conflict between "the saint and the artist," or the dichotomy between the "truthful, formless figure" and the "form-maker." She mentions Tallis Browne and Julius King in *A Fairly Honourable Defeat*, Ann and Randall Peronett in *An Unofficial Rose*, and Hugo Belfounder and Jake Donaghue in *Under the Net* as examples. She believes that Plato's life exemplifies this conflict: "We can see played out in that great spirit the peculiarly distressing struggle between the artist and the saint." The true or "good" artist must avoid the "ruthless subjection of characters" to his will and should use symbolism judiciously in a "natural, subordinate way" that attempts to be "perfectly realistic." In her fiction, Murdoch's artist-figures are often demonic individuals who manipulate people in real life without regard for their well-being or independence as persons. Her "saint" figures have a corresponding lack of form, or sense of self, and are frequently unable or unwilling to act in any way. Douglas Swann's comment in *An Unofficial Rose* that "nothing is more fatal to love than to want everything to have form" is also true of Murdoch's attitude toward art.

Many of Murdoch's characters attempt to find form in their own lives in order to explain the apparent chaos that surrounds them. In her essay "Vision and Choice in Morality," Murdoch talks about the need at times to stress "not the comprehensibility of the world but its incomprehensibility" and says that "there are even moments when understanding *ought* to be withheld." In *Flight from the Enchanter*, John Rainborough experiences a moment of joy when he feels "how little I know, and how little it is possible to know," but this happiness in a lack of knowledge is rare in Murdoch's fiction. In the same novel, Rosa Keepe, a much more representative Murdoch character, listens to the sound of the machines in the factory, hoping to hear a "harmonious and repetitive pattern," just as Michael Meade in *The Bell* expects to find "the emergence in his life of patterns and signs." At the end of the novel, he regretfully concludes that the apparent pattern he had observed in his life was merely his own "romantic imagination. At the human level there was no pattern."

The search for rational, discernible causal relationships is the major structuring principle in *An Accidental Man*, a novel concerned with the discovery of, in Gracie Tisbourne's words, "a world . . . quite without order." In "The Sovereignty of Good Over Other Concepts," Murdoch says that "there are properly many patterns and purposes within life, but there is no general and as it were externally guaranteed pattern or purpose of the kind for which philosophers and theologians used to search," and she has also stated her desire to write novels that, because they contain more of the contingent, accidental dimensions of life, are more realistic than "patterned" fiction.

Murdoch's reservations about form in life and art are paralleled by her suspicions about language. A fervent defender of literature and language who has said in "Salvation by Words" that "words constitute the ultimate texture and stuff of our moral being. . . . The fundamental distinctions can only be made in words" and in *The Fire and the Sun* that "the careful responsible skillful use of words is our highest instrument of thought and one of our highest modes of being," Murdoch has also voiced suspicions about the ironic nature of language, its potential to distort the truth and to create false pictures of reality. This distrust of language is evident in her first novel, *Under the Net*, and has continued to inform her fiction. In this respect, Murdoch has been greatly influenced by Ludwig Wittgenstein; direct references and sly, sometimes ironic allusions to Wittgenstein appear repeatedly in her novels.

In spite of these reservations, however, Murdoch has mounted one of the most eloquent defenses of art and literature in modern times in *The Sovereignty of Good* and *The Fire and the Sun*. She claims in "The Sovereignty of Good Over Other Concepts" that art "can enlarge the sensibility of its consumer. It is a kind of goodness by proxy," and in "On 'God' and 'Good,'" she asserts that art, rather than being any kind of playful diversion for the human race, is "the place of its most fundamental insight." According to Murdoch, literature is the most important art because of its unique ability to shed light on the human condition: "The most essential and fundamental aspect of culture is the study of literature, since this is an education in how to picture and understand human situations." This statement in "The Idea of Perfection" obviously places an enormous burden on the novelist, a burden which Murdoch's prolific output, technical virtuosity, and moral vision appear to be capable of bearing.

Jake Donaghue, the narrator-protagonist of *Under the Net*, informs the reader early in the novel that the story's central theme is his acquaintance with Hugo Belfounder. The relationship between the two men illustrates Murdoch's philosophical and aesthetic concerns, for the Hugo-Jake friendship represents the saint-artist dichotomy; this "philosophical novel" allows her to explore the problem of theoretical approaches to reality, the issue of contingency, the realization of the otherness of individuals, and the ambiguities of language and art.

The character of Hugo Belfounder is based in part on that of the enigmatic Elias Canetti, winner of the Nobel Prize for Literature in 1981; the Bulgarian-born Canetti, who has lived in England since 1939, appears in various guises in several of Murdoch's early novels. Hugo, some of whose precepts also suggest the influence of Wittgenstein, is Murdoch's first "saint" figure, and he embodies many of the qualities of the "good" characters who appear later in her fiction. Hugo's saintliness is a result of his truthfulness and his lack of desire for form or structure in life and art. Opposed to him is Jake, who, fearing that he may actually tell the truth to Mrs. Tinckham about being evicted by Madge, delays telling his story until he can present it in a "more dramatic way . . . as yet it lacked form." Form, as Jake tacitly admits, is a kind of lying, an imposition of structure that distorts reality. Hugo, on the other hand, is attracted by the ephermerality and formlessness of the firework displays he has created, and he abandons them when they receive the attention of art critics who begin to classify his work into styles. Hugo is also characterized by a selflessness that Jake finds astonishing: it does not occur to him that he is responsible for the concepts discussed in Jake's book *The Silencer*, or that Anna Quentin's mime theater is based upon her interpretation of his beliefs.

The difference between the two men is also evident in their attitude toward theory. After his conversations with Hugo, Jake concedes that his own approach to life is "blurred by generalities," and he is entranced by Hugo's refusal to classify the world around him or to adopt any kind of theory about it. Annandine, Hugo's persona in *The Silencer*, says that "the movement away from theory and generality is the movement towards truth. All theorizing is flight. We must be ruled by the situation itself and this is unutterably particular." Theories, like form, distort what they attempt to explain and understand.

Hugo's lack of a general theroretical framework for his ideas, the "net" of the novel's title, makes everything he encounters "astonishing, delightful, complicated, and mysterious."

Part of Jake's education and development as a potential artist is dependent upon relinquishing the need for theories and generalizations. In his first meeting with Anna, he notices that she is in "the grip of a theory," and one of the most important episodes in the novel is Jake's realization that Jean-Pierre Breteuil, whose work he has previously translated into English, has finally written a good novel—a feat Jake had believed impossible. He understands that he has incorrectly "classed" Jean-Pierre and says that "It wrenched me, like the changing of a fundamental category." Similarly, when Jake becomes aware that Hugo is in love with Sadie Quentin rather than Anna, he says that "a pattern in my mind was suddenly scattered and the pieces of it went flying about me like birds." At the end of the novel, Jake has abandoned attempts to impose his own ideas onto his environment; rather, he decides to sit quietly and "let things take shape deeply within me," noting that he can "sense," beneath the level of his attention and without his conscious aid, "great forms moving in the darkness."

Jake's initial need to perceive form and to create theories is paralleled by his fear of contingency. One of Murdoch's major quarrels with Sartre is his inability to deal with the contingent, or, in her words, the "messiness" and "muddle" of human existence. Rather than rejecting Sartre's concept of viscosity, Murdoch frequently forces her characters to come to terms with the physical world and the accidental and apparently chaotic nature of reality. Early in the novel, Jake announces that "I hate contingency. I want everything in my life to have a sufficient reason," and later, in a reference to Sartre's *Nausea*, observes that Hugo's Bounty Belfounder movie studio is situated in a part of London "where contingency reaches the point of nausea." The novel ends with Jake's laughingly admitting that he does not know the reason why Mrs. Tinckham's kittens look as they do. "I don't know why it is," he says, "It's just one of the wonders of the world." In this scene, Jake focuses on the particular—the kittens—and is able to accept that their appearance cannot be explained by him, two actions which show that he has moved much closer to Hugo's position. Hugo had earlier advised Jake that "some situations can't be unravelled" and, as a result, should be "dropped."

This acceptance of contingency implies a realization that life cannot be completely controlled by human will. Jake also learns that other individuals exist independently of him and resist his efforts to explain and categorize their behavior. When he introduces his close friend Peter O'Finney to the reader, he claims that "Finn has very little inner life," and that, while Finn is an inhabitant of his universe, "I . . . cannot conceive that he has one containing me." Events in the novel force Jake to move out of his solipsistic consciousness, and at the conclusion he acknowledges that for the first time

Anna exists "as a separate being and not as a part of myself," an experience he finds "extremely painful." She becomes "something which had to be learnt afresh," and he then asks if it is possible ever to know another human being. He answers himself in a statement that clearly belongs to his author: "Perhaps only after one has realized the impossibility of knowledge and renounced the desire for it and finally ceased to feel even the need of it." In the same way, Jake also grants Hugo a final mysteriousness and impenetrability, comparing him to a monolith whose purpose remains obscure.

Murdoch's suspicions about the nature of language are also evident in *Under the Net*. In a conversation between Hugo and Jake, Hugo maintains that, by definition, language lies: "The whole language is a machine for making falsehoods." Language is also vulnerable because of man's tendency to distort and to exaggerate experiences when attempting to articulate them; Hugo notes that when he speaks he does not state precisely what he thinks but rather what will impress Jake and force him to respond. Only actions, says Hugo, do not lie. This is not, however, Murdoch's final word on language and literature, for Jake's development as a human being during the course of the novel culminates in his realization that he will be able to write creatively. The "shiver of possibility" that he feels at the novel's conclusion is his knowledge that his earlier writing has been merely a preparation for his emergence as a novelist.

Murdoch's first novel is clearly a *Künstlerroman* and her most overtly "philosophical" novel. In an interview in 1978 with Jack Biles, in *Studies in the Literary Imagination*, she said that she does not want to "promote" her philosophical views in her novels or to allow them to "intrude into the novel world." This attitude certainly seems more descriptive of the novels written after *Under the Net*. Although she paints an ironically amusing portrait of the novel's only professional philosopher, Dave Gellman, her major concerns in her first novel are clearly philosophical; *Under the Net* contains in more obvious form the philosophical issues which are transmuted into the fictional material of her subsequent work.

Speaking of *A Fairly Honourable Defeat* in her interview with Michael Bellamy, Murdoch said that the "defeat" of the novel's title is the defeat of good by evil. She calls the novel a "theological myth" in which Julius King is Satan, Tallis Browne is a Christ-figure, and Leonard Browne is God the Father. Another trichotomy, however, is suggested in *A Fairly Honourable Defeat*, for Julius and Tallis, like Ann and Randall Peronett in *An Unofficial Rose*, embody the saint-artist opposition that is so common in Murdoch's fiction; and Rupert Foster represents the rationalist philosopher's approach to experience, an approach which ultimately fails because it does not take into consideration the reality of evil and the formlessness of good. The relationship among these three men is one of the most important thematic concerns of the novel.

A Fairly Honourable Defeat begins with Hilda and Rupert Foster enacting a scene common in Murdoch's fiction, that of the happily married couple whose contentment has insulated them from their less fortunate friends. Like Kate and Octavian Gray in *The Nice and the Good*, Rupert and Hilda feel as if their happiness has granted them a privileged and protected status. Rupert's statement that "Anything is permitted to us," ominously similar to Friedrich Nietzsche's "all is permitted," signals that for the moment they live in the "old world" of pleasure and stability that is so frequently shattered in the course of a Murdoch novel. The agent of destruction in *A Fairly Honourable Defeat* is Julius King, a scientist who considers himself an "artist" whose art works consist of manipulating the lives of people around him, forcing them to "act parts" and in the process become "educated" about their moral failures.

Julius King's reaction to Rupert's philosophy of life is the catalyst for the events of the novel. Although Rupert, like Murdoch, calls human existence "jumble" and castigates his sister-in-law Morgan Browne for her "love and do as you please" attitude toward people, Rupert believes that "complete information and straight answers and unambiguous positions . . . clarifications and rational policies" are possible and desirable; for Rupert, goodness is a fairly simplistic concept that can be experienced directly and articulated eloquently. His statement to Morgan after Julius has orchestrated their ostensible "love affair" that "nothing awful can happen" summarizes his inability to grasp the kind of evil that Julius represents, and the destruction of the manuscript of his book on moral philosophy symbolizes the fragility of his world view, a fragility underscored by his death. Rupert's major error is believing that his own rationality can prevail; he hypocritically thinks that "the top of the moral structure was no dream, and he had proved this by exercises in loving attention: loving people, loving art, loving work, loving paving stones and leaves on trees." In reality, as Julius later observes, Rupert is in love with his own image of himself as a good, loving, and rational man who can control any urge that threatens the "moral structure" of his world; while he espouses many theories about the nature of love, he lacks the "direct language of love" that makes real action possible.

Unlike Rupert, who believes that his duty is to love others, Julius' attitude toward human beings is one of contempt, an emotion the narrator describes as "the opposite extreme from love: the cynicism of a deliberate contemptuous diminution of another person." One of the major reasons for his low valuation of people is the very quality that makes them vulnerable to his manipulation—their malleability, or, as he phrases it, the easiness with which they are "beguiled." In a conversation with Tallis, Julius says that most individuals, motivated by fear and egotism, will cooperate in almost any deception. The most obvious examples of his theory in *A Fairly Honourable Defeat* are Morgan Browne and Simon Foster. Morgan, titillated by Julius' boast that he can "divide anybody from anybody," first encourages him in his plan to separate Simon and Axel and later unknowingly becomes one of his victims; Simon, afraid that Julius will destroy his relationship with Axel, unwillingly allows Julius to "arrange" a relationship between Rupert and Morgan. In fact, Julius' claim that he is an "artist" and a "magician" depends upon the moral weaknesses of the characters whose lives he carefully "plots."

Both Leonard Browne and Julius King mount verbal assaults on the world; in some respects, their diatribes sound remarkably similar. Like Leonard, Julius believes that the human race is a "loathesome crew" who inhabit a "paltry planet"; he goes further than Leonard, however, in his statement that human beings "don't deserve to survive," and, more important, in his desire to see the reification of his ideas. Julius' theory that people are merely puppets who need to be educated becomes, in practice, a tragedy. Although, like Hugo Belfounder, he claims that philosophy is the subtlest "method of flight" from consciousness and that its attempted truths are "tissues of illusions." In *Theories*, he is entranced with his own theorizing as is Rupert. Good, he says, is dull, and what passes for human goodness is a "tiny phenomenon" that is "messy, limited, truncated." Evil, by comparison, "reaches far far away into the depths of the human spirit and is connected with the deepest springs of human vitality." Good, according to Julius, is not even a "coherent concept; it is unimaginable for human beings, like certain things in physics."

One of Murdoch's saintlike characters, James Tayper Pace in *The Bell*, also discusses the difficulty of comprehending goodness while he emphasizes the need for the individual to seek the good beyond the confines of his own consciousness: "And where do we look for perfection? Not in some imaginary concoction out of our own idea of our own character—but in something so external and so remote that we can get only now and then a distant hint of it." In "The Sovereignty of Good Over Other Concepts," Murdoch talks about contemplating goodness, and, like James Tayper Pace, defines it as an "an attempt to look right away from self towards a distant transcendent perfection, a source of uncontaminated energy, a source of *new* and quite undreamt-of virtue." Unlike Pace and Murdoch, Julius is unwilling to waste his energies in the contemplation of a concept so "remote" and "transcendent" and is instead beguiled by the immediacy and vitality of evil.

Tallis Browne, the "saint" of *A Fairly Honourable Defeat*, is one of the strangest characters in Murdoch's fiction. Early in the novel, his wife Morgan, talking about the human psyche, complains that "it stretches away and away to the ends of the world and it's soft and sticky and warm. There's nothing real, no hard parts, no centre." This description of human consciousness also explains Morgan's dissatisfaction with her husband, who is completely lacking in the qualities she so admires in Julius King: form and myth. With Tallis, says Morgan, "there were no forms and limits, things had no boundaries"; he lacks any kind of personal "myth," while she characterizes Julius as "almost all myth." Like Julius, Tallis does not believe in theories, and at one point he correctly accuses Morgan of being "theory-ridden" and chasing "empty abstractions"; unlike Julius, however, he has no theories about human nature or behavior, a fact that Julius acknowledges when he tells Tallis that Rupert probably feels that "theorizing would be quite out of place with you." While Julius manipulates the relationships of those around him according to his ideas about human weakness and Rupert writes a text on morality and goodness, Tallis nurses his dying father and helps to feed and shelter the poverty-stricken immigrants in his neighborhood.

The formlessness of Tallis' goodness causes him to have no desire to analyze the tragedy of Rupert's death or to assign reasons or blame. He grieves "blankly" over what appears to have been a "disastrous compound" of human failure, muddle, and sheer chance, and mourns Rupert by attempting to remember him simply with a kind of mindless pain. His reaction to the loss of his wife is similar. Rather than indulging in anger, grief, or speculations about their future relationship, he simply lets her "continue to occupy his heart." His unwillingness to impose any kind of form or to structure his surroundings in any way extends to his feelings for his father Leonard, who is dying of cancer. Tallis cannot find the appropriate moment to tell his father of his impending death because, as he tells Julius, "It seems so arbitrary, at any particular instant of time, to change the world to that degree." Rather than seeing human beings as puppets, as does Julius, Tallis has reached a crisis state in which he fears that any action may have a deleterious effect on those around him. Significantly, however, in spite of Tallis' passivity he is the only character in the novel who is capable of positive action. As Axel phrases it, he is "the only person about the place with really sound instincts." In the Chinese restaurant, he strikes the young man who is abusing the Jamaican, and later he forces Julius to telephone Hilda Foster to explain that it is Julius who has created the "affair" between Morgan and Rupert.

At the end of the novel, Tallis has abandoned the idea of prayer, which the narrator notes could only be a "superstition" for him at that point, and has instead become a completely passive and receptive consciousness. He catches hold of objects "not so as to perform any act himself, but so as to immobilize himself for a moment to be, if that were possible, perhaps acted upon, perhaps touched." The similarity of this statement to Simone Weil's definition of "attention" in *Waiting for God* (1951), where she describes the act of attention as "suspending our thought, leaving it detached, empty, and ready to be penetrated by the object . . . our thought should be empty, waiting, not seeking anything," is clear. Much earlier in the novel, Morgan has grabbed an object, a green paperweight belonging to Rupert, in an attempt to escape from the formlessness of the psyche. Tallis, on the other hand, uses objects as a way to attend to reality, as a means of opening himself up to the world outside himself.

A Fairly Honourable Defeat ends with Tallis weeping over his father's approaching death and Julius, after contemplating his choices of Parisian restaurants, concluding that "life was good." The conversation between the two men which precedes this, however, is much more ambiguous. Julius, in an apparent attempt to win Tallis' approbation for his actions, reveals a great deal about himself personally and asks Tallis to agree that he is "an instrument of justice." Tallis' attitude toward Julius is one of detached tolerance, and his response to Julius' statement is merely to smile. A parallel to his calm acceptance of Julius' evil is his response to the "weird crawling things," apparently rats, mice, and insects, which inhabit his house; he feels for them "pity rather than disgust" and has advanced far beyond Rupert's claim to love "paving stones and leaves on trees." Tallis' acceptance of the world, which has grown to embrace even its most despicable and horrible elements, makes him the most saintlike character in Murdoch's fiction. He is her answer to Jean-Paul Sartre's Roquentin in *Nausea* (1938): instead of becoming nauseated by the world's plethora of objects and the muddle of existence, as does Roquentin, Tallis, at the end of *A Fairly Honourable Defeat*, is capable of feeling only pity and acceptance for everything that surrounds him.

In *An Accidental Man*, Murdoch presents a chaotic world of accident and unpredictability in which several of her characters search for—and fail to find—any kind of pattern or causal relationships in their lives. Perhaps Murdoch's fear that form in fiction can hinder the characters' development as complex and fully realized individuals and that intricately patterned fiction sometimes prevents the author from exploring "the contradictions or paradoxes or more painful aspects of the subject matter" led her to write a novel in which the narrative voice is almost completely absent: in *An Accidental Man*, the characters appear to have taken over the novel. In an interview with W. K. Rose, in *Shenandoah* (Winter, 1968), Murdoch expressed the desire to write a novel "made up entirely of peripheral characters, sort of accidental people like Dickens' people," and mentioned that the author "might go so far as starting to invent the novel and then abolishing the central characters." *An Accidental Man* is the result of these speculations about fiction, for it contains a Dickensian sweep of characters and lacks any kind of "protagonist." The inclusion of more "accident" in Murdoch's work is one aspect of her wish to write realistic fiction, for she believes that the novelist should portray the world as "aimless, chancy, and huge." *An Accidental Man*, a brittle comedy of manners which contains four deaths, two attempted suicides, and more than twenty characters, some of whom are suffering from mental retardation, schizophrenia, and brain damage, is Murdoch's vision of a contingent, random, and godless world.

Many characters in the novel share this vision. At the conclusion, Matthew Gibson Grey notes that Austin's appropriation of Mavis Argyll "has been, like so many other things in the story, accidental." Charlotte Ledgard, contemplating suicide, sees herself as "the slave of chance" and the world as being made up of "chaos upon which everything rested and out of which it was made." Ludwig Leferrier senses that "human life perches always on the brink of dissolution," and Gracie Tisbourne, who is usually not given to philosophical speculations, has "a sense of the world being quite without order and of other things looking through." The characters in *An Accidental Man* wander through mazes in which they lack important information about their own and others' lives, or they become the victims of "accidents" which radically transform their existence. London's labyrinthine streets become symbolic of their ignorance and blindness as they pass and miss one another, and, in the instance of Rosalind Monkley, symbolic of accidental death itself. Garth Gibson Grey, Matthew Gibson Grey, Ludwig Leferrier, and Mavis Argyll all hope to find some kind of logical order and rationality in the world, but are finally defeated by the "absolute contradiction . . . at the heart of things," and instead encounter what Garth calls "the rhetoric of the casually absent god."

Although Murdoch is generally not interested in experimentation in form, *An Accidental Man* shows her moving beyond the traditional narrative form of her earlier work in search of new structures to embody the philosophical assumptions that underlie the novel. Conspicuously missing in this novel is an authoritative narrative voice; instead, one tenth of the book is in epistolary form and a significant portion consists of chapters of untagged dialogue. In *An Accidental Man*, Murdoch, who has stated her wish to expel herself from her fiction in order to avoid imposing "the form of one's own mind" on the characters, creates a work in which the narrator is frequently not privy to the inner thoughts or reactions of the characters and can only report their spoken and written words without comment or elucidation. The disappearance of the narrator in certain sections of the novel parallels the absence of god; Murdoch creates a novelistic world in which the reader must search for his own patterns and conclusions without the guiding presence of the authorial voice which was present in her earlier fiction. In addition, the narrator's refusal to pass judgments or give information about the thoughts of the characters, despite the fact that he has shown himself to be omniscient in certain situations, results in a coldly detached tone which refuses to grant a fundamental importance to any act.

Like the chapters of dialogue, the epistolary sections of the novel create a voyeuristic situation for the reader which parallels the voyeurism which takes place several times during the narrative. The reader is privileged to read correspondence and to overhear important conversations while being denied access to the characters' thoughts, just as the characters in *An Accidental Man* have a noticeable penchant for eavesdropping on one another's conversations and reading other people's letters. The epistolary sections also create comically ironic effects because the reader knows more about the entire situation than any of the individual letter-writers, and the ignorance, lies, and exaggerations of the writers are juxtaposed in ways that underscore the limited and fallacious viewpoint of each individual. These chapters also give Murdoch an opportunity to open up the novel, expanding its boundaries to encompass more and more territory—a narrative technique which corresponds to her desire to write fiction that depicts reality as "a rich receding background" with "a life of its own."

The widening framework of the novel creates a constantly changing perspective, for when the narrator withdraws from a direct presentation of events in order to present the reactions of peripheral or uninvolved characters, the importance of these events is reduced through distancing and in the process rendered comic. The same technique is used in the chapters of pure dialogue, where events which have been treated seriously in earlier episodes become the subject of comically trivial cocktail-party conversations. The dialogic and epistolary sections are central elements in the novel, for Murdoch uses them to advance the narrative through fragmentary bits of information which are often necessary for a complete understanding of what is happening; her belief that "reality is not given whole" is expressed in her narrative technique.

The self-acknowledged "accidental man" of the novel's title is Austin Gibson Grey. Neurotically obsessed with his older brother, Matthew, and unable to keep either his wife or his job, Austin is nevertheless a survivor who depends upon his own egotism for his continued well-being. One aspect of Austin's ability to survive is his refusal to allow the catastrophes of others to affect him. He observes that "a man can see himself becoming more callous to events because he has to survive," and his reaction to the death of Rosalind Monkley, whom he has killed in an automobile accident, is typical. He writes to his wife, Dorina, that "I will survive and recover, I have had worse blows than this"; he does not mention any guilt he may feel about the incident or the pain Rosalind's death may have caused her family. Similarly, after Dorina's accidental death, Austin tells Matthew that "Poor old Dorina was just a sort of half person really, a maimed creature, she had to die, like certain kinds of cripples have to. They can't last." In spite of Austin's selfishness, however, he is merely the most exaggerated example of egotism in *An Accidental Man*. The statement by an unnamed character at the novel's conclusion that "Austin is like all of us only more so" is, unfortunately, correct.

Austin Gibson Grey resembles several other characters in Murdoch's fiction, all of whom show a talent for survival and an ability to turn unfortunate incidents to their account. In the same way, Austin's wife Dorina is representative of another character-type which recurs throughout Murdoch's novels: the individual who functions as a scapegoat or assumes the consequences of the sins of others. Frequently, through no fault of their own, such characters cannot cope with the events happening around them and either choose suicide or become the victims of an "accidental" death that appears to be inevitable.

Traditionally, the scapegoat or *pharmakos* figure is an individual who must be expelled from society in order to maintain its continued existence and vitality. Dorina Gibson Grey is a *pharmakos* who manifests all of these characteristics. Early in the novel, she feels as if "something were closing in for the kill," and after her death, her sister Mavis voices the opinion that "she has died for me," telling Matthew that "she has somehow died for us, for you and me, taking herself away, clearing herself away, so that our world should be easier and simpler." Dorina's death enables Garth Gibson Grey to feel love once again for his father. Her death also rejuvenates her husband, as Matthew ironically observes: "Something or other had . . . done Austin good. Perhaps it was simply Dorina's death." Her death has an almost ritualistic dimension in *An Accidental Man*, and it ensures the rejuvenation of several of the characters.

The ending of *An Accidental Man* is one of the darkest in Murdoch's fiction, and very few of the defeats suffered in this novel can be termed "honourable." In fact, several characters, including Matthew Gibson Grey, Garth Gibson Grey, and Charlotte Ledgard, appear to have settled for what Julius King in *A Fairly Honourable Defeat* calls a "sensible acceptance of the second rate." Matthew, en route with Ludwig Leferrier to the United States, where Ludwig will receive a prison sentence for refusing to fight in Vietnam, realizes that "he would never be a hero. . . . He would be until the end of his life a man looking forward to his next drink"; Garth is metamorphosed into a self-satisfied, successful novelist whose former social conscience and pursuit of goodness have been abandoned in favor of marriage to Gracie Tisbourne and all that she represents; and Charlotte chooses to remain with Mitzi Ricardo in spite of her knowledge that what she feels for Mitzi is merely "a fake dream love." These failures contrast with the fates of Austin and Clara Tisbourne, both of whom are described as looking "radiantly juvenile." Austin, in particular, has been completely rejuvenated by the misfortunes of others and is finally able to move his fingers, which have been rigid since his childhood "accident"; his inability to do this heretofore has symbolized his problems with dealing with the world, just as his new physical flexibility reflects the rebirth of his psyche.

The darkly comic final chapter of *An Accidental Man*, which consists solely of untagged dialogue, furnishes important information while it trivializes the events of the entire novel. The fact that Ludwig Leferrier is now in prison in the United States after his decision to leave his idyllic and protected situation in England, the real moral dilemma of the novel, is mentioned in passing and then dropped by an unnamed character who incorrectly says that he has been imprisoned for "Drugs or something." In this final section of the novel, unlike the earlier chapters of letters and dialogue, the reader becomes less and less certain about who is actually speaking. In fact, the dialogue appears to be spoken by a group of eerie, disembodied voices which create an ominous atmosphere from which the narrator and the main characters have departed, leaving the reader to overhear the mindless gossiping of strangers. At the conclusion of *An Accidental Man*, contingency and "the rhetoric of the casually absent god" have triumphed.

In *The Sea, the Sea*, Murdoch focuses on a type of character who has appeared throughout her fiction, the artist or would-be artist who confuses life and art with unfortunate (and sometimes tragic) consequences. In Murdoch's earlier novel, *The Black Prince*, Bradley Pearson's quiet life is suddenly shattered by a series of revelations and catastrophes which include an affair with the teenage daughter of his best friend. These real-life events cause Bradley to create the novel he had been unable to write previously; at the same time, Bradley is consciously aware of his movement from experience to the expression of experience in aesthetic form and realizes the difference between the two, even though he takes great pride in his "artistic" consciousness throughout the story. In *The Sea, the Sea*, however, Charles Arrowby, the famous and ostensibly "retired" theatrical director who is unable to leave behind the artifice and dramatic structure of the stage, begins to "direct" life offstage, ignoring the boundaries between fact and fiction. His theater becomes the small seaside village to which he has moved, and his actors are the people around him.

Published one year before *The Sea, the Sea*, *The Fire and the Sun*, Murdoch's study of Plato's objections to art and artists, is instructive to read in the light of her portrayal of Charles Arrowby. Although Murdoch disagrees with several of Plato's fundamental assumptions about the nature of art, her narrator in *The Sea, the Sea*, embodies many of Plato's—and Murdoch's—suspicions about the artistic sensibility. In *The Fire and the Sun*, Murdoch discusses the Platonic doctrine that art and the artist "exhibit the lowest and most irrational kind of awareness, *eikasia*, a state of vague image-ridden illusion"; in Plato's myth of the cave, this state corresponds to the prisoners who, facing the wall, can see only the shadows cast by the fire. Charles Arrowby, called the "king of shadows" several times in the novel, exemplifies the "bad" artist, the "naive fantasist" who "sees only moving shadows and construes the world in accordance with the easy unresisted mechanical 'causality' of his personal dream life." Throughout the novel, James Arrowby, Charles's cousin and the "saint" figure in *The Sea, the Sea*, tries to convince Charles that the woman he is pursuing is only a "dream figure," just as Hartley Fitch, the sixty-year-old woman who was Charles's adolescent girl friend and is now married to another man, tells Charles that their love is a "dream" that does not belong in the real world. Near the end of the novel, Charles acknowledges the truth of their interpretations, calling his novel "my own dream text."

Charles Arrowby's psychological state, one that combines tremendous egotism with an obsessional need to control other people while remaining almost completely deluded about what is happening around him, closely resembles

Murdoch's description of Plato's idea of the "bad" man. The "bad" or mediocre man is "in a state of illusion, of which egoism is the most general name. . . . Obsession, prejudice, envy, anxiety, ignorance, greed, neurosis, and so on *veil* reality." Similarly, Plato says that the human soul desires "omnipotence" and erects barriers between itself and reality so that it can remain comfortably within a "self-directed dream world." Although on the novel's first page Charles claims that he has come to his retirement home "to repent of egoism," his realization that Hartley is living in the same village results in his jealously obsessional need to "capture" her from her husband. Although he views himself as a Prospero-like magician-artist who can effect any kind of magical transformation, he gradually reveals his incorrect evaluations of himself and others. Charles's novel, the chronicle of his delusions and errors, is a portrait of the "bad" man who refuses to acknowledge the unpredictability and intransigence of reality.

Charles tells the reader that his last great role as an actor was as Prospero in William Shakespeare's *The Tempest* (1611), and he believes he has much in common with Shakespeare's magician. Despite his statement early in the novel that "Now I shall abjure magic and become a hermit," he soon begins the direction of his final "drama." His theatrical vision of the world often obscures reality; not surprisingly, he is overjoyed to discover that what he first called a "diary," "memoir," and "autobiography" has become a novel. The change from a journalistic mode of writing to a fictional one parallels his growing tendency to dramatize and fictionalize events, and soon after his announcement that he is indeed writing a novel, he begins to construct an elaborate "story" about Hartley and her marriage. James fails in his attempt to convince his cousin that he is fighting for a "phantom Helen" and that his wish to rescue her is "pure imagination, pure fiction." Although Charles later admits to the reader that he has created an "image" of Hartley which does not correspond to reality, he denies that his "image" is untrue. His kidnaping of Hartley reveals his need to hold her prisoner in his imagination, to create an aesthetic image he can manipulate for his own purposes. Unlike Bradley Pearson, who finally admits that any kind of final possession of human beings is impossible, Charles continues to believe that he can force Hartley to concede to the planned denouement of his "drama."

Charles's attitude toward his novel is related to his dramatic theories, and both have implications for the way his story is interpreted by the reader. He defines the theater as "an attack on mankind carried on by magic," and its function as being "to victimize an audience every night, to make them laugh and cry and suffer and miss their trains. Of course actors regard audiences as enemies, to be deceived, drugged, incarcerated, stupefied." Although he claims to take painstaking care to relate events in his novel as truthfully as possible, at one point even reassuring the reader that he is rendering the dialogue almost verbatim, he is delighted by his sudden discovery that language, like dramatic art, can create illusion and veil truth. He says that anything written down is "true in a way" and gloats over the fact that he could write down "all sorts of fantastic nonsense" in his memoir and be believed because of "human credulity" and the power of the written word. He takes an increasing pleasure in fictionalizing his life and in transforming the people around him into "stylish sketches," acts which reveal his desire to cast his friends and enemies into a drama he can both write and direct. Like Bradley Pearson in *The Black Prince*, he finds that verbalizing experience can be a way to control what is happening; he also believes that he can dramatically intensify his feelings by writing them out "as a story." When he writes out his account of the visit of another former girl friend, Lizzie Scherer, he observes that it would be "rewarding" to "write the whole of one's life thus bit by bit as a novel. . . . The pleasant parts would be doubly pleasant, the funny parts funnier, and sin and grief would be softened by a light of philosophic consolation." Murdoch, who has said that the function of art is to reveal reality rather than to console its creator or consumer, portrays Charles as the "bad" artist who attempts to use art and the creative process for solace instead of revelation.

Just as Murdoch's characters often misuse art and their own creative impulses, they frequently fall in love suddenly and violently, an experience that produces a state of delusion and neurotic obsession. Although she says in *The Fire and the Sun* that the "lover" can be shocked into an awareness of "an entirely separate reality" during the experience of love, the lover's ego usually causes him to wish to "dominate and possess" the beloved. The lover, rather than wishing to "serve and adore," instead wants "to de-realize the other, devour and absorb him, subject him to the mechanism of . . . fantasy." Charles Arrowby's "Quest of the Bearded Lady," as one character terms his pursuit of Hartley, exemplifies this dimension of falling in love; his feelings for her are typical of the obsessive, self-centered, fantasy-ridden love that Murdoch believes is antithetical to an objective, free apprehension of others. He admits that he is "like a madman" and compares himself to a "frenzied animal." Later, he says that "I was sane enough to know that I was in a state of total obsession and that I . . . *could only* run continually along the same rat-paths of fantasy and intent." Unlike his cousin James, who has cultivated the intellectual and spiritual detachment of Eastern philosophy combined with a concern for the well-being and "otherness" of individuals, Charles's passion for Hartley Fitch is, at bottom, an obsession with his own past and loss of innocence.

In two earlier novels, *An Accidental Man* and *The Black Prince*, Murdoch uses narrative devices such as epistolary and dialogic chapters and the addition of "postscripts" by other characters to alter the reader's perspective and interpretation of events. In *The Sea, the Sea*, she allows Charles Arrowby to add a "revision" to his novel that qualifies and contradicts much of his earlier narrative. At the end of the "History" section of *The Sea, the Sea*, he closes his story on a note of repentance and revelation, goes to sleep hearing "singing," and awakens to see the seals he had previously been unable to sight.

Murdoch believes that fiction should reflect the "muddle" of reality, and thus she adds a postscript by the narrator appropriately entitled "Life Goes On." Charles begins by mocking his "conclusion" and observing that life, unlike art, "has an irritating way of bumping and limping on, undoing conversions, casting doubt on solutions"; he then decides to continue his story a while longer, this time in the form of a "diary" in which he alters his own version of events and reveals that he has learned very little from them. In this way, Murdoch further reduces the stature of her "failed Prospero," and the picture of Charles that emerges in the postscript is that of a rapidly aging man with an incipient heart condition. Another addition to the group of "power figures" in Murdoch's fiction who believe that they can "invent" reality and manipulate other people for aesthetic purposes, Charles Arrowby represents Murdoch's belief in the final impossibility of one human being's controlling another. In *The Sea, the Sea*, the would-be director who thought himself a "god" or "king" is revealed as a relatively powerless individual over whom the formlessness and unpredictability of "transcendent reality" triumphs.

Murdoch's most critically acclaimed novel of the 1980's is *The Good Apprentice*, a novel that reflects her continuing desire to write fiction whose length and complexity embody her belief in a contingent, infinitely particularized universe in which goodness is easily discussed but achieved, if at all, with great difficulty and pain. The "good apprentice" can refer to either of two characters in the novel. Edward Baltram has recently been responsible for the death of his best friend and is attempting to deal with his resulting guilt and self-hatred; Stuart Cuno, his stepbrother, is, like many other Murdochian characters, seeking goodness and finding it a problematical goal.

Murdoch make Stuart Cuno the mouthpiece of some of her most cherished ideas about the nature of goodness. Like Murdoch, Stuart acknowledges that goodness is often an unimaginable concept that involves inaction rather than action, and several times in the story he is referred to as a "negative presence." Stuart has rejected the entire concept of God and instead attempts to meditate blankly, to empty his mind out in order to perceive clearly, what Murdoch calls "an instinctive craving for nothingness which was also a desire to be able to love and enjoy and 'touch' everything, to *help* everything." Psychoanalyst Thomas McCaskerville, who stands in direct opposition to Stuart's nontheoretical approach to goodness, catechizes the younger man at length in an important conversation that reveals Thomas' dependence on the cozy theories of psychoanalysis that Murdoch has mocked in her earlier novels. Thomas has a conceptual framework for almost any idea or event, and his discovery that his wife Midge has been having an affair with Stuart's father Harry Cuno only temporarily shocks him out of his comfortable mental and emotional world. His further realization that his supposedly psychotic patient Mr. Blinnet is actually quite sane and has been faking mental illness for years is another blow at Thomas' carefully constructed theoretical world.

It is the artist Jesse Baltram, Edward's father, who best represents one of the most enduring and interesting figures in Murdoch's fiction, the magician-artist power figure who mysteriously spellbinds those around him and functions as a catalyst for many important events. Edward goes to Seegard, Jesse's home, to be "healed" and "purified" of his friend's death. In the process he meets May Baltram, Jesse's wife, his two half sisters, and, finally, his father, who has been reduced by an unspecified illness to childlike behavior and incoherence. Jesse's difficulty in making rational conversation is another alternative in the novel to Stuart's "blankness" and "whiteness" and Thomas' frenziedly articulate philosophizing: it signifies that the logical ordering principle of language ultimately cannot describe or explain a reality that is always "boiling over" with energy and creativity. Jesse's description of the world and the relationship between good and evil, in which syntax and logic break down, is directly opposed to the other characters' slick facility with language. He tells Edward, "What I knew once—about good and evil and those—all *those* things—people don't really have them, meet them—in their lives at all, most people don't—only a few—want that—that fight, you know—think they want—good—have to have evil—not real, either—of course—all inside something else—it's a dance—you see—world needs power—always round and round—it's all power and—energy—which sometimes—rears up its beautiful head—like a dragon—that's the meaning of it all—I think—in the shadows now—can't remember—doesn't matter—what I need—is a long sleep—so as to dream it all—over again."

Jesse's connection with the supernatural and paranormal dimension of Edward's stay at Seegard reveals Murdoch again experimenting with the limits of realistic fiction. As in *The Sea, the Sea*, she is willing to force the reader to accept the unexplained and acknowledge the thin line between the natural and the supernatural, between distortion of perception and a glimpse into another world where the usual rational rules no longer apply. *The Good Apprentice* shows Murdoch at the height of her powers as a novelist, combining her "moral psychology" with her long-held aesthetic theories in a work that proves the undiminished fecundity of her imagination and intelligence.

Angela Hague

Other major works

PLAYS: *A Severed Head*, 1963 (with J. B. Priestley); *The Italian Girl*, 1967 (with James Saunders); *The Servants and the Snow*, 1970; *The Three Arrows*, 1972; *Art and Eros*, 1980; *The Black Prince*, 1989.

NONFICTION: *Sartre: Romantic Rationalist*, 1953; *The Sovereignty of Good*,

1970; *The Fire and the Sun: Why Plato Banished the Artists*, 1977; *Acastos: Two Platonic Dialogues*, 1987.

Bibliography

Bloom, Harold, ed. *Iris Murdoch*. New York: Chelsea House, 1986. Bloom's collection of essays, a representative selection of some of the best articles and book chapters on Murdoch, includes his introductory analysis of *The Good Apprentice* and Murdoch's essay "Against Dryness."

Byatt, Antonia S. *Degrees of Freedom: The Novels of Iris Murdoch*. London: Barnes & Noble Books, 1965. This excellent and frequently quoted early study focuses on the different types of freedom found in Murdoch's novels. The book has extended discussions of *Under the Net*, *The Flight from the Enchanter*, *The Sandcastle*, *The Bell*, *A Severed Head*, *An Unofficial Rose*, and *The Unicorn*.

Dipple, Elizabeth. *Iris Murdoch: Work for the Spirit*. Chicago: University of Chicago Press, 1982. The most thorough and comprehensive of the studies of Murdoch, Dipple's book addresses the aesthetic, moral, and philosophical dimensions of all of Murdoch's writings through *Nuns and Soldiers*.

Hague, Angela. *Iris Murdoch's Comic Vision*. New York: Associated University Presses, 1984. This work defines Murdoch as a comic novelist in the light of her aesthetic and philosophical theories, focusing on extended analyses of *An Accidental Man*, *The Black Prince*, and *The Sea, the Sea*.

Johnson, Deborah. *Iris Murdoch*. Bloomington: Indiana University Press, 1987. Johnson uses Anglo-American and French feminist theories to analyze Murdoch from a feminist perspective, focusing on Murdoch's male narrators, the issue of confinement, the symbol of the cave, and the problem of endings in the fiction.

Todd, Richard. *Iris Murdoch: The Shakespearian Interest*. New York: Barnes & Noble Books, 1979. Murdoch's frequently noted debt to Shakespeare is explored in this study, which pays particular attention to *The Black Prince*, *Bruno's Dream*, *A Word Child*, *The Nice and the Good*, and *A Fairly Honourable Defeat*.

Wolfe, Peter. *The Disciplined Heart: Iris Murdoch and Her Novels*. Columbia: University of Missouri Press, 1966. Wolfe's early study of Murdoch is an excellent introduction to the philosophical dimension of her novels, covering all her fiction through *The Italian Girl*.

VLADIMIR NABOKOV

Born: St. Petersburg, Russia; April 23, 1899
Died: Montreux, Switzerland; July 2, 1977

Principal long fiction

Mashenka, 1926 (*Mary*, 1970); *Korol', dama, valet*, 1928 (*King, Queen, Knave*, 1968); *Zashchita Luzhina*, 1929 (serial), 1930 (*The Defense*, 1964); *Podvig*, 1932 (*Glory*, 1971); *Kamera obskura*, 1932 (*Camera Obscura*, 1936; revised as *Laughter in the Dark*, 1938); *Otchayanie*, 1934 (serial), 1936 (*Despair*, 1937, revised 1966); *Dar*, 1937-1938 (serial), 1952 (*The Gift*, 1963); *Priglashenie na kazn'*, 1935-1936 (serial), 1938 (*Invitation to a Beheading*, 1959); *The Real Life of Sebastian Knight*, 1941; *Bend Sinister*, 1947; *Lolita*, 1955; *Pnin*, 1957; *Pale Fire*, 1962; *Ada or Ardor: A Family Chronicle*, 1969; *Transparent Things*, 1972; *Look at the Harlequins!*, 1974.

Other literary forms

Vladimir Nabokov began, as many novelists do, as a poet. As a youth, he published privately what now would be called a chapbook and a full book of poetry before emigrating from Russia. Throughout his life, he continued to publish poetry in periodicals and several book-length collections, including *Stikhotvoreniya: 1929-1951* (1952, *Poems: 1929-1951*); *Poems* (1959); and *Poems and Problems* (1970). Some critics even consider the long poem "Pale Fire" (an integral part of the novel *Pale Fire*) as a worthy neoromantic poem in itself. Nabokov also published a good deal of short fiction, first in a variety of short-lived émigré publications such as *Rul'*, *Sovremennye Zapiski*, and *Russkoe ekho*, and later in such prominent magazines as *The New Yorker*, *The Atlantic*, *Playboy*, *Harper's Bazaar*, and *Tri-Quarterly*. His stories were collected in *Vozvrashchenie Chorba* (1930, *The Return of Chorb*, which also included twenty-four poems), *Solgyadatay* (1938, *The Eye*), *Nine Stories* (1947), and *Nabokov's Dozen* (1958), among others. His plays include: *Smert'* (1923, *Death*); *Tragediya gospodina Morna* (1924, *The Tragedy of Mister Morn*); *Chelovek iz SSSR* (1927, *The Man from the USSR*); *Sobytiye* (1938, *The Event*); and *Izobretenie Val'sa* (1938, *The Waltz Invention*). He also worked on a screenplay for the film version of *Lolita*. Besides translating his own works from Russian to English (and vice versa, as well as occasionally from French to Russian to English), he often translated the works of other writers, including Lewis Carrol's *Alice in Wonderland*, and poetry of Alexander Pushkin, Arthur Rimbaud, Rupert Brooke, William Shakespeare, and Alfred De Musset. In nonfiction prose, Nabokov's fascinating life is recalled in three volumes of memoirs, *Conclusive Evidence* (1951), *Drugie Berega* (1954, *Other Shores*), and *Speak, Memory* (1966, a revision and expansion of the earlier works). Throughout his life, his often idiosyncratic criticism was widely published, and the recent publication of several volumes of his lectures on world literature provoked much discussion among literary scholars. As a lepidopterist, Nabokov published a number of scholarly articles in such journals as *The Entomologist*, *Journal of the New York Entomological Society*, *Psyche*, and *The Lepidopterists' News*.

Achievements

An extraordinary individual, Nabokov's strength as a writer lay in his control and mastery of style. Writers are sometimes successful in a language other than their native language, but only a select few are capable of writing equally well in two languages, and Nabokov may be alone in his ability to master the insinuations of two extraordinarily different and subtle languages such as Russian and English. Under the pen name "V. Sirin," Nabokov was recognized as a noteworthy émigré novelist and poet in Berlin and Paris. After fleeing the rise of Nazism and settling in the United States, he became recognized as a major English-language author with the publication of *Lolita* in 1955. As was the case with Gustave Flaubert, James Joyce, and D. H. Lawrence, all of whose international sales were aided by the controversies surrounding their works, Nabokov received worldwide attention as critics debated the morality of *Lolita*, prompting the republication and translation of many of his earlier works. Few writers with such an uncompromising style achieve such popularity. Nabokov was often in financial difficulty before *Lolita*, yet he always remained the consummate craftsman. He has come to be regarded as one of the literary giants of his generation.

Biography

Vladimir Vladimirovich Nabokov was born to Vladimir Dmitrievich and Elena Rukavishnikov Nabokov in St. Petersburg, Russia, the eldest of five children. He grew up in comfortable circumstances, tracing his ancestry back to a Tartar prince of the 1380's and through a number of military men, statesmen, Siberian merchants, and the first president of the Russian Imperial Academy of Medicine. His father was a noted liberal who had helped found the Constitutional Democratic Party, was elected to the first Duma, and coedited the sole liberal newspaper in St. Petersburg. In his childhood, the young Nabokov was taken on trips to France, Italy, and Spain, and summered on the country estate of Vyra, accumulating memories which would become woven into his later writings. His father, an Anglophile, provided governesses who taught the boy English at a very early age. He once remarked that he had learned to read English even before he had learned Russian. He was also taught French.

Entering puberty, Nabokov attended the liberal Prince Tenishev School, where he first developed a hatred of coercion, but played soccer and chess, started collecting butterflies, and showed some artistic talent. He began writing poetry, and a now-lost brochure of a single poem "in a violet paper cover" was privately published in 1914. In 1916, he privately published a recollection that provoked his cousin to beg him to "never, never be a writer," and in 1918, he collaborated on a collection with Andrei Balashov. Nabokov inherited an estate and the equivalent of two million dollars when his Uncle "Ruka" died and seemed to be on his way to the comfortable life of a Russian bourgeois when history intervened. His father became part of the Provisional Government in the March Revolution of 1917, but in October, when the Bolsheviks displaced the Alexander Kerensky government, the Nabokov family fled, first to the Crimea and then, in 1919, into permanent exile in the West on an old Greek ship ironically named *Nadezhda* ("Hope").

Nabokov studied at Trinity College, Cambridge University, paying little attention to anything but soccer, tennis, and girls. He did, however, do many translations (of Rupert Brooke, Seumas O'Sullivan, W. B. Yeats, Lord Byron, and others) and came under the influence of English poetry. He also read and was influenced by James Joyce. Despite his claim that he never once visited the library, he was graduated with honors in French and Russian literature in 1923. This was shortly following his father's assassination in Berlin in March, 1922, as two reactionaries shot the elder Nabokov in error as he was introducing their intended victim. After Cambridge, the twenty-five-year-old Nabokov moved to Berlin, where, in 1925, he married Vera Evseevna Slonim, and a year later published his first novel, *Mary*, under a pseudonym. He felt that his father had prior claim to the name "Vladimir Nabokov" and wrote all of his early Russian works as "V. Sirin."

With very little money, Nabokov published poems, stories, and essays in Berlin's émigré newspapers, and later, as the Nazis grew in power (his wife was Jewish), in similar Parisian publications. He survived by teaching tennis, devising crossword puzzles in Russian, making up chess problems, teaching Russian, and translating. He sold the Russian translation of *Alice in Wonderland* (1923, *Anya v strane chudes*), for example, for the equivalent of five dollars. In 1934, his only son Dmitri was born, and four years later, Nabokov fled to Paris. As early as 1935, he decided to emigrate to the United States, probably recognizing that Europe was no longer safe. He was invited by the Soviet government during the 1930's to return to Russia several times, but he refused.

Nabokov's novels in Berlin and Paris had been relatively successful and several had been translated into English with and without his assistance. He made the remarkable and difficult decision to abandon the language in which he had written so well. "My private tragedy," he later wrote, "which cannot, indeed should not, be anybody's concern, is that I had to abandon my natural idiom, my untrammeled, rich, and infinitely docile Russian tongue for a second-rate brand of English." Stanford University invited him to teach in the summer of 1940, and he set sail for America on the liner *Champlain* in May, just ahead of the German invasion. He had already begun writing his first English novel, *The Real Life of Sebastian Knight*, while in Paris, and, in 1941, it was published in the United States after several friends helped him edit it. He taught Russian grammar and literature at Wellesley College from 1941 to 1948, also serving as a research fellow at the Museum of Comparative Zoology at Harvard University. He became a prominent lepidopterist, publishing many monographs, articles, and reviews. He spent summers roaming America searching for butterflies and discovered several species and subspecies, including "Nabokov's Wood Nymph." After seeing praise for his work on the Lycaeides genus in a field guide, Nabokov is said to have remarked, "That's real fame. That means more than anything a literary critic could say."

In 1944, Nabokov published a critical book on Nikolai Gogol, and in 1947, his first novel written in the United States, *Bend Sinister*, appeared. From 1948 to 1959, he taught at Cornell University, carefully writing out his lectures, combining his attacks upon such intellectual touchstones as Karl Marx, Charles Darwin, and especially Sigmund Freud with dramatic classroom readings. Well before the publication of *Lolita*, he was recognized as a remarkable talent in certain quarters, as is indicated by his receipt of grants from the Guggenheim Foundation in 1943 and 1953, and by an award from the American Academy of Arts and Letters in 1953; students in his classes at Cornell, however, were often unaware that their teacher was also a writer, although he published stories and articles in *The New Yorker*, *The Atlantic*, *Hudson Review*, and others. *Lolita* changed all that. Rejected by several American publishers, it was brought out by publisher Maurice Girodias' Olympia Press in Paris in 1955. As one of the most controversial books ever published— banned for a while in France, debated in the British Parliament, and forbidden in many American libraries—it swept the best-seller lists and freed Nabokov from teaching. Besides the royalties, he received $150,000 and a percentage on the film rights and wrote a screenplay (which was later substantially changed) for Stanley Kubrick's 1963 film.

In 1960, Nabokov moved to Montreux, Switzerland, where he and his wife lived in a sixth-floor apartment in the Palace Hotel overlooking Lake Geneva, in order to be near their son Dmitri, who was having some success as an opera singer. In the wake of *Lolita*, Nabokov and his son translated many of his earlier novels into English, and introduced several collections of his short stories to American readers. His novels *Pale Fire*, *Ada or Ardor*, *Transparent Things*, and *Look at the Harlequins!* were all published during this period. He was regularly discussed as a possible recipient of the Nobel Prize until his death of a viral infection in 1977.

Analysis

In 1937, Vladeslav Khodasevich, an émigré poet and champion of "V.

Sirin's" work, wrote, "Sirin [Nabokov] proves for the most part to be an artist of form, of the writer's device, and not only in that . . . sense of which . . . his writing is distinguished by exceptional diversity, complexity, brilliance, and novelty." Khodasevich went on to say that the key to all of Sirin's work was his ability to put all his literary devices on display, with little or no attempt to conceal them, thus entertaining his readers more with the revelation of how the magician performs his tricks, than with the trick itself. "The life of the artist and the life of a device in the consciousness of an artist—this is Sirin's theme." Khodasevich, although he had not yet read *The Gift*—purported to be Vladimir Nabokov's greatest Russian novel—had discovered the most important element of Nabokov's fiction.

Throughout his entire life, although Nabokov underwent great changes in his circumstances, he was consistent, whether writing in Russian or English, in his unflagging delight in literary devices of all sorts, art for it's own sake, and a contempt for mimetic conventions, simplistic psychological motivation, ordinary plot structure, and anything that inhibits the literary imagination. He can, in many respects, be called an aesthete, but his rejection of most schools of thought makes him difficult to classify. He strove for and achieved a uniqueness that runs as a thread throughout his oeuvre. Clarence Brown once commented in a critical essay that "For well over a quarter of a century now . . . [Nabokov] has been writing in book after book about the same thing," and Nabokov is said to have admitted that Brown was probably correct.

Nabokov's first novel, *Mary*, is rather sentimental and probably based on Nabokov's regret for a lost love, but it already contains two elements he would use repeatedly—the love triangle and uncertain identity. *King, Queen, Knave*, however, is an even more obvious reflection of the Nabokov canon. In it, a character named Franz Bubendorf, a country bumpkin on his way to the city, apparently to be corrupted by the bourgeois life, is, in fact, already corrupted by his distaste for his own class, which distorts his perception. As if to emphasize this distortion of perception, Franz steps on his glasses and Berlin becomes a blur. Again, there is a love triangle, and each of the participants is, in his or her own way, unable to perceive reality. The melodrama of a love triangle and a planned murder is handled with the authorial detachment which is one of Nabokov's hallmarks. The novel becomes a parody of traditional forms, and the characters become obvious contrivances of the author. Derived from a Hans Christian Andersen work of the same title, the novel consists of thirteen chapters, as there are thirteen cards in each suit in a deck of cards. The card metaphor is carried throughout the work, even in the description of clothes.

Laughter in the Dark opens with a parody of the fairy tale revealing the entire plot, here a relatively conventional bourgeois love-story that Nabokov typically manipulates. The main character, blinded by love, becomes literally blinded and trapped in a love triangle which results in his murder (accomplished in a scene that is a parody of motion-picture melodrama). This type of parody, which partially represents Nabokov's delight in mocking inferior art, can also be seen as a parody of the reader's expectations. Nabokov constantly thwarts the reader who wants a nice, comfortable, conventional novel. The writer is always in control, always tugging the reader this way and that, never allowing a moment of certainty. Perceptions are distorted on all levels. The characters have distorted perceptions of one another. The reader's perception of events is teasingly distorted by the author. Nabokov operates a house of mirrors. If a reader expects realism, there will be no pleasure in the warped mirrors Nabokov presents. One must delight instead in the odd shapes and obvious deformities in the mirrors he has shaped.

Character-types in the Russian novels also recur throughout Nabokov's career, so much so that some critics have attempted to pair earlier Russian novels with later English ones. Usually, the central figure is an outsider, an unusual person in his milieu. Bubendorf of *King, Queen, Knave* is a country boy in the city. In *The Defense*, the chess master Luzhin does not fit in with his family or his school, and is sent into exile after the Revolution. Martin Edelweiss of *Glory* is in exile in London.

What is more important, however, is that these and many more of Nabokov's characters are isolated as much by their mental states as by their physical surroundings. Their fantasies, dreams, ambitions, and obsessions set them utterly apart from the ordinary world. Luzhin, for example, is so obsessed with chess that he cannot deal with the disorder of life. Cincinnatus in *Invitation to a Beheading* is thought peculiar by his fellow workers in the doll factory. In later English novels, immigrant Timofey Pnin is thought mad by his academic colleagues; Humbert Humbert and Adam Krug are seen as dangers to society; and Charles Kinbote intrudes and imposes on people. Generally, the main characters of Nabokov's novels are perceived as talented men, in some sense more valuable than the soulless people and society that persecute them. They are outsiders because they are extraordinary. They are free, imaginative, and capable of a kind of heroism that ordinary people lack: the ability to remake the world according to their own obsessions.

The Gift is generally thought of as Nabokov's best Russian novel. Originally published serially in *Sovremennye Zapiski*, an émigré periodical, the fourth section was not included (for political reasons) in a complete edition until 1952. In *The Gift*, the central figure is Fyodor Godunov-Cherdyntsev, a brilliant émigré poet. As the book opens, he has just published a collection of poems, and much of the early part concerns his literary career. Later, his obsession with the memory of his father begins to dominate his everyday life, and he becomes caught in the typical confusions of the biographer: What is the truth and how can one see it? He feels an obligation to write a biography of his father, but becomes trapped in assessing the various versions of his father's life. Later, he does succeed in writing a biography of Nikolai Gavrilovich Chernyshevski, a so-called "poetic history" based upon the idea that reconstructing the past is essentially a creative act—history only exists in the historian's imagination—and that the best biographies are literary creations.

The Gift has been seen as the summing up of Nabokov's experiences as an émigré writer, and similarities have been seen between the author's biography and the events and people in the novel. The book is heavy with allusions to Russian literature and has been called the Russian counterpart to *Ada or Ardor* (1969), an extremely allusive and complex book that also focuses on the nature of the writer. In *The Gift*, many of Nabokov's favorite devices are employed: the love triangle, the ironic suicide, and the heightened perception of the hero, in which he imagines conversations with the dead.

After his decision to begin writing in English, Nabokov produced two novels before the *succès de scandale* of *Lolita*. *The Real Life of Sebastian Knight* was begun in Paris and is ostensibly the biography of a fiction-writer, Sebastian, narrated by his brother, "V." "V" is shocked to discover upon his brother's death in 1936 that there was more to learn of Sebastian from his novels than he had learned in person. Once again, Nabokov introduces the theme that art surpasses reality. "V" fights the various distortions of Sebastian's life, yet, at the end of his biography, confesses that "Sebastian's mask clings to my face." "V" created Sebastian, so Sebastian is "V" (as both characters were created by Nabokov). Again, the novel is characterized by the use of parodistic techniques and distorted characters. One can easily recognize this novel as a Nabokov work, yet because of Nabokov's uncertainty at writing in the English language at this stage, the work is not completely satisfying. Nabokov admitted, for example, to having had native speakers help him with the editing, something he would never permit later.

Many resemblances have been noted between Nabokov and his brother Sergei, and "V" and his brother Sebastian. Sergei, unlike Vladimir, stayed in Europe during the Nazi period and died of starvation in a concentration camp near Hamburg on January 10, 1945. These events perhaps explain the harsh allegorical tone of *Bend Sinister*, a novel that is, in some ways, better than its predecessor and perhaps one of the most accessible of Nabokov's novels. The hero, Adam Krug, is an intellectual whose ideas are largely responsible for the new regime in an Eastern European country. Krug, however, refuses to swear allegiance to the ruler of the regime, a fellow student from childhood named Paduk. "I am not interested in politics," he says. Inexorably, the ring of tyranny tightens around Krug, resulting in the arrest of friends, the death of his son, and Krug's death as he attempts to attack Paduk in a mad vision of schoolyard life.

The artist, the literary craftsman in Nabokov, was incapable, however, of writing a straightforward novel of outrage against Fascists or Communists. The country is not specified; numerous vague descriptions of setting give the work a Kafkaesque flavor. The regime is tyrannical—it wants the souls of its people as well as their cooperation (not unlike Big Brother in George Orwell's *Nineteen Eighty-Four*, 1949)—yet it is not a specific ideology which is being attacked. Any form of coercion that limits the imagination of the artist or the intellectual is the target. Although some critics have argued that Krug's flaw is that he refuses to become involved in politics, it is difficult to imagine *Bend Sinister*, in the light of other works, as being a call to commitment. Krug has made a commitment to his own intellectual life. He, like many Nabokov heroes, does not "fit in," and, like many Nabokov heroes, comes to a tragic end. The supremacy of the individual imagination is Nabokov's "message"; art is his morality. There is an abundant helping of satire and parody directed against the intellectual community and the "great" political leaders of the world. Paduk is shown as a sniveling, ugly weakling who craves Krug's approval, but the alternatives to his tyranny are shown to be equally preposterous. Even in reacting to the horrors of dictatorship, Nabokov remains the detached artist.

Lolita, the novel that would provide a comfortable living for the author for the rest of his life, has been called everything from pornography to one of the greatest novels of the twentieth century. Today, when virtually every sexual predilection has been the subject of motion pictures and television, it is hard to appreciate the whirlwind of controversy that was stirred up by *Lolita*'s publication. Humbert Humbert, the central character and narrator, has an obsession for young girls which he has hidden by unhappy affairs with older women. He comes to the United States after inheriting a business and separating from his childish wife Valeria. Eventually, he becomes the boarder of Charlotte Haze and falls in love with her twelve-year-old daughter Lolita. He marries Mrs. Haze to be near Lolita, and when the mother is killed, takes the girl on a trip across the United States. She is eventually stolen by Clare Quilty, who is, in many ways, Humbert's double, and Humbert goes on a two-year quest to rescue her. He finds the sad, pregnant Lolita married to a man named Richard Schiller and, in revenge, shoots Quilty. The novel is allegedly Humbert's manuscript, written as he awaits trial. According to the Foreward, Humbert died in jail of a coronary thrombosis and the manuscript was transmitted to one John Ray, Jr., Ph.D., who prepared it for publication.

As in all of Nabokov's works, however, a plot summary is absurdly inadequate in characterizing the book. *Lolita* is protean in its directions and effects. It has been seen as a satire on the United States (though Nabokov denied it), as a psychological study (although Nabokov called Freud a "medieval mind"), and as a parody of the romantic novel. Lionel Trilling argued that, since adultery was such a commonplace in the modern world, only a perverse love could cause the adequate passion mixed with suffering characteristic of great romantic loves: Tristan and Isolde, Abélard and Héloise, Dante and Beatrice, Petrarch and Laura. Humbert often justifies his pedophilia by references to the courtly love tradition. There is also much reference to the story of Edgar Allan Poe's love for Virginia Clemm (Humbert's first teenage love was a girl named Annabel Leigh).

Although many critics attempted to justify *Lolita* as having an important moral message, Nabokov rebuked the notion by saying, "I am no messenger boy." His aesthetic philosophy would never have permitted him to subordinate his art to a moral. He once said that Lolita was about his love for the English language, but even that is an oversimplification of an immensely complex book. Among the various elements critics have noted are the *Doppelgänger* relation of Quilty to Humbert, chess metaphors, puns on names, the question of the masks of the narrator (the probably unreliable Humbert through the clinical Ray through the mischievous Nabokov), and the supposed immortality of Humbert's love, a love that becomes timeless through a work of art. It has even been argued that Nabokov's description of Lolita very much resembles his description of a certain species of butterfly in his scientific studies. While *Lolita*'s place in the canon of world literature is still debated, there is little doubt that it may be the finest example of the author's "gamesplaying" method of artistic creation.

In *Pale Fire*, readers were once again amused, perplexed, or horrified with Nabokov's ironic wit. This experimental novel inspired extremes of praise—such as Mary McCarthy's judgment that "it is one of the great works of art of this century"—and mockery. The novel is presented in the form of a scholarly edition of a poem entitled "Pale Fire" by John Shade, with commentary by Charles Kinbote. Both worked at Wordsmith University, where Kinbote seems to have believed that Shade was writing a poem but Kinbote's obsession with Charles Xavier Vseslav, "The Beloved," the King of Zembla who was forced to flee the revolution that replaced him. *Pale Fire* can be described as a series of Russian dolls, one enclosed within another. John Shade's poem (as edited by Kinbote) is explained by Kinbote, who intends to give life to the extraordinary personality of Shade. He writes in the Foreward, "without my notes Shade's text simply has no human reality at all," but the reader soon recognizes that Kinbote is a madman who either is, or imagines himself to be, the displaced King of Zembla, and whatever human reality Shade may have exists only through his colleague's warped interpretation of events. On another level, the reader finds some of Shade's "reality" in the text of his poem, and reads much into and between Kinbote's lines as the madman gradually exposes his own madness. Yet, Nabokov never wants his reader to forget that all this invention is entirely of his making. Much more is intended than a mere parody of scholarly editions, scholars and neoromantic poetry. Once more, Nabokov wittily develops his lifelong theme that reality exists only in the eyes of its interpreter.

J. Madison Davis

Other major works

SHORT FICTION: *Vozvrashchenie Chorba*, 1930; *Soglyadatay*, 1938; *Nine Stories*, 1947; *Vesna v Fialte i drugie rasskazy*, 1956; *Nabokov's Dozen: A Collection of Thirteen Stories*, 1958; *Nabokov's Quartet*, 1966; *A Russian Beauty and Other Stories*, 1973; *Tyrants Destroyed and Other Stories*, 1975; *Details of a Sunset and Other Stories*, 1976.

PLAYS: *Smert'*, 1923; *Dedushka*, 1923; *Polius*, 1924; *Tragediya gospodina Morna*, 1924; *Chelovek iz SSSR*, 1927; *Sobytiye*, 1938; *Izobretenie Val'sa*, 1938 (*The Waltz Invention*, 1966).

SCREENPLAY: *Lolita*, 1962.

POETRY: *Stikhi*, 1916; *Dva puti*, 1918; *Gorny put*, 1923; *Grozd'*, 1923; *Stikhotvorenia, 1929-1951*, 1952; *Poems*, 1959; *Poems and Problems*, 1970.

NONFICTION: *Nikolai Gogol*, 1944; *Conclusive Evidence: A Memoir*, 1951; *Drugie berega*, 1954; *Speak, Memory: An Autobiography Revisited*, 1966 (revision of *Conclusive Evidence* and *Drugie berega*); *Strong Opinions*, 1973; *The Nabokov-Wilson Letters, 1940-1971*, 1979; *Lectures on Literature: British, French, and German*, 1980; *Lectures on Russian Literature*, 1981; *Lectures on Don Quixote*, 1983; *Vladimir Nabokov: Selected Letters, 1940-1977*, 1989.

TRANSLATIONS: *Anya v strane chudes*, 1923 (of Lewis Carroll's novel *Alice in Wonderland*); *Three Russian Poets: Translations of Pushkin, Lermontov, and Tiutchev*, 1944 (with Dmitri Nabokov); *A Hero of Our Time*, 1958 (of Mikhail Lermontov's novel, with Dmitri Nabokov); *The Song of Igor's Campaign*, 1960 (of the twelfth century epic *Slovo o polki Igoreve*); *Eugene Onegin*, 1964 (of Alexander Pushkin's novel).

Bibliography

Appel, Alfred, Jr., and Charles Newman, eds. *Nabokov: Criticism, Reminiscences, Translations, Tributes*. Evanston, Ill.: Northwestern University Press, 1970. A good introduction to Nabokov's writing, including a varied sampling of material about the man, about the writer, and about his several unique works. Perhaps a hodgepodge, but an early collection that contrasts dramatically with later criticism, which suggested that Nabokov was a humanist if also a kind of verbal magician.

Bader, Julia. *Crystal Land: Artifice in Nabokov's English Novels*. Berkeley: University of California Press, 1972. The focus of this exclusively critical work is often narrow and technical. Deals with the complexities of Nabokov's contrived, playful plot and character development in six novels: *The Real Life of Sebastian Knight*, *Pale Fire*, *Lolita*, *Pnin*, *Bend Sinister*, and *Ada or Ardor*.

Clancy, Laurie. *The Novels of Vladimir Nabokov*. New York: St. Martin's Press, 1984. An assessment of Nabokov's entire creation of novels focusing on style and thematic development. Challenges the charge of what might be called moral isolationism or isolated artistic purpose ("art for art's sake") by earlier critics, claiming that his most significant work blends art and life. Of particular additional value is an extensive bibliography of his novels and other writings as well as books about his life and works.

Field, Andrew. *Nabokov, His Life in Part.* New York: Viking Press, 1977. An intimate portrait written by an author who was often very close to Nabokov during the latter part of Nabokov's life. The book may also suggest to would-be biographers some of the difficulties of writing a biography while enjoying an intimate relationship with the subject. Follows Field's critical work, *Nabokov, His Life in Art: A Critical Narrative* (Boston: Little, Brown, 1967).

Pifer, Ellen. *Nabokov and the Novel.* Cambridge, Mass.: Harvard University Press, 1980. Uses as an epigraph Flannery O'Connor's "All novelists are fundamentally seekers and describers of the real, but the realism of each novelist will depend on his view of the ultimate reaches of reality" to develop a critical dialogue about Nabokov's technique, not surprisingly including realism. Ends in a discussion on Nabokov's humanism. Robert Alter called this book "poised and precise," and it is excellent for serious, critical readers of Nabokov.